'Bang up to date with its coverage of British politics – taking in the aftermath of the 2016 referendum and the 2017 general election – and the recent academic literature, this text offers a balanced, wide-ranging and, above all, crystal-clear overview.'

– Andrew Hindmoor, University of Sheffield, UK

'A comprehensive and insightful look at the ever changing landscape of British politics. As in their previous writing, the authors' thorough and engaging manner makes this textbook an informative guide for students at all levels.'

– Victoria Honeyman, University of Leeds, UK

'*British Politics* has always been my 'go-to' textbook and this latest edition shines a light on the changing nature of British politics, not least in terms of devolution and multi-level governance and set against the backdrop of the 2016 EU Referendum result. The companion website is a treat for those with different learning styles and is packed with videos, quizzes and flashcards. Highly recommended for academics and students alike.'

– Cathy Gormley-Heenan, University of Ulster, UK

'Just what's needed: approachable, well-organised, and very much on-point, this new edition keeps pace with events, yet continues to provide readers with the essentials they really need to know. Highly recommended.'

– Tim Bale, Queen Mary University of London, UK

'UK politics seems to be changing daily to reflect economic, political, and constitutional crises. It is difficult, but necessary and profoundly important, to produce a comprehensive textbook that remains authoritative and up to date on so many developments. Therefore, Griffiths and Leach should be congratulated for providing such a rich account of British politics.'

– Paul Cairney, University of Stirling, UK

'An excellent new edition to a definitive text. It provides an engaging and accessible introduction to British politics, from established academic debates to the volatility of the contemporary political setting. An essential starting point for any student interested in British politics.'

– Ian Stafford, Cardiff University, UK

# BRITISH POLITICS

## THIRD EDITION

SIMON GRIFFITHS

ROBERT LEACH

 palgrave

First published as *Contemporary British Politics* in 1989
Second edition 1994
Third edition 1998
Fourth edition 2003

First published as *British Politics* in 2006
Second edition 2011

Third edition published 2018 by
PALGRAVE

Palgrave in the UK is an imprint of Macmillan Publishers Limited, registered in England, company number 785998, of 4 Crinan Street, London, N1 9XW.

Palgrave® and Macmillan® are registered trademarks in the United States, the United Kingdom, Europe and other countries.

ISBN 978–1–137–60302–9 hardback
ISBN 978–1–137–60300–5 paperback

This book is printed on paper suitable for recycling and made from fully managed and sustained forest sources. Logging, pulping and manufacturing processes are expected to conform to the environmental regulations of the country of origin.

A catalogue record for this book is available from the British Library.

A catalog record for this book is available from the Library of Congress.

# Brief Contents

# Contents

## PART I: FROM PAST TO PRESENT

## PART II: GOVERNMENT AND GOVERNANCE

# Lists of Illustrative Material

## Key Figures

## Timelines

## Figures

## Tables

## Maps

# TOUR OF THE BOOK

### Politics in Action video
Watch video interviews showcasing different opinions on political ideas and theories in practice.

### Opening vignette
Kick-start your reading with a concise example exploring key issues

## POLITICS IN ACTION

In this video Simon Griffiths, one of the authors of this book, provides an overview of some of the key questions and themes in this Part.

Emily Robinson talks about some of the historical and social events that have shaped politics since 1945, and reflects on why such an understanding is useful for politics students today.

Watch the videos at www.macmillanihe.com/griffiths-brit-pol-3e

British politics seems to be in flux. In a BBC Radio 4 programme called *Tearing Up the Politics Textbook* (BBC, 2016a), political scientist Rosie Campbell asked: 'How should we understand this new landscape ... And what should go in the new politics textbooks?' This book tries to answer some of those questions

## ⊞ COMPARING BRITISH POLITICS 5.2

### Amending constitutions

Procedures for amending the US Constitution are described in Article 6 of the Constitution. Congress can propose amendments that have been approved by a two-thirds majority in each House. Any such amendment must also be approved by three-quarters of the state legislatures before it takes effect. Thus, amending the US Constitution is very difficult. Even so, a number of important amendments have been passed. These include:

» The Bill of Rights, the name given to the first ten amendments, ratified in 1791, which includes a number of basic citizen rights,

» The limitation of the presidential period of office to two terms (22nd amendment, 1951).

In Australia, constitutional amendments require the support of both houses of parliament, then a referendum which must receive majority support overall and in a majority of states.

In Germany, constitutional amendments need a two-thirds majority in both houses of parliament, but the federal system and the rights of German citizens cannot be amended.

France has two methods for making constitutional amendments:

### Spotlight On ...
Dive deeper into a particular example or case study

### Comparing British Politics
Take a look at how Britain stacks up against other nations

## SPOTLIGHT ON ...

### Conditions for representative democracy          1.1

» Full adult franchise: all adults have the right to vote

» A secret ballot: helps ensure voting without intimidation or bribery

» Regular elections: governments and parliaments must not be able to postpone elections

» Fair elections: each vote should count equally

» An effective choice of candidates and parties for voters

» A level playing field between rival parties and candidates contesting elections

» A free and diverse media enabling a wide expression of views

---

*Power is the capacity to achieve desired goals.*

---

*Authority is the rightful or legitimate use of power.*

---

*Influence involves the ability to shape a decision or outcome through various forms of pressure.*

---

### Glossary
Solidify your understanding of important terminology

### Timelines
Recap key dates and events

### Timeline 2.1 The welfare state: key developments

| | |
|---|---|
| 1942 | The Beveridge Report, *Social Insurance and Allied Services* |
| 1944 | Education Act |
| 1944 | White Paper on employment policy (high and stable level of employment) |
| 1945 | Family Allowances Act |
| 1946 | National Insurance Act (implemented Beveridge Report) |
| 1948 | Establishment of the National Health Service |

## 👥 KEY FIGURES 2.1
John Maynard Keynes

**John Maynard Keynes (1883–1946)** had been a brilliant critic of interwar economic policy. *The General Theory of Employment, Interest and Money* (1936), his key work, argued that governments could secure full employment, stable prices, steady economic growth and a healthy balance of payments by influencing total (or aggregate) demand for goods and services, through fiscal and monetary policy, without requiring direct intervention, or controls on particular firms and industries (often described as 'Keynesian demand strategies'). So, whenever unemployment appeared to be rising above politically acceptable levels, government could stimulate demand in the economy by reducing taxation and/or increasing government spending (if necessary running a budget deficit).

### Key Figures
Learn about leading individuals and their contributions to the field

**FURTHER READING**

The first chapter of Heywood's (2013) *Politics* addresses the question 'What is Politics?' It includes a particularly useful brief discussion of power. There is also a brief discussion of alternative views on the nature of politics in Leach and Lightfoot (2018, pp. x–xx) *The Politics and IR Companion*. The same subject is treated in more depth from different perspectives by several authors in Leftwich (ed.) (2004) *What is Politics?*

Older classic texts include Lasswell (1936) *Politics: Who Gets What, When, How?* and Crick (1993) *In Defence of Politics*, which is thought-provoking, if a little idiosyncratic. French political scientist Duverger's *The Study of Politics* (1972) is still worth reading. Arblaster (1987) provides a readable short introduction to *Democracy*. Macpherson's almost as brief *The Life and*

The distribution of power in Britain is, inevitably, a controversial subject. One readable personal view is provided by Sampson (2005) *Who Runs This Place?*, the last of a series of studies of the 'Anatomy of Britain' which he began in 1962. For a more theoretical discussion of power, see Lukes (1974/ 2005). Classic texts on participation and representation are also worth reading, notably, Carole Pateman *Participation and Democratic Theory* (1970) and Hanna Pitkin, *The Concept of Representation* (1967).

Dunleavy and O'Leary's (1987) *Theories of the State* provides a clear account of most of the models of power (pluralism, elitism, Marxism, etc.) briefly described in this chapter.

On the issues around the widespread current disillusionment with politics and democracy, there are two provocative prizewinning books:

**Further Reading**
Widen your knowledge by exploring other works on key issues

**Summary**
Review the key points covered in the chapter and check your understanding

 **SUMMARY**

» Politics involves far more than government and party politics. It is about power and decision-making that affect all our lives and determine how scarce resources are allocated – 'who gets what, when, how.'

» There are disagreements over the legitimate scope of politics. Some distinguish between a public or political sphere and a private sphere, between the state and 'civil society.' Others would deny that politics can or should be excluded

few, others that it is widely dispersed. Theories or 'models' of power reflect conflicting underlying assumptions and look at different kinds of evidence.

» Although politics is about the conflicting interests of different social or ethnic groups, it is also about ideas. Political differences commonly reflect contrasting underlying ideological assumptions.

**Questions for Discussion**
Join in the debate yourselves and consolidate your comprehension of chapter themes

 **QUESTIONS FOR DISCUSSION**

» What is politics? Why do many people seem to show distaste for politics? Or are people 'fed up' with politicians or the political process?

» Should we distinguish between a political (or public) sphere and a private sphere from which politics should be excluded?

» What do you understand by democracy? How far is Britain a democracy?

» Who governs Britain? Where does power lie in Britain? Is power highly concentrated in the

» Is political change driven by ideas and principles, or by economic and social change?

» Is it possible, or desirable, to take such issues as education, health, defence or law and order out of politics?

» Does it still make sense to study British politics, particularly when the British state is apparently in the process of being eroded from above and below?

**Useful Websites**
Tap in to useful online sources for further information

 **USEFUL WEBSITES**

The Political Studies Association exists to develop and promote the study of politics in the UK. It also blogs on many issues on the study of British politics: www.psa.ac.uk.

*Tearing Up the Politics Textbooks*, Rosie Campbell's programme referred to at the start of this chapter, can be heard at: www.bbc.co.uk/ programmes/b07w9km7.

**Online Teaching and Learning Materials**
Access a wide range of ancillary resources to support the book

 *Further student resources to support learning are available at*
**www.macmillanihe.com/griffiths-brit-pol-3e**

# Teaching and Learning Resources

To support the use of this book, the companion website contains a host of interactive and ancillary content that can be used during lectures and seminars, or as a self-study aid. These can be found at www.macmillanihe.com/griffiths-brit-pol-3e.

## Teaching Resources:

Lecturers using this book on their course can take advantage of the following materials to support their teaching:

» Lecture slides

» Testbank of assessment questions

## Learning Resources:

Students using the book have access to interactive learning aids, including:

» Politics in Action video interviews

» Interactive Timelines

» Flashcard quizzes

» Content updates

# POLITICS IN ACTION VIDEO INTERVIEWS

Accompanying this textbook is a series of video interviews with key figures in the field, who offer their thoughts on a number of important issues. Bringing politics to life, these videos invite you to expand your learning beyond this textbook.

## PART 1: FROM PAST TO PRESENT

EMILY ROBINSON

Emily Robinson is Senior Lecturer in Politics at the University of Sussex and a Fellow of the Royal Historical Society. Her publications include *The Language of Progressive Politics in Modern Britain* (Palgrave, 2017) and *History, Heritage and Tradition in Contemporary British Politics* (Manchester University Press, 2012).

## PART 2: GOVERNMENT AND GOVERNANCE

CATHERINE HADDON

Dr Catherine Haddon is the Institute for Government's resident historian. She joined in November 2008 from academia and leads the Institute's work on the history of government and civil service, general elections, changes of government, constitutional issues and government reform. She often features as a commentator on radio and TV.

## PART 3: PEOPLE AND POLITICS
ROSIE CAMPBELL

Professor Rosie Campbell is a Professor of Politics at Birkbeck University of London. She is the principle investigator of the ESRC funded *Representative Audit of Britain*, looking at the 2015 and 2017 British General Elections, and co-investigator of a Leverhulme funded study of British parliamentary candidates and MPs from 1945–2015. Rosie has presented four episodes of RadioFour's *Analysis* programme on British politics.

## PART 4: POLITICS AND POLICYMAKING
PATRICK DIAMOND

Dr Patrick Diamond has held positions at the University of Manchester, and Nuffield College, Oxford and is currently Senior Lecturer in Public Policy at Queen Mary, University of London. He was a local councillor in the London Borough of Southwark and Chair of the think-tank *Policy Network*. Patrick held a number of senior posts in British central government between 2000 and 2010, and was formally Head of Policy Planning in 10 Downing Street. He comments regularly on national media outlets.

# ABOUT THE AUTHORS

 **Simon Griffiths** is a senior lecturer at Goldsmiths, University of London, UK. He has also worked in parliament and for various think tanks. Simon has written for several newspapers and regularly appears on TV and radio to discuss British politics.

 **Robert Leach** is visiting reader at Leeds Metropolitan University, UK. He has written extensively on British government, local government and ideologies. Recent publications include *The Politics and IR Companion* (2018) and *Political Ideology in Britain* (2015).

# PREFACE

Since the last edition of this book, British politics has been in turmoil. Some of this instability can be traced back to the effects of the global banking crisis of 2007–08, which soon turned into a full-blown economic slump. In the UK, this was the end of a long period of sustained growth. Debates suddenly shifted from how the state should invest money wisely in public services to how to rein in spending. The unexpected crash led political parties across the world to shift to a politics of 'austerity', which often meant deep cuts to public spending in order to rebalance the economy (Lodge and Hood, 2011). This was the language that dominated the Conservative–Liberal Democrat coalition, for example, in government from 2010 to 2015. For many other people, the crisis raised new questions about the fairness and stability of the political and economic system and led to a renewed search for alternatives.

Economic worries seemed to be linked to a crisis in 'politics as usual'. In June 2016, against the advice of the leadership of every significant party in the House of Commons, the UK population voted to leave the European Union (EU), scuppering the UK's main economic strategy for the previous half century.

Party politics in the UK has been just as volatile. Experts and pollsters confidently predicted that the 2017 general election would lead to a significant Conservative victory. Instead, it resulted in Prime Minister Theresa May losing her majority in parliament and controversially relying on the support of Northern Ireland's Democratic Unionist Party (DUP) to keep the Conservatives in power.

The 2017 election was just one example of the unpredictability that has come to define contemporary party politics in the UK. Two years earlier, just before the 2015 general election, a group of experts put the Conservative's chance of having a majority of seats in the House of Commons at 200 to 1. When the Conservatives unexpectedly won the 2015 election outright, the position of their leader, David Cameron, seemed impregnable. Just over a year later he had resigned, after leading the UK into a referendum on membership of the EU and backing the losing side.

In the aftermath of the 2015 general election, Labour ditched their electoral strategy of the previous 30 years – which had seen leaders taking the party to the political centre – by electing Jeremy Corbyn, a veteran socialist, as leader. Corbyn had spent much of his time in Parliament on the backbenches rebelling against his own party. Some Labour MPs were so unhappy at the direction Corbyn was taking the party that they forced a leadership election. Just a few months later people were starting to take the idea of Prime Minister Corbyn seriously.

North of the border, the dominance of the Scottish National Party (SNP) broke the two-party duopoly in 2015. The SNP won all but three seats in Scotland at that election, increasing their representation from 6 to 56 MPs (although they dropped back again in 2017). Politics, in recent years, is nothing if not unpredictable.

*British Politics* is the first textbook to really try to make sense of these dramatic changes. It has been extensively revised to take account of these, and many more, recent developments. It sets out to try and understand the interplay of individuals, groups, institutions and ideas that shape and reshape politics, as well as understanding their history, so we know better how we got to where we are today. For that reason, Part I, 'From Past to Present', sets out some of the main trends in British politics since the Second World War, taking us up to the present day. It ends with a snapshot of contemporary UK society in all its diversity.

Part II explores questions of 'Government and Governance' in the UK. It sets out the changing constitution within which British politics operates and explores some of the key institutions, from Parliament to the law. It also examines the various tiers of government in the UK from local to European, ending with an exploration of Britain's relationship with Europe after 'Brexit' and the ensuing desperate wrangling for a deal with the EU.

Part III, 'People and Politics', examines how politics is organised and carried out. It explores voting behaviour and the systems used to elect representatives in the UK. It also examines the nature of political parties and ideology, and looks at how we participate – or don't participate – in the political process. It concludes with a discussion of how the media affects politics – including exploring the way in which new media (such as Facebook or Twitter) and traditional media (like newspapers) feed off one another.

Part IV, 'Politics and Policy-making', explores the policy-making process in more detail, setting out some of the theoretical approaches to policy and examining the framework in which it operates. It then explores some of the big policy questions the UK faces today: how to create a successful economy; provide welfare and public services; and protect the environment. It concludes with an exploration of foreign policy and an analysis of Britain's place in an increasingly globalised world.

There is never an ideal time to produce a new book on British politics – authors and publishers always risk being overtaken by events, particularly given the fast pace and unpredictable direction of recent changes discussed above. However, we have tried to more than simply update the text to include recent developments.

This book builds on the success of previous editions, but pays more attention to the changing nature of politics and society. This means that there is a greater focus on questions of gender, ethnicity, nationalism and other important forms of identity, as well as an attempt to show not only what political institutions have been, but also how they are changing. There is also a renewed focus on how mainstream politics in the UK has historically excluded certain groups, such as women and ethnic minorities.

It is always a challenge writing for a wide audience and this is particularly true of textbooks such as this one. We hope that this book is rewarding for all readers. For students who have studied British politics and history before, we hope that after the introductions, we have pushed the analysis far enough to challenge you.

At several points in the book, we have included links to videos on our website, where leading experts in the field give their perspectives on the issues discussed. We hope these sections challenge all readers. We include questions at the end, which are still the subject of debate in the academic community, and which we hope will stimulate further debate. We also link to wider reading if you want to go further. Many of these new pedagogic features are set out in the 'Tour of the Book', above, which introduces the book's various exciting new features. Inevitably, we can't please everyone, but we hope that there is enough here to introduce you to some of the most engaging and tricky questions in British politics.

For students who are unfamiliar with British politics, we have focused on making sure that the most important issues and debates are set out clearly and in an engaging and accessible way.

Bill Coxall and Lynton Robins deserve the credit for establishing this textbook. They wrote its predecessor, *Contemporary British Politics* (1989, 1994, 1998). Robert Leach took the lead in producing the fourth edition of *Contemporary British Politics* (2003) and the fully revamped text, *British Politics* (2006, 2011). Simon Griffiths and Robert have taken responsibility for this third edition. Many people have invested their time in making this book as good as it can be. We would both like to thank Niki Jayatunga, Lloyd Langman and Georgia Park at Palgrave, Maggie Lythgoe for her work copyediting the text, Elizabeth Evans for her helpful and careful comments across many chapters, and several anonymous reviewers who commented insightfully on all or parts of the draft script. Although any errors remain the authors' own, there are far fewer of them thanks to the help, support and advice of this group.

# ABBREVIATIONS

*Please note: these are some of the most frequently used abbreviations.*

| | | | |
|---|---|---|---|
| AMS | additional member system | NAO | National Audit Office |
| AV | alternative vote | NATO | North Atlantic Treaty Organization |
| BAME | black, Asian and minority ethnic | NEC | National Executive Committee (of the Labour Party) |
| BME | black and minority ethnic | | |
| CAP | Common Agricultural Policy | NHS | National Health Service |
| CBI | Confederation of British Industry | NPM | new public management |
| CCT | compulsory competitive tendering | NUM | National Union of Mineworkers |
| CND | Campaign for Nuclear Disarmament | OBR | Office of Budget Responsibility |
| Defra | Department for Environment, Food & Rural Affairs | ONS | Office for National Statistics |
| | | PAC | Public Accounts Committee |
| DSC | departmental select committees | PCA | Parliamentary Commissioner for Administration |
| DUP | Democratic Unionist Party (Northern Ireland) | | |
| | | PCT | primary care trust |
| GDP | gross domestic product | PFI | private finance initiative |
| EC | European Community | PLP | Parliamentary Labour Party |
| ECHR | European Convention on Human Rights | PMQs | Prime Minister's Questions |
| ECtHR | European Court of Human Rights | SCS | Senior Civil Service |
| ECSC | European Coal and Steel Community | SDLP | Social Democratic and Labour Party (Ireland) |
| EEC | European Economic Community | | |
| ERM | Exchange Rate Mechanism | SDP | Social Democratic Party |
| EU | European Union | SMP | single member plurality |
| FSA | Financial Services Authority | SNP | Scottish National Party |
| GLC | Greater London Council | STV | single transferable vote |
| IMF | International Monetary Fund | TUC | Trades Union Congress |
| IRA | Irish Republican Army | UK | United Kingdom |
| IS | 'Islamic State' | UKIP | United Kingdom Independence Party |
| LCC | London County Council | UN | United Nations |
| LGBT+ | lesbian, gay, bisexual, transgender | USA | United States of America |
| MEP | Member of the European Parliament | USSR | Union of Soviet Socialist Republics |
| MP | Member of Parliament | UUP | Ulster Unionist Party (Ireland) |
| MPC | Monetary Policy Committee | WMDs | weapons of mass destruction |
| MSP | Member of the Scottish Parliament | WTO | World Trade Organization |

# PART I

# FROM PAST TO PRESENT

Part I introduces you to the study of politics in the UK. We examine the history of politics in the UK from the Second World War onwards, arguing that it is impossible to understand contemporary politics without understanding the recent past. It ends by providing a snapshot of contemporary politics and society, and examining the diversity of the UK today.

1   The Study of British Politics
2   The Shadow of the Past I: From War to Welfare
3   The Shadow of the Past II: Thatcher and After
4   Life in Contemporary Britain

## POLITICS IN ACTION

In this video Simon Griffiths, one of the authors of this book, provides an overview of some of the key questions and themes in this Part.

Emily Robinson talks about some of the historical and social events that have shaped politics since 1945, and reflects on why such an understanding is useful for politics students today.

Watch the videos at **www.macmillanihe.com/griffiths-brit-pol-3e**

1

# 1

# THE STUDY OF BRITISH POLITICS

British politics seems to be in flux. In a BBC Radio 4 programme called *Tearing Up the Politics Textbook* (BBC, 2016a), political scientist Rosie Campbell asked: 'How should we understand this new landscape … And what should go in the new politics textbooks?' This book tries to answer some of those questions.

In the last two decades, British politics has entered a period of transformation and unpredictability. The uncodified British constitution, which for decades grew organically, has gone through more change in the past 20 years or so than any other stage. New, devolved parliaments and assemblies were created in Scotland, Wales and Northern Ireland, passing control of significant areas of policy over to the territories that make up the United Kingdom (UK). In 2014, Scotland voted on whether it wanted to remain a part of the UK at all. The answer was hardly a resounding 'yes' and the Scottish nationalists are pushing for a second vote.

Other constitutional changes have shaken politics in the UK. In 1999, the House of Lords ceased to be a hereditary body, whose members were mainly the sons of white, aristocratic families. The Human Rights Act incorporated the European Convention on Human Rights (ECHR) into UK law in 1998. Britain's relationship with the rest of the world is also changing. In 2016, the UK voted to leave the European Union, breaking the dominant approach to British foreign and economic policy for much of the previous half century.

Party politics also seems more volatile than ever. While 2017 appeared to be a return to normality, with Labour and the Conservatives dominating the general election, the result masks a long-term rise in multiparty politics within the UK. The Scottish National Party hold most of the seats north of the border, in both Scottish and Westminster elections. Voters are less wedded to the old parties. In 1900, 99% of voters in the general election supported one of the big three parties – the Conservatives, Labour or the Liberals. Over a century later, in 2005, this figure was almost unchanged: 94% of the population supported one of those parties or their contemporary successors. By the 2015 general election, however, that figure had fallen to 77%. Smaller parties squeezed out bigger ones. The United Kingdom Independence Party (UKIP) gained votes from the bigger parties, particularly in large parts of England and Wales. The Scottish National Party (SNP) all but wiped out the other parties in Scotland (BBC, 2016b), although they made something of a recovery in 2017.

The behaviour of electorates also seems to be becoming more unpredictable. In 2015, Jeremy Corbyn took over as leader of the Labour Party. Just weeks before his election he was 100/1 with some bookmakers to win the leadership. He set about taking a radically different approach to many of his predecessors; ignoring their lesson that elections are won from the centre, he offered a radical, populist manifesto at the 2017 general election that his critics argued would be a disaster and would force his resignation. Instead, Labour hugely increased its share of the popular vote and the number of seats cast. Politics in the UK has rarely been so surprising.

In this chapter, we examine some issues that will inform the rest of this book.

## THIS CHAPTER:

- » Asks what 'politics' is, and sets out some of the ways in which the term is used in this book.
- » Explores 'power' in British politics, and the related concepts of 'authority' and 'influence'.
- » Sets out some of the main views on 'democracy' – the power of the people – the principle on which our parliamentary system is now said to be based.
- » Looks ahead to some of the big issues in policy, such as how we end discrimination or promote social justice, run our public services, or conduct foreign policy, discussed later in the book.
- » Asks if it still makes sense to talk about something called 'British' politics, as opposed to local, regional or national politics, after all the changes of recent years.

## WHAT IS POLITICS?

Politics fascinates many people and the volatility of recent years makes it all the more interesting. The numbers of students studying the subject reflects this. Yet the fascination is far from universal. Colin Hay (2007), British academic, wrote *Why We Hate Politics*, in response to evidence among some sections of society of increasing apathy, alienation and disillusion from mainstream politicians and political parties. This alienation is disturbing, not least because the UK, along with most other countries in the world, claims to be a democracy, a system of government that requires a widespread degree of public political interest and involvement. (This is discussed further in Chapter 13.)

Perhaps we should not be surprised that politics inspires such contradictory feelings. The subject is bound up with controversy, which is one reason why it both attracts and repels. Some of this controversy will surround the current political issues facing the UK, which are often deeply divisive. Recent examples include an ongoing economic crisis, the decision to leave the European Union, terrorism and climate change, among many others. Other areas of controversy concern the mechanics of government and the political process, such as reforming the electoral system and parliament, or re-examining the relationship between the constituent nations of the UK. Some of it relates to deeper questions over ideas and values that have long exercised philosophers and political scientists: the distribution of political power, and the nature of politics itself, which is the subject of this chapter.

Before we begin to explore British politics in more detail, it would make sense to ask 'what is politics?' Various interpretations have been given (see Leftwich, 2004 and Heywood, 2013, Ch. 1 for good summaries). The answer we choose – from a focus on the mechanics of government to a study of power relations in British society – will inform what we consider the appropriate focus of this book.

## POLITICS AS THE STUDY OF THE STATE AND GOVERNMENT

The first interpretation of politics is derived from the word itself. 'Politics' is from the Ancient Greek word, *polis*, literally meaning city-state. Thus, politics is 'what concerns the *polis*' or in modern terms, the state. The study of politics from earliest times has focused largely on a unit of government called the 'state'.

---

*A state is a political and governmental unit – a compulsory association that is sovereign over a particular territory.*

---

States have differed considerably in geographical extent and population size over space and time, from the small 'city-states' of Ancient Greece, through more recent nation states and colonial empires, such as the British Empire, to the considerable variation in size and wealth of modern independent sovereign states. The state that is the focus of this book is the United Kingdom of Great Britain and Northern Ireland, one of 193 independent sovereign states that today are members of the United Nations (UN).

The term 'independent sovereign state' is commonly used to stress that the state has supreme (or sovereign) power within its own borders, and no external power can interfere in its internal affairs. No particular system of government is implied – it can be a hereditary monarchy, a military dictatorship or a representative democracy.

Max Weber (1991, p. 78), German sociologist, argued at the end of the First World War that: 'The state is a human community that (successfully) claims the monopoly of the legitimate use of physical force within a given territory.' Without this exclusive right to employ force, individuals and groups could take the law into their own hands with impunity, leading to lawless chaos; countries where this is the case are often termed 'failed states'. Weber also stresses that the force is legitimate (or lawful). This may mean simply that the state is widely accepted as legitimate and acts within the law that it has itself established. In the UK, it is only the state that can, after due process, imprison

us (or, until the 1960s, even execute us) if we have broken the state law. In practice, even states established through violent usurpation or conquest – including the United States – often acquire legitimacy over time, through the acquiescence or willing acceptance of their subjects and through their acceptance by the governments of other states.

Under this view, therefore, politics is the study of the state and government. This interpretation makes its way into our everyday use of the term: people are said to be 'in politics' if they hold public office. Indeed, it can sometimes narrow to a simple equation of politics with party politics. While MPs are in politics, a common criticism of the Civil Service or judiciary made by politicians is that they are getting 'too involved in politics' (an issue we discuss in Chapters 8 and 9). Academic study is more likely to acknowledge the political role of these state actors, with a focus on the institutions and process associated with government or government policy. These are, of course, all legitimate subjects for academic study, and are an important part of this book.

However, 'British politics' is surely broader than the study of the British state or its government. This definition implies that politics is a rather remote activity, distinct from the lives, activities and input of ordinary people. How far does politics include the governed as well as those doing the governing? Although the state and government are important, this understanding of politics is too narrow for our interpretation of British politics in this book.

## POLITICS AS THE STUDY OF PUBLIC AFFAIRS

A second, broader view interprets politics as public affairs. As such, British politics is not limited to the study of the British state or what goes on in government, but involves all of 'public life'. This implicitly contrasts the public sphere with the private sphere. It leads to an immediate question. Where should the distinction between public and private be made?

Some liberals and conservatives would draw a clear distinction between the state and civil society. This contrasts a public or political sphere and a private sphere of life from which politics should be excluded, for example the family, private business and other voluntary clubs and associations. The Wolfenden Report, which was published in 1957 and paved the way for the decriminalisation of homosexual acts in England, implicitly drew on this distinction, arguing that: 'It is not, in our view, the function of the law to intervene in the private life of citizens.' Champions of the free market would also seek to exclude politics from much economic activity, and place firm limits on government intervention.

Drawing this neat line of distinction has been controversial. Many feminists, for example, have objected that the equation of politics with 'public affairs' ignores the impact of politics in our private lives. They have argued that 'the personal is political'. They are not just concerned with formal legal equality in the public sphere, but with gender relations in the family, home and bedroom, because these are seen as central to the types of injustice and oppression suffered by women. Consequently, personal and sexual relations and the division of labour within the home are not purely private matters but a legitimate sphere for political engagement. The hard distinction therefore between a public political world and a private non-political one excludes many

*Source*: iStock.com/violinconcertono3

For feminists, in particular, politics is understood broadly, to include both personal and public life.

personal issues that are within the scope of politics, as we understand it in this book.

## POLITICS AS A PROCESS OF COMPROMISE

A third, rather different account of politics argues that it is about compromise. This conception of politics is less interested in the *arena* of politics – the state or the public sphere, for example – and more in the way in which politics is conducted. Under this view, politics is seen as a means of resolving conflict, through compromise, and reaching a peaceful resolution. To the British Conservative politician 'Rab' Butler (1971), politics was 'the art of the possible'. Butler hints at the constraints involved in the political process. Compromise is often necessary because different sections of the community want different and often conflicting things. Thus, political decisions commonly produce winners and losers. Bernard Crick (1993), British socialist political scientist, made a similar argument in his book, *In Defence of Politics*, originally published in 1962, which focused on the necessity of compromise.

This definition of politics is also found in our everyday use. For example, Jeremy Corbyn (BBC News, 2017a) argued that military action was not the answer to the crisis in Syria and called for a 'political solution'. However, this account of politics is, to some degree, limited to parliamentary democracies like the UK, with free elections and multiple political parties. Clearly, an account of politics that excludes any state which does not meet such standards cannot be a far-reaching one. However, Crick's argument is a useful reminder that politics is about processes of reaching decisions, as well as the study of the state or the public sphere, for example. The focus on process is an element of the view of politics we draw on in this book.

## POLITICS AS THE STUDY OF POWER

A fourth, much broader account equates politics with power. This view is associated with radical French philosopher Michel Foucault ([1975] 1991). Under this interpretation, politics is not confined to a particular arena – the government, the state or the 'public' realm – or a process, such as compromise. It takes place in our social interactions with families and friends, as much as it does in our dealings with government. This interpretation has found its way into common use too. People often talk about 'the politics of the boardroom' or the 'lecture hall'. A lecturer standing at the front of a room is in a position of power. However, under this view, politics becomes conflated with the study of power relations in society. It raises the question, what is distinctive about *political* activity compared to any other form of social behaviour?

A useful, workable definition of the term 'politics' comes from Harold Lasswell (1936), American political scientist, who defined the subject as the study of 'who gets what, when, how'. This concise definition suggests that politics is about choosing between different possibilities. Individuals, communities and governments must determine their priorities – they cannot have everything they want. Politics is therefore about conflict, but it is also about the distribution of scarce resources. Politics is not only about the struggle for those scarce resources, but also an analysis of the process of getting them. We return to Lasswell's question (who gets what, when and how?) at various points in this book.

## POWER IN BRITISH POLITICS

Politics is clearly in part about power, but this key concept is difficult to define. Power suggests a capacity to achieve desired results and compel obedience. It may be lawful or unlawful. An armed criminal may force his victims to do things they would not choose to do. He is clearly exercising power, although unlawfully. Others, such as a government minister or a judge, may also wield effective power, but power that is generally recognised as lawful. (For a classic analysis of power, see Lukes (1974 [2005]), discussed in more detail in Ch. 18.)

*Source*: Getty Images/Vetta/Clerkenwell

If politics is about power, then many everyday situations, from lectures to relationships, are 'political'.

The term authority is widely used to describe the rightful use of political power, or legitimate power. Power may compel obedience, while authority is widely accepted by those over whom it is exercised. We voluntarily obey those in authority because we accept the legitimacy of their power. Max Weber asked many of these questions (discussed further in Key Figures 1.1).

Power is sometimes also distinguished from influence. While power implies a capacity to determine outcomes directly, influence suggests the ability to shape outcomes indirectly, to exert pressure on those who are taking the decisions, persuading them to change their opinion and behaviour. The study of politics therefore involves examining not just the formal institutions and offices directly involved in government, but also the influences on government and the policy process, including, for example, the role of business organisations and trade unions, religious sects, voluntary bodies and cause groups. Many policy decisions taken by politicians or civil servants may have their origin and explanation in the successful influence of groups outside government (see Chapter 18, pp. 379–81).

---

**Power** *is the capacity to achieve desired goals.*

---

**Authority** *is the rightful or legitimate use of power.*

---

**Influence** *involves the ability to shape a decision or outcome through various forms of pressure.*

---

# KEY FIGURES 1.1
## Max Weber

**Max Weber (1864–1920)**, German sociologist, asked why we choose to obey those in authority. He argued that it was because we accept the legitimacy of their power. He distinguished between three main types or sources of authority: traditional, charismatic and legal-rational:

» *Traditional authority* rests on long established custom – the authority of a tribal chief or hereditary monarch, for example.

» *Charismatic authority* derives from the compelling personal qualities of an individual – the authority exercised by a Napoleon, Hitler or (more positively) Nelson Mandela. They are obeyed because of *who* they are, rather than *what* they are.

» *Legal-rational authority* is based on formal rules. An elected politician or appointed government official may be obeyed, not because of custom, nor because of their personal qualities, but because it is acknowledged that they legitimately hold their office under accepted rules and procedures. It is the office or post rather than the person occupying it whose authority is obeyed.

Weber considered that legal-rational authority is the characteristic form of authority in the modern world. Both modern bureaucracy, such as that embodied by the UK's Civil Service, and representative democracy involve legal-rational authority.

## DEMOCRACY: POWER TO THE PEOPLE?

Britain, along with most states in the modern western world, and many others elsewhere, claims to be a democracy. This near universal approval of democracy as a system of government is relatively recent. A form of democracy had flourished in the small city-state of Ancient Athens nearly 2,500 years ago, where direct rule by the people themselves (or at least those men who were not slaves) was just about possible. However, with the emergence of extensive empires and larger nation states, democracy was regarded as a remote and essentially impractical system of government.

*Democracy is a term derived from Ancient Greek to mean the rule or power of the people. 'Our constitution is called a democracy because power is in the hands not of a minority but of the whole people' (Pericles of Athens, 431 BCE, as reported in Thucydides' History of the Peloponnesian War [5th century BCE] 1972, p. 145).*

Democracy became more feasible with the development in the nineteenth century of the idea of **representative democracy**, that is government by the elected representatives of the people, rather than **direct democracy**, or government by the people themselves (such as had existed in Ancient Athens). It is representative democracy rather than direct democracy that has become the approved system of government over much of the modern world, although some advocate extending direct citizen participation in the political process beyond voting, infusing representative democracy with elements of direct democracy.

Democracy may have become widely approved, but it has often been accorded only faint praise by some influential modern thinkers and politicians. Whether modern representative democracy does ensure real government 'by the people', as Abraham Lincoln asserted, is far from clear. Indeed, it does not even invariably result in a government chosen by the majority of the people. Yet despite their limitations, mature democracies do offer an element of real choice between rival parties and programmes, divergences of opinion and a process of resolving dispute that renders opposition respectable rather than treasonable, as well as providing for the peaceful transfer of power between governments (as Crick, 1993, argued).

*Representative democracy involves indirect government by the people through representatives elected by the people. In 1863, in his Gettysburg Address, US President Abraham Lincoln defined democracy as 'government of the people, by the people, for the people'.*

*Direct democracy involves the direct and continuous participation of citizens in government, for example, through regular referendums.*

While the British like to think they invented modern representative democracy, the Americans and the French have a rather better claim. Britain only came to terms with democracy rather later (as shown in Timeline 1.1). Although England boasts an ancient Parliament with over 700 years of near continuous existence since it was established in 1265, even the lower house of that Parliament, the House of Commons, was not democratically elected until recently. Even today, it is questionable how far Britain satisfies all the conditions to qualify as a full and fair system of representative democracy (see Spotlight 1.1).

### Timeline 1.1 The emergence of democracy in Britain

| Date | Event | Implications for democracy |
|---|---|---|
| 1776 | Declaration of Independence by American rebels against the British state and crown | Creation of the first modern democracy, although voting limited by gender and race |
| 1789 | French Revolution | Replaced (initially only briefly) the autocratic monarchic system with the ideas of popular sovereignty and liberty, equality and fraternity |
| 19th century | Reform Acts in Britain | Extended the vote to most men |
| 1918 | Representation of the People Act in Britain | Women over the age of 30, who met minimum property qualifications, gained the right to vote |
| 1928 | Extension of the Representation of the People Act in Britain | All women over the age of 21 could vote, equalling the terms for men |

## Conditions for representative democracy       1.1

» Full adult franchise: all adults have the right to vote

» A secret ballot: helps ensure voting without intimidation or bribery

» Regular elections: governments and parliaments must not be able to postpone elections

» Fair elections: each vote should count equally

» An effective choice of candidates and parties for voters

» A level playing field between rival parties and candidates contesting elections

» A free and diverse media enabling a wide expression of views

## POWER IN THE UK

It would be generally conceded that elections in the UK do involve a choice and that they are not patently rigged (as they are in some countries). Yet, regardless of the extent of the right to vote and the mechanics of the electoral system, there are many who would question whether 'government of the people, by the people, for the people' is a reality in Britain. Are the elected representatives of the people the real rulers of Britain? Do these elected representatives really serve the interests of the people, or simply their own interests? If Britain is a democracy that, in theory, gives power to the many, not the few, how far do ordinary people have any real control or influence over those who govern them?

Voting offers only a limited choice. Those who bother to use their vote in a general election may determine which of the rival teams of politicians occupy government posts for the next five years, but does this give voters significant influence over key government decisions and policies? What other opportunities do citizens have to participate in the political process? How far can 'ordinary people' hope to have a real voice in the many decisions that affect them?

Do elected politicians make the real decisions that affect the British people? Perhaps the real decision-makers are not the politicians who tend to dominate the news but relatively faceless civil servants or advisers (discussed in Chapter 8). Alternatively, more real power and influence may be exercised by individuals who are not part of the formal political process at all – businessmen (and they are usually still men), bankers, or owners of newspapers, television companies and other media, some of whom may not even be British. Newspapers and magazines sometimes attempt to compile lists of the most powerful people in Britain. These may generally be headed by the prime minister, as one might expect, but often include prominent businesspeople, media magnates, appointed officials, even sports personalities and pop idols, interspersed among some other elected politicians. Such lists are hardly scientific and may reflect little more than the highly subjective views of the journalists who compose them. However, they do suggest that power is dispersed more widely than those who hold some formal position in government.

One cynical conclusion might be that 'money talks'; those with substantial wealth and income can use it to buy (sometimes literally) political influence. Yet there is no simple correlation between wealth and power. Newspapers also sometimes list the wealthiest people in Britain, but some of the names near the top of such lists, such as the Duke of Westminster or the Queen, do not figure prominently, if at all, in the lists of those with power. Celebrities, such as footballers or pop stars, may avoid any formal association with politics and lack significant economic power, but could still have enormous influence as role models for behaviour, and perhaps contribute more to changing political attitudes on key issues than professional

*Source*: BEN STANSALL/AFP/Getty Images
Where does power lie in the UK? Critics of capitalism have argued that the multinational corporations, and in particular the financial sector, hold too much power in the UK.

politicians. Yet again, it are possible that real power and influence are exercised by many who are not celebrities – 'faceless bureaucrats' or anonymous figures, global capitalists perhaps – pulling strings behind the scenes.

However, this whole approach may make too much of the power of particular individuals. Ministers and company chairs come and go, but the organisations they head generally last much longer. Perhaps we should be looking at the power of institutions or corporate power. Perhaps the Civil Service, the financial centre of the City of London or multinational corporations exercise far more effective power and influence in the British political process than any single personality. Alternatively, power may not lie with particular institutions but with more amorphous **elites**, such as **the ruling class** or **the establishment**, or interests around 'big business' or 'global capitalism'. Those

who hold formal positions of power, such as elected politicians, are perhaps driven by interests outside their control. Indeed, this kind of argument has been made with great success in recent years by Nigel Farage, when he was leader of UKIP, and Donald Trump in his successful campaign to become president of the USA. Both men presented themselves as outsiders who would take on the 'elite' who ran 'the establishment'.

---

An **elite** *is a small dominant group. Elite theorists argue that power is inevitably exercised by the few (or by an elite or elites), even in nominally democratic organisations or states.*

---

The **ruling class** *is a term used particularly by Marxists to describe those who own and control capital, and whose economic power gives them political power.*

*The establishment is a term sometimes used to describe the British elite, an unaccountable dominant social group largely educated at leading private schools and ancient universities.*

Alternatively, we can seek to identify those who are effectively excluded from power. Thus, it is often suggested that certain groups or interests might be marginalised in the political system – the unemployed, ethnic minorities, teenagers, women, or those who live and work in the countryside. Entire groups may be excluded from the political process.

All this implies that power may be rather, or very, unevenly distributed. Some, perhaps a small minority, appear to have a great deal of power, others relatively little influence, while others again may be virtually excluded from any effective participation in the decisions that affect their lives. Yet, while *elitism* suggests that political power is narrowly concentrated, *pluralism* implies that ordinary people do have the capacity to influence and even determine key outcomes, in accordance with notions of democracy.

*Elitism suggests power is substantially concentrated in the hands of an elite or ruling class.*

*Pluralism involves the belief that power is widely dispersed through society.*

The distribution of power may also change over time. Journalist Anthony Sampson wrote a series of books examining power in Britain, the first in 1962, the last in 2005. He suggested that over that period some institutions, such as trade unions and universities, had lost influence, while the media had become more important than ever. He thought power had become more centralised and the prime minister and the Treasury more dominant, while the Cabinet and the civil service were less influential. Looking back with a more sceptical eye, Sampson (2005, p. xii) had become 'more impatient and intolerant of the humbug and deceptions of democracy', which is, of course, only one person's view and not necessarily right. Moreover, he died before the financial and economic crises of 2007 onwards and the

2010 coalition government that might have suggested further changes in the distribution of power and influence in Britain.

## WHO RULES BRITAIN? PERSPECTIVES ON POWER

The question, 'Who then rules Britain?' is a simple one, to which a variety of simple answers may be given: Cabinet or prime ministerial government; parliamentary sovereignty; an elected dictatorship; government by bureaucracy; business or corporate power; an 'establishment' or 'ruling class'; men. All these answers, and others besides, have some plausibility and are worth serious consideration. Yet, although it is certainly possible to provide a wealth of relevant information and analysis that should help towards an appreciation of who rules Britain, it should be acknowledged right away that it is impossible ultimately to give an authoritative and definitive answer to the question. Those answers that are given inevitably reflect different interpretations of the facts, contrasting perspectives on politics and varied underlying ideological assumptions.

The term 'model' is often used in social science to describe a simplified version of reality. We try to make sense of a wide range of possibly relevant information by constructing simple hypotheses about the relationship between key variables, and see how far the real world fits the resulting models. Some simple models of the possible distribution of power in society are shown in Table 1.1. The crucial question is how far power is dispersed or concentrated in the political system, but the different models also provide alternative explanations of the institutions and mechanisms involved.

These are not the only possible models and, indeed, different names or versions of these models may be encountered elsewhere. Moreover, not all the models are mutually exclusive. 'Pluralism', 'liberal capitalism' or 'liberal democracy' are the names often given to a composite version of the first three models listed in Table 1.1, suggesting a model where power is dispersed through a mixture of elections, the free market and the influence of group interests on the policy process. Certainly, these institutions and processes can be seen as playing a mutually reinforcing role. Yet they

Table 1.1 Competing models of possible power distributions

| Name of model | Key players | Power | Evidence | Thinkers |
|---|---|---|---|---|
| Representative democracy model | Individual voters through the ballot box | Dispersed | Formal political mechanisms, electoral system, written constitutions | Bentham, John Stuart Mill |
| Market model | Individual consumers and producers through the free market | Dispersed | Classical economic assumptions: evidence of working of the market | Adam Smith, Hayek, Friedman |
| Pluralist model | Pressure groups and parties | Relatively dispersed | Influence of groups in case studies of decision-making | Bentley, Truman, Dahl, **neopluralists** (e.g. Lindblom) |
| Elitist model | Elites: social, business, military, or bureaucratic | Concentrated | Reputation of key figures and their interrelations | Pareto, Mosca, Michels, Wright Mills |
| Marxist model | Ruling class, 'bourgeoisie' in a capitalist society | Highly concentrated | Distribution of income and wealth: working of capitalist system | Marx, Lenin, Trotsky, Gramsci, Ralph Miliband |

also reflect different and sometimes competing perspectives. Some old-fashioned liberals (or those on the modern New Right) place far more emphasis on the free market than the verdict of the ballot box, particularly if that leads to interference with free-market forces. Similarly, they may fear that group influences represent selfish sectional interests and illegitimate power that may distort the market. While pluralists assume a role for elections and representative institutions, they regard these as only providing a limited, occasional and blunt instrument for popular political participation, and place more emphasis on the continuous influence of countless pressure groups on the policy process.

---

**Neopluralism** *is a modified version of pluralism, which still emphasises the dispersal of power while acknowledging the influence of key interests (e.g. business).*

---

How persuasive are these models? Which is the most convincing? The obvious answer is to look at the evidence, but the problem here

is that each model begins from rather different assumptions, employs different methodologies and looks at different sorts of evidence. The representative government model largely assumes that political power lies where the constitution, laws and other official documents say it does, so here it is important to examine the theory and practice of the key institutions. The market model derives its key assumptions from classical economics. It is countless individual producers and consumers operating through the market who determine the crucial questions of 'who gets what, when, how'. The role of politics in this economic process is (and, they argue, should be) strictly limited, as government intervention can only distort the operation of the free market and lead to a less efficient allocation of resources. Evidence in support of these assumptions comes from analyses of market forces and government intervention in practice. Pluralists cite case studies in decision-making to demonstrate the role of large numbers of different groups in the political process. Elitists, by contrast, identify key individuals or groups who dominate decision-making in their communities. Marxists, finally, infer political power from economic power. They document the massive inequalities in income and wealth in modern capitalist society and assume that it is those who control the means of production who will also control the political process.

At this point, a reader coming to the study of politics for the first time might ask: 'Is this description or prescription? Political science or ideology?' The answer is, inevitably, both. While writers on politics may conscientiously strive to provide an accurate picture of the way in which the political process actually operates, they are inevitably influenced by their own fundamental assumptions, and sometimes also by their ideals. Marx believed he was providing a dispassionate analysis of the underlying forces within capitalism, but it is difficult to divorce this analysis entirely from his condemnation of capitalism and hopes for a future socialist revolution. Marx (*Theses on Feuerbach* XI, in Tucker, 1978) wrote: 'The philosophers have only interpreted the world ... the point, however, is to change it.' There is a similar mixture of analysis and prescription among modern free marketeers. Like Marx, they too want to change the world, although in a quite different direction. Moreover, while much of the debate between pluralists and elitists apparently involves dispassionate social scientific research into the distribution of power, most of those involved are also defending or advancing theories of democracy, and implicitly or explicitly criticising or defending the processes they describe.

## Policy: Who Gets What, When, How?

The academic discipline of politics has previously concentrated on political ideas, institutions and processes, but often neglected the decisions, policies and outcomes that are the product of the political system. Yet it is through policies that politicians try to implement their values and priorities. Thus, it is almost impossible to understand British conservatism without examining some of the policies that Conservative politicians have pursued and continue to do so under the current government of Theresa May. How policies are made tells us

much about the political system in action (see Chapter 18). Where did the initiative come from? Who influenced the policy process and affected the outcome? How far did wider public opinion play a part? How was the policy implemented? How far did the policy meet its proclaimed objectives? What explanations can be offered for its apparent success or failure? Who ultimately gained and who lost? Some of the answers to these questions may provide suggestive clues to the distribution of political power and influence.

Questions about who gets what, when and how are also related to issues of equality and social justice. Whole communities within the general population, including women, ethnic minorities, faith groups, the disabled, gays and others, may be more systematically excluded from power and a share of general prosperity as a result of blatant or more subtle forms of discrimination, injustice and prejudice. The proposed remedies often reflect not only alternative values, but different perspectives on the nature of the problem.

The question of who gets what, when and how is also affected when some of the most important areas of policy may be subject to forces partially or substantially outside the control of domestic politics. Commonly, governments are judged by how they manage the economy. While they claim credit for the good times, they often blame economic disasters on global circumstances outside their control, as with the ongoing economic crisis, which stemmed from a global financial crisis in 2007–08. Opposition politicians naturally take a different view, condemning the government for their mismanagement. Apportioning responsibility is not easy. Apparent success may be due as much to good luck as good judgement, with the converse applying to failure. Yet even in an increasingly globalised economy, governments by their actions or inactions can help or hinder national prosperity (see Chapter 19).

Public services such as health and education are now at the centre of political debate in Britain. Upon the quality of these services depends an important element of the quality of life of individuals and communities. Poor education in schools, colleges and universities ultimately affects everyone, not just the unfortunate recipients. Thus, it has long been recognised that such services cannot be left to the free market. Yet how far the state should intervene, the level of service and the method of control, delivery and finance of services remain acutely controversial (see Chapter 20).

Can governments eradicate poverty? If the rich are getting richer, is that necessarily a bad thing? How far is it the role of government to promote equality and social justice? Such questions are at the centre of debate between socialists, liberals and conservatives, and the answers depend inevitably on ideological assumptions as well as economic analysis. Yet the relative poverty of some can affect people generally, obviously from the payment of taxes to fund social security benefits, less directly from the possible knock-on effects on national economic prosperity, health, education and crime. Child poverty, the problems of low income and one-parent families, rundown housing estates and deprived urban areas are problems that successive British governments have tried to tackle in different ways.

Foreign policy manifestly has causes and consequences beyond national boundaries. While Britain has not been involved in a major war since 1945, British troops have been engaged in active combat in (among other places) Korea, the South Atlantic, the Persian Gulf, Kosovo, Afghanistan and Iraq. Britain's membership of the North Atlantic Treaty Organization (NATO), a military alliance initially covering the leading states of North America and Western Europe, has determined much of its foreign policy. There has also been a tension between the 'special relationship' with the USA, on the one hand, and ties with nearer neighbours in the European Union (EU) on the other. A more fundamental problem, however, for Britain and other advanced capitalist countries are the gross and intensifying differences in living standards across the world, which could now threaten a political explosion.

However, it is no longer only the threat of violent conflict between the 'haves' and the 'have nots' that now endangers the future of the planet. The relationship of humankind with its environment has only been widely recognised as a serious issue in relatively recent times, but for some this has become the supreme political problem facing this country and the world generally. Finite resources are being used up, and various forms of environmental pollution threaten irreversible changes to soil, seas and climate. At best, future generations may suffer a heavy burden from our extravagance. At worst, our planet could be heading for catastrophe. The rising scepticism of current politicians in many cases, particularly many members of the Trump administration in the USA, elected in 2016, about human responsibility for global warming in the face of scientific evidence makes this considerably more likely. The politics of the environment has added a new dimension to ethical and political debate (see Chapter 21).

## 'BRITISH' POLITICS

This is a book that focuses primarily on British politics. This may appear unduly narrow and insular, particularly in the light of the discussion in the previous section, which raises some questions about the whole future of independent sovereign states in circumstances of increasing globalisation. If many of the problems facing us are substantially global, surely we should be focusing our attention on global politics, rather than the institutions, processes and policies of a single state?

There is still much to be said for the in-depth study of a particular political system, either in parallel or prior to other studies. This helps to explain the special characteristics of British politics, and the interdependence of features of the British political system as a whole. Moreover, a close study of British politics does not preclude the study of comparative politics, international relations and global politics. Thus, while this book, as the title suggests, focuses on British politics, it is not wholly confined to Britain, partly because much of politics in Britain is influenced by wider forces, including globalisation.

Specific aspects of British government and politics can only be appreciated in comparison with practices elsewhere. Both the similarities and the differences with other states can be instructive. It is, for example, helpful to discuss the system of voting in Britain, its advantages and disadvantages, and proposals for reform, with reference to voting systems in other countries (see Chapter 13). In this book there will be frequent references to politics and government in other countries, some in Comparing British Politics boxes. Of course, none of this can be a substitute for a systematic analysis of comparative politics, but it may perhaps help foster an interest in other political systems, as well as setting British political institutions and practices in a broader context.

Needless to say, the level at which decisions should be taken is often an acutely controversial political question. Some fear British national sovereignty is being eroded and British citizens are losing control of decisions that affect them, while others seek to devolve power downwards to the nations, regions and localities within the UK or even to break away, as many Scottish nationalists hope to do. If these hopes or fears are fully realised, this could even mark the end of British politics as it has traditionally been understood.

Indeed, the very term 'Britain' and the notion of 'British politics' is itself increasingly contested (Davies, 2000, pp. 853–86). The official name of the state (since 1922) is the United Kingdom of Great Britain and Northern Ireland, often described more simply as the United Kingdom or by the acronym UK. This book tends to follow convention and uses 'British Politics' as shorthand for the politics of the entire UK, although we recognise this is problematic at times. Where we refer to matters in a part of the UK, we try and make that explicit. Northern Ireland remains part of the UK, although its inhabitants remain fiercely divided in their political allegiance. A narrow majority insist they are 'British', often rather more passionately than most people who live across the Irish Sea in Great Britain. A large minority consider themselves Irish rather than British, and wish to belong to the Irish Republic rather than remain within the UK or British state. The remarkable power-sharing agreement, signed in 1999 between republicans (who wish Northern Ireland to be part of a wider Irish state) and unionists (who want to remain a part of the UK), provides grounds for optimism that whatever transpires need not involve further bloodshed and violence, although the frequent difficulty that both sides have in working together since then leads to caution. The political future of Northern Ireland

remains acutely controversial, particularly after Theresa May's controversial deal with the Democratic Unionist Party after the 2017 general election (discussed in Chapter 3). These difficulties are discussed in more detail in Chapter 11.

Even without the long-running problem of Northern Ireland, the future of Britain and the British state is an increasingly open question. England is the largest of the constituent parts of Britain in territory and by far the largest in population. Many of those who live in England describe themselves almost interchangeably as 'English' or 'British', a confusion that can infuriate those who live in Scotland or Wales. Wales was absorbed by the English Crown in the Middle Ages and was formally politically united with England in 1536. Scotland was an independent state until King James VI of Scotland became also James I of England in 1603, although this Union of the Crowns did not involve full political union until 1707. The notion of a British state and the image of 'Britannia' effectively date from then. Some inhabitants of Scotland and Wales consider themselves to be both Scots or Welsh and British. Others consider themselves primarily or exclusively Scots or Welsh, and a significant minority, particularly in Scotland, would prefer to be part of an independent country (see Chapter 11). Indeed, some have long forecast the imminent 'breakup of Britain' (Nairn, 1981, 2000).

The 'breakup of Britain' has become rather more likely since the Scottish National Party (SNP) gained power in Scotland in 2007 (first as a minority administration and since 2011 with a majority of seats in the Scottish Parliament). They delivered on their promise of a referendum in Scotland for full independence in 2014, which resulted in a relatively narrow victory for those voters who wanted to remain part of the UK. The continuing dominance of the SNP in Scottish politics makes possible a second referendum on Scottish independence in the next few years. Meanwhile, Plaid Cymru, the Welsh nationalist party, became the second largest party in the Welsh Assembly after Labour in 2016. If the majority of those in Scotland and/or Wales clearly wished to be part of a separate state, it would be impossible to maintain the union. 'Britain' would no longer exist as a meaningful political entity, although it would probably survive as a useful geographical term to describe the island. 'British politics' would be confined to the history books, to be replaced by the study of English (or Scottish or Welsh) politics.

Yet, for the present, 'British politics' remains a convenient shorthand term to describe politics and government at various levels inside the UK, and the growing two-way influences between the UK and other levels of government, including – for the time being – European and international. This is sometimes described as **multi-level governance**. While many of the crucial decisions that affect British citizens are still resolved within Britain's central government around Whitehall and Westminster, others are effectively taken elsewhere. Some decisions are made above the level of the British state; for example, by the UN,

the International Monetary Fund, the World Trade Organization, NATO or (especially) the EU. Other decisions are taken below the level of the central UK government based in Whitehall and Westminster, by devolved parliaments and assemblies (see Chapter 11) or local councils (see Chapter 10). Even with Britain's planned withdrawal from the EU, British politics is increasingly multilayered. Pressure for the breakup of Britain and an unknown future outside the EU make British politics more unpredictable than ever before.

---

*Multi-level governance is the idea that there are many interacting authority structures at work in the emergent global political economy and that domestic and international levels of authority are entangled.*

---

## SUMMARY

» Politics involves far more than government and party politics. It is about power and decision-making that affect all our lives and determine how scarce resources are allocated – 'who gets what, when, how'.

» There are disagreements over the legitimate scope of politics. Some distinguish between a public or political sphere and a private sphere, between the state and 'civil society'. Others would deny that politics can or should be excluded from many areas previously considered private.

» Although politics is clearly about power, this is difficult to define and measure. A distinction can be drawn between power and authority (or legitimate power). Those without formal power may still have influence over decisions that affect them.

» Britain is called a representative democracy, implying that the people or the majority have effective influence over government and over decisions that affect them. Britain satisfies most of the conditions commonly laid down for representative democracy.

» There is disagreement over the distribution in power in Britain. Some argue that it is effectively concentrated in the hands of the

few, others that it is widely dispersed. Theories or 'models' of power reflect conflicting underlying assumptions and look at different kinds of evidence.

» Although politics is about the conflicting interests of different social or ethnic groups, it is also about ideas. Political differences commonly reflect contrasting underlying ideological assumptions.

» Many crucial political decisions that affect people in Britain are made both above and below the level of the British state, for example by international institutions, the EU, devolved governments in Scotland, Wales and Northern Ireland, local councils and other public bodies. There is no longer a single British government, but rather a complex system of multi-level governance. However, most British citizens are still principally affected by political decisions made in Westminster and Whitehall.

» The very future of British government and politics is now uncertain, particularly as a result of increased support for Scottish, Welsh and Irish nationalism within the UK, which could lead either to a quasi-federal or fully federal system of government, or the end of the union.

## QUESTIONS FOR DISCUSSION

» What is politics? Why do many people seem to show distaste for politics? Or are people 'fed up' with politicians or the political process?

» Should we distinguish between a political (or public) sphere and a private sphere from which politics should be excluded?

» What do you understand by democracy? How far is Britain a democracy?

» Who governs Britain? Where does power lie in Britain? Is power highly concentrated in the hands of the few, or relatively widely dispersed?

» Is political change driven by ideas and principles, or by economic and social change?

» Is it possible, or desirable, to take such issues as education, health, defence or law and order out of politics?

» Does it still make sense to study British politics, particularly when the British state is apparently in the process of being eroded from above and below?

 ## FURTHER READING

The first chapter of Heywood's (2013) *Politics* addresses the question 'What is Politics?' It includes a particularly useful brief discussion of power. There is also a brief discussion of alternative views on the nature of politics in Leach and Lightfoot (2018, pp. x–xx), *The Politics and IR Companion*. The same subject is treated in more depth from different perspectives by several authors in Leftwich (ed.) (2004) *What is Politics?*

Older classic texts include Lasswell (1936) *Politics: Who Gets What, When, How?* and Crick (1993) *In Defence of Politics*, which is thought-provoking, if a little idiosyncratic. French political scientist Duverger's *The Study of Politics* (1972) is still worth reading. Arblaster (1987) provides a readable short introduction to *Democracy*. Macpherson's almost as brief *The Life and Times of Liberal Democracy* (1977) might also be consulted. Fuller and more ambitious is Held (1987) *Models of Democracy*.

The distribution of power in Britain is, inevitably, a controversial subject. One readable personal view is provided by Sampson (2005) *Who Runs This Place?*, the last of a series of studies of the 'Anatomy of Britain' which he began in 1962. For a more theoretical discussion of power, see Lukes ([1974] 2005). Classic texts on participation and representation are also worth reading, notably, Carole Pateman *Participation and Democratic Theory* (1970) and Hanna Pitkin, *The Concept of Representation* (1967).

Dunleavy and O'Leary's (1987) *Theories of the State* provides a clear account of most of the models of power (pluralism, elitism, Marxism, etc.) briefly described in this chapter.

On the issues around the widespread current disillusionment with politics and democracy, there are two provocative prizewinning books: Stoker (2017) *Why Politics Matters* and Hay (2007) *Why We Hate Politics*.

 ## USEFUL WEBSITES

The Political Studies Association exists to develop and promote the study of politics in the UK. It also blogs on many issues on the study of British politics: www.psa.ac.uk.

*Tearing Up the Politics Textbooks*, Rosie Campbell's programme referred to at the start of this chapter, can be heard at: www.bbc.co.uk/programmes/b07w9km7.

 *Further student resources to support learning are available at*
**www.macmillanihe.com/griffiths-brit-pol-3e**

# 2    THE SHADOW OF THE PAST I: FROM WAR TO WELFARE

A country's politics is shaped by its history. Key features of the British system of government examined in this book are centuries old. The monarchy dates back to the tenth century, Parliament to the thirteenth century and Cabinet government and the post of prime minister to the eighteenth century. Although none operate in the same way as they did in the eighteenth or nineteenth centuries, Britain retains a monarchy, a prime minister, a Cabinet and two Houses of Parliament. British politics, as it is today, is only understandable through understanding the context in which it emerged (see Comparing British Politics 2.1).

In this chapter and Chapter 3 we focus on the evolution of British politics from the Second World War. The recent political history of the UK is worth examining. First, although the Second World War is beginning to fade from living memory, it had a massive and lasting impact on British society, economy and politics. Many of the practices and institutions that survive to this day, such as the National Health Service (NHS) and the welfare state, were the product of the immediate postwar years. And while these have been greatly reformed since their conception, the legacy of their creation can still be seen in the way they work today. The worldview of many contemporary politicians, including Theresa May and Jeremy Corbyn, was also shaped in the postwar world.

Second, the historical view is worth examining because an appreciation of the recent history of British politics also shows us that things do not have to be the way they are. The institutions we examine in this book are the result of contingency rather than inevitability. Had the factors that shaped our current society come together differently, we would not be where we are today. The NHS and the welfare state, for example, are the products of the actors, events and interests that came together after the Second World War. British politics and society could have been different, and it will be in future.

## THIS CHAPTER:

» Introduces the shadow of the Second World War on later politics.

» Sets out some of the main polices of the 1945 Labour government, including much greater state involvement in the economy and social life.

» Examines the period of postwar 'consensus'.

» Explores Britain's place in the world, the decline of empire, and introduces some of the tensions between the different territories that make up the United Kingdom.

» Introduces some of the factors that led to the collapse of the postwar consensus.

## WARFARE TO WELFARE

The declaration of war in September 1939 was not welcomed by cheering crowds, as some previous wars had been. Most British citizens had been relieved when Prime Minister Chamberlain returned from Munich in 1938, believing he had secured 'peace for our time' (quoted in Self, 2017, Ch. 13). However, following Hitler's invasion of Poland in September 1939, most accepted with resignation rather than optimism that war was inevitable. To that extent, the country was reasonably united.

Previous wars in which Britain had been engaged were largely fought on foreign soil, with little direct impact on the civilian population, apart from higher taxation and shortages of imported produce. Even the monstrous carnage of the First World War most directly affected the British armed forces, who discovered when they returned on leave that those at home had little conception of the horrors of the front line. The Second World War was different. Although mainland Britain was never invaded and to that extent suffered less than much of the European continent, its cities were extensively bombed, with heavy casualties. Hundreds of thousands of urban children were evacuated to the relative safety of the countryside. Yet despite the privations of wartime rationing of food and clothing, some of the poor actually enjoyed a healthier although limited diet, and no one starved. High unemployment, which had caused so much deprivation in the 1930s, was no longer a problem. Indeed, the shortage of male labour,

caused by conscription into the armed forces, led to women being recruited for all kinds of work previously performed almost exclusively by men. In a real sense, the whole country was in it together.

The sense that all parties, at least, were 'in it together' was replicated at Westminster, with the formation of a coalition government from 1940 under Winston Churchill, whose own long political career had survived two changes of party, and included periods of high office and isolation in the political wilderness. Once bitterly hostile to socialism and the Labour Party, Churchill welcomed its leading figures into a new government of national unity.

Labour had only previously experienced two brief and frustrating spells of government in 1924 and 1929–31, the latter abruptly terminated by a global financial crisis, in which the party's erstwhile leader Ramsay MacDonald formed a new 'National Government' (largely made up of Conservatives), which then defeated Labour at the polls, but had little success in reducing the long recession of the 1930s. In the wartime coalition, Labour's leading figures, including Clement Attlee, Herbert Morrison, Stafford Cripps and Hugh Dalton, and key trade unionists, such as Ernest Bevin, leader of the huge Transport and General Workers' Union, gained vital experience of government and a new political credibility, transforming the party's standing and, ultimately, its electoral prospects. They were all to figure prominently in Attlee's postwar Labour government, with Bevin as foreign secretary. (Attlee is discussed further in Key Figures 2.2 on p. 23.)

At home, the war involved a massive expansion of government power and control, and a commensurate increase in taxation and expenditure. In the midst of a desperate battle for survival, time was also devoted to using these new powers and resources for future postwar reconstruction, as we will explore later in this chapter.

Britain survived, initially precariously, particularly after the defeat and occupation of its ally France in 1940, when the country stood alone against Nazi Germany and fascist Italy, which had overrun much of Continental Europe. Britain's 'finest hour' involved its air force winning the 'Battle of Britain'. Yet what turned the tide was, first, Hitler's invasion of the Union of Soviet Socialist Republics (USSR), which brought it into the war on the same side as Britain, and, second, the Japanese attack on Pearl Harbour, which led to the USA joining the allied cause. Although final victory over Germany and, later, Japan was greeted euphorically as a triumph in Britain, it was largely the USSR and the USA that had won the war, and it was these countries that were to dominate international relations in the postwar world (as we discuss further below).

## COMPARING BRITISH POLITICS 2.1

### Continuity and change in Britain and other countries

British politics may seem a model of stability and continuity, as compared with many other modern states. France, for example, has experienced a succession of revolutions and regime changes over little more than two centuries, including several forms of monarchy, two periods of empire and five republics. Italy and Germany, which only became nation states in the late nineteenth century, went through similar upheavals, culminating in the fascist and Nazi dictatorships, before the restoration of parliamentary democracy following the military defeat of those regimes in 1945. Spain, Portugal and Greece have only more recently re-established democracy after periods of dictatorship. Eastern European countries only escaped from communist dictatorship with the fall of the Berlin Wall in 1989. Most states now represented at the United Nations (UN) did not even exist in 1945; many were former colonies that have since gained their independence, while other new countries have emerged from the partition of larger states.

While Britain experienced violent civil war and political revolutions in the seventeenth century, from then on its politics has evolved largely peacefully. The bullet has not generally been a feature of the politics of mainland Britain (although Ireland is another matter). Yet the appearance of stability and continuity is, in some respects, illusory. Power has shifted, and the substance of British politics has profoundly changed. Further changes, some even threatening the continuation of the UK, are far from unthinkable, particularly following the 2016 referendum vote to leave the EU, with the Scots and Northern Irish preferring to remain. Thus, the appearance of stability and continuity is illusory: the British state and British politics are in a state of flux, as will be apparent in some later chapters.

### 'THE NEW JERUSALEM': LABOUR, THE WELFARE STATE AND THE MIXED ECONOMY

Churchill had won huge credit for winning the war, as much for his oratory and indomitable spirit, as for any critical decisions (where in truth his record was more chequered). Thus, there was considerable surprise abroad and even at home when he was swept from power in the postwar Labour election landslide of 1945. There was perhaps more fondness among voters for Churchill than the Conservative Party – although Churchill was never universally popular, and was remembered by many working-class voters for his hostility to striking workers during the interwar period. There was also lingering hostility to the Tories for their failure to rearm the country under Conservative Prime

Minister Neville Chamberlain in the run-up to the Second World War and their willingness to appease German expansion. Finally, there was a sense of radicalism among voters who had felt let down by the interwar governments, which had promised a 'land fit for heroes' after the First World War (1914–18), but had presided over economic crises and high unemployment. It was Labour that seemed to mark a decisive break with the politics of the past. Attlee's Labour government promised a 'new Jerusalem' – a phrase taken from William Blake's poem – that is, a fair society, particularly for the less affluent majority.

It was during the war that the Archbishop of York (and later Canterbury) first popularised the term welfare state, which he contrasted positively with a 'warfare state' (Bandelj and Sowers, 2013, p. 88). While some of the foundations of the welfare state had been laid in wartime, including the Butler Education Act 1944 and the payment of family allowances to mothers (1945), it was the 1945–51 Labour government that was substantially responsible for its establishment. They drew, above all, on the wartime Beveridge Report (1942) – officially entitled *Social Insurance and Allied Services* – to form the basis for the postwar welfare state. Labour rapidly implemented Beveridge's national insurance scheme. To help ensure the maintenance of full employment, the government relied on 'demand management' techniques, advanced by economist John Maynard Keynes. Thus, the ideas of the Liberals, Beveridge and Keynes (discussed in Key Figures 2.1) remained critical to Labour's welfare programme. However, it was left-wing socialist Aneurin Bevan, who was responsible for the most substantial and enduring legacy of the postwar Labour government, the establishment in 1948 of the new NHS, initially opposed by the Conservatives and many doctors (Thomas-Symonds, 2014). It was to receive strong support from the wider public, both then and ever since.

*A* **welfare state** *is one in which the government takes responsibility for providing for the social and economic security of its population through the provision of pensions, unemployment insurance, healthcare and so on.*

# KEY FIGURES 2.1
## John Maynard Keynes

**John Maynard Keynes (1883–1946)** had been a brilliant critic of interwar economic policy. *The General Theory of Employment, Interest and Money* (1936), his key work, argued that governments could secure full employment, stable prices, steady economic growth and a healthy balance of payments by influencing total (or aggregate) demand for goods and services, through fiscal and monetary policy, without requiring direct intervention, or controls on particular firms and industries (often described as 'Keynesian demand strategies'). So, whenever unemployment appeared to be rising above politically acceptable levels, government could stimulate demand in the economy by reducing taxation and/or increasing government spending (if necessary running a budget deficit).

In the Second World War, Keynes rejoined the Treasury, and his economics became the new orthodoxy. His 'managed capitalism' was attractive to leading postwar politicians across the political spectrum, including Conservatives such as Harold Macmillan and 'Rab' Butler, and Labour's Hugh Gaitskell and Anthony Crosland (see Chapter 15, p. 319), in what some described as a Keynes-Beveridge consensus, involving both Keynesian economic demand management and the pursuit of social welfare. Subsequently, and especially from 1979 onwards, the Conservative New Right blamed Keynesian economic policies and increased welfare costs for rising government spending and fuelling inflation. However, the 2008 banking and subsequent economic crisis briefly assisted a revival of some of the ideas and prescriptions of Keynes. (See Chapter 19, pp. 406–08 for a discussion of Keynesian economics.)

It was anticipated that the costs of the NHS would initially rise until the backlog of untreated ill health in the community was cleared (because hitherto some were too poor to afford medical treatment). However, it was expected that thereafter costs would fall. In practice, a steadily rising population of the elderly (in part a consequence of better healthcare) and the development of new forms of treatment led to ever higher demands and costs. These have been a headache for successive governments from the beginning (as Chapter 20 explores in more detail).

It was Attlee's government that was later responsible for the first significant exception to free healthcare. Charges for dental and eye care were introduced by Chancellor of the Exchequer Hugh Gaitskell in 1951, partly to help pay for Britain's involvement in the 1950–53 Korean War. This provoked the resignation of Bevan together with Harold Wilson, a future Labour leader, and initiated the split between Bevanites and Gaitskellites, which continued to divide the party through the 1950s and after, long after its leading figures died (Bevan in 1960, Gaitskell in 1963). Later governments have extended charges to a few other services, and have encouraged some further private provision of some NHS services, but the broad principle of a health service substantially free at the point of use has been maintained. Even some Conservatives, critical of the growth of the state and public spending, such as Margaret Thatcher, maintained their public commitment to Britain's free NHS, as we see in Chapters 3 and 20.

### Timeline 2.1 The welfare state: key developments

| | |
|---|---|
| 1942 | The Beveridge Report, *Social Insurance and Allied Services* |
| 1944 | Education Act |
| 1944 | White Paper on employment policy (high and stable level of employment) |
| 1945 | Family Allowances Act |
| 1946 | National Insurance Act (implemented Beveridge Report) |
| 1948 | Establishment of the National Health Service |

Labour was committed to some form of economic planning, but although Attlee's government maintained some rationing in the face of postwar shortages, they did not attempt detailed controls of production and labour. Nor did Labour pursue the wholesale nationalisation of industry, implied in clause IV of its own constitution, in which the party proclaimed its commitment to the 'common ownership of the means of production, distribution and exchange'. Instead, Attlee's government proceeded to take into public ownership what were sometimes described as the 'commanding heights' of the economy, the Bank of England (1946), coal (1947), electricity, gas and rail (all 1948), and finally steel and road haulage (1949), thus establishing a mixed economy with a substantial state sector. Moreover, of these measures, only steel and road haulage were acutely controversial. The other nationalised industries were either already substantially state owned (electricity, gas) or declining (railways, coal).

---

**Nationalisation** *is the transfer of private assets into public ownership, in the UK usually through a public corporation. In the UK, many industries and the public utilities – gas, electricity, water and so on – were taken into public ownership after 1945.*

---

### THE END OF EMPIRE AND THE BEGINNING OF THE COLD WAR

Although Britain emerged from the Second World War as a victor, escaping the defeat and occupation that was the fate of much of Continental Europe, and still appeared a great power, one of the 'big three' (along with the USA and the USSR) determining the shape of the postwar world, its great power status was largely illusory. The British economy, which had lost its status as the world's biggest earlier in the century, was further damaged by the war, and the British manufacturing industry was ill-equipped to compete effectively with the USA, and later subsequently with the fast-recovering economies of Western Europe and Japan. The once extensive British Empire was to be substantially liquidated within 25 years of the war, starting with the independence of India and Pakistan, followed by most of its

# KEY FIGURES 2.2
## Clement Attlee

**Clement Attlee (1883–1967)** was ranked Britain's most successful prime minister in a survey of academics specialising in post-1945 British history and politics (Cowburn, 2016). His government introduced the NHS, nationalised one-fifth of the British economy and oversaw the transition to independence of India. He was the Labour leader for almost 20 years, and prime minister from 1945–51.

Attlee had a conventional, middle-class upbringing. He went to Oxford University and began a career as a barrister. However, he later abandoned this path to become a social worker, managing Haileybury House, a youth charity, in Limehouse, east London. The experience had a deep impact on Attlee, and the poverty he saw in the East End shaped his political views. He joined the Labour Party in 1908. During the First World War, he served in the army, rising to become a major, a title that would stay with him throughout his life. Attlee was elected as MP for Stepney in east London in 1922 and became a junior minister in the brief 1924 and 1929 Labour-led governments. He became party leader in 1935, partly because several of his more charismatic rivals lost their seats at the 1931 election.

As leader in the 1930s, Attlee became an increasingly strong opponent of appeasing German expansion under Hitler. He took Labour into the wartime coalition, led by the Conservative Winston Churchill, in 1940 and was appointed deputy prime minister in 1942. Attlee and Churchill worked together surprisingly harmoniously during the war, with Attlee handling much of the domestic policy and detail, as Churchill focused his attention on diplomacy and military policy.

The coalition government was dissolved with victory in Europe in May 1945. For the Conservatives, Churchill (2013, p. 188) expected to be rewarded for leading Britain during 'its darkest hour'. To many people's surprise, however, Attlee led the Labour Party to a landslide victory, securing 48% of the vote and 393 seats to the Conservative's 213. Attlee's tenure as prime minister was hugely active. Labour implemented nearly all their 1945 manifesto pledges, changing the direction of British policy for a generation and creating a new consensus about the direction postwar Britain would take.

Attlee was modest and unassuming, largely ineffective at public relations, which mattered less then than today, and lacked Churchill's charisma. Attlee's leadership style was collective, but once the Cabinet had voiced their opinions, he would make decisions quickly with military precision. Attlee saw his role as that of a cricket umpire, reconciling the opinions of 'big beasts' in the Cabinet, such as Ernest Bevin, Aneurin Bevan and Herbert Morrison. After Labour's defeat in the 1951 general election, Attlee's authority was undermined by infighting between left and right in the party and his effectiveness declined (Radice, 2008). He resigned in 1955, and remains, by some distance, the longest serving Labour leader. Through the policies of his government, Britain was a different place from when he was elected Labour leader 20 years before.

remaining African and Asian colonies in the 1950s and 60s, some painfully and reluctantly abandoned, following losing struggles against nationalist revolts (e.g. Kenya, Malaya, Cyprus), others more readily conceded.

The former British Empire was rapidly converted into a Commonwealth of independent states – a loose group of nations formerly part of the British Empire. The loss of the empire was regretted by many in Britain, particularly on the right of the Conservative Party, although it was celebrated by others active in organisations such as the Movement for Colonial Freedom – a civil rights group founded in 1954, which had the backing of many senior Labour MPs. However, the transition from empire to Commonwealth,

*Source*: Arvind Yadav/Hindustan Times/Getty Images
The end of British rule is a cause for celebration in many parts of the world. Here, schoolchildren celebrate 70 years of independence at the Red Fort in New Delhi, India on 15 August 2016.

while it involved some violence and bloodshed, was largely achieved without military conflict by UK forces. This is in stark contrast to French withdrawal from Indochina and Algeria, which involved bloody and prolonged wars of independence and traumatic consequences for French domestic politics. Even so, there was a painful process of adjustment, as Britain lost much of its influence in wider geopolitics. As former US Secretary of State Dean Acheson famously observed: 'Great Britain has lost an empire and not yet found a role' (quoted in McKercher, 2017, p. 75).

Britain's postwar foreign policy was largely shaped by the **Cold War** between the two superpowers, the USA and the USSR. Although both had been Britain's wartime allies, there was never any doubt that Britain would side with the USA, becoming one of the founding members of the North Atlantic Treaty Organization, a military alliance between several North American and European countries, established in 1949, where each member state agrees to

mutual defence in response to an attack by any external party. The most obvious threat at the time was the USSR, which followed suit in 1955 by creating the Warsaw Pact, an opposing alliance of states allied with the Soviets. The UK positioned itself as America's most reliable ally. The policy was largely bipartisan, pursued and maintained by Conservative and Labour governments, although the Labour Party contained a significant minority that favoured greater neutrality and, subsequently, nuclear disarmament.

*The Cold War describes the long tension from the end of the Second World War (1945) to the fall of the Berlin Wall (1989) between the USSR and its allies, on the one hand, and the USA and its allies, on the other. It was a 'cold' war because it never involved direct armed conflict between the two major powers, despite periodic crises when the Cold War threatened to become a hot war. Some argue this was only prevented by the fear of war between the two major nuclear powers.*

* Date when independence was recognised. The white settler government of Ian Smith had earlier made a unilateral declaration of independence in 1965.

However, what became known as the 'special relationship' between the UK and the USA was always an unequal one, with the UK very much a junior partner (see Chapter 22, pp. 463–64). Although Britain became a nuclear power, in practice its independent nuclear deterrent became increasingly dependent on American rockets and submarines. On the one occasion when a British government engaged in a foreign policy adventure opposed by the USA, the Anglo-French attack on the Suez Canal in 1956, they were forced into a humiliating climb-down, entailing the resignation of Anthony Eden, the prime minister responsible. However, the illusion among many in the governing class that the UK still had its 'great power' status, the 'special relationship' with the USA and

the continuing concern with the empire and Commonwealth effectively deterred British governments from closer engagement with Continental Europe in the years following the war. Neither Labour nor the Conservatives were interested in joining the European Coal and Steel Community (ECSC), set up by the 1951 Treaty of Paris, or the European Economic Community (EEC), established by the 1957 Treaty of Rome. Britain thus missed the opportunity to help shape the new Europe (see Chapter 12).

## THE 1950S ONWARDS: AN AGE OF CONSENSUS?

### 'YOU'VE NEVER HAD IT SO GOOD'

The Conservatives returned to power in 1951, but apart from the denationalisation of steel and road haulage in 1953, there was no sharp reversal of policy by the incoming Conservative administration under the now elderly Churchill. Indeed, Labour's Dick Crossman observed in his diary: 'the general make-up of the Churchill Cabinet means that it will be only very slightly to the right of the most recent Attlee Cabinet. Just as Attlee was running what was virtually a coalition policy on a Party basis, so Churchill may well do the same' (Morgan, 1981, p. 30).

Both parties built on, but were constrained by, the legacy of the past. Both were determined to turn their backs on the policies of the interwar years, which had failed to deal with unemployment at home or the rise of the fascist dictators Hitler and Mussolini abroad. It was no accident that it was first Labour and then former Conservative rebels such as Churchill, Eden and Macmillan, who dominated the politics of the early postwar years. Indeed, many of the policies pursued by Labour and Conservative postwar governments had their roots in the experience of war, and the wartime coalition government (Page, 2015, Ch. 3).

There appeared so little difference between the economic policies pursued by Labour Chancellor Hugh Gaitskell and his Conservative successor R.A. Butler that *The Economist* in

1954 coined the term 'Butskellism' to describe their approach (Dutton, 1997, p. 57). This involved continuing to pursue Keynesian demand management (see below for more on Keynes). These policies apparently succeeded in maintaining close to full employment, in marked contrast to the interwar period. Thus, it has been claimed that there was a substantial consensus (or agreement) between the major parties on economic and social policies in the postwar period. Key elements of agreement included the system of government, the welfare state and the mixed economy, with a substantial state sector. All this substantially persisted until the government of Margaret Thatcher (see Chapter 3). Even so, the extent and even the reality of the postwar consensus has been questioned (see Spotlight 2.1).

In some respects, Harold Macmillan personified the apparently dominant 'one-nation' conservatism in the 1950s and early 1960s – a centrist form of conservatism, which stressed the responsibility of those at the top of society for those at the bottom (see Chapter 15, pp. 312–14). As housing minister, Macmillan proudly boasted that he had built 300,000 houses a year (many of them council houses). Later, as prime minister, he accepted the resignation of his entire Treasury team who demanded cuts in public spending. To Macmillan and his supporters, the Conservative Party was quite at peace with Labour's 'new Jerusalem'.

## SPOTLIGHT ON ...

### Consensus politics: myth or reality?

2.1

The postwar consensus was said to be the agreement between the main parties in Westminster from the 1940s until the 1970s about certain key principles, including full employment, a mixed economy in which the state controlled certain important industries, active government in which the state would use Keynesian techniques to boost demand, a strong welfare state, conciliation with trade unions and the role of the expert civil servant in running government and the economy.

The mainstream view on the consensus is put forward by Paul Addison ([1975] 1994) in *The Road to 1945*, who claimed that the new consensus 'fell like a plum' into the lap of the Attlee government, who arrived to find the Beveridge Report and other White Papers written and public demand for change ripe. Even before the term 'consensus' was much used, Canadian academic Robert McKenzie (1955) claimed that there were minimal differences between the major British parties, while British observers saw much in common between the social democracy of Gaitskell and Crosland and the one-nation conservatism of Macmillan and Butler. American political scientist Daniel Bell (1960) suggested that the West was witnessing the 'end of ideology'; policy-makers used modern social science to find practical solutions to problems, rather than relying on old ideological assumptions.

Later historians have questioned the extent of consensus. Ben Pimlott (1994) talked about the 'the myth of consensus', arguing that the term minimises differences between parties and the population, and was only ascribed to the first two or three postwar decades by politicians and commentators viewing the postwar years from the more divisive 1980s.

Kevin Hickson (2004) has provided a more qualified account of consensus. He argued that the consensus was limited to the leadership in the Labour and Conservative Parties. There was plenty of dispute among backbenchers and within society as a whole. He also argued that consensus was limited to policy, not ideology. Both one-nation Conservatives and Labour socialists supported the building of council houses, for example. But they did so for different reasons: Labour to create good homes for the working class as part of a more equal society; one-nation Conservatives because they saw it as the responsibility of those at the top to care for those at the bottom. Consensus, to Hickson, was more limited than earlier accounts showed.

## FOREIGN RELATIONS AND SEXUAL AFFAIRS

Churchill's second administration survived until 1955, when he was succeeded as prime minister by Anthony Eden, whose political experience was largely in foreign affairs, which, ironically, was to end his premiership and ruin his political reputation. In July 1956, President Nasser of Egypt nationalised the Suez Canal, which had, in practice, been managed by the French and British and provided them with a quick sea route from Europe to trading partners in Asia and elsewhere. After intense international debate had failed to resolve the crisis, Britain and France invaded Suez. In a highly controversial and at the time top secret piece of foreign policy, this was carried out with the collusion of Israel, which had launched an attack on Egypt at the same time. Ostensibly, Anglo-French involvement was meant to keep the combatants apart, but was universally interpreted as a reoccupation and reseizure of the canal, and was condemned by international opinion, including the USA and the Labour opposition at home. One upshot was that the Suez Canal was effectively blocked for months by ships sunk by the retreating Egyptians. Following continued international pressure, including more pertinently the threat to withhold a loan from the USA to the UK, the Anglo-French forces withdrew, to be replaced by a UN contingent. (An unfortunate side effect of the world's distraction was the reoccupation of Hungary by Russian forces, following a popular revolt.) Altogether, it was perhaps the most discreditable episode in Britain's postwar foreign policy. Eden was eventually obliged to resign, officially on health grounds, early in 1957, to be succeeded by Harold Macmillan. (The Suez crisis and its effect on UK foreign policy are discussed in more detail in Chapter 22.)

Macmillan initially restored his party's fortunes, healing the transatlantic alliance damaged by Suez, after a successful Anglo-American summit in Bermuda in 1957. His Edwardian manner proved surprisingly popular. (As a young man, Macmillan had been wounded in the First World War and, as he got older, he projected a charming, aristocratic and rather genteel persona.) When the cartoonist Vicky satirised him as 'Supermac', a kind of comic superman, the image worked in his favour. He capitalised on rising living standards, boasting: 'You've never had it so good!' In the 1959 election, the Conservatives claimed: 'Life's better under the Conservatives. Don't let Labour ruin it.' They were returned with a larger majority.

After the election Macmillan further strengthened the transatlantic alliance following summits with the new US President Kennedy at Bermuda in 1961 and Nassau in 1962, which substantially preserved Britain's independent nuclear deterrent. Yet at home, the government's popularity was falling, following economic problems and by-election defeats. Macmillan had boldly decided to seek British membership of the EEC in 1961, but negotiations dragged on. Macmillan's difficulties worsened after a major Cabinet reshuffle (described as the 'night of the long knives') backfired in 1962.

Macmillan was not helped by the scandals that enveloped the last years of his government, particularly after his minister of war, John Profumo, was forced to resign after he admitted lying to the Commons over an extramarital relationship with Christine Keeler, who had also been involved – at the height of the Cold War – with a Russian naval attaché. Rumours of further scandals surrounded other public figures and to some extent the whole establishment. Macmillan seemed suddenly old and out of touch, facing criticism within his own party. Moreover, in 1963, the long negotiations over UK membership of the EEC were abruptly terminated, effectively by the veto of the French President Charles de Gaulle. (Britain's difficult relationship with Europe is discussed in more detail in Chapter 12.) Following the death of Gaitskell and the election of Harold Wilson as Labour leader, Macmillan now faced an agile younger opponent who was surprisingly successful in reuniting his previously divided party and restoring its electoral fortunes. In October 1963, Macmillan resigned, ostensibly on grounds of ill health, to be eventually succeeded by Lord Home, who resigned his peerage, and fought a by-election to win a seat in the Commons (a process that finally confirmed that the prime minister should be a member of the lower elected house). Home did not last long, as he was obliged to call a general election in October 1964, when the Conservatives were narrowly defeated. This meant that Harold Wilson became Britain's first Labour prime minister for 13 years, and only the second to enjoy an (initially small) majority in the House of Commons.

## FROM EMPIRE TO EUROPE

Both Conservative and Labour governments had failed to deal with Britain's persistent economic problems. Both came to see entry to the EEC, the forerunner to today's EU, as a possible solution to those issues. The six countries that originally formed the EEC in 1957 were all apparently growing much faster than Britain. West Germany and Italy, in particular, went through rapid periods of industrial development, with the expansion of manufacturing companies like Volkswagen in Germany and Fiat and Zanussi in Italy. British membership was increasingly seen as a potential answer to slow economic growth and lack of competitiveness. Macmillan's Conservative government applied to join in 1963 and Wilson's Labour government in 1967; both attempts were effectively vetoed by de Gaulle, who feared the economic and cultural influence the UK would have over the EEC. After de Gaulle's departure from office, Heath's government successfully negotiated entry in 1973. Membership was subsequently endorsed by two-thirds of British voters in a referendum in 1975, after some minor renegotiation of the terms of entry by the incoming 1974 Labour government.

The time finally seemed ripe for Britain to engage with Europe. Earlier obstacles to membership, including ties with the British Empire, the Commonwealth and the wider world, no longer seemed so important. Most former colonies had achieved, or would very soon achieve, full independence. British forces had been withdrawn from east of Suez, in line with a scaling down of defence commitments, and sterling was no longer the most powerful currency in international trade. The leaders of all three parties had supported entry, and those politicians who had opposed it largely

accepted that the 1975 referendum had settled the issue for the immediate future.

However, the British commitment to Europe was less than wholehearted, while entry into the European Community (EC) provided no instant answer to Britain's economic problems. The timing was unfortunate. The UK missed out on the years of growth and rising living standards that the original six member states had experienced. It joined in 1973, the year of the energy crisis, when major industrial countries faced substantial petrol shortages, due to instability in the oil-exporting Middle East. This crisis precipitated an international economic downturn. Moreover, the UK had joined the club too late to affect the development of its rules, which did not always suit British needs. Thus, Britain's small but comparatively efficient agricultural sector did not benefit much from the cumbersome Common Agricultural Policy, which initially consumed three-quarters of the EC's total budget. This led to early complaints that Britain was paying in far more than it was getting in return, and Margaret Thatcher's subsequent and ultimately successful demand for a budget rebate.

Only the then tiny Liberal Party were consistently in favour of EC membership. Labour was divided. Broadly speaking, the social democratic right were in favour and the more socialist left, who regarded it as a rich man's club, were against, although there were exceptions to this generalisation on both sides. Wilson had finally and reluctantly agreed to a referendum on the issue to avoid splits in his own party, yet under the leadership of Michael Foot, Labour was to fight the 1983 election committed to withdrawal from Europe without a referendum. Although the end of empire initially made it easier for many Conservatives to accept Europe as a practical alternative, a significant minority remained opposed to the implications for Britain's national sovereignty. From the early 1990s the Conservatives became an increasingly Eurosceptic party, opposing EU expansion and aiming ultimately to pull the UK out of the EU. Ironically, over the same period, the majority of the Labour Party became more positive towards Europe (see Chapter 12).

# THE 1960s AND AFTER: CONSENSUS TO CRISIS

## SOCIAL CHANGE AND THE POLITICS OF PROTEST

Living standards rose continuously in the postwar decades. Rationing was phased out in the early 1950s and wartime shortages abated. There was a greater range of goods on which to spend money, including durable consumer goods such as cars, washing machines and television sets, increasingly within the range of ordinary working people. Some argued that increased prosperity was affecting political allegiances. Workers in the then flourishing car industry acquired middle-class lifestyles, and perhaps attitudes, for the middle-class vote was then overwhelmingly Conservative. Conservative election posters in 1959 showed happy middle-class families with father,

*Source*: The Conservative Party Archive/Getty Images

For many Britons, the 1950s were a time of economic growth. It was the Conservatives who were the main electoral beneficiaries.

mother and two children enjoying their new home and car.

Increasing prosperity was accompanied by other social change, less consistent with traditional family values. It was becoming easier for men and women to choose alternative lifestyles. The 1960s have been associated with increased personal liberation: contraceptive pills enabled couples to plan or avoid parenthood; more couples lived openly together unmarried and having a child outside marriage lost much of its earlier stigma; abortion was largely decriminalised in 1967; and divorce law was reformed, making divorce easier and cheaper. Homosexual acts, previously punishable by law, were legalised between consenting adults in private, although it took much longer for public attitudes to homosexuality to change. State censorship for obscenity was relaxed, allowing classic novels like D.H. Lawrence's *Lady Chatterley's Lover* to be legally sold in the UK for the first time. Some critics deplored increased social and sexual permissiveness and the effects it had on the traditional family. Others countered that easier divorce enabled some women, in particular, to escape from violent marriages and freed couples from long, unhappy relationships. Women's increased earning power gave them more freedom to choose and control their own lives.

The families portrayed in election posters, commercial advertising and in the media generally remained overwhelmingly white until the last years of the twentieth century. Yet one largely unintended consequence of empire had been substantial immigration into Britain from its former colonies, particularly from the West Indies, the Indian subcontinent and parts of Africa. The growing black and Asian population faced considerable prejudice and discrimination, and in the largely inner urban areas where most of them settled, there were ethnic tensions and sometimes serious riots. Politician Enoch Powell courted controversy and destroyed his own chances of ever leading the Conservative Party with his 'rivers of blood' speech in 1968, which was widely seen to be racist, and in which he warned against the UK's immigration policy. In spite of discrimination, over the postwar years Britain was transformed into an increasingly multicultural society, accommodating a range of different religions, languages and lifestyles (see Chapter 4). Ethnic minorities undoubtedly brought a new dimension to British politics, but there was still tension and conflict. The children and grandchildren of immigrants, while often assimilating much of British culture, were less prepared to accept casual discrimination and prejudice.

Social change provoked political change. Largely outside the parties, the politics of protest grew in the 1960s and 70s. The Campaign for Nuclear Disarmament (CND) organised a series of massive marches against nuclear weapons, while they and other groups demonstrated against the American war in Vietnam, as part of a growing peace movement. Others became active participants in the developing environmental movement (see Chapter 21). The continuing economic, social, legal and political inequality suffered by women inspired a powerful feminist movement, which by the 1970s would help secure significant changes in the law and some real advances in employment opportunities, childcare and political representation. (Many of these legal advances are set out in Chapter 9.) In response to the racist agitation stimulated by some far-right groups, and tacitly endorsed

by a few mainstream politicians, the Anti-Nazi League and ethnic minority groups sought to counter racial prejudice and discrimination, and champion the rights of minorities. Much of this politics of protest involved a reaction against the political mainstream and the established traditional parties, and cut across old class divisions. The relative homogeneity of British society and culture, proclaimed by some earlier British and foreign observers, seemed to be breaking down.

## NORTHERN IRELAND, SCOTLAND AND WALES

To some observers in the 1970s, the main threat to the integrity and sovereignty of the UK came not from Europe but from within, from the resurgence of Irish, Scottish and Welsh nationalist desires to break off from the UK, linked perhaps with the relative political and economic decline of Britain, now neither a world power, nor the centre of an extensive overseas empire. Some Scots and Welsh felt that they were no longer partners in a great imperial enterprise, but neglected second-class citizens of a shrunken British state. Economic problems hit the more peripheral areas of the UK particularly hard – Northern Irish shipbuilding, the coal and steel industries of South Wales and the industrial belt of central Scotland. Those nationalists who had always questioned union with England now had additional economic arguments to support their case.

Northern Ireland posed the first and most immediate threat to the British state (see Chapter 11). Following persistent Irish nationalist pressure in the nineteenth and early twentieth centuries, Ireland had been partitioned, substantially on religious lines, in 1922, with the majority of the country becoming an independent Irish state. The predominantly Protestant six counties of the province of Northern Ireland remained part of the British state. It had its own devolved government and Parliament (at Stormont), but also sent MPs to the Westminster Parliament. While the Protestant majority maintained a fierce allegiance to the British crown, most Catholics were nationalists who sought a united Ireland. Even so, despite periodic disturbances, the province had been fairly

*Source*: The Campaign for Nuclear Disarmament
The threat of nuclear war loomed large and spurred many citizens, particularly younger people, into action and protest. The first CND badges were made using clay and distributed with a note explaining that in the event of a nuclear war, these fired badges would be among the few human arte-facts to survive.

quiet since the war. The Ulster Unionist Party, then affiliated to the Conservatives, dominated both the Stormont Parliament and Northern Ireland representation at Westminster. The nationalist party, Sinn Féin, won odd seats in predominantly Catholic areas, but declined to take them up, as they did not recognise British rule. Unionist (and Protestant) domination of the province seemed complete, while Catholics were a disadvantaged minority.

From the mid-1960s, Catholics, dissatisfied with their second-class status, demanded civil and political rights. This led to political disturbances. Concessions announced by the unionist government upset many 'loyalist' Protestants without winning support from Catholics. The two communities became increasingly polarised. Riots became frequent. A new hard-line Protestant unionism, in which Ian Paisley was to become a key figure, emerged. Troops sent in by the British government to restore order in 1969 were at first welcomed by the Catholics, who had suffered attacks by loyalists. However, perhaps inevitably, these troops soon became targets for nationalists who saw them as representatives of an alien occupying force. The Provisional Irish Republican Army (IRA) began a violent campaign to secure the withdrawal of British troops and ultimately a united Ireland. In 1972, the events of 'Bloody Sunday', when British troops fired on demonstrators, killing 13 civilians, led to the suspension of the Stormont government and the imposition of direct rule from Westminster. Violence, involving sectarian murders, revenge attacks and bombings, was to remain a feature of Ulster life for a quarter of a century, and was periodically exported to the mainland of Britain. A series of political initiatives failed to end the cycle of violence.

The Irish nationalist challenge to the historic union of Great Britain and Northern Ireland was paralleled by a resurgence of Scottish and Welsh nationalism, although these were almost entirely nonviolent. Parliamentary by-election victories for nationalists led to a more marked advance for the Scottish National Party and (to a lesser extent) Plaid Cymru in the two general elections of 1974. Disturbed by the threat to its support in Scotland and Wales, Labour promised a new elected Scottish Parliament and Welsh Assembly, involving some devolution of power rather than the independence pursued by nationalists. This first attempt at devolution foundered with the failure to secure sufficient support in referendums in 1979, an outcome that precipitated the fall of Callaghan's Labour government. The Conservatives had long been the party of the union, and the later governments of Thatcher and Major made no concessions to nationalist pressures. These seemed to recede for a time in Scotland and Wales, although not in Northern Ireland (see Chapter 3).

## 'THE CRISIS OF THE 1970s': UNDERPERFORMING ECONOMY, 'STAGFLATION', TRADE UNIONS AND INDUSTRIAL RELATIONS

Despite continuing political stability, coupled with the establishment and maintenance of full employment, a mixed economy and the welfare state, all did not seem well with the British economic and political system in the 1960s and 70s. Britain's economic growth was only modest in comparison with that of major competitors in North America, Western Europe and Japan. Low growth was blamed on 'stop-go' policies, under which expansion led to inflation and a balance of payments crisis, followed by cuts in public spending, recession and increased unemployment, sparking reflation and a recurrence of excess demand and rising prices. Thus, governments seemed incapable of pursuing steady growth. Britain's competitiveness also appeared to be undermined by relatively low labour productivity, exacerbated by strikes and other problems with industrial relations, and outdated management.

After 13 years of Conservative rule, the new Labour government under Harold Wilson in 1964 was pledged to modernise the economy and secure an annual rate of economic growth of 4% to pay for further social reform and increased spending on public services. Yet the government was handicapped by a deteriorating balance of payments and increasing pressure on the exchange rate of the pound sterling, which eventually forced devaluation in 1967, an event from which Wilson's reputation never quite recovered. Both his government and the following Conservative government under Heath (1970–74) attempted to reform trade unions and industrial relations, but failed. Increasing numbers of days were lost to industrial action, culminating in the miners' strike of 1973–74 that effectively brought down the Heath government.

The Keynes-Beveridge consensus was under threat. While some criticised the rising cost of the welfare state, others questioned its effectiveness. Problems such as homelessness, failing schools, child poverty and inner-city decline showed that the system was not providing effective social security 'from the cradle to the grave'. Moreover, although Keynesian theory recommended contrasting policy remedies to cope with inflation, on the one hand, or economic stagnation with rising unemployment, on the other, by the 1970s governments were confronted with rising prices *and* rising unemployment. Journalists coined the term stagflation to describe this apparently new phenomenon.

---

**Stagflation** *is persistent high inflation combined with high unemployment and stagnant demand in a country's economy.*

---

Politicians from both parties concluded that unreasonable wage increases were pushing up prices. So governments from Macmillan's to Callaghan's tried to restrain inflationary pressures through various forms of incomes policy. This entailed making deals with the leaders of business and organised labour. Some observers discerned a new system of making policy involving government, the Confederation of British Industry and the Trades Union Congress, a process described as 'tripartism' or 'corporatism'. These terms described who was involved, but said little about the power relationships between them. While some saw corporatism as a new political system involving partnership with business and labour, others saw it as an essentially top-down process, bypassing Parliament and people. Some socialist critics thought the

apparent participation of the unions in policy-making was essentially cosmetic; the reality involved restraints on workers' wages in the interest of business profits. By contrast, critics on the right thought the unions had been given too much power, and that incomes policies interfered with free-market forces, damaging Britain's competitiveness. In practice, incomes policies appeared to restrain wage rises in the short term, but were difficult to maintain on a longer term basis.

The Heath government's attempts to control inflation were not helped by the 1973 energy crisis, which saw a quadrupling of oil prices. This underlined the continued importance of Britain's coal industry and the industrial muscle of the miners, who began a national strike in 1973. Heath responded by imposing a three-day working week to save energy costs. The crisis provoked an early election in February 1974, which the government narrowly lost, producing a hung parliament. This allowed Wilson to return as the prime minister of a minority Labour government, which acquired a slim majority in a second election the same year.

---

*A **hung parliament** (or a hung council) is one where no single political party can command a majority, implying coalition or minority government.*

---

Inflation continued to rise steeply under Labour (Dutton, 1997, p. 102). The government initially sought to maintain its spending plans by borrowing. In 1976, after Callaghan had replaced Wilson as prime minister, mounting debts forced the government to seek a massive loan from the International Monetary Fund under conditions that required major cuts in public spending. Confidence in Keynesian solutions was undermined, as Callaghan (1987, p. 426) mournfully acknowledged to the Labour Party conference in 1976:

> We used to think that you could just spend your way out of recession and increase employment by cutting taxes and boosting government spending. I tell you, in all candour, that that option no longer exists, and that in so far as it ever did exist, it only worked ... by injecting a bigger dose of

inflation into the economy, followed by a higher level of unemployment as the next step.

Savage deflationary policies eventually enabled the Labour government to control spending and reduce inflation, but at considerable political cost, alienating voters and many in the unions, and dividing the Labour Party. Callaghan could have called a general election in late 1978, and seemed close to doing so, but decided to wait until after the winter in the hope that the economy would improve and voters would return the Labour government. It was a mistake (Dorey, 2016). The last version of the incomes policy introduced by the Callaghan government culminated in a series of strikes by key public sector workers, dubbed the winter of discontent by newspapers (Shepherd, 2013). While the Conservative Party and other anti-Labour groups did much to exaggerate the extent of the crisis, the strikes fatally undermined Callaghan's Labour government (Hay, 2009). The government collapsed in March 1979, after losing a vote of 'no confidence', and on 3 May 1979, Labour were defeated at general election. It was to be the last Labour government for almost 18 years, by which time the Conservatives, under Thatcher for much of that time, set about dismantling much of the postwar consensus.

---

*The* **winter of discontent** *was a series of public sector strikes during the winter of 1978/79 that undermined the Labour government.*

---

 **SUMMARY**

» Although British politics from 1939 to 1979 was clearly shaped by past history, and showed a marked stability and continuity with the past, it was extensively transformed by the Second World War and its aftermath.

» Key features included the development of the welfare state at home, the Cold War between the USA and the USSR abroad, coupled with the decline of empire.

» Although the British people continued to enjoy rising standards of living and relatively low unemployment, Britain continued to suffer relative economic decline.

» The declining British Empire and the 'special relationship' with the USA were obstacles to Britain engaging with the movement for closer European economic and political integration on the European continent. When Britain finally joined the EEC in 1973, it was too late to shape its rules or share early benefits, and the commitment was less than wholehearted.

» From the late 1960s onwards, the UK faced threats to the maintenance of the union from nationalist movements in Northern Ireland, Scotland and Wales. The first attempt of Labour to establish greater devolution in Scotland and Wales did not attract sufficient support in referendums in 1979.

» Changes in population, living standards and lifestyles raised new political issues, and involved some rejection of traditional values. It helped spark a politics of protest largely outside the traditional party system.

 **QUESTIONS FOR DISCUSSION**

» How does war change society?

» How far was Britain's great power status an illusion after the Second World War?

» Should politicians have focused on the economy or welfare in the years after the Second World War?

» Was there a political consensus in the period after the Second World War, and if so, on what was it based?

» Why were British governments not involved in closer European integration in the 1950s? Why have British governments, and the British people, not engaged more closely with Europe?

» How was the unity of the United Kingdom apparently threatened in the 1970s and why?

» How far was 'the crisis of the 1970s' a real crisis that Britain had to face?

 FURTHER READING

There are several useful books on postwar British politics. Kynaston's series, *Austerity Britain 1945–51* (2008), *Family Britain, 1951-1957* (2010) and *Modernity Britain, 1957–62* (2015) provide an excellent social history. Black's (2010) *Redefining British Politics: Culture, Consumerism and Participation, 1954–70* explores the ideas, moments, identities, organisations and individuals that created social change. Hennessy's *Never Again: Britain 1945-1951* (1993) and *Having It So Good: Britain in the Fifties* (2006) are also good accounts. Sandbrook produced a readable series, *Never Had It So Good: A History of Britain from Suez to the Beatles* (2005), *White Heat: A History of Britain in the Swinging Sixties* (2006) and *State of Emergency: The Way We Were: Britain, 1970–1974* (2010). From a different political angle to Sandbrook, Judt's (2005) *Postwar: A History of Europe Since 1945* provides a valuable broader European perspective and a particularly useful brief comparison of the German and British economies in the postwar period (pp. 354–59). On the experience of particular groups, Clair Wills, *Lovers and Strangers: An Immigrant History of Post-War Britain* (2017) and Jane Lewis, *Women in Britain Since 1945* (1992) are well worth a read.

 USEFUL WEBSITES

The journal *Contemporary British History* has many relevant articles: www.tandfonline.com/toc/fcbh20/current.

 *Further student resources to support learning are available at* **www.macmillanihe.com/griffiths-brit-pol-3e**

# 3 THE SHADOW OF THE PAST II: THATCHER AND AFTER

Margaret Thatcher broke decisively from the 'consensus' politics set out in the last chapter. She declared in 1979: 'I am a conviction politician. The Old Testament prophets did not say, Brothers I want a consensus' (quoted in Dutton, 1997, p. 110). Over the next 11 years, her government decisively rejected Keynesian economics, the part-nationalisation of the economy, full employment as a policy aim and aspects of the 'cradle to grave' welfare state that had been created by the 1945 Labour government. Instead, Thatcher's government used the power of the state to create a free economy that they believed would set Britain on a path to prosperity. It marked a change in direction that governments have continued along to this day.

The Conservative election victory in 1979, which inaugurated 18 years of Conservative rule, can be seen as a reaction against much of the social and political change outlined in Chapter 2. Margaret Thatcher, Britain's new prime minister, spoke the language and reflected the values of the white English middle classes. She was to prove the most controversial figure in postwar British politics. Her legacy is still hotly contested. To her admirers, she was a great leader who restored the British economy, confronted and defeated enemies at home, while resolutely defending and advancing Britain's interests abroad. To her critics, including not only Labour and the trade unions but some Conservatives (see, for example, Gilmour, 1992), her government was harsh and divisive, with disastrous implications for Britain's social harmony, its manufacturing industry and its public services. Thatcher's legacy arguably still shapes contemporary politics. This chapter examines Thatcher, her legacy and the subsequent Conservative government of John Major. We also discuss the rise of New Labour, whose politicians accepted many of Thatcher's reforms, before concluding with a discussion of the Conservative-led governments from 2010 to the present day, with Theresa May's flawed decision to hold an election in 2017.

## THIS CHAPTER:

» Introduces the key policies and debates surrounding Thatcher and Thatcherism.

» Examines the significance of the 'New Labour' government elected in 1997, focusing on their constitutional reforms, and the financial and economic crisis that is now affecting politics around the world.

» Provides an overview of the Conservative-led governments that have been in power since 2010, first under David Cameron, in coalition with the Liberal Democrats until 2015, and from July 2016 under Theresa May as she struggles with the challenges of Brexit and of heading a minority government after the 2017 general election.

## CONSERVATIVE DOMINANCE: THATCHERISM AND THE FREE MARKET

The 1979 election was not the only, nor the principal, cause of the changes in the British state, economy and society in the last decades of the twentieth century. As we have seen, some roots lay earlier. The previous Labour government had already largely abandoned Keynesianism and introduced public spending cuts. (Keynesian economics are discussed in more detail in Chapter 19.) Both the Wilson and Heath governments had attempted to reform industrial relations, anticipating some of the Thatcher curbs on trade unions. To an extent, what came to be called 'Thatcherism' was a response to worsening economic conditions in Britain and the wider world and the 'crisis of the 1970s' (discussed in Chapter 2). Western governments of various political colours pursued similar policies. Despite these qualifications, it is worth recording the verdict of Nigel Lawson, Thatcher's former chancellor and once close ally, who resigned after quarrelling with his chief over exchange rate policy. She had, he said: 'transformed the politics of Britain – indeed Britain itself – to an extent that no other Government has achieved since the Attlee Government of 1945–51' (cited in Hennessy, 2000, p. 151) (see Spotlight 3.1, overleaf).

### THE RISE OF THATCHER

Thatcher's right-wing radicalism was not so apparent in her earlier political career. As secretary of state for education in Ted Heath's government, 'she approved more schemes for comprehensive schools, and the abolition of more grammar schools, than any other Secretary of State before or since' (Young, 1989, p. 68). Here, she was largely following an educational movement that was already well under way, but it is striking that she did little to defend the grammar school education that she had experienced, which presents an interesting contrast with the next female Tory prime minister, Theresa May. Nor was she a rebel in Heath's Cabinet.

It was only after Heath narrowly lost the election of February 1974 that she began to show signs of dissent in his Shadow Cabinet, and even then she did not take the lead in articulating a more right-wing, free-market conservatism. That role was taken by Keith Joseph, who was increasingly influenced by the ideas of right-wing think tanks, such as the Institute of Economic Affairs and the Centre for Policy Studies. Joseph was an important influence on Thatcher, and was briefly seen as a possible successor to Heath. (Thatcherism as a distinct ideology is debated overleaf.) Heath himself began to favour a 'government of national unity', with support from the Liberal Party, which would clearly involve a further watering down of what Joseph, and increasingly also Thatcher, regarded as true conservatism. When Heath lost the second election in 1974 in October, Joseph put himself forward as a candidate for the party leadership, but he was always a thinker prepared to think the unthinkable

# SPOTLIGHT ON ...

## Thatcherism as an ideology?

Few prime ministers have an 'ism' appended to their name: Thatcher did. This seems to imply that Thatcherism is an ideology, in the same way that socialism or liberalism are ideologies. (For more on ideology, see Chapter 15.) Under this view, Thatcher was a conviction politician, motivated by various values about how the country should look. The term 'Thatcherism' was first used by the left. Sociologist Stuart Hall, who popularised the term, saw Thatcherism largely in this way (Hall and Jacques, 1983). Perhaps the best-known summary of Thatcherism came from Andrew Gamble (1979, 1988), who argued that Thatcherism was about 'the free economy and the strong state', that is, that Thatcher's governments were seeking to use the power of the strong central state to create a free-market economy. However, many members of Thatcher's own party also saw Thatcherism in these terms. Ian Gilmour, a one-nation Conservative (of the kind discussed in Chapters 2 and 15), wrote a book called *Dancing with Dogma* (1992), in which he attacked the dogmatism of Thatcherism and the damage that it was doing to the institutions created during the postwar period, such as the NHS.

Other accounts of Thatcherism take a less 'ideological' interpretation. Some commentators argue that Thatcher was just doing what any prime minister would have had to have done to meet the challenges raised by the crisis of the 1970s, including rising unemployment, inflation and trade union militancy (discussed in Chapter 2). Under this view, Thatcherism is much more about Thatcher's personality (Riddell, 1991) or her 'iconoclastic instinct' (Bale, 2010) than a set of ideas. The debate about whether Thatcherism is a clear ideological programme or a summary of various characteristics associated with Thatcher goes on to this day.

rather than an ambitious practical politician, and he stood down, after arguing that poorer people should have fewer children, for which he was denounced as advocating selective breeding. Edward du Cann, another candidate hostile to Heath, also stood down to deal with personal financial issues, leaving only Thatcher to mount a serious challenge from the right. In the first round, Thatcher outvoted Heath, who then stood down in favour of the conciliatory Whitelaw, who also lost. So she became Conservative Party leader in 1975, and eventually prime minister in 1979.

## THATCHERISM: ECONOMIC AND WELFARE POLICIES

Thatcher was a firm believer in the free-market economics of Hayek, Friedman and Adam Smith, the founder of classical economics. (Hayek is discussed in Key Figures 3.1). Like Friedman, Thatcher saw control of the money supply as the key to controlling inflation and, early on, the term monetarism was used to describe her philosophy.

*Monetarism involves controlling inflation by controlling the money supply. More broadly, monetarists reject interventionist Keynesian policies and increased government spending, which, they argue, fuel inflation, particularly if financed by budget deficits and borrowing. Instead, they favour 'rolling back the state' and reducing government spending, to promote free enterprise and a healthy economy.*

In practice, Thatcher's government was not particularly effective in controlling the money supply; high interest rates damaged the manufacturing industry and substantially increased unemployment. Nor was it particularly successful in cutting total state spending, partly because the rise in unemployment increased the cost of welfare benefits. But, her free-market views did inspire the policy with which she became most associated: privatisation.

*Privatisation involves the transfer of ownership of assets from the public sector to the private sector.*

# KEY FIGURES 3.1

## Hayek, neoliberalism and the New Right

**Friedrich von Hayek (1899–1992)**, born in Austria, spent many years teaching in Britain at the London School of Economics, and was eventually naturalised as British. He was a fervent opponent of economic planning, not only Soviet communist planning but also the moderate state intervention favoured by social democrats, New Liberals and one-nation Conservatives. State interference with the free market informed *The Road to Serfdom* (1944). Hayek's ideas were later taken up with enthusiasm by Margaret Thatcher, Keith Joseph and the New Right in Britain and America. Significantly, Hayek sometimes described himself as a liberal rather than a conservative, but his liberalism was the older, free-market *laissez-faire* liberalism of the nineteenth century, rather than the social liberalism advocated by many twentieth-century liberals.

Under Thatcher, huge areas of the economy, formerly run by the state, were sold off to private investors. Timeline 3.1 shows the wave of privatisation implemented by Thatcher and her successor John Major. Advocates of privatisation claimed significant gains in economic efficiency, arguing that the state has no incentive to provide better services for citizens, whereas the market provides a profit motive for companies to provide a cheaper service. However, among other things, critics noted that these public assets were undervalued and sold at a loss. For the Conservatives, privatisation produced political dividends, by promoting 'popular capitalism'.

Another massive transfer of property ownership from public to private sector was secured by legislation obliging local authorities to sell council houses at substantial discounts to tenants; in ten years 1.3 million council houses were sold under the 'right to buy' scheme, turning Britain into what the policies' supporters described as a 'property-owning democracy' (Francis, 2012) and ensuring for the Conservative Party that many working-class families remembered Thatcher as the prime minister who allowed them to own their house for the first time.

While there were some real cuts in public services, the welfare state was not substantially reduced. Thatcher declared 'the NHS is safe in our hands' (quoted in Seldon and Collings, 2000, p. 72), and spending on education per pupil slightly increased. However, these services were exposed to increased competition through the introduction of an internal market in the NHS and similar developments in education. Moreover, some ancillary health and local government services were subjected to compulsory competitive tendering (CCT), whereby services such as cleaning, catering, laundry, refuse collection and ground maintenance were put out to tender to the lowest bidder, which was often a private sector firm (CCT is discussed in Chapter 18, p. 389). The state, at local and national level, was shedding many of the responsibilities that it had taken on after the Second World War.

Timeline 3.1 The main privatisations involving former public enterprise under Thatcher and Major

| Date | Company or undertaking |
| --- | --- |
| 1981 onwards | British Aerospace |
| 1984 onwards | British Telecom |
| 1986 | British Gas |
| 1987 | British Airways |
| 1988 | British Steel Corporation |
| 1989 | Water authorities |
| 1990 | Electricity distribution |
| 1991 | Electricity generation |
| 1995 | British Rail |

*Source*: PA/PA Archive/PA Images

Thatcher enthusiastically embraced free-market ideas and sought to apply them in government.

The Thatcher government also took on the trade unions. Strikes by public sector workers during the 1979 'winter of discontent' were thought by many to be harming British industry and hurting the public. Their impact had been a significant factor in the Conservative election victory. Curbs on union powers, such as compulsory strike ballots and restrictions on picketing, were initially popular, while rising unemployment weakened effective trade union resistance. But when the government's fight with the unions reached its climax with the miners' strike of 1984–85, public sympathy began to switch to the coal miners, who suffered increasing hardship the longer the strike lasted. This sympathy increased when it appeared that Thatcher's government was determined to secure the miners' total defeat, perhaps in revenge for the humiliation the National Union of Miners (NUM) had inflicted on a previous Conservative government in 1974, when its decision to strike had undermined the economic authority of the Heath government. Thatcher was better prepared to confront the NUM than Heath, and, crucially, Britain was now less dependent on coal. The shift towards oil and later gas to provide the bulk of Britain's power needs undermined the NUM's leverage.

## THE 'IRON LADY': FOREIGN POLICY

It was, however, Thatcher's image and record in foreign affairs that earned her the nickname 'Iron Lady'. She secured a rebate in the British contribution to the European Community (EC) budget, establishing a reputation for defending British interests abroad. Her style of diplomacy hardly endeared her to the UK's European partners, although she had earlier supported Britain's entry into the EC, and later signed the Single European Act in 1986 (near the end of her premiership), allowing British entry into the Exchange Rate Mechanism (ERM). More to her taste was the special relationship with the USA and her political ally President Ronald Reagan, to whom she was a reliable ally in the last years of the Cold War. The end of the Cold War appeared as a victory for their joint vision of free-market capitalism over communism.

The Argentine invasion of the Falkland Islands (Las Malvinas to the Argentinians), a British colony in the South Atlantic, could have brought down Thatcher's government, who were caught totally unprepared; the entire Foreign Office team of ministers accepted responsibility and resigned. Instead, the war greatly helped her premiership. The radicalism of Thatcher's domestic policy had led to unpopularity and protest. The Falklands War boosted her flagging support and gained her a reputation as a strong leader. A substantial task force sailed to the Falklands to recapture the islands. (The Falklands War is discussed in Chapter 22.) What began as a political disaster became a personal triumph for the prime minister, if an expensive and divisive one, and Thatcher went on to win the 1983 election by a landslide.

The Falklands and the miners' strike typified Thatcher's leadership style as warrior rather than healer. She was reluctant to compromise at home or abroad. She was also essentially an English politician, who showed little sympathy or understanding for Scottish and Welsh interests and susceptibilities. Thus, she opposed devolution, while support for her party steadily declined in Scotland and Wales. She also took on local government, which was largely in the hands of opposition parties, abolishing the Greater London Council (GLC), led by Ken Livingstone, and the metropolitan counties, including what had become colloquially known as the 'Socialist Republic of South Yorkshire'. She curbed local government spending and, to the initial delight of her party, she replaced domestic rates – the taxation levied by local authorities based on the rentable value of a home, with the flat rate community charge (or 'poll tax' as it became known). This especially hit some poorer households and provoked serious riots in protest. This contributed to her eventual fall in 1990.

By then Thatcher had won three elections and served as premier for over 11 years, a longer continuous term than any of her predecessors since Lord Liverpool in the early nineteenth century. She might have lasted longer still had she not antagonised both the political opposition and also a substantial section of her own party, with whom she was increasingly domineering, leading to the eventual resignation of senior ministers, including Michael Heseltine, Nigel Lawson and Geoffrey Howe. It was Howe's devastating resignation speech that precipitated Heseltine's challenge to her leadership and opened up an election for leader of the Conservative Party, which John Major eventually won (see Key Figures 3.2).

# KEY FIGURES 3.2
## Margaret Thatcher

**Margaret Thatcher (1925–2013)** has a good claim to be the most important prime minister of the twentieth century (the only serious rivals being Churchill for his role in the Second World War and Attlee for the postwar consensus). Thatcher led the Conservative Party from 1975 until 1990 and was prime minister from 1979 to 1990. She was the longest serving UK prime minister in the twentieth century, as well as being the first woman to hold the role. Despite being the first woman to hold this role, a considerable achievement, many feminists do not believe that Thatcher advanced the interests of women.

Thatcher was born to middle-class parents. Her father was a grocer and Methodist preacher. She went to Oxford University to study Chemistry, and later retrained as a barrister. She was elected an MP in 1959. In 1970, Prime Minister Edward Heath appointed her secretary of state for education. The Conservatives lost power in 1974. A year later, with his position severely weakened, Thatcher defeated Heath to become the leader of the party and leader of the opposition.

In office, Thatcher was seen as a 'conviction' politician, who rejected the politics of the post-war consensus. Her policies were a blend of social conservatism and free-market liberalism. To her supporters, she saved Britain from domination by the trade unions and made the country a force to be reckoned with. To her critics, she undermined the welfare state, created inequality and destroyed British industry. She was forced to resign as prime minister by Conservative ministers in 1990, who feared that she was heading for defeat at the upcoming general election. She remains perhaps the most divisive British politician of the modern age.

## THATCHER'S LEGACY

John Major, Thatcher's successor, had a difficult act to follow, his six-and-a-half-year premiership seeming, in retrospect, little more than a prolonged coda to Thatcherism, despite his less dogmatic leadership style. Although the Major government replaced the poll tax with the council tax, it otherwise maintained and extended Thatcher's competition and privatisation policy. Major inherited the American-led first Gulf War, launched in response to Saddam Hussein's invasion of Kuwait. In Europe, he negotiated opt-outs for Britain from the single European currency and the Social Chapter at the Maastricht Treaty, but this did not appease growing Conservative Euroscepticism.

Britain's role in Europe had been a Conservative achievement, yet opinion in the party increasingly moved against the EU, at the very time when the previously divided and hostile Labour Party was moving in the other direction. (Britain's relationship with Europe is discussed in more detail in Chapter 12.) The dramatic events of 'Black Wednesday', in which property speculators made millions of pounds by gambling on a fall in the value of the pound, led to Britain's forced exit from the ERM and the effective devaluation of the pound, in autumn 1992. (Black Wednesday and its consequences are discussed in Chapter 19.) This dealt a blow to Major's government from which it never recovered and contributed further to the growing Eurosceptic divisions within the Conservative Party. Previous economic crises had occurred largely on Labour's watch, while the Conservatives had enjoyed a reputation for economic competence. This was shattered almost overnight. Major's government was also undermined by a series of scandals involving low-level corruption ('cash for questions') and sexual misbehaviour, rendered more serious by Major's call to 'get back to basics', widely interpreted to mean traditional family values. Major delayed the election as long as he could, and the economy did substantially recover, but this was already too late for the prime minister and his party.

## 'NEW LABOUR': BLAIR AND BROWN (1997–2010)

The 1997 election produced a massive reversal of party fortunes. Labour, whose chances of ever returning to power were once almost written off after their third consecutive election loss in 1992, swept to victory with the biggest election landslide since 1945. In the intervening years, Tony Blair, who had led the party since 1994, moved it to the political centre and rebranded it as 'New Labour' (see Chapter 15, pp. 319–20). The new government was dominated by Blair and his chancellor, Gordon Brown, who was given wide authority over economic and social policy – and perhaps a promise that Blair would step aside for Brown to take over. Brown had been widely tipped to become leader and was more experienced than Blair in 1994. Rivalry between the pair was a significant story of the New Labour years. (Blair is discussed in Key Figures 3.3.)

*Source*: PAUL VICENTE/AFP/Getty Images

Tony Blair and 'New Labour' were hugely popular in 1997, the year they won an electoral landslide.

A shell-shocked and much reduced Conservative parliamentary party went on to elect William Hague, the then relatively unknown former Welsh secretary, as their new leader. Meanwhile, the Liberal Democrats doubled their parliamentary representation (on a smaller proportion of the total vote), becoming a credible third parliamentary force. The Liberal Democrats had only been formed in 1988 after a merger between the once powerful Liberal Party, which had gone into decline after the First World War, and the Social Democratic Party (SDP). The SDP had been created in 1981 after a group, made up almost entirely of former Labour MPs unhappy with the party's leftward direction, attempted to 'break the mould' of British politics, by creating their own centre-ground political party.

The dramatic changes in the relative strength of parties made 1997 a landmark election, which transformed the political geography of Britain with a massive 10% swing in support from Conservative to Labour, unprecedented in postwar elections. The Conservatives won no seats in Scotland or Wales, while Labour won parts of the south of England that had previously been alien territory for them. The Conservatives failed to make any appreciable recovery in the ensuing 2001 election, another landslide victory for Labour. Hague resigned, to be replaced briefly by Iain Duncan Smith, and then, in 2003, by Michael Howard. The Conservatives appeared doomed to ineffective opposition following a third consecutive election defeat in 2005. Howard in turn resigned, to be succeeded eventually by David Cameron.

 ## KEY FIGURES 3.3
### Tony Blair

**Tony Blair (1953–)** is known by many students today as the prime minister who took Britain into war with Iraq and for his lucrative business activities after stepping down from Parliament. Blair was, however, by far the most electorally successful Labour prime minister. Until Blair, no previous Labour prime minister had won re-election with a workable majority in parliament. Blair won three general elections in a row, with substantial majorities.

Blair was educated at the fee-paying Fettes School, and became a barrister after attending Oxford University. He was elected an MP in 1983 and became the Labour leader in 1994 after the sudden death of John Smith. Smith and Neil Kinnock, his predecessors as leader, had begun the process of moving the Labour Party to the political centre in an effort to win power. Blair moved to rebrand the party more thoroughly than his predecessors. After being elected leader Blair unofficially renamed the party 'New Labour' to distance it from its 'old', left-wing past.

In 1997, Labour won a landslide general election, making Blair, at 43 years of age, the youngest prime minister since 1812. Under Blair, New Labour invested significantly in health, education and other public services. Blair was a charismatic media performer and was highly popular for the first years of his premiership. However, his strong support for the American-led invasion of Iraq in 2003 undermined public support. He was replaced by his chancellor, Gordon Brown, in 2007.

## LABOUR POLICIES: 'NEW LABOUR', OLD CONSERVATIVE POLICIES?

The 1997 election had a more marked impact on party fortunes than on policy. To the disappointment of many Labour supporters, the new government did not reverse the Conservatives' trade union reforms and privatisation policies, but extended market reforms of the public services. Some even concluded that Blair was Thatcher's heir. But New Labour also introduced other reforms that the Conservatives had opposed, such as a national minimum wage. Labour's record in social policy was contentious. Increased spending on health and education produced some improvements, notably reduced waiting times for operations and better exam results in schools. Yet there were some questions over value for money, and rather more over management regimes and the increased role of the private sector. Moreover, Labour largely failed to reverse significantly the growth of inequality manifest under the previous Conservative administrations (a damning failure from a socialist perspective). Yet Brown's management of the economy appeared to have achieved steady growth, low inflation and low unemployment. Incautiously, he claimed to have ended 'boom and bust'.

Labour's foreign policy proved far more controversial, particularly the close alliance with the USA, involving British forces in several wars, over Kosovo, Afghanistan and Iraq. The last two followed the 9/11 New York terrorist attacks, and were justified as part of the 'war on terror'. The invasion and subsequent occupation of Iraq from 2003 onwards proved particularly divisive. Although this policy was supported by most Conservatives, it split Blair's own party and the country, sparking massive protest marches. (The Iraq invasion and its consequences are discussed in Chapter 22.)

## CONSTITUTIONAL CHANGE: REFORM AND DEVOLUTION

Labour's most enduring legacy is likely to be the sweeping changes in the system of government (many of which are discussed in Chapter 5). Not all of their ambitious programme of constitutional reform was successfully implemented. The failures to fully change the House of Lords or the voting system for the House of Commons particularly disappointed reformers, who also criticised the lack of overall vision and coherence. Despite these shortcomings, the transformation of British government has been substantial and almost certainly irreversible. The Freedom of Information Act 2000 and the Human Rights Act 1998 have had massive implications, not least for the Labour government, allowing the judiciary to hold government to account much more easily (see Chapter 9). The Supreme

Court, created in 2009, was a major reform, enhancing the independence of the judiciary and the separation of the powers of the state. The new voting systems involving more proportional representation introduced for the European Parliament and devolved institutions were not only important in themselves but increased the pressure for reform of the electoral system for Westminster.

The peace settlement in Northern Ireland and the devolution of powers to Scotland and Wales are likely to prove the most important of Labour's constitutional reforms. Blair built on earlier initiatives of the Major government in Northern Ireland, but gained enormous credit for his skill in persuading the main republican and loyalist groups to renounce violence and commit to democratic means. Few could have foreseen that the old irreconcilable DUP leader Ian Paisley could be persuaded eventually to head an executive with the former IRA brigade commander Martin McGuinness in 2007. Yet this unlikely partnership endured, and was continued under other party leaders until 2016, by which time the unexpected referendum vote to leave the EU put fresh pressures on the Irish peace settlement (see Chapter 11).

Developments in Scotland and Wales were initially less dramatic. Plans for devolution in Scotland were substantially agreed between Labour and the Lib Dems in the Scottish Constitutional Convention before the 1997 election. The Blair government swiftly introduced referendums in which Scottish voters emphatically and Welsh voters narrowly endorsed devolution. This provided popular authority for the substantive legislation that followed, establishing a new Scottish Parliament and Welsh Assembly, both elected by the additional member system (for more on this system of voting, see Chapter 13, pp. 272–73). Labour also restored an elected government for London, leading to the election of the maverick Labour MP Ken Livingstone, who had led the old GLC before it was abolished by Thatcher. It was soon clear that devolution was here to stay, once it was accepted by the previously opposed Conservatives.

The consequences of devolution for Labour were initially mixed and, in Scotland, ultimately disastrous for the party. The first elections for the new devolved bodies left them without a majority in either the Scottish Parliament in Holyrood or the Welsh Assembly in Cardiff. Even so, from 1999 to 2007, Labour was the largest party in the Scottish Parliament and took the lead in a coalition government with the Lib Dems. Donald Dewar, who had long advocated devolution, became first minister at Holyrood. In 2011 the Scottish National Party gained the overall majority at Holyrood that had eluded Labour, and Alex Salmond, their then leader, went on to introduce a referendum in 2014 on Scottish independence. This was lost, but the 45% in favour was higher than earlier opinion polls had suggested. In the 2015 general election, Labour was reduced to a single seat, while the SNP won 56 out of 59 seats, although they lost some of that ground to the Conservatives and Labour in 2017. The vote to leave the EU in the 2016 referendum, with a majority of Scots voting to remain, increases the prospects of a second referendum on Scottish independence, and the breakup of the UK. Nicola Sturgeon, the leader of the SNP, campaigned in the 2017 general election on the basis of holding a new referendum on independence, although reigned back on the drive to push that commitment through immediately after losing seats in the election. Whatever the eventual outcome of Scottish independence, British politics and government has already become more multilayered, complex and problematic as a result of devolution.

## FROM BROWN'S BOOM TO THE FINANCIAL CRISIS AND LABOUR'S DEFEAT

What secured for Labour a second and third election victory was probably none of the above, but its apparently successful management of the economy from 1997 to 2007, with Chancellor Gordon Brown presiding over relatively high employment and economic growth with low inflation. It was this economic success that facilitated the substantial growth in public services. Blair finally resigned as Labour leader and prime minister in 2007, in favour of Brown, who was chosen by the party without a challenge.

Although some hoped, and others feared, that Brown's government would involve a marked change of direction, and perhaps a return to 'old Labour', in practice the differences in government personnel and policy were marginal. Brown promoted some of his own followers and advisers, but many of Blair's closest associates survived the departure of their leader. Brown enjoyed a brief honeymoon period in which he toyed with an early general election in the autumn of 2007 to secure a personal mandate. He hesitated, the opportunity passed, and the 'election that never was' began a slide in support for his party from which it never quite recovered (Kavanagh and Cowley, 2010, pp. 1–17). Moreover, although all parties suffered from the parliamentary expenses scandal of 2009 (see Chapter 16, p. 330), which further eroded already low public confidence in politicians, it was Labour, as the party in government, that was most adversely affected.

However, far more critical was the banking crisis and ensuing economic recession of 2008–09 (discussed in more detail in Chapter 19). Although this was a global crisis, the enduring earlier support for the Labour government substantially reflected the economic prosperity of the Blair and Brown years. The recession inevitably called into question Labour's management of the economy and Brown's own record as chancellor. Critics argued that some of the specific problems in Britain could be attributed to Brown's stewardship: the boom had been fuelled partly by the growth of government and consumer spending, the latter financed by often rash lending by banks only subject to the 'light touch' regulation endorsed by Brown.

Brown earned some credit with other world leaders for his energetic response to the crisis and the massive injection of government, and ultimately taxpayers', money to avoid a complete meltdown in public confidence in the whole global financial system. But the crisis had happened on his watch and British voters were rather less impressed with the leadership he showed in responding to it. While his own standing in the country plummeted, many (ultimately unsuccessful) plots arose within the Labour Party to replace him as leader and prime minister. In desperation, Brown surprisingly brought Peter Mandelson, the key architect of New Labour, back into the Cabinet following years of some enmity between the two men dating back to Blair's election as Labour leader in 1994. The new business secretary played an important role in limiting a threatened Cabinet revolt to save Brown's premiership, after disastrous European and local elections for Labour in 2009.

Yet beyond the immediate effect of the crisis on British party politics, the recession had already had much more important consequences for the British economy and society, highlighting once again Britain's overdependence on financial services and the weakness of manufacturing. It dramatised major weaknesses in the regulation of banks and publicised the huge rewards Britain's bankers had reaped in salaries, bonuses, share options and pensions, illuminating the massive and increasing inequality in income and wealth within Britain that successive governments had either encouraged or failed to check. One surprising by-product of the crisis was the temporary return of nationalisation. The Labour government nationalised Northern Rock in 2007 and subsequently bailed out and maintained a stake in much larger banks, including RBS, Lloyds and HBOS. It also renationalised the east coast rail route (later again privatised by the Conservatives). While all this was temporary, it involved a partial reversal of the privatisation associated with the previous quarter of a century under Thatcher and Major. Moreover, the need for more government management of the economy was, for a time, widely accepted. To an extent, the theories and prescriptions of Keynes enjoyed a temporary renaissance.

## CONSERVATIVES, COALITIONS AND CRISIS?

David Cameron was elected Conservative leader in 2005, after the party had lost three general elections in a row. The party was perceived negatively by many voters. Theresa May, who became Cameron's home secretary, had earlier told the members that some voters thought of the Conservatives as 'the nasty party' (May, 2002). For many voters, the party was associated with harsh economic policies, divisions over Europe and several scandals dating back to the 1990s. Cameron (2005) needed to change this image, arguing when he launched his leadership bid that: 'This party has got to look and feel and talk and sound like a completely different organisation.' In his first few months as leader Cameron distanced himself from Thatcherism. He talked about 'diversifying' the party in terms of gender and ethnicity. He apologised for the Conservative's failure to implement economic sanctions on the racist apartheid regime in South Africa, for their introduction of the unpopular 'poll tax' a year earlier in Scotland than in the rest of the UK, and for the privatisation of British Rail under Major, which was widely seen as a failure. While Margaret Thatcher (1987) had argued 'there is no such thing as society', which was seen to reflect an uncaring, individualistic approach, Cameron disagreed and talked about building a 'big society'. Cameron's party proclaimed an interest in social justice, and even the promotion of greater social equality, as well as a concern for the environment. Cameron and Osborne initially promised to match Labour's spending, a pledge that did not survive the financial crisis, which they now blamed on Labour's profligacy (Griffiths, 2014).

Opinion polls in 2009 forecast a decisive Conservative majority at the forthcoming general election, with Brown's personal standing and that of his party hitting new lows. A partial recovery in Labour fortunes early in 2010 proved insufficient for the party to retain power. The result of the 2010 election effectively closed one chapter in British postwar political history, the 13 years of New Labour, and began another, apparently involving a very different kind of coalition government and politics.

The election produced the first 'hung' parliament since the 1970s, and prolonged negotiations over a new coalition government between the Conservatives and Lib Dems, whose leader Nick Clegg had seen his personal ratings soar after the UK's first televised party leaders' debates during the election campaign. His party was rather disappointed to win only 57 seats, fewer than the 62 in 2005, but enough for a comfortable majority added to the Conservatives' 307. Other outcomes briefly appeared possible: a minority (Conservative or conceivably Labour) government, as in 1974, or a 'traffic-light coalition' of Labour, Lib Dems, the solitary Green and others. There was brief discussion of the last option, but it was hardly a viable alternative. The Conservatives and the press would have cried 'foul' and perhaps most voters would have agreed. While the Conservatives had failed to win the election, Labour had clearly lost it, even if not as disastrously as some party supporters feared. The sums did not add up sufficiently to create a viable alternative government with more than a vestigial paper majority. Moreover, the continuing financial and economic crisis was widely considered to require tough measures that only a stable government with solid parliamentary support could deliver.

The Lib Dems disliked the term 'hung parliament', which they argued was pejorative, and preferred 'balanced parliament'. They had a point – a 'hung jury' is one that fails to agree on a verdict. Interestingly, the Northern Ireland Assembly is not described as 'hung'; perhaps because its electoral system and other institutional arrangements were deliberately designed to prevent single-party rule and encourage power-sharing. Similarly, the Scottish Parliament and Welsh Assembly are rarely termed 'hung', even though elections for these bodies have rarely produced a clear majority for a single party.

David Cameron eventually entered 10 Downing Street as the first Conservative prime minister for 13 years, heading the first UK coalition government since the exceptional challenges of the Second World War, with the Lib Dems as junior partners. Soon afterwards, in 2011, the new government introduced fixed-term parliaments, which set the regular dates for general elections that can only be changed under certain conditions. This gave some hope of the coalition lasting until 2015, which it did. (The Fixed-term Parliaments Act and the ease with which it was side-stepped in 2017 by Theresa May's government are discussed in Chapter 7, p. 140.)

Thus, the perpetual third-party outsiders achieved their first share of power in UK government since the war. Nick Clegg, their leader, became deputy prime minister, and Lord President of the Council. This gave him a high profile, but he might have done better to have insisted on a major department. He had few reliable allies in Cabinet. Almost immediately, David Laws, one of his senior colleagues, was obliged to resign as chief secretary to the Treasury, following allegations that he had incorrectly claimed parliamentary expenses for accommodation in his partner's flat. He was replaced by a less experienced Lib Dem, Danny Alexander. The other leading Lib Dem with a major post, Vince Cable, secretary of state for business, innovation and trade, was effectively isolated, as the other economic ministries were in the hands of Conservatives. (Cable was elected leader of the party in 2017, but by this stage the party had lost most of its MPs in the 2015 general election.) In retrospect, Clegg might have struck a tougher bargain, giving his party more clout in government, and a promise of support for their campaign pledges.

Although the Lib Dems were in office, it is questionable how far they were in power. Indeed, it could be argued that their main function was to give Cameron a plausible alibi for disappointing his own backbenchers. Some predicted the coalition government would not survive five years, even after the introduction of fixed-term parliaments. But the Lib Dems had already alienated many of their former voters after they supported the introduction of university tuition fees that they were pledged to oppose in the election campaign. Another major blow was the defeat of a referendum on the alternative vote in 2011 (discussed in Chapter 13), following a strong campaign against the measure by their Conservative partners in government. Even so, the coalition survived until 2015.

Compared with previous postwar Conservative governments, it was inexperienced. Churchill, Eden, Macmillan, Home, Heath, Thatcher and Major had all had ministerial careers, some of them lengthy, before they entered 10 Downing Street. Neither Cameron nor Osborne had been in government, nor had any of their Lib Dem colleagues. Only Kenneth Clarke, who was Lord Chancellor and justice secretary under Cameron, had extensive experience of high office.

The early focus of the coalition government was the reduction of the public deficit resulting from the banking crisis, economic recession and (they would argue) Labour's profligacy. In an analogy that resonated with the public, Labour was accused of failing to fix the roof when the sun was shining, leaving the new government to clear up Labour's mess. It was soon manifest that the coalition was determined to cut the deficit sooner rather than later, and mainly by reductions in public spending rather than increases in taxation. This involved potentially massive implications for public services, and arguably also for equality and social justice.

The key figures in the new government were drawn from a narrow social elite. Prime Minister David Cameron was Eton educated and Chancellor George Osborne had attended Westminster (another leading public school). Both Cameron and Osborne, together with Boris Johnson, the London mayor (and future foreign secretary under Cameron's successor) had been members of the Bullingdon Club at Oxford University, notorious for trashing the expensive restaurants where they dined and paying for the damage they caused. This made it easy for critics to argue that they did not understand – or care – how their government's spending cuts affected the majority of people around the country.

Osborne's critics deplored the damage they felt his budgets caused the economy. Indeed, while some of his budgets were enthusiastically endorsed by Cameron, his party and some financial journalists, they sometimes contained details that later unravelled, particularly the so-called 'omnishambles' budget of 2012, in which a series of policy announcements caused problems for the chancellor after closer inspection (*Hansard*, 2012, HC Deb, 18 April, col. 301). Thus the overall final verdict was rather less complimentary. However, Cameron and Osborne continued to show each other total confidence and mutual support. Indeed, only on one decision did Osborne privately disagree with his chief, on the pledge of a referendum on the EU.

The Labour opposition was eventually headed by Ed Miliband, following the resignation of Gordon Brown and a lengthy party leadership election, in which the frontrunner, former Foreign Secretary David Miliband, was defeated by his younger brother. Labour argued that the pace and scale of the proposed spending cuts put economic recovery at risk and threatened a second recession. They also claimed that behind the government's plans lay a broader ideological agenda to 'shrink the state' and the public sector, reflecting Thatcherite ideas. This placed increasing strains on the Conservatives' coalition partners. While some Lib Dems who had entered government seemed broadly sympathetic to the economic liberalism of their Conservative coalition partners, for example David Laws, many Lib Dem MPs and party members saw themselves as on the left, and committed to the social liberalism that had become the dominant political philosophy of the party.

Cameron (2006) had warned his party against 'banging on over Europe' soon after being elected leader. In government, this warning continued to fall on largely deaf ears, both on the Conservative backbenches and in constituency parties where Euroscepticism continued to flourish. Moreover, under Nigel Farage, UKIP had grown in popularity and appeared to pose a threat to Conservative support, which might cost the party dear at the next election. Finally, in 2012, Cameron agreed to introduce a referendum on Britain's membership of the EU, ignoring the doubts and concerns of his chancellor. Cameron felt fairly sure he would never have to fulfil his pledge, as he knew only too well that his fervently pro-Europe coalition colleagues would never agree. Indeed, they would not, while they were partners in government. However, after the 2015 election, Cameron won an overall majority and was able to form a single-party Conservative government. This unexpected triumph proved a poisoned chalice and ultimately led to Cameron's demise. It meant that he was now honour-bound to implement his referendum promise.

## FROM CAMERON TO MAY

The 2015 election decimated the Lib Dems, who were reduced to eight seats, after voters punished them for coalition with the Conservatives and the compromises to their earlier policies this had forced. The 2015 election also led to considerable turmoil within the Labour Party. Following an election that some thought might make Miliband prime minister, he resigned as party leader, and under a new system for electing Labour's leader that left the final say to party members, Jeremy Corbyn, outsider and former serial rebel, won the leadership, and won it again, after facing a new challenge. He retains the enthusiastic support of most Labour Party members, but not of some of his MPs, nor many of Labour's traditional working-class voters. Labour is further weakened by the massive drop in its support in Scotland, where the SNP controls the Scottish government in Edinburgh and holds almost all Scottish seats at Westminster.

## BREXIT AND THE END OF THE 'CAMEROONS'

Cameron's new Conservative government closely resembled his old coalition government, minus the Lib Dems. Otherwise, most of his old Conservative ministerial colleagues stayed in the same jobs, headed by Osborne at the Exchequer and Theresa May at the Home Office. For a time it looked like the continuation of business as usual. However, the issue of Britain's relationship with the EU was now inescapable. Cameron first tried to win significant concessions from the other member states that would enable him to sell Britain's EU membership to voters. Although he came back with nothing of substance, he was still confident he would be able win the referendum.

Indeed, it was widely expected that British voters would choose to remain. The 'remain' cause was backed by most of business, finance and establishment opinion generally. It was supported by the clear majority of the Cabinet and many Conservative MPs as well as the SNP, the Lib Dems and most of the Labour Party. On the other side were, of course, UKIP, some long-standing Conservative Eurosceptics and, perhaps crucially, Boris Johnson and

Michael Gove, as well as the bulk of the press. Those who favoured 'remain' warned of dire economic consequences if Britain voted to leave. Those who campaigned to 'leave' argued that the costs of membership (which they considerably exaggerated) would be better spent on the NHS. They warned of the ongoing impact of immigration into Britain from the free movement of labour within the EU. Some of them argued that Britain could retain many of the benefits of EU membership by adopting the Swiss or Norwegian arrangements.

In the event, voters opted to leave the EU by 52% to 48%. Cameron almost immediately resigned, and soon afterwards also resigned his seat in Parliament. It was a sudden fall from power, particularly following his surprise majority in 2015. Johnson and Gove, the leading members of the government who had campaigned to leave the EU, fell out explosively when Gove explicitly failed to back Johnson as the next Tory leader. Theresa May – Cameron's home secretary for the previous six years – became leader unopposed, after all other contenders dropped out. While Johnson was rewarded with the Foreign Office by the new prime minister, Gove did not re-enter the cabinet until after May's poor election performance in 2017 – and then perhaps so that May could stop one of her rivals seeking to undermine her from the backbenches. George Osborne, the other main 'Cameroon' (a supporter of Cameron), was never close to May and was immediately removed by her from his job as Chancellor. He stepped down as an MP at the 2017 election, after having taken on numerous highly paid consultancies in the private sector and the editorship of the *Evening Standard*.

## THERESA MAY AND THE 2017 GENERAL ELECTION

Theresa May had been a quiet 'remainer' who did not play a significant part in the referendum debate. She soon made it clear that she intended to implement the decision of the British people, and pursue exit from the EU, declaring 'Brexit means Brexit' (May, 2016a). While Philip Hammond was moved from the Foreign Office to the Treasury, the ministers in charge of pursuing Britain's exit from the EU were all committed 'Brexiteers'. (The nature of Britain's relationship with Europe after Brexit is discussed in more detail in Chapter 12.)

It is no longer just the future of the EU which is at stake but the union of the United Kingdom itself. While England and Wales voted to leave the EU, Scotland and Northern Ireland voted to remain. A particular immediate concern is the future of the peace settlement in Northern Ireland, which once seemed secure. Relations between Northern Ireland and the Republic became a key sticking point in phase one of the UK's Brexit negotiations. By December 2017, the UK committed itself to avoiding a 'hard' border between Northern Ireland and the Republic (although details on how this would be achieved in the wider context of Brexit were hazy). The future of Scotland within the UK is even more problematic. If special conditions for Scotland cannot be negotiated, there is the very real possibility of a second referendum on Scotland's independence, and a customs border between England and Scotland. The United Kingdom could ultimately break up into its component national parts (something discussed in more detail in Chapter 11).

May initially provoked comparisons with Margaret Thatcher, although largely because of her gender. However, in some ways, it is remarkable that the Conservative Party, not known as being generally supportive of feminism, has produced not just one but two female leaders and prime ministers. Both have been described, in an aside by Ken Clarke, the only male politician to have served in Cabinet with both of them, as 'bloody difficult women' (cited in Mason and Asthana, 2016), which perhaps reveals the highly gendered nature of political discourse and style in UK politics, particularly in the Conservative Party. It is also true that May identifies as a feminist, even if she is a divisive figure within the women's movement.

However, in other respects May and Thatcher do not seem similar. Thatcher favoured the free market and wished to rein back the state, seeking to reverse much of the work of her Labour and Conservative predecessors in welfare reforms and economic management. May, by contrast, arguably supports the protective role of the state, perhaps reflecting her Home Office background (Davies, 2016). She favours the 'smart state' rather than the minimal state (Cowley, 2017). She has showed concern for those who are 'just about managing' (the 'jams') (cited in Sodha, 2016) and seems more prepared to use state powers to promote social housing (and renting). Remarkably, May admires aspects of Attlee's government, in marked contrast to Thatcher who sought to destroy much of his legacy. By contrast, one area where May is less favourable to the postwar political consensus is on education: whereas Thatcher's educational policy broadly followed support for comprehensive schools shown by both Labour and Conservative ministers, May wants to bring back more grammar schools, of the type she and Thatcher attended. Yet, while May is not an unqualified advocate of the free market either at home or abroad, Thatcher in office fully supported the single market, whatever she thought of other aspects of the EU. Both Conservative and Labour former prime ministers supported Britain's membership of the EU. May was a quiet 'remainer' before the referendum. Now she has already signified that her priority is restoring Britain's borders and controlling immigration, which seems to mean Britain cannot belong to the single market (Davies, 2016; Cowley, 2017).

In the months after becoming prime minister, May's dominance of British politics seemed to be absolute. By spring 2017 the party were often 20% ahead in opinion polls. When asked who would make the best prime minister, May had a 38% lead over Corbyn in one poll – the highest between UK party leaders ever recorded (Smith, 2017). Over Easter 2017, May decided to go back on her previous promise not to hold a general election until 2020, believing that there would be no better chance to extend her Commons majority, which would make negotiations over Brexit less vulnerable to attacks from rival parties (or her own backbenchers). The decision was disastrous. May promised 'strong and stable' leadership, and placed herself at the centre of the campaign. However, she failed to connect with voters and had to reverse unpopular pledges mid-campaign, notably over long-term care for the elderly. Corbyn's Labour Party, by contrast,

*Source*: Kate Green/Anadolu Agency/Getty Images

After 2017, the Conservative Party relied on a controversial deal with the Northern Irish DUP to secure a majority in the House of Commons.

exceeded almost all expectations. Labour set out a series of popular policies and Corbyn largely benefitted from increased television exposure and pictures of hugely well-attended rallies with passionate supporters around the country. After a six-week campaign, May lost her majority in the House of Commons, although the Conservatives remained the largest party.

After several weeks of negotiations, the Conservatives managed to form an agreement with Northern Ireland's Democratic Unionist Party (DUP), who won ten seats at the election. This gives the Conservatives enough votes in theory to survive in power. The deal with the DUP was, and remains, hugely controversial. First, the party's views on issues such as homosexuality and abortion are deeply conservative, run counter to popular opinion and are offensive to many more socially liberal voters. Second, the deal seems to threaten the Northern Ireland peace process, because the government can no longer realistically claim to be neutral between Irish nationalists and British unionists in the Northern Ireland Assembly

(discussed in more detail in Chapter 11). Finally, the DUP extracted significant financial promises from the government. In return for their support, the government promised over £1 billion pounds of extra investment in Northern Ireland, much to the annoyance of politicians in Scotland and Wales, who did not get similar treatment. May had criticised Labour policies in the election with the line that there is no 'magic money tree' to fund the extra spending (Bush, 2017). Critics responded that May seemed to have found one growing in Belfast. The agreement with the DUP seemed to fatally undermine May's claims for financial competence. May's government staggered on after 2017. George Osborne, her former Cabinet colleague, described her as a 'dead woman walking' (cited in Elgot, 2017). May is severely weakened, although the DUP agreement has provided her with some space. Rivals in the Conservative Party are waiting for their moment to make a leadership challenge. British politics seems to be facing a new period of change and uncertainty.

# SUMMARY

» The Thatcher government brought a marked shift away from the politics of the postwar decades, involving a rejection of Keynesian economics and a renewed emphasis on market forces.

» Major faced increasing differences over Europe within his own party, particularly after Black Wednesday.

» Politics under New Labour showed elements of both change and continuity. Labour's constitutional reform programme has transformed the system of government, with unclear implications for the future, particularly in the UK outside England.

» The credit crunch and recession called into question both Labour's apparent success in managing the economy and the free-market ideas associated with Thatcherism. Keynesian ideas enjoyed a brief modest renaissance.

» The 2010 election unusually resulted in a hung parliament and coalition government between Cameron's Conservatives and the Lib Dems. It is, however, difficult to identify a significant Lib Dem contribution to the coalition. Austerity dominated.

» Cameron's unexpected majority in 2015 was a personal triumph that became a political disaster, as he was obliged to implement his pledge of a referendum on the UK's membership of the EU.

» The referendum vote to leave the EU in June 2016 immediately led to Cameron's resignation, and soon afterwards the emergence of Theresa May as party leader and prime minister. May has repeatedly reaffirmed her commitment to take Britain out of the EU.

» Opposition to Brexit in Scotland and Northern Ireland could eventually lead to the breakup of the United Kingdom.

» The Conservative Party under May lost their majority in the 2017 election and signed an agreement for support with the Northern Irish Democratic Unionist Party. May's position was severely weakened by the election result, while that of Jeremy Corbyn, the Labour leader, has been greatly strengthened by his performance.

# ? QUESTIONS FOR DISCUSSION

» What was 'Thatcherism'? How far did it involve a repudiation of the postwar consensus? How far has Thatcherism survived Thatcher's resignation?

» Was John Major's government simply a continuation of Thatcherism? Why was he defeated so badly in 1997?

» How far did the election of a Labour government in 1997 involve a turning point in British history, comparable to the election of the Attlee government in 1945 or the Thatcher government in 1979?

» How far did New Labour mark the reversal or continuation of Thatcherism?

» Did the hung parliament and coalition government represent a problem or an opportunity?

» Why did Cameron pledge a referendum on EU membership?

» What are the differences and similarities between May and Thatcher?

» Does the 2017 general election show that politics is entering a new, more divisive stage? If so, why, and what are the main issues at stake?

## FURTHER READING

There are many good, popular and readable accounts of this period. In particular, Turner's two books: *Rejoice! Rejoice! Britain in the 1980s* (2013) and *A Classless Society: Britain in the 1990s* (2014) are well worth reading. Journalist Andy McSmith also covers the 1980s well in *No Such Thing as Society: A History of Britain in the 1980s* (2011).

The literature on Thatcherism has become voluminous. Kavanagh (1990) provides a very readable introduction. Beatrix Campbell is still fascinating on Thatcher's support among women voters (1987). Thatcher's (1993) own account of her premiership, *The Downing Street Years*, is worth consulting, while Moore (2013, 2016) has produced an authorised biography, currently running to two volumes. Kavanagh and Seldon (1994) provide a useful survey of the early part of Major's government, while Major's (1999) own autobiography is frank and readable.

The literature on Blair and New Labour is also substantial. Chadwick and Heffernan's *New Labour Reader* (2003) provides a useful, early overview of various materials. Meg Russell's *Building New Labour* is also a useful source (2005). Journalist

Andrew Rawnsley (2001, 2010) provides a useful account of the rise and fall of New Labour. Blair (2010) has now published his own account of his party leadership and premiership. Journalist Steve Richards (2010) provides a good account of Gordon Brown.

There was some extensive discussion of Cameron's conservatism well before he became prime minister, partly because he had already been Conservative Party leader for several years, and was increasingly viewed as a prime minister in waiting. Bale (2010) provides a full account of Conservative 'modernisation'. Theresa May's own brand of conservatism aroused little interest until she expectantly succeeded Cameron. Davies's (2016) article 'Home Office Rules', *London Review of Books*, 38(31): 3–6, explores how her Home Office background shaped her political outlook. A broader piece by Cowley (2017), 'The May Doctrine', *New Statesman*, 8 February, discusses her attitude to the state, the common good and the new realism.

There are more detailed discussion and fuller references on many of the issues discussed in this chapter in some subsequent chapters.

## USEFUL WEBSITES

The journal *Contemporary British History* has many relevant articles:
www.tandfonline.com/toc/fcbh20/current.

The main 'broadsheet' newspapers often contain good analyses of contemporary politics. These include: *The Times*: www.thetimes.co.uk; *The Guardian*: www.guardian.co.uk; *The FT*: www.ft.com; and *The Telegraph*: www.telegraph.co.uk.

There are also important weekly current affairs magazines: *The Economist*: www.economist.com; *The Spectator*: www.spectator.co.uk; *The New Statesman*: www.newstatesman.com; as well as purely online sites, such as: Buzzfeed: www.buzzfeed.com; and *The New European*: www.theneweuropean.co.uk.

*Further student resources to support learning are available at*
**www.macmillanihe.com/griffiths-brit-pol-3e**

# 4 LIFE IN CONTEMPORARY BRITAIN

In a book first published in 1941, Sir Ivor Jennings ([1941] 1966, pp. 8–9), a leading expert on British politics in the mid-twentieth century, wrote:

> Great Britain is a small island with a very homogeneous population. Few think of themselves as primarily English, Scots or Welsh. The sting has long been taken out of religious controversy. The country is so interdependent that there is little economic agitation on a regional basis, as there sometimes is in a large country like the United States. There are class divisions and (what is often the same thing) economic divisions, but they are not wide or deep, and they are tending to disappear through heavy taxation at the one end and high wage rates at the other. We are a closely knit economic unit, with a large measure of common interests and a long political tradition.

Anyone studying contemporary British politics will realise that this description of Britain is hardly valid today. When it was first written, it reflected reasonably accurately the mood of national unity at the height of the Second World War. Moreover, it preceded many of the substantial changes in society and in political attitudes that have taken place in Britain since the Second World War, often reflecting global changes.

These changes have included large-scale immigration into Britain and the emergence of a multi-ethnic and multi-faith society, second- and third-wave feminism and the women's movement (discussed in Chapter 15), the rise of nationalism and devolution, the decline of mining and manufacturing, together with manual trade unionism, and massive changes in the management of the economy. The financial crisis and the ensuing economic recession of 2007–09 has inflicted a more recent shock to the system, with major ongoing economic and political implications. Politics is not static but dynamic. British society and British politics have changed dramatically in the years since the Second World War. They are still changing, and will continue to change, perhaps in directions that it is difficult to foresee.

The economic and social circumstances of a country have significant implications for its politics. Marxists have long argued that political power reflects economic power and economic inequality drives political change. Many British political scientists have acknowledged the importance of economic class divisions especially for party allegiances and voting. But, it is also clear that other social divisions based on national identity, ethnicity, religion, culture, gender and age increasingly affect political perceptions and allegiances and the extent of political participation.

Politics is, therefore, substantially shaped by economic and social factors. Yet it is also widely claimed that politics can transform economies and societies. Governments employ a variety of policies to influence the economic and social behaviour of their citizens; for example, to seek employment, avoid antisocial behaviour, increase saving or consumption and avoid discrimination on grounds of gender, ethnicity or religion. State-sponsored services, such as education, health, social and environmental services, aspire to influence the economy and society.

In this chapter the main emphasis is on the economic and social influences on British politics; the policy chapters in Part IV will focus more on the influence of British political activity on the economy and society.

## THIS CHAPTER:

- » Reflects on the divisions between the nations and regions of Britain and within the cities and regions of the UK.
- » Explores the changing British economy.
- » Investigates inequalities in income and wealth, including those around occupation and social class, Britain's changing class structure, property ownership and the relation between economic inequality and political power.
- » Explores the changing sense and relevance of 'Britishness' and unpicks the social fabric of Britain today, with its various constituent divisions and identities, including gender, ethnicity, religion, age and family life.

## NATIONS, REGIONS AND BRITISHNESS

Although the United Kingdom is made up of four main component national territories (England, Wales, Scotland and Northern Ireland), most of its inhabitants (54.8 million out of 61.5 million) live in England. Thus the union inevitably appears a rather lopsided affair between the English and the much less numerous peoples inhabiting Scotland, Wales and Northern Ireland (see Figure 4.1). Historically, the terms 'England', 'Britain' and 'the United Kingdom' have often inaccurately been used interchangeably, to the annoyance of the Scots, Welsh and Northern Irish.

Each country has its own religious traditions and divisions. Wales, in particular, has its own language and an associated distinctive culture. Scotland has always had a separate legal system. In addition, since the creation of the Scottish Parliament and Welsh Assembly in 1999 and the reopening of what is now the Northern Irish Assembly in the same year, these territories not only continue their own political traditions but all enjoy varying degrees of self-government. There are also important economic differences too. Agriculture is rather more important to the economies of Scotland and Wales than England. Heavy industry in central Scotland, South Wales and Northern Ireland was adversely affected by Britain's industrial decline. Levels of income per head in Wales and Northern Ireland are substantially below the UK average, although there are disparities within each region and territory of the UK.

## Figure 4.1: Population (millions) of the UK, mid-2016

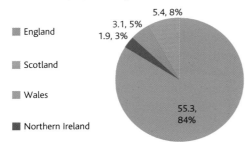

- England
- Scotland
- Wales
- Northern Ireland

5.4, 8%
3.1, 5%
1.9, 3%
55.3, 84%

Total: 65.6

*Source*: Data from ONS (2016a) *Statistical Bulletin: Population Estimates for UK, England and Wales, Scotland and Northern Ireland: mid-2016*, p. 8, www.ons.gov.uk/peoplepopulationandcommunity/populationandmigration/populationestimates/bulletins/annualmidyearpopulationestimates/latest. Contains public sector information licensed under the Open Government Licence v3.0, www.nationalarchives.gov.uk/doc/open-government-licence/version/3/

There are also significant differences in income and other economic indicators, such as unemployment, between English regions. There are marked variations in prosperity between a wealthy London and, to a lesser extent, the southeast, which has seen substantial economic growth in recent decades, often driven by the growth of financial and other services sector, and the poorest English region, the northeast, which has been hit by the long-term decline of heavy industry and manufacturing. Such regional disparities fuel demands for more favourable treatment by government, assistance for inward investment and improvements to basic infrastructure.

These economic disparities in the performance of Britain's nations and regions have some implications for political allegiances. The 'North–South divide' in social, cultural and economic differences between the north and south of England has become something of a cliché, albeit with some basis in economic and political reality. Not only is the south richer than the north, but Labour's main political support still comes from the working-class populations in the industrial north of England, central Scotland, South Wales and inner London, while Conservative strength lies in the south of England and particularly the southeast. The Midlands are politically contested. Although economic inequality and relative deprivation partly explain the distinctive political allegiances of Wales, Northern Ireland and parts of Scotland, cultural factors and the politics of identity have long been more significant in Northern Ireland, and are increasingly important in Scotland and Wales. (This is discussed in detail in Chapter 11.)

There remain, however, more significant differences in economic activity and thus in income and wealth within nations and regions. Yorkshire and the Humber, for example, is among the poorest of Britain's regions, but it contains the city of Leeds, which is relatively booming as a major financial, commercial and administrative centre, at least compared with neighbouring Bradford, Sheffield and Hull. Bradford is now unhappily known for its deprivation, racial tension and riots rather than the woollen industry on which its former wealth was based. Yet within the boundaries of the Bradford Metropolitan District is the small commuter town of Ilkley, overwhelmingly white, middle-class and as comfortably prosperous as parts of the Surrey 'stockbroker belt' in the wealthy southeast. Ilkley is, in turn, part of the parliamentary constituency of Keighley, a formerly prosperous woollen town, now inhabited mainly by distinct groups of poor working-class Asian communities on one hand and predominantly white communities on the other, with only rare interaction between the two. Similar comparisons between neighbouring areas of prosperity and deprivation could be drawn all over Britain.

Thus there are generally marked differences in wealth and living standards between inner urban areas on the one hand and outer suburbs and 'dormitory' (i.e. commuter) towns on the other. Some of the political implications of these economic differences can be charted in the party representation of parliamentary constituencies and local government wards. It is still broadly true that the more deprived urban areas are more likely to be represented by Labour, and the more prosperous outer suburbs and semi-rural areas by Conservatives. However, where economic deprivation is particularly significant, there may also be more serious political consequences in terms of alienation, antisocial and criminal behaviour, disturbances to public order, intercommunity conflict and the rise of fundamentalist parties and movements, such as the far-right English Defence League.

Where people live is less significant for politics than how people think about where they live and the nations or communities to which they think they belong, that is, the question of 'identity'. *The Guardian* newspaper ran a series of stories in 2011 entitled *Disunited Kingdom?*, reporting the weakness of British identity around the UK as a whole. If voters were forced to choose, 52% of English voters choose 'British' as their self-identification first compared to just 19% of Scots and 30% of Welsh (Carrell, 2011). Of course, such felt identities and allegiances can shift further over time, but they have some clear implications for the future of UK and British politics generally. Support for independence is strongest in Scotland and Northern Ireland, although there is considerable nationalist support in parts of Wales too, as well as in Cornwall. Scotland rejected independence in September 2014, with 55% of voters wanting to remain a part of the UK, although pressure continues from many nationalists for a new referendum. The recent history of Northern Ireland has been more violent, with conflict between unionists, who support Northern Ireland's continuing membership of the UK, and republicans, who do not. However, recent polling showed 22% of voters supported a united Ireland, while 63% wanted to stay in the UK (Ipsos MORI, 2015). (For more discussion, see Chapter 11.)

## Economic Division

### THE CHANGING ECONOMY

Britain was the first country to industrialise, beginning in the eighteenth century, and by the nineteenth century it was seen as the 'workshop of the world'. Yet even before the end of the nineteenth century, Britain was already being overtaken by the new industrial strength of the USA and Germany, and commentators noted British economic decline (Gamble, 1981, pp. 13–14). The decline was relative. In the postwar period, growth and living standards continued to increase, but at a slower rate than leading competitors (Gamble, 1981, pp. 18–23; Gamble, 2000, pp. 2–10). In the aftermath of the Second World War millions of British workers were still employed in mining, iron and steel, shipbuilding, textiles and clothing, and motor manufacturing.

Since then output and employment in all these industries has declined dramatically, and the British share of world production has shrunk. The UK still has the fifth largest economy in the world (in terms of current gross domestic product (GDP), a measure of what is produced in an area in a particular period) behind the USA, Japan, China and Germany (World Bank, 2017). Yet, taking account of the number of people in the UK (GDP per capita), the UK is behind all these, as well as being behind all the Scandinavian and Benelux countries, some Gulf states, Australia, Canada and the Irish Republic. Explaining British economic relative decline has become a major subject of political debate. Depending on the political analysis, it has been attributed to faults in Britain's entrepreneurs and workers, company structure, trade unions, banking system, education system, government intervention and the welfare state.

Some communities, cities and regions were harder hit than others by relative economic decline. The collapse in shipbuilding particularly hit Clydeside in Scotland, Belfast in Northern Ireland and Tyneside in northeast England. Pit closures have decimated employment in the coalfields of central Scotland, South Wales and Yorkshire. The rundown of the textile industry has seen the closure of Lancashire cotton mills and Yorkshire woollen mills, and the blighting of the once prosperous towns and cities in which they were based. The contraction of the iron and steel industries has particularly affected cities like Sheffield and, more recently, Swansea. In recent decades, problems in motor manufacturing have had particularly adverse consequences for the West Midlands.

So Britain, like other western countries, is adjusting, sometimes painfully, to a postindustrial society, with an economy increasingly centred on services rather than mining and manufacturing. Most British workers are no longer employed in making tangible objects – clothes, cars and 'white goods', such as fridges and washing machines. Instead, they provide services to each other and the wider world, including education, health and social care, retailing, hotels and catering, maintenance and cleaning, and professional and financial services.

Until recently, the one apparent success story in the British economy was the continuing growth of its financial services, particularly in London and the southeast. Successive governments sought to preserve and enhance London as a world financial centre, replacing controls with 'light-touch' regulation. Easier credit supplied by banks fuelled much of Britain's economic boom from 1992 to 2007. Although the financial and then economic crisis of 2007–08 onwards highlighted the overdependence of the British economy on its financial sector, politicians hesitated to introduce more controls, fearful of 'killing the goose that lays the golden eggs' and risking the transfer of London's financial services to other countries. The rest of the economy suffered for the bankers' mistakes, and for politicians' failure to regulate their activities appropriately, with some parts of the country worse affected than others. (The economic crisis is discussed in Chapter 19.)

## INEQUALITIES IN INCOME AND WEALTH

With changes in the economy, new patterns of inequality emerge in income and wealth. The division between the rich and the poor has been seen as the crucial political divide. Commonly, the rich have constituted a tiny minority, and poverty has been the common experience of the majority. In the nineteenth century, industrialisation raised living standards and redistributed income and wealth between groups, but it did not reduce inequality within

society as a whole, and indeed may have increased it. However, particularly after the Second World War, it was no longer necessarily assumed that governments could or should do nothing about poverty and inequality. Although only a minority in Britain advocated an immediate radical redistribution of wealth and income, postwar Labour and Conservative governments up until the 1970s largely agreed that redistribution to eliminate poverty should be a key principle of social policy. In practice, this meant reducing relative poverty rather than the absolute poverty suffered by many in the wider world. Taxation was progressive, with the better-off paying much greater percentages of their incomes in tax than the less well-off. Tax revenues were used by governments to provide a 'social wage' – including free education, free healthcare, pensions and other benefits for all, but particularly benefiting the poor. Thus, from 1945 to 1979, wealth and income became significantly more equally distributed (Mullard and Swaray, 2008, pp. 36–8).

Relative poverty means people cannot afford things that most of the population in Britain take for granted. Relative poverty changes over time. In the early 1950s, most Britons did not own a car, television, refrigerator or telephone, but were not considered poor, although they would be today. Some critics on the right argue that relative poverty is a term invented by the left to describe inequality, which they claim is inevitable and essentially desirable as an incentive to labour and enterprise.

Absolute poverty involves the lack of basic necessities of life: food, clothing, shelter and so on. While many millions around the world experience absolute poverty, very few do in advanced western economies like Britain.

From the 1970s onwards, politicians associated with the 'New Right' challenged the former progressive consensus that increased equality was good in principle, arguing that high taxation reduced incentives to work and enterprise, while state welfare produced a 'dependency culture'. Cutting taxes and reducing welfare would release enterprise and energy that would result in the creation of more wealth. The fear of poverty, no longer cushioned by generous welfare benefits, would encourage many poor people to 'get on their bikes' in search of work. The poor would benefit from the 'trickle down' of prosperity from the rich. Creating new wealth would assist the poor more than redistributing existing wealth. (The New Right is discussed in Chapter 15.)

This change in attitudes to economic and social inequality underpinned changes in public policy under Conservative administrations from 1979. Inequalities in income and wealth that had been declining in the postwar decades increased sharply in the 1980s and 90s. Income differences in the UK grew 40% from the mid-1970s until the early 1990s (Wilkinson and Pickett, 2010, pp. 239–41). The widening gap between rich and poor was partly the consequence of deliberate changes in the tax and benefit system, including a shift from direct to indirect taxation and cuts in the higher rates of income tax. It also reflected other developments, including rising unemployment, the decline of mining and manufacturing and the reduced membership and power of the trade unions. The effects of inequality in society are examined in Comparing British Politics 4.1.

## 🇬🇧 COMPARING BRITISH POLITICS 4.1 🌍
### Inequality and social problems

Wilkinson and Pickett (2010, pp. 15–19) review the distribution of income in 23 rich countries with a population over 3 million, using UN figures to compare the gap between the richest and poorest 20%. The UK is the fourth most unequal society, behind Singapore, the USA and Portugal. The most equal societies in this survey were Japan followed by the Scandinavian countries, Finland, Norway, Sweden and Denmark. Wilkinson and Pickett go on to correlate inequality with a wide range of health and social problems, showing that the most unequal countries have lower levels of trust and lower life expectancy with high infant mortality. They also have more mental illness (including drug and alcohol addiction), more obesity, teenage births, homicides and people in prison, and lower children's educational achievement and social mobility. Thus the most unequal societies are worse off in other respects. UK policies, targeted to reduce health or educational inequality, have largely failed because they are tackling symptoms rather than accepting 'the glaringly obvious fact that these problems have common roots in inequality and relative deprivation' (Wilkinson and Pickett, 2010, pp. 238–9).

Britain continues to be characterised by wide disparities in the distribution of wealth, as Figure 4.2 demonstrates. The richest 10% of households have wealth of well over £1 million, while the poorest 10% have £12,600 – almost a hundred times less. For much of the population, the only significant wealth they own is bound up in their houses (as we see in Figure 4.3 on p. 63). In the next section, we examine in rather more detail the nature and extent of these social divisions by exploring the contentious concept of social class.

### Occupation and social class

It is sometimes suggested that Britain is already, or well on the way to becoming, a classless society. Others, however, not only suggest that class differences are persistent, but that social inequality is increasing. Some foreign observers are struck by the extent to which Britain remains a class-conscious country. Class remains an important concept in social science in general and political science in particular. It is, for example, still regarded as an important factor in explaining voting behaviour and party allegiance (see Chapter 13, pp. 278–79). It is most commonly defined and measured in terms of occupational categories, but different categories are used for different purposes, hinting at problems and ambiguities in fundamental concepts.

Class is a particularly important aspect of the Marxist perspective on power and the state. 'The history of all hitherto existing society

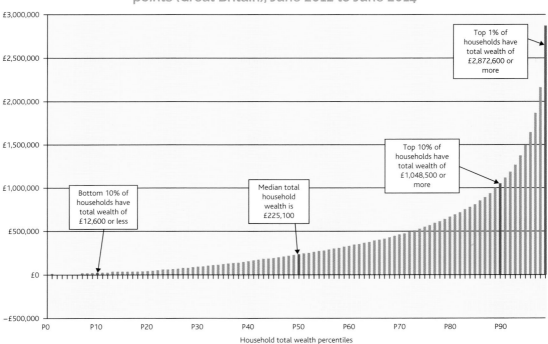

Figure 4.2: Distribution of total household wealth, percentile points (Great Britain), June 2012 to June 2014

*Source*: ONS (2015a) *Main results from the Wealth and Assets Survey: July 2012 to June 2014*, Figure 2, p. 3, www.ons.gov.uk/peoplepopulationandcommunity/personalandhouseholdfinances/income andwealth/compendium/wealthingreatbritainwave4/2012to2014/mainresultsfromthewealthand assetssurveyjuly2012tojune2014. Contains public sector information licensed under the Open Government Licence v3.0, www.nationalarchives.gov.uk/doc/open-government-licence/version/3/

is the history of class struggles' (*Communist Manifesto*, Marx and Engels, [1848] 2017). Marx, however, used the term 'class' in a distinctive way, linking it with the ownership of productive wealth rather than occupation. He assumed that there was a fundamental conflict of interest in a capitalist society between those who owned and controlled the 'means of production' – the capitalists or *bourgeoisie* – and those who owned only their own labour, the proletariat. These were the two key classes that mattered in a capitalist society – others such as the old landed gentry, the *petit bourgeoisie* (shopkeepers etc.) and the peasants were becoming progressively less significant.

Some argue that actual ownership of the means of production may be less important in a modern capitalist society, where ownership can be divorced from effective control, and the key decisions are made by managers. Marx

may also have underestimated the power of the professions and the growing state bureaucracy. These developments were more fully appreciated by Max Weber, writing in the early twentieth century. While Weber acknowledged that the ownership of property was a key element in understanding social inequality, he also attached importance to differences in status between, in particular, occupational groups. Our modern understanding of class often owes more to Weber than to Marx.

A long-established three-class distinction – upper, middle and lower (or 'working') – is linked in popular usage to hierarchies of social status. The 'upper class' is often linked with the old aristocracy and landed gentry, or used in a quasi-Marxist sense to mean those who are sufficiently wealthy not to have to depend on their own labour for a more than adequate income. The terms 'middle class' and 'working class', particularly the former, cover too wide

*Source*: Dan Kitwood/Getty Images News/Getty Images
A fire in Grenfell Tower, a high-rise block in North Kensington, London, in June 2017 caused 71 deaths. Residents had expressed concerns about fire safety before the event, which highlighted the disparities of wealth in one of the most affluent areas of the UK.

a range to be of much practical value unless broken down into further subcategories. Thus, the middle class is commonly taken to include business owners and directors, both salaried and self-employed professionals, clerical workers, shopkeepers and own account workers (such as small builders). While some work in the private sector and some own their own businesses, many others work in the public sector. It should be clear that many of this diverse 'middle class' scarcely share the same economic and political interests. Some have a strong interest in low taxation and reduced regulation of business enterprise; others have a vested interest in high public expenditure and thus high taxation. Some are professionally involved in the state intervention and regulation that other members of the middle class complain about.

The distinction between the middle and working class in the popular understanding is most commonly associated with the division between 'white-collar' (or non-manual) work and 'blue-collar' (or manual) work, and it also underpins some formal classifications for statistical purposes and much academic analysis. However, the division between manual and non-manual work is not always closely aligned with differences in income and wealth. Some 'white-collar' jobs (e.g. junior clerical workers) are relatively poorly paid, while in parts of Britain some manual workers (plumbers and builders) enjoy comparatively high wages. Moreover, the distinction between a manual working class and a non-manual middle class in no way corresponds to the Marxist distinction between the working class and the '*bourgeoisie*', despite the fact that this term is often loosely translated as 'middle class'. From a Marxist perspective, both blue-collar and white-collar workers are 'working class'. The (essentially non-Marxist) British Labour Party similarly referred to the familiar distinction between manual and non-manual work, but rejected its significance, in the phrase 'workers by hand or by brain' in the old clause IV of its constitution (discussed in Chapter 15 on ideology).

Academic commentators have often grouped junior white-collar workers with the working class, along with various categories of manual workers, and this makes a great deal of sense in terms of income and economic inequality. Even so, the distinction in assumed social status between white-collar and blue-collar work has proved remarkably persistent, with implications for political behaviour. Thus, many poorly paid white-collar workers have declined to identify themselves with the 'interests of labour', which the Labour Party and its trade union allies claimed to champion.

Nevertheless, it is increasingly questionable whether this distinction between manual and non-manual work means much anymore. Because of the decline of mining and heavy manufacturing industries, and the increased application of technology, most work no longer involves heavy physical labour. At the same time, some white-collar and blue-collar occupations have experienced an element of 'deskilling', while others require more complex skills and training than before.

The social class categories used by political scientists are for the most part reasonably objective – depending chiefly on occupation. One common classification came originally from the Institute of Practitioners in Advertising, to help understand the market, but it has been widely adopted by many political scientists, particularly in the analysis of voting and party allegiance. It consists of:

A   Higher managerial, administrative or professional

B   Intermediate managerial, administrative or professional

C1  Supervisory or clerical, and junior managerial, administrative or professional

C2  Skilled manual workers

D   Semi-skilled and unskilled manual workers

E   State pensioners or widows (no other earnings), casual or lowest grade workers, long-term unemployed.

But individuals may think of themselves as working class or middle class, and this 'self-assigned' class may not correspond with the categorisation of statisticians. Thus a manual worker who earns high wages, owns his own house and car and adopts a middle-class lifestyle may think of himself as middle class. Similarly, some university lecturers (middle class by classifications based on occupation) may identify with the working class. Self-assigned class may be significant for political behaviour. For example, a manual worker who considers himself middle class may be more likely to vote Conservative, while many self-proclaimed working-class lecturers will be on the left politically.

## Changing class structure?

There has been much academic debate on how Britain's class structure may be changing (including some innovative new attempts to classify Britain's social class system, such as Savage et al., 2013). Some argue that the old manual working class is now relatively far smaller and more fragmented – 'class fragmentation'. Others claim that inequalities in income and wealth are as significant as ever and the basic class structure of Britain has not altered – 'class persistence'. Others again believe that old class divisions are being replaced by new ones – 'class realignment'.

These disagreements relate back to differences in theoretical assumptions and classifications (discussed above). If the working class is identified with manual workers formerly employed in mining and manufacturing, it is clear that numbers have declined in line with these industrial sectors. Moreover, many new jobs in the services sector are commonly counted as middle class, because they appear to be 'white collar' and 'non-manual'. However, it is at best questionable whether, for example, work in call centres (one major growth area), should be regarded as 'middle class'. It is poorly paid, relatively unskilled work often undertaken on a short-term or casual basis.

It is certainly true that there is a larger proportion of the population now employed in management. Moreover, it is also true that the working class appears more fragmented between employed and unemployed, part time and full time, public sector and private sector, as well as along increasingly important gender and ethnic lines. These differences have clearly reduced traditional working-class solidarity, with political repercussions for the organisation of labour through the trade union movement and for the Labour Party, which historically relies heavily on working-class support. Moreover, as a consequence, partly of the decline of traditional manual occupations and partly of changes in the law, far fewer workers are now members of trade unions. By 2015, only just under a quarter (25.8%) of all workers were unionised. Today, union density is higher among women workers than men, a remarkable turnaround from the days when the British trade union movement was heavily male dominated (BIS, 2015). This is due in part to the fact that women are more likely to be employed in highly unionised professions, such as schools and in healthcare.

It has been persuasively argued that there are now significant new cleavages in British society, based not on differences within the production process but on differences in the consumption of goods and services. It is claimed that there are significant differences in interest between those who are substantially reliant on public services – particularly transport, education, health and housing services – and those who

own their own homes and cars and use private healthcare and private schools. The former have a vested interest in public services and in higher public spending and taxation, the latter in lower public spending and taxation. Indeed, the poorer public services are, the more their decision to opt out of them seems justified.

## Housing tenure and the distribution of property

One of the most significant of these 'consumption cleavages' used to be housing tenure. A key distinction was between 'homeowners', who owned their house outright or were buying it on a mortgage, and those who were renting a house from the local authority. While many 'working-class' people lived in council houses, owner occupation was a badge of middle-class respectability. The council estate was among the most reliable sources of Labour votes, while homeowners were far more likely to vote Conservative. However, the sale of council houses and the transfer of substantial local authority housing to other landlords, both encouraged by Conservative governments after 1979, substantially altered the pattern of housing tenure (see Figure 4.3).

Figure 4.3: UK household tenure: 1977 to 2014

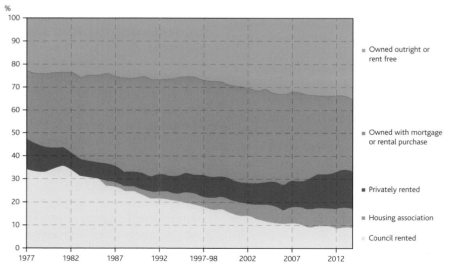

*Source*: ONS (2016b) *Economic Review: April 2016*, Figure 15 p. 16, www.ons.gov.uk/economy/nationalaccounts/uksectoraccounts/articles/economicreview/april2016. Compiled using data from Living Costs & Food Survey, Expenditure & Food Survey, National Food Survey. Contains public sector information licensed under the Open Government Licence v3.0, www.nationalarchives.gov.uk/doc/open-government-licence/version/3/

So the number of council houses had been more than halved, a trend that continued under New Labour, when some remaining council estates were transferred to housing associations – private, non-profit organisations, which provide low-cost 'social housing'. Owner occupation has become easily the majority form of housing tenure. The substantial rise in house prices was a major factor in the consumption and credit boom that culminated in the financial crisis of 2007–08. However, since then, credit has become tighter and, as a result, many young adults are now finding it difficult to obtain the substantial down payments required for mortgage loans to get a foot on the property ladder. The result is that more young people live with parents for longer than before, particularly in the south east of England, or end up renting property for many years rather than buying.

## Economic inequality and political power

The growth of homeownership is one aspect of what might be seen as a deliberate attempt to give more people a stake in property. A growing proportion of the population has now acquired a large, if indirect, stake in the stock market through the growing market in pension and life insurance funds. However, the most high-profile stimulus to wider shareholding was provided through the heavily promoted privatisations and flotations of shares in former nationalised industries by the Thatcher and Major governments. The initial flotations were so successful that they were substantially oversubscribed. The cumulative effect was that shareholders outnumbered the (declining) trade union members, which could not have been anticipated in the very different economic and political climate in the years immediately after the Second World War.

This suggests that 'popular capitalism' has arrived. Yet the extent of the change can be exaggerated. While many more people seemed to have acquired a stake in property or capitalism, for most of them that stake has remained very small. As Figure 4.3 on p. 63 indicates, property ownership has not been significantly spread, but remains heavily concentrated. Income inequality has widened since the 1970s. Little significant progress has been made towards either the old Labour ideal of a more equal society or the Conservative 'property-owning democracy'.

The relationship between economic inequality and political power remains contentious. The norms of representative democracy – one person, one vote, one value – suggest political equality and the rule of the majority. To Marxists, the concentration of income and wealth in the hands of the few reflects the effective concentration of political power in the hands of the ruling class. To right-wing liberals, inequality in income and wealth simply reflects market forces and the effects of the unequal distribution of talents and enterprise in society. Both Marxists and neoliberals assume the primacy of economics over politics. Social democrats, by contrast, implicitly assume that the political power of the majority can be mobilised to create a more equal society through the ballot box and representative government (Judt, 2010). These very different views of power are discussed in Chapter 15. They lead to very different ideas about the role of the state and are worth bearing in mind throughout this book.

However, economic inequalities only tell part of the story. From the 1960s and 70s onwards, this was coupled with strenuous efforts to reverse the discrimination and disadvantage that some suffered, by reason of their sexuality, gender, race or disability. There appeared to be a gradual shift in emphasis away from the class politics of the first half of the century towards identity politics, that is, politics concerning the groups or communities with which individuals subjectively identified. This reflected extensive evidence of discrimination on these grounds in Britain, clearly visible in official statistics, but illustrated further by the evidence of campaigning groups and commissioned reports. Some of this involved equal opportunities legislation, assisted by the creation of new official bodies such as the Race Relations Board, the Equal Opportunities Commission and the Disability Rights Commission. However, this also provoked some political backlash, with criticism of 'politically correct' ('PC') values and attitudes, particularly in the popular press.

# ALLEGIANCE AND IDENTITY

## ETHNICITY

The British are the product of waves of invasion and immigration from different ethnic groups over the centuries – Celts, Angles, Saxons, Vikings, Norman French and so on. Although sometimes surviving in place names and surnames, these ethnic origins generally have had no lasting political implications. Seventy years ago, British society was relatively ethnically homogeneous. With the partial exception of the Jewish and Irish communities, ethnic minorities were too small to be politically significant.

In sharp contrast, contemporary Britain is characterised by ethnic diversity, particularly in most major cities, largely as a result of relatively recent immigration from former British colonies, from Europe and, to some degree, from the rest of the world. Britain's new multicultural society offers a rich variety of experience and opportunity to the general benefit, although it has also brought some tension within and between communities. Many ethnic minorities suffer from discrimination and prejudice.

The definition of 'ethnicity' and how it is distinguished from terms such as 'nation', 'culture', 'community' and 'race' is problematic. Ethnicity generally refers to shared cultural practices and heritage that set one group of people apart from another. It could include a shared ancestry, sense of history, language or religion, for example. The more contentious and problematic term 'race' is generally used to refer to groups of people who are perceived to possess certain physical characteristics that are then ascribed social significance, such as skin colour (see, for example, Wilson and Wilson, 2002). The term 'ethnic minorities' today generally refers to non-white ethnic groups. But not all ethnic minorities are 'non-white'. Long-resident Jewish communities and Poles and Ukrainians who settled in Britain after the Second World War are sometimes categorised as ethnic minorities. There are also more recent (mainly white) economic migrants from Eastern Europe, resulting from the free movement of labour within the EU.

Politicians, journalists and political and social scientists often use terms such as BAME (black, Asian and minority ethnic) or BME (black and minority ethnic) as a label for members of these groups. However, these terms are increasingly controversial. Trevor Phillips (2015), former chair of the Commission for Racial Equality, argued that these phrases have become outdated, existing 'to tidy away the messy jumble of real human beings who share only one characteristic – that they don't have white skin'. He argued that the acronyms could be divisive and served to mask the different experiences of particular ethnic and cultural groups. The experiences of the grandchildren of Christian immigrants from the Caribbean is likely to be very different to that of immigrant Muslims from Pakistan, for example. To Phillips, placing all these groups in one category is unhelpful.

Those who did not describe themselves as 'white' made up 14% of the UK population in the 2011 census (the last UK-wide census) – an increase from around 9% in 2001 and 6% in 1991 (ONS, 2011a). Indian was the next largest ethnic group, with 1.4 million people (2.5%), followed by Pakistani (2.0%), as shown in Figure 4.4 (overleaf).

Issues of identity and allegiance can be complicated for ethnic minorities. It is hardly surprising that many relatively recent immigrants and their immediate descendants should have some continuing positive sentiments towards their country of origin, particularly where they retain contacts with relatives there. In the UK, there are thriving Indian, Pakistani, Caribbean, Irish, Polish, Italian and many other communities in most British towns and cities. These dual identities suggest that allegiances are not mutually exclusive – it is, of course, possible to be, for example, Asian and British, and such a dual allegiance is clearly felt by many. These hybrid identities are reflected in the latest census and shown in Figure 4.4.

Figure 4.4: Ethnic groups, England and Wales

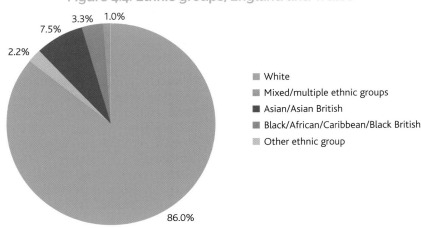

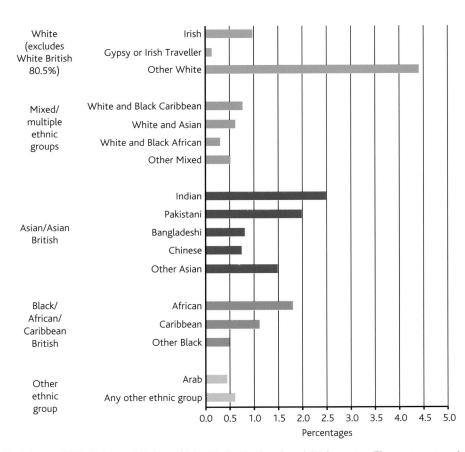

*Source*: ONS (2011a) *Ethnicity and National Identity in England and Wales: 2011*, Figure 1, p. 3, using 2011 census data. Accessible from www.ons.gov.uk/peoplepopulationandcommunity/culturalidentity/ ethnicity/articles/ethnicityandnationalidentityinenglandandwales/2012-12-11. Contains public sector information licensed under the Open Government Licence v3.0, www.nationalarchives.gov.uk/doc/ open-government-licence/version/3/

*Source*: Stu Forster/Getty Images Sport/Getty Images

Sporting events, such as the 2012 London Olympics, can help to forge national identity.

Overall, ethnic minorities and different faith communities have contributed hugely to the British economy and culture. The arts, the media, sport, fashion, cuisine and numerous other areas would be immeasurably poorer without the variety and vitality of the contributions of Britain's ethnic minorities. Yet this is far from being universally agreed. Some see it as a threat to the traditional 'British' way of life and national identity. Norman Tebbit, the Conservative politician, claimed that 'most people in Britain did not want to live in a multicultural, multiracial society, but it has been foisted on them' (quoted in Solomos, 2003, p. 218). Some members of the white working class have felt uncomfortable about the effect of immigration on jobs and hold a more general grievance that the social, cultural and economic changes that have occurred in the UK in recent years have not helped them (Kenny, 2011). This group were seen as key actors in the decision to leave the EU in 2016, voting 'out' in order to limit the free movement of labour that comes as a condition of membership. (For more on the EU, see Chapter 12.) However, although there are areas where different communities freely intermingle in a genuinely multicultural society, residential segregation and mutual misunderstanding and suspicion are also common.

Postwar immigration is largely a legacy of empire, and many immigrants felt close ties to the UK (Hammond Perry, 2016). Immigration to the UK, free to Commonwealth citizens until 1962, has been progressively tightened since then. Earlier postwar governments only acted when racial prejudice and conflict involved civil disorder. In the late 1950s, Britain experienced its first major 'race riots', which were an unexpected shock. In response, successive governments introduced increasingly tough restrictions on immigration. These restrictions appeared racist, as effectively they targeted non-whites, but they were not tough enough to satisfy the far right and even some mainstream politicians, who sought a virtual halt to black immigration and the 'repatriation' of those already in Britain.

Restrictive immigration policies have generally been accompanied by more liberal policies towards ethnic minorities already resident within Britain. The Race Relations Acts of 1965, 1968 and 1976 outlawed direct and indirect discrimination in widening areas of public life and provision such as housing, employment and education.

But anti-discrimination legislation has not ensured equality for ethnic minorities. Recent surveys have shown that child poverty is much higher in some ethnic minority groups than in the rest of the population. Over 40% of Bangladeshi and Pakistani children are growing up in poverty, compared with 31% of Chinese, 22% of black Caribbean and 15% of children in the white majority population (Understanding Society, 2016). Black children perform significantly worse in schools and are far more likely to be excluded from school than white children. Unemployment levels remain significantly higher for most ethnic minorities, particularly those of black, Pakistani or mixed ethnicity. Young people from ethnic minorities are also less likely to be in education, employment or training after school, and find it much more difficult to secure jobs than their white counterparts. Black and Asian citizens are less likely to be employed in occupations appropriate to their qualifications, and are more likely to be employed in part-time or casual labour, often involving working unsociable hours. They also encounter discrimination in the housing market. They are more likely to be victims of certain kinds of crime and are far more likely to be stopped by the police and questioned (Ministry of Justice, 2015). Yet the picture is more mixed than this analysis suggests. Chinese and Indian pupils, for example, outperform white children in schools. Within and between ethnic groups, generalisations can be misleading.

Allegations of racism in the police and other institutions persist. In schools, racism has been blamed for the underperformance of black pupils. Young black males are still much more likely to be excluded from schools than their white counterparts. Predominantly white teachers may unconsciously have low expectations of black pupils, which contribute to low self-esteem and poor behaviour among the students themselves, who lack positive role models to inspire them.

## RELIGION

Religious conflict, once a major source of political division, was a running thread in British political history from the sixteenth to the nineteenth centuries. Yet apart from the persecution of the relatively small Jewish minority, religious divisions then were between variants of Christianity. Following the Protestant reformations in England and Scotland in the sixteenth century, Roman Catholics became a feared, hated and persecuted minority in Britain, and an oppressed majority in Ireland. The further division between high Anglicanism and Puritanism (or, later, nonconformism) in the seventeenth century was the major cause of the English Civil Wars (1642–51), contributing significantly to subsequent political differences between the rival Tory and Whig parties. While the Church of England was dubbed the 'Tory Party at prayer', it was the 'nonconformist conscience' of Methodists, Baptists and other non-Anglican Protestants that was the bedrock of British nineteenth-century liberalism, and a key strand in the early Labour Party. (Some of these issues are discussed in more detail in Chapter 14.)

Yet if religion was once important as a source of political inspiration and conflict, its political significance declined rapidly for most of the twentieth century. Today, Anglicans, nonconformists, Catholics and Jews can be found among the supporters of all modern mainstream political parties (in Britain, if not Northern Ireland). Secularism is on the rise in Britain. Between 2001 and 2011, there was a decrease in people who identified as Christian (from 71.7% to 59.3%) and an increase in those reporting no religion (from 14.8% to 25.1%) (ONS, 2011b). Many of those who still routinely claim to be Christian do not attend church services. Christian affiliation has ceased to be an indicator of political allegiance for most of England, apart from areas such as Liverpool, where the Protestant/Catholic divide remains important in sporting loyalties and has a significant if diminishing influence on party support. In Scotland, especially Glasgow, parts of Edinburgh and the Western Isles, religious differences remained a key factor in explaining political allegiances. In Northern Ireland, however, religious affiliations still correlate closely with political loyalties, particularly for the fundamental unionist/nationalist divide (discussed in Chapter 11).

Leaving Northern Ireland aside, there are some signs that religious differences may once again become more politically significant in twenty-first-century Britain, not because of divisions within Christianity, but due to the increasing importance of other religious faiths. The Jewish faith (0.5% of the population) retains a high profile; a strong Jewish identity is still felt by many of Jewish descent, even those with little or no religious belief. Physical evidence of the multi-faith society Britain has become is provided by the Muslim mosques and Hindu and Sikh temples in British cities. Of these faiths, Islam is the most visible and important, in terms of numbers of adherents (over 2.7 million or 4.8% of the population), places of worship and political significance. Religion may be more important in the lives of those belonging to non-Christian faith groups. Many are heavily concentrated in specific localities within London and other large urban areas (ONS, 2011b).

Conflict arose from the publication in 1989 of Salman Rushdie's *The Satanic Verses*, a book that Muslims regarded as offensive to their faith, leading to death threats against the author, who was obliged to go into hiding with police protection. For western liberals the principle of freedom of speech was at stake. For many Muslims, the Rushdie affair symbolised a wider lack of respect for their religion and culture. It has sharpened other issues over Muslim dress and religious observance. However, such issues remain less divisive in Britain than in France, where Muslim girls are forbidden to wear the veil (or hijab) in state schools (see Parekh, 2000, pp. 249–54). The debate about multiculturalism is introduced in Spotlight 4.1.

Until recently, these religious affiliations had a relatively marginal significance for politics. But following the 11 September 2001 attacks in the USA, and the ensuing 'war on terror', there was a much greater discussion of the role of religion in contemporary society. In the UK, there have now been several terrorist attacks associated with Islamic fundamentalism, killing scores of people, notably the London bombings in 2005,

the murder of Fusilier Lee Rigby in 2013, and in 2017 a van and knife attack in Westminster, a bomb attack at an Ariana Grande concert in Manchester, and another van and knife attack on London Bridge. To some in the West, these terrorist atrocities chillingly confirmed the predictions of Samuel Huntington (1996), who had argued that the old Cold War ideological conflict between two superpowers would be replaced by broader struggles between rival cultures, such as between Islam and the West. While US President George W. Bush and UK Prime Minister Tony Blair insisted that the invasion of Afghanistan (2001) and Iraq (2003) involved a 'war against terrorism', not 'a war against Islam', many Muslims believed that Britain and America were indeed involved in such a war.

# SPOTLIGHT ON ...    Multiculturalism    4.1

Political theorist Bhikhu Parekh (2000) argued that western liberals wrongly assumed their ideas had universal validity. Thus western liberal values embodied in declarations of rights conflicted with other communities' cultures, which involved other values, such as 'social harmony, respect for authority, orderly society, a united and extended family and a sense of filial piety' (Parekh, 2000, p. 137). Human beings are not the same everywhere, but 'culturally embedded in the sense that they are born into, raised in and deeply shaped by their cultural communities'. The distinctive cultures of minority communities should be respected by the majority, even where they appear to conflict with universal human rights.

British political philosopher Brian Barry (2001, p. 58) argued that respecting minority rights 'is liable to be harmful to women and children in minority communities and to those within them who deviate from prevailing norms'. Respecting the values of other cultures might

entail accepting discrimination on grounds of gender or caste, and legitimating prejudices against different sexual orientations. The appeal to universal principles and rights helped to abolish slavery and transform the status of women, while hitherto prevailing cultural norms had justified discrimination on grounds of race and gender. The cultural values of minority communities may even involve restricting rights to free speech (see the Rushdie affair above).

Parekh (2000, p. 196), however, acknowledged inevitable tensions between the norms of majority and minority communities. Any society 'should foster a strong sense of unity and common belonging among its citizens'. The problem is how to reconcile unity with diversity. Parekh went on to discuss sensitively several controversial issues, including female genital mutilation, polygamy, Muslim and Jewish methods of slaughtering animals, arranged marriages, initiation ceremonies and exemption from legal or school requirements on dress.

Inevitably, the conflict provoked divided loyalties for British Muslims and, for some, further weakened their British allegiance and identity. At the same time, fears aroused by

al-Qaeda and later so-called 'Islamic State' (IS) atrocities inflamed popular prejudice and suspicion against British Muslims, even though leading British Muslim organisations had roundly condemned extremism. In the UK, extremist groups and parties exploited popular fears, suggesting that Muslims were a potential 'enemy within'. There were some 'revenge attacks' against Muslims and their mosques, notably a van attack in Finsbury Park, London in 2017. This indiscriminate Islamophobia has seriously damaged intercommunity relations.

Compared with the problems associated with Islamophobia, other religious controversies appear less serious. Even so, some other minority faiths, such as Hindus and Sikhs, have concerns over issues of dress and diet, while some Jewish people detect a revival of anti-Semitism. Even some Christian groups have issues around aspects of gender equality, such as women priests and bishops, and gay rights, for example the rights of same-sex couples to adopt children. Meanwhile, secular humanists continue to criticise what they consider to be the unreasonable privileges of faith groups, such as subsidies for faith schools, and the established church in particular.

## GENDER

For women, despite some legal advances, postwar Britain remained profoundly unequal. They had far fewer opportunities in education and employment than men, particularly in the professions and business. Even where they were doing the same work, they were commonly paid much less. Most married women were financially dependent on their husbands. They were widely expected to be responsible for all the domestic chores and child-rearing, even if they were also undertaking paid work outside the home. Despite the right to vote, women remained grossly underrepresented at every level of British politics. The House of Commons long remained an overwhelmingly male-dominated chamber, while the House of Lords was all-male until the 1960s.

Some changes in the 1960s were the product of the 'permissive society', although these were never quite as permissive as legend suggests. The widespread availability of new forms of contraception (principally the pill), controlled by women rather than men, made it easier for married and unmarried women to avoid pregnancy. Many 'career women' sought to delay motherhood, and some chose to avoid

it altogether. The legalisation of abortion in 1967 and the reform of divorce laws in 1969 both reflected changes in social attitudes and assisted further change. Women did not always gain from the new social and legal climate. Men were arguably the main beneficiaries of sexual liberation and increased marital breakdown. Yet most women did have more choice in relationships and sexual behaviour.

Women from the 1960s onwards also drew attention to a long-standing evil that had long been virtually ignored, the evidence of persistent violence against women, and the sexual abuse of women and children. However, despite some change in public attitudes, just 5.7% of rape cases end in conviction and two women a week are killed by a current or former partner (Kelly et al., 2005). Women's groups have also established refuges and other forms of support for abused women (although cuts to public spending since the economic crisis in 2008 have seen many refuges close).

Women's economic position also changed, particularly as traditional male employment in mining and heavy manufacturing declined and opportunities for employment grew in the services and professions. Many more women entered, and advanced in, the traditionally male-dominated professions of law, medicine, accounting and education, and to some degree in banking, business and the media, even if a 'glass ceiling' often seemed to prevent them from rising to the highest levels (although entrance to the professions was overwhelmingly dominated by white, middle class women). At the same time, women still dominate lower paid industries, sometimes summarised as the five Cs: cleaning, catering, childcare, cashiering (retail) and clerical (administrative roles). Opportunities in higher education expanded markedly for both sexes. From being a tiny minority of university graduates, women over time achieved near equality.

While men still outnumber women in the workforce, the gap is fast closing, as Figure 4.5 shows. Yet these figures are rather misleading, as women are much more likely than men to be working part time – 42% of women were in part-time work compared to 12% of men (ONS, 2013). Moreover, women still undertake a disproportionate share of the burden of domestic work and childcare, even when both members of a heterosexual relationship are in full-time paid work. They are also far more likely to be involved in the care of elderly relatives.

Women's dual caring burden may be one reason (besides discrimination) why relatively few women reach the highest and most well-paid managerial and professional posts. Women's average pay still lags well behind that of men, despite equal pay and equal opportunities legislation (shown in Figure 4.5). While the gender pay gap between men's and women's earnings is relatively low for people under 30, it increases substantially after that, as women taken on roles as primary carers. Moreover, differences in income extend into retirement. The overall gender pay gap in Britain is over 18% (EHRC, 2017).

*The **gender pay gap** is a measure of the difference between men's and women's average earnings across an organisation or the labour market. It is expressed as a percentage of men's earnings.*

Figure 4.5: UK employment rates for men and women aged 16–64, 1971–2013

The employment rates for men and women have changed over time:

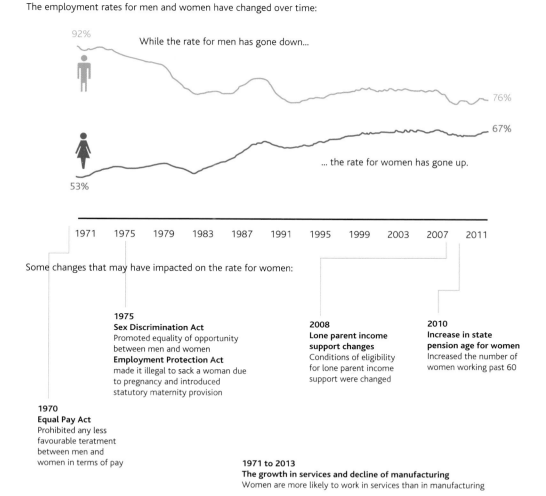

Some changes that may have impacted on the rate for women:

**1975**
**Sex Discrimination Act**
Promoted equality of opportunity between men and women
**Employment Protection Act**
made it illegal to sack a woman due to pregnancy and introduced statutory maternity provision

**2008**
**Lone parent income support changes**
Conditions of eligibility for lone parent income support were changed

**2010**
**Increase in state pension age for women**
Increased the number of women working past 60

**1970**
**Equal Pay Act**
Prohibited any less favourable teratment between men and women in terms of pay

**1971 to 2013**
**The growth in services and decline of manufacturing**
Women are more likely to work in services than in manufacturing

*Source*: ONS (2013) *Women in the Labour Market: 2013*, p. 3, compiled using data from Labour Force Survey. Accessible at: www.ons.gov.uk/employmentandlabourmarket/peopleinwork/ employmentandemployeetypes/articles/womeninthelabourmarket/2013-09-25. Contains public sector information licensed under the Open Government Licence v3.0, www.nationalarchives.gov.uk/ doc/open-government-licence/version/3/

As we shall see in subsequent chapters, men still substantially outnumber women in formal involvement in politics and government, although that is changing. One consequence of this continued male dominance of the political process, feminists would argue, is that policies are still skewed towards male interests and economic dominance. While gender divisions have not often been expressed in terms of separate political parties (with the notable exception of the Women's Equality Party, founded in 2015), they have been politically expressed in a number of other ways. Thus women have worked in pressure groups, through and across existing parties and through the women's movement as a whole to secure better representation in politics and government and specific reforms to improve the position of women. Yet numerous other divisions, including class, age, ethnicity and religion, cut across the gender divide. Inevitably, women find themselves on opposite sides on many political issues (see, in particular, Chapter 15 on feminism and Chapter 6 on women's representation in Parliament).

## FAMILIES AND SEXUALITY

Families are the smallest social group, but one that, to an extent, transcends divisions of gender and age. As an institution, 'the family' is changing rapidly. The period 1945 to 1970 is often caricatured as the age of the 'nuclear family', a heterosexual couple and their dependent children, although there were always exceptions to this and the period is historically unusual, rather than the norm. The era of the nuclear family also contained higher rates of relationship breakup, marital unhappiness and violence towards women and children than is realised, partly because divorce was financially and legally inaccessible to all but middle- and upper-class men. Indeed, it was not until 1978 that men were fully legally restrained from beating their wives (Thane, 2010). More recently, as a result of both changes in the law from the 1960s onwards and slower and partial changes in public attitudes more recently, there is now a diversity of lifestyles and families where once the values of traditional marriage and the small nuclear family predominated.

Cohabiting without marrying is now common and accepted – a change from a time when unmarried couples that cohabited were described as 'living in sin'. There is no longer a stigma attached to children who are born outside marriage, so that couples who have children feel less obligation to marry. Marriage remains popular, however, with some trying it two or three times or more, as hope triumphs over experience. Moreover, many same-sex couples now seek to regularise their union, with civil partnerships introduced in 2004 and legislation to allow same-sex marriage in England and Wales passed by the Parliament of the UK in 2013 and Scotland in 2014. Same-sex marriage is still not possible in Northern Ireland.

As divorce and remarriage have become common, many families have become more complex, with a web of step-parents, step-grandparents and step-siblings. And, while many extended families operate amicably, family breakdown can be a source of trauma for children, and can lead to economic and social problems requiring intervention by social services and other state agencies. Thus issues around the family have become increasingly political. Particularly on the political right, strengthening 'family values' has become a political mantra.

There is also more freedom for individuals to pursue their own lifestyle. This includes freedom to pursue homosexual relationships. Once sexual activity, even between consenting men, was a criminal offence (homosexuality was never criminalised for women – as it was not thought possible for women to have sex without a man involved). Gay men were imprisoned for having sexual relationships. It was not until 1967 that private homosexual acts between men were decriminalised, and then only in England and Wales. (Decriminalisation did not happen until 1980 in Scotland and 1982 in Northern Ireland.) However, the age of consent for gay men was 21. It was not until 1994 that this age was lowered to 18 and 2001 before it was lowered again to 16 – making it the same as the age of consent for heterosexuals.

However, the change in attitudes towards homosexuality is not universal. Younger people are more likely to report that they are homosexual than older people, perhaps because of greater prejudice among the older generation (ONS, 2015a). Nor has this acceptance extended to all communities. Homosexuals can still suffer homophobia and abuse, which has even extended to murder. Catholic adoption agencies are unwilling to consider adoption by same-sex couples. Some ethnic minorities and non-Christian faiths remain particularly intolerant of same-sex relationships. Yet, compared with a half a century ago, homosexuals today face far less discrimination and prejudice.

## AGE

As a social division, age groups may seem obvious, as we may share interests and

*Source*: iStock.com/oversnap

The London Underground, decorated in the colours of the rainbow, to mark 50 years since the decriminalisation of homosexuality.

## KEY FIGURES 4.1

### The 'average' Briton

The Office for National Statistics (ONS, 2010) has found that:

» The *'average' British woman* is 40 years and seven months old and has 42 years left to live. If she works full time, she works 34 hours a week, earns £22,151 a year, and is educated up to GCSE A*–C level. If she lives in England or Wales, she will have 1.96 children during her lifetime. If she lives in England, she is 161.6cm tall and weighs 70.2kg.

» The *'average' British man* is 38 years and 4 months old and has 41 years left to live. If he works full time, he works 39 hours per week and earns £28,270 a year. He is educated up to A-level standard. If he lives in England, he is 175.3cm tall and weighs 83.6kg.

» When a *British family goes shopping*, the five items most likely to be put in the typical weekly grocery shopping basket are a two-pint carton of semi-skimmed milk, pre-packed sliced ham, unsweetened breakfast cereal, bacon and a bar of milk chocolate.

» The *'average' household size* in Great Britain in 2009 was 2.4 people per household compared with 2.9 people per household in 1971.

Of course, any average is, to some degree, misleading. The UK, as we have seen, is highly diverse. But statistics are vitally important for government. The information above raises huge challenges for policy-makers. Smaller families need smaller houses, for example, while an ageing population has different healthcare needs. Who we are matters to policy-makers.

attitudes with those who have had similar life experiences. Yet age groups are an unusual division, as we move between statistical age categories in the course of our lifetime. The old may remember how it feels to be young, while the young may anticipate how their needs, capacities and circumstances will change with age. Even so, the elderly can be the victims of negative stereotypes and they may experience

some of the same kind of discrimination and prejudice felt by some other groups.

There have been significant changes in the age structure of the British population from the nineteenth and even the mid-twentieth century, with considerable implications for politics and economic and social policy. As a result of increasing longevity and decreasing birth rates, in 2008 for the first time those of pensionable age (11.8 million) exceeded the numbers of those under 16 (11.5 million). The ageing population has enormous implications for policy-makers, in almost every area of policy – including health and social care, employment, education and welfare. The state pension age, which was set at 60 for women and 65 for men, is now being gradually raised as people live longer. Between 2010 and 2020, it is planned that the age of retirement for women will be brought up to the same age as men (65) and thereafter the state pension age for both sexes will rise in three stages to 68 in 2046.

Older people have growing political weight. They not only outnumber younger voters, but are more likely to use their vote (see Chapter 13, pp. 280–81). They also have the time and leisure to involve themselves in other political activities, in political parties and a range of pressure groups. The implications of an ageing population are particularly obvious for pensions and health, and it is no accident that these two issues have shot up the political agenda in recent years. Adequate pensions and good healthcare are critical for the quality of life of the elderly, but have massive implications for public expenditure and taxation.

It should not be assumed, however, that older people have homogeneous interests. They are a diverse group. Thus older people who are largely or wholly reliant on state benefits, for example, may experience real poverty, while those with good occupational pensions and who own their own home may enjoy a better quality of life than when they were younger. However, both categories of pensioners may, as they age further, suffer physical and mental deterioration, to the extent that they become dependent on the care of others, perhaps relatives or professional careers in their own home, but more commonly in nursing homes. While such care is increasingly expensive, raising major issues of how the costs should be met, some older people suffer not only loneliness and boredom but also increasing physical discomfort and pain.

Younger adults constitute a smaller proportion of the population than formerly. In recent years, younger people have had relatively low involvement in conventional politics; although some would argue that this is balanced by their involvement in single-issue pressure groups. The election of Jeremy Corbyn as Labour leader led to a significant increase in the proportion of young people voting in the 2017 general election, as the party managed to pull together a message that clearly enthused younger voters. (The Corbyn surge among younger voters is discussed in more detail in Chapter 13.) As with older people, generalisations are dangerous, as there are many significant divisions among young adults; between the growing number of university students and graduates and those not involved in higher education, between the full-time employed, casually employed and unemployed, along with differences associated with gender and ethnic divisions. Thus there is some active resentment of students among some poor working-class communities where relatively few have attended university. While some younger adults are much more comfortable within a multicultural environment than their elders, others from both the white majority and ethnic minorities are attracted to more extremist or exclusive political involvement, such as racist parties or various forms of religious fundamentalism.

There are clear differences of attitude between age groups on a range of issues, some essentially economic, others based on formative influences when young, such as drugs, crime, sexual orientation and race relations. Different generations may have different expectations because of the experiences they have gone through. Prevailing values in society when people were young may condition their own attitudes for a lifetime. There is some evidence to support the assumption that, as they age, people become more set in their ways, less open to change and conservative (with a small 'c', but perhaps with a large 'C' as well), although there are some conspicuous exceptions to this generalisation.

There is some potential for increased intergenerational conflict, as former Conservative minister David Willetts sets out in his book, *The Pinch: How the Baby Boomers Took Their Children's Future – And Why They Should Give it Back* (2010). Willetts argued that the baby boomers born between 1945 and

1965 run the country and by virtue of their sheer demographic power have fashioned policies in a way that meets their housing, healthcare and financial needs at the expense of younger citizens in particular. Recent and current students who have piled up debts to finance their higher education are also entitled to regard with some envy an earlier generation who enjoyed not only free tuition but fairly generous maintenance grants. But current and future workers will have to pay increased taxes to support the steadily rising financial costs of maintaining the elderly. Many will also find there is little prospect of inheriting much from parents and grandparents, as their houses and savings are utilised to help pay for their care.

## DISABILITY

The prevalence of disability rises with age. While only around 6% of children are disabled, 16% of working age adults and 45% of adults over pension age are disabled. This means that there are over 11 million people in Britain with a limiting long-term illness, impairment or disability. Most commonly, this will include impairments that affect mobility, lifting or carrying (Department for Work and Pensions/ Office for Disability Issues, 2014).

A substantially higher proportion of individuals who live in families with disabled members live in poverty, compared to individuals who live in families where no one is disabled: 21% of children in families with at least one disabled member are in poverty, a significantly higher proportion than the 16% of children in families with no disabled member. Disabled people remain significantly less likely to be in employment than non-disabled people, are less likely to be out of work or hold a qualification. There is substantial regional variation in the number of people reporting a disability, with a strong link between disability and economic inequality.

Disabled people frequently experience unfair treatment and discrimination. Until relatively recently, disabled people had no rights that could be enforced in courts and so suffered extensive discrimination. Those considered mentally disabled were often shut away in remote 'lunatic asylums'. The physically disabled fared little better. There were few jobs available, as employers were not obliged to provide facilities for the disabled, nor to employ them at all. There were severe problems of access to shops and services as there was no obligation to provide ramps, lifts, or even doors sufficiently wide to take wheelchairs. Both physically and mentally disabled people suffered from discrimination and prejudice and were often treated as if they were invisible.

Their position has improved somewhat as a result of government legislation and some changes in public attitudes. The Disability Discrimination Act 1995 made it illegal to discriminate against the disabled in employment, the provision of goods and services, education and transport. From 2004, service providers were supposed to provide improved physical access to facilities. There have been further Acts (2005) and amending legislation to extend rights and services to disabled people. In 2000, the Disability Rights Commission was established, replacing the former National Disability Council (since replaced by the Equality and Human Rights Commission in 2007). Campaigners have helped to change public attitudes, although this has been further assisted by the growth in the numbers of elderly disabled, as the population ages.

Who are the British today? Clearly, they are not the homogenous population that Sir Ivor Jennings described at the start of this chapter, if they ever were. The Britain of today is more diverse, with a multicultural and multi-ethnic population. It is also a more open and accepting place than a generation ago. But, Britain is a far from equal place. There are significant differences of wealth within and between regions, with some areas of the UK still struggling to adapt to the long-term decline of manufacturing and industry. In terms of social values, while women, gay people and ethnic minorities face less discrimination than was once the case, sexism, homophobia, racism and other forms of prejudice are still common. How society and governments respond to the challenges of the next generation remains to be seen.

## SUMMARY

» British politics is shaped by ongoing changes in economy and society, although this is a two-way process, as government and politics can in turn influence economic and social change.

» While most of the population of the UK live in England, Scotland, Wales and Northern Ireland retain their own distinctive economic interests, cultures and identities.

» There are substantial inequalities between the English regions, between the north and south of England, and within regions and cities.

» The decline in mining and manufacturing, and the increased importance of (particularly financial) services has major ongoing implications for the distribution of wealth and income and for political attitudes and behaviour.

» After the end of the Second World War, a cross-party consensus accepted that government had a responsibility to reduce poverty and inequality.

» Income and particularly wealth remain unequally distributed in Britain, with some obvious implications for political power, although the relationship remains contentious.

» Changes in occupational class structure overlaid by other social differences have had contentious implications for politics. Differences based on the consumption (public or private) of key goods and services (particularly housing) may be of increased significance.

» This progressive consensus was increasingly challenged by New Right (or neoliberal) analysis that suggested that welfare benefits encouraged a dependency culture that reduced incentives and harmed the poor they were supposed to help.

» Evidence of the social problems associated with a wider gulf between rich and poor has helped revive the case for more economic equality. However, the post-recession economic climate may not help to reduce income inequality.

» There has been less focus recently on reducing economic inequality, and more on remedying the discrimination and disadvantage suffered by particular categories or groups of people – women, people who are gay or disabled, ethnic and faith minorities.

» A growing ethnic minority population has resulted from immigration from the 'new Commonwealth' and more recently from Eastern Europe. Ethnic differences reinforced by social and educational segregation have fed prejudice and discrimination, and created some political tension between communities.

» Political differences related to variants of Christianity have declined in significance. However, non-Christian faiths are practised by an increasing minority. Many Muslims have suffered from Islamophobia.

» The role of women continues to change in the workplace, but less in the home. Gender divisions have had only a limited impact on party political allegiances, but women continue to suffer discrimination in many fields, including politics, and there is an ongoing struggle to secure equal rights for women.

» Changes in the age structure of the UK population mean that pensioners now comfortably outnumber children. The 'grey vote' is of increasing political significance and, especially after the 2016 referendum on membership of the EU and the 2017 general election, stark differences were clear between how older and younger people voted.

## ? QUESTIONS FOR DISCUSSION

» Why are more people in Scotland and Wales identifying themselves as Scots or Welsh rather than British? What might be the political implications?

» How far and in what respect has Britain declined in relation to other states?

» Is social class still important for British politics? How might changes in the class structure have affected political allegiances?

» Why was there an apparent reduction in inequality from the Second World War onwards and an increase in inequality after 1979?

» How far should it be the business of government to reduce inequality?

» How far do ethnic minorities suffer continuing prejudice and discrimination in Britain? Are ethnic tensions rising or declining?

» How significant for politics are differences in religious belief? Should politicians pay more attention to 'faith politics', and if so, why? What are the causes and consequences of Islamophobia?

» How far does the more extensive participation of women in the paid workforce indicate there is no longer significant discrimination against them? Why might gender differences remain important for politics?

» Explain the increasing differences in voting behaviour between younger and older citizens.

 ## FURTHER READING

Many of the implications of the social and economic divisions explored here for British politics as a whole are addressed in later chapters of this book; see particularly Chapter 11 on devolution, Chapter 19 on the economy and Part III, which covers chapters on 'people and politics'.

The most authoritative and detailed statistics on the UK population are to be found in the full official census, undertaken every ten years. However, up-to-date statistics will not be obtainable until the results of the 2021 census are available. Even the census is not particularly helpful on some divisions within the UK population, for example on religious allegiances and observance.

Evans and Tilley (2017) provide an interesting account of *The New Politics of Class: The Political Exclusion of the British Working Class*. Wilkinson and Pickett (2010) compare the extent of inequality in the UK with other states, and correlate this with a range of other social characteristics and problems, as does Marmot (2015) in *The Health Gap: The Challenge of an Unequal World*. Piketty's (2013) masterful tome *Capital in the Twenty-First Century* provides an analysis of inequality of wealth and income in Europe and the USA since the eighteenth century and was a surprising bestseller when it was released. Celebrated reports on racism in Britain include Scarman (1981) and Macpherson (1999). Kelley, Khan and Sharrock's *Racial prejudice in Britain today* (2017) is a useful contemporary summary of social attitudes on this issue. On ageism and intergenerational conflict, see Willetts (2010). The Fawcett Society has produced a series of reports on discrimination against women in politics and society more broadly, including *Sex Equality: State of The Nation 2016* (2016).

 ## USEFUL WEBSITES

The most easily accessible source for up-to-date statistics is from the Office for National Statistics (ONS): www.ons.gov.uk.

 *Further student resources to support learning are available at*
**www.macmillanihe.com/griffiths-brit-pol-3e**

# PART II

# GOVERNMENT AND GOVERNANCE

Part II explores government and governance in the UK, setting out the changing constitution and exploring some of the UK's key institutions, from Parliament to the law. It also examines the various tiers of government in the UK from local to European, ending with an exploration of Great Britain and Northern Ireland's relationship with Europe after Brexit.

## POLITICS IN ACTION

Simon Griffiths, one of the authors of this book, provides an overview of some of the key questions and themes in this Part.

Catherine Haddon discusses the UK's changing constitution, reflects on the principle of parliamentary sovereignty and Brexit, and examines the role of the prime minister, cabinet and civil service.

Watch the videos at **www.macmillanihe.com/griffiths-brit-pol-3e**

# 5

# THE CHANGING CONSTITUTION

The British constitution is in a state of rapid change. Both the Labour government that took office in 1997 and the Conservative-led governments that followed pledged constitutional reform. Since 2010, for example, politicians have promised to give voters the right to recall wayward MPs, sought to reduce the number of MPs and reform the House of Lords on a more democratic basis. The cumulative impact of recent and proposed constitutional change involves a massive change to Britain's traditional system of government.

To its defenders, however, British government has long appeared a model of stability in a changing and unpredictable world. Since the upheavals of the seventeenth century, culminating in the so-called 'Glorious Revolution' of 1688, and the 1707 Act of Union, Britain has not experienced the revolutions and regime changes that have characterised, for example, French government and politics for over 200 years. Instead, for its proponents, the British system of government evolved gradually towards a constitutional monarchy and later a parliamentary democracy, a process substantially completed at the end of the First World War. Its defenders argued that reforms were grafted onto traditional institutions and the new was painlessly absorbed into the old and familiar. There appeared to be no need to spell out the functions of different parts of government, nor the rights of citizens in any authoritative written constitution, such as other states possessed. With the spread of empire, Britain's system of government was exported around the world (see Comparing British Politics 5.4 on p. 90). Indeed, what was sometimes described as 'the Westminster model' was widely admired at home and abroad.

Have recent reforms superseded the Westminster model? Do the recent reforms make sense? Or have they been grafted onto traditional institutions and principles without much apparent thought being given to the implications for the system as a whole. Is the current constitution such a mess that the tensions and ambiguities inherent in this still evolving new system of government can only be resolved by a written constitution?

## THIS CHAPTER:

» Sets out the key features or principles of the British constitution.

» Examines the 'uncodified' British constitution and asks how constitutions change.

» Reviews the changing positions of the main political parties on constitutional issues, from the stability of the postwar period to the time of flux we are in today.

» Concludes by asking if the traditional constitutional principles discussed at the outset still accurately describe the current constitution, and whether those principles are appropriate for today's political problems.

## THE NATURE OF THE CONSTITUTION

In the analysis of any system of government the powers of the state are widely grouped under three headings: **legislative**, **executive** and **judicial**.

In many other countries the separation of legislative, executive and judicial powers has long been established as an important constitutional principle. It is a key feature of the American Constitution, and many other constitutions that have been established since. In the USA, the executive is the presidency, the legislature, Congress, while the Supreme Court heads an independent judiciary. There are checks and balances in the American Constitution that are designed to prevent any part of government from becoming too powerful.

Back in the eighteenth century, British government appeared to involve a **separation of powers** between king, Parliament and an independent judiciary. In practice, the executive was increasingly not so much the king but a Cabinet of leading ministers dependent on a parliamentary majority. This effectively involved a fusion of executive and legislative powers. Today, the British executive remains a parliamentary executive, dependent on a continuing Commons majority, but dominating the work of Parliament. Moreover, until 2009, Britain's highest court was a committee of the upper house of the legislature, the House of Lords, so the separation between legislative and judicial roles was blurred. While recent reforms appear to have strengthened the independence of the judiciary, Britain's new Supreme Court lacks the prestige and power of the US Supreme Court.

---

*The **legislature** is responsible for making law.*

---

*The **executive** is charged with the day-to-day government of the country, responsible for making policy and administering law.*

---

*The **judiciary** is responsible for adjudicating on the law and legal disputes.*

---

*The **separation of powers** is the principle, used in many countries, that the executive, legislative and judicial powers of a government should be kept apart to provide a system of checks and balances of power. The UK is described as having a weak separation of powers, as the executive is derived from the legislature.*

---

A constitution provides a framework of rules and principles for the conduct of government and politics in a particular state, setting out its legislative, executive and judicial powers. For almost all states today these are contained in a single written document, which commonly proclaims key political values, details the functions and powers of institutions and the rights and responsibilities of citizens.

Britain, unusually, lacks such a single authoritative written document on its system of government. Instead, some of these rules are written down, as part of the law of the land, contained in Acts of Parliament, or decisions on cases decided in the courts. Some written sources for the constitution include:

» *statute law*: that is, law passed by Parliament

» *common law*: in practice, the law as determined by decisions of courts

» *the law and custom of Parliament*: these are listed and described in Erskine May's *A Treatise on the Law, Privileges, Proceedings and Usage of Parliament* (1844)

» *European law*: which, until the UK leaves the EU, is binding.

Strictly speaking, therefore, the British constitution is uncodified – in the sense that it has not been collected into a single document – rather than unwritten.

Some key aspects of the British system of government, however, are unwritten, as they are not contained within any formal written document, but rest on 'conventions' – agreed usages that are so widely accepted they have long been undisputed, largely because of the political difficulties that would follow if they were not observed. Most of the powers relating to the prime minister depend on convention. Conventions may evolve over time and may be difficult to date precisely (e.g. the convention that a prime minister must sit in the House of Commons). However, these conventions, 'unwritten' in the sense that they have not been authoritatively recorded in some law or charter, have been extensively analysed and dissected by constitutional lawyers and political scientists. These works by eminent experts on the British constitution are often consulted, notably those of Walter Bagehot, *The English Constitution* ([1867] 1963), and A.V. Dicey, *An Introduction to the Study of the Law of the Constitution* ([1885] 1959), as well as Erskine May (2011), now in its 24th edn, on parliamentary procedure. (For more on Dicey and Bagehot, see Key Figures 5.1 on p. 86.)

Although constitutions (written or unwritten) are sometimes treated with great reverence (note the veneration of the US Constitution by large numbers of Americans), they are not 'above politics'. Constitutions embody the current rules of the political game. These advantage some interests and disadvantage others, so they can become acutely controversial. Thus some politicians and political activists may seek to modify, radically reform or, if they are revolutionaries, overthrow the existing constitution. Yet, even if there is a broad consensus supporting key elements of the existing constitution, ongoing technological and social change may inevitably require amendments to institutions, procedures and, sometimes, constitutional principles.

So constitutions are not immutable, although it is widely agreed that they should not be altered lightly. Outside the UK, constitutional law often has the status of a higher form of law, only alterable by special procedures. In many countries, more than a simple parliamentary majority is required for a constitutional amendment – Article 5 of the US Constitution specifies a two-thirds majority in both legislative houses, the House of Representatives and the Senate (see Comparing British Politics 5.1). Some constitutions additionally stipulate the support of the people in a referendum. Federal systems of government will normally require the support of all or most of the member states for a constitutional amendment.

Britain's 'unwritten', or more accurately 'uncodified', constitution remains highly flexible. Indeed, interpretation of the constitution has altered almost imperceptibly over time. Thus, at one time, a prime minister could come from either of the Houses of Parliament, and in the nineteenth century most came from the House of Lords. In the twentieth century, this seemed incompatible with democratic assumptions, and over a period it has become a convention that the prime minister must sit in the House of Commons, although this has not been officially laid down in any law. Some parts of the British constitution found in Acts of Parliament (e.g. those relating to the powers of the House of Lords) can be changed, effectively by a simple majority in the House of Commons. While a number of issues with constitutional implications have been submitted for a popular vote in a referendum, there is no obligation on government to hold such referendums, nor was Parliament bound by the results of

## 🇬🇧 COMPARING BRITISH POLITICS 5.1 🇺🇸
### The American Constitution

The American Constitution was originally drawn up in 1787. It was specifically written as a response to the tyranny of the British monarchy. Much of the text still accurately describes features of the US system of government, including the separation of legislative, executive and judicial powers. To this day, the USA has a much stronger separation of powers than the UK, where the executive – notably the Cabinet and prime minister – are drawn from the legislature. The US constitution states:

> All legislative Powers herein granted shall be vested in a Congress of the United States, which shall consist of a Senate and a House of Representatives (Article 1, Section 1)

> The Executive Power shall be vested in a President of the United States (Article 2, Section 1)

> The Judicial Power of the United States shall be vested in one Supreme Court (Article 3, Section 1).

However, although the constitution was proclaimed in the name of 'We the people of the United States', it was not a document originally designed to give much real power to the people. But, over time, the USA became more democratic, in part because some features of the system, such as the Electoral College for choosing the president, never operated as the Founding Fathers intended. A conspicuous flaw in American democracy was the survival of slavery until the American Civil War, and the treatment of black Americans as second-class citizens for more than a century afterwards.

The US Constitution continues to be treated with reverence by US politicians and citizens. It is a constant reference point when major disputes over government arise. Even so, it is not always an accurate guide to US government and politics. On other important issues such as the rights of the states, city and local government, political parties and organised groups, the constitution is vague or silent.

Note: The text of the US Constitution and amendments is reproduced in many books on American politics and also available online, for example: www.archives.gov/founding-docs/constitution.

---

referendums on Europe (in 1975 and 2016) or electoral reform (in 2011) (see below).

A flexible constitution may enable a system of government to evolve with the times, but may appear vulnerable to ill-considered change or subversion. By contrast, a constitution that can only be changed with great difficulty may lack the capacity to adapt to new pressures and altered circumstances, perhaps of a kind that its original designers could hardly anticipate. Yet judicial interpretation can lead to significant change even in countries with an apparently 'rigid' constitution. Thus the US Supreme Court's interpretation of the constitution has evolved with the times, with, for example, considerable implications for racial segregation and civil rights (see Comparing British Politics 5.2 overleaf).

## KEY FEATURES OF THE BRITISH CONSTITUTION

Written constitutions commonly contain some statements of principle, for example a commitment to democracy, or a republic or an established religion (e.g. the Islamic Republic of Iran). In Britain, there is no authoritative statement of the principles on which the (uncodified) constitution rests and, in practice, these have been inferred by constitutional lawyers and other experts. The British

## COMPARING BRITISH POLITICS 5.2

### Amending constitutions

Procedures for amending the US Constitution are described in Article 6 of the Constitution. Congress can propose amendments that have been approved by a two-thirds majority in each House. Any such amendment must also be approved by three-quarters of the state legislatures before it takes effect. Thus, amending the US Constitution is very difficult. Even so, a number of important amendments have been passed. These include:

» The Bill of Rights, the name given to the first ten amendments, ratified in 1791, which includes a number of basic citizen rights, including free speech and religious toleration, the right to a fair trial and the notorious second amendment, the right to bear arms.

» The abolition of slavery (13th amendment, 1865).

» Prohibition of the manufacture, sale, or transportation of intoxicating liquors (18th amendment, 1920, subsequently repealed in the 21st amendment, 1933).

» The enfranchisement of women (19th amendment, 1920).

» The limitation of the presidential period of office to two terms (22nd amendment, 1951).

In Australia, constitutional amendments require the support of both houses of parliament, then a referendum which must receive majority support overall and in a majority of states.

In Germany, constitutional amendments need a two-thirds majority in both houses of parliament, but the federal system and the rights of German citizens cannot be amended.

France has two methods for making constitutional amendments:

1 Amendments can be made by a majority in both houses of the French parliament voting on an identical motion, followed by ratification of three-fifths of Congress (the two houses combined). The Fifth Republic has been amended seven times using this method.

2 Amendments can also be made by a constitutional referendum, after an identical motion passed in both houses of parliament.

Note: For more on amending constitutions, see Hague et al. (2016) Ch. 7.

---

constitution has long been described in terms of the following key features or principles:

» A unitary state – rather than a federal state

» A constitutional monarchy – rather than a republic

» Parliamentary sovereignty – rather than a separation of powers

» Representative democracy – rather than direct democracy

» The rule of law.

All these principles require some further explanation and discussion. Some are contentious, particularly in the light of relatively recent and proposed changes in UK government (discussed later in the chapter). This section outlines how the principles have been traditionally explained and interpreted,

and goes on to explore some of the questions and ambiguities now surrounding them.

## A UNITARY RATHER THAN A FEDERAL STATE?

The United Kingdom is, as its name suggests, theoretically a unitary rather than a federal state. Besides the separation of executive, legislative and judicial powers, some constitutions divide the functions of the state between different levels. Under a federal system, sovereignty is deliberately divided between two or more levels of government. Each level of government is, in theory, sovereign (or supreme) in its own sphere.

**Federalism** was virtually invented by the 'Founding Fathers' of the American Constitution. Some earlier political thinkers like Thomas Hobbes (1588–1679) had declared that **sovereignty** (or supreme authority) could not be divided. Yet those who devised the American Constitution had to reconcile the rights of the original thirteen American states with the need for some overall coordination of (especially) defence, foreign policy and interstate trade. So powers were effectively divided between the federal government and state governments. This solution was attractive to other countries where there was a similar need to accommodate both unity and diversity, particularly where different ethnic, cultural and national groups were located within the same territories. Today, there are many federal states, including the USA, Canada, Switzerland, Australia, Germany, India and Belgium (Hague et al., 2016, Ch. 7).

---

**Federalism** *involves the division of sovereignty between two or more levels of government. In a federal system, each level of government is sovereign (or supreme) in its own sphere.*

---

**Sovereignty** *means supreme authority. Within a state, it refers to the ultimate source of legal authority. When used of states in their external relations, sovereignty means a state's ability to function as an independent entity – as a sovereign state.*

---

A federal state virtually requires a written constitution. If each level of government is supreme in its own sphere, there has to be some authoritative document determining those spheres, laying out the functions of the federal and state governments. This could involve listing the functions of each (perhaps with some powers exercised 'concurrently'), or merely listing the functions of one level, and ascribing all remaining powers to the other level. Thus the American Constitution details the powers of the federal government, reserving all other powers to the states. Inevitably, this does not preclude tensions between the levels of government. A major theme of the history of American government has been the alleged encroachment of the federal power on states' rights.

Most states are not federal states. Some particularly emphasise their unity. The French Fifth Republic is 'one and indivisible'. This does not preclude other levels of government

(regional and local), but these are legally subordinate to the sovereign state. The UK (like France) is still a unitary state, at least in legal form. Legally and constitutionally, the recent **devolution** of power to Scotland, Wales and Northern Ireland affects neither the unity of the UK nor the sovereignty of the Westminster Parliament. However, some argue that devolution in practice involves a quasi-federal system of government. Devolution is discussed further in Chapter 11.

---

**Devolution** *describes the delegation of powers in the United Kingdom downwards to institutions in Scotland, Wales and Northern Ireland. Devolution is distinguished from federalism because it does not, in theory, involve any transfer of sovereignty, nor any breach of the constitutional principle of the unity of the United Kingdom.*

---

## A CONSTITUTIONAL MONARCHY

The United Kingdom, again as its name implies, remains a monarchy, but a limited or constitutional monarchy. It is generally reckoned that the Queen 'reigns but does not rule' and has little or no political power. The personal political power of the monarch has been eroded gradually over the centuries and is now largely symbolic. Constitutional experts used to debate the monarch's discretion over the choice of a prime minister, or a requested dissolution of Parliament, but the circumstances in which there might be scope for discretion now seem remote. After the inconclusive result of the 2010 election, for example, advisers and experts agreed that the Queen must in no way be personally involved in the making of a new government. She had to wait for the main parties to resolve the deadlock, and for Brown to resign, before she could ask Cameron to form a government whose shape had already been determined. The monarch, in the words of Walter Bagehot, the nineteenth-century authority on the constitution (see Key Figures 5.1), retains the right to be consulted, the right to encourage and the right to warn. The prime minister still has regular meetings with the sovereign, and the present Queen's experience of successive governments and prime ministers from Churchill onwards may well sometimes make her advice worth listening to.

# KEY FIGURES 5.1
## A.V. Dicey and Walter Bagehot

**Albert Venn Dicey (1835–1922)** founded the scholarly discipline of constitutional law. His best-known book, *Introduction to the Study of the Law of the Constitution*, was first published in 1885. The principles set out in that book are still considered part of the uncodified British constitution. Dicey saw the rule of law as a fundamental characteristic of the British constitution – of equal importance to the doctrine of parliamentary sovereignty.

**Walter Bagehot (1826–77)** provided the basis for many later political scientists' accounts of the constitution. Bagehot was the editor of *The Economist* magazine for many years and greatly expanded its influence. His best-known work is *The English Constitution*, first published in 1867. Despite the title, the book explores the wider UK constitution, and particularly the role of the monarchy and Parliament. Bagehot argued against Dicey's claim that the constitution involved a balance between monarch, aristocracy and commons. Instead, Bagehot distinguished between the 'dignified' and the 'efficient' versions of the constitution. The dignified parts of the constitution, such as the monarchy, were ancient, ceremonial and complex – revered by the people. The efficient parts were modern, simple and functional. The distinction explains how an 'efficient' modern system of government was able to emerge from the shell of an ancient constitution.

Hulton Archive/Getty Images

However, if the personal power of the monarch is too negligible to be a live political issue, the institution of the Crown and the royal prerogative are more contentious. Ministers, members of the armed forces and civil servants are officially servants of the Crown rather than the public or 'the state'. There is no positive injunction to serve the people or the public interest. Moreover, some of the former powers of the sovereign, which are no longer exercised by the Queen, have not been abolished but transferred, mainly to the prime minister. Thus it was the prime minister who effectively inherited the former 'royal prerogative' powers to declare wars, make treaties and dissolve Parliament. A prime minister, until very recently, could involve Britain in war without seeking ratification from Parliament. There was no vote on UK intervention in Suez in 1956, the Falkland Islands in 1982, the first Gulf War in 1991, Kosovo in 1999 or Afghanistan in 2001. It was only with the invasion of Iraq in 2003 that Parliament voted in favour of action before the invasion. (These episodes are discussed in more detail in Chapter 22.) While some of these prerogative powers are now being restricted or abolished, others remain.

The monarchy has rarely been a political issue since the later nineteenth century, even if the removal of the principle of heredity from the second chamber may be thought to have implications for a hereditary head of state. No major political party has dared propose the abolition of the monarchy, although many MPs have done so. If Britain were to become a republic, a president or formal head of state would probably be necessary, in addition to the prime minister as head of government, as in most other modern democratic republics (see Comparing British Politics 5.3).

## PARLIAMENTARY SOVEREIGNTY

Parliamentary sovereignty has long been considered a key British constitutional principle. Parliamentary sovereignty effectively denies

## ⬛ COMPARING BRITISH POLITICS 5.3 🌍

### Constitutional monarchies and republics

**Constitutional monarchies**

While the retention of the institution of monarchy is rare, it is not unique among countries with a reasonable claim to democracy. Belgium, the Netherlands, Sweden, Denmark and Spain are among examples in Europe, and Thailand and Japan in Asia, of democratic states that retain hereditary monarchs, who are heads of state but in all cases have negligible personal political power. In addition, several Commonwealth countries still acknowledge the Queen as their head of state, although the issue has often become politically contentious; for example, after years of protest, Australia held a referendum in 1999 on whether to maintain the monarch as head of state, eventually voting in favour.

**Republics**

In France, the USA and most other countries regarded as democratic, republicanism is regarded as the natural corollary of democracy. The retention of the principle of heredity for filling the post of head of state appears incompatible with democratic values. So, many democracies have a non-hereditary head of state. Sometimes, the head of state is also head of the government, as the president is in the USA. More commonly, there is a separate formal head of state with little effective power, either directly elected by the people, or indirectly elected by parliament.

---

the principle of the separation of powers. The executive in Britain is a parliamentary executive, whose existence depends on the continuing confidence of Parliament. The judiciary is bound to accept law passed by Parliament.

What parliamentary sovereignty means in practice is that, in formal terms, parliamentary authority in the UK is unlimited. William Blackstone ([1827] 1979, p. 117), the eighteenth-century jurist, declared that Parliament 'can do everything that is not naturally impossible'. According to the principle of parliamentary sovereignty, statute law, that is, law passed by Parliament, is supreme over other kinds of law. No person may question its legislative competence and the courts must give effect to its legislation. Part of the principle is that no Parliament can bind its successors. This looks like a limitation on the power of Parliament, but clearly if an Act of Parliament contained a clause that it could not be repealed, this would effectively end parliamentary sovereignty.

## REPRESENTATIVE DEMOCRACY

Representative democracy may be considered an even more fundamental principle of the British system of government than parliamentary sovereignty, even if it is a principle less discussed by constitutional lawyers. It is a mark of the evolutionary nature of the British system of government that it is difficult to pin down precisely when Britain became a democracy (and some critics would deny that it is, in some important respects, even now). Yet the extension of the vote was accompanied by a gradual acceptance of democratic principles over time, and this in turn prompted the emergence of new conventions embodying the spirit of democracy. Thus it came to be established that the peers in the House of Lords should not frustrate the will of the democratically elected House of Commons, particularly on issues that had been submitted to the people in a manifesto by the governing party. Similarly, it became an unwritten rule that the prime minister and head of government should be a member of the House of Commons, and, normally, the elected leader of the majority party.

Of course, British democracy involves representative (or parliamentary) democracy rather than direct democracy. There is an implied contradiction here between the principles of **parliamentary sovereignty** and **popular sovereignty**. It is elected representatives of the people rather than the people themselves who decide. How far these representatives are truly representative of the people is itself a contentious issue (see for example, Spotlight 6.1: Substantive and descriptive representation, p. 113). But it is clear that parliamentary decisions do not always coincide with public opinion. For example, Parliament legislated to abolish capital punishment by hanging even when opinion polls suggested continuing public support for it.

---

*Parliamentary sovereignty means that Parliament has supreme authority.*

---

*Popular sovereignty means that supreme authority rests with the people. There is clearly potential for tension or open conflict between these two doctrines. The views of the elected representatives of the people may not always coincide with the views of the people themselves.*

---

## THE RULE OF LAW

Although in strict constitutional terms, the rule of law is subordinate to parliamentary sovereignty, the rule of law remains of key significance. It affirms that, while the executive and legislative branches of the state are 'fused', the judicial branch is largely independent and separate and can check the executive. Second, the rule of law enshrines principles such as natural justice, fairness and reasonableness that can be applied by the courts through the process of judicial review. (For more on this, see Key Figures 5.1 on Dicey.)

The fundamental principle is that people are subject to the rule of law, not to the arbitrary will of their governors. No one is above the law. Ministers and public authorities are bound by the law. Actions without the authority of law can be challenged in the courts. Citizens should have redress for illegal or arbitrary acts by public authorities, through the ordinary courts, administrative tribunals or other special machinery, such as complaints to the various 'ombudsmen' over what is termed 'maladministration'. (For more on the rule of law, and its application, see Bingham, 2010.)

The constitutional principles described above, particularly the unitary state and parliamentary sovereignty rather than a separation of powers, also emphasise the centralisation of political power on Westminster and Whitehall. This model, to its admirers, delivers strong, responsible and responsive government, and promotes national unity and homogeneity. Indeed, features of the system of government have been admired and sometimes imitated in other countries, particularly former British colonies (see Comparing British Politics 5.4). More recently, however, as we shall see, the Westminster model has been much criticised.

## THE WESTMINSTER MODEL

The Westminster model is a shorthand description of the traditional British system of government, derived ultimately from the analysis of Bagehot ([1867] 1963). The centre and focus of British government is Westminster and Whitehall. Constitutional principles associated with the Westminster model include the unitary state, parliamentary sovereignty and strong government derived from the virtual fusion of executive and legislative functions, rather than a separation of powers. It is also taken to involve some features of relatively recent political practice, including the two-party system and single-party majority government, both facilitated (but not necessarily produced) by a disproportionate electoral system, the single member plurality system. (For a discussion of the Westminster model, see Flinders, 2006; see also Moran, 2015, p. 2.)

## BRITISH PARTIES AND THE CONSTITUTION

While constitutions can be acutely contentious, consensus in British politics has often extended to constitutional issues. Thus, after a period of intense constitutional controversy in the years leading up to the First World War, there appeared to be a substantial consensus between the two major parties in support

*Source*: Brand X

Although the Houses of Parliament at Westminster date back to 1265, much of the present building only dates back to the middle of the nineteenth century. In this photo, the chamber of the House of Commons is on the right of the picture, while the Lords is on the left.

of the system of government lasting up until the 1970s. However, this apparent agreement conceals some very different assumptions on the constitution that help to explain the marked differences in attitude to constitutional reform that subsequently emerged between the parties in the late twentieth and early twenty-first centuries.

Throughout their history, Conservatives have generally defended the existing constitution and its traditional institutions, including the monarchy and the House of Lords. However, they rarely sought to reverse any constitutional reforms introduced by their opponents. So they came to accept the principle of representative democracy by the end of the nineteenth century, although 'Tory democracy' continued to emphasise the need for firm government and strong leadership. They have sometimes initiated changes of their own (e.g. the introduction of life peers in 1958). It was also a Conservative government (Heath's) that finally negotiated

UK entry into the European Community (later Union). However, Conservatives in government and opposition resisted other changes to Britain's system of government. From the nineteenth century, when they strongly opposed home rule for Ireland, Conservatives were strongly committed to the preservation of the union; they opposed Labour's devolution proposals from 1974–79 and in the 1997 elections, although devolution, once implemented, was subsequently accepted. The party has also generally resisted electoral reform.

For much of its history, the Labour Party was surprisingly uninterested in radical constitutional reform, although it intermittently pursued House of Lords reform, and occasionally toyed with other constitutional changes. Labour wished to capture and control the state rather than reform it. Their priorities were social and economic reform, and it was assumed that this could be achieved through the existing state apparatus (Bogdanor, 2001, pp. 139–42).

## 🇬🇧 COMPARING BRITISH POLITICS 5.4 🇮🇳 🇵🇰 🇱🇰 🇲🇾 🇳🇵

### Westminster versus 'Eastminster'

The spread of empire exported the British parliamentary model around the world. While it is most frequently identified with countries like Australia, Canada and New Zealand, these are dwarfed by the numbers of people living under Westminster-influenced systems in Asia. The British model dominates in India, Pakistan, Sri Lanka, Malaysia, Nepal and elsewhere. In 1950, the population of the UK, Canada, Australia, South Africa and New Zealand was just a fifth of the population of the Asian states of India, Pakistan, Nepal and what are today called Sri Lanka and Malaysia.

As the Westminster system is largely based on convention rather than rigid rules, the same system applied in different contexts could produce very different results, often with problematic consequences. For Harshan Kumarasingham (2016), the export of the model to Asia has produced what he describes as an 'Eastminster' model. While they have clear resemblances to the UK, these states have developed significant constitutional and cultural deviations from Westminster, as well as from other former parts of the British Empire. Kumarasingham argued that the main differences could be identified as:

» *Settler states versus the Asian Raj*: Unlike countries such as Canada and Australia, Eastminster states in Asia contained no substantial 'settler' populations. Civilisations, governance traditions and social divisions already existed. This made a simple imposition of the Westminster model frequently problematic.

» *Ceremonial versus interfering heads of state*: The Westminster model in the UK, Canada, New Zealand or Australia relegates the monarch (or their representative, such as the governor general) to a ceremonial role, if any. In contrast, Eastminster heads of state – although modelled on the British monarchy – frequently engaged in political activities, such as sacking and selecting prime ministers and ministers, commanding the military, formulating policy and so on. In

Pakistan, under Governor-General Ghulam Mohammad, cabinet decisions were seen as advice, which he was free to reject. This level of intervention is almost unheard of in UK and other 'West'minster systems.

» *Elective versus selective dictatorship*: Lord Hailsham (BBC, 1976) famously described British government as an 'elective dictatorship', because of the substantial powers of the executive. This tendency to centralise power became a feature of Eastminster models too. However, Eastminster states often did not exhibit the conditions to make a two-party system functional. It was more common that one party dominated politics, such as the Indian National Congress, or that elites limited the role of the political opposition, such as Malaysia's Alliance.

» *Majority systems versus minority rights*: Eastminster models, Kumarasingham argued, provided few incentives to the majority to protect minorities. The first past the post electoral system (discussed in Chapter 13) created majority governments that suited Eastminster leaders, who invariably came from the dominant group in their society. In Sri Lanka, for example, the linguistic rights of a major minority were removed in parliament on a show of hands, without breaking the constitution.

» *Colonial continuities*: Upon independence, many provisions were simply transferred from the colonial arrangements to the new constitution: almost two-thirds of the articles in India's 1950 Constitution of India had been transferred across from the colonial Government of India Act. These included controversial elements, such as emergency provisions, which could be used to suppress democracy.

While frequently neglected in the academic literature, the 'Eastminster' states should be significant in any assessment of the wider influence of the Westminster model.

Labour, like the Conservatives, endorsed strong government, but for different reasons. Once they had achieved a parliamentary majority and a mandate from the people, Labour wanted to be able to enact their social and economic programme unchecked (Dorey, 2008). Labour, like the Conservatives, also benefitted from an electoral system that protected the two major parties from third-party competition (see Chapter 13 on elections).

While Conservatives have strongly defended the existing constitution and Labour was generally content to work within it, Whigs, Liberals and, more recently, Lib Dems have placed more emphasis on constitutional reform. Thus, in the nineteenth century, Liberals championed parliamentary reform and, from 1886 onwards, Irish 'Home Rule' (that is, self-government for Ireland within the empire) and subsequently 'Home Rule All Round'. In the early twentieth century, the Liberal government took on and defeated opposition from the House of Lords and reduced its powers. After the Second World War, the Liberal Party was the first to support entry into the European Economic Community, and they continued to support devolution to Scotland and Wales as well as English regional government. They have sought to defend civil liberties and individual rights, and to strengthen the role of Parliament. Unsurprisingly, they have consistently campaigned for electoral reform, as the simple single member plurality system has particularly penalised them. The Lib Dems maintained this commitment to constitutional reform.

On the fringes of British politics there were always those who sought to overthrow rather than reform the state. These have included small groups on the far right or the far left of the political spectrum, but also, and increasingly significantly, varieties of nationalists, who rejected most of the key institutions of the British state. It was the growing support for separatist nationalism in Ireland that led to the establishment of the Irish Free State (and later Republic). Nationalism in Scotland and Wales took longer to make an impact, and was generally committed to peaceful change, although they also sought the breakup of the British state. They only began to make an impact after nationalist pressures reignited in Northern Ireland in the late 1960s and early 1970s, at around the same time as the debate over British membership of the European Community was raising concerns over British national sovereignty.

These pressures had a particular impact on the Labour Party. The rise of nationalism threatened its own heartlands in Scotland and Wales, and converted Labour to devolution. At the same time, Labour was split from top to bottom by the issue of Europe and opted for a referendum on European Community (later Union) membership in 1975 as a way out of its own divisions, before referendums were also held (and lost, in 1979) on Labour's devolution plans for Scotland and Wales. The introduction of referendums was a significant development for parliamentary sovereignty and representative democracy. In opposition after 1979, Labour became increasingly committed to constitutional reform, with important implications when they finally exchanged opposition for power in 1997.

## INCREMENTAL CONSTITUTIONAL REFORMS IN THE UK, 1945–97

Although neither of the major parties that dominated British postwar politics put forward radical programmes for constitutional reform, there were important incremental changes in the system of government. Clement Attlee's Labour government further reduced the delaying power of the Lords in the Parliament Act 1949. Of rather more significance was the introduction of life peers in 1958 by Harold Macmillan's Conservative government. This, over time, was to transfer the upper house from an almost entirely hereditary chamber to a largely appointed one (for more on the reform of the House of Lords, see Chapter 6, pp. 118–22). Wilson's 1964–70 Labour government (rather unsuccessfully) sought further parliamentary reform, including the introduction of more specialist Commons committees to scrutinise the government. (It was under the Thatcher government that committee scrutiny became more permanent and comprehensive.)

Moreover, the introduction of a popular referendum to resolve the issue of UK membership of the EU (and divisions within the Labour Party) also created a precedent, with significant constitutional implications, as we found after Britain voted in a referendum to withdraw from the EU in 2016 (see Chapter 12).

## NEW LABOUR AND CONSTITUTIONAL REFORM, 1997–2010

Constitutional reform was a cause that became increasingly fashionable from the late 1980s onwards. Compared with earlier proposals in the 1960s and 70s, which had been limited to specific issues, this new phase was about fundamentals and produced radical proposals for reform. An important step was the formation of Charter 88, the influential pressure group, symbolically 300 years on from the Revolution of 1688. The organisation campaigned for, among other things, a written constitution, a democratic second chamber and electoral reform. Charter 88 merged with other groups to form Unlock Democracy in 2007.

The movement for constitutional reform found fertile ground in the atmosphere of the late 1990s. John Major's Conservative government had been dogged by 'sleaze' allegations, including sex scandals in the popular press and accusations of backbenchers taking cash for asking questions in Parliament. There was a growing sense that politicians, and the system as a whole, should be subject to much greater scrutiny, with stronger safeguards to protect the interests of citizens.

Most of the interest in constitutional change then came from the centre and left of the political spectrum (Hutton, 1996, Ch. 11; Barnett, 1997). In March 1997, Labour and the Lib Dems, the two centre-left parties, which had already been cooperating closely in the Scottish Constitutional Convention (on devolved Scottish government), produced an agreed raft of proposals for constitutional reform, including:

» Select committee on modernisation of House of Commons

» Abolition of hereditary peers

» A Scottish Parliament and Welsh Assembly elected by proportional representation

» Referendums on an elected London authority and elected English regional assemblies

» Incorporation of European Convention on Human Rights into UK law

» An electoral commission to recommend alternative to present voting system

» Freedom of Information Act.

Labour enacted a substantial part of this reform programme in government after 1997. There were referendums on devolution in Scotland and Wales (1997) and Northern Ireland (1998), and on a new system of government for London. Support for change was soon followed by legislation for a new Scottish Parliament, a Welsh Assembly, a Northern Ireland Assembly and Executive, and a directly elected mayor and authority to govern London. Thus Labour fulfilled its commitment to devolution, but only partially met pledges on electoral reform. While the additional member system was introduced for the new assemblies in Scotland, Wales and London, the single transferable vote system for Northern Ireland and regional party lists for elections to the European Parliament, Labour did not introduce its promised referendum on a new system of voting for Westminster. However, other pledges were met. The Labour government legislated to incorporate the 1950 European Convention on Human Rights into British law and eventually passed the Freedom of Information Act 2000. All this amounted to a significant reform of the British constitution.

However, other proposed constitutional reforms ran into trouble. Labour had originally intended to complement Scottish and Welsh devolution with some devolution to the English regions, and although new regional development agencies were introduced, plans for elected regional assemblies were abandoned after they were rejected in the single region (the northeast) where a referendum was held in 2004. More seriously, the government's plans for Lords reform (after they had removed most hereditary peers) were rejected but no new alternative proposals for the composition of the second chamber

*Source*: Andrew Cowan/Scottish Parliament. Image © Scottish Parliamentary Corporate Body www.scottish.parliament.uk/Fol/ScottishParliamentLicence20160404.pdf

Devolution, which created the Scottish Parliament (pictured here), raises profound questions about the relevance of the 'Westminster model' as a description of contemporary UK politics.

could be agreed upon. Blair's government did eventually proceed with plans in its second term to replace the judicial functions of the Lords with a new Supreme Court, finally established in 2009. While some changes were introduced to the timetables and procedures of the House of Commons, these had rather less impact and did nothing to reduce executive dominance of the legislature.

A number of criticisms have been levelled at Labour's constitutional reforms. An early criticism was that they were insufficiently 'joined-up' and not informed by any coherent vision (Bogdanor, 2001, pp. 149–50). So Labour did not seek to introduce a written constitution, which would have required resolving fundamental issues, over parliamentary sovereignty and the unitary state, that the government preferred to avoid. Flinders (2006, pp. 117–37) described it as

a 'half-hearted revolution', which failed to transform the old Whitehall and Westminster model of the constitution into 'a new multi-level polity'. Evans (2008, p. 87) compared Blair to the 'sorcerer's apprentice in Walt Disney's *Fantasia*, desperately trying to stem the flood of unintended consequences that flow from constitutional reform'.

## FROM THE COALITION TO THE CONSERVATIVES, 2010–

The coalition government elected in 2010 was also committed to constitutional reform. The parliamentary expenses scandal of 2009 (see below) had given renewed impetus to reform. Although all the major parties were affected by the scandal, it was Labour as the party in power who were most tarnished by it, and the opposition parties who were better placed to profit from renewed calls for reform.

However, there were also potential stumbling blocks to a coalition deal between the Lib Dems and the Conservatives. The Lib Dems have been long-term advocates of a fairer voting system, involving proportional representation, which the Conservatives firmly rejected. Moreover, the parties differed sharply over future UK relations with the EU, with the Conservatives proposing the repatriation of some powers to Westminster, while the Lib Dems remained fully committed to the EU and sympathetic, in principle, to the single currency, the euro.

When the 2010 election produced a hung parliament, both parties agreed a constitutional reform programme. (Hung parliaments are introduced on p. 32.) This resulted in the introduction of the Fixed-term Parliaments Act 2011, which (theoretically) fixed the date of future general elections as the first Thursday in May, five years from the date of the previous election. Thus, the 2015 general election, which the Conservatives won outright, was held on 7 May 2015. Before this legislation, the incumbent prime minister was able to determine the date of a general election (providing it was within five years of the time Parliament was last 'summoned to meet'). Many, including the Lib Dems, felt that this gave sitting governments far too much power to hold a general election at a time that advantaged them. However, the law made it clear that an election could be held with two-thirds support from the House of Commons, as happened when Theresa May decided to hold an early general election in 2017 (making the Act largely redundant, as it became clear an opposition party would be unlikely to oppose a call for an election).

The coalition also agreed, much to the scepticism of many Conservatives, a referendum on voting reform. In the event, the population overwhelmingly rejected a move to the 'alternative vote' during a referendum in May 2011 – nearly 68% of voters voted against any change to the current system, with only around 42% of the electorate voting. (For more on the electoral reform referendum, see Chapter 13, pp. 273–76).

Other constitutional reforms set out in the coalition agreement largely fell by the wayside. The Conservative leadership was unable to deliver backbench support for the creation of a largely elected House of Lords. As a result, the Lib Dems pulled out of an agreement to reduce the number of seats in Parliament and create constituencies that had more equally sized electorates (a change that would have helped the Conservatives at the 2015 general election). There was also further devolution to Scotland and Wales (see Chapter 11). To Martin Loughlin and Cal Viney (2015), the lessons of the 2010–15 coalition were stark. Although the Lib Dems were successful in getting their commitments to constitutional reform recorded in a formal agreement, they did not buck one of the most basic laws of parliamentary politics: 'that there exists a considerable gulf between promise and realisation and without continuous active political support, both within Parliament and among the electorate, even the noblest of aspirations will count for little' (Loughlin and Viney, 2015, p. 86).

## THE BRITISH CONSTITUTION TODAY

The changes to the British system of government introduced over the last few years, coupled with other reforms still in progress, already amount to a constitutional revolution that calls in question some of the key features or principles of the British constitution described in this chapter. Britain is still a constitutional monarchy, and the rule of law has, if anything, been strengthened by the growth of judicial review, the incorporation of the ECHR into British law and the clearer separation of the legislative and judicial functions of the state. However, the description of the UK as a unitary state with parliamentary sovereignty is more questionable.

### THE END OF THE UNITARY STATE?

The official orthodoxy is that the UK remains a unitary state, despite devolution. One obvious consequence of devolution, however, is increasing diversity within the UK, as devolved executives increasingly exercise their powers in different ways. This diversity was less evident from 1999 to 2007, when Labour ruled at Westminster and dominated the devolved governments of Scotland and Wales. Yet an SNP government in Scotland from 2007 and a Labour mayor of London from 2016 have led to increased disagreements and some demarcation disputes between different levels of government. Britain is already arguably a 'quasi-federal state' and, as pressures for more devolution of powers increase, could be en route to a fully federal state.

A fully federal Britain is, however, only one possible longer term outcome of the constitutional reform process. For Irish, Scottish and Welsh nationalists, devolution and federalism are only stages on the road to separation and the breakup of Britain. Some who have opposed devolution all along (including many Conservatives and some Labour critics, like Tam Dalyell) have feared that it is a 'slippery slope' on the road to independence, as indeed nationalists wish. By contrast, Labour and the Lib Dems hope that devolution will satisfy the legitimate demands of many in Scotland and Wales to have a greater say in decisions that affect them, and that devolution will ultimately strengthen rather than weaken the British state. The rise in popularity of the SNP in Scottish politics makes this claim questionable. The various peoples of the UK have embarked on a journey where the final destination is unknown.

## THE END OF PARLIAMENTARY SOVEREIGNTY?

Parliamentary sovereignty has been eroded by at least four developments in recent decades: UK membership of the EU, the employment of referendums, the Human Rights Act and devolution.

First, the 1972 European Communities Act recognised that in areas of EU legislative competence, EU law is supreme and is given precedence over national UK law where the two conflict. The implications were not perhaps fully appreciated at the time, but became clearer when UK and EU law clashed (as we see in the discussion of the 'Factortame case' in Chapter 12). The decision to leave the EU in the 2016 referendum appears to be a reversal of this trend.

Second, referendums, such as the 2016 vote to leave the EU, are a threat to the principle of parliamentary sovereignty. Following the precedent of the 1975 referendum on European Community membership – the first nationwide referendum in the UK – British governments have had recourse to popular referendums on essentially constitutional issues. So, referendums were held on devolution to Scotland and Wales (1979, and again in 1997), London government (1998), the Northern Ireland agreement (1998), a projected elected assembly for the northeast (2004), electoral reform (2011), further Welsh devolution (2011), Scottish independence (2014) and continued membership of the EU (2016). The referendum has become (an increasingly frequent but significant) part of the UK constitution.

Referendums require the passing of a specific Act of Parliament, and the result of a referendum remains theoretically advisory, so the principle of parliamentary sovereignty is officially maintained. Yet it would be politically suicidal to hold a referendum and ignore the result. Vernon Bogdanor (2001) argues that, in practice, 'a referendum which yields a clear outcome on a reasonable turnout binds Parliament'. The sovereignty of the people is substituted for the sovereignty of Parliament. The more referendums become a regular part of the British system of government, the further the principle of parliamentary sovereignty is eroded.

Third, the Human Rights Act 1998 does not give judges power to reject Westminster legislation, but 'nevertheless alters very considerably the balance between Parliament and the judiciary' (Bogdanor, 2001, p. 146), so that Parliament will feel obliged to respond to judicial decisions that a statute is incompatible with the ECHR. The status of the ECHR after leaving the EU remains to be seen.

Fourth, while the sovereignty of the Westminster Parliament is theoretically unaffected by devolution, in practice English MPs have lost responsibility for legislation on devolved functions, particularly in Scotland. Bogdanor (2009) argues that the Human Rights Act and the Scotland Act have the characteristics of fundamental laws. In practice, they limit the rights of Westminster as a sovereign parliament, and provide for a quasi-federal constitution.

The official answer here is clear. Devolution is not the same as federalism. Power devolved is power retained, because sovereignty or supreme power is unaffected, and thus any functions that are devolved can be called back. Devolution itself may be reversed, as the suspension of the Stormont Parliament in 1972 and the resumption of direct rule of Northern Ireland after 50 years of devolved government demonstrate. Indeed, following the Good Friday Agreement (1998), the Northern Ireland Assembly and Executive were suspended four times, reinforcing the point.

Nevertheless, Northern Ireland is a special case. Any reversal of devolution to Scotland and Wales now seems inconceivable, unless wanted by a clear majority of Scots and Welsh. However, all the pressures are now the other way – for more devolution to the Scottish Parliament and Welsh Assembly. Thus it is arguable that Britain is evolving towards a quasi-federal system of government, which entails the end of UK parliamentary sovereignty (these points are discussed further in Chapter 11).

The political impossibility of reversing devolution illustrates the practical limitations on the power of the Westminster Parliament. Yet it is not just devolution that illustrates the limitations of the legislative authority of Westminster. Sometimes Acts of Parliament apparently embodying the full force of law can become virtually unenforceable. Trade union resistance wrecked the 1971 Trade Union Act and widespread popular revolt helped destroy the poll tax (introduced by the Thatcher government and abolished by Major, Thatcher's Conservative successor). This suggests that parliamentary sovereignty can, in practice, be limited by what the people will stand (or, effectively, by democracy).

## DIRECT DEMOCRACY RATHER THAN REPRESENTATIVE DEMOCRACY?

Parliamentary sovereignty implicitly places limits on the sovereignty of the people. It is the representatives of the people who ultimately decide, not the people themselves, whose role was traditionally confined to choosing the representatives who would control the government.

While the use of referendums has given individual voters a say on a few specific (essentially constitutional) issues, their use arguably undermines representative democracy. The 2016 EU referendum is a particularly clear example. The overwhelming majority of elected representatives in the House of Commons were, at that time, in favour of remaining in the EU, yet the British people narrowly voted to leave. Although referendums are, in theory, only advisory, as we saw above, MPs are unlikely to ignore that advice.

The 2009 parliamentary expenses scandal was also the catalyst, not only for a loss of public trust in elected representatives, but also for a range of new reforms. For example, the Recall of MPs Act 2015 enables voters to force a by-election if over 10% of constituents demand it in a petition, after their MP is successfully convicted of a crime resulting in time in jail, suspended from the House of Commons for an extended period, or found to have given false or misleading information in claiming parliamentary allowances. This would, it is argued, give the electorate more power to continuously hold the person they elected to account. Since the 2010 general election, another reform to empower the electorate is being trialled by the Conservative Party, which in a few constituencies has opened up the selection of candidates to the wider public with the introduction of primary elections (as in the USA), rather than selection by relatively few local party members. This would, it is argued, help to bring into Parliament MPs from different, less conventional backgrounds, less constrained by party machines and it would help a wider number of local people feel 'more invested' in the candidate and therefore more likely to vote for them in the general election.

Other responses to a decline in support for the major parties, in terms of voting and particularly active membership, advocate a democracy less dependent on political parties. This might involve increased use of referendums (which could be demanded by the initiative of voters, another US practice). It might involve more direct popular participation in decision-making through citizens' juries, perhaps selected by lot, an ancient Athenian practice. All these projected reforms reflect a widespread public distrust of Parliament, parties, MPs and the whole traditional system of representative democracy as it has operated in Britain. (For more on alternative forms of participation, see Chapter 16, p. 339ff.)

## THE DISINTEGRATION OF THE BRITISH STATE, OR TOWARDS MULTI-LEVEL GOVERNANCE?

Although writers may not fully agree over exactly how and why the British state has changed, there is widespread agreement that it has changed, and profoundly. Instead of a unified, highly centralised state with its traditional core institutions in Westminster and Whitehall, there is a fragmented and multilayered system of government and politics that is still evolving. This more complex pattern of governance operates at a range of levels – international, European, UK, devolved national, regional, local and institutional (see Table 5.1). While some levels remain more important than others, the balance is clearly shifting over time. Key decisions affecting the lives of British citizens are not just made in London but in Brussels or Edinburgh, within local authorities, city regions, hospital trusts or chains of academy schools, and across a range of other devolved agencies, units and networks.

**Table 5.1 The new multi-level governance, as applied to Britain**

| Level | Institutions |
| --- | --- |
| Global | UN, IMF, WTO, G8, G20, multinational organisations and companies, NGOs |
| Transatlantic | North Atlantic Treaty Organization |
| European (although withdrawal from the EU will remove a large part of this level) | European Union, European Commission, European Parliament, European Court of Justice, Council of Europe, European Court of Human Rights |
| UK | Cabinet and core executive, Westminster Parliament |
| Devolved national | Scottish Parliament and government, Welsh Assembly and Executive, Northern Ireland Assembly and Executive |
| Regional | Government offices, regional development agencies, regional chambers (both facing abolition) |
| Local | County, district, unitary and parish councils, non-elected local government |
| Institutional | Hospital trusts, universities and colleges, academy schools, 'free schools', etc. |

For some, this trend towards multi-level governance is natural and inevitable in the modern world. It is the old nation state that is obsolete (Giddens, 1998; Pierre and Peters, 2000; Pierre and Stoker, 2002). For others, who cherish the traditional, unitary British state, British national independence and the sovereignty of the Westminster Parliament, the changes are deeply unsettling. From their perspective, the growing importance of the EU, on the one hand, and the devolution of power to sub-UK nations and regions, on the other, represents a danger to the British state that could prove terminal.

In part, the question comes down to functional efficiency and effectiveness. It might seem appropriate to decentralise some decision-making down from the UK government level to local communities or even institutions in the interests of improved delivery of (for example) education and health services.

There are other issues, such as international trade, disarmament, global pollution and conservation, which can only be effectively tackled at a supranational and global level. Yet for many services and functions, there are many levels at which decisions may be appropriately taken, and multi-level governance appears almost inescapable.

However, issues of functional efficiency are bound up closely with the politics of identity and allegiance. The demands for closer European union, for a Scottish Parliament, and even for successive UK local government reorganisations were not just driven by expectations of more efficient government and service provision, but by political ideals and loyalties. Much of the debate over Europe, or devolution, or local authority boundaries is ultimately about how people feel about who they are, and the communities they identify with. Do they feel part of Europe or the English-speaking world? Are they Scots or British? Do they identify with their city or county? Other identities – ethnic, religious, class – may cut across spatial boundaries.

Some are comfortable with loose, multiple overlapping identities and allegiances. Prime Minister Theresa May (2016b) talked dismissively of these 'citizens of the world' as 'citizens of nowhere', without strong identity or commitment. To others a particular identity may appear exclusive and all-important. For them we are either British or European, either Scots or Brits; we have to choose between UK national sovereignty or a European superstate, between allegiance to the UK or an independent Scotland. The whole notion of multi-level governance is hardly compatible with more exclusive identities and allegiances.

There is much that seems confusing and contradictory about this emerging system of multi-level governance, which explains some of the range of competing terms that have been employed to describe it (see Table 5.2). Is the new British politics all about devolution and decentralisation, or does it more plausibly involve a new concentration of power? Has the state been 'hollowed out' or 'joined-up'? Has the welfare state been replaced by a regulatory state? In part, different answers reflect different assumptions and partisan viewpoints, yet they also reflect genuine uncertainty. Clearer answers to such questions may be available to historians with the benefit of hindsight but it is difficult to spot the truly significant trends in an era of extensive political and institutional upheaval.

#### Table 5.2 From the old Westminster model to the new British governance

| The Westminster model | The new British governance |
| --- | --- |
| The unitary state | The 'differentiated polity' |
| Parliamentary sovereignty | The devolution of power (Chapter 11) |
| Ministerial responsibility (Chapter 8, pp. 152–53) | Delegation of management (Chapter 18, pp. 389–92) |
| Central–local relations | Multi-level governance |
| Homogeneity, uniformity, 'Fordism' | Diversity, fragmentation, 'post-Fordism' |

*Source*: Adapted from Leach and Percy-Smith (2001), p. 7. Reproduced with permission of Palgrave

## BEYOND THE WESTMINSTER MODEL

The Westminster model has long provoked criticism. For some critics, the term no longer describes the system we have today. For others, the Westminster model is no longer suitable for the world we live in, and it should be updated by a more appropriate system. This has led some commentators to talk of the need to move 'beyond the Westminster model' (Diamond, 2011). Features of the Westminster model have been criticised by constitutional reformers advocating devolution and decentralisation, a clearer separation of powers, a proportional electoral system, and popular rather than parliamentary sovereignty, involving more direct or participatory democracy. Chapter 6 sets out the argument that accounts of 'multi-level governance' better explain where we are today, rather than an account of a unitary state or parliamentary sovereignty. These criticisms of the values and ideas implicit in the Westminster model were and are essentially normative. Yet they have helped inspire constitutional changes that, allied with the developments in political practice discussed in this chapter, have transformed British government to such an extent that it is questionable whether the Westminster model remains an accurate description of British government today (Dunleavy, 2006).

The constitutional reforms and political changes that have taken place have been grafted onto the traditional British system of government rather than replacing it. Formally, the UK remains a unitary rather than a federal state, and the parliamentary sovereignty of Westminster is unaffected. Moreover, the media continue to focus on the old familiar confrontation between the government and opposition. To many casual observers, it may appear that nothing has fundamentally changed.

Yet there are now significant tensions, even contradictions, in the new British system of government. Some constitutional reforms have had unforeseen consequences. Mark Evans (2008) talks of 'spill-backs' and 'spill-overs'. These tensions and spill-overs may be resolved in various ways. Reformers continue to urge the need for a written constitution that would lay down the principles and institutional framework for a modernised system of government. If this was a constitution like most others, the constitution rather than Parliament would be sovereign, and the various powers of the state would be classified and defined. This could involve a fully federal system of government, although it would be difficult to accommodate England, with 84% of the UK population, easily within a federal state (see Chapter 11 for more on the dominance of England within the union). But, as the result

of the 2011 referendum on electoral reform perhaps indicates, there seems to be little public appetite for a protracted and divisive debate about constitutional issues.

Additionally or alternatively, separatist nationalists in Scotland, Wales and Northern Ireland may ultimately achieve their objectives, and the unity of the United Kingdom would be formally dissolved. One possibility is that a separate English state, freed from its quasi-federal elements in non-English territories, could maintain or reassert the principles and practices of the traditional Westminster model, including the unitary state, parliamentary sovereignty (strengthened by withdrawal from the EU) and the two-party system with single-party majority government. The latter would be facilitated by the disappearance of separatist nationalist parties at Westminster, and probable dominance by a Conservative Party traditionally sceptical about constitutional reform. The relatively close independence referendum in Scotland in 2014, and the continuing dominance of the SNP north of the border and their opposition to the UK's withdrawal from the EU, make this a strong possibility.

It is also possible, however, that the British system of government will continue to muddle along, with all its current tensions and contradictions. Indeed, similar tensions and contradictions are a feature of many states with written constitutions, including between the federal government and the states in the US Constitution. Ambiguity can help to contain awkward differences over principle. Constitutional myths may have some value. Bagehot, considered the original source of the Westminster model, famously distinguished between the dignified and efficient elements of what he called the English constitution. However, he did not conclude that the dignified elements, such as the monarchy, were useless, but assisted confidence and legitimacy. Some analysts consider the Westminster model still shapes the behaviour of ministers and civil servants (Richards and Smith, 2004, p. 777). Although key parts of the Westminster model now appear to some more dignified than efficient, if many inside and outside government continue to accept its validity, it will continue to influence the way British politics is practised.

# SUMMARY

- » Britain does not have a written constitution. There is no authoritative description of the British system of government contained in a single document.

- » In the absence of a written constitution, major sources of the British constitution include relevant statute law, case law, conventions and the law of the EU.

- » Key constitutional principles include constitutional monarchy, parliamentary sovereignty, representative democracy and the rule of law. In contrast to the USA and many other countries, there has been no clear separation of executive, legislative and judicial powers in the UK.

- » There was a two-party consensus on most aspects of the constitution until relatively recently. This consensus was broken when Labour became committed to specific constitutional changes amid a growing movement for extensive constitutional reform.

- » The New Labour government initiated major constitutional reform, although the pace slowed subsequently, as some initiatives failed or ran into substantial difficulties.

- » An extensive programme of constitutional reform was promised by the Conservative and Lib Dem coalition that took office in 2010. Despite some significant changes, for example the Fixed-term Parliaments Act and further devolution, further reform fell by the wayside.

- » The decision to leave the EU has profound constitutional implications, which are as yet unknown.

- » The final outcome of recent and ongoing changes to the UK system of government remains unclear, but the future of the 'Westminster model' is questionable. Britain could be moving towards a quasi-federal system of government. Another possibility is the breakup of Britain.

# ? QUESTIONS FOR DISCUSSION

- » What is parliamentary sovereignty? Why is there a potential conflict between parliamentary sovereignty and popular sovereignty? Will Brexit revive parliamentary sovereignty or not?

- » How far were Labour's constitutional reforms after 1997 part of a coherent vision for the future government of Britain? Why did the reforms appear 'insufficiently joined-up'?

- » On which points did the Conservatives and Lib Dems agree and disagree over constitutional reform between 2010 and 2015 and why?

- » Is the United Kingdom still a unitary state? Should it be?

- » Does Britain need a written constitution, and if so, what should be included in it?

- » What are the strengths and weaknesses of the Westminster model? Does the model still describe the British system of government with reasonable accuracy?

# FURTHER READING

Britain's constitution and constitutional reform has become a difficult and fast-changing topic. Loughlin's (2013) *The British Constitution: A Very Short Introduction* provides a useful, largely historical introduction. King (2007) *The British Constitution*, is

a good overview. Bogdanor (2009) *The New British Constitution* is now a key source. For commentary on the coalition, Bogdanor (2011) *The Coalition and the Constitution* is worth consulting, as is Loughlin and Viney (2015). For earlier commentary on Labour's reforms, see works by Hazell, such as *Constitutional Futures* (1999), *The State and the Nations* (2000) and *The State of the Nations 2003* (2003), and Bogdanor (2001). Newspapers, periodicals and the internet provide early material on the coalition government reforms, pending the appearance of journal articles and books.

Thoughtful although now dated reflections on the principles and practice of the traditional British constitution include Mount (1992) *The British Constitution Now*, Marr (1996) *Ruling Britannia*, Hutton (1996) *The State We're In* (Ch. 11) and Barnett (1997) *This Time: Our Constitutional Revolution*. Chapter 7 in Hague et al. (2016) *Comparative Government and Politics* (10th edn) provides some useful comparative background against which the unusual British constitution can be assessed.

 ## USEFUL WEBSITES

On arguments for constitutional reform, see the publications of the pressure group Unlock Democracy and its website: www.unlockdemocracy.org.

The Constitution Unit at University College, London pulls together the latest in research in this area: www.ucl.ac.uk/constitution-unit.

 *Further student resources to support learning are available at* **www.macmillanihe.com/griffiths-brit-pol-3e**

# 6 PARLIAMENT AND THE LEGISLATIVE PROCESS

In 1976, Lord Hailsham, a one-time Conservative leadership contender, described the UK's system of government as an 'elective dictatorship' (BBC, 1976). The weakness of Parliament, he claimed, meant that a government with a majority is able to behave like a dictator.

In academic terms, there is 'executive dominance' of the legislature. Traditionally, the electoral system ensures a government with a majority in the House of Commons (although interestingly, not in 2010 or in 2017). And, although sometimes rebellious, MPs tend to support their party, particularly on the most important votes. Defeats in the House of Commons for a sitting government are rare. The last time a government lost a vote of confidence, triggering a general election, was in 1979. The executive in Westminster seems to have far fewer constraints than the US president, for example, whose party does not necessarily have a majority in Congress. In this chapter we examine the Westminster Parliament and its relationship with the executive.

## THIS CHAPTER:

» Assesses the functions of both chambers of the Westminster Parliament in more detail and in particular examines Parliament's legislative function.

» Examines how far and in what sense Parliament is representative of the British people, in terms of identity, and explores the representative role of Parliament.

» Looks at the linked issues of the composition and powers of the upper chamber within the context of the ongoing reform process.

» Discusses the future of the Westminster Parliament in a multi-level system of representative bodies.

# THE FUNCTIONS OF THE HOUSE OF COMMONS

The House of Commons has five main functions:

» Legislation

» Recruitment and maintenance of a government

» Scrutiny of the executive

» Forum for national debate

» Representation.

## LEGISLATION

Legislation, or law making, is ostensibly the most important function of Parliament, which is, after all, a legislature. Law passed by Parliament remains supreme over other forms of British law, such as common law (that part of law made through custom and judicial precedent), although while the UK is a member of the EU, it also has to accept EU law. But while Parliament devotes much of its time to considering legislation, it may be questioned whether Parliament effectively makes the law, unlike the US Congress (see Comparing British Politics 6.1). Westminster legislation today is substantially an executive function. Government dominates the legislative process from start to finish. Although ordinary backbench MPs retain some limited opportunities to initiate legislation, they normally have little chance of converting their draft bills into law. Most of the time devoted by Parliament to the scrutiny of legislation is spent on government **bills**, and it is almost entirely government bills that are ultimately successful in passing through all their stages to become **Acts**. Parliament's effective influence on the principles and even the details of government legislation is usually limited. Although significant amendment and, very occasionally, even defeat of a government bill remains a possibility, the government's majority normally ensures that its legislation emerges from its passage through Parliament more or less in the form intended.

---

*A **bill** is a draft Act of Parliament. It remains a bill until it has passed all its stages.*

---

*An **Act** of Parliament, also known as a Statute, is a bill that has passed though all its stages and received royal assent.*

---

Parliament, it may be said, legitimates rather than legislates. Although it is government rather than Parliament that substantially makes law, Parliament's assent remains vital to the establishment of the legitimacy of that legislation. Thus the formal parliamentary stages of legislation – the process through which bills or **delegated legislation** become an Act of Parliament – remain important (see Table 6.1 below). But they do not tell us very much about how law is really made in Britain. Where do the ideas for new laws come from? Who decides that legislation is necessary? Which interests influence the shape and content of legislation, and how? Is the formal completion of the parliamentary stages with royal assent really the end of the process? How are Acts implemented and adjudicated upon? How far are they successful in fulfilling the intentions of the legislators? To answer such questions, it is important to go beyond the formal parliamentary stages of legislation, to consider the crucial formative pre-parliamentary stages of the legislative process, the extra-parliamentary influences on the formal parliamentary stages, and the all-important process of implementation, adjudication and review.

---

*Delegated legislation is sometimes referred to as 'secondary or subordinate legislation' – the technical name is Statutory Instruments. Many Acts are outline in form, giving authority to ministers or to other public bodies to make necessary orders or regulations under the authority of the parent Act. Thousands of Statutory Instruments are published every year.*

---

## 🇬🇧 COMPARING BRITISH POLITICS 6.1 🇺🇸

### The legislative roles of the UK Parliament and the US Congress

The US Congress is a legislature in the full meaning of the term. It makes laws. 'All legislative powers herein granted shall be vested in a Congress of the United States' (US Constitution). Both houses of Congress, the House of Representatives and the Senate, play an important role in the legislative process and both have to agree before legislation can go forward for presidential approval. If the president declines to approve laws passed by Congress, this veto can be overridden by a two-thirds majority of both houses of Congress. Although the president can propose laws, these may be substantially modified or rejected by Congress, which is quite often controlled by a different party to that of the president, as they are elected separately and for different terms. The system is one of 'checks and balances', deriving from the separation of powers in the US constitution.

By contrast, the executive dominates the legislative process in the UK Parliament.

Virtually all government bills are passed, while most bills introduced by ordinary MPs fail, and can normally only succeed if the government gives them tacit support and space in the schedule of parliamentary proceedings. The subordinate role of the British Parliament stems from the fusion of executive and legislative powers in the Westminster system (discussed in more detail in Chapter 5), compared with the separation of powers in the US Constitution. Thus, the British Parliament is controlled by the government by means of its (usually) disciplined majority in the House of Commons. The British Parliament, like most in Western Europe, is essentially a reactive, policy-influencing assembly that may modify or even (very exceptionally) reject government legislative proposals, but has negligible opportunities to initiate legislation. Unlike the US Congress, it is not a legislature in the full meaning of the term.

### Introducing new laws

Where does the legislative process really start? Normally, not in Parliament. The initial idea may come from a variety of sources, perhaps from a government department or an official report such as a Royal Commission, or possibly from a party manifesto or a pressure group or media campaign. Whatever the initial inspiration, the idea for legislation will not normally get far unless it wins government favour and eventually receives the backing of the Cabinet, and finds a place in the government's legislative programme.

Before a government decides to legislate, it will consult widely across departments and other relevant public bodies, and often extensively with outside interests (see Chapter 18, pp. 378–83). This process of consultation not only provides the government with more information and expert opinion, but also may be crucial in winning the argument in Parliament and the country. If the government is able to claim that they have consulted widely with

affected interests and secured their support, this reduces the scope for effective opposition. In some cases, the government seeks not just the acquiescence of key interests but their active cooperation. For example, the coalition's 2012 Health and Social Care Act, which led to significant reform of the NHS, needed at least a degree of support from medical professionals before it was implemented. Indeed, early scepticism from many medical professionals led then Prime Minister David Cameron to initiate a 'Listening Exercise', which led to significant amendments to the Bill before it was passed.

Only after much initial consultation will the department principally concerned begin the process of drafting a bill using the services of expert parliamentary law drafters, Parliamentary Counsel. Drafts are circulated to other interested departments and consultation with outside interests will continue. It may take a year or two before the government feels ready to introduce a bill in Parliament. Thus much activity will often have taken

*Source*: Carl Court - WPA Pool/Getty Images
The ceremonial role of the monarch in the parliamentary process is still important. Here, the Queen reads her government's priorities for the coming year.

place before Parliament has the opportunity to consider a government bill. Debates on the Queen's Speech (in which the monarch reads a prepared speech to MPs when a session is opened, outlining the government's agenda for that session) may provide some opportunity to comment on proposals to legislate, and sometimes the government will announce its intentions through a **Green** or **White Paper**. Normally, however, Parliament's first opportunity to debate a bill is at the Second Reading, as the First Reading is purely formal.

---

A **Green Paper** *is a consultative document, implying the government has not finally made up its mind.*

---

A **White Paper** *normally involves a firmer statement of government intention. However, sometimes ministers may observe that a particular White Paper 'has green edges', indicating a readiness to listen to arguments and make changes.*

---

## Parliamentary scrutiny of government legislation

Bills can be first introduced into either the Commons or the Lords, although more controversial measures are normally introduced in the Commons (see Table 6.1). The First Reading of a bill is purely formal, with no debate. A dummy copy of the bill is placed on the Speaker's table, and a date announced for the Second Reading. Only after the First Reading is the bill printed and circulated. (However, some

draft bills are now published for Parliament's consideration.) The Second Reading normally involves a full debate on the principle of the bill. If it passes its Second Reading, the bill proceeds to the committee stage, normally taken by a committee of MPs responsible for scrutinising a particular bill, although a 'Committee of the Whole House' may consider very important bills with constitutional implications, or at the other extreme, relatively simple and noncontroversial bills. It is also now possible for bills to be referred to a **select committee**, or a special committee, enabling a more rigorous examination of the evidence and contributions from outside witnesses, although these procedures remain uncommon (Norton, 2005, pp. 86–7, 255).

---

**Select committees** *check and report on areas ranging from the work of government departments to economic affairs.*

---

During the committee stage, the bill is considered in detail, line by line and clause by clause, and amendments may be proposed, either by the government, seeking to tidy up and improve the bill, or by government or opposition party MPs. The process of consultation with outside interests will continue throughout the committee stage. Friendly committee members may sometimes be prepared to introduce amendments drafted by such outside groups. If the governing party has a substantial majority in the Commons as a whole, it will have a commensurate majority on all committees. Thus most of the amendments passed by the committee will be the government's own amendments, although it may accept amendments proposed by its own backbenchers and, occasionally, even an opposition amendment. This process may help improve the legislation, closing loopholes, removing obstacles to successful implementation, and perhaps securing the goodwill of important interests whose full cooperation may be crucial to ensure that the Act achieves its intentions.

After the committee stage comes the report stage when the amended bill is reported back to the House of Commons as a whole. Further amendments may be considered here, before

## Table 6.1 The formal parliamentary stages of legislation

| Stage | Where taken | Comments |
|---|---|---|
| First Reading | Floor of House of Commons (unless introduced in Lords) | Purely formal – no debate |
| Second Reading | Floor of House of Commons | Debate on principles – very unusual for a government bill to be defeated at this stage |
| Committee stage | Normally in bill committee on which government has a majority. Some bills taken in Committee of the Whole House | Considered in detail, clause by clause – amendments can be made but only those introduced by ministers have much chance of success. Can take weeks |
| Report stage | Floor of House of Commons | Report on amended bill; further amendments can be made |
| Third Reading | Floor of House of Commons | Debate (often short) on final text, and approval of bill – generally a formality |
| Lords stages (or Commons stages if bill introduced in Lords | Bill passes through similar stages in other chamber. Committee stage normally taken on floor of Lords | Lords may amend bill (some further amendment may be introduced by government). If bill is amended it returns to the Commons for consideration |
| Consideration of Lords (or Commons) amendments | Floor of House of Commons | Lords' amendments may be accepted, if not the Lords usually give way. Otherwise bill can be reintroduced and passed without Lords' consent under the Parliament Act |
| Royal assent | Monarchy | Last refused in reign of Queen Anne |

Note: Following changes made in October 2015 to introduce 'English Votes for English Laws' (EVEL), additional parliamentary stages are added to Bills that only affect England. This means that, before the Third Reading, these Bills are considered only by MPs representing English constituencies, effectively giving English MPs a veto over Bills that only affect England (which could previously have been pushed through with the support of MPs from Scotland, Wales or Northern Ireland).

the Commons proceeds immediately to a debate on the Third Reading. If the bill passes its Third Reading, it proceeds to the House of Lords (assuming the bill was initiated in the Commons) and follows similar stages there, with further opportunities for consultation and amendment. After a bill has passed all its stages in both Houses of Parliament, it goes to the monarch for royal assent (last refused in the reign of Queen Anne, three centuries ago). It then becomes an Act, and the law of the land.

It looks like a thorough scrutiny, yet it is not always as effective as it appears. Governments normally seek to push through a large and complex legislative programme as quickly as possible without significant concessions. So MPs on the government side in a committee on bills often appear to have taken a vow of silence. By contrast, opposition MPs are only too voluble, speaking at length on numerous amendments – some essentially 'wrecking amendments' undermining the whole principle of the bill – to delay proceedings as long as possible. This may go on until the government loses patience and 'guillotines' debate through a timetabling measure. Often this can mean that important parts of a bill are never scrutinised in committee, although sometimes the omission is remedied in the Lords. However, governments normally get their way.

## Implementation of legislation

While royal assent may seem to mark the end of the legislative process, a new Act often requires extensive subsequent delegated legislation if it is to be successfully implemented. This happens when the Act confers on ministers or other public bodies the authority to lay detailed regulations and orders having the force of law. Thousands of such Statutory Instruments are published annually. Although critics have been unhappy that they do not have to be voted through by Parliament, they are generally no longer regarded as a sinister threat to the power and sovereignty of Parliament, but as an essential adjunct to modern governance, allowing regulations to be amended with changing circumstances, and permitting useful experiments. Often they will involve further consultation with affected interests. For example, a change in the list of harmful substances that cannot be sold over the counter might involve discussions with chemists, doctors and the police.

With or without the addition of delegated legislation, Acts still have to be implemented. Often implementation is not the responsibility of the central government but of other agencies, such as local authorities, which may proceed slowly and reluctantly, arising from their own opposition to a particular measure. Alternatively, they may complain they have been given statutory responsibilities without adequate resources. Thus some Acts are not fully implemented, and a few have never been implemented at all. On other Acts there may be considerable discretion given over methods of implementation. Problems with implementing law may be reported to Parliament but Parliament has no formal responsibility for overseeing implementation. Finally, Acts are open to interpretation and adjudication in courts of law. Although judges must accept an Act of Parliament, they have to interpret it. In such judicial interpretation, only the wording of the Act will be taken into account, not the pronouncements of governments or speeches in Parliament. Moreover, as Britain is a signatory to the European Convention on Human Rights (ECHR), a judge may now declare that an Act 'appears inconsistent' with the ECHR, effectively requiring its amendment (see Chapter 9, pp. 171–77).

So, the legislative process in Britain is largely executive-dominated from start to finish. Parliament has a negligible role in the origination and formulation of legislation, with the exception of Private Members' bills (see below), and no role in implementation beyond its generally inadequate scrutiny of delegated legislation. On the parliamentary stages of legislation, government backbenchers generally have more influence than the opposition, for the simple reason that the opposition cannot normally threaten the government's majority, while dissent in its own ranks can. Thus governments may be prepared to make some concessions to critics on their own side. Beyond that, governments can expect to carry most of their legislative proposals substantially unchanged: 'Once bills have been introduced by government, they are almost certain to be passed' (Norton, 2005, p. 102). We examine several criticisms of the legislative process and attempts to reform it below.

## Private Members' legislation

The only partial exceptions to executive control of the legislative process are Private Members' bills. These are bills introduced by MPs who are not members of the government, including backbench members of the governing party or parties and members of the opposition. They can be introduced under various procedures, but the only method that normally stands any chance of success is through the annual ballot under which up to 20 backbenchers secure the right to introduce bills on a number of Friday sittings set aside for Private Members' measures. They then go through the same stages as government bills. But there are a number of practical limitations on Private Members' bills:

» They are not supposed to entail the expenditure of public money (which requires a money resolution).

» Lack of time is a crucial constraint. Ordinary backbenchers lack the procedural devices used by the government to curtail debate, and thus most bills run out of time. Normally, only the first half-dozen or so of the 20 bills introduced have a chance of passing all their stages and becoming law.

» Bills are unlikely to make progress if the government is opposed, because the government with its majority can use the whip system to destroy a bill. In practice, some Private Members' bills may be government measures in disguise, with the government offering its own facilities and benevolent support for a backbencher sponsoring a bill the government favours but has no time for in its own legislative programme.

» Even if the government is not opposed, a bill that arouses strong animosities among a minority of MPs may often be blocked. It may be 'talked out' by 'filibustering' from opponents, and thus run out of time, or be 'counted out' because too few MPs can be persuaded to attend on Fridays (in the absence of pressure from party whips).

Thus only a small proportion of Private Members' legislation reaches the statute book. Even so, some Acts introduced by Private Members have been important, transformed lives and changed attitudes. Private Members' legislation changed the law on capital punishment, homosexuality, divorce and abortion in the 1960s; compelled front-seat passengers to wear seat belts and restricted advertising on cigarettes in the 1980s; banned cruelty to wild animals in the mid-1990s, and strengthened the laws dealing with female genital mutilation in the 2000s. In 2015, the House of Commons rejected a Private Members' bill that proposed doctors could help terminally ill people end their lives. Such controversial social issues with a strong moral dimension often cut across normal party lines, so both government and opposition parties find it more convenient to leave them to a free vote.

## RECRUITMENT AND MAINTENANCE OF A GOVERNMENT

A key (but often insufficiently emphasised) function of the House of Commons is the recruitment and maintenance of a government. The executive in Britain is a parliamentary executive, as discussed in Chapter 7. Members of the government are drawn from Parliament and must retain the confidence and support of a majority in the House of Commons. It might be assumed that this would render governments weak, dependent on parliamentary support that might be withdrawn at any time. In practice, governments normally dominate Parliament and control its business, as we saw in the introduction to this chapter. It is virtually impossible in normal circumstances (i.e. government possession of a working majority) to bring a government down and, in practice, difficult to engineer a significant government defeat in the House of Commons. Thus executive dominance of Parliament is the general rule.

Government control of the House of Commons rests on four main factors:

1 *Possession in normal circumstances of a majority, allied with the habit of loyal voting by its own supporters*: Out of 20 general elections between 1945 and 2017, only in February 1974, 2010 and 2017 did one party fail to win an overall majority of seats, although in four others (1950, 1964, October 1974, 1992) the governing party enjoyed only small majorities. Far more commonly, governments have enjoyed comfortable majorities, coupled with generally strong party discipline. The guarantee of a 'payroll vote', that is, support from anyone who holds government positions, including ministers and junior ministers, will generally provide a significant number of the votes needed to retain power.

2 *Power to determine the parliamentary timetable*: Although some Commons business is initiated by opposition parties and backbenchers, three-quarters of Commons time is devoted to the consideration of government business (but see House of Commons Reform Committee reforms, below).

3 *Ability to curtail debate*: The government can restrict debate by employing a 'guillotine'. The guillotine – an 'allocation of time' motion regulating the amount of time to be spent on a bill – is normally used when the government considers that progress on a major piece of legislation is unsatisfactory at committee stage. In recent years, guillotine motions have been used more frequently.

4 *Control over legislation*: The legislative process, from initiation to completion, is dominated by the Cabinet, Cabinet committees and the departments, and is essentially now a function of the executive (see section on legislation).

Although an opposition can make life awkward for a government in a number of ways, they normally lack the numbers to defeat the government on their own. The only time since the Second World War that a government has suffered defeat on a motion of confidence was in March 1979, when Jim Callaghan's Labour government, which had already lost its overall Commons majority, was defeated by one vote on a censure motion. The resulting general election brought the Conservatives led by Margaret Thatcher to power. In more normal circumstances, when a government enjoys a comfortable majority, it can only be defeated if some of its own backbenchers combine with the opposition. Backbench rebellions have increased in size and frequency in recent decades. Conservative rebellions seriously embarrassed John Major's 1992–97 government, whose small initial majority of 21 declined steadily as a result of by-election defeats and removal of the party whip from rebel Conservatives. Blair's government, cushioned by substantial majorities, was able to survive sizeable Labour rebellions, most notably on Iraq, when the main opposition party supported its policy. His government came closer to defeat over university tuition fees, when Labour rebels combined with Conservatives and Lib Dems (Cowley and Stuart, 2008). The 2010–15 Parliament was, in terms of the number of rebellions, the most rebellious in the postwar era (Cowley, 2015). Taken as a whole, from 2010 to 2015, coalition MPs rebelled in 35% of votes. That comfortably beats the previous record of 28%, held by the Blair/Brown government between 2005 and 2010. The likely cause was tension in the coalition government between Lib Dems and Conservatives, including some high-profile rebellions over tuition fees, for example, as well as dissatisfaction from more Eurosceptic Conservative politicians over the direction Cameron was taking the Conservative Party.

Although in Britain it is taken for granted that ministers are drawn from Parliament, and predominantly from the House of Commons, it is not necessarily the case in other democratic states. Indeed, in some countries where there is a stricter separation of executive and legislative powers, government ministers are not even allowed to serve as members of the legislative assembly. Elsewhere, it is more common than in Britain for some ministers to be drawn from the worlds of business, finance or academia, without serving as elected representatives. One consequence is that the prime minister is effectively limited in choosing ministerial colleagues by the pool of party talent available in Parliament and particularly the House of Commons. Prime ministers have sometimes sought to recruit ministers from outside Parliament, but such ministers have been obliged by convention to obtain a seat in the Commons (through a parliamentary by-election) or in the House of Lords. However, such appointments have been few, and not always successful. Businesspeople and trade unionists without prior experience of Parliament have often found it difficult or frustrating to cope with parliamentary conventions and procedures.

Anyone seeking high office in government must normally first seek election to the House of Commons, and gain recognition there. Election to, and successful performance in, the House of Commons are the main criteria for political advancement and promotion into government in the British political system. It is in the Commons that ambitious politicians first attempt to make, and then as ministers sustain, their reputations. However, the skills of parliamentary debate are widely acknowledged to be no real preparation for running a department, nor are the two kinds of ability invariably present in the same person. Outstanding parliamentary orators do not necessarily make good ministers. Some potentially outstanding ministers may not be discovered through the British system of recruiting and training for government office.

## SCRUTINY OF THE EXECUTIVE

Governments are accountable to Parliament, and through Parliament to the voters. So it is in Parliament that the government must explain and defend its actions. Major opportunities for scrutinising and influencing the government through the procedures of the House of Commons are parliamentary questions, general, adjournment and emergency debates, early day motions, select committees and correspondence with ministers (see Table 6.2).

### Table 6.2 Main methods of Commons scrutiny of the executive

| | |
|---|---|
| Questions | • Backbenchers may submit oral and written questions to ministers<br>• Written questions and replies are recorded in *Hansard*, the official record of what is said in Parliament<br>• Ministers reply to oral questions daily, Monday to Thursday<br>• Prime Minister's Question Time 1–1.30pm, Wednesday: MPs may ask one (unscripted) supplementary question |
| Debates | • General: on Queen's Speech, no-confidence motions (rare) and motions tabled by government and opposition<br>• Adjournment debates: opportunity to raise general or constituency issues<br>• Private Members' bills: 11 days per session allocated to these<br>• Emergency debates: can be demanded but rarely conceded by Speaker |
| Early day motions | • Proposing and signing early day motions enables MPs to express their views: gains publicity, but no debate follows |
| Select committees | • Able to scrutinise executive away from the floor of the Commons<br>• Powers to send for 'persons, papers and records': can interrogate ministers<br>• Include 16 departmental select committees and others (e.g. Public Accounts, Public Administration, Statutory Instruments, Standards and Privileges)<br>• Party balance on select committees reflects that of the Commons as a whole: unanimity difficult – may divide on party lines |
| Letters to ministers | • Main way in which MPs pursue cases and issues raised by constituents |

Parliamentary questions remain the most celebrated means of calling the prime minister and ministers to account for their conduct of government. Questions for written answers enjoy less publicity, but can be a useful means of extracting information from government. Not all questions for oral answer can be dealt with in the time allotted, and ministers together with their civil servants have plenty of time to prepare answers to the pre-submitted questions, although ministers can sometimes be embarrassed by unexpected supplementary questions. Overall, the effectiveness of Question Time as a means of providing effective scrutiny of the executive is rather diminished by party point-scoring – particularly in Prime Minister's Question Time.

Further opportunities for backbenchers to raise issues are provided through general debates initiated by government and opposition, Private Members' motions and adjournment debates, and through the largely symbolic device of signing early day motions. However, more effective scrutiny is provided not so much by the Commons as a whole but by select committees.

An old and important select committee is the Public Accounts Committee (PAC), which has a central role in the Commons' scrutiny of government expenditure. Control of finance was once considered a crucial function of the Commons, but today, in as far as the Commons has any effective influence over government finance, it is largely through the PAC. It is composed of 15 members and chaired by a senior member of the opposition, and is particularly concerned to ensure that taxpayers get value for money from public spending. Since 1983, the PAC has been powerfully assisted by the National Audit Office (NAO), an independent body directed by the comptroller and auditor-general with a staff of 900, which produces around 50 'value for money' reports every year. Reports of both the PAC and the

NAO are sometimes extremely critical of government departments.

Parliamentary reformers from the 1960s advocated the greater use of departmental select committees (DSCs) to improve scrutiny of the executive. A new system of DCSs to provide regular scrutiny of the work of every government department was implemented in 1979. The task of these new DSCs was 'to examine the expenditure, administration and policy in the principal government departments ... and associated bodies' and to make reports with recommendations. In conducting their investigations, they can send for 'persons, papers and records'.

*Source*: PA/PA Archive/PA Images

Select committees sometimes make the headlines through their investigations, but they lack the power of their US rivals. Here, the BIS select committee interviews the controversial businessman Sir Philip Green, who was accused of selling off his company, British Home Stores, cheaply to avoid liability for the company's troubled pension scheme.

DSCs undoubtedly constitute a marked improvement on the Commons machinery for scrutinising the executive available before 1979. However, critics point out that, despite the frequent excellence of their reports and the occasional publicity achieved by their investigative sessions, they lack real clout. For example, in 2016, the select committee for what is now the Department of Business, Energy and Industrial Strategy carried out inquiries on several controversial aspects of UK business, including: the future of the steel industry, after the closure of Tata Steel's Port Talbot plant in South Wales; the sale and acquisition of retail chain British Home Stores after the company's collapse; and poor working practices at Sports Direct after several high-profile news reports. While generating headlines for this work, they frequently lack real impact to change policy. They are still part of an executive-dominated parliamentary system and lack the resources or prestige to sustain the powerful inquisitorial role that US congressional committees have long enjoyed. Some of the advantages and limitations of DSCs are set out in Table 6.3.

## Table 6.3 Advantages and limitations of DSCs

| Advantages | Limitations |
|---|---|
| • Powers to send for 'persons, papers and records' improve scrutiny and accountability of executive<br><br>• Coverage of proceedings aids open government<br><br>• DSCs may have pre-emptive or deterrent effect, deterring ministers and civil servants from behaviour they might be unable to justify before committee<br><br>• Committee investigation and reports may ultimately persuade government to change course<br><br>• Committee membership helps develop specialisation and expertise, and committees can seek outside advice and assistance | • Party whips' influence on membership of DSCs has compromised their independence<br><br>• Many members of DSCs lack necessary motivation, knowledge and skills<br><br>• Most DSCs lack the staff and budgets for substantial independent research<br><br>• Limited powers: ministers normally attend when requested, but are not obliged to answer questions. Civil servants may withhold information in the interests of 'good government' or national security<br><br>• Lack of influence: few DSC reports are debated on the floor of the House of Commons, and ministers can, and generally do, ignore them |

## FORUM FOR NATIONAL DEBATE

In addition to the functions outlined above, the Commons is also reckoned to provide a forum for national debate. On occasions, the Commons has appeared to rise above party conflict to change the course of history. A celebrated instance was when the Conservative Leo Amery famously called out 'Speak for England, Arthur' to Labour's Arthur Greenwood in the 1940 Norway debate, which was to bring down Neville Chamberlain and make Churchill head of a coalition government. On this occasion, a debate in Parliament had momentous consequences, which decisively transformed the conduct of the Second World War and perhaps changed the course of history. Critics suggest, however, that such occasions are very much the exception. More commonly, debates take the form of relatively narrow, almost ritualistic combat between rival teams of party gladiators urged on by compact stage armies of supporters. The proceedings in Parliament often seem to amount to little more than episodes in a continual election campaign, rather than offering a more open and wide-ranging forum of national debate.

Indeed, Parliament is not always even given the opportunity to debate issues of national importance. Parliament is not in session for substantial periods of the year, including some three months in the summer. While events may lead to demands for a recall of Parliament, this is rarely conceded. However, Parliament was recalled, for example, in June 2016 to pay tribute to Jo Cox, the Labour MP who was murdered by a member of a far-right group with psychiatric problems; in August 2013 to discuss Syria and the use of chemical weapons; and April 2011 for tributes to be paid following the death of Margaret Thatcher, former prime minister.

Even when Parliament is in session, it is not easy to organise an extensive debate on some unanticipated development. Much of the parliamentary timetable is determined well in advance. While emergency debates may be demanded, they are rarely conceded by the Speaker. Explicit parliamentary approval is not required for some of the most momentous decisions that a government can take. The British prime minister has inherited most of the old prerogative powers of the crown and does not need express parliamentary sanction for crucial and potentially far-reaching acts, such as signing treaties and even declaring war. As Hennessy (2000, p. 89) has observed: 'here, the royal prerogative is all. Unless primary legislation is required, Parliament does not have to be routinely involved at all.'

In practice, a wise prime minister will normally try to involve Parliament as much as possible over national crises and war. During his wartime premiership, Churchill treated the Commons with 'high respect', addressing numerous 'secret sessions', which gave MPs 'a sense of being privy to special knowledge' (Jenkins, 2001, p. 622). Eden, by contrast, failed to carry Parliament with him over Suez in 1956, refused a request for the recall of Parliament from the leader of the opposition (Hennessy, 2000, p. 245), and (it is now clear) lied to the House of Commons on the crucial issue of foreknowledge of Israeli plans. Mrs Thatcher wisely agreed to an exceptional Commons debate on a Saturday over the Falklands crisis, and this perhaps helped her to maintain a level of bipartisan support for the subsequent task force. There were major Commons debates on the eve of the Iraq War on 26 February and 18 March 2003, when Blair secured a parliamentary majority despite the opposition of 139 Labour rebels. It is now accepted that Parliament must debate and vote before British forces are sent into action.

However, Parliament does not always provide an effective forum for national debate. Even if Parliament is generally given the opportunity to debate issues of national importance, it no longer appears to be at the centre of national debate. The proceedings of Parliament are now much less reported even in the 'broadsheet' press, such as *The Times*, *The Guardian* or *The Telegraph*. Although the Commons reluctantly let in the TV cameras in 1989 after decades of debate, and it is now possible for members of the public to follow parliamentary proceedings on minority channels, the main BBC coverage and commercial news and current affairs programmes devote only cursory treatment to Parliament.

## REPRESENTATION

The 'representative' character of the House of Commons underpins its other roles. The House of Commons has long been held to represent the common people of Britain, and this claim was strengthened by the extension of the vote to the whole adult population in the nineteenth and early twentieth centuries. In this section, we examine three ways in which the Commons is formally representative: its representation of constituencies; its representation of parties; and its representation of different interests. In Spotlight 6.1, we discuss how Parliament should represent the diverse society in which we live.

## SPOTLIGHT ON ...

## Substantive and descriptive representation    6.1

How does Parliament represent us? In *The Concept of Representation* (1967), Hanna Pitkin distinguished between different types of representation. Perhaps the most important distinction she drew was between 'substantive' and 'descriptive representation'. Substantive representation occurs where a representative seeks to advance a group's policy preferences and interests. After the Second World War, the Labour Party was led by Clement Attlee (see Chapter 2). Attlee came from a reasonably prosperous family, but the postwar policies that Labour pursued, such as the creation of the NHS and the welfare state, were designed primarily to help the working class. It could be said, therefore, that Attlee provided substantive representation for this group.

Descriptive representation is based on the extent to which the representative 'resembles' the represented. Here the focus is on the politics of 'being' rather than 'doing'. Attlee's wealthy background meant that he did not descriptively represent many of his working-class voters. The House of Commons could only be said to be descriptively representative if it was a microcosm of society as a whole, in terms of class, gender, ethnicity, religion, ability and other forms of identity (discussed in more detail in Chapter 4).

Does it matter if the House of Commons is not descriptively representative, providing that each group's interests are represented substantively? For British feminist Anne Phillips, in *The Politics of Presence* (1998), the answer is yes (as the book's title implies). For Phillips, both descriptive representation and substantive representation are needed. Phillips wrote with women's representation in mind, but her argument can be applied to other groups as well. She argued that parliaments should look like society as a whole for several reasons, including the importance of role models, because justice demands it, because different groups have specific interests that are not clear without representation, and because representing different groups could impact upon the style of politics in a positive way.

How descriptively representative is the Commons today? The 2017 general election resulted in a Parliament that was far more diverse than a generation before (BBC News, 2017b):

» There were 208 women elected in 2017, and women now make up 32% of the Commons (but over 50% of the UK population). Labour has the most women with 45%, while the Tories have 34%. Of the two next biggest parties, the SNP have 34% and the Lib Dems 33%

» There were 52 ethnic minority MPs elected in 2017. (It was not until the general election of 1987 that the first black MPs were voted into the House of Commons.) Of the 2017 intake, 32 are Labour, 19 Conservatives and 1 Lib Dem. It is an increase from 41 in 2015 and the highest number ever. They include Preet Gill, the first female Sikh MP, and Shadow Home Secretary Diane Abbott (see Key Figures 6.1), who became the first ever black female MP in 1987, and Afzal Khan, Manchester's first Muslim MP.

» Forty-five MPs openly define themselves as lesbian, gay or bisexual. (No MPs currently identify as transgender.) That is a 40% increase in LGBT+ MPs from the 2015 election – when there were 32 – and includes 19 from Labour, 19 from the Tories and 7 from the SNP. However, of the 9 transgender candidates who stood, none were elected.

» While there are no definitive figures on the number of disabled MPs, it appears there has been an increase in the 2017 Parliament. Labour has two new MPs in the Commons who have disabilities. Marsha de Cordova, who represents Battersea, is registered blind and used her victory speech to champion disabled rights.

» In terms of school background, which correlates strongly with social class, 51% of MPs in the new Commons went to comprehensive schools, while 29% went to private schools and 18% to selective state schools. The analysis found 45% of all Conservative MPs elected in 2017 were privately educated, compared to 14% of Labour MPs and 6% of SNP MPs. By contrast, the number of MPs attending private school was still far higher than the general population, which stands at 7%.

Parliament is hardly descriptively representative of the society it serves, although it is has become more so in recent years.

# KEY FIGURES 6.1
## Diane Abbott

Diane Abbott in 1987

**Diane Abbott (1953–)** is a British Labour Party politician. She was born to working-class Jamaican parents in west London. She was first elected as MP for Hackney North and Stoke Newington in 1987, becoming the first black woman ever to be elected to the House of Commons. On the left of the Labour Party, Abbott voted against the Labour leadership under Tony Blair on several occasions, notably opposing the Iraq War, the introduction of ID cards and the renewal of Britain's Trident nuclear deterrent. She stood to become leader of the Labour Party in 2010, but was comfortably defeated. She was appointed shadow home secretary in October 2016. Although MPs often experience abuse from the public, Abbott has experienced particularly hostile treatment as a black woman.

## The representation of constituencies

The House of Commons consists of 650 MPs, elected by single-member parliamentary constituencies. Candidates for Parliament may stand as representatives of a party but, once elected, each MP is expected to represent the interests of the constituency as a whole and to be at the service of all constituents. Through this constituency role MPs collectively may be said to represent the entire country, which would not be true of their roles as party and group representatives.

Yet if each MP represents a particular constituency, that does not necessarily mean that they have to represent the views of their electorate, at least according to the influential trustee theory of representation derived from Edmund Burke, eighteenth-century Whig politician and thinker: 'Your representative owes you, not his industry only, but his judgement; and he betrays, instead of serving you, if he sacrifices it to your opinion. [Parliament is] a deliberative assembly of one nation [rather than] a congress of ambassadors from different and hostile interests' (Burke, speech to his electors in Bristol, 1774, quoted in Burke, 1975, p. 158). Burke was cited by several MPs after the vote to leave the EU, when they voted in Parliament to remain in the EU against the majority of voters in their constituency. Thus Parliament should be entrusted to lead public opinion rather than simply reflect it. This contrasts with the more radical delegate theory of representation in which the elected representatives are considered to be the agents of, and directly accountable to, their constituents.

Most MPs take their constituency responsibilities seriously and the burden of work can be considerable. MPs' constituency work falls into two main categories. First, there is the local welfare officer/social worker role, dealing with a wide variety of problems, such as housing, education, health and social security, on behalf of individual constituents. MPs tackle the problems at the appropriate level, conducting a voluminous correspondence with ministers, government departments, local authorities and other local offices and so on. Also, MPs can raise constituents' grievances through parliamentary questions and debate.

Second, MPs seek to look after the interests of the constituency as a whole. So they may try to attract new commercial and industrial investment, get roads built, find solutions for local industrial disputes and prevent local factories, schools and hospitals from closing. Cowley (2006, pp. 38–41) argues that the constituency role of MPs has grown substantially in recent years.

## The representation of parties in the House of Commons

MPs are elected (almost always) as representatives of a party, and that party underpins their activities once in the Commons. However, although MPs clearly represent parties, the distribution of seats is not proportional to the distribution of support for parties in general elections (as we see in Chapter 13). Nor do parliamentary parties necessarily closely mirror the opinions of the party members who selected them as candidates, or the voters who elected them, although MPs with markedly different views may face criticism and ultimately perhaps deselection. Alternatively, MPs who become unhappy with their party may leave it and seek to join another party.

Several important institutions help to organise parties in the Houses of Parliament. These include:

» *Cabinets and Shadow Cabinets*: The Cabinet is normally drawn from the party (or,

occasionally, such as during the coalition of 2010–15, parties) with a majority in the Commons, and thus provides a collective leadership for the governing party or parties. The inclusion of ambitious potential rival leaders in the Cabinet renders a dangerous backbench revolt less likely and reinforces party unity. Shadow Cabinets provide collective leadership for the official opposition party. When the Conservatives are in opposition, the leader chooses their Shadow Cabinet. When Labour is in opposition, its Shadow Cabinet is elected by the Parliamentary Labour Party, although the leader allocates Shadow Cabinet portfolios and appoints additional shadow ministers.

» *The whip system*: The prime minister appoints some MPs to act as 'whips'. Whips play a central role in linking the party leaderships with the backbenchers. The whips try to ensure that backbenchers support party policy in divisions (or votes) of the House of Commons. Party MPs are sent a weekly outline of parliamentary business with items underlined once, twice or three times, depending on whether an MP's attendance is merely requested (described as a 'one-line whip'), expected (a 'two-line whip') or regarded as essential (a 'three-line whip'). Defiance of a three-line whip constitutes a serious breach of party rules. But whips are personnel managers rather than disciplinarians. They rely mainly on persuasion, which may sometimes include veiled inducements and hints of honours or promotion. The ultimate sanction against a party rebel – withdrawal of the party whip, that is, expulsion from the parliamentary party – is rarely used, and can prove counterproductive, as the Major government discovered when the whip was withdrawn from eight Conservatives in 1994, only to be restored in 1995. More recently, the whip has been suspended for two Conservative MPs: Nadine Dorries in 2012, when she left the country to take part in a reality TV programme, and Anne Marie Morris for using racist language in 2017.

» *Party meetings*: Meetings of the parliamentary party provide an important channel of communication between party leaders and backbenchers, allowing the airing of grievances and concerns. The Conservative Party's '1922 Committee' (discussed in more detail in Chapter 14) meets weekly when Parliament is sitting, and includes all MPs except the leader when the party is in opposition. Historically, when the party was in government, only backbenchers attended, but Prime Minister David Cameron attempted to involve all Conservative MPs including ministers, a move that upset backbenchers who valued the freedom to meet away from the watchful eye of the leadership. Under a compromise, ministers can now attend but not vote. The chairman of the '1922 Committee' plays a key role in the party especially in times of controversy and crisis. When in opposition, the Parliamentary Labour Party (PLP) is attended by all Labour MPs including members of the Shadow Cabinet. When the party is in government, Labour ministers attend meetings of the PLP when the work of their departments is under discussion.

» *Specialist party committees*: Each major party also forms a large number of specialist committees, which may enable backbenchers to influence party policy on specific subjects. (These purely party committees should not be confused with all-party committees, such as the increasingly important DSCs, which may lead to a cross-party consensus that could erode discipline and cohesion within parties.)

Government is party government; consequently, it is crucial for governments to retain their parliamentary majority by maintaining the support of their parliamentary party, or parties (and preferably the party members around the country). Discipline and cohesion, especially in formal activities such as voting in Parliament, are almost as important for opposition parties as for the government if they are to have parliamentary and electoral credibility. Open divisions are damaging to a party and encouraging to its rivals. For a government, they may jeopardise the passing of legislation and, for an opposition, destroy any chance to embarrass or defeat the government. The worst eventuality is that a party will split and, as may happen as a result, suffer electoral defeat – as Labour did from 1983 to 1992 after splitting in 1981. Thus each parliamentary party appoints whips to maintain party discipline (see above). However, although there are strong inducements for MPs to maintain party loyalty, the number and size of rebellions has increased (Cowley and Stuart, 2008, pp. 103–19).

Party, then, dominates Parliament, but the reverse is also true. Parliament equally clearly dominates party. Virtually all UK parties accept the legitimacy of Parliament, and have as their major aim the winning of seats in the House of Commons. The parliamentary party generally assumes far greater importance than the party in the country. The stand-off in summer 2016 between the PLP, which passed a vote of 'no confidence' in Labour leader Jeremy Corbyn, and party members around the country, who had overwhelmingly supported Corbyn as leader in 2015, is a notable exception to this rule. Parliament provides the main arena for the party battle between elections, and this parliamentary conflict, through the media, influences the shifting public support for rival parties.

## The representation of interests

MPs not only represent parties, they also, less formally (and sometimes less openly), represent a range of interests. Some of this arises naturally from their past (and sometimes continuing) occupations, their membership of a range of organisations, their personal and family connections and leisure pursuits. It is only to be expected that a former teacher or miner will retain not just an interest in their old occupation but also useful experience and expertise to contribute to debates on the subject. Similarly, MPs who are keen churchgoers or ramblers have an interest they will naturally seek to defend and promote where relevant. They may hold a position (honorary or otherwise) in an organisation that gives them an additional obligation to look after its interests. Much of this is relatively uncontroversial, and indeed may enrich the deliberations of Parliament.

## SPOTLIGHT ON ...

## MPs and the representation of interests: some areas of concern

6.2

» *Payment of fees to MPs to serve as advisers, consultants or directors*: in 1995 the Nolan Committee found that 168 MPs, including 145 Conservatives, 15 Labour and 6 Lib Dems, shared 356 consultancies. (Publicity has led to a marked reduction in the number of such consultancies.)

» *Access to the Commons as MPs' research assistants and aides*: the use of House of Commons photo-identity passes by organisations as a cover for commercial lobbying activities, in return for services to the MP concerned, first became evident in the late 1980s.

» *Lobbying of MPs by professional consultancy firms*: this kind of lobbying developed into an important industry by the 1980s and now involves many consultancy groups lobbying governments to take account of their position.

» *Financing of all-party parliamentary groups by outside interests*: such as individual businesses,

groups of companies, trade associations, lobbying firms and charities.

» *Specialist assistance on an ad hoc unpaid basis*: a wide range of groups provide information and support for MPs' parliamentary activities, such as select committees and Private Members' bills.

» *MPs' pursuit of outside occupations*: outside interests are represented in the House of Commons through MPs' part-time occupations as, for example, journalists, lawyers and company directors.

» *Sponsorship of election candidates through a particular party*: such as Labour Party candidates by trade unions. This practice ended in 1995. Formerly, unions could not instruct MPs how to speak or vote (as that would be a breach of parliamentary privilege) but they did expect MPs to watch over their interests.

*Source*: iStock.com/njmorgan

Lord Hailsham once commented that Conservatives prefer fox hunting and religion to politics. Many politicians use their influence to defend their interests in Parliament.

However, some representations of interests by MPs have raised rather more concern (see Spotlight 6.2).

## REFORM OF THE HOUSE OF COMMONS

While the House of Commons is, in theory, the centre of democracy in Britain, it has often seemed to operate more as a private club determined to keep the public at arm's length. When TV cameras were finally allowed in and the public could hear and see their representatives, they were unimpressed by MPs' behaviour and the quality of debate in an often near-empty chamber. The Commons remains cramped and ill-equipped, and its procedures antiquated. Thus while town halls have long used push-button voting, votes in the Commons are decided first by acclamation (shouting) and then by queuing in the division lobbies to be counted manually by tellers, a process that can take 20 minutes or more. For long periods, particularly over the summer, the Commons does not meet and, until 2003, its daily timetable began at 2.30 and continued without an official break until 10.30, and sometimes on into all-night sittings. Although some of its more meaningless jargon has been simplified, quaint language and rituals continue to bewilder outsiders.

Reform of the Commons has been long debated, and indeed some important reforms have been carried through in recent decades. As we have seen, DSCs were introduced in 1979, with a Standards Committee to provide more effective safeguards against corruption and 'sleaze', although it failed to stop the MPs' expenses scandal (discussed in Chapter 16). Improved office and secretarial facilities have been provided to help MPs to work more effectively. Recent reforms have focused on the Commons timetable and methods of working. The Blair government reduced the frequency of Prime Minister's Questions from twice to once a week, which some critics thought weakened the prime minister's accountability to Parliament, even though the total time given to them remained the same. Norton (2001, p. 54) maintained that Blair gave 'less time to parliamentary activity than his predecessors'. Partly in answer to such criticisms, Blair inaugurated, in 2002, twice-yearly prime ministerial appearances before the Liaison Committee of the House of Commons, composed of chairs of select committees. This has proved a more successful innovation.

The Select Committee on the Modernisation of the House of Commons, appointed in 1997, recommended a number of reforms. Some of these have been implemented. Thus Westminster Hall, located in the Houses of Parliament, has been utilised as a 'parallel chamber' for debates not involving votes, increasing speaking opportunities for MPs. Modernisation of the Commons was revived in 2009 and a new Select Committee on Reform of the House of Commons chaired by MP Tony Wright was appointed. Their report, *Rebuilding the House* (House of Commons Reform Committee, 2009), proposed the following:

» A reduction in the number and size of DSCs

» Chairs and members of DSCs and similar select committees to be elected by secret ballot of MPs

» Backbench business to be determined by the Commons rather than the government

» One backbench motion to be debated each month.

These proposals were generally approved by the Commons, and the coalition government agreed that they should be fully implemented in May 2010. The reforms have improved the independence and effectiveness of DSCs, and enhanced the control of the Commons as a whole, and backbenchers in particular, over its own business (Russell, 2011).

In addition, the coalition agreement in 2010 between the Conservatives and Lib Dems committed the government to four major pieces of reform that would have a considerable effect on parliament: the equalisation of constituency sizes and a significant reduction in the number of MPs; an elected House of Lords; a referendum on the electoral system (discussed in Chapter 13), and five-year fixed-term parliaments. Only the last of these policies was passed, removing the power of the prime minister to call a general election at the time of their choosing. On the other proposals, the electorate voted 'no' to electoral reform much to the Lib Dems' annoyance, Conservative backbench rebels blocked Lords reform and in return the Lib Dems vetoed boundary changes, arguing that they were mainly being pushed through to benefit the Conservatives electorally. After the Conservative victory in the 2015 election, most of these reforms were shelved. Electoral reform is not on the party's agenda. Nor is Lords reform a priority for the Conservative Party, as we shall see below, despite the events raised in the introduction to this chapter.

## THE HOUSE OF LORDS

The British Parliament, like many, but by no means all, legislatures around the world, is bicameral; in other words, it has two chambers or houses. In many other countries the second chamber has a significant role. Thus the US Senate is actually rather more powerful and prestigious than the US lower house, the House of Representatives. However, the British upper house, the House of Lords, because of its bizarre composition (until recently composed largely of hereditary peers), has long been of marginal significance to British government and politics. One indication of its declining role is that while in the nineteenth century many prime ministers and other leading ministers came from the House of Lords, since 1902 there have been no prime ministers who have sat in the Lords, and very few senior ministers. The powers of the Lords are limited. Although it can delay legislation for up to a year, its undemocratic composition has generally inhibited their lordships from exercising even this limited power too often.

## POWERS AND FUNCTIONS OF THE LORDS

The main functions of the House of Lords are as follows:

» *Legislation*: revision of House of Commons bills, giving ministers the opportunity for second thoughts; initiation of non-controversial legislation, including government bills, bills by individual peers, private bills (promoted by bodies outside Parliament, e.g. local authorities), and consideration of delegated legislation.

» *Deliberation*: the provision of a forum for debates on matters of current interest.

» *Scrutiny*: the Lords subject government policy and administration to scrutiny through questions and through the work of its select committees (e.g. European Communities, Science and Technology).

## Legislation

Constitutionally, despite its reduced powers, the upper house remains an essential part of the legislative process, and spends over half its time on legislation. By the Parliament Act 1911, the Lords completely lost their power to delay or amend money bills, which receive royal assent one month after leaving the House of Commons, whether approved by the Lords or not. It retained the power to delay non-money bills for up to two years (reduced to one by the Parliament Act 1949).

In practice, the Lords has accepted further limitations on its own power of delay. The main guiding rule – firmly established by Conservative opposition peers in the immediate postwar period – is that the upper house does not oppose measures included in the governing party's manifesto at the previous election (the Salisbury/Addison doctrine). In addition, the Lords rarely press an amendment or delay a measure to the point where the Parliament Acts have to be invoked.

The House of Lords can cause political embarrassment to the government of the day, but no more. The upper house has on numerous occasions impeded government legislation and forced concessions, although generally on minor issues. Although it is far from being a major constitutional obstacle to the party in power, during periods of substantial government majorities and weak opposition in the House of Commons, the Lords have sometimes offered more substantial if ultimately ineffective resistance to government.

A significant trend in recent decades has been the greater use made of the Lords by governments to revise and generally tidy up their legislation – carefully thinking through how it is written and its consequences. Because much of the process of passing legislation has to be done hurriedly at the end of sessions in the Commons, one peer in the Lords has described the upper chamber as 'a gilded dustpan and brush' (*Hansard*, 25 April 1990, HC Deb, col. 614). Suggested causes for this development include inadequate consultation, government indecisiveness and poor drafting in the early stages of legislation, but whatever the reasons, it has made the House of Lords an increasingly attractive target for pressure groups seeking to influence the detailed amendment of bills (as we discuss in Chapter 16).

## Deliberation and scrutiny

The House of Lords, which devotes approximately one day a week to general debate, is often praised for the quality of its debates but their overall impact is questionable. Its exercise of its scrutiny functions (through Questions and select committees) is of greater consequence. For example, the House of Lords EU Select Committee, which considers initiatives proposed by the EU Commission, is well staffed, able to consider EU proposals on their merits and has considerable expertise in the area. It produces over 20 reports a year, which, like other Lords select committee reports but unlike their equivalents in the Commons, are all debated. Overall, however, the House of Lords has made no attempt to establish through its select committees a mechanism for consistent, comprehensive scrutiny of government but has rather used them to fill gaps left by the Commons select committee system.

## The end of the Lords' function as the supreme court of appeal

One important historic function of the Lords has recently been abolished. Until 2009, the Lords not only contributed to making the law, but also adjudicated on the law in its role as the supreme court of appeal. In 2005, the Constitutional Reform Act transferred the Lords' judicial powers to a new UK Supreme Court, which became effective in 2009. This has contributed to a clearer separation of the legislative and judicial powers of the state.

### THE COMPOSITION AND REFORM OF THE HOUSE OF LORDS

If the powers of the Lords have been controversial, the traditional composition of the upper chamber has come to be regarded as unsustainable in a modern democratic era. The House of Lords long consisted of lords temporal (holders of hereditary titles) and lords spiritual (the archbishops and senior bishops of the Church of England). In the nineteenth century, specialist Law Lords, appointed for life, were added to assist the upper chamber in its (then) judicial capacity as the highest court in the land. The composition of the House of Lords was more significantly affected by the Life Peerages Act 1958, which empowered the Crown (effectively the prime minister) to create life peers. The Peerages Act 1963 allowed hereditary peers to disclaim their titles, and admitted hereditary peeresses

into the House of Lords in their own right. These two Acts had the effect of introducing a small proportion of women to what had been an all-male chamber. By 2016, women still only made up around 25% of membership of the House of Lords. The 1963 Act also transformed the Lords over a period from an almost entirely hereditary chamber to a chamber in which appointed life peers outnumber hereditary peers in the work of the Lords. This occurred because, whereas most of the hereditary peers did not attend regularly, many of the life peers were 'working peers' and they constituted the bulk of the active membership. However, the hereditary peers retained a nominal majority, which could become effective when a subject dear to their hearts was debated.

However, the composition remained bizarre, and not only because the majority of members still claimed their seats from an accident of birth. The only religion represented as of right is the established Church of England, which hardly seems appropriate in what has become multi-faith Britain. Moreover, while appointment may constitute an advance on heredity as a qualification for membership, the life peers owe their appointments to prime ministerial patronage (although the prime minister normally accepts recommendations from the leaders of opposition parties), which hardly seems much more democratic. In practice, retired ministers and long-serving MPs are among those who are commonly offered peerages. Thus debates in the Lords often feature elderly politicians, who were once household names but are now largely forgotten, giving substance to a quip of Jo Grimond, the former Liberal leader, that the House of Lords proves there is life after death.

A final objection to the composition of the unreformed upper chamber was its unbalanced representation of political parties. Although a substantial minority of peers are crossbenchers who are independent of party allegiance, among those who took a party whip, Conservative peers outnumbered Labour peers by 300 up to 1997. (For the current political composition of the House of the Lords, see Figure 6.1c on p. 122.) This built-in Conservative advantage had a marked effect on the Lords' function as a revising chamber. On average, whereas the Lords inflicted 70 defeats a year on Labour governments between 1974 and 1979, it defeated Conservative administrations only 13 times a year between 1979 and 1997. Unsurprisingly, the Labour government that took office with a huge Commons majority in 1997 sought to correct this party imbalance, as part of an intended comprehensive reform of the second chamber.

While it has long been recognised that the hereditary second chamber is indefensible in a democratic era, reform of the Lords has proved difficult. As Robert Hazell (1999, p. 114) has observed: 'it is impossible to decide a satisfactory system for Lords' membership without first deciding what interests peers are there to represent'. This is not easy in Britain. The key function a second chamber performs in a federal state is to represent the interests of the states, as the Senate does in the USA or the Bundesrat in Germany. It is more difficult to establish such a clear function in a unitary state, as the UK remains, at least in theory. It would be easier to devise a logical role for a second chamber if British government evolves towards a quasi-federal or ultimately perhaps a fully federal system. Although Lords reform is long overdue, and some would argue that it has come a century late, it is perhaps premature while the final outcome of the devolution process remains unclear.

Another solution to the Lords reform dilemma is simply abolition. Unicameral legislatures have become more common. In 2015, about 60 per cent of the world's legislatures had just one chamber, after some mature democracies abolished their second chamber (Hague et al., 2016, p. 133). Indeed, China, the world's most populous nation, and large parts of Africa have unicameral systems. The devolved assemblies and parliaments in the UK in Scotland, Wales and Northern Ireland are also unicameral. Bicameral legislatures are used in most of the UK's former colonies, where the 'Westminster model' was exported, North America and much of Europe (as we discussed in Chapter 5). The abolition of the Lords to create a unicameral system has never found much favour in Westminster, although Labour proposed it for

a time. It is commonly argued that a second chamber provides an opportunity for second thoughts on over-hasty legislation from the lower house. If it is accepted that some kind of revising chamber is necessary or desirable, it is then a question of deciding how that chamber should be composed. While many favour a wholly or largely elected second chamber, a problem here is that this could challenge the legitimacy and primacy of the House of Commons.

Because previous reform proposals had foundered on the failure to agree on the composition and powers of the second chamber, Blair's Labour government opted for a two-stage model of reform. Stage one was to involve simply removing the hereditary peers, stage two a more long-term and comprehensive reform. The government moved quickly towards the abolition of the right of hereditary peers to sit in the Lords, but faced with the prospects of a prolonged battle with the upper house, instead reached a compromise. This allowed the hereditary peers to elect 92 of their number to remain as members of the transitional upper house pending a more fundamental final reform. After the 92 peers were chosen, the rest of the hereditary peers lost their powers to speak and vote in the Lords. The interim composition of the half-reformed House of Lords, compared with its former composition, is shown in Table 6.4 and Figure 6.1.

### Table 6.4 Old and interim composition of the Lords, after House of Lords Act 1999

| | Old | Interim new |
|---|---|---|
| Spiritual peers (archbishops and senior bishops of Church of England) | 26 | 26 |
| Hereditary peers | 777 | 92 |
| Law Lords | 27 | 27 |
| Life peers | 525 | 525 |
| Total | 1,355 | 670 |

## Figure 6.1: Composition of House of Lords

(a) Unreformed, pre-1999

(b) Interim, 1999

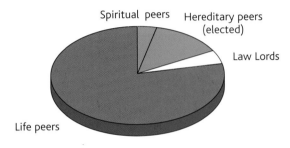

(c) Party affiliations, 2016

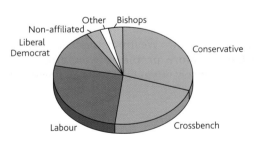

*Source*: Parliament website: www.parliament.uk

The projected second stage of Lords reform has proved far more difficult. The government adopted a time-honoured device for dealing with politically awkward questions, appointing an independent Royal Commission chaired by Lord Wakeham, a former Conservative minister. The Wakeham Report (2000) favoured a largely appointed house with only a minority of elected peers, but a government White Paper in 2001 (Cabinet Office, 2001) that largely endorsed

Wakeham's proposals met wide-ranging opposition. The government then set up an independent joint committee of both houses to undertake widespread consultation and propose options for reform. But, in 2003 when both houses were given the chance to vote on seven options ranging from a wholly appointed to a wholly elected upper chamber, none commanded a clear majority. The government then proposed simply removing the remaining hereditary peers, but following opposition in the Lords this too was abandoned.

Following the 2010 general election, the Conservative–Lib Dem coalition agreement set out further plans for a reformed second chamber, elected by proportional representation. Nick Clegg, Lib Dem leader and deputy prime minister, introduced the House of Lords Reform Bill in June 2011. This set out plans for a mainly elected second chamber with members serving 15-year terms. In July 2011, Clegg announced that the government was abandoning the bill due to opposition from Conservative backbench MPs, and claimed that the Conservatives had 'broken the coalition contract' (BBC News, 2012). Smaller reforms were introduced later in the Parliament. In 2014, it became possible for members to resign from the Lords, often to retire. Further reform in 2015 authorised the Lords to expel or suspend members. However, significant Lords' reform had faltered once again. The Lords did, at least, appear to be more assertive and powerful in its semi-reformed state (Russell, 2013).

## THE WESTMINSTER PARLIAMENT AND DEVOLUTION

Although the Westminster Parliament remains at the centre of British politics, formally at least, in the sense that its sovereignty remains a key principle of the unwritten (or uncodified) British constitution, it is no longer the only parliament with which British politics is concerned. The Westminster Parliament now coexists with an increasingly powerful Scottish Parliament with legislative powers, and assemblies for Wales and Northern Ireland (see Chapter 11). There is also a Greater London Assembly, as well as newer experiments in local democracy, such as the 'Northern Powerhouse' (see Chapter 10, pp. 210–11). Additionally, while Britain remains a member of the EU, representatives are also elected to the European Parliament. While this used to be dismissed as a mere 'talking shop', its influence on EU decision-making, and hence on decisions that affect Britain, has grown steadily in recent years (see Chapter 12). Indeed, some would argue that it has become a more effective policy-influencing body than the Westminster Parliament. Thus the Westminster Parliament may increasingly appear as one of many representative assemblies in the evolving British system of governance. The existence of these other parliaments and assemblies have considerable and potentially increasing implications for the role and functions of the Westminster Parliament, and requires significant liaison and coordination.

The EU referendum in June 2016 was, in part, a debate about sovereignty. Since 1973, UK membership of the EU had involved considerable if contentious implications for the sovereignty of the Westminster Parliament. Under the Treaty of Rome and subsequent treaties, EU law is binding on member states. Parliamentary sovereignty seemed increasingly circumscribed, despite attempts to improve the legislative accountability of the EU to national parliaments. With an increasing proportion of legislation emanating from the EU, Westminster surveillance of European directives and regulations is a matter of some importance. The task involves both Houses of Parliament. In the Commons, the European Scrutiny Committee, the select committee on European legislation, refers EU legislation that it sees as requiring further scrutiny and debate to one of the two **bill committees**. The House of Lords also has a scrutiny committee, the EU Select Committee, whose task is to decide which of the hundreds of EU documents deposited with it each month require scrutiny because they raise important questions of policy or principle or for other reasons. Six subcommittees, whose reports are normally debated by the House, undertake this scrutiny. The attempt to disentangle this element of Britain's multilayered form of governance is causing constitutional experts considerable difficulty, but can be seen, at the very least, as a partial reassertion, at least for the time being, of the sovereignty of the Westminster Parliament (see Chapter 12).

---

*A public or private **bill committee** is appointed for each bill that goes through Parliament. Until 2006, they were called standing committees.*

---

The longer term consequences of the devolution of power to the Scottish Parliament and Welsh and Northern Ireland Assemblies also have profound implications for the role and, perhaps ultimately, for the composition of the Westminster Parliament. Much of the law passed at Westminster will now be English (or English and Welsh) law rather than UK law, while law passed in the devolved assemblies may have knock-on implications for Westminster. At the very least, there is a need for considerable liaison between the various parliaments and assemblies. Initially, the potential for serious conflict between parliaments was somewhat lessened by Labour or Labour-dominated governments at Westminster, Edinburgh and Cardiff. More problems were predicted when a Conservative–Lib Dem majority at Westminster in 2010 faced a minority SNP government in Edinburgh and a Labour–Plaid Cymru coalition in Cardiff. Indeed, the idea that a Westminster Parliament, where the Conservatives have been the largest party since 2010 and in a majority since 2015, should be sovereign over a Scottish Parliament dominated by parties of a quite different political hue was a powerful motivator for Scottish independence and a source of considerable tension. Some of the implications of these developments for long-established British constitutional principles, particularly the sovereignty of the Westminster Parliament and the unity of the UK, are discussed in Chapter 9.

## SUMMARY

» Although the Westminster Parliament is old, retains a certain amount of prestige and is constitutionally sovereign, critics allege that, in practice, it is not very powerful, nor particularly effective.

» MPs represent electoral areas called 'constituencies'. They tend not to be socially representative of those who elect them, nor are they expected to reflect their views. Almost all represent parties, and all of them also reflect a range of outside interests. While this can be useful, some outside interests raise ethical questions.

» Government is recruited from and maintained by Parliament (and largely from the House of Commons). There has long been a close interdependence between the executive and legislature in British politics. In practice, the government dominates the Commons.

» Traditional means of parliamentary scrutiny of the executive have been supplemented by the development of departmental select committees that oversee all ministerial departments.

» Most of the legislation examined in the Commons and almost all the laws that are passed are government measures. Legislation is, in practice, substantially an executive function.

» The upper house only has powers of delay over legislation. Its undemocratic composition restricts its legitimacy and authority.

» Although most hereditary peers have been removed, detailed proposals for further reform of the upper house have failed to secure broad support, and it remains a mainly appointed chamber. Further promises of reform, such as those made during the 2010–15 coalition government, have always faltered through lack of a clear agenda or lack of support, particularly from the Conservative Party.

» The former judicial functions of the House of Lords have been transferred to a new Supreme Court.

» The Westminster Parliament is no longer the only representative assembly elected by UK voters. There is, at the time of writing, still need for more liaison with the European Parliament and the new devolved Scottish Parliament and Welsh and Northern Irish Assemblies. The results of recent elections, particularly the rise of the Scottish National Party after 2015, may potentially lead to increased tensions between devolved institutions and Westminster.

## QUESTIONS FOR DISCUSSION

» How might the House of Commons be given more effective influence over the executive?

» How might MPs be given a more effective role in the legislative process?

» Should MPs vote according to their constituents' wishes?

» Should MPs be full time? What restrictions (if any) should be placed on MPs' pursuit of outside interests?

» How representative are MPs of those they are elected to serve? How does this compare with other parliaments and assemblies around the world?

» How might the Commons become more socially representative? Why does descriptive representation matter?

» Why does Britain need an upper house? Should the House of Lords simply be abolished?

» If members of the second chamber should be wholly or mainly elected, how should they be elected, and whom should they represent?

**FURTHER READING**

Norton's (2013) *Parliament in British Politics* can be recommended as an up-to-date introduction to the subject by a leading academic who is also a Conservative peer. Kelso's (2013) *Parliamentary Reform at Westminster* is a reasonably up-to-date review of recent reforms. Leston-Bandeira and Thompson's (2018) *Exploring Parliament* provides a detailed overview of the workings of Parliament in theory and practice. Emma Crewe provides an interesting, alternative account in *Commons and Lords: a short anthropology of Parliament* (2015). There was much analysis of the composition of the 2010 post-election House of Commons in the press. Criddle (2010) has since provided a more authoritative analysis of party election candidates and elected MPs. On representation, Norris and Lovenduski's (1995) foundational text on representation, *Political Recruitment: Gender, Race and Class in the British Parliament*, is still worth consulting, as is Phillips (1998) *The Politics of Presence: Political Representation of Gender, Ethnicity, and Race*.

 **USEFUL WEBSITES**

Parliament (links to House of Commons and House of Lords): www.parliament.uk.

*Further student resources to support learning are available at*
**www.macmillanihe.com/griffiths-brit-pol-3e**

# 7

# THE CABINET AND PRIME MINISTER

In 1962, the Scottish politician, John Mackintosh summed up the UK political system in the following way: "The country is governed by the Prime Minister who leads, coordinates and maintains a series of ministers, all of whom are advised and backed by the civil service. Some decisions are taken by the Premier alone, some in consultation between him and the senior ministers, while others are left to heads of departments, the Cabinet, Cabinet committees or the permanent officials. Of these bodies the Cabinet holds the central position because, although it does not often initiate policy or govern in that sense, most decisions pass through it, and Cabinet ministers can complain that they have not been informed or consulted". (Mackintosh, 1962)

Aside from the gendered language, this description of the executive, now over 50 years old, still seems broadly accurate. Today, one might additionally mention the Cabinet Office (that did exist then) and the Prime Minister's Office (which did not), and the increasing number of special advisers independent of the permanent Civil Service brought in by successive governments. (See Chapter 8, pp. 158–60 for more on special advisers.) But otherwise John Mackintosh captures well the complexity and ambiguity surrounding British government at its centre, which is why some more recent writers prefer to avoid a misleading focus on prime minister and Cabinet by employing broader, more neutral terms such as 'the central executive territory' (Madgwick, 1991) or 'the core executive' (a term coined by Dunleavy and Rhodes, 1990) for British central government, avoiding more familiar but loaded definitions such as 'Cabinet government' or 'prime ministerial government'.

Finally, another obvious and crucial point is that today the government associated with Whitehall and Westminster is now only part (although still the most important part) of a complex system of multi-level governance that affects the lives of British people. There is a Scottish government in Edinburgh (something John Mackintosh powerfully argued for), a Welsh executive in Cardiff and a Northern Ireland executive in Stormont. Effectively, the UK government no longer has executive authority for powers that have been devolved to these governments, and the likelihood is that further powers will be transferred over time. (See Chapter 11 for further discussion of devolved government in the UK.)

The extent of the executive, and the distribution of power and influence within it, have long been contentious, as we explore in this chapter.

## THIS CHAPTER:

» Discusses the way in which Cabinet works and examines many of its core functions.

» Explores the crucial convention of 'Cabinet responsibility'.

» Examines some of the most important roles prime ministers (PM) play, focusing on the huge power of patronage ('hiring and firing') they enjoy, their power to provide direction to government and manage Parliament, and their role as a 'national leader' – a role that is changing with the arrival of 24/7 media (discussed in Chapter 17).

» Reviews the PM's often-tense relationship with their own party.

» Concludes with a debate about how much power the PM has in politics today.

## THE CABINET

The **Cabinet** is the country's top executive committee. After the general election in June 2017, Cabinet was attended by 28 members, 27 from the House of Commons and 1 from the Lords.

---

*The **Cabinet** is the supreme decision-making body in government, dealing with the big issues of the day and the government's overall strategy.*

---

*Source*: Zoe Norfolk/Handout/UK Government via Getty Images

The Cabinet May appointed immediately after the 2017 general election was still largely 'pale, male and stale'. Things have changed in recent years, however. John Major's first Cabinet in 1990, was exclusively white and male.

The role of the Cabinet includes:

» *Formal approval* of decisions taken elsewhere

» *Final court of appeal* for disagreements referred from below

» *Crisis management* of emergencies and issues of major political controversy

» *Debating forum* and sounding board for leading ministers

» *Legitimiser,* conferring full legitimate authority upon government decisions

» *Symbol of collective executive* rather than single person executive in Britain.

Status within the Cabinet is not equal and most Cabinets divide into a small circle of ministers who may expect to be frequently consulted by the PM and an outer circle who count for less. The 'plum' jobs are the posts of chancellor of the exchequer, foreign secretary and home secretary, which a victorious party's leading politicians may hope to occupy. Alongside the prime minster, these three roles are often referred to as the 'great offices of state'. For the first time in 2016, half of these were held by women, when Theresa May appointed Amber Rudd as home secretary. Immediately following the June 2017 election, eight Cabinet ministers were women, marking an advance on previous Conservative Cabinets, which, between 1979 and 1990, generally contained just one woman, the prime minister, Margaret Thatcher, while John Major's first Cabinet was all male. Claire Annesley and Francesca Gains (2010) have argued that the **core executive** of Cabinet and prime minister is widely recognised as the locus of power in Westminster-style parliamentary democracies. As such, they are critical that studies on women's representation have tended to focus on other institutions, notably Parliament. They argued that there should be much more attention paid to gender in analysis of the 'core executive' (Annesley and Gains, 2010).

Other important posts today are justice secretary (combined with the traditional post of Lord Chancellor) and business secretary. Other posts

*Core executive refers to the key institutions at the centre of government. Its exact range depends on the priorities of the government, the prime minister and their allies, but generally refers to the prime minister, the Cabinet and its committees, the Prime Minister's Office and the Cabinet Office, coordinating departments such as the Treasury, the government's law officers and the security and intelligence services.*

may become particularly important because of external circumstances or special government priorities. Some cabinets are dominated by 'big beasts' – powerful politicians – who have to be managed by the PM (some of these 'big beasts' are discussed in Key Figures 7.1).

# KEY FIGURES 7.1
## 'Big beasts' in the Cabinet

Sometimes leading members of the government are dubbed 'big beasts' by the media. Who are the big beasts in the Cabinet? And what distinguishes them from lesser politicians? Andrew Heywood (2009) has argued that three factors are important:

1   Big beasts have a significant power base within their party.

2   Big beasts are figures of a certain public standing. They are known by the general public. They also generally have a record of competence or policy success.

3   The big beasts *know* they are big beasts. They are aware of their political leverage and they are willing to use it to advance their positions. Perhaps there is a gendered, macho element to this. Those described as 'big beasts' tend to be men.

Ultimately, according to Heywood, a big beast is a minister whose resignation would seriously weaken the PM, either/or by undermining party support or damaging the PM's public image. Recent big beasts have included Heseltine, Brown and Johnson.

**Michael Heseltine (1933–).** A charismatic media and Commons performer and ambitious politician, Heseltine had resigned as defence secretary from Margaret Thatcher's Cabinet in 1986 when he believed that the prime minister had sided with a rival. A pro-European, Heseltine proved a dangerous presence on the backbenches for Thatcher until he challenged for the leadership in 1990. His challenge forced her resignation, but Heseltine was ultimately defeated by John Major in his quest to be leader of the Conservative Party (partly because Thatcherite MPs did not forgive him for undermining their leader). Heseltine returned to the Cabinet under Major, eventually becoming his deputy prime minister.

Derek Hudson/Hulton Archive/ Getty Images

**Gordon Brown (1951–).** Brown was the only serious rival to Tony Blair, after Blair became prime minster in 1997. Brown was one of the most significant Labour 'modernisers', who moved Labour to the centre in the 1980s and early 90s. In power, Blair tried to keep Brown, his chancellor, onside by ceding vast areas of responsibility over domestic affairs to him. Brown was able to build up an unprecedented power base among Labour backbench MPs. His reputation was helped by good economic fortune, which saw significant growth until the financial crash. Blair was unable to find a rival to Brown in the Cabinet, who might balance some of his power. Blair's management of Brown was largely successful for Blair's first two terms as PM. However, Brown eventually forced Blair out in 2007, midway through his third term.

**Boris Johnson (1964–).** A former journalist and a well-known media performer, notably through performances on the BBC's satirical news quiz, *Have I Got News for You*, Johnson took over Heseltine's Henley constituency after the latter's retirement. He was quickly promoted into the Conservative Shadow Cabinet, but forced to resign after lying about an extramarital affair. He stepped down as an MP after being elected mayor of London from 2008 to 2016, ensuring enormous public recognisability. In 2015 he was again elected an MP and returned to the Cabinet under David Cameron. He was perhaps the best-known public face of the campaign for leaving the EU. This was after a very late public decision to support Brexit, which many critics saw as opportunism to align himself with the increasingly anti-European Conservative backbenches. After Cameron's resignation, Johnson's campaign to take over fell apart when Michael Gove, another instrumental Eurosceptic Tory, pulled his support. Johnson was made foreign secretary by Theresa May in 2016 – a role leaders have often given their rivals: it ensures they have little control of domestic policy and are out of the country for extended periods.

There are, however, signs that big beasts are becoming an endangered species. Harold Wilson's Cabinets in the 1960s had several, including Anthony Crosland (see Chapter 15, p. 319), Dennis Healey and Roy Jenkins. Clement Attlee's Cabinet in the 1940s included Aneurin Bevan, Ernest Bevin and Herbert Morrison (see Chapter 2). Today, perhaps, the big beasts are rarer than they once were.

On occasion, and notably in times of war, a small inner Cabinet has been formed, as in the Falklands War, for example. Thus, although the decision to commit the task force in 1981 was taken by the full Cabinet, Margaret Thatcher formed a small war Cabinet of five to run the war on a day-to-day basis. Blair similarly formed what was effectively a smaller war Cabinet over Kosovo in 1999, although there were regular reports to the full Cabinet (Hennessy, 2000, p. 504). Some have called for a smaller Cabinet in peacetime, arguing that a Cabinet of over 20 is too large for the efficient conduct of business. However, political difficulties would arise if a major department and its associated outside interests were not seen to be represented at the 'top table', or if particular areas of the country or sections of the population, or important strands within the party were excluded.

## CABINET BUSINESS AND MINUTES

Full Cabinet meetings became more numerous throughout the twentieth century until the 1960s but declined thereafter, slowly at first but then dramatically under Thatcher to a much lower level, which was continued under her successors. The full Cabinet normally now meets once a week when Parliament is sitting, although in times of crisis it may meet more frequently. Under Blair, the length of Cabinet meetings noticeably shortened, commonly to an hour or less (Hennessy, 2000, p. 481).

Very few decisions in the modern Cabinet system are actually *made* by full Cabinet, although virtually all the major policy issues come before it in some form. Its agenda over a period of time consists predominantly of three kinds of matter:

» *routine items*: such as forthcoming parliamentary business, reports on foreign affairs and major economic decisions

» *disagreements referred upwards for Cabinet arbitration*: e.g. from Cabinet committees or from departmental ministers in dispute

» *important contemporary concerns*: a broad range, including national crises such as a war, issues of major controversy such as a large-scale strike and other matters of political sensitivity.

Cabinet minutes are the responsibility of the Cabinet Secretariat. Like the minutes of most meetings, they involve a brief record of decisions and conclusions rather than a full account of any preceding discussion. As such, they are very important as they are binding on the whole government machine. Controversy has occurred over the extent of prime ministerial involvement in the process, with certain members of past Labour Cabinets suggesting that this could be considerable (Castle, 1980, p. 252). But Harold Wilson, the then prime minister, denied it, maintaining at the time (1970) that only 'very, very occasionally' was he consulted about the minutes before issue. Wilson (quoted in King, 1985, p. 40) later provided what is now widely accepted as the correct account of routine procedure: 'The writing of the conclusions is the unique responsibility of the Secretary of the Cabinet ... The conclusions are circulated very promptly after Cabinet, and up to that time no minister, certainly not the Prime Minister, sees them, asks to see them or conditions them in any way.'

## CABINET COMMITTEES AND THE CABINET OFFICE

Because of the sheer volume and complexity of modern governmental business, the bulk of decisions within the Cabinet system are taken by Cabinet committees. These consist of groups of ministers who can take collective decisions that are binding across government. Cabinet committees reduce the burden on Cabinet by enabling collective decisions to be taken by a smaller group of ministers. The composition and terms of reference of Cabinet committees are a matter for the PM. Cabinet committees either take decisions themselves or prepare matters for higher level decisions, possibly at Cabinet. Official committees (of civil servants) underpin ministerial committees and prepare papers for their consideration (Burch and Holliday, 1996, p. 44). Cabinet committee decisions have the status of Cabinet decisions and normally a matter is referred to full Cabinet only when a Cabinet committee cannot reach agreement. The PM or a senior Cabinet minister chairs the most important committees. The committee chair must agree any request to take a dispute to full Cabinet, but such appeals are discouraged. In 1975, however, Treasury ministers gained the right of automatic appeal

to Cabinet if defeated on public spending in committee (James, 1992, p. 69).

The establishment, composition, terms of reference and chairmanship of Cabinet committees are the responsibility of the prime minister. Before 1992, their structure was supposedly a secret, although details did gradually come to light from the 1970s as a result of ministerial memoirs and partial statements by the PM. After the 1992 general election, John Major decided to make public the entire system of Cabinet standing committees and the subjects they deal with. This information has been routinely available since.

Cabinet committees have become central to decision-making in the postwar period. Thatcher and Major reduced the number of committees and the frequency of meetings. Blair and Brown maintained the system of Cabinet committees but also set up a number of ad hoc working groups, while Blair in particular often relied on bilateral discussions with relevant departmental ministers. The relative informality of this decision-making (dubbed 'sofa government') aroused some criticism (e.g. in the Butler Report, 2004). The Conservative–Lib Dem coalition reduced the number of full Cabinet committees, but introduced some new ones, notably the Coalition Committee, of which the party leaders were co-chairs. Otherwise, most committees were chaired by Conservatives with Lib Dem deputies. (These arrangements did not survive the 2015 election and the return of a majority Conservative government.)

The Cabinet Office is another institution at the heart of the core executive that has developed in response to the large growth in the volume of government business. Dating from 1916, its most important component is the Cabinet Secretariat, a group of some 30 senior civil servants on secondment from other departments working under the direction of the Cabinet secretary. Over the years, a number of new special offices and units have been brought within it, such as the Efficiency and Reform Group (which is meant to drive government savings), often covering policy issues that cut across departmental boundaries. The Cabinet Office now works closely with the Prime Minister's Office.

## COLLECTIVE RESPONSIBILITY

The doctrine of **collective responsibility**, which holds that all ministers accept responsibility collectively for decisions made in Cabinet and its committees, is the main convention influencing the operation of the Cabinet. The first Cabinet paper a new minister is handed is the *Ministerial Code* (Cabinet Office, 2016), previously *Questions of Procedure for Ministers*. This declares: 'Decisions reached by the Cabinet or Ministerial Committees are binding on all members of the Government' (not just the Cabinet). The argument behind the doctrine is that an openly divided government could not work together and could not command the confidence of Parliament or the wider public.

---

**Collective responsibility** *refers to the convention of Cabinet government requiring all ministers to support publicly decisions of Cabinet and its committees, or resign from office.*

---

The doctrine of collective responsibility is clearly of value to the prime minister in the control of Cabinet colleagues. On the other hand, it does lay reciprocal obligations on the PM, first, not to leak decisions and, second, to run the government in a collegiate way, making sure that ministers have reasonable opportunities to discuss issues. One problem for ministers is that they often play a limited part in making the decisions to which they are required to assent. This latter point has implications not only for the conduct of Cabinet itself but also for the composition of Cabinet committees, which – if they are to take authoritative decisions in the name of the Cabinet – must be representative of the Cabinet as a whole (see Spotlight 7.1).

Cabinet collective responsibility obliges all ministers to support government policy or resign. Although such resignations are relatively uncommon, when they occur they can have serious and sometimes devastating implications for the future of the government and the prime minister in particular, especially if senior figures with a following in the party and Parliament are involved. So, the resignations of Defence Secretary Michael Heseltine (1986), Chancellor of the Exchequer Nigel Lawson (1989) and finally Deputy Prime Minister

## SPOTLIGHT ON ...

### The practical implications of (Cabinet) collective responsibility

7.1

» *Cabinet solidarity:* Ministers may disagree until a decision is made, but are then expected to support it publicly or, at least, not express their lack of support. If they feel they must dissent publicly, they are expected to resign. If they fail to resign, it falls to the prime minister to require them to do so. The underlying purpose of this is to create and maintain the authority of the government, which public squabbling between ministers could be expected to damage.

» *Cabinet secrecy:* A precondition of Cabinet solidarity is that Cabinet discussion is secret. Ministers need to feel free to speak their minds, secure in the knowledge that their views will not be divulged to the media. Ministers who are known to disagree with a policy may be expected to have little commitment to it: well-publicised disagreements, therefore, have potentially damaging consequences for public confidence in government.

» *Cabinet resignation:* If defeated on a Commons vote of confidence, convention requires that the Cabinet – and therefore the entire government – should resign. Thus when the Labour government elected in October 1974 was defeated on a vote of confidence on 28 March 1979, Prime Minister James Callaghan immediately requested a dissolution. However, such defeats are very rare, because governments usually enjoy a comfortable overall Commons majority.

Geoffrey Howe (1990) progressively damaged the Conservative government of Margaret Thatcher and substantially contributed to her fall. The resignation of Leader of the House Robin Cook in 2003 over the decision to invade Iraq was a serious blow to Blair's government, particularly as Cook had been foreign secretary from 1997 to 2001, and could speak with some authority on the subject. The resignation of more Cabinet ministers would have indicated a significant Cabinet split. However, Clare Short, the international development secretary, who had openly expressed disquiet over Blair's 'recklessness', was persuaded to stay on to assist in the rebuilding of postwar Iraq. She eventually resigned, but the delay reduced the impact and limited the damage to the government.

There were two earlier occasions when the principle of collective responsibility was formally suspended. In 1932, there was an 'agreement to differ' over tariffs among members of the national government. In 1975, members of Wilson's Labour government were allowed to campaign on opposite sides of the referendum on whether the UK should remain in the European Community.

These precedents were significant for the Conservative–Lib Dem government from 2010 to 2015. Although a substantially common programme for government was agreed, involving concessions and compromises by both parties, there remained some issues on which the coalition partners were divided, particularly on relations with Europe and electoral reform. While there was an agreed commitment to a referendum on the introduction of the alternative vote (AV), the coalition parties campaigned vigorously on opposite sides, which worsened relations between them, particularly after AV was decisively rejected. Subsequently, the failure of the coalition to pursue agreed Lords reform was followed by the refusal of the Lib Dems to support reform to the number of seats in the House of Commons. Despite these significant differences, the coalition continued to the end of the Parliament in 2015.

After 2015, Cameron's Conservative government suspended Cabinet collective responsibility, allowing ministers to take different sides on the issue of the UK's membership of the EU, as Wilson had similarly agreed, back in 1975. In both cases, the governing party was so divided that any other course would have been politically disastrous. Once the vote was held, Cabinet collective responsibility was restored, and it remained so under May, despite the public knowing the very public differences within her Cabinet over whether Britain should have remained a member of the EU.

## THE PRIME MINISTER

At the centre of the executive is the prime minister. The PM is the effective head of British government (rather than head of state). The post of PM emerged in the course of the eighteenth century, although it long remained an unofficial position, and the title only found its way into parliamentary debate in the nineteenth century. Sir Robert Walpole, the leading minister from 1721 until 1742, is generally regarded as the first prime minister. The government then was still the sovereign's government in more than name, but the Cabinet, consisting of senior ministers, had become the effective executive. The role of chairing Cabinet meetings fell to the leading minister. Walpole's official post was First Lord of the Treasury (a title retained by modern prime ministers). This crucially put him in charge of patronage – the distribution of jobs in government – and gave him pre-eminence in the Cabinet. In the course of the eighteenth century, Cabinets became increasingly dependent on parliamentary support rather than royal favour, and the prime minister became the real head of government. In the process, the prime minister effectively acquired the right to exercise most of the old prerogative (or personal) powers of the crown, while the hereditary monarch (king or queen) remained the legal and ceremonial head of the state.

Prime ministers in the eighteenth and nineteenth centuries could come from either House of Parliament, and many sat in the Lords: Lord Salisbury, who resigned in 1902, was the last peer to serve as PM for any length of time,

## COMPARING BRITISH POLITICS 7.1

### Prime ministers and presidents

The position of a UK prime minister is often compared with heads of government in other democratic countries:

» The US president is directly elected by the American people and combines the role of head of government with head of state. They are the acknowledged head of the armed forces, and the focus of national loyalty. Yet, as head of government, the US president may often have less control of policy than a British prime minister, particularly if they do not have a majority in Congress, which is not uncommon. The main reason that a UK prime minister can seem more powerful is because of the fusion of the executive and legislature in Britain compared with the constitutionally separate executive and legislature in the USA.

» Many other 'presidents' around the world are formal heads of state, not heads of government, with little political power, for example the presidents of Germany, Italy and Israel. This makes the US president rather unusual. Most presidents are not subject to direct popular election. In Germany, for example, the president is chosen every five years by a Federal Convention made up of elected members of the lower house of parliament and representatives of the federal states that make up Germany.

» The French Fifth Republic comes somewhere between the US and German models. It is sometimes characterised as a 'dual executive', because it has both a directly elected president with significant powers, particularly in foreign affairs, and a prime minister (who has to command a majority in the French Assembly) largely responsible for domestic policy.

*Source*: Cole et al. (2013)

---

although Alec Douglas-Home was also in the Lords when he became PM in 1963, albeit for less than a month. However, the post had long required the support of a majority in the House of Commons, and, increasingly, democratic assumptions required a head of government who had been elected as an MP. Even so, the convention that a prime minister must sit in the House of Commons only gradually emerged in the twentieth century.

## THE ROLES OF THE PRIME MINISTER

The modern office of prime minister involves a formidable concentration of power, although much of this depends on convention rather than law. The lack of formal codification of the roles of the PM gives them considerable leeway in shaping the job as best they are able. Among other things, the PM is responsible for forming a government; for directing and coordinating its work; and for general supervision of the Civil Service. The PM also has special responsibilities in the sphere of national security. Alongside these formal responsibilities, the PM can, in practice, exercise a strong influence over any specific policy or service, and many recent holders of the position have taken a particular interest in defence, foreign affairs and the management of the economy. Finally, the prime minister is the national leader, as evidenced by their role in representing the country at international conferences and meetings, signing treaties and playing host to leaders of other states.

### Patronage ('hiring and firing')

The most important element of prime ministerial patronage is the power to select the hundred or so politicians – normally drawn mainly from the majority party in the Commons but including some from the Lords – who at any given moment form the government. The prime minister appoints not just the Cabinet, but also ministers of state, under-secretaries of state, whips and law officers such as the attorney-general. Occasionally, a prime minister may wish to appoint a minister who is not already an MP, but convention dictates that such individuals have to become MPs or peers. Gordon Brown, in particular, appointed several ministers who were not MPs in his 'Government of All the Talents' (GOATs as they were dubbed by the press). These included Lord West, former admiral; Lord Malloch Brown, ex-UN deputy secretary-general; Lord Digby Jones, former director-general of the Confederation of British Industry; and Lord Myners, wealthy fund manager.

The 2010–15 coalition government imposed some further restraints on the PM's freedom of action, as the distribution of posts agreed in 2010 involved negotiations with coalition partners (as it had done previously in 1915, 1931 and 1940, when new coalition governments were formed). The PM of a coalition government also faces constraints in dismissing and replacing ministerial colleagues who do not belong to their party. However, even with single-party government, there are significant practical political constraints on appointments and dismissals, as all parties involve coalitions of views and interests and a PM must be wary of upsetting influential factions and tendencies within their party.

Whether the government is drawn from a single party or a coalition of parties, a substantial proportion of MPs (normally from a quarter to a third) of the governing party or parties can expect to be in office. By no means all politicians seek ministerial office but most probably do. The continuing power to 'hire and fire' is a formidable source of control for the prime minister.

The prime minister also plays a key role in the selection of individuals to fill a wide variety of other leading posts in national life. This influence extends over the creation of peers as well as over the appointment of top civil servants at the permanent secretary and deputy secretary levels, the heads of the security services and the chairmen of royal commissions. In addition, they have ultimate responsibility for recommendations of honours (peerages, knighthoods and other awards). Between 2010 and 2015, David Cameron appointed 236 new members of the House of Lords or 'peers', which is more than any PM has created since the current system was set up in the 1950s. (It is also controversial that just over 60% of Cameron's appointments have been Conservative. By comparison, only 43% of Blair's new peerages were Labour.) Some recipients are substantial contributors to party funds: David Lloyd George, PM from 1916 to 1922, notoriously sold honours to boost his election fund, but more recent prime ministers have also ennobled generous party supporters. The PM's use of patronage is a powerful tool and just one way in which they have significant power in the UK political system.

## Direction and organisation of the government

The prime minister is responsible for directing and organising the work of the government at the highest level. This involves setting broad policy objectives (within the framework of party ideologies and party manifestos) and devising short-term and long-term strategies for attaining these goals. The leadership, of course, is always in the collective context of the Cabinet system: the prime minister is not a single person executive like the US president. Within that framework, there are clearly differences in style. Thatcher is well known for having led from the front, and the same might be said of Blair. Harold Wilson (particularly from 1974 to 1976) and John Major both had a more consensual style, as did David Cameron. However, the PM normally expects all ministerial colleagues to support government policy according to the convention of collective responsibility (discussed earlier).

The prime minister not only has overall responsibility for government, but can take a particular interest in key policy areas. Thus, many prime ministers (particularly Gordon Brown, but not his predecessor Tony Blair) have taken a decisive role in the determination of economic policy in consultation with the chancellor of the exchequer and the Treasury. Others, notably Churchill, Thatcher and Blair,

Timeline 7.1 Prime ministers since 1945

| Entered office | Prime minister | Party |
|---|---|---|
| 2016 | Theresa May | Conservative |
| 2010 | David Cameron | Conservative |
| 2007 | Gordon Brown | Labour |
| 1997 | Tony Blair | Labour |
| 1990 | John Major | Conservative |
| 1979 | Margaret Thatcher | Conservative |
| 1976 | James Callaghan | Labour |
| 1974 | Harold Wilson | Labour |
| 1970 | Edward Heath | Conservative |
| 1964 | Harold Wilson | Labour |
| 1963 | Alec Douglas-Home | Conservative |
| 1957 | Harold Macmillan | Conservative |
| 1955 | Anthony Eden | Conservative |
| 1951 | Winston Churchill | Conservative |
| 1945 | Clement Attlee | Labour |

have played a leading part in foreign and defence policy, sometimes overshadowing their foreign and defence secretaries. However, the PM can choose to get involved in any government issue in which they have an interest. Thus prime ministers in the 1960s and 70s were unavoidably involved in industrial, trade union and pay policies. Thatcher took a direct personal interest in the management of the economy, in Europe and foreign policy generally, in trade unions and industrial relations, in changes to the Civil Service and the NHS, and in the introduction of the poll tax in local government. Major and Blair were both centrally involved in the development of the peace process in Northern Ireland. Brown, because of his long experience of economic policy, continued to play a leading

role nationally and internationally in coping with the credit crunch and recession after he became PM.

The prime minister draws up the Cabinet agenda, and decides the composition, terms of reference and chairs of Cabinet committees: in the case of Cameron's 2010–15 coalition government, this involved consultation with the Lib Dems. As well as playing a key part in deciding the nature, timing and ordering of issues reaching the Cabinet, the PM chairs Cabinet meetings. This can give them considerable influence over the direction and outcome of Cabinet discussions, by making their views known before and during the meeting, determining who is called to speak and in what order, and summing up 'the sense of the meeting'. In the process, they may deploy various manipulative 'arts' of chairmanship, including delay, verbosity, deliberate ambiguity, sheer persistence and authority. Votes are rarely taken in Cabinet: they encourage division, dilute collective responsibility and are vulnerable to 'leaks' and misleading reports in the media. But it is the task of the PM to summarise the decisions reached in the way they see fit, taking into account the weight of opinion for or against a course of action.

Finally, the prime minister has overall responsibility for the work of the Civil Service. Developments since 1979 have seen a significant strengthening of the PM's position in relation to Whitehall. The Thatcher–Major era saw large-scale changes in the organisation and management of the Civil Service. Blair continued and expanded the practice of his predecessors in bringing in external special advisers on fixed-term contracts and establishing special cross-departmental units, which upset some senior permanent civil servants, some of whom felt marginalised (Norton, 2008, p. 95). (Chapter 8 examines the Civil Service and the role of special advisers in more detail.)

## Managing Parliament

As the prime minister heads a parliamentary executive, must be an elected MP and depends for survival on maintaining a majority in the House of Commons, the management of

Parliament is clearly an important concern. The PM's performance in Parliament is always the subject of close scrutiny. Every Wednesday for 30 minutes the premier appears in the House of Commons to answer 'Prime Minister's Questions' (PMQs). This was the result of a change introduced by Blair; formerly it was two 15-minute sessions a week. This is by far the most common prime ministerial activity in Parliament. Prime ministers can expect to answer about 1,000 questions per year, a large proportion of them on economic and foreign affairs. Many of the questions appear as 'supplementaries' that are more difficult to prepare for. PMQs is a testing ordeal, at which much is at stake, including personal reputation, command of party and the authority of the government. In particular, the verbal duels between the prime minister and the leader of the opposition can attract considerable media publicity, and may affect the morale of their respective parties. While Blair excelled in verbal sparring with his opposite number, Brown was frequently worsted in his weekly duels with David Cameron. As PM, Cameron was only occasionally in trouble with Ed Miliband, or more his successor, Jeremy Corbyn. May's performances have been reported more negatively since the 2017 election, which made her position as PM far less secure.

When Parliament is sitting, premiers may expect to be constantly preoccupied with it in other ways, too. Their concerns include the progress of government legislation, set-piece speeches in parliamentary debates and, more generally, the state of party morale. 'Parliamentary business' is always an item on the Cabinet agenda. However, modern prime ministers only attend the Commons for a specific purpose, and normally only for brief periods. Indeed, Blair was criticised for devoting little time and attention to Parliament (Norton, 2005, p. 243) and having 'the worst voting record of any modern Prime Minister' (Norton, 2008, p. 97). Yet it was Blair who introduced twice-yearly meetings of two and a half hours with the Liaison Committee, which consists of the chairs of the parliamentary select committees, who were able to question him in depth over a wide range of topics (Cowley, 2006, p. 47).

## National leadership

The prime minister occupies a special role in the life of the country that quite distinguishes the occupant of the office from other Cabinet members – as national leader. This is always the case but becomes especially apparent at times of national crisis such as war, natural or man-made disasters or serious economic problems, such as the world banking crisis and economic recession of 2008–09. Winston Churchill's role as national leader during the Second World War is a good example of this. Churchill's defiant speeches provided leadership at a time of national uncertainty and potentially imminent invasion by Nazi Germany. More recently, Blair was praised at the time for his response to the 9/11 terrorist attacks in New York in 2001, and Brown received plaudits for providing leadership in his response to the economic crash in 2007–08 (see Chapter 19, pp. 412–15). Prime ministers are expected to provide leadership in such circumstances and may be criticised if they fail to do so. An important element of leadership comes from the way in which they manage the media and communication. This is discussed further in Spotlight 7.2.

## PRIME MINISTERS AND THEIR PARTIES

Modern prime ministers derive much of their authority and democratic legitimacy from their position as elected leader of the majority party in the House of Commons, although the formal election of party leaders only developed in the course of the twentieth century. Gordon Brown (PM, 2007–10) won neither a general election, nor a contested Labour leadership election, although he was formally elected by his party. Some argued his position was weaker as he lacked a personal mandate. Indeed, prime ministers gain considerable informal authority from electoral success (as Heffernan's analysis, discussed below, shows). May was significantly weakened as prime minister in her authority

**SPOTLIGHT ON ...**

## The role of the prime minister as communicator

7.2

Contemporary prime ministers need to pay particular attention to the way they and their governments are presented. Indeed, Richard Toye (2011) has argued that to understand the power of the British PM, we should pay attention to a PM's use of 'rhetoric' – how they seek to persuade people – as an important element in understanding how the PM can maintain power and achieve their policy aims. This is as important as a study of the formal instruments of control exercised within Whitehall – the roles set out in this section, for example. Toye (2011) uses the term 'rhetorical premiership' to denote the ways in which prime ministers use public speech to augment their formal powers – from set-piece speeches to soundbites used for 24/7 media. How effectively prime ministers get their message across is an important part of their success.

over her Cabinet after a poor performance at the 2017 general election. However, the British executive is a parliamentary executive, and the head of government has never been directly elected by the people (in contrast with US or French presidents: see Comparing British Politics 7.1 on p. 133). Many prime ministers, like Brown, have succeeded to the position in mid-Parliament, without a general election (e.g. since 1945, Eden, Macmillan, Home, Callaghan, Major, Brown and May: of these only Callaghan and Major won a contested leadership election in the majority parliamentary party). Others became PM as

**Table 7.1 Prime ministerial power and constraints on prime ministerial power: a summary**

| Prime ministerial power | Constraints on prime ministerial power |
| --- | --- |
| • PM's power of patronage, to 'hire and fire', appointment of Cabinet, junior ministers, other posts, recommendation of honours etc. | • Political constraints on exercise of patronage: need to satisfy powerful rivals, sections of party, interests in the country etc. |
| • PM's position as majority party leader (normally following a party election) | • Party a constraint on power as well as source of power: potential party revolts and challenge from party rivals |
| • PM's parliamentary majority and dominance of parliamentary business | • Problems in managing Parliament: increasing backbench rebellions (PMs devote little time to Parliament beyond PMQs) |
| • PM's position as chair of Cabinet: heading whole machinery of government | • PM can be outvoted in Cabinet, and can face Cabinet revolts and threats of resignation |
| • PM's control over Civil Service (e.g. as the Minister for the Civil Service) | • PM's limited authority over Civil Service, which has a tradition of political neutrality |
| • PM's power to intervene personally in any area of government | • Opportunity costs to PM's intervention in any policy area: cannot intervene everywhere |
| • PM's standing in country enhanced by modern communication through mass media | • PM can be undermined by failures in communication |
| • PM represents the country at home and abroad | • PM is not a head of state (cf. US president) |

leaders of a party that subsequently won a general election (Attlee, Churchill, Wilson, Heath, Thatcher and Blair). Since 1945, only Cameron and May have emerged as PM following inter-party negotiations when no party secured an overall majority, although Wilson briefly headed a minority government in 1974, before securing a small majority at a second election the same year.

Thus it is normally as the leader of the majority party that a prime minister gains office in the first place; it is the continuing regular support of that party in Parliament that maintains the PM's authority to govern. Relationships with the party, therefore, are of the greatest significance and these are two-way. The prime minister seeks to maximise control of the party, while the party strives for influence over the prime minister.

Faced by potentially recalcitrant backbenchers, the prime minister can appeal to personal ambition (the power of patronage is a potent weapon) and party loyalty (a general desire to do nothing to assist the opposition). In general, prime ministers are strongest in their relations with their parties in the months following victory in a general election or leadership election. Such 'honeymoon' periods may be brief indeed, as John Major's experience in 1992 showed. His unexpected election victory in April was a personal triumph, but by early November he had become, according to pollsters, the most unpopular PM since records began. Blair, by contrast, remained well ahead in the opinion polls from his election victory in 1997 until the unexpected fuel protests of September 2000, by which time he had enjoyed a 'honeymoon' of over three years. Brown's brief honeymoon period was abruptly terminated by 'the election that never was' in September 2007, when Brown decided at the last minute not to hold an early general election. May's honeymoon period with the electorate ended abruptly after the disastrous election performance of 2017, after almost a year of dominating in the polls.

While the party is a source of support for a prime minister, it is often a constraint on freedom of action. Thus Europe has caused serious problems of party management for PMs from Macmillan onwards. Wilson suspended collective responsibility and held a referendum to avoid splitting his party. Major resigned the party leadership in 1995 and successfully sought re-election, in an attempt to end incessant Cabinet and party dissension over Europe. Cameron first agreed to hold a referendum on Britain's continuing membership of the EU, in an attempt to appease Eurosceptics within his own party and then, like Wilson, felt obliged to allow his ministers to campaign on opposite sides. Ultimately, the parliamentary party may even force the resignation of a prime minister, but this has only happened once since the war, to Thatcher in 1990.

Prime ministers are at their weakest when government policies seem not to be working and provoke popular hostility and opposition. It was Thatcher's mounting unpopularity, as a result of high interest rates, a stagnant economy and the local government poll tax, that led the party to revolt against her in November 1990. Economic problems and increasing divisions over Europe provoked a formal challenge to Major in 1995. The Iraq War, foundation hospitals and student tuition fees caused increasing problems for Blair from the Parliamentary Labour Party and the public from 2003 onwards (leading him to contemplate stepping down in the early summer of 2004). Falling poll ratings for Brown during the financial crisis and economic recession led to unsuccessful plots against his leadership in 2008 and 2009 (Rawnsley, 2010). May's 2017 election pledge on funding social care for the elderly through the sale of their homes was dubbed 'the dementia tax' by critics and led to an immediate backlash, which damaged her election campaign and substantially weakened her position after the election (Asthana and Elgot, 2017). However, the failure of plots against Brown, and of many similar challenges to former PMs, indicate the difficulty in unseating an incumbent premier (further discussed in Spotlight 7.3).

# SPOTLIGHT ON ...

## Removing prime ministers

7.3

» *Election defeat*: Most commonly, prime ministers are brought down by a defeat in a general election. Since the Second World War, Prime Ministers Churchill (1945), Attlee (1951), Home (1964), Wilson (1970), Heath (1974), Callaghan (1979), Major (1997) and Brown (2010) were effectively removed by the electorate. It was once fairly common for defeated prime ministers to return for a second or subsequent period in charge, but since 1945 only Churchill and Wilson have returned for a second premiership. Some defeated prime ministers have resigned their party leadership immediately (Major, Brown) or soon afterwards (Home, Callaghan).

» *Death or serious illness*: No postwar prime minister has died in office. Illness was the ostensible reason for the resignations of Churchill (1955), Eden (1957) and Macmillan (1963), although political difficulties played a part in the departures of the last two in particular, and all three lived for many years after resigning.

» *Resignation after a challenge or threat of challenge from colleagues*: Thatcher was the only prime minister to resign after a formal challenge to her position as party leader in 1990. Major provoked and defeated a similar challenge in 1995. Neither Blair nor Brown ever faced a formal challenge to their leadership. Cameron resigned as

*Source:* Howard McWilliam/The Week

In 2016, Theresa May toppled rivals to become Conservative Party leader after David Cameron was forced to resign.

prime minister in 2016 after Britain voted to leave the EU, although he almost certainly would have faced a challenge if he had not stepped down. May replaced him after all other contenders stepped aside before a formal ballot. Her poor performance at the 2017 general election makes her much more vulnerable to a challenge from her colleagues.

The management of more than one party creates more complications for a prime minister. Coalition government from 2010–15, common over most of Continental Europe and much of the rest of the world, was a new experience for politicians at Westminster, who had experienced single-party government from 1945. In 2010, Cameron, as leader of the largest party, became prime minister with the support of the Lib Dems, but faced some problems in controlling his own parliamentary party in his first term as PM, because he had failed to win a majority. The need to accommodate his coalition partners in government reduced the scope of his patronage, which disappointed the ambitions of some restless backbenchers, and also led to compromises over aspects of policy. Thus there followed a succession of damaging revolts by disaffected Conservative MPs in votes on issues ranging from Lords reform to the EU, Syria and immigration. After the 2017 general election, May is reliant on the support of the Democratic Unionist Party (DUP) to pass legislation, who have their own agenda and who can hold the government to its commitments on Northern Ireland, regardless of other priorities.

While Cameron faced persistent rebellions from his own backbenchers from 2010 to 2015, he had far fewer splits and resignations within his 2010–15 Cabinet than his immediate predecessors, Brown, Blair, Major or Thatcher. Brown and Blair's Cabinets were split over tensions between supporters of the two leading New Labour figures. Major's Cabinet and government were divided over Europe, while Thatcher's Cabinets were divided between moderate 'wets' and more radical, right-wing supporters of the prime minister. Cameron had no real difficulties with his Conservative Cabinet colleagues. Indeed, three key figures, Chancellor George Osborne, Home Secretary Theresa May and Secretary of State for Work and Pensions Iain Duncan Smith, not only remained for the whole Parliament, but were re-appointed to the same posts in 2015. Cameron's coalition partners posed few problems. Perhaps Nick Clegg, the Lib Dem leader, erred by declining to take responsibility for a major department, instead becoming deputy prime minister, with a special concern for constitutional reform, which became something of a poisoned chalice, after the rejection of electoral reform and the ditching of Lords reform. The Lib Dems were further weakened by the early resignations of senior colleagues such as David Laws and especially Chris Huhne, who had been a close rival of Clegg's in the 2007 party leadership election. (Laws ultimately returned to office, but Huhne's political career ended in scandal.) Only Secretary of State for Business, Innovation and Skills Vince Cable remained as a significant independent Lib Dem voice in Cabinet.

The coalition with the Lib Dems was strengthened by the introduction of fixed-term parliaments of five years, which was part of the coalition agreement between the two parties on entering government. Up until 2010, prime ministers had the exclusive right to recommend to the monarch the timing of the dissolution of Parliament at any time within a five-year period. This meant that they effectively controlled the date of the general election, as the monarch could not refuse such a request without appearing to take sides in party politics. The introduction of fixed-term parliaments removed the PM's power to call an election at the time of their choosing, a significant surrender of power, as prime ministers were formerly able to choose an election date most favourable for their party's prospects (e.g. soon after a generous budget or a diplomatic triumph). Indeed, without the commitment to fixed-term parliaments, Cameron would have been free to recommend a further dissolution of Parliament after a few months in office, in the hope of securing an overall Conservative majority, when other parties, including the Lib Dems, would be financially ill-equipped to fight another election. However, May's decision to hold a snap general election in 2017 showed the weakness of the Fixed-Term Parliament Act. An election could be called if a government lost a vote of confidence, or more than two-thirds of the House of Commons supported a call for new elections. Labour were not going to be put in a position where they refused the challenge of May's election call, so supported May, easily providing enough votes for new elections.

## THE PRIME MINISTER'S OFFICE

Although prime ministers wield extensive powers, and normally dominate the entire governmental system, they do not head a large department but are directly served by a Prime Minister's Office (sometimes referred to as 'Downing Street' or 'Number 10'). It was only in 1974 that a Policy Unit was established within the Prime Minister's Office at Number 10 to give the prime minister an independent source of policy advice. Prime ministers have also gone outside Downing Street for advice, notably to party research offices, think tanks and independent experts. Under Thatcher and Major, the staff at Number 10 serving the PM had numbered around 90 people. The Blair government expanded and reformed Downing Street, introducing a new Strategic Communications Unit in November 1997 to coordinate press relations of the various departments and ministers, which led to some tension between the Labour Party's 'spin doctors' and the permanent civil servants responsible for government information. The number of staff also increased. By 1998, there were 121 people working in Downing Street, and by 2005 this peaked at nearly 226. Within this group, a big increase took place in the special advisers serving the PM. Major had 8, Blair in 1998 had 16, rising to a peak of 28 in 2004 (Blick and Jones, 2010).

The expansion and higher status of what has become the Prime Minister's Office have increased the PM's capacity to oversee government strategy, to monitor departmental work and to initiate policy from the centre. Contemporary prime ministers are better informed about what is happening across the whole range of government and there is a greater tendency for business to flow to the Prime Minister's Office and for ministers to consult Number 10 before launching policy initiatives.

Some argue that the Prime Minister's Office has effectively become a Prime Minister's Department of the kind that some centralising reformers have advocated (Hennessy, 2000, pp. 485–6). Holliday (2002, pp. 94–6) claims the increased integration and coordination of the Prime Minister's Office and the Cabinet Office (see below) 'makes them, in effect, a single executive office'. Yet Riddell (2001, pp. 31–2) points out that 'the Number 10 operation is still small by comparison with the executive offices in presidential systems, such as the United States and France, and even in Prime Ministerial systems such as Australia and Canada'.

## PRESIDENTS, CABINETS OR JUST PRIME MINISTERS?

How much power do prime ministers have? Do they dominate the core executive or is it the other way around? Writing in the mid-Victorian period, Walter Bagehot ([1867] 1963) identified the Cabinet as the 'efficient secret' of the constitution. Yet, on reviewing Bagehot's classic text almost a century later, the Labour Cabinet minister Richard Crossman (1963) declared that 'Prime Ministerial government' had replaced 'Cabinet government'– the PM was now the centre of power in the British

political system. Much of the debate at the time focused on Wilson's 1964–70 government of which Crossman himself was a leading member. Crossman's diaries (1975, 1976, 1977), the writings of other Cabinet ministers and Wilson himself (1976) contributed further to the controversy.

Subsequently, academics revived the debate during the contentious government of Margaret Thatcher. In his book *The British Prime Minister*, Anthony King (1985, p. 136) claimed that Thatcher had 'been pushing out the frontiers of her authority ever since she took office in 1979', but King was suitably cautious as to whether she had 'fundamentally changed the office of Prime Minister'. Indeed, there is strong evidence that the role of Cabinet as a formal decision-making body has been in decline since the Second World War and that the political personality of the PM is increasingly important. To give one indication of this, *The Economist* magazine made 415 mentions of Clement Attlee during his premiership from 1945 to 1951, but over 1,000 mentions of his chancellors. By the 1980s, the relative standing of PM and chancellor had been reversed – Thatcher was mentioned more than 4,500 times, while her chancellors only merited 1,033 mentions (Parker et al., 2010, p. 38).

Despite this, it was a parliamentary party and Cabinet revolt, precipitated by former ministers with whom she had acrimoniously parted, which brought Thatcher down in 1990. This suggests significant constraints on prime ministerial power.

The debate about prime ministerial power was taken to another level when Michael Foley (1993, 2000, 2013) claimed that modern UK prime ministers wielded 'presidential' authority, rather than the traditional view that the prime minister is simply the 'first among equals' in the Cabinet. Early commentators on the post-1997 Labour government freely used the term 'President Blair'. Journalist Andrew Rawnsley (2001, p. 50) claimed that from the beginning, Blair's premiership 'was designed to be a presidential premiership' (see also Hennessy, 2000). Philip Norton (2008, p. 99), constitutional historian, suggested that Blair 'exhibited the characteristics of presidentialism ... on an unprecedented scale'.

One facet of the presidentialisation thesis is the increasing focus on the personality of the PM and, in the modern age, their ability to convey this via the media. Thus, in the 1960s, Harold Wilson came over well, particularly on TV, while Ted Heath often appeared more wooden in the 1970s. In the 1980s, Thatcher modulated her hairstyle, clothes and voice to become a very effective parliamentary and public performer. While Blair excelled as a communicator, Brown failed to convert his successful platform and parliamentary style to the homelier demands of TV. Cameron's public relations skills generally served his party well, while May has been criticised for her rather 'robotic' performances (Peck, 2017).

Yet, despite the focus on the prime minister above their Cabinet, claims that we have moved to a more presidential system of government are increasingly out of fashion. From 2010 to 2015, Cameron was constrained by the compromises of coalition government (Bennister and Heffernan, 2011), and, after winning outright victory for his party in 2015, by having to make concessions to powerful backbench Conservative MPs with their own agenda – notably Britain's membership of the EU. After the 2017 election, when the Conservative Party failed to secure a majority in Parliament, May was constrained by her Cabinet, backbenchers and the DUP, upon whom she relied for a majority. The constraints of Cabinet collective responsibility for policy perhaps demonstrate the limits of the 'presidentialisation' thesis.

Today, there is a backlash against the idea that we are moving towards a system where the PM looks increasingly like a president. Keith Dowding (2013) has claimed that: 'The presidentialisation of the Prime Minister thesis should be expunged from political science vocabulary.' Making a limited comparison with the US president, Dowding argues that the roles of the prime minister and the president as leaders of their parties are entirely different. He concludes, however, that the British prime minister is often more powerful within their systems than the US president, who is deeply limited in what they can achieve: testament

to that are President Trump's failure to guide healthcare reform through Congress and the Supreme Court's decision to overturn his order preventing nationals from certain countries entering the USA.

To others, the idea that we have a more 'presidential' prime minister confuses personality politics with institutional differences. Ana Langer (2011) argues, for example, that the personalisation of politics – which may well be happening and was part of the claims for Blair or Thatcher being viewed in presidential terms – is very different from an institutional comparison of the offices of the prime minister or a president.

In retrospect, much of the debate over prime ministerial or presidential power drew on the earlier years of the Wilson, Thatcher and Blair premierships. The Wilson government of 1974–76, and the later years of both Thatcher and Blair suggest more limitations to prime ministerial power, as did the governments led by Callaghan, Major, Brown, Cameron and May. Thus the power of the prime minister inevitably fluctuates with the personality of the holder of the post and the political circumstances of the time. As the first postwar coalition prime minister, Cameron faced new constraints from 2010 to 2015, although his largely unexpected election victory in 2015 not only restored single-party government but enhanced his own authority in the Conservative Party.

In practice, prime ministerial power can vary considerably, depending on the ability of the individual prime minister to exploit the capacities of the office, as well as political circumstances, such as the size of the parliamentary majority and simply how 'events' fall out. Constitutional, political, administrative and personal constraints prevent the prime minister from achieving the degree of predominance suggested by the prime ministerial government thesis.

Richard Heffernan (2013) argues that debates around presidentialisation, 'prime ministerial' government and 'Cabinet' government are misleading. He suggests that a more helpful categorisation in understanding the power of the prime minister would be an analysis of which prime ministers are *pre-eminent* and which become *predominant*. Pre-eminence, he argues, is assured – all prime ministers are pre-eminent due to the institutional power resources they have. These include:

1  Being the legal head of the government, using the crown prerogatives, and being involved, either directly or not, in all significant matters concerning government policy.

2  Having the political and administrative means to access knowledge and expertise and extend their reach and grasp across central government.

3  Being able to influence and shape the preferences of other actors and institutions.

4  Being able to frame the policy agenda through leading the government and the party and by controlling the government's 'official' news media operation.

However, for prime ministers to be *predominant*, they have to go beyond this and possess and make effective use of the following personal power resources:

1  Being an entrenched party leader with a reputation for being 'prime ministerial'.

2  Being associated with actual or anticipated political success.

3  Being electorally popular.

4  Having a high standing in their parliamentary party.

It is only once these resources are effectively used that a pre-eminent politician can become predominant. The predominant prime minister is, in short, electorally popular and (potentially at least) politically successful. To Heffernan (2013), this division explains prime ministerial power better than any other.

In summary, the British prime minister has very considerable powers – and these were stretched to the limit by a dynamic prime minister such as Thatcher and more recently by Blair. But the constraints upon the premier make presidentialism or 'prime ministerial government' an inappropriate description. Is 'Cabinet government' a more apt one? Our earlier discussion suggested that the Cabinet itself neither originates policy nor takes more than a small proportion of major decisions. Most policy decisions in British government are taken in departments and Cabinet committees. However, the Cabinet retains what may be described as 'a residual and irreducible' authority; it has not sunk into merely 'dignified' status (Madgwick, 1991, p. 259). It remains strong enough to help depose a once-dominant prime minister, as it did with Thatcher in 1990. The British system of decision-making at the top has grown more complex, diffuse and extensive but, arguably, it is still a collective executive in which the prime minister provides leadership within a Cabinet system.

Although the argument over whether Britain has Cabinet or prime ministerial or perhaps even presidential government has rumbled on for 50 years, it seems increasingly irrelevant to the understanding of political and governmental power in modern Britain, as Heffernan (2013) has shown. Indeed, in assuming a bipolar struggle between PM and Cabinet, the traditional debate oversimplifies the complexity of Britain's core executive, and the role of other players within that core executive, including the Treasury, departmental ministers, senior permanent civil servants, special advisers and Cabinet committees. It fails to distinguish sufficiently between the power of Cabinet ministers as heads of departments with real resources at their disposal and interests behind them, and the power of the Cabinet as a collective body. By focusing on the debate between the institutions of Cabinet and prime minister, this approach also underestimates the importance of relationships between key players and the resources they can deploy in bargaining – resources which may shift significantly over time. It also underestimates the importance of the context in which conflicts within government are fought out. Factors such as the size of a government's majority (or lack of one), the governing party's discipline and cohesion, and the poll standing of the prime minister and leading rivals are not minor incidental features, but crucial to power relationships. Finally, focusing on the struggle between prime minister and

Cabinet focuses too much on the traditional centre of British government in Whitehall and Westminster, ignoring the shift towards multi-level governance, in which the prime minister and Cabinet are only operating at one level (Rhodes, 1997). So it is suggested that the prime minister now has 'more control over less' (Rose, 2001). Indeed, Smith (2003, p. 79) has cautioned against focusing too much on the power of the PM, noting that: 'While a Prime Minister may be increasingly powerful in the Whitehall world, policy making in the real world has increasingly shifted from that arena ... power has shifted upwards to the international arena, outwards to the private and voluntary sector, and downwards to agencies, quangos and devolved institutions.'

## SUMMARY

» The Cabinet is chaired by the prime minister and consists of some 20–23 ministers. Most head major government departments. Most are members of the House of Commons, although a few (normally only one or two) may come from the Lords.

» Alongside the Cabinet, a complex system of Cabinet committees has grown up. Some of these are chaired by PMs, others by senior ministers. Junior ministers as well as Cabinet ministers may be members of Cabinet committees. Many decisions are taken in committees and not referred to Cabinet.

» All members of the government are bound by the principle of (Cabinet) collective responsibility. They are expected to support all government policy in public (or at least refrain from public dissent). Any member of the government who wishes to make public their disagreement with any item of government policy is required to resign their ministerial post.

» The prime minister, the head of government, is not directly elected by the people. Their authority derives normally from being leader of a party that gains a parliamentary majority in a general election.

» The PM's key powers include appointments to government and public office, steering and organising government, and giving leadership to the nation.

» The prime minister is served directly by the Prime Minister's Office, which has grown in size and importance but is relatively small compared with the staff of many other heads of government.

» Although it is widely alleged that the power of the prime minister has grown at the expense of the Cabinet, there remain important constraints on the exercise of prime ministerial power, which has, in any case, fluctuated markedly between and within premierships, according to personalities and circumstances.

## QUESTIONS FOR DISCUSSION

» Has the growth of Cabinet committees involved the bypassing of Cabinet?

» Why is there an apparent need for collective responsibility, and what are the implications in practice?

» Has Cabinet government been effectively replaced by prime ministerial (or presidential) government?

» What are the sources of the power of the British prime minister?

» In what respects might a British prime minister sometimes seem to have more power within their country's governmental system than an American president?

» Why might the debate over prime ministerial power be regarded as only marginally relevant to the real issue of power in British government?

## FURTHER READING

On the PM, Blick and Jones (2010) *Premiership: The Development, Nature and Power of the Office of the British Prime Minister* is a short, readable guide. A key source is Hennessy (2000) *The Prime Minister: The Office and its Holders since 1945*. Older useful sources include King (1985) and Foley (1993, 2000). Diamond (2014), a former special adviser to Tony Blair, has published a fascinating account of tensions in, and power of, the core executive: *Governing Britain: Power, Politics and the Prime Minister*.

A series of short articles in *Parliamentary Affairs*, 2013, 66(3) cover the debate over the 'presidentialisation' of the office of PM. Dowding leads the attack with 'The Prime Ministerialisation of the British Prime Minister' (pp. 617–35); presidentialisation is defended by Webb and Poguntke in 'The Presidentialization of Politics Thesis Defended' (pp. 646–54) and by Foley in 'Prime Ministerialisation and Presidential Analogies: A Certain Difference in Interpretive Evolution' (pp. 655–62).

Beech and Lee have edited a series of books that shed light on the work and policy of PMs from Blair to Cameron, including: *Ten Years of New Labour (2008)*, *The Conservatives under David Cameron: Built to Last?* (Lee and Beech, 2009), *The Brown Government: A Policy Evaluation* (2010) and *The Conservative-Liberal Coalition: Examining the Cameron-Clegg Government* (2015).

## USEFUL WEBSITES

Useful websites include 10 Downing Street: www.gov.uk/government/organisations/prime-ministers-office-10-downing-street, and the official Twitter account: @number10gov.

You can read all about the current Cabinet here: www.gov.uk/government/ministers.

The website of the Cabinet Office is: www.gov.uk/government/organisations/cabinet-office. They tweet @cabinetofficeuk.

*Further student resources to support learning are available at*
**www.macmillanihe.com/griffiths-brit-pol-3e**

# 8

# MINISTERS, DEPARTMENTS AND THE CIVIL SERVICE

Midway through David Cameron's first term in office, *The Times* newspaper reported that an increasingly bitter power struggle between ministers and civil servants was poisoning relations and undermining the then prime minister's reforms. A Conservative Cabinet minister commented that the working relationship had descended into a 'cold war'; ministers felt blocked at every turn by an unwieldy and unwilling Civil Service uncomfortable with Cameron's policies. The newspaper spoke to dozens of ministers and senior civil servants: 'They think it's their job just to say "No"', one Cabinet minister said.

In *The Times* piece, former Conservative Prime Minister David Cameron and former Labour Prime Minister Tony Blair both referred to the classic 1980s television satire *Yes Minister* (and subsequently *Yes, Prime Minister*). The fictional series focuses on Sir Humphrey Appleby, a senior civil servant, and his invariably successful battles with his minister – and later prime minister – Jim Hacker. Cameron and Blair both argued that the series seemed more a documentary than a comedy. Some ministers quoted Jim Hacker's observation that: 'The Civil Service are the Opposition in residence' (Sylvester et al., 2013).

While Chapter 7 focused on the central direction and coordination of policy by the PM and the Cabinet, relatively few government decisions are sufficiently important or controversial to be taken at this level. Most are made in departments. What's more, whenever new government responsibilities are created by legislation, Parliament confers them upon ministers and departments, not on the Cabinet or the PM. How decisions are taken within departments is consequently of vital significance in British government, as the controversies discussed above make clear. Are ministers the real decision-makers? How far does power lie with permanent, neutral civil servants or politically appointed special advisers? These are some of the debates discussed in this chapter.

## THIS CHAPTER:

» Examines the relationship between ministers and civil servants, and the tensions between them.

» Discusses what are sometimes seen as the traditional features of the Civil Service; looks at who it recruits in terms of expertise, ethnicity and gender; and examines various claims of bias made against it.

» Reflects on the idea of individual 'ministerial responsibility' and asks if the convention is still relevant today.

» Examines various attempts to reform the Civil Service over the past 40 years.

» Provides an account of the radical changes made to the Civil Service in the 1980s under the Thatcher governments, and explores the importance of ideas of new public management in explaining those reforms.

» Discusses Blair's 'New Labour' government's use of 'special advisers', which challenged the traditional Civil Service model and introduced constitutional reforms that changed the role of the Civil Service.

» Looks at Civil Service reform after 2010 and the radical moves towards a smaller Civil Service, which is focused on commissioning services rather than administering them, and has lost its monopoly on policy advice to ministers.

» Concludes with the question that opened this chapter: Where does the balance of power and influence lie between ministers and civil servants?

## THE ORGANISATION OF CENTRAL GOVERNMENT

The central government of the United Kingdom is organised into a number of departments of varying size and importance. Ministries or departments have emerged rather haphazardly over the centuries, and particularly over the last century, as the responsibilities of government have expanded. Moreover, ministries or departments have frequently been merged or subdivided in periodic reorganisations, and often renamed in the process.

Is there any coherent rationale behind these departmental reorganisations? Back in 1918, the Haldane Report into the machinery of government argued that there were two main principles under which the tasks of government might be grouped: by function (education, health, transport) or by client group (children, pensioners, disabled, unemployed). Haldane (1918) came down in favour of the functional principle. However, the actual organisation of British central government does not entirely reflect this. While most departments follow Haldane's functional (or service) model, there are also others that deal with particular areas of the United Kingdom – Scotland, Wales and Northern Ireland (but see below for the impact of devolution). In addition, ministers (if not departments) have sometimes been appointed for particular client groups. Thus we have had ministers for the disabled, a minister for women and, during Gordon Brown's period as prime minister (2007–10), a Department for Children, Schools and Families.

Administrative fashion has sometimes influenced organisational change. In the 1960s and 1970s, there was a general preference for large-scale organisation in the private and public sectors. 'Big was beautiful', it was argued – it could yield economies of scale, and lead to better coordination of policy. Thus a number of 'giant departments' were created that merged previously separate ministries, for example the Department of Trade and Industry (DTI), the Department of Health and Social Security (DHSS), the Department of the Environment (DoE). Subsequently, there was a reaction against 'big government', and also against large departments. Now they were seen to produce problems for effective management, and diseconomies rather than economies of scale. So the DHSS and, for a time, the DTI were redivided, while a separate Transport Department was hived off from the DoE. After 1988, disaggregation went further with the introduction of executive agencies (see below).

More often, organisational change seems to have reflected political factors rather than administrative theory. The creation of a new department may be intended to signal the importance the government attaches to a particular responsibility. So Harold Wilson formed a new Ministry of Technology in 1964, while Tony Blair established a separate Department for International Development in 1997. Occasionally, a new department has been created to provide a senior post for a particular politician, such as John Prescott, deputy leader of the Labour Party, for whom a special Department of the Environment, Transport and the Regions (DETR) was created in 1997, although it was subsequently broken up from 2001 onwards. The Cameron and May governments largely continued the departmental responsibilities of their Labour predecessors, sometimes with simpler titles (such as the Department for Education).

The Civil Service is still widely associated with London, and more specifically with Whitehall, the street that is home to many departments. While it remains true that the great majority of the most senior civil servants remain London-based, it is increasingly geographically dispersed. Just 16% of UK-based civil servants work in London and a further 10% work in the rest of the southeast, while almost three-quarters work in other English regions, Scotland, Wales and Northern Ireland, or overseas.

---

*The Civil Service includes all those directly employed by government departments and executive agencies. These civil servants are 'Servants of the Crown, other than holders of political or judicial offices, who are employed in a civil capacity and whose remuneration is paid wholly and directly out of moneys voted by Parliament' (Tomlin Commission, 1931).*

---

## THE INTERNAL ORGANISATION OF GOVERNMENT DEPARTMENTS: POLITICIANS AND CIVIL SERVANTS

Departments are officially directed and run by politicians drawn mainly from the House of Commons, although a few come from the Lords. Today, virtually all the ministers who head departments are of Cabinet rank (by convention most of these are given the title of 'secretary of state', although others – notably the chancellor of the exchequer – are not). Below the secretary of state, each department frequently contains at least one minister of state and two or more parliamentary under-secretaries of state. These junior ministerial appointments are the route by which aspiring politicians gain experience of government and often lead to promotion to more senior ministerial ranks. Memoirs of junior ministers, however, suggest that some do not feel they have much power or influence (see Mullin, 2009).

Ministers are the political and constitutional heads of departments. Departments are largely composed of permanent officials – members of the Civil Service. The top officials are 'senior civil servants'. The concept of the Senior Civil Service (SCS) is about 25 years old. The SCS consists of the permanent secretaries in central Whitehall, and heads of other government executive agencies, departments and the top tiers of management below them – about 4,000 people in total. (Executive agencies are discussed in more detail below.) The SCS is subject to a degree of centralised management through the Cabinet Office. Terms and conditions, including the pay structure, are determined centrally, with departments having only limited discretion at the margins to vary those terms and conditions. This is in contrast to lower grades, where, theoretically, departments have much greater freedom, although recent attempts by the Treasury to curb government spending have curtailed this freedom over pay.

The Cabinet Office seeks to ensure common titles for senior civil servants. In each department, the highest tier is made up of the permanent secretary. (A couple of the more prestigious departments such as the Treasury may have two people at that level, with the more junior known as the 'second permanent secretary'.) Officials below them are usually called 'director general'. A few people at that level with specialist functions might have different titles (e.g. chief economist or chief scientist). Below that are directors and deputy directors.

The head of each department's internal management structure is the permanent secretary. The permanent secretary is also the accounting officer, which means they are directly accountable to Parliament for ensuring the department's funds are properly spent. All departments also now have a management board, which will normally be chaired by the departmental secretary of state. In most cases, this meets monthly and includes non-executive members (who volunteer their time, often while holding senior roles elsewhere) and executive members (civil servants from the department). Non-executives are meant to provide external experience and insights and challenge the organisation's decision. Below the management board, as in any large organisation, officials will have a number of other management committees, covering areas such as finances or human resources.

The 'engine room' of policy-making is just below the SCS, where officials are expected to know their subject area inside out. (At this level, each department has freedom to decide their own titles. There are a range of terms, such as 'assistant directors', 'team leaders', 'team members', 'policy advisers' and so on.) It is officials below the SCS who will handle the day-to-day 'stuff' of politics and policy-making – drafting replies to parliamentary questions, ministerial correspondence; gaining interdepartmental clearance on new proposals; drafting policy announcements; checking the

detail of press releases; and preparing the briefing for ministerial meetings, visits and speeches (Waller, 2014).

## TRADITIONAL FEATURES OF THE BRITISH CIVIL SERVICE

British constitutional theory has always made a clear distinction between the *political* role of ministers and the *administrative* role of civil servants. Ministers are in charge of departments and responsible to Parliament for running them, while civil servants advise ministers on policy and implement government decisions. Three features of the civil service have been traditionally linked to this distinction: permanence, political neutrality and anonymity:

» *Permanence*: While ministers are temporary, subject to the patronage of the PM and electoral fortunes, civil servants are career officials enjoying security of tenure. Unlike the position in the USA (see Comparing British Politics 8.1), where large numbers of administrative posts change hands when the make-up of the government changes, civil servants in Britain are expected to serve governments of any party.

» *Political neutrality*: British civil servants are required to be politically impartial, not allowing their own political opinions to influence their actions and loyally carrying out government decisions, whether they agree with them or not. Senior civil servants are still not permitted to engage in any open partisan political activity.

» *Anonymity*: Because ministers are constitutionally responsible for policy and accountable for their departments to Parliament and the public, civil servants have traditionally been kept out of the public eye. It was the role of civil servants to offer confidential advice to ministers; if they became public figures, this might compromise their neutrality and undermine the frankness of the advice offered to ministers.

All these features are now under threat, as we will see below.

Although senior civil servants are not allowed to play a formal (party) political role, as key ministerial advisers they have always been heavily involved in the politics of bargaining for influence *within* departments, *between* departments, *with* outside interests and *in their relations with* ministers. Moreover, in recent decades, the traditional neutrality and anonymity of the Civil Service has been significantly eroded, as we explore throughout this chapter.

## RECRUITMENT AND BIAS

In the early nineteenth century, civil servants were recruited by a system of patronage, by *who* they knew rather than *what* they knew, which was hardly likely to promote efficient government. Following the Northcote-Trevelyan Report (1854) on the organisation of the Civil Service, competitive examinations were introduced and promotion was to be on merit, with the aim of recruiting the best and brightest graduates into the higher Civil Service. This aim was substantially achieved. In the twentieth century, British higher civil servants generally had outstanding academic records with first class degrees from the older and more prestigious universities. However, in the latter part of the twentieth century, there were increasing criticisms of top British civil servants on two main grounds: their lack of relevant skills and expertise, and their narrow and unrepresentative social and educational background.

While there was little doubt that the senior civil servants recruited by the rigorous selection process were, in general, exceedingly able, critics argued that they usually lacked relevant knowledge of the services they were called on to administer and appropriate managerial skills. Nor were these deficiencies systematically addressed through in-service training. Moreover, as most were recruited straight from university, they had little direct experience of the outside world, particularly commerce and industry. The professional and technical expertise of British senior civil servants was compared unfavourably with their French equivalents (see Comparing British Politics 8.1).

## ⊞ COMPARING BRITISH POLITICS 8.1 ▤ ▮ ▮

## Public bureaucracies in the USA, France and Britain

» *USA*: The American public bureaucracy is highly complex, fragmented and, at higher levels, more politicised than the British. The complexity partly reflects the US federal system and division of powers. Bureaucracies exist at federal, state and local levels, but there is also a bewildering proliferation of departments, bureaus and agencies, often with overlapping responsibilities. Whereas British higher civil servants are expected to be politically neutral, many senior posts in the USA change hands when control of government changes (the 'spoils system'). American senior bureaucrats do not generally enjoy the same prestigious status as their British or French equivalents.

» *France*: A strong, technocratic and highly prestigious bureaucracy serves the French 'one and indivisible' Republic. While senior British civil servants had the reputation of being able generalists without much specialist background or training, senior French public officials tend to be specialists with technical or professional expertise. However, the French public service is not necessarily a career service on the lines of the British Civil Service. Although leading bureaucrats are recruited from the elite *Ecole Nationale d'Administration* (whose graduates are referred to as *énarques*), some subsequently move into politics, and others transfer into the private sector, and sometimes back into the state service. This more specialist education combined with a greater breadth of experience may help to account for the prominent role of French officials in modernising the economy and implementing prestigious projects.

» *Britain*: Changes in the British system of government (devolution, executive agencies, special units) have increased the complexity of the British bureaucracy. Moreover, changes in recruitment (more special advisers, short-term appointments, secondments to and from industry) have reduced the permanence and uniformity of the traditional higher British Civil Service.

The Fulton Report (1968) called for changes in Civil Service recruitment, promotion and training. The report was partly a response to the criticism that the Civil Service was too reliant on well-educated generalists, but lacked staff with the specialist knowledge in sciences and social sciences needed to deal with the modern age. Lord Fulton recommended the recruitment of graduates with more relevant degrees (in the sciences for example), a considerable expansion of late entry in order to enable people from many walks of life to bring in their experience, and the widening of the social and educational base from which top civil servants were recruited. The idea of demanding 'relevance' was rejected but, although expansion of late entry had disappointing results, from the mid-1980s there was a significant programme of two-way temporary secondments between Whitehall and industry, commerce and other institutions (Hennessy, 1990, pp. 523–4). By 1996, there had been a dramatic increase in recruitment from the private sector, with a quarter of the 63 posts advertised in the SCS going to private sector applicants. Secondments outside Whitehall had also increased, with 1,500 civil servants on medium- to long-term attachments in 1996. The Blair government established a new group headed by the Cabinet secretary and the (pro-business) president of the Confederation of British Industry to oversee the development of shorter, more flexible secondments from the Civil Service into industry, especially of junior level civil servants from outside London.

A rather different criticism was that the SCS was socially and educationally unrepresentative of the public they served. A persistent bias in favour of the recruitment of Oxford and Cambridge graduates tended to reinforce the rather exclusive and distinctly untypical social and educational background of senior civil servants. Broadening the base of recruitment away from elite-educated arts graduates has occurred very gradually, although canvassing for recruits at other universities intensified from 1991.

Another concern has been the gender and ethnic bias. Women make up just over half (54%) of the total number of civil servants, but they are still disproportionately employed at lower levels, although this gender balance is fast changing. Broadly speaking, the percentage of women employed declines progressively through the higher levels of the Civil Service (ONS, 2015b), reflecting a wider social trend in professional careers. Women constitute only 39% of senior civil servants and only six of the seventeen top permanent secretaries (Byrne, 2017). While these figures could obviously be further improved, they compare favourably with the gender balance at the higher levels in the private sector, particularly in company boardrooms, as well as in politics more generally (see Chapter 6, p. 113).

The Civil Service is also recruiting more among ethnic minorities. In 2016, 11.2% of all civil servants declaring their ethnicity identified as BAME (black, Asian and minority ethnic), up from 9% in 2010, and 4% in 1988. However, this is still lower than the national population figure of 14% from the 2011 census. Progress to top jobs is worse, with just 7.1% of senior civil servants from an ethnic minority. There are also no permanent secretaries from an ethnic minority in charge of a Whitehall department. BAME civil servants are still more likely to experience discrimination (Byrne, 2017).

The composition of the highest Civil Service ranks almost inevitably reflects patterns of

*Source:* Lefteris Pitarakis – WPA Pool/Getty Images
David Cameron addresses civil servants at the Home Office in 2010. The Civil Service has been criticised for its lack of technical experience in industry, and its gender and ethnic bias.

recruitment 20–30 years ago from a society that was different in important respects. As senior civil servants advise ministers and influence policy-making, it is a matter of some continuing concern that important sectors of the community are underrepresented in their ranks. If relatively few top civil servants have had direct experience of state schools or universities other than Oxford or Cambridge, they may be less competent to advise on education. If relatively few have had to juggle the demands of their professional work with the domestic work, childcare or care of the elderly or disabled, which remains disproportionately a female responsibility in British society, they will have little direct insight into the problems of working women. If they have never felt at first hand the prejudice and discrimination that is the routine experience of many people who are not white, heterosexual, able-bodied men, then they can scarcely appreciate, say, the attitudes and behaviour of ethnic minority communities and the problems of living in modern multicultural Britain. While senior civil servants may strive to give disinterested and impartial advice, their attitudes will inevitably reflect their own educational and social background, and their ignorance of very different environments. They have also sometimes been accused of other forms of bias, including:

» *Party bias*: Although senior civil servants have sometimes been accused of a Conservative bias, Labour minsters have testified to the loyal support they received from the Civil Service after 1997. More recently, members of the SNP were critical of the perceived pro-union stance of the Civil Service in the run-up to Scotland's referendum on independence in 2014. (The referendum is discussed in more detail in Chapter 11.)

» *Establishment bias*: Radical critics have argued that the untypical social and educational background of senior civil servants gives them a bias in favour of establishment (or elite) values and interests. There are still concerns that the SCS is socially unrepresentative.

» *Liberal arts and social science bias*: Other critics suggest that the restricted academic background from which most top civil servants are drawn means that few have knowledge or understanding of business, science or technology (see also Comparing British Politics 8.1).

» *Consensus bias*: Both left-wing socialists and right-wing Conservatives have sometimes accused civil servants of a bias in favour of moderate consensus politics, and hostility towards radical reform. Civil servants, obliged to serve governments of different parties, may prefer continuity to change, and may react negatively to radical proposals from the left or the right.

» *Bias towards their own interests*: New Right thinkers argue that civil servants primarily pursue their own self-interest, and favour policies most likely to preserve and enhance their own pay, conditions and prospects.

## INDIVIDUAL MINISTERIAL RESPONSIBILITY

The convention of **(individual) ministerial responsibility** governs relations between ministers, civil servants and Parliament. Ministerial responsibility means that individual ministers are required to inform Parliament about their work and explain their own and their departments' actions. Individual ministers constantly explain and defend departmental policy before Parliament – during parliamentary questions, during the committee stage of legislation, before select committees and privately to MPs. Ministerial answers to political questions are not always entirely full or satisfactory and sometimes they are downright evasive. Nonetheless, individual ministerial responsibility, in its first meaning of 'answerability' or 'explanatory accountability', still applies.

---

**(Individual) ministerial responsibility** *is the constitutional convention by which each minister is responsible to Parliament for the activities of their department, and 'carries the can' for failure.*

---

Ministerial responsibility used to mean that individual ministers – and ministers alone – were responsible to Parliament for the actions of their departments. However, the delegation of managerial responsibility, a key aspect of executive agencies, clearly implies some reduction of direct ministerial responsibility. Chief executives of agencies have been summoned to appear before parliamentary committees, and their replies to parliamentary questions are published in *Hansard* – the official record of what is said in the Houses of Parliament. Of course, ministers remain in charge of policy, but there is a difficulty in dividing responsibility neatly between 'policy' and 'operations' (for which chief executives are responsible).

In the last resort, ministerial responsibility may entail the resignation of a particular minister, yet relatively few have felt obliged to take full responsibility for policy failure. The most celebrated example of such resignations was that of the foreign secretary, Lord Carrington and the whole Foreign Office team of ministers who resigned in 1982 for failure to foresee and prevent the Argentine invasion of the Falklands, although the defence secretary, John Nott, survived. Under Blair, Estelle Morris resigned as education secretary in October 2002, following a series of embarrassing failures in the service and department over which she presided, culminating in the A-level marking scandal, in which thousands of students were given the wrong grade. It is not entirely clear how far the failings here were the fault of the minister or officials, but the minister accepted responsibility. There is no more recent case of a minister resigning for mistakes made by officials.

While there has indeed been a stream of forced ministerial resignations in recent decades, most of these have been due to personal rather than policy failings, commonly sexual misconduct or financial impropriety, while some others might be ascribed to political misjudgements and mistakes. In a few instances, there was a fairly clear breach of the ethical principles governing the holding of public office (and formalised by Lord Nolan in 1995). In other cases, resignation followed lurid publicity of a minister's private life and a prolonged media 'feeding frenzy', which made the minister's position untenable.

The principle of individual ministerial responsibility should be distinguished from the convention of collective Cabinet responsibility, requiring all ministers to support government policy in public (discussed in detail in Chapter 7). But the distinction is by no means always clear-cut in practice. Thus, a policy that was the collective responsibility of the government as a whole may be treated as a matter of individual responsibility to minimise loss of public confidence in the government. Accordingly, an individual minister may feel obliged to accept responsibility for a policy that was really a collective decision.

# REFORMING THE CIVIL SERVICE

The Civil Service has long been regarded as the core of what was described as public administration in Britain, with a distinctive public sector ethos quite different from the practice and principles of the private sector. More recently, however, there have been persistent attempts to introduce some of the characteristics of the private sector into the management of the public sector. The term 'new public management' (NPM) is often applied to the extensive changes inspired by the private sector introduced into managing public services, not only in Britain, but in many other western countries (see Spotlight 8.1 overleaf). Indeed, many of the theoretical assumptions behind NPM, and many key initiatives, originated elsewhere, particularly in the USA. In Britain, it is argued that NPM has increasingly displaced the values and processes associated with traditional public administration in the Civil Service and other parts of the public sector.

## THE THATCHER AND MAJOR GOVERNMENTS

NPM was particularly associated with the Thatcher and Major governments, although it was largely maintained by Labour from 1997 to 2010, and subsequently by Conservative-led governments. Many of these reforms were inspired by free-market assumptions, involving distrust of big government and the public sector. They assumed that public sector organisations not subject to market competition were inherently wasteful and inefficient. Following free-market economists

# SPOTLIGHT ON ...    The new public management: main features    8.1

» A managerial culture that reflects private sector norms and practices rather than those of traditional public administration

» The promotion of competition, markets and quasi-markets within the public sector

» More managerial delegation, decentralisation and organisational disaggregation

» An emphasis on economy, efficiency and effectiveness – the three Es

» Performance measurement, involving published standards and targets

» Flexibility of pay and conditions; sometimes including performance-related pay

» A greater emphasis on customer choice and service quality

» The contracting out of some service provision to the private sector, with the separation of purchaser and provider (or client and contractor) roles

» Privatisation of some former public services, with state regulation rather than state control

such as Buchanan, Tullock and Niskanen, they considered that senior civil servants essentially pursued and protected their own interests rather than the wider public interest. The remedy was to cut the public sector down to size, and expose it to competition, introducing private sector norms and practices (see Spotlight 8.2).

Conservative reforms between 1979 and 1997 constitute the most radical change in the Civil Service since the Northcote-Trevelyan reforms of 1854. They substantially reduced the numbers of civil servants from 735,000 to 494,300 between 1979 and 1996, a drop of over 32%, although some of this involved the reclassification of jobs rather than their disappearance. (See Figure 8.1 on p. 156 for the long view on Civil Service decline.) From 1979, an Efficiency Unit headed by Sir Derek (later Lord) Rayner initiated a series of scrutinies of departments with the aim of reducing costs and streamlining procedure. From 1982, a variety of management information systems, such as the Financial Management Initiative, were designed to enable ministers to discover 'who does what, why and at what cost?' The overall aim was to transform the Civil Service culture along business lines, to enhance the role of civil servants as managers of people and resources and to downgrade their role as policy advisers. This was to be done in the context of drastic cost-saving measures to be introduced under austerity, which would significantly reduce the number of civil servants. Indeed, Steve Hilton, Cameron's special adviser, is said to have argued that a 70% reduction in civil servant numbers was possible (Sylvester et al., 2013). Facing a future of job insecurity, the civil servants' rocky relationship with the executive and ministers – discussed in the introduction to this chapter – becomes very easy to understand.

## Next steps and the new agencies

In 1988, Sir Robin Ibbs produced a report entitled *Improving Management in Government: The Next Steps*. This argued that there had been insufficient focus on the delivery of services, even though the vast majority of civil servants (95%) were in service delivery rather than policy advice roles. The report advocated the division of the Civil Service into a small 'core' engaged in supporting ministers with policy advice within traditional departments, and a wide range of executive agencies responsible for the delivery of services. Departments would set the policy and budgetary objectives and monitor the work of the agencies, but within that framework, each agency, headed by a chief executive, would have considerable independence from Whitehall, with control over the recruitment, grading, organisation and pay of their staffs. By the time New Labour

# SPOTLIGHT ON ...

## Critiques of the Civil Service: bureaucratic oversupply

8.2

The *bureaucratic oversupply model* came to the fore in the 1970s and is mainly but not exclusively linked with the New Right critique of government and Civil Service growth in previous decades. (The rise of the New Right is discussed in more detail in Chapter 15.) It drew on the analysis of public or rational choice theory advanced by William Niskanen and others. Niskanen (1971, 1973) applied classical liberal economic assumptions of the pursuit of individual self-interest to the public sector. In the absence of market constraints and the profit motive, public sector bureaucrats would seek to maximise the size of their own 'bureau' or department and its spending, because this would favour their own pay, promotion prospects, conditions of service and status. Such growth would involve the supply of more public services and more public spending and a bloated, inefficient and wasteful bureaucracy (bureaucratic oversupply). New Right analysis was not just descriptive but prescriptive, and pointed to its own solutions: both the bureaucracy and 'big government' needed 'cutting down to size', through transferring some activities to the private sector

and subjecting others to competition. So the bureaucratic oversupply model provided much of the theoretical underpinning for the Thatcher government's programme of Civil Service reform.

One influential study (Dunleavy, 1991) has applied public choice assumptions to argue that bureaucrats will engage in bureau *shaping* rather than bureau *maximising*. Size (of budgets or staff) does not necessarily matter to senior bureaucrats, who do not always like managing large numbers of (sometimes difficult) junior staff. Indeed, the most prestigious departments are often among the smallest (e.g. the Treasury). Cuts in public spending and institutional change have rarely affected senior bureaucrats. While competition and market testing has often adversely affected the pay and conditions of routine manual and clerical workers, it has generally involved increased opportunities and more managerial autonomy for senior officials. In pursuit of their own self-interest, they do not necessarily want or need 'big government'.

---

were elected in 1997, three-quarters of civil servants were working in what by then were called Next Steps agencies (compared to none in 1988). Today, most civil servants are employed in what are now called executive agencies (see Spotlight 8.3 for an example).

---

*Executive agencies (sometimes still referred to as 'Next Steps' agencies) are organisations with some managerial autonomy within the Civil Service that are responsible for the management of a specific function or service (see below for more on executive agencies).*

---

It was argued that the new agencies improved service delivery, increased cost-effectiveness and produced significant savings. Another advantage claimed for the transfer of activities

to executive agencies was a reduction in ministerial overload, although critics argued it also weakened ministerial accountability and effective political control, particularly in politically controversial area such as the Prison Service or the Child Support Agency.

The Conservatives increasingly involved the private sector in the delivery of public services. During the 1980s, compulsory competitive tendering (CCT) was introduced in local government and the NHS, allowing the private sector to bid for contracts to provide certain public services (see Chapter 18, p. 389). Following a White Paper *Competing for Quality* (HM Treasury, 1991), market testing was extended to the Civil Service. By January 1995, over £1 billion of work had been transferred to the private sector. Privatisation of some

## SPOTLIGHT ON ...

### Example of an executive agency: The Driver and Vehicle Licensing Agency (DVLA)   8.3

» Sets itself clear targets; e.g. to reduce average waiting time for driving tests and reduce delays in issuing driving licences

» Has shown considerable enthusiasm for marketing; e.g. customised number plates

» Has cut costs by putting provision of security and cleaning services out to private tender

agencies had been envisaged by the Ibbs Report (1988) from the outset, although only eight small central government organisations were transferred to the private sector between 1992 and 1995.

The implicit and often explicit criticism of public service in these reforms was demoralising for public sector workers. John Major's Citizen's Charter involved a rather more positive campaign to raise standards in public services, although critics suggested that it was more cosmetic than substantial. Each service was required to publish

performance targets and results against set targets and establish well-publicised and readily available complaints and redress procedures. By 1995, nine agencies had published individual charters specifying standards that customers and clients were entitled to expect (e.g. the Jobseekers' Charter). The move away from civil servants as top-down providers of services to commissioners has led to a significant reduction in their number over the long term, as shown in Figure 8.1.

The changing nature of service delivery is discussed in more detail in Chapter 20, which

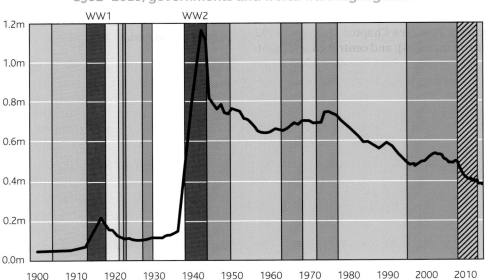

Figure 8.1: Civil Service staff numbers (full time equivalent), 1902–2016, governments and world wars highlighted

Source: IfG analysis of CO, Civil Service stats 1902–90; ONS PSE 1991–8 annual, 1999–2016 quarterly. Excl Central Govt Security from 1999. Reproduced with permission from the Institute for Government. Available at: www.instituteforgovernment.org.uk/publication/whitehall-monitor-2017/workforce

looks more at the provision of services by nongovernmental organisations.

## Standards in public life

The reform programme from 1980s onwards was primarily about improving the *efficiency* of government. The *probity* (or integrity) of government was more often taken for granted. However, a series of scandals in the 1990s reawakened concerns over ethical standards among politicians and office holders. Some of the concerns were over the conduct of MPs (see Chapter 14, p. 303). Several ministers were forced to resign, some for personal or sexual misconduct that had little to do with their government duties, although others had wider implications. Beyond these scandals, there were also concerns over the rules and principles covering those who held public office, whether as ministers or civil servants, and the relations between them. So Prime Minister John Major set up the Nolan Committee on Standards in Public Life in October 1994. Nolan's terms of reference were to examine current concerns about standards of conduct in public office holders and to make recommendations as to any changes required to ensure the highest standards of propriety in public life. His brief covered Parliament; ministerial appointments to 'quangos', such as the Environment Agency or Jobcentre Plus (see Chapter 18, pp. 389–92 for more on quangos); and central government. The subsequent Nolan Report (1995) laid down the 'seven principles of public life':

1  *Selflessness*: Holders of public office should take decisions solely in the public interest. They should not do so in order to gain financial or other material benefits for their family or their friends.

2  *Integrity*: Holders of public office should not place themselves under any financial or other obligation to outside individuals or organisations that might influence them in the performance of their official duties.

3  *Objectivity*: In carrying out public business, including making public appointments, awarding contracts or recommending individuals for rewards and benefits, holders

of public office should make their choices on merit.

4  *Accountability*: Holders of public office are accountable for their decisions and actions to the public and must submit themselves to whatever scrutiny is appropriate to their office.

5  *Openness*: Holders of public office should be as open as possible about all the decisions and actions they take. They should give reasons for their decisions and restrict information only when the wider public interest clearly demands it.

6  *Honesty*: Holders of public office have a duty to declare any private interests relating to their public duties, and to take steps to resolve any conflicts arising in a way that protects the public interest.

7  *Leadership*: Holders of public office should promote and support these principles by leadership and example.

The Nolan Report (1995) made a number of more specific recommendations regarding the conduct of ministers and civil servants, which were largely accepted and incorporated into a non-statutory *Civil Service Code* in 1996 and a revised *Ministerial Code* (Cabinet Office, 1997), setting expectations about how civil servants and ministers should behave. Both codes are regularly updated.

## NEW LABOUR AND THE CIVIL SERVICE: COMPETITION AND COORDINATION

Labour policy towards the Civil Service largely involved the consolidation and extension of Conservative initiatives, rather than their reversal. Thus the Blair government accepted most of the Conservative reform programme, including the introduction of competition and market values into the management of the public sector and administrative decentralisation through executive agencies.

There was also an important shift in emphasis towards more coordination between departments and agencies, and towards a wider cooperation between the public, private and voluntary sectors in the interests of 'joined-up government'. 'Departmentalism' is a familiar difficulty of government. Problems and policies are viewed through the often narrow perspectives of individual departments. But specific issues (e.g. drugs, child poverty, care of the elderly) frequently transcend departmental and agency boundaries, and require people from different organisations to work together.

Coordination may sometimes be improved by the reorganisation of government departments, such as the replacement of the former Ministry of Agriculture, Fisheries and Food with the new Department for Environment, Food & Rural Affairs. But no matter how far functions are reshuffled between different departments, there will always remain a need for cooperation across departments on specific issues (see Spotlight 8.4). Labour attempted to ease the problem by creating a number of special cross-departmental units (e.g. the Social Exclusion Unit, the Women's Unit, the UK Anti-Drug Coordination Unit). However, to an extent, the new coordinating machinery increased the sheer complexity and, ironically, even the fragmentation of government. Responsibility and accountability were blurred.

## SPOTLIGHT ON ...

### The need for departmental and agency coordination: the case of food

8.4

Food production was long seen as the almost exclusive responsibility of the old Ministry of Agriculture, Fisheries and Food, with its understandable concern for British farming. The Department for Environment, Food & Rural Affairs (Defra), established by the Blair government, involved a more explicit focus on food production and its relationship with broader environmental concerns. However, other departments retained a strong interest in aspects of food. For example, the Department of Health clearly had an interest in the safety and quality of food. Other aspects of food production and marketing raised issues for the Department of Business (e.g. the dominance of major supermarkets over food retailing), the Department of Transport (e.g. the long-distance carriage of live animals) and the Department of International Development (e.g. the impact of agricultural subsidies on food exporters from poorer countries). While the UK remains a member of the EU, European regulations governing food and animal safety also come into play. Many of these departments have their own associated agencies and outside interests to consider. Thus food policy in the fullest sense requires cooperation between a number of government departments and agencies and extensive consultation with all kinds of groups and interests outside government.

Moreover, there was a continuing tension between the New Labour 'third way' approach to management, emphasising networks, mutual trust and cooperation and the earlier New Right-inspired emphasis on markets, competition and consumer choice, which Labour substantially endorsed. Thus schools and hospitals were still encouraged to *compete* for pupils and patients to promote more efficiency and value for money in the delivery of public service, but also urged to *cooperate* with their main rivals by sharing information and methods, which might reduce their own competitive advantage. (See Chapter 20 for more on competing views of the state and policy-making.)

### The rise of special advisers

The 1997–2010 Labour governments, like their Conservative predecessors, were no longer content to rely on the permanent Civil Service for most of their policy advice. What New Labour required of the Civil Service was similar to what the Thatcher government wanted – loyal and effective *delivery* of government policy.

"OH, PLEASE! CAN WE CALL A SPAD A SPAD?"

*Source*: Reproduced by kind permission of *Private Eye* magazine/Richard Jolley

There has been a significant increase in political advice from outside the Civil Service in recent years.

Labour preferred to draw its policy *advice* from a range of sources, including party research, independent think tanks and, most important of all, its own special advisers (spads for short), appointed on fixed-term contracts and brought into the centre of the government machine.

Special advisers were not new. They were employed alongside the permanent Civil Service by successive governments. However, their number and more particularly their influence has steadily grown. Although still heavily outnumbered by senior civil servants, special advisers were, by repute, hugely influential on key areas of Labour government policy. Indeed, some special advisers, such as Ed Balls, Ed Miliband and Andrew Adonis, were later to become ministers and influential figures in Brown's Cabinet. (On the Conservative side too, being a special adviser was often seen as a route to parliamentary election. David Cameron was, for example, the special adviser to the Conservative chancellor and home secretary in the mid-1990s.) Under New Labour, the role of special advisers

became increasingly controversial, particularly for the way in which they dealt with the media. Several special advisers acquired a high media and public profile as New Labour's spin doctors (Waller, 2014).

Some of the special advisers who had served earlier governments (such as Harold Wilson's in the 1960s and 70s) had found themselves isolated and effectively neutralised by the permanent Civil Service. More recently, special advisers have become some of the most influential figures at the heart of government, while top civil servants have found their traditional pre-eminence in policy advice considerably eroded. Smith (2003) observes: 'To some extent, top officials have been excluded almost completely from policy making.' Even with the qualifications, this is an exaggeration. A permanent secretary's length of experience, and first-hand knowledge of past policy failures and difficulties remains enormously valuable to ministers. But the permanent secretary is no longer necessarily the most important voice in the minister's ear, and some permanent secretaries have felt their role has been significantly diminished.

Some see the growing influence of special advisers as contributing to a decline in the traditional neutrality of a permanent career Civil Service. It is not unreasonable, however, for a government to bring in some experts who share their general political philosophy to give advice on policy. In many other countries, there is a far larger turnover in officials when the government changes hands. But the rise to prominence of special advisers caused tension with permanent civil servants in some departments. *The Times* report that started this chapter provides an example of unnamed special advisers being physically locked out of policy meetings held by civil servants. Special advisers have the ear of ministers but are outside the hierarchy of permanent staff, which led to demands for more clarification of their role. In October 2015, the Conservative government issued new guidance clarifying that special advisers were able to issue instructions to civil servants. This shifts power to the political appointees and creates the possibility of tensions between advisers and permanent civil servants.

## KEY FIGURES 8.1
The special advisers

**Alastair Campbell (1957–)** is the best-known New Labour 'spin doctor' (see also Chapter 17). He was Downing Street press secretary (1997–2000) and then director of communications (2000–03). He resigned in August 2003 during the Hutton Inquiry into the death of David Kelly. Campbell began his journalistic career as a trainee reporter and moved to the London office of *The Daily Mirror* in 1982 – the only Labour-supporting popular newspaper. He became a political correspondent, before moving to a new newspaper, *Today*, as a news editor in 1986. He left *Today* to become Tony Blair's press secretary, soon after Blair was elected leader of the party in 1994, where he was said to have coined the term 'New Labour'. In the run-up to the Iraq War (see Chapter 22, pp. 470–74), Campbell was involved in the preparation and release of controversial dossiers making the case for war. He resigned in August 2003 during the Hutton Inquiry, even though it ultimately exonerated him of wrongdoing. His colourful language and domineering personality when dealing with journalists and ministers is said to be the inspiration for the character Malcolm Tucker in the BBC political comedy, *The Thick of It*.

**Steve Hilton (1969–)** is a former director of strategy for David Cameron. After graduating, he joined Conservative Central Office and became friends with Cameron. While the party was out of office, Hilton talked of the need to 'replace' the traditional grassroots membership of the Conservative Party, which he saw as preventing the party from embracing a more 'metropolitan' attitude on social issues. He sought to rebrand the Conservative Party as green and progressive, and was a significant factor in David Cameron's modernisation programme after 2005. Hilton was also satirised in *The Thick of It*, as the generally relaxed, 'blue-sky' thinker, and herbal-tea drinking special adviser.

**Nick Timothy (1980–)** was joint Downing Street chief of staff, alongside Fiona Hill, to Prime Minister Theresa May from 2016 to 2017. He also worked in the Conservative Research Department, and a variety of private sector jobs, before becoming special adviser to May when she was home secretary. After briefly working elsewhere, he rejoined May's office when she became PM.

**Fiona Hill (1973–)**, who had a career in journalism, working for *The Scotsman* and *Sky News*, became May's media adviser at the Home Office between 2010 and 2014.

Both Hill and Timothy were criticised for the level of control they had over access to the PM and their attitude towards ministers. Both advised May to call a snap general election in early 2017, in order to capitalise on her lead in the opinion polls and strengthen her position in the upcoming Brexit negotiations. The Conservative Party performed far worse than expected – losing its parliamentary majority – and Hill and Timothy were forced to resign as a result, taking the blame for the poor campaign.

## Constitutional reform and the organisation of central government

New Labour's constitutional reform programme after their election in 1997 had a more fundamental impact on the organisation of UK central government. Devolution to Scotland and Wales inevitably reduced the role and importance of the secretaries of state for Scotland and Wales, and the Scottish and Welsh Office. (For more on devolution in the UK, see Chapter 11.) Most of the staff were transferred to the new Scottish and Welsh executives, while the ministerial posts were effectively downgraded, although David Cameron and Theresa May gave full Cabinet posts without additional responsibilities to the secretaries of state for Scotland, Wales and Northern Ireland, despite the ongoing transference of additional powers to their devolved governments. Yet the secretary of state for Northern Ireland has retained extensive administrative responsibilities – particularly as the Northern Ireland Assembly and Executive were frequently suspended (see Chapter 11 for more on this) – as well as a delicate political role in maintaining the impetus of the peace process. (Responsibility for policing was finally transferred in 2010.)

The Blair government's reorganisation of the Lord Chancellor's Department was more controversial. The original intention was simply to abolish the post, as part of a package of reforms, which included the introduction of a new Supreme Court, and a clearer separation of executive, legislative and judicial powers. A new Department for Constitutional Affairs was established, which in turn was swallowed up, along with some former Home Office responsibilities in the new Ministry of Justice in 2007. The title of Lord Chancellor is now combined with that of secretary of state for justice.

## THE CIVIL SERVICE SINCE 2010

The economic downturn in 2008 (discussed in more detail in Chapter 19) and the election in 2010 of a coalition government in Britain created new challenges for the Civil Service. The 2010 general election produced the first peacetime coalition since the 1930s, and the end of a long period of Labour administration. It involved a complete change of ministerial personnel and special advisers. However, the new government continued to work with most of the top civil servants who had served the Brown government. Some of the latter were perhaps more influential and others less so with the coalition government, depending on their own areas of expertise and their developing personal relations with new ministers. An additional problem, or perhaps opportunity, for top civil servants was having to work with ministers drawn from two parties. Although initially the new coalition team of ministers appeared particularly harmonious, there were inevitably some differences of emphasis arising from their respective party backgrounds.

There is an established tradition of top civil servants talking to the opposition before an election, as well as studying their manifesto and other available party policy documents, so as to enable the smooth transition, if the former opposition take office. However, the hung parliament and complex prolonged negotiations between the two opposition parties involved the ditching or delay of some Conservative commitments, the acceptance of some Lib Dem policies, and many compromises. Thus the new government's programme was not the same as that foreshadowed in the Conservative manifesto. Nor did the Lib Dem manifesto, to which civil servants paid little close attention until the party's surge in the election campaign, provide a reliable guide either. So civil servants were required to help implement a programme that was only cobbled together in the feverish days after the election. Yet the machinery of government managed the transition to a novel coalition calmly and without manifest difficulty.

Although coalition is unfamiliar at Westminster and Whitehall, it is the norm in most other western democracies, and there is ample experience of it elsewhere in the UK, in the devolved administrations in Scotland, Wales and Northern Ireland and in local government, and civil servants may have to get used to it, even though the 2015 election saw a, largely unanticipated, return to single-party government.

### *Civil Service Reform Plan*: a smaller civil service with a different role

In 2012, the coalition government announced its *Civil Service Reform Plan* (HM Government, 2012). It was set against the backdrop of the economic downturn and, like Thatcher's reforms a generation before, stressed the need for money-saving cuts to the size of the Civil Service. In this respect, the period from 2010 to 2015 was remarkably radical. The Civil Service shrank by around 90,000 jobs — almost 20% of its total size. By 2015, it was at its smallest since before the Second World War.

Moving staff to less expensive premises, often away from Whitehall and central London, also reduced costs.

The *Civil Service Reform Plan* also saw a rethink of the main functions of civil servants. It pointed out that 7 out of 10 civil servants work in 'operation delivery' – often in executive agencies – ranging from working at borders, administering pensions and benefits, to working in prisons and courts. Much earlier, the Fulton Report (1968) had noted a lack of expertise in the social sciences and science. Similarly, today's Civil Service also needs new skills. Public services are increasingly contracted out, normally to private sector organisations. The plan argued that the Civil Service needed more commercial and commissioning skills as it moves towards a model where civil servants commission more advice from alternative sources. Fewer civil servants were administering services directly.

The *Civil Service Reform Plan* also challenged another traditional role of Whitehall civil servants: offering policy advice to ministers. It advocated a move towards 'open policy-making', where ministers were not solely reliant on civil servants, but could seek policy advice from other sources, including academics, think tanks or consultancies. This opens up advice to ministers even further than had already occurred with the rise of special advisers. Taken together, these reforms constitute a radical attack on the traditional model of the Civil Service.

## Government, the Civil Service and the private sector

Governments since Thatcher not only imported some private sector ideas and techniques into the management of government, they also favoured advice from the business world, and additionally began recruiting those with business experience into the Civil Service and executive agencies on secondments, short-term contracts and more permanent appointments. Indeed, there seemed to be considerable advantages to both sides from these arrangements. The private sector found out more about government thinking, while the Civil Service could learn from hard-nosed practical business skills and experience. Yet some argue that the private sector has been the main winner from these exchanges between the Civil Service and the private sector.

Owen Jones (2015) argues that the big accounting firms 'were not simply offering governments their expertise: they were advising governments on tax law, and then telling their clients how to get around the laws they had themselves helped to draw up'. While the big four accounting firms claimed to be only providing 'technical advice', they gained a 'huge insight into the nature of Britain's tax laws' and 'a massive advantage when it comes to telling their clients how to get around the legislation' (Jones, 2015, pp. 212–13).

While ministers emphasise the benefits of the free market, critics allege that the reality is often extensive state subsidy of the private sector paid for out of taxation. Thus the Brown government felt obliged to bail out the banks that were considered 'too big to fail' with over a trillion pounds of public money. The government's continuing close relationship with the banking industry has been subjected to widespread parliamentary and media criticism. There are also extensive and rising state subsidies of those who now operate Britain's privatised rail system, and also large state subsidies for the arms industry. The former Conservative and UKIP MP Douglas Carswell is quoted by Jones (2015, p. 179) claiming that this was not capitalism but corporatism: 'It's big business and big government getting together and carving up a large slice of the economic pie for their advantage.' To such critics, both ministers and civil servants are no longer involved simply in the neutral regulation of the private sector, but are inextricably implicated in furthering business interests.

## 2015 onwards

Despite the departure of the Lib Dems, there was a marked element of continuity in the policy and personnel of the new Conservative government that took office in 2015. Indeed, not only was the same PM in charge, but the new Cabinet (minus the Lib Dems) was largely composed of the same politicians in the same jobs. Contingency preparations by civil servants for a government led by Ed Miliband, the then Labour leader, were immediately discarded. There was little need to adjust to serve new political masters with new ideas. Moreover, civil servants no longer had to satisfy ministers drawn from two parties. So, in some respects, for Britain's bureaucracy, it was back to normal. However, the problems facing the new Conservative government were as severe as those under the coalition. After a brief period of single-party normality under David Cameron, the Civil Service is now having to renegotiate and untangle its approach to policy as the UK pulls out of the EU – a scenario it had done little if any planning for before 2016. This was complicated after 2017 by a weakened minority government, relying on the support of the DUP to survive.

Robert Pyper and June Burnham (2011) have argued that there are two predominant characterisations of the British Civil Service. It is either in decline, overwhelmed by the challenges posed by the reforms and perhaps now by cuts to its size; or it is in the vanguard of adopting modernising reforms and adapting to new public service values. They argue that taking the long view shows that the British Civil Service has a long history of being 'progressively modernised' – becoming less corrupt, more accountable, more pluralist and more responsive to citizens' needs along the way. Pyper and Burnham conclude that civil servants have often been sceptical about the changes their political masters introduce, but nevertheless they do move with the times.

## THE IMPACT OF REFORMS ON KEY ATTRIBUTES OF THE CIVIL SERVICE

These reforms have affected some of the historical attributes of the UK Civil Service in important ways:

» *Permanence*: Traditionally, the Civil Service was a career service, characterised by security of tenure. The permanence of the Civil Service underpinned its public service ethos and commitment to impartial service of the government of the day. The majority of civil servants now work for executive agencies, which have substantial responsibility for recruitment, pay (sometimes involving an element of payment by results) and conditions. Approximately one-quarter of agency chief executives and some top civil service posts are appointed from outside the service, while ministers have appointed more special advisers to provide the policy advice formerly given by senior civil servants. Today, a unified, career civil service with a single hierarchical organisation, and common pay and conditions, no longer exists.

» *Neutrality*: In traditional theory, top civil servants are politically neutral, obliged to give ministers honest and impartial advice. However, the 1983 Armstrong Memorandum asserted that the Civil Service lacked 'constitutional personality or responsibility separate from the duly elected government of the day' (cited in Blick, 2016, Ch. 2, I.B) and stressed that the duty of the civil servant was first and foremost to the ministerial head of department (rather than Parliament or the public). This overriding duty of responsibility to a (party) government inevitably creates problems for their political neutrality. Critics argue that the Civil Service has become progressively politicised under recent governments, Conservative and Labour, who are accused of involving permanent civil servants in the promotion of policies for partisan objectives.

» *Anonymity*: Individual civil servants are increasingly named and blamed. Some of the chief executives who head the more controversial executive agencies attracted considerable media attention and, sometimes, personal criticism. They are also more directly accountable to Parliament and summoned for interrogation by departmental select committees. The idea that civil servants should remain anonymous was removed from the *Civil Service Code* in 2006.

## WHERE DOES POWER LIE?

How does this review of the main themes and issues concerning ministers and civil servants help us to answer the questions set out in the introduction to this chapter? Who has the power to make policy in the UK?

The constitutional position is that ministers make policy and civil servants implement it. Yet it has sometimes been argued that, in practice, senior civil servants have a much larger role in the making of British public policy and, indeed, are the real decision-makers. Ministers and civil servants, this argument runs, have an adversarial relationship, in which the latter have distinct advantages in terms of numbers, permanence, information, expertise and time. Ministers are often not well prepared for office, lacking time to learn on the job because of frequent Cabinet reshuffles, and have too many other parliamentary, party and constituency duties to concentrate fully on running their departments (see Spotlight 8.5). As we saw in the introduction, this notion of top civil servants as the real rulers of Britain might be termed the *Yes Minister* view of politics (Weir and Beetham, 1999, p. 167). Judging from the surprising success of sales of the 1980s series abroad, the theme evidently struck a chord in many other countries too.

## SPOTLIGHT ON ...

### Constraints on the effective power of ministers

8.5

» *Numbers*: Ministers are substantially outnumbered by leading civil servants.

» *Permanence*: Civil servants are permanent, while ministers are 'birds of passage' who change jobs frequently (average tenure of ministerial office since 1945 is just over two years). It takes ministers a lengthy period to master the business of their departments (according to Richard Crossman, postwar Labour minister, about 18 months) and during this time they are largely dependent on official briefings.

» *Weak preparation for office*: Few ministers, on taking office, have specialised knowledge of their departments, and frequent moves do not help them acquire expertise. Ministers rarely come to office with clearly defined policies, priorities or objectives. Unexpected situations that arise during their terms of office further increase their dependence on officials.

» *Ministerial workload*: Ministers face multiple demands upon their time – from Cabinet, Parliament, party, constituency and media, in addition to their departments; on average, they spend about two-thirds of their working week on responsibilities other than departmental matters.

» *Control of information*: Top civil servants retain substantial influence over information going before ministers, the way in which it is presented and its timing, all of which gives them a formidable capacity to shape decisions.

» *Coordinating role*: Both formally through official committees and through informal contacts with their opposite numbers in other departments, top civil servants prepare and, to a varying extent, predetermine the work of ministers.

» *Implementation*: Civil servants can employ a variety of tactics to thwart implementation of policy, including delays and finding practical difficulties.

Ironically, the *Yes Minister* take on the relationship between ministers and civil servants acquired widespread acceptance in Britain at a time when the power and influence of civil servants was already under sustained attack, particularly from the Thatcher government (see above). In recent decades, ministers, both individually and collectively, appear to have increased capacity to control policy-making, partly as a result of the growing numbers of special advisers, appointed by politicians, who often break the monopoly of advice traditionally held by civil servants. Indeed, the reality has always been more complicated than the simple adversarial view of the minister–civil servant relationship portrayed in *Yes Minister*. In a world of complex government often wrestling with intractable problems, the relationship has become more interdependent; civil servants may find strong ministers not only more interesting to work for, they are also more likely to be successful in fighting the department's battles in Cabinet and Cabinet committees (this classic view was set out by Bruce Headey, 1974, pp. 140 ff.).

There is no simple answer to the question of who rules, ministers or top officials. Government today is far more complex. It no longer consists of a set number of great Whitehall departments, each headed by a minister and a permanent secretary. Instead, it has evolved into a mosaic of departments,

executive agencies, cross-cutting units and task forces, often operating at different levels of government, from the local to the European. Recent research has shown that, to get things done, there have to be trade-offs and alliances built across departments, with more give and take on all sides (Rhodes, 1997, 2015; Bevir and Rhodes, 2003). The key personnel may include not only elected politicians and career civil servants, but also many other appointed public officials, special advisers, as well as representatives of powerful outside interests who have the ear of ministers. Government is in a constant state of flux, so that the real movers and shakers at any one point of time may no longer be influential soon afterwards. A civil servant as powerful and long-serving as *Yes Minister*'s Sir Humphrey Appleby would appear only in fiction today.

 **SUMMARY**

» Traditionally, the bulk of decisions made by central government were made in departments, by ministers and civil servants, rather than by the Cabinet. This has been changing with, among other things, the move to 'joined-up government', which cuts across departments.

» Most departments are based on the function or service principle, although there is no single coherent rational principle behind the structure of central government. Departments have been frequently reorganised for a mixture of administrative, political and personal reasons.

» Departments are headed by politicians, usually a secretary of state and several junior ministers. They are staffed by civil servants. The most senior civil servants who advise ministers are permanent secretaries.

» The traditional characteristics of the British Civil Service include permanence, neutrality and anonymity, although changes over the past 40 years call much of this into question.

» Although women and ethnic minorities are well represented among the Civil Service as a whole, they are underrepresented among senior civil servants, whose social and educational background remains restricted in other ways.

» The unrepresentative character of the Civil Service may influence their outlook. Although it is generally conceded that senior civil servants do not show a party bias, it is sometimes argued they show other forms of bias.

» The Civil Service has been extensively reformed over the past 40 years, along the lines of the new public management (NPM). This has involved a reduction in size, administrative decentralisation and increased competition. Senior civil servants are expected to concentrate more on the management of departments and agencies and the delivery of services rather than advice to ministers.

» Renewed concern over ethical standards, prompted by scandals in the 1990s, led to the formalisation of principles and codes of practice for both ministers and civil servants.

» The Blair and Brown governments largely maintained previous Conservative reforms but emphasised the need for increased coordination and cooperation ('joined-up government') alongside competition.

» The rise in numbers and importance of special advisers to ministers and the implications for the responsibilities of career civil servants have raised some concerns.

» Although civil servants unusually had to serve ministers drawn from two parties in the 2010–15 administration, this seemed to cause few problems. There was already extensive experience of working with coalitions in other countries, and some precedents also in UK local and devolved government.

» The Civil Service is in a new stage of reform. There are now around 400,000 civil servants, geographically dispersed around the UK, although the majority of senior civil servants continue to work in London. The number of civil servants fell rapidly under the Conservative government of 1979–97, stabilised under New Labour, and has fallen again since 2010. Government is increasingly opening up policy advice to new sources – including academics, think tanks and consultancies – which challenges the traditional Civil Service advisory role.

» There is no easy answer to the question, where does power lie, ministers or civil servants? The relationship is often more collaborative than competitive. Permanent civil servants may have ceded some influence to ministers and special advisers, but government has become more complex, shifting and multilayered, so generalisations are difficult.

## ? QUESTIONS FOR DISCUSSION

» Why are government departments so frequently reorganised in Britain?

» How far is the higher Civil Service unrepresentative? Does it matter? How might it be made more representative?

» In what ways, if at all, might senior civil servants show bias?

» How far are senior civil servants in Britain suitably qualified for the work they are required to do?

» In what ways have changes introduced into central government and the Civil Service over the past 40 years affected the traditional permanence, neutrality and anonymity of senior civil servants?

» How is the principle of individual ministerial responsibility upheld in practice? Who is responsible for policy failure? For what reasons are ministers obliged to resign?

» How far are senior civil servants the real rulers of Britain?

» Should ministers be reliant on civil servants for policy advice? Or should ministers be turning to academics, think tanks and consultancies?

## FURTHER READING

For some recent debates, see Massey (ed.) (2011) *International Handbook on Civil Service Systems*. On the history of the Civil Service, see Hennessy (1990) *Whitehall* and Lowe (2011) *The Official History of the British Civil Service: Reforming the Civil Service, Volume I: The Fulton Years, 1966–81*. In *Everyday Life in British Government* (2015), Rhodes uncovers the everyday life of ministers and civil servants, to try to understand how the British political elite thinks and acts. For the emerging role of special advisers, Yong and Hazell's (2014) *Special Advisers: Who They Are, What They Do and Why They Matter* discusses the recent debates.

## USEFUL WEBSITES

The government's official site on the Civil Service contains a range of important documents: www.gov.uk/government/organisations/civil-service.

The Institute for Government carries out important work on the effectiveness and composition of the Civil Service, as well as

analysing contemporary changes: www.instituteforgovernment.org.uk.

The Constitution Unit at University College, London runs a government research programme that looks at, among other things, ministers and special advisers: www.ucl.ac.uk/constitution-unit.

*Further student resources to support learning are available at*
**www.macmillanihe.com/griffiths-brit-pol-3e**

# 9 THE LAW, THE STATE AND THE JUDICIAL PROCESS

In 2016, Gina Miller, a wealthy British investment manager, brought a private case before the High Court, arguing that the government's plans for Britain to leave the European Union should not go ahead without the support of a majority in Parliament. Three judges agreed and were immediately vilified by much of the popular press and some politicians for appearing to thwart 'the will of the people' in the June referendum. 'Judges vs the people' was the headline in *The Daily Telegraph*. The government immediately declared that it would appeal against the decision to the Supreme Court. Others, however, strongly criticised the PM and the Lord Chancellor for not defending the crucial principle of judicial independence.

The case reflected the tensions between executive, legislature and judiciary in the British system. Miller was, in effect, using the law to uphold the constitutional principle of parliamentary government. Parliament, as the legislature, must be allowed a vote on whether the UK remained part of the EU; it could not just be a decision made by the executive on the basis of a referendum. Miller's legal success meant that the government had to go back to Parliament to gain its explicit support for leaving the EU. The final stages of that bill passed in March 2017.

Some maintain that the executive, legislative and judicial functions of the states should be kept strictly separate. While this separation of powers has been enforced, as far as practicable, in some state constitutions (notably the US Constitution), in Britain the executive and legislature have long been interdependent. Moreover, although there is a clear assumption that government and Parliament should not interfere with judges and the judicial process, there was no clear separation of powers here either. On the contrary, until very recently, the Lord Chancellor was not only the head of the judiciary but a leading member of the Cabinet (the executive) and also presided over the proceedings of the House of Lords (the 'upper chamber' of the legislature). However, constitutional reforms, first announced in

2003, involved the introduction of a separate Supreme Court, which was finally established in 2009. Changes in the system for appointing judges and the reform of the office of Lord Chancellor were also intended to re-emphasise the independence of the judiciary from both the executive and legislature.

These reforms seemed to involve a significant shift in constitutional theory and practice. They appeared to separate the administration of the law further from government and politics. However, in Britain the law and politics remain closely interrelated. The language of the law and legal concepts permeate the theory and practice of politics. Lawyers still play a leading role in government and Parliament, and figure prominently in public bureaucracies and business. Court judgments can have significant political consequences, affecting governments and the lives of ordinary people, particularly following the substantial growth in the practice of judicial review of executive decisions. Judges themselves continue to wield considerable power and influence, not just through the courts but in politics and government generally, and questions can and perhaps should be asked about their social and educational background and their personal and political views. These are among the issues that we seek to address in this chapter.

Questions can also be asked about the efficiency and effectiveness of the judicial system in Britain. Does it deliver justice, fairly, quickly and reasonably economically? How might it be improved? There are other vital questions about the protection of human rights and civil liberties in Britain, and the effectiveness of the various channels for securing redress of grievances against the state and public authorities. Finally, there are also important issues surrounding the enforcement of law and the pursuit of prosecutions by the police.

## THIS CHAPTER:

»  Examines the concept of the 'rule of law', one of the most important principles in the British and other constitutions.

»  Discusses human rights and how our human rights are protected by the European Convention on Human Rights.

»  Explores how the law protects civil liberties and provides redress when things go wrong.

»  Assesses the development of English, Scottish and European law, and the structure of the court system.

»  Looks at the judiciary, the judicial system and the police, and asks who provides these services and what background they are from.

## THE RULE OF LAW

The **rule of law** has long been considered one of the fundamental principles of the unwritten (or uncodified) British constitution. It has, however, been variously interpreted over time. Today, the rule of law involves a number of assumptions, although each of these involves some qualifications or raises additional questions (as discussed in Table 9.1 overleaf).

---

*The **rule of law** is the principle that no one is above the law. The principle is intended to guard against arbitrary government.*

---

Law is conventionally subdivided into a number of categories, such as criminal, civil

Table 9.1 The rule of law

| The principle | Explanation | Qualification |
|---|---|---|
| Everyone is bound by the law | No one is above the law. Ministers and public officials are subject to the law and have no authority to act beyond the powers conferred on them by law – the ultra vires principle | British ministers are in a strong position to change the law because of executive dominance of the parliamentary legislative process, coupled with the traditional principles of parliamentary sovereignty and the supremacy of statute law (discussed in Chapter 6) |
| All persons are equal before the law | All citizens have legal rights and can have recourse to the law, which is supposed to treat all citizens on an equal basis | There are some doubts over equality before the law in practice. One cynical judge at the turn of the twentieth century commented that: 'In England, justice is open to all, like the Ritz Hotel' (cited in Hayes, 2010, p. 29). Legal proceedings can be expensive, and although legal aid is available for those with limited means, it is restricted (e.g. it is not available for libel cases). Some would also argue that the law in practice has systematically favoured property owners and established interests |
| Law and order must be maintained | The state has a monopoly on the legitimate use of force within its borders. Citizens should be protected from violence, theft and disorder, but should be restrained, forcibly if necessary, from taking the law into their own hands | The maintenance of law and order may lead to restrictions on individual liberty. Emergencies may involve limits on freedom of movement and detention of suspects without trial. Recently, the rise of Islamic fundamentalism has been used to justify restrictions on civil liberties, particularly after the London bombings of July 2005, when four suicide bombers with rucksacks full of explosives killed 52 people and injured hundreds more on public transport in London |
| Legal redress must be provided | Anyone with complaints against the state, public bodies or government is provided with a way of seeking compensation | Doubts are still expressed over the effectiveness of some of these remedies (see below) |
| The law, legal processes and personnel should be independent and free from political interference | The courts are generally reckoned to be free from political pressures in practice. Labour's Constitutional Reform Act 2005 was supposed to establish more formally the separation of powers and the independence of the judiciary (see below) | Judges still complain about the interference of politicians, particularly over judicial sentencing and, more recently, over constitutional issues (see below) |

and administrative. In Britain, these involve distinctive terms and procedures:

» *Criminal law* provides standards of conduct as well as institutions (police, courts system) for dealing with those who commit *crimes*. Crimes are normally classified as against the state (treason, public order), against the person (murder, assault, rape), and against property (robbery, malicious damage). A successful *prosecution* in a criminal case leads to a *sentence* (e.g. fine, imprisonment, community service, probation).

» *Civil law* is concerned with the legal relations between persons. Normally, proceedings in a civil court depend upon a *plaintiff* pursuing an *action* against a *defendant* and they generally result in some *remedy*, such as damages, specific performance (where the defendant has to keep his side of the bargain), or a 'declaration' of the plaintiff's legal rights. While cases in criminal law have to be proved 'beyond reasonable doubt', actions in civil law are decided on the 'balance of probabilities'.

» *Administrative law* is the set of general principles that govern the exercise of duties and powers by any public authorities. Administrative law is more systematically developed in Continental Europe. (It is discussed in much more detail below.) However, this sphere of law has grown considerably in Britain over the past century, with the growth of the welfare state and public services, which we explore more fully in the last part of the chapter. A variety of judicial and quasi-judicial institutions (the ordinary courts, tribunals, the ombudsman) apply a framework of rules within which public authorities act. Administrative law is particularly involved in citizen rights and the redress of grievances.

## CIVIL LIBERTIES AND HUMAN RIGHTS

The hallmark of a liberal democratic state, it is often said, is the effectiveness with which a range of basic citizen rights or civil liberties is guaranteed. These rights or liberties have long been enthusiastically extolled by British people, and it is vital, therefore, to examine to what extent this confidence in the security of such rights is justified. Virtually all British civil liberties stem from a fundamental principle: that people may do what they like, so long as no law prevents them. Legal protections against infringements of this fundamental freedom in specific instances (e.g. freedom of expression, meeting, association and so on) have been established gradually throughout British history, and many commentators trace their roots back to the *Magna Carta* of 1215 (see Spotlight 9.1 on p. 173). Civil liberties were not codified or enshrined in any particular statute until the 1998 Human Rights Act, which came into force in 2000. Table 9.2 outlines some of the main civil rights that have been established in the UK and notes their limitations.

---

**Civil liberties** *are the political liberties (or freedoms) that must be available to us, in order for us to be able to say that we live in a society that adheres to the principle of representative, or democratic, government.*

---

**Habeas corpus** *is, among other things, the legal principle guaranteeing trial before the law.*

---

### Table 9.2 Civil rights established over centuries in the UK (and some limitations)

| The right | Explanation | Limitations |
| --- | --- | --- |
| Political rights | Includes the right to vote, guaranteed by the Representation of the People Acts 1918, 1928, 1948, 1969 | In general elections, the right to vote is not extended to people who are under 18, not British citizens, prisoners and anyone recently convicted of electoral corruption |

*(Continued)*

| The right | Explanation | Limitations |
|---|---|---|
| Freedom of movement | Includes the right to move freely within, and the right to leave, Britain. The Free Movement Directive of the European Parliament gives rights to move freely for citizens of the EU within EU (and some other) countries | But note powers to detain suspected terrorists, and police powers to stop and search on suspicion |
| Personal freedom | Includes freedom from detention without charge (*Magna Carta*, 1215, **habeas corpus** legislation in eighteenth century). Also guaranteed by the UK decision to sign the European Convention on Human Rights (ECHR) | There are exceptions, especially detention without charge in Northern Ireland and, more recently, for suspected terrorists in Britain |
| Freedom of conscience | Includes the right to practise any religion, the right of parents to withdraw children from religious instruction in state schools, and the right to conscientious objection to conscription into the armed forces | |
| Freedom of expression | Includes the rights of individuals and the media to communicate information and express opinions. Protected by Article 10 of the ECHR | Freedom of expression is limited by laws on treason, sedition, blasphemy, obscenity, libel, incitement to racial hatred, defamation, contempt of court and the Official Secrets Act |
| Freedom of association and meeting | Includes the right to meet, march and protest freely. Protected by Article 11 of the ECHR | Some restrictions by police etc. on public order grounds, and restrictions on 'secondary picketing' in industrial disputes |
| Right to property | Includes the right to property and to use it, and not be deprived of it without due process | Compulsory purchase orders, planning restrictions etc. |
| Right to privacy | A general right to privacy is contained in Article 8 of the ECHR, now incorporated into UK law through the 1998 Human Rights Act | There are exceptions in interests of state security, which is used to justify political surveillance, phone tapping etc. |
| Rights at work | Includes protection against unfair dismissal, the right to a satisfactory working environment, and freedom from racial and sexual discrimination: all embodied in a series of Acts of Parliament and the Social Chapter of the Maastricht Treaty | |
| Social freedoms | Includes freedom to marry and divorce, to practise contraception and seek abortions, to practise homosexuality between consenting adults: contained in several postwar Acts of Parliament and the ECHR | |

## SPOTLIGHT ON ...    Over 800 years of the *Magna Carta*    9.1

The *Magna Carta* (or Great Charter) was agreed by the English King John, at Runnymede on 15 June 1215. It was meant to bring peace between the King and his rebellious barons. It promised church rights, trial by jury and habeas corpus – protection from illegal imprisonment – for the barons, as well as limiting the king's demands for tax. Neither the King nor his barons stood by their commitments, and the treaty was soon annulled by the pope, leading to civil war in England.

After John's death, his son Henry III reissued the document. It formed part of the peace treaty agreed at Lambeth, London, ending the 'first baron's war'. His son Edward I renewed it once more in 1297, confirming it in statute law.

In the late sixteenth century, there was a renewed interest in *Magna Carta*. Historians and lawyers claimed that it was the essential basis for the powers of Parliament, and for legal principles such as preventing trial without justice. It was also used to argue against the divine right of monarchs. The political myth of *Magna Carta* later influenced the US Constitution. The charter became, rather late on, a symbol of English freedom against the despotic rule of the monarchy.

*Magna Carta* is still an important symbol of liberty to this day. It is cited by politicians and campaigners as a symbol of 'Britishness', despite its English origins. The year 2015 marked the 800th anniversary of the charter and a renewed interest in the document, now taking on a new life as an inspiration for constitutional reform through the UK (Hazell and Melton, 2015; Atkins, 2015).

---

Civil liberties and human rights are sometimes seen as opposite sides of the same coin. On some accounts, a civil liberty is generally expressed in negative ways: it is a freedom from interference in your rights – for example freedom from arbitrary arrest. A right, by contrast, is often expressed as something you are entitled to from someone else: in that sense, it is 'positive' – for example the right to health through a good health service. Human rights are generally also expressed in much broader terms than civil liberties. The European Convention on Human Rights (ECHR), for example, protects the 'Right to liberty and security'. Table 9.3 lists the rights available under the ECHR and its Protocols.

---

*The* European Convention on Human Rights (ECHR) *was drafted in 1950 and came into force in 1953. It protects the human rights and fundamental freedoms of people in countries that belong to the Council of Europe. The Council of Europe (founded 1949) has 47 member states, 28 of which are EU members. Membership is open to any European country, provided they meet specific democratic and human rights standards.*

---

*The* European Court of Human Rights (ECtHR), *based in Strasbourg, France is a supranational or international court established by the ECHR. It has jurisdiction to decide complaints ('applications') submitted by individuals and states concerning violations of the ECHR in any of the signatory nations. It currently has 47 member states, including many that are not part of the EU, such as Russia, Switzerland and Norway.*

---

The UK ratified the ECHR in 1951 and allowed individuals to petition it from 1966. The European Court of Human Rights (ECtHR) has the jurisdiction to decide complaints ('applications') submitted by individuals and states concerning ECHR violations. (It is not to be confused with the European Court of Justice, discussed in Chapter 12.) It has long played a part in upholding and enlarging civil liberties in Britain. However, although the UK government normally complied with ECtHR judgments, these rights were not enforceable in British law for many years, because the UK did not incorporate the ECHR into British law.

This changed in 1998, when the Labour government passed a Human Rights Act, which came into force in 2000 (Wadham, 1999; Lester and Clapinska, 2004; Wadham et al., 2007). This means that British citizens who consider that their rights have been infringed are now able to take their cases to British courts rather than to the ECtHR in Strasbourg. The Act makes it illegal for public authorities to act in a way incompatible with the ECHR (see Tables 9.3 and 9.4).

In theory, the Human Rights Act preserves parliamentary sovereignty. Judges do not have

**Table 9.3 Summary of selected articles from the ECHR**

| | |
|---|---|
| Article 1 | Obligation to respect human rights |
| Article 2 | Right to life |
| Article 3 | Prohibition of torture |
| Article 4 | Prohibition of slavery and forced labour |
| Article 5 | Right to liberty and security [i.e., if you are arrested, you have the right to know why. If you are arrested or detained, you have the right to stand trial soon, or to be released until the trial takes place] |
| Article 6 | Right to a fair trial |
| Article 7 | No punishment without law |
| Article 8 | Right to respect for private and family life |
| Article 9 | Freedom of thought, conscience and religion |
| Article 10 | Freedom of expression |
| Article 11 | Freedom of assembly and association |
| Article 12 | Right to marry |
| Article 13 | Right to an effective remedy |
| Article 14 | Prohibition of discrimination [i.e., you have these rights regardless of your skin colour, sex, language, political or religious beliefs, or origins] |
| Article 15 | Derogation in time of emergency [i.e., in time of war or other public emergency, a government may do things that go against your rights, but only when strictly necessary] |
| Article 16 | Restrictions on political activity of aliens [i.e., governments may restrict the political activity of foreigners, even if this would conflict with other articles] |
| Article 17 | Prohibition of abuse of rights [i.e., nothing in this Convention can be used to damage the rights and freedoms in the Convention] |
| Article 18 | Limitation on use of restrictions of rights |
| Articles 19 to 51 | These articles explain how the European Court of Human Rights works |

*Source*: Full text of European Convention on Human Rights available at www.echr.coe.int/Documents/Convention_ENG.pdf

### Table 9.4 Selected Protocols to the ECHR

| | |
|---|---|
| Article 1, Protocol No. 1 | Protection of property [i.e. you have the right to own property and use your possessions] |
| Article 2, Protocol No. 1 | Right to education |
| Article 3, Protocol No. 1 | Right to free elections |
| Article 2, Protocol No. 4 | Freedom of movement [i.e., if you are lawfully within a country, you have the right to go where you want and to live where you want within it] |
| Article 1, Protocol No. 6 | Abolition of the death penalty |
| Article 2, Protocol No. 7 | Right of appeal in criminal matters |
| Article 3, Protocol No. 7 | Compensation for wrongful conviction |
| Article 1, Protocol No. 12 | General prohibition of discrimination [i.e., you cannot be discriminated against by public authorities for reasons of, for example, your skin colour, sex, language, political or religious beliefs, or origins] |

*Source*: Full text of European Convention on Human Rights available at www.echr.coe.int/Documents/Convention_ENG.pdf

the power to strike down Acts of Parliament (as they do in Canada, for example). Instead, they are able to declare a law 'incompatible with the Convention', which should prompt the government and Parliament to change the law through new fast-track procedures. However, Bogdanor (2001, pp. 146–8) argues that the Act 'alters considerably the balance between Parliament and the judiciary' and enables judges 'to interpret parliamentary legislation in terms of a higher law, the European Convention'. The Human Rights Act had some significant immediate implications for British politics and law; some of the more significant decisions are set out in Spotlight 9.2.

On top of this, the UK is increasingly influenced by international law and conventions. Thus critics of the Iraq War argued that it was illegal under international law without clear UN authorisation. The attorney general, a member of the government and its official legal adviser, eventually declared that the war was legal, although it was alleged that the short published version of his advice omitted qualifications and reservations indicated in an earlier longer judgement. It remains a

*Source*: Nikini Jayatunga

Do you have a right to demonstrate your private beliefs in public? For example, is it acceptable to wear religious symbols in a public job?

contentious issue, and is examined further below. However, even after the UK does finally leave the EU, there is nothing to suggest that it will leave the European Court of Human Rights. All of this has meant that the judiciary has been accused of becoming increasingly active, and less subordinate to the executive and Parliament (see Spotlight 9.3 on p. 177).

**SPOTLIGHT ON ...**

## Some European Court of Human Rights rulings that have affected the UK

9.2

The Strasbourg-based European Court of Human Rights (ECtHR) rules on cases brought by citizens from any one of the Council of Europe's 47 member states, who accuse their own country of violating one of the fundamental rights laid down in the European Convention on Human Rights (ECHR).

| Religious discrimination | *Eweida* v. the *United Kingdom* [2013] ECHR 37 | 15 January 2013 | The ECtHR ruled in favour of Nadia Eweida, 60, who took her employer British Airways to court for forcing her to stop wearing a cross around her neck. Lawyers for the government, which contested the claim, argued that her right to freedom of thought, conscience and religion had not been violated. But ECHR judges disagreed by five votes to two | Breaches of Article 9 or 14 |
|---|---|---|---|---|
| Abu Qatada | *Othman (Abu Qatada)* v. *The United Kingdom* [2012] ECHR 56 | 17 January 2012 | The ECtHR blocked the deportation of radical cleric Abu Qatada to Jordan, because of fears that evidence obtained under torture would be used against him in his home country. The ruling, based on the right to a fair trial, forced the then Home Secretary Theresa May to agree a new treaty with Jordan, guaranteeing him a free trial. This eventually convinced the court to allow his deportation in July 2013 | Risk of unfair trial through admission of evidence obtained by torture: breach of Article 6 |
| Prisoners' votes | *Hirst* v. *The United Kingdom* (No. 2) [2005] ECHR 681 | 6 October 2005 | The ECtHR ruled that banning prisoners from voting – in the UK and in other countries – was a breach of their human rights and unlawful. Parliament has so far resisted implementing the ruling | Breach of Article 3 of Protocol No.1 |
| Gay rights | *Dudgeon* v. *The United Kingdom* [1981] ECHR 5 | 22 October 1981 | The ECtHR decriminalised male gay sex in Northern Ireland as a result of a case brought by Jeff Dudgeon, who was interrogated about his sexual behaviour by the Royal Ulster Constabulary police force | Breach of Article 8 |

*Source*: European Court of Human Rights, http://hudoc.echr.coe.int/

# SPOTLIGHT ON ...

## Judicial activism

9.3

The claim that judges are taking an increasingly active political role is common. They seem more prepared than ever before to challenge Parliament and the executive. The term 'judicial activism' is often contrasted with 'judicial restraint', where judges limit the exercise of their own power and only strike down laws if they are obviously unconstitutional. Judicial restraint seemed to have been the norm in the UK from the 1880s to the 1960s (Malleson, 2016, Ch. 2).

Judicial activism has often meant that the judiciary finds itself in conflict with Parliament or the executive. For some politicians, this is a serious concern. Michael Howard (2005), leader of the Conservative Party from 2003 to 2005 and a former barrister, argued that 'aggressive judicial activism' could put the country's safety at risk, and undermine public faith in the justice system. Howard cited the Law Lords' decision in 2004 that the indefinite detention without trial of foreign terror suspects under the 2001 Anti-Terrorism Act contravened the Human Rights Act, and referred to the difficulties the latter Act creates for deporting extremists. To Howard, Parliament must be supreme. In the UK, the principle of parliamentary sovereignty should mean that Parliament, not the judiciary, can make, unmake and amend law – a constitutional principle set out in Chapter 6.

Two important developments help explain the rise in 'judicial activism'. First, there has been a staggering rise in the number of cases being brought to judicial review, in which citizens can apply to the courts if they object to a decision of the state, public bodies and officials. As citizens, we seem more confident to challenge government than ever before (Griffiths et al., 2009). For example, in 1981, there were under 600 cases of judicial review. By 2013, there were 15,600, the majority of which were on immigration issues. Some of these cases have led to a change in government policy. For example, Michael Gove, the former education secretary, was found to have acted unlawfully by a judge in failing to consult local authorities when he decided to abolish the Building Schools for the Future programme (Shepherd, 2011).

A second reason for the rise in judicial activism is the introduction of the Human Rights Act in 1998, which incorporated the ECHR into UK law. This represented a major constitutional reform, because it codified a set of individual rights in UK law. This gave the judiciary greater powers to protect civil liberties and check executive power. Several cases have demonstrated the potential for the Human Rights Act to generate conflict between the judiciary, Parliament and the executive. Perhaps the most controversial cases have involved disputes over deportation of religious fundamentalists, such as Abu Qatada. (Some key cases are summarised in Spotlight 9.2.)

Despite these public conflicts, the judiciary in the UK is still subordinate to Parliament and the executive. Judges in Germany or the USA, for example, where there is a much stricter separation of powers, have more authority. (See Chapter 5 for more on the separation of powers.) In both countries, human rights and civil liberties are protected by the constitution, which has a higher status than ordinary law. Because of this, the constitution can significantly constrain the executive. In the UK, by contrast, if the judiciary challenges a piece of legislation using the Human Rights Act, it can only make a 'declaration of incompatibility'. This simply sends the legislation back to Parliament for revision; it does not dismiss it. Despite this, judicial activism, as the introduction to this chapter on Gina Miller shows, does not seem to be going away (Malleson, 2016, Ch. 2).

*Source*: Dan Kitwood/Getty Images News/Getty Images

In 2016, Gina Miller successfully used the law to force the government to put the decision to leave the EU before Parliament.

## THE UK'S LEGAL SYSTEMS

There are three distinct legal jurisdictions in the United Kingdom: England and Wales, Northern Ireland and Scotland. The English and Welsh legal and judicial system differs markedly from that prevailing over most of Continental Europe. While continental law is generally based on written codes deriving ultimately from Roman law, English and Welsh law is based on common law, assumed to be the immemorial but uncodified law of the English people, and declared by judges in court cases. Thus common law is essentially contained in decisions on past cases, which are binding on subsequent cases of a similar nature. Although judges are theoretically only *declaring* the law, they can, in effect, make new law, particularly when new circumstances arise. However, statute law is supreme over common law, so the law made by Parliament (and largely initiated by the government) overrides judge-made case law.

Within the UK there are marked differences. The greatest difference is between the English and Welsh systems and the Scottish one, which predates the 1707 Act of Union between England and Scotland. In contrast with English and Welsh law, Scottish law is more like Continental European law, influenced by Roman law and involves distinctive principles and practice and a separate system of administration. Although Scottish law, like English and Welsh law, remains bound by the theoretical sovereignty of the Westminster Parliament, the devolution of legislative powers to the new Scottish Parliament has already led to some further significant divergences between English and Scottish law, and these differences seem likely to become more marked over time. Northern Ireland has a third system, with its own court system, dating from the partition of Ireland in 1921. In practice, this has led to different laws, with abortion, for example, still illegal in almost all cases in Northern Ireland, but not the rest of the UK.

## THE JUDICIAL SYSTEM

The orthodox view is that the judicial system is impartial, symbolised by the iconic figure of Justice above the Central Criminal Court (the Old Bailey). Judges balance the scales of justice fairly, without fear or favour (Gee et al., 2015). The acknowledged impartiality of the judiciary legitimises the whole administration of justice in the UK. Moreover, judges are also sometimes seen as stout defenders of the rights and freedoms of citizens against arbitrary and unjustified acts by governments and public authorities. The growth of judicial review over the past half-century or so (see below) provides some support for this perspective. The 1998 Human Rights Act has provided further opportunities for judicial intervention against government.

Yet critics argue that judges are almost inevitably biased in their attitudes and decisions because of the kind of people they are. While they may strive earnestly to appear impartial, their own highly restricted and exclusive social background is almost bound to affect their assumptions and outlook, which is inevitably conservative with a small 'c' and, critics allege, generally with a large 'C' too (Griffith, 1997). More disquietingly, judges sometimes appear more sympathetic to white-collar criminals than their working-class counterparts and have, on occasion, demonstrated racism and sexism.

Governments are now committed to increased diversity within the judiciary, although this was not made explicit in the 2005 Constitutional Reform Act. By contrast, the Scottish and Northern Ireland commissions for appointing judges were required to bring about a judiciary more reflective and representative of the community, and less overwhelmingly male and white. Although it could be argued that juries composed of 'ordinary' citizens provide protection against the (perhaps largely unconscious) bias of an unrepresentative judiciary, jury trials in which a jury of randomly selected citizens makes a decision or findings of fact, which directs the actions of a judge, are only used in a minority of cases, and there are proposals to restrict their use still further.

Trial by jury was enshrined as a principle in 1215 in *Magna Carta* and is still widely regarded as an important right and the essence of a 'fair trial' (see Spotlight 9.1). Yet most trials no longer involve a jury. Jury trials are expensive and time-consuming, not least for those summoned for jury service. Indeed, it is sometimes alleged that juries no longer represent a fair cross-section of the community because some of those who are summoned successfully plead to be excused. In criminal cases, many police believe jury trials lead to more acquittals of defendants they 'know' are guilty. There are also cases where jurors have been threatened or intimidated. It is sometimes argued that juries are not competent to decide on complex legal issues, such as fraud cases. Anecdotal evidence suggests that the deliberations of some juries may involve a muddled compromise between diametrically opposed gut reactions of individual jurors, even if most of the time juries seem to follow the guidance of the judge. Juries can sometimes show an obstinate independence and perhaps more common sense than legal experts, so the declining use of juries remains a concern.

### The courts

The UK system of courts is complicated. Scotland and Northern Ireland have their own rather different court systems. Most of what follows applies particularly to England and Wales (see Figure 9.1). Minor criminal cases are tried without a jury in magistrates' courts. More

*Source*: iStock.com/TonyBaggett

Justice, with her scales weighing up the truth, above the Old Bailey criminal court in London.

serious criminal cases for 'indictable' offences, as well as appeals from the magistrates' courts, are heard in the Crown Court before a judge and jury (unless the defendant pleads guilty, which is often the case, when a jury is not required). Appeals from conviction in the Crown Court are usually to the Criminal Division of the Court of Appeal. A further appeal on a point of law may be allowed to the Supreme Court, which became operative in 2009 (formerly, appeals were made to the House of Lords, sitting as a court).

A few minor civil cases are heard in magistrates' courts but most minor cases are heard by county courts. More important cases are heard in the High Court, which is split into three divisions – Queen's Bench Division, dealing with common law, Chancery Division, dealing with equity, and the Family Division, dealing with domestic cases. Appeals from lower courts are heard in the appropriate division of the High Court. Appeals from the High Court can be made to the Civil Division of the Court of Appeal, and from there to the new Supreme Court (see Figure 9.1).

Figure 9.1: The system of courts in England and Wales

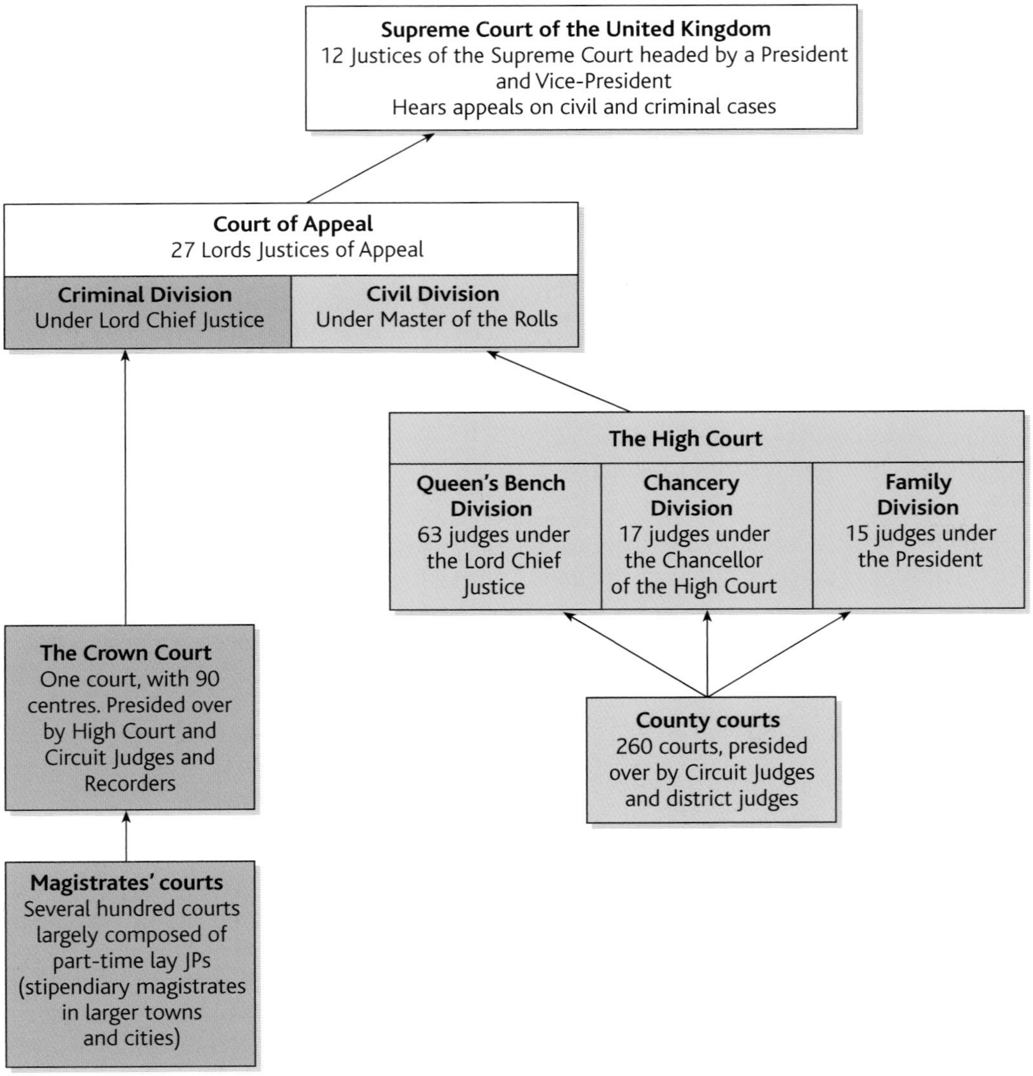

**Supreme Court of the United Kingdom**
12 Justices of the Supreme Court headed by a President and Vice-President
Hears appeals on civil and criminal cases

**Court of Appeal**
27 Lords Justices of Appeal

| **Criminal Division** | **Civil Division** |
| Under Lord Chief Justice | Under Master of the Rolls |

**The High Court**

| **Queen's Bench Division** | **Chancery Division** | **Family Division** |
| 63 judges under the Lord Chief Justice | 17 judges under the Chancellor of the High Court | 15 judges under the President |

**The Crown Court**
One court, with 90 centres. Presided over by High Court and Circuit Judges and Recorders

**County courts**
260 courts, presided over by Circuit Judges and district judges

**Magistrates' courts**
Several hundred courts largely composed of part-time lay JPs (stipendiary magistrates in larger towns and cities)

## Recent reforms to the justice system

Until the Constitutional Reform Act 2005, the head of the judicial system had long been the Lord Chancellor, a political appointment, who was also the presiding officer in the upper house of the legislature (the House of Lords) and a full member of the Cabinet. The most important judges, besides the Lord Chancellor, were the Law Lords (or Lords of Appeal in Ordinary), appointed by the Crown on the advice of the PM, specifically to exercise the judicial functions of the House of Lords. Other judges were appointed by the Crown, on the advice of the Lord Chancellor, which made those appointments appear subject to political influence. This entanglement of the judicial functions of the state with its executive and legislative functions appeared thoroughly confusing and even downright dangerous to critics familiar with the stricter separation of powers in other constitutions (see Chapter 5 for more on the separation of powers). Although many commentators in the UK conceded that, in practice, the judiciary was independent and largely free from political interference, the unreformed system did not guarantee the principle of judicial independence. The Constitutional Reform Act 2005 created the Judicial Appointments Commission, an independent commission that proposes a candidate, over which the secretary of state for justice has a veto.

---

*Judicial independence is the constitutional principle that in order to protect individual freedom, the judiciary should be independent from the other branches of government, the executive and the legislature.*

---

The Constitutional Reform Act 2005 also announced the transfer of the judicial functions of the House of Lords to a new Supreme Court. The former Law Lords would no longer sit in the House of Lords but would become the first justices of the Supreme Court. The Supreme Court has jurisdiction over English and Welsh law, Northern Irish law and Scottish civil law. The Supreme Court also has jurisdiction to settle disputes relating to devolution in the UK. The proposals were highly contentious. Traditionalists lamented the projected abolition of the Lord Chancellor (subsequently, the title was maintained but the role transformed and reduced), while critics suggested that the Labour government's reforms did not go far enough.

The new Supreme Court began operating in October 2009. It is housed in the refurbished Middlesex Guildhall in Parliament Square, close to the Houses of Parliament and some of the great departments of state. It comprises 12 justices, 10 of whom are male, and its current president is Lady Hale (see Key Figures 9.1 overleaf).

The 'Supreme Court of the United Kingdom' has jurisdiction over Scotland with its distinctive legal system. Accordingly, there are two Scottish justices (Lord Reed and Lord Hodge), although the Supreme Court does not receive appeals on criminal cases from Scotland, as the Law Lords did not hear such cases in the past. (The High Court of Justiciary remains the court of last resort for criminal law in Scotland.) The only new powers transferred to the Supreme Court not previously exercised by the Law Lords were over appeals on jurisdiction under the Devolution Acts, previously the responsibility of the Judicial Committee of the Privy Council. It is only on such devolution issues that decisions of the Supreme Court are binding throughout the UK. Moreover, the UK Supreme Court does not closely resemble some other supreme courts. Unlike the US Supreme Court, it is not able to invalidate legislation for contravening the constitution, as this would undermine the principle of parliamentary sovereignty (discussed in Chapter 6). Thus the Supreme Court has not been seen as the protector of the rights enshrined in the constitution, as it is in the US (see Comparing British Politics 9.1 on p. 183). Recent reforms have, however, created a greater separation of powers between judiciary, executive and legislature. The creation of an independent Supreme Court and reduction in the Lord Chancellor's role in the 2005 Act have had significant constitutional implications, unpicking some aspects of the fusion of powers that marked out the Westminster system.

# KEY FIGURES 9.1
## Brenda Hale

**Lady Hale (1945–)** became president of the Supreme Court in 2017 – the first woman to be appointed as the UK's top judge. From a middle-class background, Hale went to Cambridge University, before going on to be the youngest person and first woman to be appointed to the Law Commission during a career as a barrister and university academic. In 2004, she became the first woman to be appointed as a Law Lord, earning the title Lady Hale. With the establishment of the UK Supreme Court in 2009, she became its first female justice.

Lady Hale played a significant role in introducing a number of reforms to the law, including the Children Act 1989, which is widely acknowledged as the UK's most important piece of legislation protecting children. In 2011, in the housing case *Yemshaw* v. *LB Hounslow*, she gave the lead judgement ruling that domestic violence was not limited to physical violence.

She is seen as a 'champion of diversity' (BBC, 2017c), arguing that judges must be drawn from a diverse group within society. She criticised the background of her fellow senior judges, who have moved from public school to Oxbridge colleges, to the Inns of Court, as being 'from quadrangle, to quadrangle, to quadrangle'. She argued that gender and ethnicity of judges matters 'because democracy matters … We are the instrument by which the will of Parliament and government is enforced upon the people. It does matter that judges should be no less representative of the people than the politicians and civil servants who govern us' (cited in BBC, 2017c).

## The legal profession

The legal profession is divided between barristers, who alone can plead cases in the higher courts, and many more solicitors who deal directly with the public and, among their other duties, prepare the cases for barristers to plead. This division of labour is relatively unusual in other countries, and some critics suggest that it is, in effect, a restrictive practice that benefits lawyers by creating two sets of fees, including some to highly paid barristers, rather than benefiting their clients.

*Source*: Getty Images/Caiaimage/Paul Bradbury
More women are now being appointed to the judiciary, but at the highest level appointments are still dominated by men.

The cost and length of training for barristers, in particular, and the uncertain rewards in the early years in the profession have tended to restrict entry to those from well-to-do family backgrounds. Yet if barristers become successful, the rewards can be huge. Thus while lawyers may frequently have to defend the interests of the poor and marginalised in British society, very few successful barristers share the social background of their clients.

It is from the ranks of senior barristers that judges are mainly drawn. Once appointed, they are virtually irremovable before the obligatory retirement age, which was reduced from 75 to 70 in 1993. Unsurprisingly, senior judges are drawn almost exclusively from the ranks of the white, male upper middle class. Rather more women are now being appointed as judges, but few to the higher ranks of the judiciary (see Table 9.5 on p. 184). As judges are normally only recruited after a long career as a barrister and are still not obliged to retire at the same age as most of the working population, they

## 🇬🇧 COMPARING BRITISH POLITICS 9.1 🇺🇸

### The US and the UK Supreme Courts

The UK Supreme Court differs from its better known US counterpart in several important ways:

» The US Supreme Court was established in 1789, whereas the UK Supreme Court only dates from 2009. Before that, the highest court of appeal for the UK was found in the House of Lords, sitting as what was formally known as the Appellate Committee of the House of Lords.

» The US president appoints justices (subject to congressional approval) based on merit, record, experience and political affiliations. Justices in the US are therefore far more politicised and often labelled as 'liberal' or 'conservative'. In the UK, Supreme Court judges have considerable experience and are appointed by an independent panel after an open application.

» The UK Supreme Court justices are less diverse than their American counterparts: in the UK, all are white and 10 of 12 are male,

whereas in the US, 6 are men and 3 are women and they are from a mix of ethnicities.

» In the UK, judges are expected to retire at 70 in most cases, while in the US new vacancies arise only with death, resignation, retirement, or conviction of impeachment.

» Both courts hear a similar number of cases each year – about 90 in the UK and slightly fewer in the US – where this is a point of law of particular public importance. In the US, all nine judges hear cases; in the UK, it is normally five.

» The US Supreme Court has the power to determine whether legislation is constitutional. The UK does not have single written constitution, but its Supreme Court can decide that certain legislation is incompatible with the Human Rights Act 1998 or the European Convention on Human Rights. The UK Supreme Court does not strike down the legislation in question, but leaves it for Parliament to decide what to do about resolving any incompatibility.

---

are also predominantly elderly. This raises the same kind of challenges about bias in the legal system that we discussed when it comes to barristers.

Judges are powerful and often controversial figures. They may become celebrated or notorious because of their sentences in criminal cases, their comments during the course of a trial and their observations in summing up (for which they cannot be sued). Politicians and the media have sometimes criticised judges for passing sentences that are considered too light, or occasionally too heavy. Judges, in their turn, have deplored mandatory sentences for certain categories of crime, which reduce judicial discretion, and have roundly criticised interference by politicians. As law and order is an emotive political issue, it is perhaps unsurprising that politicians and judges are sometimes drawn into conflict. Because of their role in declaring (and sometimes effectively

making) the law, judges are inevitably helping to shape public policy and influence public attitudes. In addition to their judicial activities, judges, because of their public standing and legal expertise, are often invited to conduct or chair major inquiries into controversial political areas. Examples include the Scott Inquiry on the arms to Iraq scandal in 1996 or the 2003 Hutton Inquiry into the circumstances surrounding the death of the weapons inspector David Kelly (see Spotlight 17.1).

## ADMINISTRATIVE LAW: PROTECTING CIVIL LIBERTIES AND REDRESSING GRIEVANCES

What channels for the **redress of grievances** do citizens, groups and organisations have if they feel they have been illegally, unfairly, unreasonably or arbitrarily treated by a public official or public authority? How are the rights

Table 9.5 Primary appointment of judges in courts in England and Wales, by gender and ethnicity, as at 1 April 2017 (where declared[3])

| Appointment name (ordered by tier of court) | Total in post | Gender | | Ethnicity[1] | | | of which: | | | |
| | | Male | Female | White | Total BAME[2] | Asian or Asian British | Black or Black British | Mixed | Other Ethnic Group |
|---|---|---|---|---|---|---|---|---|---|
| Heads of Division | 5 | 5 | - | 3 | - | - | - | - | - |
| Lords Justices of Appeal[4] | 38 | 29 | 9 | 28 | - | - | - | - | - |
| High Court Judges[5] | 97 | 76 | 21 | 82 | 4 | 2 | - | - | 2 |
| Deputy High Court Judge[6] | 66 | 52 | 14 | 25 | 4 | 2 | 1 | - | 1 |
| Judge Advocates, Deputy Judge Advocates | 6 | 6 | - | 6 | - | - | - | - | - |
| Masters, Registrars, Costs Judges and District Judges (Principal Registry of the Family Division) | 32 | 23 | 9 | 25 | - | - | - | - | - |
| Deputy Masters, Deputy Registrars, Deputy Costs Judges and Deputy District Judges (PRFD) | 58 | 38 | 20 | 31 | 2 | - | 1 | - | 1 |
| Circuit Judges | 635 | 463 | 172 | 551 | 24 | 10 | 3 | 4 | 7 |
| Recorders[7] | 920 | 738 | 182 | 670 | 57 | 21 | 12 | 17 | 7 |
| District Judges (County Courts) | 438 | 272 | 166 | 378 | 33 | 20 | 4 | 6 | 3 |
| Deputy District Judges (County Courts) | 595 | 382 | 213 | 455 | 35 | 14 | 6 | 9 | 6 |
| District Judges (Magistrates' Courts) | 138 | 90 | 48 | 111 | 8 | 6 | - | 2 | - |

| Appointment name (ordered by tier of court) | Total in post | Gender | | Ethnicity[1] | | | of which: | | | |
|---|---|---|---|---|---|---|---|---|---|---|
| | | Male | Female | White | Total BAME[2] | Asian or Asian British | Black or Black British | Mixed | Other Ethnic Group |
| Deputy District Judges (Magistrates' Courts) | 106 | 70 | 36 | 73 | 6 | 3 | 1 | 1 | 1 |
| Total | 3,134 | 2,244 | 890 | 2,438 | 173 | 78 | 28 | 39 | 28 |

Notes:

1  Ethnicity is a non-mandatory field collected by self-declaration. Not all judges declare their information so figures are calculated as a percentage of those members of the judiciary who have agreed to provide data and from whom we have collected this information.

2  BAME stands for black, Asian and minority ethnic.

3  'Declaration rate' refers to the proportion of meaningful declarations out of the total. This is a measure of coverage and uncertainty due to non-declaration.

4  The statutory number of Court of Appeal judges was increased to 39 in 2015.

5  Twelve vacancies were being held in the High Court as at 1 April 2017.

6  Prior to 2016, only a limited number of appointments of deputy High Court judges have been made under the provisions of s9(4) of the Senior Courts Act 1981. As a result, the number of judges who hold these appointments is relatively low. However, 18 deputy High Court judges were appointed in 2016 following an open JAC selection exercise. The results of a more recent competition will be reflected in the statistics to be published in 2018.

7  The total number of recorders in post does not reflect the outcome of a JAC selection exercise that launched in February 2017.

*Source:* Derived from Table 1.1 of *Diversity Statistics 2017 Tables,* available from: www.judiciary.gov.uk/publications/judicial-statistics-2017/. © Crown copyright. Produced by the Ministry of Justice

and freedoms set out in the section on civil liberties protected in practice? Of course, aggrieved citizens will commonly first pursue a complaint with the organisation directly concerned. They may ask to see the manager, or follow a publicised complaints procedure within the organisation. However, a number of other recognised channels may be taken to achieve a remedy. While the first of these is a political channel, the others are judicial or quasi-judicial:

» Contact an elected representative: an MP or local councillor

» Appeal to the ordinary courts for judicial review and remedy

» Appeal to an administrative tribunal

» Provide evidence to a public inquiry

» Complain to an ombudsman

» Invoke the European Convention on Human Rights (discussed above).

---

**Redress of grievances** *refers to the legitimate expectation by a citizen in a democratic society that complaints against public officials will be considered fairly and impartially and that legal remedies for wrongs will be available should malpractice be found.*

---

## Judicial review

Citizens can apply to the courts if they object to a decision of the state, public bodies and officials. The grounds on which an application for judicial review can be made are as follows: *illegality, procedural impropriety, irrationality* and *proportionality*:

» *Illegality*: The exercise of power by public authorities must have specific legal authority. The fundamental doctrine invoked by the courts is *ultra vires* (beyond their powers), which prevents public servants taking actions for which they have no statutory authority, or acting illegally. When courts investigate an administrative action under an enabling statute, they consider whether the power in question was directly authorised by the statute or whether it may be construed as reasonably incidental to it. They can also consider whether a minister or other public authority abused their power by using them for a purpose not intended by statute, or whether, in exercising power, a decision-maker took irrelevant factors into account or ignored relevant factors.

» *Procedural impropriety*: The courts also allow executive decisions to be challenged on the grounds that the procedures laid down by statute have not been followed. In reviewing administrative actions, the courts may also invoke the common law principles of natural justice. These are twofold: first, the rule against bias (no one to be a judge in his own cause); and second, the right to a fair hearing (hear the other side). Under the first rule, administrators must not have any direct (including financial) interest in the outcome of proceedings; nor must they be reasonably suspected of being biased.

» *Irrationality*: This dates back to a case in 1948 when the judge held that a decision made by an authority would be unreasonable if 'it were so unreasonable that no reasonable authority could have come to it'. Although the test of unreasonableness has been used since then to strike down local authority actions, its use is rare.

» *Proportionality*: The use of proportionality was introduced in the 1990s. Thus any public action should not go beyond what is necessary to achieve its stated aims.

Judicial review has steadily increased over the past half-century or so. There are, however, some significant limitations to judicial review in Britain:

1 Judges work within the framework of parliamentary sovereignty. Because Parliament is sovereign, judges cannot strike down legislation as unconstitutional. Thus, in the UK, judicial review means preventing public authorities from doing anything the ordinary law forbids or for which they have no statutory authority. By contrast, in codified constitutions such as the USA, from the early days the Supreme Court assumed the role of striking down legislation that was deemed unconstitutional.

2 Judges in Britain cannot pronounce on the merits of legislation. They must distinguish clearly between matters of *policy*, on which Parliament is the only authority, and matters concerning *lawfulness*, on which the courts may legitimately intervene. However, as we have seen, judges can now declare that legislation appears incompatible with the ECHR and appeal to the European Court of Human Rights in Strasbourg.

3 Judicial review can be subject to statutory exclusion. Specific Acts of Parliament may rule it out.

4 The courts cannot scrutinise executive decisions made under the royal prerogative, including the making of treaties, the defence of the realm, the prerogative of mercy, the granting of honours, the dissolution of Parliament and the appointment of ministers.

## Administrative tribunals

Appeal by an aggrieved citizen to an administrative tribunal may be more appropriate where a particular decision does not involve a clear breach in the law, such as the refusal of a grant, a pension or a licence. Tribunals play an important part in the British system of administrative justice. They are normally established by legislation and cover a wide range of functions, many of them in the field of welfare. Thus, there are tribunals for national insurance, pensions, housing, education, the NHS and immigration. Claims arising out of injuries at work, industrial disputes, unfair dismissal and redundancy are dealt with by industrial tribunals.

Tribunals are usually composed of a chairman with legal qualifications (often a solicitor) and two lay members, representing interests related to the concerns of the particular tribunal. They are independent and not subject to political or administrative interference. Their functions may be described as quasi-judicial: to hear appeals against initial decisions of government agencies or, sometimes, disputes between individuals and organisations. Their role is to establish the facts of each case and then apply the relevant legal rules to it, and decide what the statutory rights and entitlements of the aggrieved actually are. They provide simpler, cheaper, speedier, specialised and more accessible justice than the ordinary courts in their specific spheres of responsibility. It is often possible to appeal against their decisions – normally to a superior court, tribunal or a minister.

Back in 1957, the Franks Committee on Administrative Tribunals and Inquiries recommended that tribunals move towards 'greater openness, fairness and impartiality'. Proceedings should be held in public and reasons for decisions should be given. The parties before tribunals should have the chance to put their own case either personally or through representatives, and should be able to appeal against decisions. Finally, proceedings should not only *be* impartial, through safeguards regulating their composition, but also *seen to be* impartial. The general trend of the last half-century has been towards making the procedure of tribunals more judicial, but without forfeiting the advantages of tribunals over ordinary courts. These are greater informality, specialisation, capacity to conduct their own investigations and flexibility.

## Public inquiries

Often, aggrieved citizens are concerned about some proposed, rather than past, action of a public authority, such as a planned new road, housing development or airport runway. The standard method for giving a hearing to objectors to a government proposal is the public inquiry. Proposals have to be adequately publicised, and third parties have to be afforded the opportunity to state their cases before decisions are taken. Decisions of inquiries may be challenged either on the grounds of procedure or the substance of the decision in the High Court within six weeks of the decision.

Courts hearing appeals from inquiry decisions have sought to safeguard the rights of the public. For example, they have ruled that objectors at an inquiry should be able to take an active, intelligent and informed part in the decision-making process and that they must be given a fair crack of the whip in putting their case. From the point of view of public authorities, major inquiries have often been unduly expensive and time-consuming. From the perspective of objectors to planning proposals, usually 'ordinary' members of the public, the dice are heavily weighted against them. They lack the expertise, time and resources available to government and developers. Often, objectors claim the terms of reference are too narrow. Thus they may be permitted to raise objections to a particular route for a road, but normally not to the need for a road. They do, however, provide a forum where objectors can make their case, and oblige planners to defend their proposals with evidence.

## The ombudsman system

As well as legal rights, citizens have a more general right to a good standard of administration. In 1967, the Parliamentary Commissioner for Administration (PCA) was established, commonly referred to as the 'ombudsman', the term long used in Sweden, from where the idea came. The ombudsman's brief is to investigate and, if possible, remedy complaints by individuals and corporate bodies who feel that they have experienced 'injustice in consequence of maladministration' at the hands of central government. 'Maladministration' relates to the way in which decisions are made, and can include:

> corruption, bias, unfair discrimination, harshness, misleading a member of the public as to his rights, failing to notify him properly of his rights or to explain the reasons for a decision, general high-handedness, using powers for a wrong purpose, failing to consider relevant materials, taking irrelevant material into account, losing or failing to reply to correspondence, delaying unreasonably before making a tax refund or

presenting a tax demand or dealing with an application for a grant or license, and so on. (de Smith and Brazier, 1998)

Appointed by the Crown on the advice of the Lord Chancellor, the PCA enjoys an independent status similar to that of a High Court judge, and has a staff of about 55, largely drawn from the Civil Service. During investigations, which are conducted in private, the ombudsman can call for the relevant files of the department concerned, and can compel the attendance of witnesses and the production of documents.

Complaints must be referred to the ombudsman through MPs. This was because MPs were concerned that the ombudsman should supplement rather than supplant their own historic role in securing redress of constituents' grievances. Normally, only a small proportion of complaints are accepted for investigation – complaints are rejected if they do not involve maladministration, or if there is a right of appeal to a tribunal. The ombudsman issues a report on each investigation to the referring MP, with a copy to the department involved. Where maladministration is found, a department is expected to correct it – for example, by issuing an apology or financial recompense to the aggrieved person – but the ombudsman has no power to compel it to do so. If the department refuses to act, the ombudsman may first bring pressure to bear on it by means of the Commons Select Committee on the PCA, and if this fails, can lay a Special Report before both Houses of Parliament.

Initially limited to the investigation of maladministration in central government, the ombudsman system was later enlarged by the addition of the Northern Ireland Ombudsman (1969), the Parliamentary and Health Service Ombudsman (PHSO; 1973), and the Local Government Ombudsman (LGO) in England and Wales (1974) and Scotland (1976). Unlike the position with regard to the PCA, direct access to these ombudsmen is allowed and both the PHSO and LGO receive a much larger volume of complaints than the PCA. As with the PCA, however, neither PHSO nor LGO commissioners

have any enforcement powers. If a local authority in mainland Britain chooses not to comply with an adverse report by a local ombudsman after various efforts have been made to persuade it, the ombudsman can require it to publicise the reasons for non-compliance.

Ombudsmen have made a less dramatic impact on British public administration than their early advocates hoped, partly because of lack of public awareness of the system, and inadequate powers of enforcement. The only powers of the ombudsmen against a recalcitrant public authority are those of publicity. However, most of their recommendations are accepted and implemented by the departments and authorities concerned, and they have, on occasion, secured substantial compensation for victims of maladministration. More usually, small-scale payments in compensation follow a report, and sometimes just an apology.

## THE POLICE

All states require police to enforce the criminal law and prevent disorder. It is the most vulnerable members of society, such as the old, the young, women and all kinds of minorities facing discrimination and prejudice, who most need the protection of an efficient and impartial police force. Yet, even more than judges, the police appear to represent the coercive role of the state. The police in many countries are treated with suspicion. Unusually, compared to other countries, ordinary police in the UK do not carry guns, indicating a degree of trust between the police and public. This trust still survives among large sections of the population. However, confidence in the impartiality and efficiency of the police in Britain was never universal and now appears lower than it used to be.

Just as there are issues over the possible bias of the judiciary, there are similar concerns over the police. This is not because the police are recruited from a restricted social and educational elite (as could be said of judges). On the contrary, most police have been recruited from lower white-collar and working-class family backgrounds. In spite (or perhaps even because) of this, it is widely alleged that the police behave in a more deferential manner towards 'respectable' people. Some senior police officers are members of the secretive Freemasons and socialise with the local elite. Moreover, it is suggested that they are less concerned, or less well equipped, to pursue white-collar crime.

However, possible class bias has received rather less scrutiny of late than the alleged sexist, homophobic and racist attitudes of sections of the police. It is sometimes alleged that women police officers, roughly a quarter of the total force (ONS, 2015c), do not fit easily into the rather 'macho' police culture, and have found it difficult to secure promotion to the highest levels. In the past, this macho culture sometimes led to the unsympathetic treatment of female victims of rape and male violence, with the police particularly reticent over intervention in 'domestic' issues. This was one factor in the reluctance of women to report rape and other crimes of violence, although more recently many police forces have made more strenuous efforts to treat such crimes sympathetically and pursue them seriously. The same macho culture has sometimes contributed to a marked lack of sympathy and sometimes hostility towards homosexuals. Again, attitudes are changing, perhaps more slowly, but sufficiently to allow a few police themselves to 'come out' and even join in 'gay pride' marches.

Allegations of police racism have received considerable publicity in recent years. It has to be said that racism in the police largely reflects racism in wider society, although the problems have perhaps been more pronounced in some forces. Relatively few blacks and Asians have been recruited into the police (less than 2%), and those who are, have often found it difficult to obtain acceptance from their white colleagues and secure promotion. This has tended to reinforce the mutual suspicions, amounting sometimes to marked antipathy, between the police and minority communities. Members of ethnic minorities are far more likely to be stopped and searched than members of the majority white community. There is also evidence of routine racist abuse of blacks and Asians, and some cases of violent maltreatment of black suspects. In 2011, the fatal police shooting of Mark Duggan, a young black man, caused widespread civil disturbance, beginning in Tottenham, London and spreading throughout cities in the UK. Duggan was unarmed when he was shot by police, who had been monitoring him, during a planned 'hard stop'. It was initially claimed by the Independent Police Complaints Commission that Duggan had fired at the police, but an inquest found that to be untrue. For some people, the Duggan case was part of a consistent use of police misinformation to legitimise their actions. While a jury concluded that Duggan was lawfully killed by police, by a majority of eight to two, the inquest raised important questions about the way the police carry out firearms operations on the streets of Britain.

Tragically, there have also been high-profile police failures to secure convictions of those responsible for black victims of crimes of violence, most notably of Stephen Lawrence (see Key Figures 9.2 overleaf) and Damilola Taylor, a boy of ten, stabbed to death in 2000.

The efficiency and effectiveness of the police has also been called into question by some high-profile miscarriages of justice and failures to solve crimes. Some miscarriages of justice were perhaps the consequence of intense media and public pressure on the police to secure convictions, leading to hasty and ill-prepared prosecutions, but in a few cases involved the extraction of dubious confessions from suspects and even the fabrication of evidence. Some former police officers have been jailed for corruption, undermining faith in the integrity of the police.

Various high-profile cases have contributed to mistrust of the police. One controversy over police tactics and behaviour was the so-called 'Battle of Orgreave' at the time of the miners' strike in 1984, in which some 6,000 police officers including some mounted police and police dogs fought with pickets from the National Union of Mineworkers

# KEY FIGURES 9.2

Stephen Lawrence and 'institutional racism'

*Source:* Metropolitan Police via Getty Images

**Stephen Lawrence** was a young black man murdered in a racially motivated attack in Eltham, southeast London in 1993, while waiting for a bus home. Flaws in the police investigation led to the setting up of the Stephen Lawrence Inquiry to investigate the way in which the police responded to the murder. The Macpherson Report concluded that the Metropolitan Police Service was 'institutionally racist' according to the Inquiry's own definition:

The collective failure of an organisation to provide an appropriate and professional service to people because of their colour, culture or ethnic origin. It can be seen or detected in processes, attitudes and behaviour which amount to discrimination through unwitting prejudice, ignorance, thoughtlessness, and racist stereotyping which disadvantage minority ethnic people. (Macpherson, 1999, p. 28)

Institutional racism suggests that racist assumptions are so embedded in organisations and society generally that discrimination can persist, even in the absence of conscious racist intentions and behaviour. The concept was developed in the USA, where it is suggested that racism was deeply ingrained as a consequence of the historical experience of slavery and racial segregation. Thus the dominant white community continue to unconsciously exclude and disadvantage blacks.

The handling of the investigation into the murder of Stephen Lawrence led to acknowledgement that there was institutional racism in the Metropolitan Police and other police forces.

(NUM), and which has yet to be re-examined. The police charged 71 pickets with riot and 24 with violent disorder, but the trials collapsed when the police evidence was deemed unreliable. Orgreave remains highly contentious. The Battle of Orgreave and the whole issue of policing in the long and bitter miners' strike were inevitably closely bound up with government and politics. Renewed calls for a public inquiry were again rejected in 2016.

A later issue was the Hillsborough disaster in 1989, when 96 football supporters, mainly young and from Liverpool, died in a crush substantially caused by ground problems but also by serious mistakes in policing. The anger of families who suffered was aggravated by police and press suggestions that the tragedy had been substantially caused by hooliganism and drunkenness among the fans. A succession of reports, inquests and inquiries, culminating in a 2016 inquest, finally established that there had been extensive police manipulation of evidence to cover up their own errors of omission and commission. In June 2017, six people in authority on the day were charged with a range of offences.

All this raises important concerns over the accountability and control of the police, an issue in many countries. It is considered important that the police should be independent from direct control by party politicians, but fully accountable to the public or their representatives. Squaring that circle is difficult and, in Britain, police accountability and responsibility is somewhat blurred. The police used to be a local authority responsibility, but control by elected councillors, never very effective, particularly on operational issues, has been progressively weakened as a consequence of police force amalgamations and a reduced councillor element on police authorities. Today, these are virtually quasi-autonomous local public bodies, often covering several local authorities. Chief constables retain substantial operational control. The former coalition government pressed ahead with proposals for elected police commissioners, with the aim of improving the public accountability of the police force, but these proposals were heavily criticised, by the police, police authorities and others. In practice, the introduction of elections for the role of police commissioners in England and Wales charged with ensuring efficient and effective policing of a local area, has involved low public interest and turnout.

If local accountability is not particularly effective, what of accountability at the centre? Nationally, the minister in charge of crime and the police is the home secretary, who only ever had direct responsibility for London's Metropolitan Police, and in 2000, even this was transferred to the Metropolitan Police Authority. So the home secretary is not answerable in the Commons for the conduct of police authorities and local police forces. Despite having overall responsibility for the police, successive home secretaries have found it difficult to pursue reorganisation and modernisation of the police.

Machinery for handling complaints against the police has improved but remains contentious. Formerly, the investigation of complaints was wholly in the hands of the police themselves (although officers from another force might be brought in for serious cases). A Police Complaints Board was introduced to supervise the process in 1976. Following the 1984 Police and Criminal Evidence Act, this was replaced by a beefed-up Police Complaints Authority,

which supervises the investigation of serious complaints, although the actual investigation is still carried out by police officers, so it is still questioned whether this amounts to a genuinely independent inquiry.

Policing, together with law and order generally, can hardly be taken out of politics. Indeed, it remains a hotly contested political issue. Thus the last Labour government tried to counter the accusation that the party was 'soft on crime'. Blair (1995) first came to national prominence as shadow home secretary, with his soundbite that Labour would be 'tough on crime and tough on the causes of crime'. New Labour's first two home secretaries, Jack Straw from 1997 and David Blunkett from 2001, were notably 'tough', and both Blair and Brown made periodic interventions on law and order issues. The coalition government sent out more mixed messages. On the one hand, former Justice Secretary Kenneth Clarke sought to reduce the numbers of the prison population (one of the highest as a proportion of the population in the western world), while other Conservatives were keen to reassert their party's traditional toughness on crime and the message that 'prison works'. The high numbers of former prisoners convicted of reoffending suggests that it does not, although those who defend prison can argue that prison at least keeps criminals off the street for a period.

As the opening sentences of this chapter show, debates about the law remain a fundamental part of politics in the UK, as ongoing disagreement about the police system, crime, human rights and the respective power of Parliament, the executive and the judiciary show. The law and politics can never quite escape one another's influence.

# SUMMARY

» Britain has not in the past accepted the need for a strict separation of powers between legislature, executive and judiciary. Reforms initiated in 2003 and completed in 2009 involved the transfer of the House of Lords' judicial functions to a new Supreme Court.

» Although Britain was an early signatory to the European Convention on Human Rights, this was only incorporated into British law in 1998. This has implications for the constitutional principle of parliamentary sovereignty, even though this is formally maintained, as judges have not been given the power to strike out laws incompatible with the ECHR.

» Judges remain unrepresentative of the communities they serve. They are predominantly elderly, white, male and come from an upper middle-class background.

» There is no clear coherent system of administrative law in Britain, although there are a number of channels for citizens wishing to make a complaint against government and public authorities, including the ordinary courts, tribunals, public inquiries and the ombudsman system.

» While the image of the police in Britain has generally been positive, parts of the police force have been accused of racist, sexist and homophobic attitudes and behaviour, although efforts have been made to remedy this.

# ? QUESTIONS FOR DISCUSSION

» Are human rights adequately protected in Britain?

» Has the Human Rights Act effectively destroyed the sovereignty of Parliament?

» How far is it possible to reconcile requirements to protect the community from terrorism with full respect for individual human rights and freedoms?

» Why was the new UK Supreme Court introduced? How far is it comparable with other supreme courts, such as the US Supreme Court?

» How far and in what respects might judges be considered to be biased?

» Should trial by jury be retained?

» How far can the police be trusted to act impartially towards all sections of the community?

# FURTHER READING

On key themes covered by this chapter, including the rule of law, the executive and the courts and redress of grievances, see Jowell et al. (2015) *The Changing Constitution* (8th edn) and the less up to date Bogdanor (2011) *The Coalition and the Constitution*. See also Barnett (2017) *Constitutional and Administrative Law* (12th edn).

On the judiciary, Griffith (2010) *The Politics of the Judiciary* (5th edn) is still well worth reading.

Contrasting views of the Human Rights Act can be found in the comments of Bogdanor (2001). Further background and critical analysis are provided by the director of Liberty, John Wadham (1999). A more detailed account, including key texts, is provided by Wadham et al. (2007) *Blackstone's Guide to the Human Rights Act 1998*.

For the UK Supreme Court and associated constitutional reforms, see Ryan (2004) 'A Supreme Court for the United Kingdom', *Talking Politics*, 17(1): 18–20. For more depth, refer to Jowell et al. (2015).

## USEFUL WEBSITES

See the Ministry of Justice: www.justice.gov.uk and www.judiciary.gov.uk for key documents and latest developments.

*Further student resources to support learning are available at*
**www.macmillanihe.com/griffiths-brit-pol-3e**

# 10 LOCAL GOVERNMENT AND POLITICS

Since 2010, the austerity agenda has shown the power of central over local government. George Osborne, chancellor from 2010 to 2016, set about making radical cuts to public spending in order to bring down the deficit. The easiest way to do this, from central government's perspective, was to pass on much of the responsibility for deficit reduction to local government. Councils in Britain – unlike local government in many other European countries – remain hugely dependent on central government for their revenue and spending decisions. This comes in the form of central grants, as well as stipulations on the amount of local tax they can raise and the services they must provide. Most local councils therefore had little choice but to bring in major reductions to services for their residents under the austerity programme. Tom Crewe (2016) writes that: 'No other area of government has been subject to the same squeeze.' The squeeze will continue under Theresa May's government, which did not reverse any of Osborne's cuts.

England is one of the most centralised countries in Europe. In practice, devolution has passed power to governments in Scotland, Wales and Northern Ireland, but in England power largely lies with the government in Westminster. For every £1 raised in taxation in the UK, 91 pence is controlled and allocated by central government (Crewe, 2016). Local government has no clear constitutional role.

Since 2010, councils have made huge cuts to budgets for transport, parks, libraries, public toilets, adult social care, housing services for the vulnerable and Sure Start centres for young children. And in general, the poorer an area is, the more the council relies on central government grants to meet its needs (Hastings et al., 2015). Some local councils will have lost more than 60% of their income between 2010 and 2020. Simon Parker (2015) describes the consequences as 'perhaps the biggest shift in the role of the British state since 1945'.

## THIS CHAPTER:

» Examines not only the strong theoretical case for local democratic institutions and the major historical contribution made by local councils to the development of social services in modern Britain, but also the serious ongoing practical problems in British local government today.

» Explores the extensive reforms to local government structure, finance and management over the past half-century or more, which have substantially complicated the whole system of local government, but have significantly failed to engage and involve the public. The austerity cuts in local government have reshaped local services.

» Discusses some of the currently fashionable remedies, including directly elected mayors and plans to devolve more powers to major provincial conurbations.

## DEMOCRATIC LOCAL GOVERNMENT?

Representative local government has been seen as crucial to the theory and practice of democracy generally. Alexis de Tocqueville declared in *Democracy in America* ([1835, 1840] 2003) that without local self-government people lacked the spirit of liberty. In *Considerations on Representative Government* ([1861] 1972), John Stuart Mill considered that local representative institutions provided a crucial education in democracy.

The case for local democratic institutions remains strong. Elected local authorities offer local communities a degree of choice and accountability over local decisions and service levels. They help disperse power and give more opportunities for citizens to participate in the political process. They allow experimentation at local level, and the development of innovative policies that may be copied elsewhere. Much of Britain's postwar welfare state owed its very existence to services developed initially by local councils, including education, social services, health services, town planning and, above all, municipal housing. While some of these services have since been taken substantially out of local authority control (health, housing and, increasingly, education), or in some cases effectively privatised, they would never have come into being without the pioneering role of elected local councils.

While the past record of local government in the UK is impressive and there is still a strong case for local democratic institutions, the reality in Britain today falls far short of the ideal. This is partly because the cumulative failure of (largely well-meant) extensive reforms to British local government over the past half-century or so has only increased public confusion about, and apathy towards, their own local councils. Surveys show that the public has a low understanding of the workings of local government (Councillors Commission, 2007, p. 9). Moreover, although many public services are delivered locally, they are no longer subject to any effective local accountability and control. Thus, an increasing proportion of UK local governance is hardly democratic.

## THE FAILURE OF LOCAL GOVERNMENT REORGANISATION

In the course of the nineteenth century in Britain, the reform and growth of local representative institutions paralleled the extension of representative democracy nationally. Local government developed haphazardly in the nineteenth century to meet the needs of fast-growing urban industrial centres and some of the acute new issues these presented. Initially, the response was to set up new, single-purpose authorities to cope with specific services, such as public welfare, public health and education. These services were largely transferred to a comprehensive system of multipurpose elected local authorities in the later Victorian period. In the cities and larger towns, they were supplied by all-purpose county boroughs; elsewhere, there was a substantially two-tier system of local government, with some of the larger services, such as education, administered by county councils, and other services run by (non-county) boroughs, urban district councils or rural district councils, with a third tier of parish councils with minor functions. From 1899, London had its own London County Council (LCC) and 28 metropolitan borough councils. In the last decades of the 19th century, local councils, acting on their own initiative, pioneered welfare provision: clearing slums and building houses, parks, hospitals, museums libraries, swimming pools and playing fields.

---

**Local government** *is conventionally understood to mean the government provided by elected local authorities (or local councils).*

---

This system of local government, developed in the Victorian era, saw only minor and largely

*Source:* iStock.com/Poohz

The grand town hall in Leeds shows the importance of local government in Victorian Britain.

incremental changes to boundaries and authorities for much of the twentieth century, although there was a considerable expansion of local services and expenditure, which put an increasing strain on local councils. By the second half of the century, there was a broad consensus among academics and politicians that British local government areas and functions required extensive modernisation. It was considered that there were too many small local authorities that no longer matched the pattern of life and work in Britain. A series of projected radical reorganisations were instituted by Conservative and Labour governments. Some of these were never, and others only partially, implemented, but all caused considerable political upheaval and controversy.

One persistent debate raged from the 1960s to the end of the century. Those who favoured a single level of unitary authorities responsible for all local services argued it would be more efficient, would improve coordination between services and make it easier for the public to understand who did what. Critics, who preferred a two-tier or multi-tier system, claimed that unitary authorities everywhere would be too large and remote from the people they served, particularly in rural areas.

Macmillan's Conservative administration transformed the government of London in 1963, creating a reformed two-tier system, with a much larger Greater London Council (GLC) replacing the old LCC and 32 London boroughs. Wilson's Labour government set up a Royal Commission on Local Government in England, and in 1969, it reported in favour of almost entirely unitary authorities (Redcliffe-Maud Report, 1969). The report was largely accepted by the Labour government, which lost office before it could be implemented. The incoming Heath Conservative government rejected the reports proposals, and introduced a new two-tier system for the whole of England and Wales in 1972, involving many wholly new local authorities, including new shire counties of Avon, Cleveland and Humberside and six metropolitan counties for the larger provincial conurbations.

The Thatcher Conservative government abolished both the GLC set up by Macmillan's government and the six Heath-created metropolitan counties, leaving only one level of elected local government in these major conurbations. John Major, Thatcher's successor, instituted a new Local Government Commission for England (1992), with a strong steer towards recommending more unitary authorities outside London and the major conurbations. After a long series of reviews, the final outcome was mixed, involving the end of Heath's new counties of Avon, Cleveland and Humberside, and the creation of 46 additional unitary authorities in England, but retained many two-tier systems. Meanwhile, unitary authorities were imposed on Scotland and Wales in 1996.

Over the past 20 years, change has been more limited (see Table 10.1). The Blair government restored a Greater London Authority (GLA) with a directly elected mayor, after a referendum in favour of the change. Although Eric Pickles (Conservative Home, 2008), a recent Conservative minister for local government (who had himself earlier been leader of Bradford Council), declared that he kept a loaded revolver in his drawer for anyone who proposed a fresh reorganisation, the Cameron government advocated more powers for new regional conurbations. Elections for these new combined authorities and metropolitan mayors finally took place in May 2017 (see later in this chapter). These new mayoral elections aroused little interest or enthusiasm among the wider public, with turnout ranging from a fifth to a third of those eligible to vote. (For more on low participation, see Chapter 16, pp. 331–39.)

### Table 10.1 The structure of elected local government in Britain

| London | English provincial conurbations | Rest of England | | Scotland | Wales |
|---|---|---|---|---|---|
| Two-tier | Unitary | Mixed | | Unitary | Unitary |
| GLA and mayor (1) | Metropolitan districts (36) | Unitary authorities (46) | County councils (34) | Unitary authorities (32) | Unitary authorities (22) |
| London boroughs (32) | | | District councils (238) | | |
| | Parish or neighbourhood councils | | | | |

Note: The establishment of new combined authorities in 2017 complicates this picture in some areas.

## WHY IS LOCAL GOVERNMENT REORGANISATION SO POLITICALLY CONTROVERSIAL?

In view of general public ignorance of, and apathy towards, local government, it may appear strange that its reorganisation has often proved politically toxic. Why should some care so much about local administrative areas, when most do not even bother to vote in local elections (as we discuss in Chapter 13)? Yet there have long been some vociferous special interests in these debates, including those strongly attached to old names and identities. Thus some campaigned to save the tiny county of Rutland, or to preserve or re-establish the ridings of Yorkshire. By contrast, newly created authorities like Humberside, which transcended old administrative areas, found it difficult to generate new identities and loyalties, similar to those associated with ancient shire counties. In addition, many inhabitants of suburban and semi-rural areas, perhaps fearing higher local taxes, strongly resisted incorporation into neighbouring towns and cities that they often relied on for employment, shopping and recreation. On top of these factions, those employed by existing local authorities provided another strong lobby against change, which threatened jobs and created uncertainty.

Among the many interests affected by local government reorganisation were political parties. Almost overnight, safe Labour or Conservative local councils could be rendered marginal or favourable to the other side by boundary changes. One reason why Labour opposed the original plans for a new GLC in 1963 was that the old LCC was a Labour stronghold, while Greater London appeared far more marginal (as recent elections continue to confirm). Similarly, it was not entirely coincidental that the GLC and the six metropolitan counties abolished by the Thatcher Conservative government were by that time all Labour controlled, with the GLC, led by 'Red Ken' Livingstone, and the so-called 'Socialist Republic of South Yorkshire' particularly arousing Tory ire. So party interests are often materially affected by reorganisation. However, there were often conflicting tensions within parties. Thus some local Conservative associations successfully resisted incorporation into enlarged predominantly urban authorities, which was not always in the electoral interests of their parties. For example, inhabitants of parts of Surrey strongly, and ultimately successfully, resisted incorporation in Greater London and in effect weakened Conservative chances of dominating elections for the new GLC and, later, the London mayoralty.

The troubled history of local government reorganisation over the past half-century or more might suggest that future national governments may hesitate before initiating any radical new changes. The existing system may be complex and illogical, but the political costs of fresh reforms appear considerable, while the potential gains are questionable, to judge by the record of the past. Central government may be well advised to leave local government alone (Leach, R. 1998). However, governments continue to ignore this advice.

## THE REFORM OF LOCAL GOVERNMENT FINANCE

If the reorganisation of local government areas was controversial, the reform of local government finance was briefly even more politically divisive. One attempt effectively brought down Margaret Thatcher, a formerly dominant prime minister who had won three elections.

Local authority current expenditure – on salaries, materials, fuel, rent, debt servicing and so on – is supposed to be met from current revenue. Local authorities have long had powers to raise their own local taxes, once in the form of property rates, briefly by Thatcher's community charge (or poll tax) and more recently through the council tax (see below). Yet while local voters often assume that the bulk of local spending is paid for by such local taxes, in truth they meet only a diminishing proportion of local government expenditure. The rest comes in one form or another out of central government grants, effectively out of receipts from national taxation.

Reliance on central grants is not ideal. Local accountability might be stronger if councils had to meet all their spending out of local taxation. But some local communities are far better off than others. If the quality of local services depended exclusively on the money that could be raised locally, the poorest areas with the greatest needs would have the least income for spending on public services. One purpose of central grants is to redistribute resources to help poorer areas with substantial problems and demands on spending. Almost inevitably, then, local government is substantially dependent on central funding in some form or other, and the old adage 'he who pays the piper calls the tune' applies. Central governments of all parties employ the rhetoric of decentralisation – devolving more autonomy to those responsible for the actual delivery of services. Yet all governments are aware that they will be judged on the effectiveness of their spending and service delivery, so money is given with strings attached, including an increasing number of centrally determined targets that have to be met. Governments are also accused of favouring councils run by their own party. Ultimately, there is no easy answer to this tension between central direction and local autonomy, which is particularly evident over spending, because local authorities rely substantially on income they do not raise themselves.

## DOMESTIC RATES

Even so, councils still raise significant revenue from local taxation. This once took the form of domestic and business rates for most of the history of UK local government. Householders and business owners paid rates based on the annual value of their property, with the actual payment varying with the rate in the pound levied by each local authority. Rates were cheap to collect, difficult to avoid and broadly progressive, particularly after the introduction of rate rebates for those on low incomes. However, domestic rates were a highly visible tax, paid for out of current income, and widely hated, particularly by those with highly valued properties.

## COMMUNITY CHARGE (POLL TAX)

The Thatcher government decided to replace domestic rates with a new community charge or poll tax. The official name 'community charge' was significant. It was deemed a *charge* on *consumers* for local government services, rather than a *tax* on local *citizens*. But it became universally known as the 'poll tax', a tax per head – similar to the poll tax that provoked the Peasants Revolt back in 1381. Almost all adult residents, rather than just householders, paid the poll tax, strengthening the link (the government argued) between taxation and representation. The government hoped that this would deter high spending by local councils, who would be punished by voters through the ballot box for their higher poll tax.

It never worked as the Thatcher government hoped. Although the new tax was popular with most Conservative Party members, many of whom, living in highly rated properties, gained from the change, critics argued the new tax was regressive and unfair because it was not linked to ability to pay. Most local voters found they were paying more, sometimes

much more. It proved a bureaucratic nightmare, three times as expensive to collect as the old rates and subject to widespread evasion. (Many councils were still chasing up defaulters years after the tax was abolished.) It was also widely seen as a tax on voting, as the annually revised electoral role was the most reliable guide to who lived where. So those seeking to evade the new tax (including many students) avoided registering to vote. This also affected local population calculations used as a basis for assessing government grants. Poorer councils thus suffered twice over – from loss of revenue from defaulters, and loss of income from grants based on an assessment of needs from population figures that were too low.

Public reaction was hostile, particularly in Scotland where the new tax was introduced in 1989, a year earlier than England. It was a prime cause of the sharp decline in Conservative support in Scotland. In England, it provoked serious riots and led to major reverses for the Conservatives in parliamentary by-elections and local elections, and contributed significantly to Margaret Thatcher's resignation later in 1990. The new Conservative government, under John Major, soon moved to scrap the poll tax, which only lasted for three years in England and four in Scotland (Butler et al., 1994).

## COUNCIL TAX

The poll tax was replaced with a new council tax in 1993, a tax on the capital values of domestic properties divided into eight bands, with a 25% rebate for one-person households. The actual tax levied depends not only on the property band (and whether or not a rebate applies) but on the money needed by each local authority for its expenditure after all other receipts are taken into account. The proportion of total revenue councils derive from the council tax can vary considerably between authorities, as well as over time, but the average council in recent years has met only around a quarter of its spending needs from the tax. Because income from other sources can fluctuate considerably from year to year, it does not necessarily follow that an above-inflation increase in council tax is the

*Source*: Richard Baker/In Pictures Ltd/Corbis via Getty Images

The introduction of the poll tax led to widespread protest and contributed to the resignation of Prime Minister Margaret Thatcher in November 1990. Here, a protester climbs onto a lamp post in London's Trafalgar Square at the height of the riots on 31 March 1990 as flames erupt from a nearby building site.

result of some commensurate increase in a council's spending, nor does a reduction in tax necessarily reflect spending cuts. As changes in council tax levels often bear little relation to changes in spending, effective accountability to the local electorate is reduced. It is difficult even for tolerably well-informed local taxpayers to know who to blame (or reward) for their council tax bills.

The council tax initially provoked surprisingly little criticism, largely because many were happy to see the poll tax abolished, while across the political spectrum there was little appetite for further change. However, opposition has grown, particularly in those parts of the country containing large numbers of retired residents, often in highly rated properties (e.g. Cornwall). The Lib Dems long advocated a local income tax, which would pose some administrative problems and inevitably create losers as well

as winners. Yet following the experience of the poll tax, any future government at Westminster may hesitate to venture again into reform of local taxation, which remains a political hot potato.

## CHANGES TO THE RUNNING OF LOCAL GOVERNMENT

### LOCAL COUNCILLORS AND LOCAL GOVERNMENT OFFICERS

Local government, like national government, involves both elected politicians and appointed officers. Some of the issues affecting relations between elected local politicians and leading local officials mirror the debate over ministers and civil servants in central government (discussed in Chapter 8). The once influential thesis that civil servants were the real rulers of Britain was matched by a widespread assumption that senior local government officers rather than elected councillors dominated town hall decision-making. Indeed, there were more differences between local politicians and bureaucrats than their national equivalents, who often came from similar educational and social backgrounds. It was argued that councillors who were (until comparatively recently) unpaid, predominantly elderly and often less educated frequently lack the relevant knowledge and skills to challenge the recommendations of professionally quali-fied lawyers, accountants, engineers or town planners, who headed local government departments.

## PARTY POLITICS IN LOCAL GOVERNMENT

Elected members of councils had always had formal responsibility and could exercise real power if they were sufficiently determined. Here, the role of party politics was an important factor. Even in the nineteenth century, party politics was significant in the government of major cities. Joseph Chamberlain established his political reputa-tion as a radical Liberal mayor and leader of Birmingham Council, where his energy and drive transformed the city, before he entered Parliament and pursued a dazzling and controversial career in first Liberal and later unionist governments. In the course of the twentieth century, local elections were increasingly fought on party labels.

Some regret this, arguing that party should have no role in local government. Yet many of the key issues in national politics are replicated at local level – particularly the balance between taxation and spending, public services or private provision. Labour, nationally and locally, have tended to support higher spending on public services, while the Conservatives emphasise the need for economy and lower taxes. Moreover, party politics has increased the number of contested elections and can raise turnout levels. Perhaps most important of all, disciplined party groups on the council provide political

leadership and make it more likely that elected members rather than appointed officers will have the final say in decisions.

Traditionally, Labour dominates in the cities, particularly in the inner urban areas, while the Conservatives have controlled the more rural and suburban authorities. Lib Dems, like lightning, can strike anywhere, including northern cities such as Sheffield, prosperous commuter territory (e.g. some of the outer London boroughs), or the Celtic fringe, particularly southwest England. By and large, Labour-controlled authorities are more likely to favour spending on core public services, while Conservatives are keener to keep council tax low, although there are some important differences within both parties as well as between them. The Lib Dems in particular may be associated with different interests in different areas, championing inner-city areas sometimes taken for granted by Labour, and competing with the Conservatives for suburban and rural votes elsewhere. Lib Dem gains in local government in the late twentieth and early twenty-first centuries led to an increasing number of hung councils, where no party had overall control, and more coalitions in local government, until 2010 when the Lib Dems joined in coalition with the Conservatives nationally and lost some of their popularity locally. Only after the end of coalition in 2015 have the Lib Dems begun a modest recovery in local elections. However, there would be many more coalitions on local councils if proportional representation was introduced into English local elections (as has already happened in Scotland), as Chapter 13 on electoral systems shows. As it is, most English councils are dominated by one party, often with little prospect of any change in control.

The evidence of recent years suggests that it certainly does matter which party or parties controls local councils. In the 1980s, some Conservative-controlled councils, such as Wandsworth or Westminster, provided a testing ground for Thatcherite policies, while Liverpool, the GLC and the county and districts of what was described as the 'Socialist Republic of South Yorkshire' defiantly challenged the policies of a Conservative government. There was then heady talk of 'local socialism'.

## LOCAL GOVERNMENT AND LOCAL INTERESTS

Local authorities are also influenced by a wide range of local interests. These include groups of local residents, parent-teacher associations, leisure groups (e.g. allotment associations, sports clubs), senior citizens, groups representing ethnic minorities and local producer interests (e.g. chambers of commerce representing business interests and trade federations representing workers and trade unions). These engage in the political process to protect their interests and secure benefits for their members – policy decisions in their favour, new equipment or facilities, often financial support of some kind. Some groups, however, have something to offer local public bodies – information, expertise, even voluntary labour in the case of some established 'third sector' groups. Gerry Stoker (1991) concluded that the

willingness of councils to respond to various types of pressure groups depended closely on their prevailing politics. Labour councils may be more prepared to listen to trade unions, tenants groups, women's groups and ethnic minority associations, while Conservative councils may pay more attention to the local chamber of commerce and business interests generally, as well as professional interests and local residents associations. Other groups may be relatively ignored.

Just as it is often alleged that power in Britain is really exercised by interests outside government, it is also suggested that real power in cities and local communities is not held by the elected members or appointed officers of the council, but by outside interests. Indeed, many celebrated attempts by political scientists in the USA, France and Britain to assess the distribution of political power focused on case studies of decision-making in towns and cities rather than nationally (see Comparing British Politics 10.1).

Interest in community power studies has declined, partly perhaps because of their

## ⚒ COMPARING BRITISH POLITICS 10.1 ▤

### The community power debate

There has been a long academic debate among scholars over power in the local community. In perhaps the classic text in what became known as the 'community power debate', American political scientist Robert Dahl studied the town of New Haven in Connecticut, USA and asked *Who Governs?* (1961). He found that power was widely distributed, citing evidence from urban decision-making to demonstrate that there is no single local elite dominating the town and its policy processes. His work is described as 'pluralist', as he argued that a plurality of groups have political influence. Others have cited different kinds of evidence to demonstrate the existence of urban elites. American radicals (e.g. Crenson, 1971) and French Marxists (e.g. Castells, 1977) have argued

that urban decision-making systematically favours business interests.

Much of this community power debate was replicated in Britain, but is similarly inconclusive. Particular case studies sometimes appeared to confirm the initial perspective of authors, finding evidence for a quasi-pluralist policy process in Birmingham (Newton, 1976), elite decision-making in Kensington and Chelsea (Dearlove, 1973) and strong business influence in Lambeth (Cockburn, 1977) and Croydon (Saunders, 1980). Although these are only case studies, at the very least the existing literature shows the complexity of the conflicting interests involved in the governance of urban areas, and dramatises some of the issues involved in the distribution of power, locally as well as nationally.

inconclusive (or sometimes contradictory) findings. However, another reason in Britain is the transfer of functions and power away from local government and local communities. Local councils are still big business and some remain the largest single employer in their area. But they have lost effective control of many key services and decisions to central government, other public agencies and the private and voluntary sectors (see below). Moreover, the private firms (and even some of the voluntary agencies) with which the council has to deal are no longer necessarily locally managed and controlled but are branches of national and, in some cases, multinational organisations. So the key players in urban development and planning may not be closely involved with the city whose future they affect.

## TRANSFORMING DECISION-MAKING IN LOCAL GOVERNMENT: FROM COMMITTEES AND PROFESSIONS TO CORPORATE MANAGEMENT

There have long been pressures to transform decision-making in local councils, which often seemed opaque to the public, while others criticised the efficiency of the system. Formally, decisions were made by a number of specialist committees of councillors, for each local government service, such as education, housing, planning, social services and so on. These meetings were open to the public, but the few who attended generally found that key issues often involved little discussion or debate, and some were simply passed through 'on the nod'. The real decisions commonly seemed to have been made elsewhere, either following recommendations of local government officers, organised in separate departments and headed by professionally qualified chief officers, or by the majority party group, which also normally dominated the membership of every committee. Up until the 1960s, there also seemed little attempt to prioritise local authority policy and expenditure between services.

A more corporate approach to management from the 1960s onwards followed a series of official reports, such as the Maud Report (1967) and Bains Report (1972). On the elected members' side, the committee system was now headed by a Policy and Resources Committee, chaired by the leader of the council, which, in theory, determined the direction of policy and expenditure across the whole council, with an officers' management team led by a council chief executive providing similar direction on the professional side. Even so, the new corporate management made little impression on the general public.

## ELECTED MAYORS?

Some argued the need for more politically prominent leadership in the town hall. So Michael Heseltine, who had been secretary of state for the environment under Margaret Thatcher and deputy prime minister in John Major's government, pushed the case for directly elected mayors. The title of 'mayor' had long been used in English local government, where it was normally a purely ceremonial role, with no political power, held for a year by a senior councillor. However, in French local government and in some leading US cities, the mayor had long been a powerful local politician, sometimes dominating the government of their town for many years. Heseltine hoped that directly elected mayors could provide similar political leadership in Britain and reinvigorate interest in local government. Such mayors were also favoured by some New Labour politicians.

So Labour's 1997 manifesto included a commitment to devolution (discussed in Chapter 11). This did not just mean passing power to the various territories that make up the UK, but also to London as well. Labour promised to reform London government, with a directly elected mayor, which became part of the Greater London Authority Act 1999 (see Spotlight 10.1 overleaf). The Local Government Act 2000 also allowed other local councils to opt for a directly elected mayor. After local referendums in 2002, eleven councils chose a directly elected mayor. By 2016, there had been 52 local referendums on the introduction of an elected mayor: only 16 voted in favour and 36 against. In addition, in 6 subsequent local referendums on whether to abolish elected mayors, they were removed in 3 and retained in the other 3.

## SPOTLIGHT ON ...

### The government of London: the mayor and Greater London Authority

10.1

Because of its sheer size and status as the UK's capital city, the government of London has long appeared distinctive from the rest of UK local government. The earlier LCC was replaced by the larger GLC in 1963, but subsequently abolished in 1986 by the Thatcher government, which detested its left-wing Labour leader, Ken Livingstone (see below). The 1997 Labour government pledged to restore a strategic authority for London. It established a new Greater London Authority (GLA) with a directly elected mayor and a 25-member Assembly, elected by the additional member system (described in Chapter 13). These proposals were endorsed in a referendum of Londoners in 1998.

The new mayor of London was given strategic (but not operational) responsibilities for transport, policing, fire and emergency planning, economic development and planning: various functional bodies, including Transport for London, the Mayor's Office for Policing and Crime, and London Fire and Emergency Planning Authority, are responsible for the delivery of the relevant service. The 25 elected Assembly members can only scrutinise the mayor's activities, but they do have the power (with a two-thirds majority), to amend the mayor's annual budget and reject the mayor's strategies.

The record so far is chequered, but hardly amounts to a ringing endorsement of directly elected mayors. For the present, the diversity of political leadership styles across local government increases the complexity of the whole system, and scarcely makes it easier for voters to understand how local government works. However, the creation of new authorities to run regional conurbations advocated by the Conservative-led governments elected after 2010 (as the section on the Northern Powerhouse below shows) depends on the acceptance of directly elected mayors, which will provide fresh impetus for this form of leadership (see Key Figures 10.1). Much depends on the new generation of mayors whether this model of local political leadership becomes more widely accepted.

## THE LOSS OF SERVICES AND POWER: FROM DELIVERING TO ENABLING

Over the past half-century or so, the structure, finance and management of local government have all been substantially and sometimes repeatedly transformed. Yet the biggest changes in British local government have been the erosion of its functions, services and powers over time. The first half of the twentieth century had seen elected local authorities in the UK that were directly responsible for an extensive range of services delivered locally. These included education, libraries and leisure services, social services and social welfare, police and fire services, environmental health and community health services, housing, highways, planning and urban development. Some authorities were also responsible for major public utilities such as water, gas, electricity and public transport. Some even developed and ran their own airports. Birmingham had its own bank and Hull its own telephone service (Wilson and Game, 2011).

In the immediate postwar period, many of the functions of local government were nationalised (and then subsequently privatised in the 1980s). These nationalisations undermined the independence of local councils: council-owned gas, water and electricity companies (and their profits) were transferred to central government control, denying councils a huge chunk of their independent income. Major

# 👥 KEY FIGURES 10.1
## The London mayors

**Ken Livingstone** won as an independent against the official Labour and Conservative candidates in the first London mayoral election in 2000. Livingstone was a committed socialist and had led the GLC in the 1980s, introducing radical policies aimed at helping the poorest Londoners. Livingstone was readmitted to the Labour Party and won a second mayoral election in 2004. He was a significant player in bringing the 2012 Olympic games to London.

**Boris Johnson** (Conservative) beat Livingstone in a closely fought contest in 2008, and defeated him again in 2012. Johnson was from a very different background to Livingstone, but his eccentric personality seemed to be well received by many Londoners. As mayor, Johnson maintained a high political profile, although critics alleged he did little for the city. In 2015, he was again elected as an MP, and retired as London mayor in 2016. He became foreign secretary in Theresa May's Cabinet.

Simon Dawson/Bloomberg via Getty Images

**Sadiq Khan**, one of eight children of a Pakistani immigrant Muslim family, who had later become a successful human rights lawyer and Labour MP, defeated the Conservative candidate Zac Goldsmith in 2016. His clear victory, despite a widely deplored attempt by the Conservative campaign to associate him with Muslim extremism, seemed emblematic of the cosmopolitan and multicultural city that London has become. Khan has robustly restated his own strong opposition to any form of racism, including anti-Semitism and is socially liberal on homosexuality and women's rights. In office, he has argued against the expansion of Heathrow Airport (a concern for many West London voters) and focused on affordable transport and air pollution.

trunk roads became a national responsibility. Social security was effectively taken over by central government, partly to ensure that all those in the same circumstances were treated similarly, regardless of where they lived. For these and other reasons, local authority hospitals and later community health services were transferred from local government to the NHS. However, it was the loss of services that was one of the main developments that led William Robson (1966) to lament that local government was in crisis.

From the 1980s onwards, local government has lost full responsibility for many more services and operational control of others. Thus, some of the once extensive education services of local councils have been substantially transferred (further education,

vocational training, academy schools). Many local authorities throughout the country once built and maintained extensive council housing estates, which have since been largely forcibly sold off to their tenants under 'right to buy' legislation, while much of the remaining rented housing stock has been transferred to housing associations or private landlords. Residential care for the old and infirm has been substantially privatised, although councils retain regulatory responsibilities. Councils also keep extensive and expensive responsibilities for supplying home care for those who need it. Former council services were made subject to compulsory competitive tendering (CCT) by Conservative governments in a series of Local Government Acts, including building construction and maintenance (1980), cleaning services, ground maintenance, vehicle maintenance, school meals and refuse collection (1988) and housing management and other white-collar services (1992). Under CCT, the council retained ultimate responsibility for the service, but it could be provided by a private firm where it submitted the lowest tender. So, refuse collection may be undertaken by outside firms rather than workers directly employed by the council.

In the late 1990s, New Labour later replaced CCT with a new 'best value' approach, which allowed councils more scope to procure services on grounds other than cost, but the provision of services continued to be mixed.

The consequence has been that elected local authorities are no longer the only form of local government for their area. As Blair (1998, p. 10) observed: 'There are all sorts of players on the local pitch jostling for position where previously the local council was the main game in town.' Local authorities in Britain have been persuaded to assume more of an 'enabling' role (Clarke and Stewart, 1988; Brooke, 1989). While local councils may retain ultimate responsibility for key local decisions and services, they should enable others, including local business, voluntary organisations and other public agencies and community groups, to participate in decisions and provide services rather than seeking to control everything. In reality, local authorities, short of powers and resources, had little choice over cooperating with other agencies, the voluntary and private sector.

This reflects much of the currently fashionable governance literature. Governance emphasises the process of governing rather than the machinery of government. Local governance involves not just the formal institutions of local government but the whole process of delivering local services and governing local communities through complex partnerships or networks of public, private and voluntary bodies and all manner of local interests (Leach and Percy-Smith, 2001).

---

Governance *is the process by which we collectively solve our problems and meet our society's needs.*

---

Government *is the instrument we use' (Osborne and Gaebler, 1992).*

---

Local governance *includes appointed agencies and other local governing bodies besides elected local authorities, but also emphasises the process of governing, rather than the institutions of government, and relations between local authorities, other agencies, voluntary bodies and local business and community groups.*

---

The enabling role requires new skills, in drawing up and monitoring contracts, inspecting and regulating. Where local councils are working with other agencies and the private and voluntary sectors in partnerships and networks, diplomatic cooperation is required, rather than the line management local government officials were used to in large hierarchical organisations. Under New Labour, this was sometimes referred to as 'third way management'. Instead of the command and control management of old large and hierarchically structured public sector organisations, or the competition and profit maximisation that drives the private sector, third way management emphasised leadership, diplomacy and collaborative joint working.

Critics complain of the erosion of local autonomy by central government and the bypassing of elected local authorities by appointed agencies, sometimes described as the 'local quangocracy' (Wilson and Game, 2011, p. 155). Indeed, there might be as many as 5,000 of these quangos in local government, with around 70,000 board members – many times the number of elected councillors (Wilson and Game, 2011, p. 19). (Quangos are discussed in more detail in Chapter 18, pp. 389–94.) There is, it is argued, a 'democratic deficit' in the running of local services. All the major parties, particularly when they are in opposition, lament the decline in local democracy and promise to restore power to local communities. But, with the exception of some specific innovations, Labour and Conservative governments have contributed to the erosion or bypassing of democratic local government by passing on spending cuts, or by taking over or giving away traditional local government functions. Conservative-led governments since 2010 have continued this trend.

However, local councils retain some advantages in this fragmented jumble of local agencies and networks. They still have extensive statutory powers, control many key resources, remain multipurpose bodies and, crucially, are the only directly elected bodies that can claim to represent their local community. This gives them a legitimacy lacking in other public agencies and in the business and voluntary sector, however public spirited they may claim to be. As the only bodies with some claim to represent the whole of their local communities, they remain well placed to take the lead on major local issues and projects. Crucially, though, they may still lack sufficient powers and resources to make things happen.

Since 2010, the functions of local government have continued to be pared back due to austerity cuts. The Conservatives have backed down on plans to convert all remaining local authority schools into privately managed and run academies, directly funded by grants from central government, although a strong steer in this direction remains. Today, while councils retain oversight of many other services, such as refuse collection, building cleaning and ground maintenance, these are now extensively privately supplied. Local public transport is operated by private bus and train companies, although partly regulated and often subsidised by local councils. Police services are controlled by independently elected police commissioners. Local authority architecture departments have largely disappeared, while planning departments are far smaller and weaker than formerly. Up and down the country, budget cuts have led to the closure of libraries, museums and leisure and sports centres. Local authorities retain extensive social service responsibilities, but overstretched and understaffed social services departments are routinely blamed for failures in child protection, social care and community relations.

*Source*: Photofusion/UIG via Getty Images
Local government still controls many important everyday services.

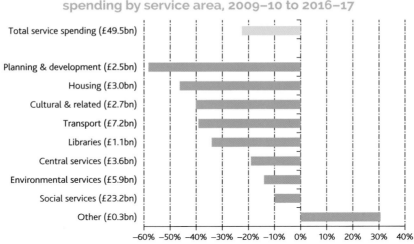

Figure 10.1: Real-terms change in local government spending by service area, 2009–10 to 2016–17

Note: 2009–10 budget in parentheses.

*Source*: IFS (2017) *A Time of Revolution? British Local Government Finance in the 2010s*, Figure 2.3, p. 12 Reproduced with permission of the Institute for Fiscal Studies. Copyright held by Institute for Fiscal Studies

The cuts to local government funding have been extensive, as we saw in the introduction. Local authority spending on public services was 22% lower in 2017 than in 2010, when the Conservative-led government was first elected and began the austerity drive in earnest (*The Economist*, 2017). Some services have been drastically reduced, as Figure 10.1 shows. The biggest cuts have been in transport and social care, such as home visits for the elderly. Both of these services are used predominately by less wealthy groups. Central government has continued its pressure on local government to think differently about what it does, in order to make savings. By 2020, central government plans to phase out the main grants through which it supports local authorities, encouraging (or forcing) them to find alternative sources of revenue and allowing them to keep a larger share of local business rates. Since 2010, one of the tools that local councils have been encouraged to use is the creation of local enterprise partnerships – voluntary partnerships between local authorities and businesses, which determine local economic priorities and lead economic growth and job creation within the local area. Economic necessity is forcing innovative approaches in local government.

# FROM CENTRAL-LOCAL RELATIONS TO 'MULTI-LEVEL GOVERNANCE'

There has long been an academic debate over what used to be called 'central-local relations', perceived as the relationship between the government at Westminster and elected local authorities. The term 'central-local relations' implies that only two levels of government matter, and is now a rather inadequate term to describe the still developing system of multi-level governance in Britain.

Among the various levels of government with which English local authorities have to relate, the most important by far remains the government at Westminster, but it is no longer the only level that counts. The EU had a large and growing impact on British local governance, both as a source of additional funding, chiefly through the European Regional Development Fund and the Social Fund, as well as specific funding for problems such as the decline of coal mining (at least until the 2016 referendum result). EU legislation also affected local responsibilities for the environment, waste management, transport and planning. Local councils were among the most vigorous lobbyists in Brussels, although the combined effect of the UK's decision to leave the EU and severe budget cuts have curtailed much of this lobbying. Similarly, local authorities in Scotland, Wales and Northern Ireland now have devolved national as well as the more remote UK government and the EU to cope with. Moreover, as we have seen, local authorities have to cooperate with neighbouring councils and a range of appointed local agencies, the local private and voluntary sectors and numerous community groups of all kinds in their own areas. The concept of the enabling authority has involved a shift to a more diplomatic rather than hierarchical relationship with partners in new complex networks.

Central-local relations have been commonly illustrated in terms of various analogies or models. Some saw local government as the 'partner' of central government, which implies a degree of equality, while others perceived local government in a position of impotent dependence as the 'agent' of the centre. A third view uses the term 'steward', which emphasises the subordinate position of local government but suggests rather more discretion than the agent model. Finally, the 'power dependence' model suggests that central and local government have resources they can use in relationship with each other (Rhodes, 1981, 1988). These models can be adapted (if somewhat awkwardly) to meet the more complex relationships arising within multi-level and inter-authority governance. If elected local authorities are too dependent on central government for their powers and finance to be regarded as 'partners', the same is even more true of other public agencies, which do not have the legitimacy of election or their own taxes. However, knowledge of local conditions and responsibility for implementation of central policies can give all kinds of local agencies considerable leverage over decisions locally and policy outcomes. In practice, there are significant differences in policies and service levels between local authorities, and some similar differences between appointed local agencies. If such bodies were simply agents implementing national policy, these differences would not exist.

It is the 'power dependence' model that can be most usefully adapted to inter-authority relations, and relations between the public, private and voluntary sectors (Rhodes, 1997). In partnerships and policy networks, for example, each participating organisation may bring in certain strengths or resources that will help to determine their influence in decision-making. Thus in a public-private partnership, a local council may contribute significant statutory powers, finance, information and legitimacy arising from its election, while a private firm may offer additional finance, commercial enterprise and experience and specific expertise. In a collaborative relationship between public agencies, such as between a local authority and health authorities over care in the community, each participant brings something that is useful to the other, and both may benefit from a fruitful cooperation (in a positive sum rather than zero-sum game).

Optimists see the new world of local governance as offering many opportunities for the development of cooperative policy networks, in which organisations from the public, private and voluntary sectors work together, drawing on a wide range of resources, and encouraging the inclusion and participation of people from across the whole local community. Both the command and control relationships typical of old-fashioned public bureaucracies and the competitive zero-sum relationships of the free market are rejected. Instead, a true 'third way' of managing and delivering services to people is envisaged, involving collaborative networks of organisations and individuals working together as equals, employing more diplomatic and less authoritative forms of leadership (Rhodes, 1997).

Pessimists, by contrast, emphasise the fragmentation of government, the potential waste, duplication and inefficiency resulting from too many agencies with overlapping responsibilities. They are more cynical over the prospects for mutual cooperation between organisations in policy networks, assuming that each will follow their own institutional interests, guided by their own organisational culture. Some formal partners will be only token participants and will offer few, if any, useful resources. The bulk of the local community will be bemused by the more complex and fast-changing institutional environment, and will become apathetic and alienated rather than engaged participants. No one will be effectively in charge and accountability will be weaker. Decisions will take longer and less will be achieved.

## THE NORTHERN POWERHOUSE, METRO MAYORS AND NEW COMBINED AUTHORITIES

It is often argued that London has become too dominant in British government and the wider British economy. While the motor of Britain's nineteenth-century Industrial Revolution had been provincial cities and regions in the north and Midlands, wealth and power have become increasingly centred on London and the southeast. George Osborne, former chancellor (2010–16), was a leading advocate of a Northern Powerhouse to reinvigorate the government and economy of provincial regions, to provide a counterweight to London and inspire more broadly based economic growth and prosperity.

The government of London, with its directly elected mayor, provided some of the inspiration for the Cameron government's proposals for transforming and re-energising the major English regional conurbations. The new Greater Manchester Combined Authority, established in 2011, with an elected mayor working with the existing council leaders within its boundaries, soon provided the model for similar developments elsewhere. Greater Manchester is now not only responsible for economic regeneration, transport and housing development but will also have a combined budget for health and social services. Moreover, the mayor will also be the police commissioner for the area. Five more new combined authorities, up and running following elections in 2017, are Liverpool City Region, West Midlands, West of England, Tees Valley, and Cambridgeshire & Peterborough.

Most of these have fewer existing powers than Greater Manchester.

It will take some time to discover how much difference these new mayors and combined authorities will make in practice, especially as George Osborne, who coined the term 'Northern Powerhouse' and backed the associated new institutions, was dismissed by Theresa May in 2016, leaving these developments without a champion at the centre of government. Moreover, the new metro mayors (also known as 'combined authority mayors'), who were elected in May 2017, will have to work closely with the leaders of constituent local authorities in their areas, and this may prove difficult, particularly as they belong to different parties and represent areas that may have conflicting interests (see Table 10.2).

The main emphasis has been on economic regeneration and stimulating the economies of the regions, in order to rebalance the British economy, making growth and prosperity less dependent on London and the southeast. To this end, there are proposals to develop transport links within and between northern city regions, and improve existing east–west communications, which are notoriously inferior to their north–south equivalents, where the gap will become wider still when and if the high-speed rail between London and Leeds/Manchester is built, unless there are major improvements to road and rail networks in the north.

What other functions besides economic regeneration and transport will be exercised by the new regional city authorities? There is much to be said for integrating health and social services, as in Greater Manchester. Currently, hospitals spend large sums of money keeping elderly and frail patients in beds needed by others, because there are inadequate facilities for social care in the local community provided by cash-strapped local councils. The problem is hardly confined to Manchester and such integration of health and social care might more logically be administered over the whole country. Perhaps if it is successful in Manchester, it will be.

## Table 10.2 Elections of metro mayors, 2017

| Combined authority | New mayor | Party | % vote | Turnout |
|---|---|---|---|---|
| Cambridgeshire & Peterborough | James Palmer | Conservative | 57% (38% on first round) | 33.6% |
| Greater Manchester | Andy Burnham | Labour | 63% | 28.6% |
| Liverpool City Region | Steve Rotheram | Labour | 59% | 26.2% |
| Tees Valley | Ben Houchen | Conservative | 51% (39% on first round) | 21.0% |
| West Midlands | Andy Street | Conservative | 50.4% (42% on first round | 26.3% |
| West of England | Tim Bowles | Conservative | 52% (27% on first round) | 29.3% |

Note: If no candidate gains more than half the votes on the first round, a second round of counting checks preferences for the two highest placed candidates from those whose first vote was for a candidate eliminated on the first round. Four mayors were elected after a second round of counting.

*Source*: Data from www.bbc.co.uk/news/election-2017-39817224

However, a substantial devolution of power to northern regional cities runs counter to the increased central control, diminished budgets and erosion of local discretion that has been a feature of British local government over the past half-century or so. Ultimately, the success of any effective regional devolution must depend on what effective powers and resources are devolved to new bodies. British governments have not in the past voluntarily given substantial powers away to local or regional bodies. Cynics might suggest that only problematic and difficult functions will be surrendered. For all these reasons, the prospects for a substantial and effective devolution of power to elected city regional authorities still seems questionable. For optimists, this is a hard, but exciting time in local government, with new structures and new forms of governance. For pessimists, local government is being hollowed out by cuts from above.

## SUMMARY

» While there is a strong case for democratic local institutions, there are problems with the practice of local democracy, including public ignorance and apathy and relatively weak local accountability.

» Although some argue there should be no place for party politics in local government, nearly all local councils (and all larger authorities) are dominated by political parties.

» Repeated reorganisations of authorities, boundaries and functions over half a century have failed to produce a structure that satisfactorily reflects community identities and ensures efficient and effective local service provision. Local government remains varied and confusing, particularly in England.

» Attempts to make local authority decision-making and accountability more transparent through (for example) elected mayors and local cabinets have, as yet, had little impact.

» Local government only finances a minority of its own spending from locally determined taxes (now the council tax), receiving the bulk of its money from central government grants. Local government taxation remains controversial. The Lib Dems have advocated a local income tax.

» Elected local authorities have lost some important functions since 1945, and no longer necessarily provide all the services themselves for which they retain responsibility. They are increasingly expected to work with (or 'enable') others, including appointed public agencies, the private and voluntary sectors, to provide local services rather than provide those services directly themselves.

» Local governance is a term widely used to cover all local community decision-making and the delivery of local public services by appointed agencies and others. It includes more than simply the elected tiers of government.

» Local public bodies of all kinds now work within a framework of multi-level governance. They have to work with other public bodies, the private and voluntary sectors within their own area, but also need to relate upwards not only to UK central government, but also to the EU, devolved national government and regional administration, and downwards to particular institutions, community and parish councils.

» The new regional conurbations with elected mayors are an interesting innovation, but throw up some awkward questions over finance and longer term central government support.

# ? QUESTIONS FOR DISCUSSION

» Why is public knowledge of, and interest in, local government apparently so low?

» Why are there 'all sorts of players on the local pitch'? Should all local public services be run by elected local councils?

» Why has it proved so difficult to reorganise local government so as to provide for local democratic accountability and efficient and cost-effective local services?

» Should the present council tax be replaced by a local income tax?

» How far are modern elected local authorities more enablers than providers? What are the implications in practice?

» In what ways are the private and voluntary sectors involved in the provision of local services? What advantages and disadvantages might there be in their involvement?

» Should local councils be headed by directly elected mayors?

» What are the obstacles to devolving more power to local councils?

» Will the devolution of power to urban conurbations, like Greater Manchester, be a success? Why has central government been open to devolution? What risks and rewards could there be in passing more power to local councils?

 # FURTHER READING

There used to be an extensive academic literature on UK local government, reflecting a vibrant specialist interest in urban politics. A succession of controversial actual and projected reforms of finance and management helped feed academic debate. Since the introduction of the council tax in 1993, the establishment of a Greater London Authority in 2000 and muted public reaction to a few additional executive mayors, the pace of change and controversy has slowed, and this is reflected in the literature.

Wilson and Game (2011) *Local Government in the United Kingdom* (5th edn) remains the best available textbook on British local government. Byrne (2000) *Local Government in Britain* can also still be recommended. Both need updating. Stoker (2000) has edited a useful reader on *The New Politics of British Local Governance*, although this and Leach and Percy-Smith (2001) *Local Governance in Britain* are now rather outdated. Stoker and Wilson's (eds) (2004) *British Local Government into the 21st Century* surveys developments in local governance and services. Tony Travers is the leading writer on London government; see his *London's Boroughs at 50* (2015) and his earlier *The Politics of London:* *Governing an Ungovernable City* (2003). Butler et al.'s (1994) *Failure in British Government: The Politics of the Poll Tax* provides a detailed analysis of the poll tax story.

 ## USEFUL WEBSITES

As always, websites provide important sources on recent and current developments, notably the Local Government Association's website: www.local.gov.uk. These and newspaper articles are the best sources on the Northern Powerhouse. Most local authorities have their own websites.

 *Further student resources to support learning are available at*
**www.macmillanihe.com/griffiths-brit-pol-3e**

# 11 DEVOLUTION

In September 2014, by a margin of 55% to 45%, the Scottish people voted 'no' to the question: 'Should Scotland be an independent country?' This result was far closer than many pundits had predicted. A rush of support for the independence campaign, in the weeks before the vote, had made the breakup of Britain seem a real possibility. The opinion polls were too close to call. It was only a late and impassioned intervention from Gordon Brown, the former UK prime minister and a Scot, the promise of greater powers for the Scottish Parliament, and a panicked final campaign push from those who wanted Scotland to remain part of the United Kingdom that gained victory.

The title of this book implicitly assumes that Britain (or the United Kingdom) should be the legitimate focus for analysing government and politics within these islands. Once, this would have been incontrovertible. Until 1921, the Parliament at Westminster and the British Cabinet exercised sovereign power over Britain and Ireland, as a unitary state. Since then, the Republic of Ireland emerged as a separate state, with Northern Ireland granted its own devolved parliament and government at Stormont. But otherwise, British government continued with full jurisdiction over England, Scotland and Wales, which were subject to the same Westminster Parliament and much the same government departments, despite some administrative devolution to the Scottish Office and, later, the Welsh Office. The same political parties (Conservative, Labour and Liberal/Lib Dem) competed in all three countries for representation at Westminster and power in Downing Street and Whitehall. British Cabinets were similarly drawn from Britain as a whole, with Scots and Welsh well represented at the highest level. Twentieth-century Scottish prime ministers included Balfour, Campbell-Bannerman, MacDonald, Home and Brown, while Lloyd George and Callaghan were Welsh. Scots and Welsh also figured prominently among the leaders of all three main UK political parties. Of postwar leaders of the Liberals and later Lib Dems, Clement Davies was Welsh, while Grimond, Steel, Kennedy and Campbell were all Scots, representing Scottish parliamentary constituencies. Swings in the fortunes of all three parties once generally appeared broadly similar across Britain as a whole, and substantially transcended internal national borders.

British politics and government now appears more fragmented and divided, particularly following significant devolution of powers to a new Scottish Parliament and some to the Welsh Assembly from 1998 onwards. While Labour and the Lib Dems initially controlled the new Scottish Parliament and government in Edinburgh, in 2007 the Scottish National Party (SNP) overtook Labour and formed a minority administration, and went on to secure an overall majority in 2011, and in so doing transformed the nature of Scottish politics. In the

2015 general election, Labour, the Conservatives and the Lib Dems, which between them had once held nearly all the Scottish parliamentary seats at Westminster, each held only a single seat in Scotland, with all the rest won by the SNP (but see the 2017 election, discussed below).

Political differences within the UK were further underlined when a majority in England and Wales voted in the 2016 referendum to leave the EU, while Scotland and Northern Ireland voted to remain. Scottish First Minister Nicola Sturgeon threatened a second referendum on Scottish independence, unless special arrangements were made for Scotland's relations with the EU. The relationship between mainland Britain, Northern Ireland and the Republic became a major issue in the first phase of negotiations over Britain's exit from the European Union. It seemed that the end of one union, between the UK and the EU, could soon be followed by the end of others. Yet, in the 2017 general election, all three main British parties made gains at the expense of the SNP, and prospects for a second independence referendum faded. Moreover, following the 2017 election, the Conservatives depended on Scottish Conservative MPs and the Democratic Unionist Party (DUP) in Northern Ireland for a majority at Westminster. Thus, even Westminster politics as a whole remains closely bound up with all the distinctive national communities that make up the UK.

Even so, the union will only continue to survive as long as majorities in its constituent parts feel that its benefits appear to outweigh the attractions of independence, especially in Scotland.

## THIS CHAPTER:

» Explores briefly the implications of the ideology of nationalism for British government and politics.

» Examines the variously expressed nationalist pressures in Northern Ireland, Scotland and Wales.

» Discusses the political background to the development of different forms of devolved government within the UK, and some of the unresolved problems, including the substantial problem of England. While some argue for an English Parliament, others hope to revive prospects for English regional devolution.

## NATIONALIST PRESSURES ON THE BRITISH STATE

At the heart of the problem are confused and conflicting national identities and interests within the UK. The very language we use is often confused, substituting the British Isles for Great Britain or the United Kingdom, for example.

For much of the nineteenth century, it appeared that nationalism and the doctrine of national self-determination had little immediate relevance to Britain. It was a principle to be applied to others – Greeks, Belgians, Italians, Hungarians and Poles – whose demands for national freedom were then regarded sympathetically by many British politicians. It was widely assumed that Britain was already a kind of nation state, although a 'British' state only really emerged after the Act of Union between England and Scotland in 1707 (following the Union of the Crowns in 1603). A new sense of British national identity was substantially forged in the eighteenth and early nineteenth centuries, symbolized by the figure of Britannia on coins and in the anthem

*Rule Britannia.* Pride and loyalty in Britain as a unitary state were strengthened by successful industrial development, imperial expansion and the visible evidence of great power status (Colley, 2003).

---

*A unitary state is a state in which sovereignty or supreme power is retained at the centre and there is no significant delegation of authority to any regional institutions. All citizens are subject to the same laws and taxes and services are administered on the basis of equal treatment for all in the same circumstances.*

---

Mainstream accounts of British history implied that the growth of the British state was a beneficial and largely voluntary process from which all Britain's peoples ultimately benefitted; thus Wales and Scotland prospered from being partners with England in a profitable commercial and imperial enterprise. There is something in the claim, particularly as far as Scotland is concerned. Scottish and Welsh nationalists, of course, tend to interpret history rather differently, arguing that their language, culture and perhaps their economy suffered as a consequence of English dominance. Indeed, British loyalties overlaid rather than replaced older Scottish and Welsh identities, while in Ireland the incompatible claims of Irish and British nationalism ultimately led to the establishment of an independent Irish state in the south of the island in the early twentieth century, following the Easter Rising of 1916, the Anglo-Irish Peace Treaty of 1921, and the conversion of the ensuing Irish Free State into the Republic of Eire in 1937.

The now reduced United Kingdom of Britain and Northern Ireland was a more awkward and less satisfactory focus for national loyalty. Historian Norman Davies (2000, p. 870) has asserted categorically: 'The United Kingdom is not, and never has been, a nation state.' Scottish nationalist Tom Nairn (2001) coined the term 'Ukania' to describe what he regards as an outdated and artificial multinational state (like the old Austro-Hungarian Empire), ripe for disintegration into its separate nations.

Irish nationalism, culminating in the establishment of an independent state from 1921, was one stimulus to stirrings of separatist nationalism in Scotland and Wales. Plaid Cymru, the Welsh nationalist party, was founded in 1925, and the SNP dates back to 1928. Yet these did not initially achieve much political impact. Sir Ivor Jennings ([1941] 1966, p. 8) still felt able to claim in 1941, in the midst of the Second World War – perhaps because of the unifying threat from Nazi Germany – that 'Great Britain is a small island with a very homogeneous population. Few think of themselves as primarily English, Scots or Welsh.'

Today, the population of Britain appears less homogeneous, and the cultural identities and political allegiances of the varied peoples living within the borders of the UK state have become particularly complex and confused. Most of the Catholic community in Northern Ireland have long continued to regard themselves as Irish rather than British, owing political allegiance to the Irish Republic, although the unionist majority passionately insisted on their British identity. Opinion polls indicate that an increasing proportion of those living in Scotland and Wales regard themselves as Scots or Welsh rather than British; one factor that helps to explain rising support for the Scottish and Welsh nationalist parties from the early 1970s onwards. England remains by far the largest part of this complex mosaic of nations and communities. Many of its inhabitants still refer to themselves interchangeably as 'English' or 'British' (to the annoyance of Scots and Welsh), although there has been some growing debate over 'Englishness' and its potential political implications (e.g. Kenny, 2014).

Postwar immigration intensified and complicated ethnic divisions that cut across these old national communities and identities. Some of the ethnic minorities in Britain's large cities maintain a complex pattern of allegiances, often retaining strong cultural or religious links with other countries and communities, alongside a sometimes-strong sense of British identity, unless they have become alienated by rejection and discrimination. In some respects, it seems easier to be 'black and British' than to be black and English, Scottish, Welsh or European (see Chapter 4).

Conflicting cultural influences resulting from the pressures of globalisation have added additional dimensions to these confusions over identity and allegiance. UK membership of the EU, along with the growth of package tour holidays to European destinations and increased sporting and cultural ties, seems to have done little to encourage a sense of a common European cultural heritage. The media reflect more the influence of the American and English-speaking world, and weaken a sense of a pan-European identity. Indeed, the press overwhelmingly favoured leaving the EU in the 2016 referendum. However, not all UK citizens would freely identify with Anglo-American, western or liberal capitalism, as the anti-globalisation movements indicate, nor would they all any longer identify with Christian values and civilisation. A multi-faith and multicultural Britain has created new tensions and divisions within society and the state.

For the future, much depends on how far these various identities are felt to be exclusive and overriding. Norman Davies (2000, p. 874) argues: 'multiple identities are a natural feature of the human condition [as] everyone feels a sense of belonging to a complex network of communities, and there is no necessary tension between them'. Indeed, multiple identities fit comfortably with the notion of multi-level governance introduced in Chapter 1 (p. 16) suggesting that it is unnecessary to choose between being (for example) Glaswegian, Scottish, British or European. Yet many nationalists remain unwilling to settle for anything less than independence and full national sovereignty. In the end, the British state is likely to last as long as the various peoples who live within its borders want it to last, and this will depend on complex issues of political identity and allegiance. Nationalism has been accommodated within the UK since 1999 by greater devolution of power to Scotland, Wales and Northern Ireland. It is an open question whether this has stalled the disintegration of the British state or provided a way in which it can survive.

## NORTHERN IRELAND, IRISH NATIONALISM AND DEVOLUTION

If Britain does break up as a political unit, Ireland began the process. It was the demand for Irish 'Home Rule' in the nineteenth century that provided the stimulus for the policy which the Gladstonian Liberal Party adopted of 'Home Rule all round', the forerunner of devolution. Irish nationalism and Irish separatism subsequently provided a precedent for Scottish and Welsh nationalism.

Ireland, as a whole, was always the least integrated part of the 'United' Kingdom. Its people had remained predominantly Catholic, while most inhabitants of Great Britain were converted to varieties of Protestantism. What has come to be called the 'Irish problem' was really an 'Ulster' or 'British problem' resulting from 'the English, and their self-serving strategies of plantation and subordination begun in the seventeenth century' (Judd, 1996, p. 49). Scottish and English Protestants were deliberately settled in Northern Ireland in the seventeenth century, creating new plantations and quelling the threat of rebellion. Formal political union between Ireland and Britain only came about in 1801 following the crushing of the revolt of the United Irishmen (known as the Irish Rebellion) in 1798, and was never a success.

The growth of British power and prosperity hardly impacted on the bulk of the Irish, who earned a bare subsistence from land rented from (often absentee) landlords. The 1845 Irish potato famine and the failure of land reform fed a growing nationalist movement, which eventually convinced the Liberal leader William Gladstone that Home Rule was the only solution to 'the Irish problem'. This led to a crisis in British politics, split the Liberal Party, and resulted in a 20-year period of dominance by the Conservatives who wanted to maintain the union. (Indeed, for a time, the Conservative Party was rebranded as 'Unionist', partly to accommodate liberal unionist defectors from Gladstone's Liberals.)

The failure to concede Home Rule to moderate nationalists before the First World War led to the Easter Rising of 1916 – an armed insurrection in Ireland during Easter Week, April 1916 aimed at bringing an end to British rule in Ireland – and its bitter aftermath, with the dominance of a new breed of nationalist who demanded full independence and were prepared to fight for it. The failure of repression led to the Irish Treaty of 1921 and the emergence of the 26-county Irish Free State, leaving the remaining 6 counties as a Northern Ireland 'statelet' within the UK.

It is often said that Northern Ireland is 'a place apart'. The people of Northern Ireland live in a distinctive political culture and support different political parties (see Table 11.1). The partition of Ireland in 1922 did not solve the 'Irish problem', since a sizeable Catholic and substantially Republican minority, now amounting to over 40% of the population, still lived in the north. In a sense, two minorities live side by side in Northern Ireland. The conflict in Northern Ireland is often oversimplified into one of religious division: the Catholic minority in Northern Ireland that feels threatened by the Protestant majority, and the Protestant minority in the island as a whole that feels threatened by Irish nationalism and Catholicism. In truth, the 'Troubles' in Northern Ireland arose from centuries of divisive historical experiences that embittered relations between the communities to an extent that is difficult to comprehend outside the province. Rulers and politicians long forgotten in Britain are celebrated in exotic murals. Quaint ceremonies, ritual marches, rival flags and symbols have become central to Northern Irish politics. Only recently has a partial measure of mutual tolerance grown between north and south, and between Catholics and Protestants within the province of Northern Ireland.

## THE TROUBLES IN NORTHERN IRELAND, 1960S–1990S

The Catholic minority in the north were effectively excluded from power, and faced discrimination over jobs and housing. There was considerable 'gerrymandering' – the manipulation of electoral boundaries to create advantage – which ensured Protestant dominance as well as brutality shown by the police – the Royal Ulster Constabulary – against the Catholic minority. This led to increasing pressure for civil rights for all members of the community from the late 1960s onwards.

### Table 11.1 Some of the political parties in Northern Ireland, 1960s to present day

| Party | Support and aims | Key politicians |
| --- | --- | --- |
| Ulster Unionist Party (UUP) | Protestant, supports union with Britain, supported the peace process, but became divided, and outflanked by DUP | David Trimble, Sir Reg Empey, Mike Nesbitt |
| Democratic Unionist Party (DUP) | Protestant, supports union with Britain, opposed power-sharing in 1998, but shared power with Sinn Féin since 2007. Provided support for the minority Conservative administration in Westminster after 2017. | Ian Paisley, Peter Robinson, Arlene Foster |
| Social Democratic and Labour Party (SDLP) | Catholic, republican and nationalist, but committed to constitutional methods. Supports peace process | Seamus Mallon, John Hume, Mark Durkan, Colum Eastwood |
| Sinn Féin (SF) | Catholic, republican and nationalist, linked with Provisional Irish Republican Army (IRA) and 'armed struggle' but signed up to peace process in 1998 and shared power with DUP in 2007 | Gerry Adams, Martin McGuinness, Michelle O'Neill, Mary Lou McDonald |
| Alliance Party of Northern Ireland (APNI) | Non-sectarian, seeks to bridge gap between two communities | John Alderdice, Sean Neeson, David Ford, Naomi Long |

Northern Ireland had its own devolved parliament and government at Stormont (since 1921), dominated by the Protestant majority, who had earlier fought to resist devolution. The emergence of moderate unionists, such as Terence O'Neill, who, as leader of the Ulster Unionist Party (UUP), was Northern Ireland's prime minister from 1963 to 1969, offered the prospect of some improvement in community relations between Catholics and Protestants. However, O'Neill's brand of progressive unionism was opposed by many Ulster loyalists, who were determined to resist change, and he was forced out of office.

Serious intercommunal rioting led to British troops being sent to restore order in 1969. Initially, Catholics welcomed these troops, but inevitably their strong-arm role became identified with supporting the Protestant state rather than defending the Catholic minority. The political condition of Northern Ireland moved close to a state of revolution. Violence against Catholics led many to accept the more militant provisional wing of the IRA as their defenders. The Troubles – a term euphemistically used to refer to the period of armed conflict – intensified after Bloody Sunday (January 1972) when British paratroopers killed 13 unarmed individuals participating in a civil rights march. Prime Minister Edward Heath announced that the Parliament at Stormont was suspended. From April 1972, Northern Ireland came under direct rule from Westminster.

Northern Ireland experienced a grim cycle of violence. Discrimination and repression won more recruits into the Provisional Irish Republican Army (IRA), who regarded British soldiers and members of the (largely Protestant) Royal Ulster Constabulary as representatives of an alien occupying power and thus legitimate targets. Loyalist paramilitaries attacked Catholics, particularly those suspected of IRA sympathies. There were well-grounded nationalist suspicions of collusion between loyalist paramilitaries and the British security forces. Much of the killing seemed more random: sometimes just the religious affiliation of the victim appeared sufficient excuse for murder. The escalation of violence led to a rising cumulative total of death and serious injury in the province, besides the economic damage caused

*Sources*: (a) Peter Turnley/Corbis/VCG via Getty Images;
(b) Robert Wallis/Corbis via Getty Images

'Loyalist' and 'Republican' views of the Troubles.

by the destruction of businesses and the deterrent to new investment. Social segregation was intensified, as Catholics living in mainly Protestant areas and Protestants in mainly Catholic areas were forced out of their homes. In some parts of Belfast and Derry (or Londonderry to unionists), virtual no-go areas were established, 'policed' by paramilitaries using punishment beatings and shootings to maintain internal discipline.

Periodically, violence was exported to the British mainland. In 1984, Margaret Thatcher narrowly escaped when an IRA bomb exploded at the Conservative Party conference, killing five and seriously injuring two senior ministers, Norman Tebbitt and John Wakeham. John Major's Cabinet survived a mortar attack on Downing Street in 1991. There were other, more random victims of IRA violence following pub bombings in Guildford and Birmingham. To the British government and the bulk of British public opinion, the perpetrators were despicable terrorists and murderers. However, IRA volunteers who died in the course of the 'armed struggle' were treated as heroes and martyrs within their own community. Such divergent perspectives are not uncommon in similar conflicts where particular communities totally reject the legitimacy of the state and its agents; examples include the Basque extremists in Spain, or Kashmiri separatists in India. However, it became increasingly clear over time that neither side could win by the use of force. The British government could not defeat the IRA, and the IRA could not achieve their goal of a united republican Ireland through the armed struggle.

Northern Ireland parties had always been distinctive, as the main British parties refrained from contesting Northern Ireland elections. In the old Stormont Parliament and in representation at Westminster until the 1970s, the dominant (almost the only) party was the UUP, then linked with the Conservatives. Republican Sinn Féin commonly won a few mainly Catholic constituencies, but the victors refused to take their seats in Westminster, seeing it as the parliament of an occupying power. From the late 1960s onwards, the Troubles led to a split in unionism.

The Reverend Ian Paisley, an intransigent Protestant, was elected as an independent unionist against the official UUP candidate in 1970 and founded the Democratic Unionist Party (DUP) in 1971 (see Key Figures 11.1). In 2003, the DUP finally overtook their UUP rivals, who suffered from periodic splits over the 'peace process'. On the Catholic or nationalist side, the most obvious division was between the peaceful constitutional nationalism of the Social Democratic and Labour Party (SDLP) and the more uncompromising Sinn Féin, linked with the IRA and the 'armed struggle'. However, the peace process also opened up fissures in the Republican ranks between the main provisional IRA and splinter movements such as 'Continuity IRA' and the 'Real IRA' opposed to the Republican ceasefire. Attempting to bridge the community divide is the small Alliance Party.

## THE SEARCH FOR PEACE IN NORTHERN IRELAND

A series of attempts to find a peaceful settlement were made in the 1970s and 80s, although in all these attempts Sinn Féin were excluded, through their connections with the IRA, while Paisley's DUP was also effectively excluded, because they regarded every new initiative as a sell-out. Instead, British governments tried to secure agreement on a new devolved government for Northern Ireland between the moderate nationalist SDLP and the moderate unionist UUP through the Sunningdale Agreement (1973–74), the Prior plan (1981–85) and the Anglo-Irish Agreement (1985).

In 1993, Major's government began a new peace process, differentiated from previous failed attempts because, for the first time, Sinn Féin (and effectively the IRA) was party to the negotiations. The SDLP could support successive plans for peace but could not end the violence. Only the IRA and Sinn Féin could do that. After 20 years of armed struggle, it was clear that the IRA could neither be defeated, but nor could it achieve victory by force. A series of public and secret communications broke the deadlock. Talks between the SDLP's John Hume and Sinn Féin leader Gerry Adams, secret messages from the Republican leadership to the British government and, finally, talks between John Major, the British prime minister, and Albert Reynolds (the Irish taoiseach or prime minister) led to the Downing Street Declaration (1993). This renounced any long-term British strategic interest in Northern Ireland and accepted the right of the peoples of north and south to unite at some time in the future. Sinn Féin would be able to join negotiations for a settlement if they renounced violence. But mutual suspicions prevented further progress.

The Labour election victory in 1997 restarted the Northern Ireland peace process. The IRA announced a restoration of its ceasefire in July 1997, and after six weeks of non-violence, Mo Mowlam, the new Northern Ireland secretary, invited Sinn Féin to join the peace talks on the long-term future for Northern Ireland. After a period of intense negotiations in which Mo Mowlam wooed the Republicans while Tony Blair reassured the fearful unionists, a formal agreement was eventually reached on Good Friday, 10 April 1998.

The Good Friday Agreement was based around a form of power-sharing in Northern Ireland, known as *consociationalism* – a model of democracy associated with Dutch political scientist Arend Lijphart. Consociationalism was designed for societies emerging from, or with the potential for, conflict and allowed power to be shared between unionist and nationalist groups. In Northern Ireland, the main consociational features are:

» Cross-community power-sharing at executive level, which means there is a joint office of first minister and deputy first minister, and a multi-party executive. The first and deputy first ministers, one unionist and one nationalist, have equal powers: one cannot be in position without the other. The multi-party executive (cabinet), or coalition, is made up of unionist and nationalist parties. The proportion of unionist and nationalist ministers within the executive is based on the number of seats a party wins in the election.

» The voting system used to elect Members of the Legislative Assembly (MLA) is single transferable vote (STV), which is a pro-portional system (see Chapter 13, p. 271). Positions of power, such as ministers, chairs and deputy chairs of committees, are allocated according to the parties' proportional vote.

» The Assembly is committed to cultural equality for the two main traditions, for example over language rights.

» There are also special voting arrangements that give veto rights to the minority community, so that certain Assembly decisions (including the election of the speaker, budget allocations, and changes to the rules of the Assembly) require cross-community – rather than simply – majority support (McGarry and O'Leary, 2006).

The Good Friday Agreement was popularly endorsed in May 1998 by a referendum majority of 94% in the Republic of Ireland and 71% in the north, where nearly all Catholics and a narrower majority of unionists voted in favour. The terms were incorporated in an international treaty, the British-Irish Agreement. Following elections to the new Northern Ireland Assembly in June 1998, the Ulster Unionist David Trimble and the SDLP's Seamus Mallon became first and deputy first ministers in July.

Arms decommissioning remained a ticking time-bomb under the peace process. After further prolonged negotiations between the British and Irish governments and the main parties, the IRA made a statement promising that it would eventually 'place its arms beyond use' in May 2000. However, progress on arms decommissioning by the IRA failed to satisfy the unionists. Fresh elections in November 2003 intensified the deadlock. Paisley's DUP, opposed to the 1998 Agreement, emerged as the largest party. On the nationalist side, Sinn Féin similarly overtook the more constitutional SDLP. However, the STV system enabled the small cross-denominational Alliance Party to retain six seats. These election results seemed most unlikely to assist any early resumption of the peace process and the return of devolved government. But, on 28 July 2005, the IRA issued a statement in which they 'formally ordered an end to the armed campaign' and instructed volunteers to 'assist the development of purely political and democratic programmes through exclusively peaceful means'. This was followed in the same year by the decommissioning of the IRA's entire arsenal of weapons, witnessed by the head of the international decommissioning body. Although the initial reaction of unionists was suspicious and cautious, ongoing talks involving the two major parties and the British and Irish governments laid the foundations for fresh Assembly elections in March 2007. This led to a remarkable new power-sharing administration, with the old irreconcilable unionist Ian Paisley as first minister and former IRA brigade commander Martin McGuiness as his deputy (see Key Figures 11.1). This once unthinkable alliance proved sufficiently warm for them to be later described in many newspapers as the 'Chuckle Brothers'. The

relationship became more formal when Paisley resigned as first minister a year later to be succeeded by Peter Robinson.

Since then, peace of a kind has survived in Northern Ireland. It may be flawed but it has already brought economic and political benefits to both communities. While not all nationalists have been prepared to renounce violence, both Sinn Féin and the IRA are now apparently committed to 'exclusively peaceful means' to achieve their long-term objectives. Sinn Féin has now shared power with unionists off and on for two decades, while the once-intransigent DUP head the governing coalition.

Most people in the province do not want a return to the past, but the longer term future remains unclear. The nationalist aim of joining the south remains diametrically opposed to the

## KEY FIGURES 11.1
### Ian Paisley and Martin McGuinness

*Source:* PAUL FAITH/AFP/Getty Images

Ian Paisley and Martin McGuinness formed an unlikely political alliance and a close working relationship that transcended religion, politics and nationalist division.

**Reverend Ian Paisley (1926–2014)** was a loyalist and a Protestant evangelical minister. On the political right, he preached against Catholicism and homosexuality. In the late 1960s, Paisley led loyalist opposition to the civil rights protests in Northern Ireland. He became MP for North Antrim in 1970 and a member of the European Parliament in 1979. In 1971, Paisley founded the Democratic Unionist Party (DUP), a party he led for nearly 40 years (and which formed an alliance with the Conservative Party after the 2017 election). Paisley opposed all attempts to resolve the conflict through power-sharing between unionists and republicans during the Troubles. In 2005, Paisley's DUP became the largest unionist party in Northern Ireland, replacing the Ulster Unionist Party (UUP). In 2007, the DUP agreed to share power with the republican party Sinn Féin. Paisley became first minister in May 2007. Paisley became a member of the House of Lords in 2010 and retired from frontline politics in 2011.

**Martin McGuinness (1950–2017)** was an Irish republican and Sinn Féin politician who became deputy first minister of Northern Ireland between May 2007 and January 2017. He was a former IRA leader, and became the MP for Mid Ulster from 1997 until 2013. His politics remained on the left. As with other Sinn Féin MPs, McGuinness never took his seat in Westminster, viewing it as a foreign parliament. He was one of the main architects of the Good Friday Agreement and the move to peace. McGuinness resigned the position of deputy first minister in 2017, plunging the Assembly into crisis, and announced in January 2017 that he would not be standing for re-election due to ill health. He died in March 2017. Between 2007 and 2011, McGuiness formed an unlikely working relationship with Ian Paisley.

unionist majority who identify with Britain. In time, demographic trends may produce a nationalist majority in Northern Ireland and Irish unification, although this prospect is distant and uncertain. Meanwhile, the Irish Republic appears less threatening to unionists with changes to its constitution. The Catholic Church has lost some of its former dominance. Moreover, until the financial crisis of 2008, Ireland had prospered economically as a member of the EU, and no longer appeared a poor relation. Thus the two Irelands have drawn closer together over time.

However, the 2016 referendum vote in favour of the UK leaving the EU poses new problems for the relations between the north and south of Ireland. It could lead to new border controls hindering trade and cross-border movement, with damaging economic and political effects, which is one reason why the majority in Northern Ireland voted to remain in the EU. It could even encourage some in the north to reassess the costs and benefits of a united Ireland. It seems unlikely, however, that there will be any fresh recourse to violence in pursuit of this political objective.

Yet the political power-sharing agreement has recently been put under threat. A simmering corruption scandal surrounding the implementation of a Renewable Heat Incentive scheme, which ran well over budget, following allegations that (among other problems) grants had been obtained for buildings that had never previously been heated, led to the resignation of Deputy First Minister Martin McGuinness in protest in early 2017. As this position was not filled, under the conditions of the power-sharing agreement, fresh elections were called for the Northern Ireland Assembly. McGuiness retired from active politics on grounds of health and died soon after. He was succeeded as leader of Sinn Féin in the Assembly by Michelle O'Neill. After these elections, the DUP only narrowly remained the largest party, with 28 seats against 27 for Sinn Féin, 12 for the SDLP, with the UUP down to just 6, behind the cross-sectarian Alliance Party's 8 (other parties picked up 4 seats between them). Thus, although the DUP remains the largest party, just, the Protestant unionist parties no longer hold the majority of seats. More seriously, the future of power-sharing now remains in the balance.

The general election of 2017 in Northern Ireland resulted in the DUP and Sinn Féin sharing the seats, with other parties not represented. Because of the loss of an overall majority by the party in the rest of Great Britain, the Conservative government became dependent for its survival at Westminster on the support of the 10 DUP MPs (Sinn Féin continues not to take up seats they have won). May's post-election agreement with the DUP promised an additional £1 billion investment in Northern Ireland, alienating nationalist parties in Wales and Scotland (as well as many other voters). Many pointed out that the Conservatives had previously insisted that extra money could not be found to fund additional investment and services. It placed further pressure on the union, by seeming to favour Northern Ireland over Scotland and Wales. The longer term future of devolution and power-sharing in Northern Ireland has therefore become problematic. The main points in Northern Ireland's devolution process are set out in Timeline 11.1 overleaf.

## NATIONALISM AND DEVOLUTION IN SCOTLAND AND WALES

The legacy of intercommunal strife and hatred in Northern Ireland and the whole history of the British engagement with Ireland as a whole and its contentious partition separate the province from the generally peaceful nationalist politics of Scotland and Wales. Both Scottish and Welsh nationalism have a long history, although internal religious, cultural and regional differences have sometimes weakened a sense of a common national identity. Moreover, many in both countries clearly felt an allegiance to the British monarchy and British state. Yet the successful achievement of Irish independence did have some influence in Scotland and Wales. Plaid Cymru, the Welsh nationalist party, was founded in 1925 and the Scottish National Party (SNP) in 1928, both only a few years after the establishment of the Irish Free State. In contrast with Irish nationalists, however, very few Scottish or Welsh nationalists were prepared to countenance violence in pursuit of their political aims.

### Timeline 11.1 Devolution to Northern Ireland

| | |
|---|---|
| 1919 | **Proposals for Home Rule in Ireland** (then entirely part of the UK). Introduced by Lloyd George, UK prime minister |
| 1922 | **Partition**. Six counties in the north of the island stay in the UK when the rest of Ireland becomes independent and later a republic. Many of the inhabitants are descended from Protestant settlers, although there is a large Catholic minority |
| 1968– | **The civil rights movement**. Catholics complain of unfair treatment at the hands of a largely Protestant political establishment, including the gerrymandering of electoral boundaries, discrimination in public services and jobs and by the Royal Ulster Constabulary |
| 1971–75 | **Internment**. Nearly 2,000 people are arrested and held without trial on suspicion of involvement in terrorism |
| 1972 | **Bloody Sunday**. A protest against internment on 30 January is fired upon by British troops, killing 14 people |
| 1972– | **Direct rule**. Edward Heath suspends the Northern Ireland parliament at Stormont (the only part of the UK with a devolved administration at the time) and introduces direct rule from Westminster |
| 1970s–1990s | **Terrorism**. Groups on both sides commit atrocities, including bombing bars and discos, killing politicians and administering 'punishment beatings' |
| 1993 | **Downing Street Declaration**. British Prime Minister John Major and Irish Taoiseach Albert Reynolds agree, in principle, talks on the future of Northern Ireland. Any party that 'renounces violence' is invited to take part |
| 1994 | **The IRA (August) and loyalist groups (October) announce a ceasefire**. Formal talks between the British government and Sinn Féin begin |
| 1996 | **The IRA declares an end to its ceasefire**. The Major government insists on the surrender or destruction of weapons by paramilitary groups. In response, the IRA explodes a bomb at Canary Wharf, killing two people in February. A bomb destroys a large part of central Manchester in June. A warning means no one is killed |
| 1997 | **The IRA announces a second ceasefire**. Tony Blair, now British prime minister, announces that decommissioning will take place in parallel with talks |
| 1998 | **Good Friday Agreement**. The deal includes the restoration of a devolved Assembly at Stormont and a role for the Republic of Ireland in the affairs of the north. A referendum later approves the deal. The Real IRA, a breakaway group, kills 29 people with a car bomb in Omagh, County Tyrone |
| 2000s | **Assembly suspended**. The NI Assembly was suspended on four occasions, including from October 2002 until May 2007, over 'loss of trust' between sides |
| 2005 | **IRA declares armed campaign over**. |
| 2006 | **IRA decommissions weapons**. Canadian General John de Chastelain announces inspectors' confirmation that all the IRA's weapons have been put beyond use |
| 2007 | **Power-sharing**. DUP leader Ian Paisley and Sinn Féin's Martin McGuinness are sworn in as first and deputy first ministers |
| 2017 | **Stormont** suspended after DUP and Sinn Féin fail to agree executive |

## SCOTTISH NATIONALISM: DEVOLUTION, FEDERALISM OR INDEPENDENCE?

Scotland had been an independent state for centuries when, on the death of Elizabeth I, James VI of Scotland succeeded to the English throne in 1603 as James I. If anything, this Union of the Crowns began as a kind of reverse takeover, in which the ruler of the smaller, less populous state also became king of the larger, after which the history of the two countries became much more closely interrelated. It only became a full union of the two states and parliaments in 1707, but the inequalities in population, wealth and power inevitably ensured that England dominated. However, Scotland retained much of its distinctive national identity, which, in the twentieth century, was reflected in a separate legal system, education system and established Church. Some Scottish affairs were handled by the Scottish Office, with a 'mini-parliament' of Scottish Westminster MPs meeting in the form of the Scottish Grand Committee.

Many Scots once fully supported the union. Scots peopled the empire, including the settlement of Scottish Presbyterians in Northern Ireland in the early years of the seventeenth century. Even as late as the 1945 general election, separatist nationalist sentiment was weakly expressed, with the SNP winning only 1.3% of the Scottish vote. The decline of Britain's empire and world role, along with industrial decline that adversely affected the Scottish mining, shipbuilding and textile industries, gave renewed significance to Scottish nationalism. The SNP began to win significant votes and seats in the 1970s. These successes worried the Labour Party, which had come to dominate Scottish politics, and helped commit the 1974–79 Labour government to Scottish devolution.

---

**Devolution** *involves the transfer of some powers and functions to nations or regions within the state from the central government and parliament, although the latter retains sovereignty or supreme power.*

---

The 1979 devolution referendum was lost because of a requirement of support from at least 40% of the Scottish electorate (not just those who voted). In the event, although 32.5% of the Scottish electorate voted 'yes', compared with 30.7% who voted 'no', the largest proportion of the electorate (37%) abstained. The failure of the referendum effectively brought down Callaghan's Labour government, and ushered in 18 years of Conservative rule, ending any immediate prospects for devolution. The SNP initially lost votes and seats, although nationalist feelings were reawakened by the discovery of oil off the Scottish coast, which greatly benefitted the British – rather than specifically Scottish – economy. The SNP campaigned under the slogan 'It's Scotland's oil' for a time in the 1970s. Margaret Thatcher's strident expression of English nationalism, and policies such as the poll tax (introduced in 1989 in Scotland, a year earlier than in England), alienated many Scots. One consequence was that the number of Conservative MPs returned for Scottish seats declined with each successive election until none at all were elected in 1997.

Labour became strongly recommitted to devolution in the 1980s. George Robertson, Scottish Labour MP and later Cabinet minister, argued that devolution would kill nationalism stone dead, although, by contrast, Tam Dalyell, a fellow Scottish Labour MP, regarded devolution as a dangerous slippery slope to independence. From 1988 to 1995, Labour joined with the Lib Dems, Scottish trade unions, local authorities and other organisations in a Scottish Constitutional Convention. This hammered out an agreed programme for devolution, which was to provide the basis for the 1998 Scotland Act. The SNP, committed to full independence, declined to join the Constitutional Convention, while the Conservative government under John Major and the Conservative Party in Scotland maintained its opposition to devolution and its support for the union. After the Labour landslide in the 1997 general election, a referendum in September 1997 gave overwhelming backing to a Scottish parliament (74.3%) with a smaller majority (63.5%) for tax varying powers. This conclusively settled the issue, rendering further Conservative opposition to the parliament fruitless. The party of the union was obliged to accept a major constitutional change they had previously argued could lead to the breakup of Britain.

## THE SCOTTISH PARLIAMENT AND GOVERNMENT

The first elections for the new Scottish Parliament were held in May 1999. Labour comfortably maintained its position as the largest party in Scotland but voting under the additional member system (AMS – see Chapter 13, pp. 272–73) failed to secure an overall majority. The electoral system benefitted the nationalists and (ironically) the Conservatives, who had always opposed devolution and proportional representation. Labour moved immediately towards a coalition administration with the Lib Dems, with whom they had worked closely in the Constitutional Convention, with Labour's Donald Dewar as first minister. Dewar, widely regarded as the 'father of the nation', did not live long to enjoy his new position. He died on 11 October 2000. His successors lacked his broad political appeal and authority.

A second round of elections in 2003 left the Conservatives and Lib Dems with the same number of seats as before. Both Labour (down from 56 to 50) and the SNP (down from 35 to 27) lost ground to various minority political groups, including the Greens (7 seats) and the Scottish Socialist Party (6 seats). However, the Labour–Lib Dem coalition, now headed by Jack McConnell, survived, albeit with a smaller overall majority. Major political difficulties were caused by the early intra-coalition differences and public outcry over the escalating cost of the new Scottish Parliament at Holyrood, although this largely evaporated once the new building was up and running, to general approval.

Following fresh elections in 2007, the SNP narrowly overtook Labour in seats and votes. As there was no basis for a workable coalition government, the largest party, the SNP, formed a minority nationalist administration with the canny Alex Salmond as the first minister. Without sufficient votes in Parliament or the country to press for an immediate referendum

on independence, their ultimate goal, the SNP was content to run devolved institutions and wait. There were some symbolic changes, however. Thus the Scottish executive was rebranded by the SNP as the Scottish government without the agreement of the other parties.

The SNP administration took over shortly before Brown succeeded Blair as UK prime minister. With an indubitably Scottish premier and a Scottish chancellor, it might have been expected that the SNP independence option would appear less attractive. Indeed, despite the growing unpopularity of Brown's government south of the border, support for Labour in Scotland substantially held. Moreover, some observers concluded that the 2008 financial crisis that particularly affected Scottish banks weakened the case for independence. Until then, Salmond and the SNP had held up the example of apparently prosperous small independent nations like Iceland or Ireland as confirmation that an independent Scotland could successfully 'go it alone'. The subsequent economic problems of those countries and the near-collapse of Scottish banks seemed to render the independence option more risky.

Yet political circumstances soon favoured the nationalists. In the 2011 elections to the Scottish Parliament, the SNP made substantial gains, winning 23 seats, a clear overall majority and a mandate for an independence referendum. This took place in 2014, resulting in defeat by a margin of 55% to 45%, after an acrimonious campaign. Independence initially appeared off the political agenda for a generation at least – Scottish voters were frequently told that they had a once in a lifetime decision. Following the referendum, Salmond resigned as SNP leader, to be replaced by his deputy Nicola Sturgeon.

This was far from the end for the SNP and its hopes for independence. In the subsequent 2015 general election, the SNP, now benefiting from the single member plurality ('first past the post') electoral system, almost swept the board in Scotland, winning 56 seats out of 59, with the main British parties securing only a seat each. The single member plurality system used for Westminster elections had previously hindered the SNP. Their rise in popularity meant that it now benefitted them, turning a lead in the popular vote into a rout in the general election. (For more on the distorting effects of the single member plurality system, see Chapter 13, pp. 267–70.)

This was an especially humiliating result for Labour in particular. Support for the party, which had previously dominated Scottish politics, plummeted. Some of the reasons were similar to those elsewhere in Britain – the decline in trade union membership and council housing. In Scotland, the now lower significance of religious divisions (the Scottish Catholic vote had been overwhelmingly Labour) also contributed to Labour's weakness. Labour was perhaps also punished for working with the Conservatives in an all-party unionist coalition to defeat the independence option in 2014. However, Labour may also have suffered from neglecting Scotland after devolution. In retrospect, it is perhaps significant that following devolution, only Donald Dewar among Scottish Labour heavyweights opted to pursue his political career at Holyrood rather than Westminster. Brown, Cook, Darling, Robertson and Reid all preferred to stay in the UK government in London. Those Scottish Labour politicians who chose to pursue their careers in Holyrood seemed to belong to the second tier.

The Scotland Act 2016 devolved further powers to Scotland (many of which are set on in Table 11.2). The Act recognises the Scottish Parliament and a Scottish government as permanent constitutional arrangements, with a referendum needed before either can be abolished. The legislation was based on recommendations given by the report of the Smith Commission, which was established in the wake of the independence referendum.

The 2016 elections for the Scottish Parliament were rather overshadowed by the bitter debate in the UK as a whole over whether to leave or remain in the EU. The SNP did less well than in the general election, substantially because of the AMS, which delivers results close to proportional representation. They won 63 seats, one less than previously, and just short of an overall majority. Labour lost 14 seats, holding just 24, and were overtaken by the Conservatives, led by Ruth Davidson, who won 31 seats. Now, all three leading parties in the Scottish Parliament were led by women. The Scottish Greens won 6 seats, gaining 4, and the Lib Dems retained 5.

But it was not these elections but the 2016 referendum result on EU membership that put Scottish independence back on the agenda, after Scots voted clearly to remain in the EU. Nicola Sturgeon moved quickly to prepare a bill for a fresh referendum. A vote for independence and the end of the union with England seemed a distinct possibility. In the event, the result of the unexpectedly called general election in June 2017 led to a partial recovery of all the established UK-wide parties and losses for the SNP. Sturgeon recognised that putting a second independence vote at the heart of her campaign during the 2017 general election had put some voters off the SNP, who went from having 56 seats in Westminster to 35. A second referendum now seems unlikely in the immediate future. However, Sturgeon has only decided to shelve plans for a second vote, and still hopes to call a referendum before 2021 and the next Scottish parliamentary vote. Few would bet against Scotland eventually becoming an independent state (see Comparing British Politics 11.1 overleaf). This remains an astonishing political turnaround compared with the years immediately following 1997, when a Labour government, including

*Source*: Ken Jack/Corbis via Getty Images

Ruth Davidson, leader of the Scottish Conservatives, has overseen a revival of the party north of the border.

## 🏴󠁧󠁢󠁥󠁮󠁧󠁿 COMPARING BRITISH POLITICS 11.1 🇨🇦 🇸🇰

### The independence option: Quebec and Slovakia

Nationalist Tom Nairn (1981, 2000, 2001) has gleefully described the breakup of Britain as virtually accomplished, assuming it is only a question of time before Scotland becomes an independent state. Iain McLean (2001, pp. 444–6) suggested two possibilities remain open, based on comparisons with Quebec and Slovakia.

Quebec is a French-speaking province of Canada where there has been persistent pressure from nationalists for an independent Quebec state. Yet voters, perhaps fearful of adverse economic consequences, have narrowly rejected the independence option in referendums. Quebec, for now, remains part of Canada.

In contrast, Slovakia, having threatened separation from the former Czechoslovakia in the aftermath of the collapse of the Eastern bloc and the end of Soviet control of Eastern Europe in the 1990s, suddenly found itself 'unexpectedly independent, to its short run disadvantage' (McLean, 2001, p. 444).

However, both the Czech Republic and Slovakia went on to join the EU in 2004. Will Scotland's future resemble the Quebec scenario (substantial home rule within a federal state) or the Slovak scenario of independence? Either seems possible.

several leading Scots politicians, successfully delivered devolution to Scotland and dominated its first government in Edinburgh.

### DEVOLUTION IN WALES

Early support for Welsh nationalism had more to do with preserving the Welsh culture and language from extinction rather than Welsh self-government. By the early twentieth century, 'English was taught as the language of advancement, and the use of Welsh was actively discouraged' (Madgwick and Rawkins, 1982, p. 67). Support for Plaid Cymru, the Welsh nationalist party, remained negligible until the late 1960s and, even after that, was substantially confined to the Welsh-speaking areas of north and central Wales. In the 1979 devolution referendum, only 11.8% of the Welsh electorate voted 'yes' to devolution, heavily crushed by the 46.5% who voted 'no' and the complacent 41.7% who did not bother to vote one way or the other. An even lower turnout marked the 1997 devolution referendum, and although the percentage voting 'yes' more than doubled and secured a wafer-thin majority for devolution, it still only represented one in four of the Welsh electorate. Welsh devolution was the by-product of the demand for Scottish devolution rather than

the result of Welsh pressure. The limited demands from the Welsh for autonomy were reflected in the relatively weak powers of the proposed new Welsh Assembly, with no tax-raising powers, and no right to pass primary legislation, especially when compared with those of the Scottish Parliament.

However, the bare majority for devolution on a low poll was enough to trigger the introduction of a Government of Wales Act in July 1998. The executive powers of the Welsh Office were transferred to the Assembly, which only had secondary legislative powers. The first elections (under the AMS, as in Scotland) took place in May 1999, and surprised expectations by failing to produce an overall Labour majority (only 28 seats out of 60). Labour formed a minority government, first under Alun Michael, then, after a successful opposition vote of no confidence in Michael, the more popular Rhodri Morgan. Morgan governed first with an informal understanding with Plaid Cymru, and subsequently with a full coalition with the Lib Dems. In fresh elections in May 2003, both Labour and the Conservatives made gains at the expense of Plaid Cymru, with the Lib Dems maintaining their share of the votes and seats. With half the seats, Rhodri Morgan's Labour Party went on to form a single-party administration.

### Table 11.2 Welsh National Assembly election results, May 2016

| Party | Constituency vote, % | Constituency seats | Regional list vote, % | List seats | Total seats |
|---|---|---|---|---|---|
| Welsh Labour | 35 | 27 | 31 | 2 | 29 |
| Plaid Cymru | 21 | 6 | 21 | 6 | 12 |
| Welsh Conservative Party | 21 | 6 | 19 | 5 | 11 |
| UKIP Wales | 12 | 0 | 13.0 | 7 | 7 |
| Welsh Liberal Democrat | 8 | 1 | 6 | 0 | 1 |

*Source*: Data from National Assembly of Wales election results, http://senedd.assembly.wales/mgManageElectionResults.aspx?bcr=1

Despite an uncertain start, support for devolution in Wales has strengthened. The Richard Commission (2004) found increased support for a Welsh Parliament, on the Scottish model, while the number wanting no elected body at all had dropped from 40% to 21%. There was a widespread view that the Assembly had been given too few powers to be effective. The new building housing the debating chamber for the Assembly, the Senedd in Cardiff, opened in March 2006. Soon afterwards, the Government of Wales Act 2006 conferred limited legislative powers on the Assembly, and separated the executive, the Welsh government, more clearly from the Assembly. Plaid Cymru attacked the Act for its failure to deliver a full Welsh parliament, similar to the Scottish Parliament. Wales gained further devolved powers as a result of The Wales Acts 2017 and 2014. The Acts drew on the Commission on Devolution in Wales, sometimes known as the Silk Commission after its chair Sir Paul Silk, established in 2011 by Cheryl Gillan, Welsh secretary in Westminster.

Since then, Labour has continued as the largest party represented in the 60-seat Welsh Assembly, but normally without an overall majority, as shown in 2016 elections (see Table 11.2). As with the Scottish Assembly elections, the AMS provides results closer to proportional representation than the single member plurality system used for the Westminster Parliament. This helps to explain the relative success of UKIP in securing seven seats, although they won no constituency seats. Another factor favouring UKIP was the timing of the election, in the middle of the campaign over the EU referendum. Apart from that, Labour performed much better and the nationalists considerably worse than in Scotland. Carwyn Jones, Labour's first minister, continued in power, despite the loss of the party's overall majority. In the 2017 general election, it was widely predicted that Labour would lose votes and seats, but instead Labour made gains, particularly at the expense of the Conservatives.

## ASYMMETRICAL DEVOLUTION IN THE UK

Although the devolution process in Wales and Scotland has run in parallel, with new assemblies and devolved governments established in each within a few years (see Timeline 11.2 overleaf), what is striking is how different the pattern of devolution in each country has been – a result known as asymmetrical devolution. 'One's overall impression of Labour's constitutional design is its incoherence' to the extent that it must be 'incomprehensible to most citizens'

---

*Asymmetrical devolution suggests that there is no common pattern to the devolution of powers within the state. Different nations or regions within the state involve very different size ranges, and involve different institutions, powers and processes*

---

### Timeline 11.2 Devolution to Scotland and Wales

| | WALES | SCOTLAND |
|---|---|---|
| 1536 | Under an Act of Union, Wales essentially becomes a region of England | |
| 1707 | | Great Britain is established through the Act of Union between Scotland and England, but the countries maintain separate legal powers and established churches |
| 1885 | | The office of secretary of state for Scotland is re-established |
| 1925 | Plaid Cymru, the Welsh nationalist party, is founded | |
| 1928 | | Scottish Office established |
| 1934 | | The Scottish National Party (SNP) is founded |
| 1964 | The Welsh Office is created, with a minister in the Cabinet | |
| Late 1960s onwards | | The discovery of North Sea oil off the Scottish coast leads to considerable resentment of London's exploitation of a 'Scottish' asset. Support for the SNP grows |
| 1969 | A Royal Commission on the Constitution meets and eventually recommends legislative and executive devolution for Scotland and Wales. The proposals are rejected as unworkable | |
| 1978 | Revised recommendations from the commission lead to the Scotland Act and the Wales Act, both subject to referendums | |
| March 1979 | Scottish and Welsh voters reject devolution in the referendums; more than 40% of Scots do not bother to vote. Shortly afterwards, the incoming Conservative government repeals both acts. Devolution is declared 'dead for a generation' | |
| July 1997 | White Paper on devolution published by the new Labour government | |
| September 1997 | Referendums held in Scotland and Wales. Both endorse proposals for an assembly in their country, the Welsh by a small majority | |
| 1998 | Scotland Act 1998 and the Government of Wales bill introduced | |
| 6 May 1999 | First elections to the Welsh and Scottish Assemblies | |
| 2007 | Government of Wales Act 2006 comes into force; the National Assembly and Welsh government are formally separated and the National Assembly gains powers to make laws for Wales in defined areas | |

| | WALES | SCOTLAND |
|---|---|---|
| 2007 | | SNP becomes largest party in Scottish Parliament and commits to a referendum on independence |
| 2011 | Wales votes in favour of giving the National Assembly further law-making powers | |
| 2014 and 17 | Wales Act devolves further powers to the Welsh Assembly | |
| 2014 | | Scotland votes in a referendum to remain in the UK by 55% to 45% |
| 2016 | | Scotland Act devolves further powers to the Scottish Parliament |
| 2016–17 | | Brexit vote in UK as a whole (but not Scotland) leads SNP to call for a second independence referendum at general election |

(Ward, 2000, p. 135). 'Each of the assemblies has a different size and composition, a different system of government, and a very different set of powers' (Hazell, 2000, p. 3).

Does this administrative untidiness matter? On the one hand, it provides supporting evidence for the view that Labour's constitutional reforms lacked any coherent overall vision; each initiative has been seemingly pursued in isolation, and some of the differences appear arbitrary. On the other hand, it could be argued that most of the more obvious differences reflect very different histories, cultures and political problems. So, an awkward collection of unique institutions with clumsy checks and balances designed to protect minorities and assuage the fears and suspicions of the majority was the minimum requirement for progress in Northern Ireland. The various devolved powers as well as the electoral systems used in each territory are set out in Table 11.3 overleaf.

Whereas Wales was effectively colonised by England, the political union of England and Scotland (whatever Scottish nationalists may now claim) began as a more equal partnership with the assent and subsequently some enthusiasm from the Scottish establishment. Scotland retained its own distinctive Church and legal and education systems, as well as a substantially separate administration, which could be readily transferred to the new Scottish government. Moreover, the demand for a Scottish Parliament was based on a distant historical precedent and a more recently established, but fairly clear consensus in favour of devolution. Detailed plans had been drawn up in the Scottish Constitutional Convention, backed by a broad swathe of Scottish opinion, and only required implementation.

The situation was very different in Wales, where devolution had been decisively rejected only 20 years before, and where popular backing remained in doubt until the last minute. It is often argued that Welsh nationalism is more commonly expressed in terms of culture and language rather than political institutions. Language was, in practice, a divisive rather than a unifying issue, with non-Welsh-speaking areas hostile to the financial and educational resources devoted to the Welsh language. It could be claimed that the Welsh voted uncertainly for devolution first, and only then began to consider what powers their new devolved institutions should have. Although the Welsh Assembly and government have acquired rather more powers over time, they still lag well behind their Scottish equivalents, and the gap could become larger if proposals

Table 11.3 Select major devolved powers

| | Scotland | Wales | Northern Ireland |
|---|---|---|---|
| **ELECTORAL SYSTEM** | | | |
| Nomenclature | Parliament | Assembly | Assembly |
| Electoral system | Additional member system | Additional member system | Single transferable vote |
| Size | 129 Members of the Scottish Parliament (MSPs); 73 represent individual geographical constituencies elected by the single member plurality system; 56 are returned from eight additional member regions, each electing seven MSPs | 60 Assembly Members (AMs); 40 AMs represent geographical constituencies elected by the single member plurality system; 20 AMs represent five electoral regions using the d'Hondt method of proportional representation | 90 Members of the Legislative Assembly (MLA); Executive selected by d'Hondt method of proportional representation to ensure unionists and Irish nationalists participate in government |
| **LAW AND ORDER** | | | |
| Justice | Devolved | Centralised | Devolved |
| Civil law | Devolved | Centralised | Devolved |
| Criminal law | Shared | Centralised | Devolved |
| Local administration, organisation and finance | Devolved | Devolved | Devolved |
| Elections | Devolved | Devolved | Devolved |
| Police | Devolved | Under consideration | Devolved |
| Prisons | Devolved | Under consideration | Devolved |
| Fire services | Devolved | Devolved | Devolved |
| **SOCIAL AND HEALTH POLICY** | | | |
| Health service | Devolved | Devolved | Devolved |
| Social services (housing and student support) | Devolved | Devolved | Devolved |
| Social welfare | Devolved | Devolved | Devolved |
| Food safety and standards | Devolved | Devolved | Devolved |

| ECONOMY, ENVIRONMENT AND TRANSPORT | | | |
|---|---|---|---|
| Taxation | Shared | Shared | Shared |
| Environment | Devolved | Devolved | Devolved |
| Housing and urban planning | Devolved | Devolved | Devolved |
| Transport | Shared | Shared | Shared |
| Economic development | Devolved | Devolved | Devolved |
| Agriculture, forestry and fisheries | Devolved | Devolved | Devolved |
| CULTURE AND EDUCATION | | | |
| Culture/language | Devolved | Devolved | Devolved |
| Primary, secondary, university and professional education | Devolved | Devolved | Devolved |
| Sport and recreation | Devolved | Devolved | Devolved |
| RESOURCES AND SPENDING | | | |
| Own tax resources | Yes | Yes | No |
| Allocation by UK government | Barnett formula – mechanism used by the Treasury to decide the distribution of UK wealth across Northern Ireland, Scotland, England and Wales | Barnett formula | Barnett formula |
| Devolved spending as % of total public spending | 63% | 60% | 50% |

*Sources*: www.gov.uk/guidance/devolution-settlement-wales; www.gov.uk/guidance/devolution-settlement-scotland; and www.gov.uk/guidance/devolution-settlement-northern-ireland

to devolve more powers to Scotland are implemented.

How far this administrative untidiness really matters is perhaps questionable. Most federal systems involve a considerable range in state populations, reflecting specific historical and cultural factors. Other countries that have pursued devolved government, such as Spain, have, like the UK, tackled the process incrementally, with considerable variations in powers and levels of autonomy for different areas. Yet it seems likely in such situations that nations and regions with fewer powers will, over time, demand functions and resources comparable to those where devolution has been extended further.

For all these reasons, devolution, in its current form, does not appear a final settlement.

Ron Davies, Welsh politician and former secretary of state for Wales, who led the devolution campaign there (until his abrupt political demise as the result of a scandal in October 1998), declared that devolution was 'a process not an event'. This was particularly true in Wales, where the case for, and extent of, devolution continues to be debated, but it is also manifestly the case for the UK as a whole. The referendums of 1997 and 1998, the Acts establishing devolved Parliaments and Assemblies in 1998 and 1999, and the elections for those devolved bodies in 1999 and onwards have not marked the achievement of devolution, but stages in the devolution process, which remains unfinished. Where it will eventually lead is unclear, and may not be so for decades.

## THE ENGLISH QUESTION

An obvious problem with devolution to date is that it is asymmetrical in another sense to that described earlier. Devolution to Northern Ireland, Scotland and Wales together only involves a small minority of the population of the UK. Of the 'four nations in one', England is much the largest in area and even more in population (see Figure 4.1). Thus England remains a massive cuckoo in the devolution nest. The growth of nationalist politics and changing national identities and allegiances pose questions for members of the majority nation, accustomed to consider themselves interchangeably English and British. Some fear a narrow and racist English nationalist backlash, while others more optimistically believe that devolution, and perhaps even the ultimate breakup of Britain, could help the English rediscover their own national culture and identity. There has been a spate of books on the rise of English national identity and what the political, social and cultural consequences of this are (e.g. Kenny, 2014).

There are more pressing political and constitutional concerns arising out of devolution. One issue concerns the number and role of Scottish MPs in the Commons following devolution. Scotland was overrepresented at Westminster, and this, always difficult to justify, became more anomalous once Scotland had its own Parliament. The implementation of the Scottish Boundary Commission recommendations has largely removed this overrepresentation. Scottish and English constituencies now have a similar average electorate. In 2015, the House of Commons attempted to correct another anomaly of devolution, when it approved the government's plans to introduce 'English votes for English laws'. In effect, this adds a new England-only committee stage for bills that are 'England-only in their entirety'. This will give English MPs a new 'veto' over laws that only affect England. This corrects that constitutional anomaly, the so-called 'West Lothian question' – after the seat of Tam Dalyell, the MP who published the problem – that non-English MPs could overturn a bill that only affects England.

### AN ENGLISH PARLIAMENT?

One apparently logical solution is the creation of a separate English Parliament in addition to the Westminster Parliament representing the whole of the UK. If the Scots, Welsh and Northern Irish are entitled to Home Rule, why not the English also? Thus each 'nation' within the union would acquire its own devolved assembly, which could also provide the basis for the development of a federal Britain. This solution, however, has not yet attracted much support. One problem is the sheer preponderance of the population of England within the UK. An English Parliament would represent 84% of the UK population. There would be damaging scope for duplication and conflict between the UK and English Parliaments.

### ENGLISH REGIONAL GOVERNMENT

Another solution is the development of English regional government, particularly if the main aim of devolution is seen as bringing government closer to people, decentralizing power and promoting regional economic development rather than satisfying nationalist aspirations. This would match initiatives in some member states of the EU, which itself established a Committee of the Regions as part of the Maastricht Treaty (1992).

The 1997 Labour government introduced regional development agencies in England, but with limited budgets and powers. Labour also promised referendums on elected regional assemblies. However, the only referendum held was for a regional assembly for the northeast, which was decisively rejected in 2004 and virtually ended any prospects for more regional devolution for the foreseeable future (Rathbone, 2005). Since then, the Conservative-Lib Dem coalition scrapped regional development agencies, although George Osborne, former chancellor, was later associated with plans for a 'Northern Powerhouse' and wider devolution of power to city regions (see Chapter 10, pp. 210–11). In particular, there has been substantial devolution of combined authorities with directly elected mayors and their own budgets. How far this new initiative is deemed successful and extended to cover other areas remains to be seen.

## DEVOLUTION, FEDERALISM OR SEPARATION?

Various future scenarios have already been touched upon. A first possibility is that the process will not go much further. The present pattern of sub-UK national devolution will more or less continue within the current complex system of multi-level governance. Extensive further powers may not be conceded to existing devolved bodies, and the sovereignty of the Westminster Parliament may appear unaffected. However, for different reasons, it seems unlikely that the present arrangements for governing Scotland, Wales and Northern Ireland can persist for long in their current form.

A second possibility is that intergovernmental relations ultimately may have to be more formalised. It is possible that the devolution process will be extended to create, over time, a quasi-federal or fully federal Britain (with or without Northern Ireland). This would end the unitary status of the UK and the sovereignty of the Westminster Parliament. The Scottish and Welsh levels of government would no longer appear conditional and subordinate, but sovereign in their own sphere. This would almost certainly require a written constitution, if only to regulate the functions and interrelationships of the various levels of government. How far the British system of government has already progressed in this direction is contentious. Bogdanor (2001, pp. 148–51) argues that parliamentary sovereignty has already been virtually destroyed and a quasi-federal system established.

Even if Scotland remains in the union, the scope for ambitious Scottish politicians in the Westminster Parliament and government is already reduced and could be constrained further. It would be virtually impossible for a prime minister at Westminster to appoint ministers sitting for Scottish parliamentary seats to preside over functions and services wholly or substantially delegated to the Edinburgh Parliament and government. One can imagine the political and media storm such appointments would provoke. The demand would be for English ministers to preside over English services. So fewer jobs in the UK Cabinet would be open to Scots. It may even or especially seem difficult to have a prime minister who is Scottish and represents a Scottish parliamentary constituency, when so many powers have been devolved: Gordon Brown could be the last Scottish prime minister of the UK. The same could apply to Wales over time, if more powers are conceded to the Welsh Assembly and executive. The union could thus be eroded steadily, without the need for any dramatic decision in a referendum or otherwise.

A third possibility is that Northern Ireland could eventually unite with the south, while Scotland (and perhaps Wales also) could become independent sovereign states, possibly within the EU. These areas of the present UK would cease to send representatives to the Westminster Parliament, which would become an English rather than a UK or British Parliament. The 'breakup of Britain' predicted and advocated by nationalists like Tom Nairn would become an accomplished fact. Today, nationalists share power in Northern Ireland, have run the government in Scotland since 2007, and were briefly junior partners in a coalition government in Wales. Few would have predicted such developments 50 years ago when nationalists were a tiny minority.

The eventual separation of Northern Ireland from Britain still seems possible. Its political system has long been distinctive, and quite different from that of the rest of the UK. The political circumstances that could lead to Scotland's separation have already been lightly indicated. It is certainly a plausible future scenario, although not the only one (see Comparing British Politics 11.1 on the Quebec and Slovak scenarios). A sizeable minority of Scots (45% in the devolution referendum) supported independence, but it would need a clear majority to succeed. It could certainly happen, as indicated by the collapse in support for the main UK parties in the 2015 general election, although the 2016 elections for the Scottish Parliament involving greater proportional representation produced a more ambiguous picture, while the general election of 2017 appeared a setback for Scottish nationalists, but they still hold the majority of Scottish seats at Westminster as well as in the Scottish Parliament. Support for independence in Wales still remains much lower than in Scotland, by any measure.

## A DISUNITED KINGDOM? THE FUTURE OF THE UK

The Conservative Party has long been associated with maintaining the union of the UK, and were only late and reluctant converts to devolution after referendums in Scotland and Wales gave them little alternative. Even today, no Conservative government would wish to preside over the dissolution of the union, and it may be assumed that a Conservative government would do everything possible to avoid such an outcome.

The current UK government appears increasingly alien to those Scots who did not vote for it. The only Scot in the Conservative Cabinet between 2015 and 2017 was David Mundell, secretary of state for Scotland, who secured the post from a shortlist of one, as the only Conservative MP representing a Scottish constituency. (This compares with the strong representation of Scots in Labour governments between 1997 and 2010.)

The Conservative Party remains committed to the union by their past history and ideology, and this commitment may increase, following the strong performance of Ruth Davidson's party in securing an unexpected increase in Scottish Conservative representation at Westminster from one to thirteen. If this proves to be a false new dawn, Conservatives may begin to question the value of a union with an increasingly awkward Scotland, if, without it, they would have a more comfortable overall majority at Westminster. If a Conservative government seeks to revise the Barnett formula (see Table 11.3) that helps finance Scottish spending, then the division of interest would be sharpened and the SNP case for independence strengthened.

There are fewer consolations for Labour. The party was founded by Scots, initially led by Scots, with a substantial Scottish presence in Labour Cabinets and the Parliamentary Labour Party. The last Labour government was headed by a Scottish prime minister and a Scottish chancellor. Despite the current parlous state of the party in Scotland, Labour must hope for a revival of the strong Labour tradition north of the border. The loss of Scotland would deprive the party of much of its tradition and roots, and leave it politically and intellectually impoverished, deprived of the heritage of many of its leading figures.

Scottish politics now appear quite different from English politics, when they were once similar. Of course, this may change, but so far it is the gloomy predictions of Tam Dalyell on devolution rather than the optimistic forecasts of George Robertson that have been fulfilled.

So the disintegration of the UK remains far from unthinkable. Whatever eventually happens will no doubt appear in retrospect 'inevitable'. But, at present, the future seems uncertain, to be influenced by events, the successes and failures of governments and politicians and, ultimately, the decisions of the people. States in a democratic era require popular legitimacy. The British state will survive as long as enough people in its constituent parts want it to survive. It will break up if and when national communities seek independence. Ultimately, what matters is the political consciousness and identities of people rather than institutional machinery, although the perceived performance of governments and parties may, of course, influence political attitudes.

## SUMMARY

» To many Britons in the nineteenth century, nationalism was a doctrine to be applied in other countries, as it was widely assumed that there was a British nation, and Britain was therefore a nation state.

» Yet British nationalism confronted Irish nationalism in Ireland, and never fully replaced older Welsh, Scottish and English identities and allegiances.

» Independence for the Republic of Ireland, divided allegiances in Northern Ireland, coupled with the rise of Scottish and Welsh nationalism, and the multi-faith and multicultural influences of immigration have contributed to the erosion of a sense of British national identity and posed problems for the long-run survival of the British state.

» In Northern Ireland, following 30 years of bitter conflict between republicans and the British state and 'loyalists', the 1998 Agreement led to new devolved institutions with power-sharing. Despite periodic crises, the peace process survives. Arms have been decommissioned and justice and policing devolved to the Northern Ireland Assembly and Executive. The breakdown in power-sharing in 2017 may prove only temporary, but could presage further problems.

» The growth of nationalism in Scotland and Wales converted the Labour Party to a policy of devolving some powers to representative bodies in those countries. After the first failed devolution attempt in 1979, Blair's Labour government established a new Scottish Parliament and Welsh Assembly.

» Devolution is 'asymmetrical', in that it involves different institutions, functions and electoral systems in Scotland and Wales.

» Devolution is also asymmetrical in that it does not cover England (with 84% of the UK population). One possible solution, a separate English Parliament, would involve too much duplication with Westminster. Another, devolution to the English regions, is only weakly supported: an elected regional assembly was decisively rejected in the northeast. However, new regional authorities with elected mayors have been established from 2017.

» Outside England, devolution is unlikely to be reversed. It is far more likely that further powers will be devolved over time. Possible future scenarios could be fully federal Britain, or the breakup of Britain into separate nation states.

» The Conservative government at Westminster may lead to increased tensions with Scotland in particular, and increase prospects for Scottish independence.

## QUESTIONS FOR DISCUSSION

»   In what sense has a British nation existed? How far does the UK still command the allegiance of its citizens? Why are national identities in Britain confused?

»   What is the real problem in Northern Ireland? Why has a solution appeared so difficult?

»   Account for the growth of Scottish nationalism. How far has devolution satisfied the demands of Scots for more control over the government of their country?

»   Why was Welsh support for an elected Assembly initially lukewarm? How far does Welsh nationalism differ from Scottish nationalism?

»   Should England have its own Parliament?

»   Account for the apparent lukewarm support for regional devolution in England.

»   What political conflicts have arisen and could arise between the Westminster government and devolved governments, particularly following the 2015 and 2017 general elections, the 2016 EU referendum result and Brexit.

»   Is devolution likely to satisfy demands in Scotland, Wales and Northern Ireland for more say in their own affairs? How far might devolution be a stage on the road to a federal Britain or the breakup of Britain?

»   How does devolution differ from federalism?

 ## FURTHER READING

There is an extensive literature on nationalism in general, rather less on nationalism in Britain. Davies (2000) *The Isles: A History* provides a stimulating history of the British Isles and its component nations, which is a corrective to Anglocentric accounts. Hall (2004) provides a brief general survey of nationalism in the UK, which is also discussed in Leach (2015).

There is a substantial literature on the Troubles and the peace process in Northern Ireland, some of which is happily more of historical interest than current relevance. Among more recent texts, see McEvoy (2008), Cochrane (2013), Tonge (2014a and b) and also Tonge's (2016) article 'The Impact of Withdrawal from the European Union upon Northern Ireland'.

On Scottish politics, Cairney and McGarvey (2013) is useful for historical background. For historical background on Scotland and the growth of nationalism, see Devine (2012) *The Scottish Nation*. Nairn (1981, 2000, 2001) provides a provocative nationalist perspective. On devolution, Jeffery

(2003) wrote a handy overview 'Devolution: What's It All For?' and another brief article 'An Outbreak of Consensus: Scottish Politics after Devolution' (2010) reviewing the then current state of Scottish devolution. The special edition of *Political Quarterly* (2016) is worth consulting. Runciman (2010) wrote a provocative short article entitled 'Is This the End of the UK?' following the results of the 2010 election. On the 2014 referendum, see Macwhirter (2013), and on the subsequent debate on Scotland's political future, see Devine (2016) *Independence or Union: Scotland's Past and Scotland's Present*.

Welsh nationalism and Welsh devolution have attracted rather less academic interest. See Morgan (2014) and Jones and Scully (2012) on the 2011 Welsh referendum. For an analysis of Plaid Cymru, see Sandry (2011).

On political identity in England, see Paxman (1998). For a more political analysis, see Kenny (2014). Gamble and Wright (2009) have edited a varied, provocative collection of essays on Britishness.

## USEFUL WEBSITES

Up-to-date information can be found on the websites of all the devolved bodies: Scottish Parliament: www.parliament.scot; Welsh Assembly: www.assembly.wales; Northern Ireland Assembly: www.niassembly.gov.uk.

The Centre on Constitutional Change is also a good resource: www.centreonconstitutional change.ac.uk/centre.

*Further student resources to support learning are available at*
**www.macmillanihe.com/griffiths-brit-pol-3e**

# 12  BRITAIN AND EUROPE

On 23 June 2016 voters in the United Kingdom voted to leave the European Union. The vote has momentous but as yet unclear implications for Britain's future political and economic relationships, not just with the EU and its member states, but also with the rest of the world. How far the UK can prosper politically and economically outside the EU remains to be seen. Much will depend on the detailed ongoing negotiations over 'Brexit', as the vote in favour of Britain's departure from the EU is now described.

There is no doubt that British politics has already been transformed as a consequence of the referendum, including David Cameron's resignation and the formation of a new Conservative government under the leadership of Theresa May, with ministers newly appointed to be responsible for negotiating the terms of the UK's exit from the EU. The longer term consequences are less clear but likely to be far-reaching, possibly for the very future of the United Kingdom itself. More than one union could be threatened by the vote to leave the EU, with voters in Scotland unhappy at the decision.

In order to understand what has happened and why, it is necessary to explain, first, the movement for closer economic and political union between European states, and second, the reasons why Britain's relationship with Europe has long been politically contentious, dividing existing parties and assisting the emergence of new ones hostile to the whole European project, such as UKIP. Indeed, it is sometimes suggested that Britain has always been 'an awkward partner' (George, 1998), and never fully committed to the European ideal. Thus the vote to leave could be seen as the culmination of some long-standing political and economic difference between Britain and Europe.

Support for membership of the EU, and its predecessor institutions, has varied over the years. In 1975, a referendum on the UK's membership of what was then generally called the 'Common Market' recorded a two-thirds majority in favour, with strong support from the unions, business and party leaders. There followed a period where attitudes turned against what became the EU, before pro-Europeanism began to dominate from the mid-1980s onwards. By the run-up to the 2016 referendum, however, the result was on a knife-edge, and the vote itself was narrow, with a substantial minority (48%) wanting to remain. This included the leadership of the Conservatives, Labour, the Lib Dems and the SNP. Some continue to hope, probably vainly, for a second referendum, which may effectively reverse the 2016 vote to leave and allow the UK to stay a member of the EU. However, even if, as Prime Minister Theresa May (2016a) has tersely declared, 'Brexit means Brexit', whatever the outcome of the detailed negotiations over

240

leaving the EU, Britain will continue to have important political, economic and diplomatic links with its closest neighbours, including the EU as a whole and its member states.

## THIS CHAPTER:

» Analyses the postwar development of the sometimes problematic relationship between Britain and what became the EU.

» Explores the run-up to the vote against EU membership in the 2016 referendum and looks at the consequences of that vote.

» Considers the EU, the role of its institutions and the history of the UK in regard to European integration.

» Examines the impact of the EU on the British political system.

» Concludes with a discussion of Britain's potential future relationship with the EU and the rest of the world.

## BRITAIN AND EUROPE: AWKWARD PARTNERS

The history of the EU is sometimes presented as a triumphal progress towards ever deeper European integration and a steady expansion in membership, population and boundaries. Yet the progress was slow and uneven, with some tension between widening and deepening the European Community/Union. Both enlargement and integration had considerable implications for the UK. Britain's vote to leave the EU in 2016 threw this view of history into crisis. (Many of the main events set out in this chapter are summarised in Timeline 12.2 on p. 252.)

### LATE TO THE PARTY: BRITAIN AND EUROPE, 1945–79

The key objective of Robert Schuman and Jean Monnet (see Key Figures 12.1), the founding fathers of the new Europe, was the prevention of future war, following centuries of destructive conflict. The Schuman Plan (1950) sought to lock the economies of France and Germany so closely together as to render another war between them impossible. It envisaged an ongoing process of integration of key policy areas that would lead, over time, to closer union, as states and peoples experienced the practical benefits of cooperation rather than conflict.

Thus, in 1952, France, Germany, Italy and the Benelux states (Belgium, the Netherlands and Luxembourg) formed the **European Coal and Steel Community (ECSC)**, with extensive powers to regulate the coal and steel industries in the member states. These same six countries went on to sign the Treaty of Rome in 1957. This inaugurated the **European Economic Community (EEC)**, which established a customs union with internal free trade and a common external tariff, and the **European Atomic Energy Authority (Euratom)**. The Common Agricultural Policy (CAP), which sets the organisation's agricultural policy and provides significant subsidies to many farmers, initially absorbed three-quarters of the EEC budget, although subsequently increasing funds were devoted to social and regional policies.

*The **European Coal and Steel Community (ECSC)** was established in 1952 following the Treaty of Paris. It was created to regulate industrial production after the Second World War. It was the precursor of the European Economic Community (and later the EC/EU).*

*The **European Economic Community (EEC)** was a European organisation that aimed to bring about economic integration among its members. It was established by the Treaty of Rome (signed in 1957, effective 1958), along with the **European Atomic Energy Community (Euratom)**, which created a market for nuclear energy in Europe.*

# KEY FIGURES 12.1
Jean Monnet

**Jean Monnet (1888–1979)** was a French political economist and diplomat. An influential supporter of European unity, he is considered as one of the founding figures of the EU. Monnet never held an elected position, but in the wake of the Second World War, he helped establish the European Coal and Steel Community (ECSC) and was appointed head of its High Authority (a forerunner of today's European Commission). The ECSC regulated industrial production in Belgium, France, West Germany, Italy, the Netherlands and Luxembourg, tying the economies of those countries more closely together in the hope that it would make future wars between these countries unthinkable. Monnet was later a significant player in the expansion of the ECSC into the European Economic Community or 'Common Market', and then into the European Community (EC) – the forerunner of today's European Union. In 1976, he was the first of just three people to have been awarded the honorary title 'Citizen of Europe', by the European Council of the EU.

*The* **European Community (EC)**, *or European Communities, resulted from the merger of the ECSC, the EEC and Euratom with the Merger Treaty (signed in 1965, effective 1967).*

*The* **European Union (EU)** *was a term adopted after the Treaty of the European Union (TEU, or Maastricht Treaty) in 1992 to describe the body that fosters cooperation between member states.*

One indication of the success of any club is the enthusiasm of new members to join it. By that token, the European Union (EU) has been very successful. There has been a progressive enlargement of what began as the EEC in 1958 (see Timeline 12.1). The EU remained fairly popular not only with the original six founding states, but among many of the states that joined from 1973 onwards. Ireland appeared to prosper economically from EU membership, at least until the 2008 recession. For Greece, Spain and Portugal, which had only recently escaped from dictatorships, joining the European club brought political and economic benefits. Following the collapse of the USSR, many Eastern European states similarly hoped for increased political stability and economic growth from being locked into the Western European political and economic system.

**Timeline 12.1  Membership of the EC/EU**

| Dates | Countries |
|---|---|
| 1952 (ECSC), 1957 (EEC) | Belgium, France, Germany, Italy, Luxembourg, the Netherlands |
| 1973 | Denmark, Ireland, the United Kingdom |
| 1981 | Greece |
| 1986 | Portugal, Spain |
| (1990) | East Germany (after German unification: no accession treaty deemed necessary) |
| 1995 | Austria, Finland, Sweden |
| 2004 | Cyprus, Czech Republic, Estonia, Hungary, Latvia, Lithuania, Malta, Poland, Slovakia, Slovenia |
| 2007 | Bulgaria, Romania |
| 2013 | Croatia |
| 2017 | UK triggers Article 50, which gives two years to negotiate exit |

British governments initially took no part in these developments. At the end of the Second World War, British concerns and interests appeared different from the countries that formed the EEC. Britain retained the illusion of great power status, one of the 'big three' that had defeated Nazi Germany, with a still extensive overseas empire. Its political system was stable, and its economic and financial interests remained worldwide. Not having experienced the miseries of defeat and occupation, British politicians saw no imperative need for closer economic and political integration with other European states. While British politicians were certainly concerned about the future of Europe, Britain's empire and Commonwealth, coupled with the transatlantic 'special relationship' with the USA, provided strong conflicting influences on Britain in the period immediately after the war (see Spotlight 22.2). Although Winston Churchill called for 'a kind of United States of Europe' in a speech in Zurich in 1946, he made

it plain that Britain would be among the 'friends and sponsors of the new Europe' rather than an integral part of it. So Britain did not join the European Coal and Steel Community (ECSC) in 1952, or the European Economic Community (EEC) in 1958. Indeed, the UK government took the lead in establishing a rival trading block, the European Free Trade Association (EFTA), which it subsequently left upon joining the **Common Market** in 1973.

---

The **Common Market** *is a term used in Britain to describe the EEC in its early years. The Treaty of Rome did involve a common market, but promised more.*

---

Political and economic developments combined to provoke a rapid reassessment of Britain's relations with the EEC from the late 1950s onwards. The rapid dissolution of the British Empire (discussed in Chapters 2 and 22) was one factor. The opposition of the USA and even some Commonwealth countries

*Source:* © European Union, 1972, EC Audiovisual Service

Prime Minister Edward Heath signs the Treaty of Accession in January 1972, with membership effective on 1 January 1973. UK membership of the EC had considerable implications for the British constitution, particularly for national and parliamentary sovereignty, and significantly affected the practice of British government and politics.

to the disastrous 1956 Anglo-French Suez expedition was a defining moment, which destroyed lingering illusions of Britain's world power status. Continuing economic problems, evidenced by low growth, adverse trade balances and recurring sterling crises, contrasted with the strong economic performance of the six EEC countries after 1958. Thus Harold Macmillan's Conservative government sought entry in 1961. Diplomatic negotiations were abruptly terminated in 1963 with the veto of the French president, General de Gaulle. Wilson's Labour government met a similar rebuff when it tried to enter the EEC in 1967. It was only the removal of de Gaulle from power that finally enabled Heath's Conservative government to join the EC, along with Ireland and Denmark, in 1973.

British commitment to Europe, however, was never wholehearted, either at elite or mass level. Insofar as EC membership was sold to the British public, it was on the basis of presumed economic benefits – higher growth and living standards. The EC's political implications, evident from its founding fathers and the Treaty of Rome, were largely ignored. This was not (as has sometimes been suggested) a deliberate conspiracy by British governments to keep people in the dark. It simply reflected a widespread UK view that joining the Common Market was essentially an economic, or 'bread and butter' issue. Indeed, opponents made much of the projected effect of entry on the price of a standard loaf and a pound of butter.

While the costs of British membership in terms of increased food prices were soon evident, the economic benefits were not immediately obvious. Partly, this was because the UK joined too late to influence the shape and early development of the EC. So the UK had to sign up to rules designed to meet the economic needs of the original six member states. The British economy, with its relatively small but efficient agricultural sector, was unlikely to benefit significantly from the Common Agricultural Policy (CAP). Moreover, 1973, the year of UK entry, was also the year of the energy crisis, which signalled the end of the postwar economic boom. While the original members of the EC had enjoyed substantial growth rates and sharply rising living standards, which ensured

the continuing popularity of European integration, the early years of UK membership were accompanied by 'stagflation' (see Chapter 2, p. 32) rather than the promised sustained higher rates of growth. It appeared that Britain had joined the party too late.

EC membership remained politically controversial in Britain. The only mainstream political party consistently in favour were the Liberals, and subsequently Lib Dems. The majority of Conservatives supported, with varying degrees of enthusiasm, membership of the EC, as sought by the party leadership, although an (initially small) minority remained strongly opposed. Thus Enoch Powell, the controversial former Conservative cabinet minister, argued that entry into the EC involved the destruction of national and parliamentary sovereignty. In the 1974 election, he even advised a vote for Labour, who had promised a referendum on EC membership, and he himself left the Conservatives for the Ulster Unionists.

Labour was initially split over Europe. Although Prime Minister Wilson had sought entry to Europe in 1967, after the unexpected election defeat in 1970, many in the party opposed entry. Much of the Labour left saw the EC as a rich men's capitalist club, providing the economic underpinning for NATO, although Labour's social democrats, led by deputy leader Roy Jenkins, remained enthusiastically pro-Europe. The return of a Labour government under Wilson in 1974 entailed a (largely cosmetic) renegotiation of the terms of entry, and a referendum in 1975 resulted in a two-thirds majority for staying in. Although the Labour government officially recommended a 'yes' vote, a third of the Cabinet campaigned on the opposite side, and Labour remained deeply divided on the issue.

## INCREASINGLY AWKWARD PARTNERS: 1979–97

Following the election of Margaret Thatcher's Conservatives in 1979, and Michael Foot, veteran Labour left-winger and Eurosceptic, becoming leader of the opposition, some pro-European social democrats deserted Labour to found the new Social Democratic Party (SDP) in 1981. Their exit further weakened Labour support for the EC. Thus, by the 1983 general

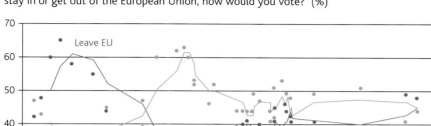

Figure 12.1: In/out EU referendum voting intentions, 1976–2014

Answers to question 'If there were a referendum now on whether Britain should stay in or get out of the European Union, how would you vote?' (%)

*Before 1999, the question was changed four times, referring to the European Community or Common Market instead of the European Union. This could have impacted on responses.

Source: Full Fact, using Ipsos MORI European Union membership-trends series, https://fullfact.org/europe/what-does-british-public-think-about-europe/. Reproduced with permission

election, Labour was pledged to withdrawal from Europe without a referendum. The party was heavily defeated at the poll, their percentage of the total vote only 2% higher than that for the pro-Europe SDP/Liberal alliance.

Most Conservatives were then far more enthusiastic about Europe. After all, Britain's membership of the EC was a Conservative achievement, strongly supported by Margaret Thatcher in her early years as leader. Although she had belligerently demanded, and obtained, a rebate from the EC budget, she went on to sign and endorse the 1986 Single European Act, regarded as the embodiment of free-market principles. It was only towards the end of her premiership that Thatcher's own reservations on European integration and the threat it presented to Britain's national sovereignty became clearer.

Part of the tension arose during Jacques Delors' presidency of the European Commission (1985–95). Delors was a French socialist, and argued that social protection went hand in hand with economic union. In 1988, Delors addressed British trade unions, promising

that the European Commission would require member states to introduce legislation to protect workers. Thatcher (1988a) responded the same year in her Bruges speech, in which she asserted: 'We have not successfully rolled back the frontiers of the state in Britain only to see them re-imposed at a European level with a European superstate exercising a new dominance from Brussels.' This became an obvious marker of the Conservative Party's increasing Euroscepticism. The Conservative-supporting popular press followed, with *The Sun* headline for 1 November 1990 reading 'Up Yours Delors' – a response to his attempts to promote greater European integration and a single currency.

Thatcher (rather reluctantly) agreed to UK entry to the Exchange Rate Mechanism (ERM) in October 1990 (discussed in more detail in Chapter 19), a system created to ensure more stability between different currencies within the EC. For Chris Gifford (2014, p. 11), in his account of the rise of Euroscepticism in Britain, Thatcher was always more concerned with the 'legitimation of a global neo-liberal economic strategy', and the EC's social policies increasingly seemed to stand in the way of that later in her premiership. However, it was only after her fall from power soon afterwards that Thatcher's public opposition to the European project intensified.

John Major, her successor, seemed more enthusiastic about Europe. However, the Maastricht Treaty was to mark further divisions with Britain's European partners, as Major's government negotiated an opt-out from the Social Chapter and monetary union. Indeed, the problems that Major's government encountered over Britain's brief membership of the ERM and the ensuing catastrophe of 'Black Wednesday' in 1992 fuelled increasing Euroscepticism on the Conservative benches. Meanwhile, over time, the Labour Party, under the leadership of Kinnock, Smith and Blair, reversed its earlier hostility and became steadily more favourable to what was now called the European Union. Labour liked the Social Chapter, which afforded some protection to workers, and approved the expansion of EU regional policy that benefitted the more deprived areas of the UK. They were not opposed in principle to European monetary integration. By 1997, the two major parties had almost reversed their positions on Europe compared with 1981–83.

The 1992 Maastricht Treaty or Treaty of the European Union (TEU) marked further progress towards closer integration, with the adoption of a Social Chapter by 11 of the 12 member states (with Britain initially opting out). It also involved agreement on a common foreign and security policy, and cooperation on justice and home affairs. The new momentum towards closer integration was maintained with the Treaties of Amsterdam (1997) and Nice (2000) and particularly with the formal inauguration of the common currency, the euro, in 1999, and the introduction of notes and coins to replace national currencies in 12 member states in 2002. However, the euro did not become the single European currency for the whole EU, as some older member states (UK, Denmark, Sweden) declined to participate, and new member states who joined in 2004 and 2007 were not ready.

## RECONCILIATION? NEW LABOUR AND EUROPE, 1997–2010

Labour leader Tony Blair came to power in 1997 with a much more positive attitude to the EU, and his government quickly signed up to the Social Chapter (from which John Major had secured an opt-out). Yet after three full terms of Labour in power, some divisions between Britain and much of Continental Europe remained, particularly on the key issue of monetary union.

There were significant enlargements to the EU in 2004 and 2007 (see Map 12.1.) Indeed, EU enlargement raised some doubts on the capacity of the EU to absorb so many new states without impeding further progress towards closer integration. Each of the previous enlargements from 1973 to 1995 had shifted the balance of power and interests between EC/EU members, and each put some strain on existing institutions and policies. The 2004 and 2007 enlargements, involving 12 new member states, required an extensive modification of existing institutions and procedures. There was also a further need for some adjustments to existing EU policies, particularly the CAP. The increased disparities between regions following enlargement also required a significant redirection of social and regional funds, which inevitably involved some reductions in regional aid directed to poorer regions of older member states, including Britain.

However, it was monetary union that was perhaps the most significant step towards European integration that has been taken since the establishment of the EC, yet Britain remained outside. While Blair insisted that the government was committed, 'in principle', to joining the euro, Gordon Brown, his chancellor, sounded a more cautious note, laying down five stringent economic conditions. Following the second landslide election victory in 2001, over a Conservative Party fighting to 'Save the pound', there were predictions that early in the new Parliament Labour would seek entry to monetary union. Yet this did not happen. The real obstacle was less perhaps Brown's economic conditions than Labour's commitment, made in opposition, to hold

Map 12.1 European enlargement

Key
1 Croatia
2 Bosnia and Herzegovina
3 Serbia
4 Montenegro
5 Former Yugoslav Republic
  of Macedonia
6 Albania
7 Switzerland
8 Moldova
9 Slovenia

Founding members (1952 ECSC; 1958 EEC and Euratom): Belgium, France, (West) Germany, Italy, Luxembourg, Netherlands. The territory of the German Democratic Republic (East Germany) was incorporated into a united Germany in 1990

First enlargement (1973): Denmark, Ireland, United Kingdom

Mediterranean enlargement (1981): Greece

Mediterranean enlargement (1986): Portugal, Spain

EFTA enlargement (1995): Austria, Finland, Sweden

2004 enlargement: Cyprus, Czech Republic, Estonia, Hungary, Latvia, Lithuania, Malta, Poland, Slovakia, Slovenia

2007: Bulgaria, Romania

2013: Croatia

*Source:* Originally used in *Global Politics* by Andrew Heywood, 2nd edn, Palgrave, 2014, p. 507.

a referendum should the government seek to join the euro. Opinion polls continued to suggest that the government would have great difficulty in winning such a referendum. The prospect of Britain joining the single currency subsequently receded.

In 2004, Blair did commit his government to a referendum, planned for 2006, but on the issue of the proposed new European constitution rather than the single currency. The unexpected rejection of the proposed new European constitution in 2005 by voters in two original member states, France and the Netherlands, not only caused an immediate crisis for the institutions and processes of the EU, but threw a long shadow over the earlier triumphs of integration. The problem was apparently solved by abandoning the controversial term 'constitution' and embodying its key provisions in a new treaty, the Lisbon Treaty, eventually approved and signed by all member states. But the change in language was symbolic. In relation to politics, a treaty in common language involves an agreement *between* sovereign states, while a constitution embodies the rules for governing *a particular* sovereign state. The ambivalent use of both terms by the EU confirms the ambiguity over whether the EU is a kind of superstate, or a federation of states.

The rejection of that constitution appeared to the Labour government to render a British referendum unnecessary. In 2007, Gordon Brown, the new Labour prime minister, along with other European leaders, signed the replacement Lisbon Treaty, which was finally ratified by all member states in 2009. Cameron, as opposition leader, had promised a 'cast-iron guarantee' on the Lisbon Treaty (Savage, 2009), but abandoned it once it became clear that the Lisbon Treaty would become law, despite concerns over the growing threat from the United Kingdom Independence Party (UKIP), as shown in the European Parliament elections in Britain in 2009, when UKIP came second with 17% of the votes and 13 seats.

## THE RUN-UP TO 'BREXIT': 2010–16

David Cameron, heading Britain's first coalition government since 1945, remained concerned about Euroscepticism within his own party, and the apparent threat from the anti-EU UKIP. Indeed, Cameron was struggling with a Conservative Party increasingly sceptical of the social elements and bureaucracy of the EU. The party had changed its outlook on Europe considerably

since a Conservative prime minister, Ted Heath, led the UK into the Common Market in 1973 (Bale, 2012). Cameron attempted to address this by offering several concessions to his backbenchers, notably withdrawing the party from the pro-European European People's Party and the European Democrats (EPP-ED) group in the European Parliament (Lynch and Whitaker, 2008), forcing them into alliance with several radical right-wing parties instead. But this was not enough to quell the political pressures. In 2012, responding to concerted pressure from sections of the Conservative Party and the rise of UKIP, Cameron pledged a referendum on Britain's membership of the EU, should the Conservatives win an outright majority at the 2015 general election, although some suspected that, with polls pointing to another hung parliament, this was a promise he felt he was unlikely to be called upon to fulfil.

Yet the 2015 election gave him an unexpected overall majority, and reduced the former coalition partners – the pro-EU Lib Dems – to just eight seats. Cameron now had to fulfil his referendum pledge, against a determined Eurosceptic minority in his own party and an increasingly vocal UKIP, led by Nigel Farage (see Key Figures 12.2). UKIP could fairly claim to have won the elections for the European Parliament in 2014, although the party only won one seat in the House of Commons at the 2015 general election.

The discrepancy in the two election results is not difficult to explain. They involved markedly different levels of public interest and voter turnout, and were fought under very different rules. While the 2015 general election was about who was to form the next government, with knock-on effects on state spending and taxation, the 2014 European Parliament elections were for an institution about which most voters knew and cared little, and with no obvious immediate effect on their lives. Thus, while 66% turned out for the 2015 general election, only 34% could be bothered to vote for elections to the European Parliament. This apathy did not extend to UKIP supporters, for these elections were bound up closely with the whole purpose of the party. So, in the European elections UKIP won 27.5% of the vote, on a

# KEY FIGURES 12.2
Nigel Farage

Daniel Leal-Olivas/AFP/
Getty Images

**Nigel Farage (1964–)** is a British politician and Eurosceptic, who was the leader of UKIP for two periods, 2006–09 and 2010–16. He was educated at Dulwich College, a fee-paying school in south London, where he was influenced by the politics of Enoch Powell. After leaving school, Farage became a commodities trader rather than going to university. He left the Conservative Party in 1992 in response to their signing of the Maastricht Treaty and became an early member of UKIP, which formed under its present name in 1993. Since 1999 he has represented the party as the Member of the European Parliament (MEP) for the South East England constituency. Politically right-wing and often blunt in his language, he is noted for his controversial speeches in the European Parliament and elsewhere.

In 2009, UKIP won the second highest share of the popular vote in the European Parliament election, defeating Labour and the Lib Dems. Farage then stepped down to contest the parliamentary seat of Buckingham at the 2010 general election, but came third. In November 2010, Farage was re-elected UKIP leader. During the 2010–15 Parliament, two Conservative MPs defected to UKIP, giving the party parliamentary representation for the first time.

Farage successfully linked membership of the EU and its requirements around free movement of people to public concerns about immigration, attracting significant support for the party. In the 2015 general election, UKIP gained 3.8 million votes, accounting for almost 13% of the popular vote and placing them third behind the two main parties. However, the party has always struggled under the UK's first past the post electoral system and a relatively large vote share only translated into one seat in Parliament.

Farage failed in his bid to gain a parliamentary seat, coming second to the Conservatives in the constituency of South Thanet in Kent. However, he threw himself into the following EU referendum campaign in 2016, acting as a prominent spokesperson for the leave camp. Farage resigned as leader after the result, claiming he had 'achieved his political ambition'. This was perhaps also reflected in UKIP's performance in the 2017 general election, at which their popular support collapsed. Often perceived as a single-issue party, their reason for existing had now seemingly been achieved.

much lower poll, compared to the 2015 general election. Moreover, because these elections were conducted under the multi-member regional party list system, which was close to proportional representation, UKIP won 24 out of 73 seats for the whole of the UK, more than any other party (see Table 12.1 overleaf).

Even so, Cameron remained reasonably confident of winning the promised referendum, as most of his party, the Parliamentary Labour Party, the Lib Dems and the SNP all supported continued membership of the EU. In the event, the issue of immigration dominated the referendum campaign. This had not been a significant issue in previous debates over

Britain's EU membership in the last quarter of the twentieth century. Although Enoch Powell had used inflammatory language in both his opposition to immigration and the EC, the two causes were not then closely connected. The immigration Powell condemned was largely from the old West Indian, Asian and African Commonwealth and empire countries, not from the EC, which he objected to on the grounds of its threat to national and parliamentary sovereignty. Yet, by 2016, Britain's membership of the EU was closely bound up with the issue of immigration, initially from new member states from Eastern Europe under the principle of the free movement of labour. Here, the issue

Table 12.1 Votes and seats for UK parties in European Parliament elections, 1989–2014

| Party | 1989 Votes | Seats | 1994 Votes | Seats | 1999 Votes | Seats | 2004 Votes | Seats | 2009 Votes | Seats | 2014 Votes | Seats |
|---|---|---|---|---|---|---|---|---|---|---|---|---|
| Con | 33% | 32 | 27% | 18 | 36% | 36 | 27% | 27 | 28% | 25 | 24% | 19 |
| Lab | 39% | 45 | 43% | 62 | 28% | 29 | 23% | 19 | 16% | 13 | 25% | 20 |
| Lib/Lib Dems | 6% | 0 | 16% | 2 | 13% | 10 | 15% | 12 | 14% | 11 | 7% | 1 |
| SNP | 3% | 1 | 3% | 2 | 3% | 2 | 1% | 2 | 2% | 2 | 2% | 2 |
| Plaid Cymru | 1% | 0 | 1% | 0 | 2% | 2 | 1% | 1 | 1% | 1 | 1% | 1 |
| UKIP | – | | – | | 7% | 3 | 16% | 12 | 17% | 13 | 27% | 24 |
| Greens | 15% | 0 | 3% | 0 | 6% | 2 | 6% | 2 | 9% | 2 | 8% | 3 |
| BNP | – | | – | | – | | – | | 6% | 2 | 1% | 0 |

Note: Elections up to 1994 are under single member plurality system, from 1999 by regional party list system. N.B. Northern Ireland elects three MEPs by single transferable vote.

was not race, but language and the perceived demands on the welfare system, housing and the threat to 'British' jobs.

In addition, from 2015, the growing numbers of refugees from Africa and the Middle East into Europe dominated the news. The EU had not encouraged this. It was an influx of desperate people from war-torn and economically destitute countries outside Europe. These refugees initially made their way into southern EU states, notably Greece and Italy. Many then travelled on to other parts of continental Europe, such as Germany. Relatively few reached Britain, but the images of people crossing the Mediterranean in boats and desperate families at border points and transit camps filled TV screens, and magnified concerns over immigration, fanned by those who favoured leaving the EU, and argued that Britain needed to regain control of its own borders.

The referendum campaign generated more heat than light. The remain camp relied chiefly on grim warnings of the economic consequences of Brexit, from leading economists, establishment figures and prominent world statesmen, including US President Obama. It was widely criticised as a repeat of Better Together, the earlier negative campaign against Scottish independence, dubbed 'Project Fear'. Few made

a positive case for European unity. Some thought that the assassination of Jo Cox, a pro-European Labour MP, just days before the vote by Thomas Mair, an anti-European nationalist and white supremacist, might lead to an increase in support for the remain campaign. The leave camp, strengthened by the last-minute support of Boris Johnson, plumbed lower depths, grossly exaggerating the costs of UK membership and exploiting fears of immigration, egged on by most of the popular press. The win for Brexit was followed by increased reports of racist abuse aimed at those perceived to be foreign immigrants and included some attacks on communities that had long appeared well integrated into British society. The immediate resignation of David Cameron as prime minister and the reconstitution of Conservative government under Theresa May, who had supported remaining in the EU but had not played a prominent role in the campaign, was a direct consequence of the largely unexpected vote to leave.

As prime minister, May initially demonstrated her commitment to withdrawal from the EU by repeating the soundbite 'Brexit means Brexit'. The government faced a legal challenge when it tried to sidestep a parliamentary vote on EU withdrawal (discussed in Chapter 9). Even then, it was some time before May began to clarify which of the many options for leaving the EU she wanted Britain to take (the theoretical options open to the UK are set out in Table 12.2 below). Eventually, the government triggered Article 50 in March 2017, which formally began a two-year process of negotiations on the terms of the UK's withdrawal from the EU. Key policies include:

» No longer being bound by EU law and European Court of Justice rulings.

» Quitting the EU single market and seeking a 'comprehensive' free trade deal in its place. This would allow the UK to end the 'free movement of people' and introduce a new, potentially tougher immigration system.

» Leaving the EU customs union and seeking a new customs agreement.

» Being prepared to walk away from talks: 'No deal is better than a bad deal' as May put it (cited on Sky News, 2017). In the absence of any deal between the UK and the EU, the UK would be required to follow World Trade Organization (WTO) rules on tariffs on goods and services it exports into the EU, as well as being vulnerable to EU states imposing rules that made it more difficult for the UK to access their markets.

» The European Union (Withdrawal) Bill (briefly known as the 'great repeal bill'), which would convert existing EU law into UK legislation, where it could then be retained or scrapped (Prime Minister's Office, 2017).

The decision to quit the single market and customs union is frequently described as a 'hard Brexit'. Many remain voters now hope for a 'soft Brexit', with arrangements as close as possible to those which previously existed. This would include access to the single market and customs union, likely to be in exchange for making a contribution to the EU budget and allowing freedom of movement of goods, services, capital and people.

May called a surprise general election in April 2017 on the specific basis that she needed to strengthen her hand in Brexit negotiations – she claimed other parties were seeking to undermine the government. She enjoyed a significant poll lead and a large Conservative majority was expected by most commentators. However, May

### Table 12.2 Potential outcomes for Brexit

| | EU membership | Norway and Switzerland | Canada | Turkey | WTO |
|---|---|---|---|---|---|
| Member of the single market | Full | Full for Norway. Close to full market access for Switzerland. | No | No | No |
| Tariffs? | None | None | A Comprehensive Economic and Trade Agreement (CETA) was approved in 2017, which eliminated tariffs on most goods, but excluded some food items and services. | None on industrial goods | Yes |
| Accept free movement? | Yes | Yes | No | No | No |
| In the customs union | Yes | No | No | Yes | No |
| Makes EU budget contributions | Yes | Yes | No | No | No |
| Option for the UK | | ← 'Soft Brexit' | | 'Hard Brexit' → | |

*Source*: Adapted from: www.bbc.co.uk/news/uk-politics-37507129

performed badly over the course of the campaign, and Labour – particularly their leader Jeremy Corbyn – outperformed predictions. As a result, the Conservatives ended up in a weaker position following the June 2017 election, losing their majority in the House of Commons. Eventually, they formed an agreement with the pro-Brexit, Northern Irish Democratic Unionist Party (DUP), giving them a workable, if small, majority.

The new arrangement provided something of a headache for May. As unionists, the DUP made it clear they would not accept any agreement with Europe that would put a border between Northern Ireland and mainland Britain. The Irish government, however, made it clear that they would veto any final agreement that put a physical, customs border between the North and the South of Ireland. May also had to be mindful of undermining the Northern Ireland peace agreement (discussed in Chapter 11). It was only in December 2017 that a compromise was reached that guaranteed no hard border between Northern Ireland and the Republic; the extent of the financial commitments that the UK still owed to the EU for projects that they had previously committed to (a figure somewhere in the region of £35 billion); and the protection of the rights of European citizens in the UK. The end of 'Phase 1' of negotiations allowed negotiations to move on in 2018 to discuss the kind of economic relationship the UK would have with the EU.

### Timeline 12.2 Europe and the UK

|  | Europe | UK |
|---|---|---|
| 1950 | The Schuman Declaration or Schuman Plan | |
| 1951 | Treaty of Paris establishes the European Coal and Steel Community (ECSC) with France, Germany, Italy and the Benelux countries, instituted in 1952 | |
| 1957 | Treaty of Rome establishes European Economic Community (EEC) and Euratom, established in 1958 | |
| 1960 | | UK and six other states form the rival European Free Trade Area (EFTA) |
| 1961 | | UK (Macmillan, Conservative government) applies to join EEC, French veto by de Gaulle terminated negotiations in 1963 |
| 1967 | | Second UK attempt to join EEC by Labour, ended by fresh French veto |
| 1973 | | UK (Heath Conservative government), Ireland and Denmark join the EEC |
| 1975 | | Labour government recommends 'yes' vote in referendum on whether UK should stay in EC after renegotiation of terms. Two-thirds vote 'yes' |
| 1979 | First direct elections for European Parliament | |
| 1981 | Greece joins the EC | |
| 1983 | | Labour party pledged to UK withdrawal from EC without a referendum |

| 1986 | Spain and Portugal join the EC. Single European Act signed | |
| 1990 | After unification of Germany, former East Germany becomes part of EC | UK (Thatcher government) joins Exchange Rate Mechanism (ERM) |
| 1992 | Maastricht Treaty (TEU) | Major secures opt-out from Social Charter and monetary integration. 'Black Wednesday' – UK forced out of ERM |
| 1995 | Austria, Finland and Sweden join EU | |
| 1999 | The euro becomes the official currency for 11 EU member states<br>European Commission resigns following fraud and corruption allegations | |
| 2000 | Nice Treaty reformed the institutional structure of the EU to withstand eastward expansion | |
| 2002 | Euro notes and coins replace national currencies in 12 EU member states | |
| 2004 | Ten more countries join the EU<br>EU leaders agree start date (October, 2005) for accession talks for Turkey | Blair promises a referendum on the new constitution for the EU |
| 2005 | Voters in France and the Netherlands reject the proposed new European constitution | Blair scraps plans for a referendum in Britain |
| 2007 | Heads of government sign up to replacement Lisbon Treaty<br>Romania and Bulgaria join EU | |
| 2008 | Irish voters reject Lisbon Treaty in referendum | |
| 2009 | Lisbon Treaty is finally ratified after a second Irish referendum | |
| 2009–14 | Financial crises in Greece and other southern EU states | |
| 2013 | Croatia joins the EU | |
| 2015 | Growing refugee crisis causes tensions within EU | |
| 2016 | | UK referendum supports leaving EU by 52% to 48% |
| 2017 | | The UK invokes Article 50 in March, formally beginning the two-year process of negotiating the terms of exit from the EU. May calls a surprise general election in April explicitly to strengthen her hand in negotiations, but is returned as prime minister of a minority government, considerably weakening her position |

# THE EU: SUPERSTATE OR INTERGOVERNMENTAL ORGANISATION?

Apart from the issue of immigration, much of the argument about the UK's relationship with the EU reflects conflicting perspectives over the nature of the institution itself. From its beginning, there has been controversy over the nature of the EC/EU and the direction in which it was going. Some talked from the start of a United States of Europe, a 'USE', whose political and economic clout would match that of the USA. They had no reservations in proposing a federal system on US lines, in which supreme power or sovereignty would be effectively divided between two or more levels of government. Yet others envisaged a weaker form of association, sometimes termed a 'confederation' rather than a federation. General de Gaulle, former French president, talked of a *Europe des Patries*, essentially an intergovernmental association of sovereign nation states. Sixty years after its original establishment, the nature and scope of Europe's political union remains both unclear and contentious.

The EU still involves a curious constitutional hybrid. Throughout its history, there has been a built-in tension between its *supranational institutions*, such as the European Parliament and Court of Justice, and its *intergovernmental* institutions and interests, which involve international cooperation between states, such as the European Council. Where the balance of power really lies is partly a matter of perception, but partly also a matter of adaptation, since it may vary over time and particularly over certain policy areas. Within the EU, there has long been an uneasy balance between institutions designed to serve the interests of the EU as a whole, and other institutions reflecting the interests of member states (see Table 12.3 for an overview of some key institutions). For the UK, this can create tension with the traditional system of parliamentary sovereignty and the Westminster model (discussed in more detail in Chapter 5).

Although Eurosceptics have lamented the power of the European Commission, which proposes laws, drafts the budget and administers laws and policies, it is widely acknowledged that this key supranational body has progressively lost its leadership role (Nugent, 2017, pp. 159–61). In contrast, the European Parliament gained some additional legitimacy following the introduction of direct elections in 1979, but is still seen as a talking shop, with little effective power. While national elections may change governments and policies within EU states, European elections do not decide very much, and they often seem to have little significant impact on the running of the EU – one factor explaining declining electoral turnout for European Parliament elections figures. Despite the talk of 'ever closer union', increasingly it appears that key EU decisions are now made by institutions representing the interest of member states: the Council of Ministers and the European Council. It is these bodies, alongside the governments of EU states, which will be of crucial importance in the negotiations over the terms of Britain's exit from the EU.

## THE IMPACT OF THE EU ON THE BRITISH STATE, GOVERNMENT AND POLITICS

Those arguing the case for Britain leaving the EU have long emphasised the alleged detrimental impact of EU membership on the British state and politics. This impact can be examined at various levels: on long-established British constitutional principles; on the machinery of government and the day-to-day process of governing; on British party politics; on pressure group politics; on the British public and UK policies.

### Constitutional impacts

The impact of EU membership on the British constitution remains contentious, and the process of disentangling the UK's membership will be a complex one. The constitutional significance of the UK to the EC (later EU) was played down when it first joined. The European Communities Act 1972 provided that EC law should take precedence over all inconsistent UK law; and it precluded the UK Parliament from legislating on matters within EC competence where the EC had formulated rules. Some argued that parliamentary sovereignty was not impaired, because membership of the EC/EU had not broken the principle that Parliament cannot bind its

## Table 12.3 Location, composition and functions of key EU institutions

| Power | Institution | Location | Composition | Functions | Comments |
|---|---|---|---|---|---|
| SUPRANATIONAL BODIES | | | | | |
| Broadly executive | European Commission | Brussels | One commissioner for each member state, serves for five years, approved by European Parliament | Proposes laws, drafts budgets, administers laws and policies | Commissioners swear allegiance to EU, head directorates |
| Judicial | European Court of Justice | Luxembourg | One judge from each state plus one additional judge | Rules on EU law, adjudicates in disputes | EU law supreme over state law |
| Broadly legislative | European Parliament | Strasbourg and Brussels | MEPs directly elected by voters in member states by regional list system | Largely consultative, but has some part in EU legislation and budget | MEPs sit in European parties, not in national blocks |
| | Economic and Social Committee | Brussels | Representatives of interests | Purely consultative | Marginalised in modern EU |
| | Committee of the Regions | Brussels | Representatives of regions of EU | Consultative role on regional policy | Set up after Maastricht Treaty |
| INTERGOVERNMENTAL ORGANISATIONS | | | | | |
| | Council of Ministers | Largely in Brussels | Relevant ministers of member states | Defends member state interests | Unanimity still needed on major issues |
| | COREPER (Committee of Permanent Representatives) | Brussels | Civil servants seconded from member states | Bureaucracy serving Council of Ministers | Do initial work for Council of Ministers |
| | European Council | Brussels | Heads of government | Forum that defines the general political direction and priorities of the EU | Crucial role since 1974 |

future action. However, while the UK remains a member of the EU, parliamentary sovereignty is certainly affected (see Spotlight 12.1 overleaf as an example).

The government's European Union (Withdrawal) Bill will repeal the 1972 European Communities Act, ending European law's precedence over UK law. It will also end the jurisdiction of the European Court of Justice (ECJ). The government plans to avoid legal disruption by copying across all existing EU legislation into domestic law as the UK leaves the EU. The UK can then 'amend, repeal and improve' those laws as necessary in future (BBC, 2017d).

*The **European Court of Justice (ECJ)** is a separate body based in Luxembourg. The ECJ is the judicial institution of the EU. It is responsible for interpreting EU laws and ensuring their equal application across all EU member states.*

# SPOTLIGHT ON ...

## Britain's legal subordination to Brussels: the 'Factortame case'

12.1

Perhaps the best-known example of Britain's legal subordination to Brussels was an important case in 1991, R. v. *Secretary of State for Transport ex parte Factortame (No. 2)* ('the Factortame case'). The ECJ in effect quashed sections of the Merchant Shipping Act 1988, which provided that UK-registered boats must be 75% British-owned and have 75% of their crews resident in the UK. The UK Act had been designed to prevent boats from Spain and other EC countries 'quota-hopping' by registering under the British flag and using the UK's EC fishing quotas. The ECJ had overturned British legislation before, but because of the effect on British fishing jobs, this case caused particular outcry and showed the power of the EU.

## Governmental impacts

Membership of the EU has had an impact on other aspects of the British system of government. The referendum was first introduced into the British political system in 1975 for a vote on whether the country should remain in the EC, and has since become an accepted, if irregular, mechanism for settling controversial issues of a constitutional nature (such as devolution and the alternative vote). EU membership also contributed significantly to the pressures for electoral reform in the UK. Thus, in 1999, the regional list system was used for British elections to the European Parliament, while the system of election used for the Scottish Parliament and Welsh Assembly (the additional member system) followed another model familiar in Germany. Although pressures for electoral reform existed prior to EU membership, they were strengthened by European precedents. Much the same could be said of demands for devolution and regional government. These demands predated membership of the EC, but were reinforced by the parallel pressures for more national and regional autonomy in other member states, and by the development of European regional policy and the establishment of the Committee of the Regions.

The machinery of government was affected less than might have been expected by EU membership – the British state has adjusted its institutions and procedures incrementally rather than radically (Bulmer and Burch, 2000). Departmental organisation has been scarcely affected. There was no separate department for Europe, nor a secretary of state for Europe in the Cabinet. As a consequence, there is also no departmental select committee for Europe in the House of Commons, although there is a European Scrutiny Committee, which examines the importance of draft European legislation to the UK. Even so, anyone studying the changing formal structures of the Cabinet, departments and Parliament before Britain's decision to leave the EU would hardly conclude that they had been much affected by EU membership. Ironically, it was Brexit that led to the greatest changes at Cabinet level, with MP David Davis as the first 'secretary of state for exiting the European Union'.

If, however, the formal structure of British government at the centre appeared little altered, the change in the working practices of ministers and civil servants has been marked. According to Hix (2002, p. 48): 'On an administrative level, most senior British ministers and many senior civil servants spend many days each month commuting to Brussels for EU meetings. Much of the rest of their time back in Westminster and Whitehall is spent tackling questions relating to the EU agenda.' This reflects the extensive consequences of EU membership for so many areas of policy (see below).

## Party system impacts

Membership of the EU has had considerable and ongoing implications for British political parties and the party system. Both the two major parties have been split over Europe.

It was the European issue that was a major factor in the 1981 SDP split from Labour (discussed in Chapter 3), but in any event helped ensure Conservative dominance for 18 years. Conservative divisions over Europe date back at least as far as Labour's, but were initially less disastrous for the party, although it was on Europe that Powell broke from the Conservatives and recommended a vote for Labour in 1974, perhaps tipping a close election in Labour's favour. Conflicting attitudes towards Europe caused tension within Thatcher's last administration, but became far more damaging under Major, threatening the survival of his government. These divisions helped undermine any immediate prospects of a Conservative Party recovery after the landslide defeat of 1997. Cameron hoped to persuade his party 'to stop banging on about Europe' (BBC News, 2006), but eventually felt obliged to promise the referendum that re-emphasised Conservative divisions and eventually led to his own political demise. Tory divisions on Europe manifestly survive his departure. The Liberals and their Lib Dem successors profited from the divisions among their opponents, but otherwise their more consistent and united support for Europe has hardly profited them electorally.

Smaller parties tended to profit from the introduction of proportional representation for elections to the European Parliament from 2009 – notably the Lib Dems (until they were punished by voters for their involvement in the coalition), as well as the Green Party and (ironically) UKIP. To some extent, this has encouraged the introduction of more proportionate elections elsewhere in the UK (e.g. for devolved government). It may yet lead to more pressure for electoral reform for UK general elections, but this pressure will be strongly resisted by the Conservatives.

The need to organise for European elections, and subsequently the need to become part of European parties in the European Parliament has had some knock-on effects for the major British parties. Labour have been consistent members of the European Socialist Party, now the Progressive Alliance of Socialists and Democrats (S&D) group. The pro-EU Lib Dems supported the Alliance of Liberals and Democrats for Europe (ALDE) group. The Conservatives found the search for ideologically acceptable and sympathetic partners in Europe rather more difficult. For a time, Conservative MEPs were linked with a few Spanish and Danish MPs in the European Democratic Group, then joined the main centre-right European People's Party (EPP) group. Following Cameron's leadership election pledge and the 2009 European elections, they became part of the small European Conservatives and Reformists (ECR) group, whose ranks included some MPs accused of anti-Semitism and homophobia.

How far closer involvement with other parties in Europe has influenced the political thinking of the major British parties is less clear. German and Swedish social democracy and, to a lesser extent, perhaps French socialism certainly helped influence the transformation of the Labour Party in the 1980s and 90s. (Labour's red rose symbol was borrowed from François Mitterrand's French socialists.) Germany's Gerhard Schroeder was for a time closely linked with Tony Blair over the third way or 'middle way'. Some of this might have happened outside the EU anyway, although the influence of European socialists perhaps contributed to the softening of Labour hostility to Europe. British Conservatism seemed rather less susceptible to influence from its various partners in the European Parliament.

## THE IMPACT OF THE EU ON PRESSURE GROUP POLITICS

As the impact of the EU on UK public policy has grown, Brussels has increasingly become a natural target for pressure group activity (Mazey and Richardson, 1993). Some of this has simply involved British groups like the CBI or the NFU or British-based firms extending their range, acquiring their own offices in Brussels or employing professional lobbyists. However, many groups have sought to combine with comparable interests in other member states to establish Europe-wide groups, with potentially more muscle to influence EU policy. It is estimated that there are some 700 of these Europe-wide groups (see Table 12.4), of which over 65% represent business, 20% public

### Table 12.4 Examples of Europe-wide interest groups

| Organisation | Acronym |
| --- | --- |
| Committee of Professional Agricultural Organisations | COPA |
| BusinessEurope – was the Union of Industrial and Employers Confederations of Europe | UNICE |
| European Trade Union Confederation | ETUC |
| Association of European Automobile Constructors | ACEA |
| European Chemistry Industry Council | Cefic |
| European Environmental Bureau | EEB |
| Council of European Municipalities and Regions | CEMR |
| European Citizen Action Service | ECAS |

interest groups, 10% the professions and 6% trade unions, consumers, environmentalists and other interests (Nugent, 2017, pp. 265–74).

The European Commission is the main target of most groups, partly because of its powers and its readiness to consult with interests, especially European groups. It is more difficult to lobby either the European Council or the Council of Ministers directly, so groups tend to seek to influence these bodies indirectly through national governments (Grant, 1993). The increase in the influence of the European Parliament on the legislative process and the EU budget has led to more intensive lobbying at Strasbourg. The Economic and Social Committee (ESC) is the EU's own institution for representing group interests, but most groups prefer to target more influential bodies directly rather than through the ESC (Nugent, 2017, p. 250).

## THE IMPACT OF THE EU ON THE BRITISH PUBLIC

It has proved much more difficult to persuade the British people to engage with Europe. There is continued evidence of widespread ignorance and confusion about the EU and over specific institutions and issues. Euroscepticism in the UK is often the result of a combination of anti-immigration sentiment, scepticism about bureaucracy and anti-elitist attitudes. Turnout levels for elections to the European Parliament have generally been among the lowest in Europe since the first elections in 1979. Although the first referendum held on Europe resulted in a substantial majority in favour of remaining in the EC in 1975, opinion surveys since then indicated a pervasive, if ill-informed Euroscepticism and, more recently, opposition to the single currency (Hix, 2002, pp. 53–8). The extent of Euroscepticism among the British public was confirmed in the 2016 referendum result.

Curiously, major parties that have aligned themselves with Eurosceptic public opinion in the past failed to profit electorally. Labour in 1983 and the Conservatives in 2001 campaigned on manifestos hostile or unsympathetic to Europe, and both managed to lose disastrously, indicating that it was not a priority issue for voters. However, the problems of winning a referendum on the single issue of joining the euro proved too daunting for Labour to risk (see above). Cameron's referendum pledge, designed to appease UKIP voters and Tory Eurosceptics, ultimately destroyed his premiership.

## THE IMPACT OF THE EU ON UK POLICIES

The actual impact of the EC/EU on UK policy has been increasingly significant but highly variable, depending on the policy area concerned. Fiscal policy has clearly been affected. UK entry to the EC involved the introduction of value added tax and conformity to EU rules that constrain taxation and expenditure. Even so, pressures to harmonise taxation have been generally resisted. Insofar as there are factors favouring greater convergence on, for example, duties on alcohol, these have more to do with the loss of revenue from smuggling than from EU regulations.

Simon Hix (2002, p. 48) claimed that while: 'The British government is still sovereign in deciding most of the main areas of public expenditure ... this is only one aspect of policy making. In the area of *regulation,* over 80% of rules governing the production, distribution and exchange of goods, services and capital in the British market are decided by the EU.' Hix argued that this severely constrained British economic policy, preventing the adoption of either neo-Keynesian demand management and pump-priming or a Thatcherite deregulatory supply side policy. The point is fair about a deregulatory supply side policy, for EU rules are designed to ensure fair competition between member states, but a boost in domestic demand fuelled by cuts in income tax appear a matter for state governments under EU rules.

As far as specific policy areas are concerned, agriculture and fisheries policy have been most dramatically affected, as EC entry required a shift from farm income support policies (with low prices) towards price support policies. Both systems involved agricultural subsidy, although the Common Agricultural Policy notoriously led to periodic overproduction, with 'butter mountains' and 'wine lakes'. Britain, with its relatively small agricultural sector, was always likely to be a net loser from the CAP. British farmers have, however, benefitted substantially from EU subsidies. Persistent efforts to reform the CAP have been partly frustrated by the strength of farming interests in some member states. However, some British criticism of continental agriculture seems exaggerated or misplaced. The bovine spongiform encephalopathy (BSE or 'mad cow disease') and foot-and-mouth crises in the UK were substantially the consequence of British farming practices and British policy, and cannot be attributed to the EU. The decision to withdraw from the EU also has significant ramifications for environmental policy in the UK (see Spotlight 21.1).

The UK has gained rather more from EC/EU regional and social policy. The net benefits to deprived regions have sometimes been less than they might have been as British governments have sometimes seen EU funding as an alternative, rather than addition, to UK spending on economic regeneration, contrary to the intentions, and sometimes the regulations, of the European Commission.

Many other policy areas have been much less affected. The management and funding of health services differ markedly between the member states of the EU. Educational policy and social security payments and social services have been only relatively marginally affected by membership of the EU, although member states increasingly face common problems (e.g. overfunding pensions), which may ultimately lead to increased convergence. Foreign and defence policy was until recently also only marginally affected. Early attempts by the original six members to develop a European Defence Community foundered in the 1950s, and defence and foreign policy has been shaped by the requirements of NATO and, more specifically, the UK's 'special relationship' with the USA (discussed in Chapter 22). Attempts to develop a common foreign policy more recently have not been conspicuously successful.

The UK has always shown a preference for certain ways of dealing with the EU and its predecessor institutions. This includes a preference for intergovernmentalism, with decisions made through negotiations between sovereign states, rather than a more 'federalist' approach through the EU Parliament or Commission. The UK has tended to support the benefits of economic union, but displays scepticism about closer political union.

## THE ROAD TO BREXIT

The relatively smooth introduction of the single European currency in 2002 appeared a triumphant culmination of the original European vision of the founding fathers, Jean Monnet and Robert Schuman. Closer European integration had taken a decisive step forward. Moreover, soon afterwards, many of the countries of Eastern Europe, long divided from the West by the Iron Curtain, became full members of the European club. Nevertheless, monetary union remains both partial and contentious. Not all the existing members of the EU joined the single currency, and the new member states that joined between 2004 and 2013 were not deemed ready. Moreover, the fall-out from the financial crisis of 2008 onwards had dire consequences for some of southern EU states, particularly Greece. The problems of combining a single currency with individual member states managing their own financial and economic policies have become more manifest.

Behind growing grievances expressed in formal referendums and other forms of protest lay more fundamental economic concerns over growth and living standards, unemployment and prospects. The old EC was popular with the original member states because it had apparently delivered economic prosperity and steadily rising living standards. Older member states have recently experienced low growth and increased economic difficulties in the new larger EU, in which they are proportionally less politically influential.

The European project already appeared to have stalled, even before the credit crunch, economic recession and the currency crisis, affecting particularly Greece, but also other countries, and ultimately the euro. A rescue package for Greece was only slowly and reluctantly agreed. The Germans, long the paymaster of the EU, contributing substantially more to the EU budget than they gain from it, are now notably reluctant to bail out less provident fellow EU members. Fears remain that the Greek problems could prove contagious, with disastrous consequences for the eurozone and the whole future of the single currency. Other major issues (further enlargement, global warming and the environment, increased cooperation on foreign policy) have been marginalised by the all-consuming economic crisis. Just a few years after the single currency and the accession of states from behind the former Iron Curtain appeared the culminating triumph for European integration, the EU is struggling to survive. Enlargement is now seen by some of the older member states as part of the problem rather than the solution. The initial enthusiasm of the new member states

## 🇬🇧 COMPARING BRITISH POLITICS 12.1 🇪🇺

### Not the only awkward partner?

The UK has been seen as an 'awkward partner' in Europe (George, 1998). From this perspective, Brexit can be seen as the culmination of long-standing British reservations over closer European integration. There is something in the argument. National independence and parliamentary sovereignty were still seen as key constitutional principles in Britain, but less so in countries that had experienced defeat and occupation in the Second World War, or domination by the USSR after it, or had themselves evolved federal institutions with multi-level governance.

Britain was far from being uniquely awkward. France at times took on the role of the 'awkward partner', particularly under President de Gaulle, who was vehemently opposed to Britain's entrance to the Common Market for a variety of economic and cultural reasons. Since then, France – generally in contrast to the UK – has often been slow to implement EU regulations. A survey in June 2016 (before the election of a pro-European president, Emmanuel Macron)

found that 61% of French voters had a negative view of the EU (BBC News, 2016).

Voters in Denmark initially rejected the Maastricht Treaty. Both Denmark and Sweden, along with the UK, initially declined to join the euro. Germany and France generally strongly resisted reforms to the CAP.

The rejection of the EU constitution in 2005 by voters in two of the original six member states, France and the Netherlands, was a major shock. Irish voters also initially rejected the constitution's replacement – the Lisbon Treaty (to be followed by acceptance in a second referendum, after reassurances). More recently, scepticism about the EU among Greeks, who reacted against German-led demands for stronger fiscal discipline in the aftermath of the credit crunch, has meant that 71% have an unfavourable view of Europe (BBC News, 2016). This might suggest that far from the UK as a special 'awkward case', its voters are expressing concerns about the EU project that regularly surface across the continent.

*Source:* Louisa Gouliamaki/AFP/Getty Images
The financial crisis highlighted the weakness of some Eurozone countries, notably Greece, whose economy was bailed out by Germany with stringent loan conditions.

that joined from 2004 to 2013 has already led to some disillusion, as the hoped-for economic and political benefits failed to materialise. The financial crisis and economic recession have damaged states that once conspicuously prospered from EU membership, such as Ireland, and those new and poorer member states, such as Latvia, Estonia, Rumania and Bulgaria. Yet it can still be argued that the problems now facing Europe are still best addressed by the cooperation of European states rather than a retreat to the pursuit of national self-interest. The problems transcend national boundaries, and so, ultimately, must the solutions.

The British role in Europe appeared problematic well before the 2016 referendum. Partly, this was because of conflicting pulls on policy, particularly the 'special relationship' with the USA, which markedly influenced Conservative and Labour governments, and has often appeared to damage the country's European credentials with its EU partners (Gamble, 2003). Many Britons seem to lack or positively reject a European identity, and may feel a closer affinity with the USA and the old Commonwealth (or 'Anglosphere'), because of a common language and a substantially shared culture. The sometimes canvassed possibility of the UK joining the North American Free Trade Agreement, even if feasible, would involve an unequal dependent relationship with a superpower inevitably preoccupied first and foremost with the interests of the Americas rather than a partnership between equals.

# SUMMARY

» Britain initially failed to engage with the movement for European integration because of the continuing illusion of world power status and interests, the special relationship with the USA, and continuing ties with the Commonwealth.

» Britain eventually joined in 1973, too late to help shape early institutions and policies, or to secure the same economic benefits that founder members (and some later members) enjoyed.

» UK membership of the EC/EU has long been a divisive issue in British politics, leading to splits in old parties and the establishment of new ones (SDP, UKIP). While enthusiasts have welcomed Britain's closer engagement with Europe, Eurosceptics were critical of the impact on national independence and parliamentary sovereignty and, more recently, immigration.

» The Conservative overall majority in the 2015 election obliged Cameron to fulfil his referendum pledge. Rising concerns over immigration were perhaps the key factor in swinging a narrow majority vote to leave the EU in 2016. The result led immediately to the resignation of Cameron and the formation of a new Conservative government to negotiate the terms of Brexit.

» The EU is a complex organisation. Some institutions represent the EU as a whole (European Commission, European Parliament, European Court of Justice), while others represent the interests of member states (European Council, Council of Ministers, COREPER).

» UK membership has contested implications for the British constitution and the principle of parliamentary sovereignty. While it has had only minor implications for the institutional machinery of British government, it has had a major impact on the process of government and on key areas of policy, as well as remaining an important issue in the minds of the British public.

» There has been some tension between the promotion of further integration of policies within the EU (deepening) and enlarging the EU to include new members (widening). Recent enlargements and proposed further enlargements have caused some problems for EU institutions and policies, and raised questions over the nature of Europe itself.

» The future relationship of the UK with the EU and the rest of the world post-Brexit remains to be determined.

# QUESTIONS FOR DISCUSSION

» Why did European statesmen seek to promote European integration? Were the motives primarily economic or political?

» Why did the UK government not seek to join the European Coal and Steel Community and the European Economic Community from the beginning?

» Account for the generally lukewarm or more recently hostile attitude to the EU shown by much of the British public, compared with the apparent enthusiasm of the citizens of other member states.

» Why did Cameron promise a referendum on Britain's membership of the EU? Why do

you think he, and the remain camp, lost the referendum?

» How far did concerns over immigration decide the outcome of the referendum? What other factors may have been important?

» How far has Britain been a significantly more 'awkward partner' than other EU member states?

» Is the EU a federal superstate, or an intergovernmental association of sovereign states? How far do specific EU institutions meet either description? Where does real power lie today within the EU, with the governments of member states or with the European Commission and other pan-European institutions?

- » How far is there a 'democratic deficit' within the EU?
- » How far is there still a tension between further enlargement and closer integration of the EU?
- » How far has membership of the EU changed British government and politics? How far is Brexit likely to restore what many see as key British constitutional principles?
- » What should the final Brexit agreement look like? Which of the possible outcomes set out in Table 12.2 on p. 251 would be best for the UK?

# FURTHER READING

The time lag in publishing means that there are almost no new editions of long-established academic texts on the EU that take into account the impact of the 2016 referendum. Green (2018) *Brexit: What Everyone Needs to Know* provides an early guide to how the UK ended up voting to leave and the options open to it outside the EU. There is, however, already a detailed analysis of the campaign itself by Jackson et al. (2016) *EU Referendum Analysis 2016: Media, Voters and the Campaign*. Owing to a similar time lag in the publication of refereed journal articles, there is little here either as yet, although there was a useful Brexit special edition of the *British Journal of Politics and International Relations*, 2017, 19(3), with several useful pieces.

Other reliable sources include Nugent (2017) *The Government and Politics of the European Union* (8th edn), long the standard guide to European institutions and procedures. See also McCormick (2017) *Understanding the European Union* (7th edn), Hix and Høyland (2011) *The Political System of the European Union* (3rd edn), and Bache et al. (2015) *Politics in the European Union* (4th edn).

On the troubled history of the UK's relationship with the EU, Young (1998) *This Blessed Plot* provides a full, if now dated, account from the perspective of a Euro-enthusiast. See also George (1998) *An Awkward Partner: Britain in the European Community*. Other slightly more recent interpretations include Geddes (2003) *The European Union and British Politics*. Gamble's (2003) *Between Europe and America* provides a stimulating analysis of the impact of these conflicting pulls on British politics. Also see Hix (2002) 'Britain, the EU and the Euro', Rosamond (2003) 'The Europeanization of British Politics' and Smith (2006) 'Britain, Europe and the World'.

# USEFUL WEBSITES

Until more considered academic analysis appears, information and comment can be obtained from the internet, such as the EU website: www.europa.eu, from political weeklies, such as the *New Statesman*: www.newstatesman.com, *The Spectator*: www.spectator.co.uk, the fortnightly *London Review of Books*: www.lrb.co.uk, and the quality daily and Sunday press. For example, see *The long read, 'How the education gap is tearing politics apart'* at: www.theguardian.com/politics/2016/oct/05/trump-brexit-education-gap-tearing-politics-apart.

*Further student resources to support learning are available at*
**www.macmillanihe.com/griffiths-brit-pol-3e**

# PART III

# PEOPLE AND POLITICS

Part III examines how politics is organised and carried out. We explore voting behaviour and the systems used to elect representatives in the UK. We then examine the nature of political parties and ideology, and look at how citizens participate – or don't participate – in the political process. In the final chapter, we explore how the media affects politics in the UK.

**POLITICS IN ACTION**

Simon Griffiths, one of the authors of this book, provides an overview of some of the key questions and themes in this Part.

Rosie Campbell discusses elections, party politics, political representation and more, and asks if the traditional way we learn about politics is still relevant in a time of political upheaval.

Watch the videos at **www.macmillanihe.com/griffiths-brit-pol-3e**

# 13 ELECTORAL SYSTEMS AND VOTING BEHAVIOUR

The Electoral Reform Society declared the 2015 general election 'the most disproportionate in UK history', a worrying trend, they argued, for 'fans of democracy' (Garland and Terry, 2015). In short, they were concerned that the electoral system used in the UK means that the proportion of voters around the UK supporting a particular party is not reflected in the make-up of the House of Commons. Although the 2017 general election returned a result that was not so distorted, the accusation was not new. Since the 1970s, general elections in the UK had tended to produce disproportionate results, which misrepresented the smaller parties in the House of Commons in terms of their popular support (Renwick, 2015).

How does the electoral system distort the popular vote? In 2015, for example, 67% of votes at the general election went to either Labour or the Conservatives. Yet when the votes were counted up and converted into seats in parliament, the electoral system used for Westminster elections gave the two big parties nearly 87% of the seats. In England and Wales, the two main parties got a 73% share of the vote, but were awarded 98% of the seats. Indeed, after 2015, the Conservative Party was able to govern with a majority of seats in the House of Commons, on less than 37% of the popular vote (or 24% of the electorate, if you include those who were registered to vote, but didn't turn up). Other parties also did well from the electoral system. The Scottish National Party (SNP) received an impressive 50% of the vote north of the border, but the electoral system converted this into 95% of Scottish seats.

By contrast, other parties faired badly from the electoral system. The United Kingdom Independence Party (UKIP) gained almost 13% of the popular vote in 2015, pushing the Lib Dems into fourth place on that measure, but they won just a single seat in the House of Commons. The Conservative Party received three times as many votes as UKIP but 331 times as many MPs as UKIP. Indeed, it took 3.8 million votes for UKIP to gain just one MP. The Green Party faced similar problems. It took 1.1 million votes to gain their one seat. By comparison, the Conservative Party required on average just 34,000 votes per MP.

How votes are counted in elections – the type of electoral system used – matters to the outcome. The electoral system used for UK general elections – 'first past the post' – does not accurately reflect popular support for the parties, as the 2015 general election in particular showed. For many critics, this is a good enough reason to reform the electoral system. Parties (including UKIP, the Lib Dems and the Greens) who feel their popular support is underrepresented, have demanded change. Indeed, a variety of more 'proportional systems', which reward seats more or less proportionally to the percentage of votes cast for a party, are already used for elections to devolved parliaments in Scotland, Wales and Northern Ireland, for the London Assembly and for UK elections to the European Parliament. These systems, relatively new in the UK but familiar in other countries, have produced markedly different results in terms of voters' behaviour, the choice and diversity of representatives, relative party strengths and the nature and style of government. Largely as a result of proportional representation, coalition or minority government has become familiar in Scotland, Wales and Northern Ireland, as it has long been almost everywhere else in Europe. Yet the current electoral system for Westminster also has its supporters, as we see in this chapter.

## THIS CHAPTER:

» Examines the merits, problems and consequences for party politics of various electoral systems, from single member plurality, which we currently use for Westminster elections, to various proportional systems used in other elections around the UK.

» Explores the possibility of further electoral reform in Britain, in light of the accusation of unfairness that some of the statistics set out above indicate.

» Analyses some of the reasons we vote for the parties we vote for (if we do at all), exploring how social class, age, gender, religion, ethnicity and nationality influence the way we vote.

## ELECTORAL SYSTEMS IN THE UK

### THE SINGLE MEMBER PLURALITY SYSTEM OR 'FIRST PAST THE POST'

There has been a long-running debate over the electoral system used for choosing members of the House of Commons in the UK – the single member plurality (SMP) system or, more colloquially, 'first past the post'. (Most political scientists prefer 'single member plurality' system as a more accurate description of the electoral system for Westminster than the more familiar term 'first past the post' used by the media.) This system is common in countries that follow the Westminster model, including Canada and India, but it is used nowhere else in Europe. SMP involves the election of a single MP for each electoral area (or constituency) into which the country is divided. The results of the 2017 general election are represented in Map 13.1 overleaf. The candidate for election who wins a plurality of votes (that

is, more votes than any rival candidate) wins, regardless of whether they have a majority of the total votes cast. This system is disproportional because there is no necessary relationship of the overall proportion of seats gained to votes won by a party over the whole country. Political scientist Maurice Duverger (1964) argued that SMP leads to a two-party political system – so-called 'Duverger's law'. However, recent research shows that this law is not as firm as once thought in countries that use the SMP system (Dunleavy and Diwakar, 2013).

The debate over the desirability of SMP has intensified in recent years, as the two main parties in the UK, Labour and the Conservatives, have been losing ground to a variety of smaller parties. This has led to an increasingly erratic relationship between the proportion of votes cast and seats won by particular parties. The pros and cons of the SMP system are set out in Table 13.1 on p. 269.

**Map 13.1 General election results 2017: constituency view**

Note: The map shows each constituency as an equally sized hexagon, regardless of its geographical size.

*Source*: Ben Flanagan, ESRI, Creative Commons license CC BY 4.0 https://creativecommons.org/licenses/by/4.0/; As shown in http://researchbriefings.parliament.uk/ResearchBriefing/Summary/CBP-7979

The case for electoral reform depends not only on the perceived defects of the SMP system, but also on the alternatives available. Ideally, an electoral system should deliver the following:

» Real choice for voters: involving a range of candidates and parties.

» Simplicity: a system that is readily comprehensible to voters.

» Fair treatment of parties and candidates: each vote as far as possible should count equally.

» Effective representation of local communities or constituencies.

» Effective representation of the gender, age, ethnic, religious and occupational class divisions in the population at large.

» Parliaments or assemblies that can sustain stable government.

» Accountable government, with a clear link between elections and the making and breaking of governments.

**Table 13.1 Pros and cons of single member plurality system**

| Arguments in defence of SMP | Criticisms of SMP |
|---|---|
| • It is arguably a simple and readily understood system, unlike many electoral systems that try to combine proportional representation with local representation | • It often produces disproportionate results in terms of seats won compared with votes cast, commonly overrepresenting the leading party (as Figure 13.1 shows) |
| • It normally produces a clear result quickly, but not in 2010, when the Conservatives ended up in coalition with the Lib Dems, or 2017 when they needed support from the DUP | • The party that wins the most votes does not necessarily win the most seats. In 1951 the Conservatives had 200,000 fewer votes than Labour but won a majority of the seats and formed the government. In February 1974 Labour won fewer votes but more seats than the Conservatives and formed the government |
| • Because it is one of a number of electoral systems to preserve a strong link between the electors in each constituency and their MP, it gives the MP a powerful incentive to listen to constituents and represent their interests and that of the area in Parliament in order to secure re-election | • It particularly penalises third and minor parties whose support is widely dispersed over the country as a whole (e.g. the Lib Dems, Greens, UKIP). In 1983 the Labour Party received 27.6% of the popular vote and won 209 seats. The recently formed Liberal–SDP alliance, close behind with 25.4% of the popular vote, won only 23 seats (3.5% of the total) |
| • It normally exaggerates the winning margin of the leading party and delivers a clear majority of seats in the House of Commons, so providing stable government, but not in 2010 and 2017 | • It can also penalise major parties in parts of the UK. The Conservatives and Labour won 3 Scottish seats between them in the 2015 general election, from a total of 59. Outside London, Labour wins few seats in the south of England |
| | • Under the system, most votes are effectively wasted. All votes for losing candidates and all surplus votes for winning candidates may be considered wasted as they do not contribute to the election of MPs. To win, a candidate only needs one vote more than the number received by any other candidate. A constituency majority of 20,000 or more may be impressive, but does not make any difference to a party's representation |
| | • Because most parliamentary seats are considered 'safe' as there was a substantial majority for the party that won last time, there is little incentive to vote in such seats (see Spotlight 13.1) |
| | • The system can distort voters' preferences. Voters may fear to vote for their main preferred candidate or party for fear of letting in the party they most dislike. Voters may vote 'tactically' (see Spotlight 13.2) for their second or third choice. Because only one candidate is selected per party, parties tend to prefer traditional candidates who they (incorrectly) assume the electorate want to vote for (who tend to be white men) |

In practice, there is no ideal system that can meet all these objectives, but a range of options, each of which offers advantages and disadvantages. There is long experience of a range of different electoral systems operating in other countries, some of which have been introduced in the UK. Elections for the European Parliament, the assemblies in Scotland, Wales and Northern Ireland, the Greater London Assembly, mayoral elections

## Turnout in general elections

13.1

One of the features of the SMP system used in general elections, and elsewhere, is that only more marginal seats are likely to change hands. This is one explanation for low turnout. Turnout can be much lower in safe constituency seats than in 'marginals', where two or more parties could realistically gain the most votes. For example, in 2015 the seat with the lowest turnout (51%) was Stoke-on-Trent Central, a safe Labour seat since it was established in 1950. By contrast, the seat with the highest turnout was Dunbartonshire East, where nearly 82% of the eligible population turned out to vote in a close-fought election. The seat has been, at various times postwar, Labour, Conservative, Lib Dem and was won by the SNP in 2015. For much of the population living in seats that rarely change hands, there is little reason to vote.

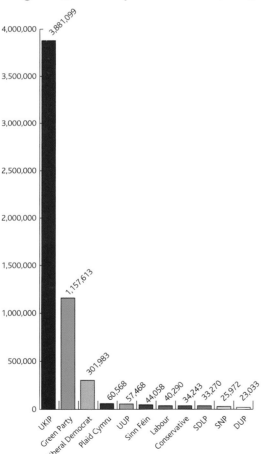

**Figure 13.1: Votes per MP elected, 2015**

*Source*: Reprinted with permission from the Electoral Reform Society from Garland and Terry (2015) *The 2015 General Election: A Voting System in Crisis*, p. 10

and local government use different systems. As John Curtice (2003, p. 100) has observed: 'Britain has become a laboratory of electoral experimentation and change'.

### ALTERNATIVE VOTE (AV)

One simple, widely advocated reform of the current single member plurality system used for Westminster elections is the alternative vote (AV). This would keep single member constituencies but allow voters to express their preferences in order. If no candidate gets 50% of the vote on the first count, the bottom candidates are progressively eliminated and their votes transferred to their second or subsequent preferences until one candidate emerges with an overall majority of the votes cast. A simple plurality of votes (more than any other candidate) would not be enough. In the USA, this system is called 'instant run-off', which sums up what AV does nicely – it delivers a run-off election if no one gets a majority of the votes after first preferences have been counted. AV is used in Australia and has created a relatively stable system. In Britain, a more limited form of preferential voting involving just second preferences (called the 'supplementary vote') is now used for mayoral elections, for example in London. In a 2011 referendum, the UK rejected shifting to AV in parliamentary elections (see below).

AV would prevent MPs being elected on a share of the vote sometimes well below 50%.

In 2015, for example, Alasdair McDonnell won Belfast South for the SDLP with just 25% of the vote and John Pugh won Southport for the Lib Dems with only 31% of the vote. It would also remove the need for tactical voting for a second or third choice candidate to prevent the election of a feared alternative (see Spotlight 13.2).

## SPOTLIGHT ON ...    Tactical voting    13.2

One explanation for the growth of multiparty politics, despite the 'first past the post' electoral system, is the emergence of tactical voting, although, of course, tactical voting is not unique to the SMP system. This can involve supporting a second or third choice party rather than one's first preference in order to prevent the election of a feared alternative. As a rational response to the current electoral system, tactical voting will continue to thrive as long as the SMP system is retained for Westminster elections. Election analysts used to be sceptical about the real extent of tactical voting, not least because it seemed to require rather more political sophistication than they assumed most voters had. However, tactical voting had long been evident in parliamentary by-elections, enabling disgruntled voters to use opinion polls to discern which opposition candidates were best placed to beat the governing party's candidate and 'send a message to Number 10'.

Tactical voting was used on a larger scale in the 1997 general election. Both the size of Labour's majority and the increase in Lib Dem seats (on a smaller national vote) can be attributed to tactical voting against the Conservatives, encouraged by pressure groups and some media publicity. In the campaign leading up to the 2010 election, which resulted in the first peacetime coalition for 100 years, even some Labour ministers advised tactical voting (Kavanagh and Cowley, 2010, p. 186), and this may have contributed to the Conservative failure to obtain an overall majority.

However, the AV would not produce proportional representation. A party obtaining 20% of first preference votes spread across the whole country might still end up with no seats, if they did not have candidates who gained a majority of support in any one constituency. Moreover, many seats would remain 'safe', with one candidate easily winning a majority of the votes in that constituency. This would reduce the incentive to vote and for parties to campaign in those constituencies. Many votes would still be 'wasted', as surplus votes for winning candidates and all votes for losing candidates would not contribute to the election of any MPs.

## PROPORTIONAL SYSTEMS

**Proportional representation** can only be achieved by other electoral systems. One option is a regional party list system, currently used for British elections to the European Parliament, as long as the UK remains a member. Another is the single transferable vote (STV) used for elections for the Northern Ireland Assembly (and the Dáil, the parliament of the Irish Republic). A third option is the additional member system (AMS) already used for elections to devolved governments in Scotland and Wales, and the London Assembly.

---

**Proportional representation** *describes an electoral system that delivers for each political party a share of elected representatives proportionate to its share of the total national vote. A 20% share of the vote for a party should produce close to a 20% share of the seats in the elected parliament, assembly or council.*

---

## Regional party list systems

A party list system can deliver a closely proportional relationship between seats and votes. Each party draws up a list of its candidates in order. So, in a national list system involving a 100-member legislature, a party securing 40% of the vote would see its first 40 candidates elected. However, larger countries that use the list system divide the country into regions, where each party has its own regional lists of candidates. Voters may be given the option of expressing their own order of preferences for candidates within parties (open list systems) rather than simply having to accept the official party list order (closed list systems). Party list systems are widely used in Continental Europe and Latin America. A closed regional party list system was introduced in Britain for the election of Members of the European Parliament in 1999, similar to that used by most other EU member states. Using a list system also allows parties to ensure that a more diverse slate of candidates is selected, for instance through 'zipping' the list by gender so women are placed, for example, in positions 1, 3, 5, 7 and 9 on a list of 10 candidates.

The system is fairly simple and delivers proportional representation. However, it does not provide effective constituency representation, and critics suggest it gives too much power to the party nationally (or regionally) responsible for drawing up lists of candidates, marginalising local party members. It may also lead to the representation of a number of small and possibly extremist parties; for example, the far-right British National Party won two seats in UK elections for the European Parliament in 2009. It can render stable government more difficult.

## The single transferable vote (STV)

The STV is a complex system that can produce results close to proportional representation. Under this system, the country is divided into a number of electoral areas that each elect a number of representatives (multi-member constituencies), but where each voter only has a single vote that is transferable between candidates. Voters number the candidates on the ballot paper in order of preference, going only as low as they want to go. To secure election, a candidate has to gain a predetermined proportion of the total vote ('the quota') in the electoral area or constituency. The quota is decided according the formula:

$$\frac{\text{Total number of valid votes cast}}{\text{Number of seats} + 1} + 1$$

Initially, only first preferences are counted. First choices on the ballot papers are counted

and any candidate who achieves the quota is elected. Once they are elected, any surplus votes above the quota are redistributed according to second preferences. If no candidate achieves the quota on the first or subsequent count, the bottom candidates are progressively eliminated and their second preferences are redistributed until all the seats are filled.

It sounds complicated, but can be best illustrated with reference to Northern Ireland Assembly elections, where the system has been used since 1998. Each constituency elects five members of the Northern Ireland Assembly. To be elected, a candidate needs (according to the formula above) one vote more than a seventh of the total number of votes. In practice, the leading parties put up not one but several candidates, hoping to get as many as possible elected in each constituency. Thus, in Belfast North in 2016, three Democratic Unionists (DUP), two Sinn Féin and one member for the Social Democratic and Labour Party (SDLP) were elected. Belfast West elected four Sinn Féin members, one SDLP and one 'People before Profit' member. In Fermanagh and South Tyrone, two DUP candidates were elected, two Sinn Féin, one UUP and one SDLP.

The system was adopted in Northern Ireland to ensure that all communities and shades of opinion were represented, as part of the ongoing peace process. There was also hope that moderate parties might profit; indeed, the small non-sectarian Alliance Party managed to retain eight seats in May 2016, while it would not have come close to winning any under the SMP system (for more on elections in Northern Ireland, see Chapter 11).

The great advantage of STV is that it combines constituency representation with overall results close to proportional representation. Broadly speaking, the more members elected for each constituency, the more proportional the whole system will be.

## The additional member system (AMS)

Under the additional member system (sometimes called 'the German system'), voters have two votes, one for their local constituency, and a second vote, designed to compensate parties that are underrepresented in the constituencies, by electing additional members through national or regional party lists. It is often referred to as a hybrid system, combining a clear link between directly elected representatives and constituencies with overall results close to proportional representation. It has long been used in Germany; however, parties can only gain additional members if they secure more than 5% of the national vote, a threshold designed to exclude very small parties and prevent the fragmentation of representation in the German parliament.

The AMS has already been used in the UK for elections to the Scottish Parliament, Welsh Assembly and Greater London Assembly, creating both a proportional system and a strong local link with the representative that has been a feature of British politics. In Scotland, the results provide a clear contrast with the general election, where Scottish MPs are still elected under 'first past the post'. In general elections from 1997 to 2010, Labour has won a comfortable overall majority of seats in Scotland (41 out of 58 in 2010). But in elections for the Scottish Parliament under the AMS, Labour fell well short of a majority in both 1999 and 2003, and formed a coalition with the Lib Dems. In 2007, the SNP won 47 seats to Labour's 46 and went on to form a minority government. They secured a remarkable overall majority, never achieved by Labour, after making sweeping gains in 2011, and incidentally demonstrating that proportional representation does not necessarily lead to minority governments or coalition. In the 2016 Scottish elections, the SNP won 63 of the 129 seats available in Holyrood (see Chapter 11).

It is worth adding that the Conservative Party has also benefitted from the AMS in Scotland. Although Conservative representation in Scotland at Westminster has been almost wiped out (no seats in 1997, only one in 2001, 2005 and 2010 and two in 2015), they have secured representation in the Scottish Parliament more proportionate to their share of the vote. By contrast, they won 17 MSPs (Members of the Scottish Parliament) in 2007, 15 in 2011 and 31 in 2016, beating the Labour Party into third place.

Arguments over proportional representation are bound up with the debate over the relative advantages and disadvantages of single-party and coalition government (see Comparing British Politics 13.1). Some argue that coalition government involves too many compromises, and often too much influence for small (sometimes extremist) parties on whose support the coalition depends for survival. So coalition government may appear weak and unstable, unable to take tough decisions. Alternatively, there may be a virtually permanent governing coalition with opposition parties effectively locked out of power, with no real viable alternative for voters. Others argue that concession and compromise are vital parts of the democratic process. Single-party governments with large majorities can behave in high-handed ways, ignoring popular opposition to policies, and riding roughshod over minorities. Critics point out that contentious British policies such as the poll tax would probably not have been implemented by a coalition government. However, the 2010–15 coalition government controversially trebled university tuition fees and raised VAT despite previous Lib Dem opposition (see Spotlight 20.3).

## APATHY TOWARDS ELECTORAL REFORM

Electoral reform only seems to excite a small section of the population, and has never been much of an issue with most voters. Yet electoral systems can make a crucial difference to the fortunes of parties and the form and nature of government, as some of the examples above indicate. Were proportional representation ever to be introduced for Westminster elections, it would lead regularly to minority or coalition government, if current voting patterns were maintained. Table 13.2 overleaf shows what the 2017 election might have looked like if votes had been counted using a different electoral system.

In practice, it might also change voting behaviour, perhaps encouraging more support for minor parties. What then are the prospects

**Table 13.2 The consequences of some different electoral systems applied to the 2017 general election**

| Party | SMP seats | AV seats | AMS seats | STV seats |
|---|---|---|---|---|
| Con | 317 | 304 | 274 | 282 |
| Lab | 262 | 286 | 274 | 297 |
| Lib Dem | 12 | 11 | 39 | 29 |
| UKIP | 0 | 0 | 11 | 1 |
| Greens | 1 | 1 | 8 | 1 |
| SNP | 25 | 27 | 21 | 18 |
| Plaid Cymru | 4 | 2 | 4 | 3 |

Note: Excludes data from Northern Ireland.

*Source*: Reprinted with permission from the Electoral Reform Society, Garland and Terry (2017), *The 2017 General Election: Volatile voting, random results*, p.34

for further electoral reform in Britain, particularly for UK general elections and local elections in England and Wales now still conducted under the SMP system?

The losers from the current system unsurprisingly advocate electoral reform involving more proportional representation. For many years, the main losers were the Lib Dems and their predecessor parties, but in 2015 they were joined by UKIP and the Greens. The Lib Dems have a reasonable grievance, as can be seen by comparing their electoral support and role in government with that of their German counterparts, the Free Democratic Party (FDP) (see Comparing British Politics 13.1).

## ⬛ COMPARING BRITISH POLITICS 13.1 ⬛
### 'Third parties' in Germany and the UK

The Free Democratic Party (FDP) have generally secured 5–10% of the vote in elections in the Federal Republic of Germany since 1949, and under the German electoral system they always received a broadly comparable proportion of seats in the Bundestag or federal parliament. Because it has been rare for a single party to secure an overall majority of seats, the FDP have held Cabinet seats in a coalition government for most of the period since 1949. In the periods 1949–57 and 1961–65 they were in coalition with the Christian Democrats and from 1969 to 1983 they partnered the Social Democrats, returning to share government posts with the Christian Democrats from 1983 to 1998. From 2009 to 2013, they were back in government as junior partners with the Christian Democrats under Angela Merkel. In 2013, they failed to win seats in the Bundestag for the first time since 1948.

The British Liberal Party and its successors have consistently won a larger share of the national vote than the FDP since 1974, sometimes achieving twice or three times the FDP's share of the vote. But the Liberals and their successors have been substantially underrepresented at Westminster and never shared in government nor held a single Cabinet post from 1945 until 2010, when the Lib Dems entered a coalition with the Conservatives for five years with catastrophic electoral consequences.

Despite calls for reform from political parties and campaign groups, there seemed little prospect of achieving this for UK general elections as the two major parties benefitted from the existing system. While the 1997 Labour government introduced a variety of new electoral systems for UK elections to the European Parliament and for devolved parliaments and assemblies in Scotland, Wales, Northern Ireland and London (the existence of which were ratified by referendums, but not the specific electoral systems used), they did not hold a promised referendum on electoral reform for the House of Commons. (For more on the creation of the Scottish Parliament and the Welsh Assembly, see Chapter 11.) It was only in the lead-up to the 2010 election that Labour indicated support for further electoral reform, and only after a hung parliament (in which no party has a majority of the seats) materialised did the Conservatives reluctantly agree to a referendum on limited reform, the AV.

In 1997, Labour set up the Independent Commission on the Voting System and planned a subsequent referendum. The Jenkins Commission (1998), named after its chair Roy Jenkins, a former deputy leader of the Labour Party and former leader of the Social Democratic Party (SDP), recommended the introduction of the AV to elect 80–85% of the House of Commons, with the rest elected by a list system. This system (sometimes described as 'AV plus') would have led to increased representation for other parties had it been in place in 1997, although Labour would have had a smaller, but still comfortable, overall majority with 44% of the vote. Thus, it fell well short of proportional representation. In practice, the report was ignored and there was no referendum.

There was some renewed debate over electoral reform leading up to the 2010 election, with Labour promising a referendum, probably just on the AV but conceivably AV plus. In the interparty negotiation that followed the election, the Conservatives under Cameron pledged a referendum on the AV, which became part of the programme of the coalition government.

AV involves only a limited reform of the voting system, yet precipitated the first full UK-wide referendum since 1975. Much more extensive and far-reaching changes have been introduced to the system of voting for the European Parliament and devolved assemblies, without any apparent need for popular endorsement. The AV referendum pledge was the minimum the Lib Dems would accept, and the maximum the Conservatives were prepared to concede in their coalition negotiations. The interests of the two parties were diametrically opposed. According to one estimate (Curtice et al., 2010, p. 417), had the 2010 election been held under AV, the Lib Dems would have won 79 instead of 57 seats, while the Conservatives would have been reduced to 281 rather than 307.

# SPOTLIGHT ON ...

## 2011 referendum campaign tactics

13.3

The referendum campaign on electoral reform in 2011 generated more heat than light. Some used it to vent their rage at the Lib Dem leader Nick Clegg for entering coalition. The 'No to AV' campaign (funded almost entirely by the Conservative Party) freely exploited Clegg's unpopularity in their material, reminding voters of his broken promises and arguing in leaflets that 'The only vote that would count under AV would be Nick Clegg's'. While supporters of AV exaggerated its advantages, its opponents employed misleading analogies, dubious evidence and highly specious cost figures. Lib Dem ministers expressed their outrage at some of these tactics in Cabinet.

The Conservatives campaigned hard against any change to the electoral system. Here, David Cameron, former prime minister, delivers 'No to AV' leaflets to voters.

The 2011 referendum involved a massive defeat for AV and an endorsement of the single member plurality system by 68% of voters on a 42% turnout. The margin of defeat would appear to rule out AV and any other electoral reform for the foreseeable future. It was a huge blow for Clegg and his party. The scale of the defeat had not been anticipated, as early polls had suggested a vote for AV. Yet electoral reform was not high on the list of voters' concerns. Party allegiance seems to have largely determined the outcome, with Conservative supporters overwhelmingly voting against change, particularly after the decisive inter-vention of David Cameron, against the (much diminished) ranks of the Lib Dems, with Labour voters as evenly divided as their MPs, despite Labour leader Ed Miliband's support for AV. So the 2015 and 2017 general elections were fought under the old rules. Although the old single member plurality system seems to be designed for an era of two-party politics, there seems little immediate chance that there will be a change for the multiparty politics in which we are increasingly a part.

## Party Allegiances: Why do we Vote the Way we do?

We move now from considering the mechanics of electoral systems to examine why people vote as they do – if indeed they do vote. Voting is perhaps the most common form of political participation (other forms are discussed in Chapter 16). Political scientists and sociolo-gists have put forward several models of why we vote the way we do.

The oldest is the *socioeconomic model*. Under this model, we tend to vote based on our social class or status. As Lazarsfeld et al. (1944, p. 27) wrote (in dated language): 'A person thinks, politically, as he is socially. Social characteristics determine political preference.' First, because members of social classes share common interests that are promoted or threatened by political parties; and second, because social classes confer norms and values on members that are shared or rejected by political parties. This is described as 'interests plus socialisation theory' (Denver et al., 2012, p. 22). People vote for what is in their interest and they are socialised in their group to do so.

More recently, the socioeconomic model has been questioned. For a start, social classes are made up of individuals, each with their own concerns and sense of values. This does not necessarily lead to a common interest in voting for the same party. We are now more aware of the idea of multiple and overlapping group memberships, including class, ethnicity, gender, disability and sexuality. This is increasingly played out in practice – we often see significant minorities within a socioeconomic group voting in unexpected ways. In the 2017 general election, for example, significant numbers of high earners voted for the Labour Party under Corbyn, even though Labour had promised to introduce higher rates of tax, which would affect many of these high earners. In the 1980s, large numbers of working-class voters supported Thatcher, although she pledged to cut spending on various public services and benefits, on which many working-class households were reliant.

A second model shifts the focus from class-based to party identification, called the *party identification model*, sometimes described as a 'social psychological model'. Here, the role of party identification (or party identity, partisanship or 'brand loyalty') is crucial. In the UK, this model is associated with David Butler and Donald Stokes' *Political Change in Britain* (1969), which drew on American research. (David Butler is discussed in Key Figures 13.1.) Social groups, such as class, are still important to Butler and Stokes' approach, because our party identification comes from our early socialisation, particularly our parents' class. However, they accept that, while we might identify with one party more than another, voting can also be shaped by short-term or tactical factors. We might identify with a particular party, but decide to vote differently because of our reservations about its leader, for example, or the fact it is not competitive in the constituency we're voting in.

 **KEY FIGURES 13.1**
David Butler

**David Butler (1924–)** spent most of his career as an Oxford academic. He has studied each election since 1945. He popularised the term 'psephology', the study and analysis of elections – from the Ancient Greek practice of voting with a pebble or *psephos*.

Butler's early work introduced the idea of electoral swings. He was asked to explain the concept to Winston Churchill, still Conservative Party leader, ahead of the 1950 general election. He became a prominent on-screen expert on the BBC's election night coverage from the 1950 election to the 1979 election, and has a good claim to be one of the inventors of the 'swingometer'. (It is now a rather more elaborate, electronic affair – see Spotlight 13.4.)

Later in his career, he brought modern American science approaches to the UK to better understand voting behaviour, particularly in *Political Change in Britain: Forces Shaping Electoral Choice* (Butler and Stokes, 1969).

Perhaps Butler's most notably works are the Nuffield Election Studies for every UK general election since 1945. These were initially co-authored with Richard Rose and Anthony King, and from 1974 to 2005, this series was co-authored with Dennis Kavanagh (who now publishes the series with Philip Cowley). They provide an invaluable guide to each and every general election.

One challenge for the party identification model is that voters are now less and less likely to identify with a particular party than they were in the early postwar period. From the 1940s to the 1960s, the majority of the electorate were strongly linked to one of the two main political parties. Although there are always exceptions, party loyalty corresponded closely with social class. Working-class voters tended to vote for the Labour Party and middle- and upper-class voters tended to vote Conservative (Särlvik and Crewe, 1983). In recent decades, this has changed, in a process described as 'partisan dealignment'. It is wrapped up with class dealignment, where we no longer identify as clearly as we once did with a particular social class. In 2017, for the first time, the link between voting and social class broke down, as we see below.

A final explanation of why we vote as we do is the *issue voting model*. Voters are much like consumers. We vote for the party we think is most likely to focus on the issues we care about. This means that long-term considerations or loyalty matter less than the short-term policies put forward by a particular party. One issue with this model is that it is sometimes difficult to know which issues matter. Here, political scientists have separated positional issues and valence issues. Positional issues are those on which voters take different positions, for example the death sentence, gay marriage or the extension of public ownership. Valence issues are those on which everyone largely agrees, for example economic prosperity or low crime rates (Clarke et al., 2004).

Many political scientists have argued that politics is increasingly about valence issues.

Parties have become more similar, with little to differentiate them on positional issues. In deciding how to vote, therefore, it is not class or identification that matters, but which party we think will be most competent at achieving widely shared goals, for example economic competence. Knowing this is not easy, so it is argued that voters often use shortcuts to help them decide, such as which leader they trust the most. More recent research (Denver, 2003, pp. 28–30) suggests that a consequence of issue voting is increased electoral volatility, with more voters prepared to switch their votes between elections, and a correspondingly weaker party identification.

We now look at how people have voted in recent elections and see if class, age, ethnicity, religion or geography affects one's likelihood of voting for a particular party.

## SOCIAL CLASS AND VOTING BEHAVIOUR

Social class has long appeared a key factor explaining voting in Britain. Labour, as the name implies, was the party established to represent the interests of the working class, particularly the manual working class who were members of trade unions affiliated to the Labour Party. The Conservative Party was associated with the interests of the property-owning middle class. Indeed, back in 1967, British political scientist Peter Pulzer (1967) claimed that 'class is the basis of British politics; all else is embellishment and detail'. Analysis of voting by class then provided substantial justification for Pulzer's bold assertion. The further down the social scale (classes C2, D and E on this common classification), the greater the support for Labour, while the professional and managerial classes (A and B) were then overwhelmingly Conservative supporters. Routine white-collar workers (C1s), often described as 'lower middle class', were twice as likely to vote Conservative as Labour. (See Chapter 4, pp. 59–63, for more on social class categories.)

Even then, however, it will be noted that significant minorities did not support the party associated with their class. So around a fifth of the middle class (A, B + C1) in postwar elections voted Labour, while around a third of the manual working class (C2, D and E)

voted Conservative. Political scientists sought to explain this 'deviant voting', particularly the working-class Conservatives. Some saw the explanation in terms of the deference of some workers to their social superiors. Others considered that affluent workers (such as Midland car workers) were increasingly acquiring middle-class characteristics and attitudes (including voting Conservative). Indeed, left-wing analysts feared that growing affluence was, over time, eroding Labour's working-class vote.

Subsequently, class allegiances have become more blurred. There has been significant class and partisan dealignment (as we saw above). Thatcher made a particular pitch for the skilled working-class vote (the C2s), with some success, although a substantial minority of skilled workers had supported the Conservatives throughout the twentieth century. From a Labour perspective, these were worrying trends. The manual working class was not only declining as a proportion of the population, but also appeared increasingly fragmented on lines of ethnicity and gender, and between public and private sector employment. Labour leaders from Kinnock to Blair took the lesson that they could no longer hope to win elections by securing most of the vote of the manual working class, but had to appeal to a wider cross-class constituency if Labour was ever to return to power (thereby prompting it to become more of a 'catch-all' party). This they seemed to achieve spectacularly in 1997, making dramatic gains across all social classes, but particularly among the C1s and C2s. Middle-class support for Labour was further consolidated in 2001 with small swings to Labour among the As, Bs and C1s, while the Conservatives made gains among the C2s, Ds and Es. (The idea of 'swing' is examined in Spotlight 13.4.)

By the 2017 election, class no longer appeared to be a good indicator of voting intention (see Figure 13.2 on p. 280). Significant numbers of middle-class voters, particularly in the cities – which tend to have younger, more multi-ethnic populations – shifted to Labour. By contrast, the Tories did well with skilled manual workers – a group that would have traditionally voted Labour. The story is more traditional when it comes to voters from social classes D and E (which cover semi-skilled and unskilled

# SPOTLIGHT ON ...

## Swing

13.4

Swing measures the shift in support between parties between elections. The two-party swing between elections can often be simply measured by adding the increase in votes for one party to the decrease in votes for the other and dividing by two. (It becomes slightly more complicated if the votes for both parties increase or decrease, because of changes in votes for other parties.) The swing needed for a party coming second in one election to win the next is more easily measured: simply halve the difference in the percentage of votes of the leading two parties. Thus, in 2017, roughly speaking, Labour won 40% of the popular vote and the Conservatives 42%. Labour would need a swing of just over 1% to win next time. In other words, just 1 voter in 100 would have to switch support between the two parties.

There is considerable evidence that the electorate is becoming more volatile. The 1997 general election was a political earthquake with an almost unprecedented swing of over 10% from Conservative to Labour (some of the reasons for this are discussed in Chapter 14). The 2010 election involved an average swing of around 5% from Labour to Conservative, considerable, but substantially less than the pro-Labour swing in 1997, and less than was required for a Conservative majority.

The average swing conceals considerable variations. Back in the 1960s and 70s, leading political scientists Robert McKenzie and David Butler used a 'swingometer' to predict the results of general elections on TV after the first handful of seats had been declared. The predictions were generally very accurate, because then the whole country appeared to swing together,

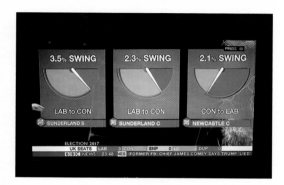

The BBC swingometer in action on general election night, 2017.

and there were only minor variations between particular constituencies.

More recently, there have been more marked differences in the size of the swing. Politics appears to be becoming more volatile. Thus the average swing in 2010 from Labour to Conservative of around 5% masked huge variations; these ranged from a Labour to Conservative swing of 14.4% in Hemel Hempstead to a 4.3% swing the other way in Cumbernauld. Local issues can still make a difference. A vigorous and effective constituency party campaign may buck the trend, as can the record and personality of individual candidates.

Indeed, in elections where several parties are competing, the two-party swing can be misleading. In the 2015 general election, Conservative and Labour dominance seemed to be challenged by other parties, such as UKIP, the SNP in Scotland, the Lib Dems and the Greens, although the collapse of UKIP and the Lib Dems by 2017 meant something of a return to the postwar norm. Thus it is less clear in which direction the swing in votes is going and the concept becomes less useful.

manual occupations, unemployed people and those in the lowest grade occupations) who still tended towards Labour. The class that people feel they belong to does not have the same partisan political consequences it once did. This is related to the big socioeconomic shifts in the UK, set out in Chapter 4, such as the decline of the manufacturing industry and the trade union movement, and the rise of the service economy. The breakdown of the link between class and voting is one of the most remarkable stories of recent years.

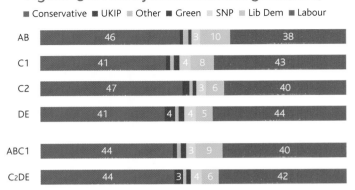

Figure 13.2: Vote by socioeconomic grade, 2017

■ Conservative ■ UKIP ■ Other ■ Green ■ SNP ■ Lib Dem ■ Labour

| | Conservative | Other | Lib Dem | Labour |
|---|---|---|---|---|
| AB | 46 | 3 | 10 | 38 |
| C1 | 41 | 4 | 8 | 43 |
| C2 | 47 | 3 | 6 | 40 |
| DE | 41 | 4 / 4 | 5 | 44 |
| ABC1 | 44 | 3 | 9 | 40 |
| C2DE | 44 | 3 / 4 | 6 | 42 |

Note: Based on a survey of 52,615 adults about their vote in the 2017 general election.

*Source*: YouGov post-election survey, 2017, https://yougov.co.uk/news/2017/06/13/how-britain-voted-2017-general-election/. Reproduced with permission

Other factors, which we look at below, seem to provide more of a guide to people's partisan support.

## AGE AND VOTING

Conservative support increases and Labour's decreases with age. In 2017, age was the strongest indicator of voting, rather than social class. The difference between age groups in their party support is stark (see Figure 13.3). Polling organisation YouGov interviewed a little over 50,000 people after the 2017 election. They found that among first-time voters (those aged 18 and 19), Labour was 47 percentage points ahead (Curtis, 2017). Among

those aged over 70, the Conservatives had a lead of 50%. This is a staggering difference. For each decade a voter ages, their chance of voting Tory increases by about 9% and the chance of them voting Labour falls by nine points. In 2017, the tipping point at which a voter is more likely to have voted Conservative than Labour was 47.

In recent elections, young people were much less likely to vote than older people. It was older voters that pushed the vote on Britain's membership of the EU towards Brexit in 2016. Lower turnout for younger voters remained true in the 2017 general election, although Corbyn's Labour Party did significantly better at getting

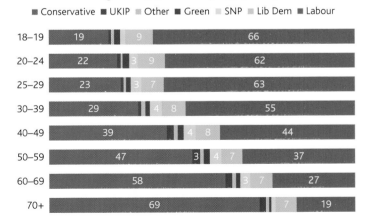

Figure 13.3: Vote by age, 2017

■ Conservative ■ UKIP ■ Other ■ Green ■ SNP ■ Lib Dem ■ Labour

| | Conservative | Other | Labour |
|---|---|---|---|
| 18–19 | 19 | 9 | 66 |
| 20–24 | 22 | 3 / 9 | 62 |
| 25–29 | 23 | 3 / 7 | 63 |
| 30–39 | 29 | 4 / 8 | 55 |
| 40–49 | 39 | 4 / 8 | 44 |
| 50–59 | 47 | 3 / 4 / 7 | 37 |
| 60–69 | 58 | 3 / 7 | 27 |
| 70+ | 69 | 7 | 19 |

Note: Based on a survey of 52,615 adults about their vote in the 2017 general election.

*Source*: YouGov post-election survey, 2017, https://yougov.co.uk/news/2017/06/13/how-britain-voted-2017-general-election/. Reproduced with permission

younger voters to turn out than his predecessor as Labour leader, Ed Miliband. Despite this improvement, only 57% of 18- to 19-year-olds voted at the 2017 election; for voters over 70, the figure was 84% (Curtis, 2017). (Turnout is discussed in more detail in Chapter 16.)

This has a huge impact on politics. Owing to increased longevity and a declining birth rate, older people are an increasing proportion of the population and they are also more likely to vote. The high turnout among older voters means that all parties compete for older voters, offering policies that will attract them; for example, Cameron and Corbyn both promised a triple guarantee that pensions would continue to rise at the 2015 and 2017 elections. Thus 'grey power' backed by the 'grey vote' is becoming increasingly significant.

## GENDER AND VOTING

A higher proportion of women than men used to support the Conservatives (see Figure 13.4). The historic ability of the Conservative Party to attract female voters perhaps lies in Labour's roots in the male-dominated, manufacturing trade unions. Throughout Thatcher's term as prime minister, women continued to prefer the Conservative Party to Labour in greater numbers than their male counterparts. It was not until 2005 that women begin to show a stronger preference than men for the Labour Party. The change was largely due to generational differences in Conservative support. Young women grew more pro-Labour

over the course of the 1980s, while middle-aged women barely waned in their support for the Conservatives. Ultimately, by the end of Thatcher's period in office, the swing away from the Conservatives among younger women was stronger than the countervailing movement among older women.

There are several explanations for women's turn away from Thatcherism, including the effect of Thatcher's policies on women in the workforce; the failure of the market economy to deliver for younger people; women's support for the peace movement; and, finally, a long-term secular trend towards greater progressivism among women born after the Second World War. The continued appeal of conservatism to a large section of British women, particularly middle-aged and older women, has, in contrast, received only slight attention (Beers, 2012).

Women – especially younger women – are now more likely to vote Labour, perhaps partly as a consequence of increases in family benefits and nursery provision under New Labour governments (Campbell, 2006). Indeed, it was women who helped to keep Labour in power with a comfortable overall majority in the 2000s and who gave disproportionate support for Ed Miliband between 2010 and 2015 and Jeremy Corbyn after 2015.

All the main parties now make significant steps to target women voters. Labour under Blair and Brown sought to include more women in politics, for example through the

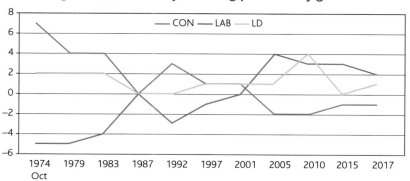

**Figure 13.4: A history of voting patterns by gender**

Note: Estimates of party vote shares among women minus share among men. LD includes predecessor parties.

*Source*: Number Cruncher Politics; Ipsos MORI data. Reproduced with permission

*Source*: Ian Forsyth/Getty Images News/Getty Images

Ahead of the 2015 general election, Labour very visually focused on women's rights by touring with a 'pink bus' – a strategy that was ridiculed as patronising by many commentators and feminist campaigners.

use of all-women shortlists (AWS), as well as by including women's perspectives and issues. AWS guarantee the return of women MPs by selecting them as candidates in held and winnable seats. Labour's position was in large part due to longstanding campaigns by women in the party – notably the former deputy leader of the party, Harriet Harman (Harman, 2017). Cameron, during his time as leader of the Conservative Party, also stressed the need for more female politicians and better access to paid work for women. This competition for women's votes led to the main parties becoming closer on 'women's issues'. Indeed, with the possible exception of UKIP, all main parties are competing to be viewed as equally *liberally* feminist (Campbell and Childs, 2015).

## RELIGION AND VOTING

In the nineteenth century, there were close links between religious and party political affiliations. It was humorously suggested by an often-used phrase that the Church of England was 'the Tory party at prayer', while Protestant nonconformists (e.g. Baptists, Methodists) provided the Liberal Party's core support. In the twentieth century, the Labour Party inherited much of the nonconformist vote – it was sometimes said that Labour owed more to Methodism than Marxism. However, with the growth of a more secular society, religion became of decreasing political importance, outside Northern Ireland of course, and with some significant exceptions elsewhere – especially

Liverpool and parts of Scotland. Catholics are more likely to support Labour in Liverpool, Glasgow and Edinburgh, although it does not necessarily follow that those with other faiths will favour Labour's opponents in these areas. Outside these areas, the religious convictions of election candidates were regarded as almost totally irrelevant. Anglicans, Roman Catholics, nonconformists, Jews and atheists can be found across all parties.

Today, religion is becoming of more political importance in some parts of Britain as a result of the increased allegiance to non-Christian faiths associated with some ethnic minorities, for whom ethnicity and religion are inseparably bound together as part of their identity. Following the 'war on terror' and more especially the Iraq War, in 2005 some Muslims deserted Labour for the Lib Dems or other anti-war parties such as Respect. By 2010, it seemed that the Muslim vote was again predominantly Labour (Curtice et al., 2016, pp. 395–6). Indeed, Sadiq Khan, a Labour MP, was elected London mayor in 2016 – the first Muslim to become mayor of a major western capital city, further cementing the link between Labour and the Muslim vote.

## ETHNICITY AND VOTING

Ethnicity hardly figured in earlier analyses of voting, as ethnic minorities were then insufficiently numerous to make much difference. Today, non-white ethnic minorities amount to around 14% of the UK population (see Chapter 4, pp. 65–70). While this is still a relatively small minority in the country as a whole, the proportion in some cities is much higher and in a few parliamentary constituencies the 'ethnic minority' population constitutes the majority.

Black and minority ethnic (BAME) voters overwhelmingly tended to support the Labour Party, with as many as 90% choosing Labour until the 1990s (Khan, 2015). But the dominance of the Labour Party is beginning to wane. For example, in the 2015 election, Labour still remained the first choice for most BME voters, with around 60% support. The Conservatives, however, are beginning to increase their share of the BME vote, from around 16% in 2010 to around 25% in 2015.

There is also increasing diversity in how different BME groups vote. The Runnymede Trust, which examines race equality in the UK, found that, generally speaking, Indian Hindus and Chinese groups are most likely to vote Conservative (Khan, 2015). One reason for this is likely to be their greater success in the labour market, their relatively higher earnings and greater levels of homeownership. This contrasts with 87% of black Africans, who supported Labour at the 2010 general election (Khan, 2015). In general, while Labour still dominates the BME vote, this is an increasingly fragmented category.

## REGIONAL AND NATIONAL VARIATION

Recent elections have seen significant regional and national variation, none more so than in 2015. The biggest change was in Scotland, where the SNP won all but three seats. Yet, as we have seen, it could be argued that the electoral system is distorting the results. For example, while Conservative popular support in Scotland is weaker than in England and Wales, the party still gained around 15% of the votes cast in Scotland. This was represented by just one seat. By contrast, the Scottish Conservatives returned 31 MSPs in the 2016 Scottish Parliament elections (gaining 22% of the popular vote). To critics, the single member plurality system exacerbates division between the nations and regions of the UK (Garland and Terry, 2015). The 2017 Westminster election saw the partial recovery of the other parties in Scotland, although the SNP still held 35 of the 59 Scottish seats.

Within England, there is significant regional variation too. The notion of a political North–South divide has some basis in reality. Even a casual perusal of the political map of Britain reveals substantial Conservative strength south of a line from the Bristol Channel to the Wash. Back in the 1980s, Labour only held a handful of seats outside London below this line. In 1997, they made significant gains in the south, but lost a few of these in subsequent elections. By 2015, Labour representation in the south was reduced once more to odd specks of red in a sea of blue, although they made significant improvements in 2017, winning traditionally conservative seats like Canterbury in Kent from the Conservatives.

Generalisations about regional party strengths conceal substantial intra-regional differences. There is also something of an urban–rural divide. Even though only 1% of the British workforce derive their living from the land, there are many more rural dwellers, some commuting into the cities, others retired or working from home. Many identify with the countryside even if they work, shop and seek entertainment in the towns. Such semi-rural areas are predominantly now Conservative in England, Wales and Northern Ireland. Thus there are strong Conservative areas in parts of a predominantly Labour north of England.

Some of these regional differences also reflect class differences. There is a rather higher proportion of manual workers in the north of England and Scotland, and rather more professional and managerial workers in the south. Yet there may also be a neighbourhood effect. Those living in strongly Labour or Conservative neighbourhoods may be influenced by the locally prevailing political attitudes. Thus manual workers in Bournemouth may be more likely to vote Conservative than manual workers in Barnsley. Similarly, doctors or solicitors in Barnsley may be more inclined to support Labour than their fellow professionals on the south coast. But it is difficult to be sure about the causal connection. It may simply be the case that doctors and solicitors with Labour sympathies are more likely to live and practise in poorer areas where they do more good.

# A NEW AGE OF ELECTORAL VOLATILITY?

Fewer people today identify strongly with political parties. As party loyalties have weakened, so electoral volatility has increased. More voters are prepared to switch to another party or decide not to vote at all. Until recently, the decline in party identification was seen in the reasonably steady fall in the percentage of the total vote won in general elections for the Conservative and Labour parties. For example, in 1951, nearly 97% of voters supported either Labour or Conservative. By 1983, with the emergence of the new centrist SDP, this figure fell to 72%. This reached its lowest level in 2010, with just 65% voting Labour or Conservative. Despite the Lib Dem collapse in 2015, support did not flow back to the big two parties. Labour and the Conservatives gained 69% of the vote in that general election.

The 2017 general election seemed to mark a revival of two-party politics in the UK, with Labour and the Conservatives achieving around 80% of the vote between them. However, this return to two-party dominance in Westminster is likely to be more to do with the unique circumstances of the UKIP collapse and the failure of the Lib Dems to make a significant recovery (factors that are discussed in Chapter 14). Volatility in voter behaviour between Labour and the Conservatives or to minor parties does not seem to be going away.

The 2017 election also called into question the single member plurality system used in Westminster elections. Its proponents argue that although the results are sometimes disproportional to party support, as we saw in the introduction, it has the advantage of producing quick, stable majority governments. In 2017, the electoral system returned a Conservative minority government, which had to rely on the DUP for support. For two of the last three general elections, the single member plurality system was failing in its own terms.

## SUMMARY

» Single-party majority UK government was the norm from 1945 until 2010 but this reflected an electoral system (single member plurality) involving a markedly disproportionate relationship between the votes and the seats won by political parties.

» Since 1997 a variety of new electoral systems have been introduced for elections for devolved assemblies, mayoral elections and, while the UK remains a member, the European Parliament. These have further stimulated a trend towards multiparty politics in the UK.

» Issue voting appears to be on the increase, although it is difficult to measure with any precision.

» There has long been a close link between social class and support for the two main parties. This has declined markedly, but there was still a clear if diminishing correlation between party support and class in recent elections.

» Some other social divisions are also significant for party support. Older people are more likely to support the Conservatives. Women, once slightly more likely to vote Conservative, are now slightly more supportive of Labour. The ethnic minority vote has been predominantly Labour, although the Iraq War alienated some Muslims, who switched to the Lib Dems or other candidates in 2005.

» There is still a pronounced North–South divide in British politics, with the Conservatives stronger in the south of England, and Labour in Scotland, Wales and the north of England, with the Midlands more closely contested. Urban Britain is more Labour, suburban and rural Britain more Conservative.

## ? QUESTIONS FOR DISCUSSION

» How far does the result of the 2015 election, in particular, advance the case for electoral reform?

» Why have so many different kinds of electoral system been introduced for various levels of government in the UK?

» What have been the effects of different electoral systems on party politics?

» How far and why does the association between voting and social class appear to be declining?

» What other social divisions seem to have important implications for voting?

» How far do issues and ideas influence voters?

» How significant is tactical voting? In what circumstances can it be effective?

» Do some electoral systems produce results that give fairer gender and BAME representation than others? If so, why?

## FURTHER READING

Denver et al. (2012) *Elections and Voters in Britain* is the best short guide to this subject. It is fuller on voting behaviour than electoral systems, although it does give a brief account of the different electoral systems now operating in the UK, with a succinct criticism and defence of first past the post. Chapter 6 of Bale (2017) is good on European comparisons. Curtice (2003) and Leach (2004) provide a critical appraisal of the effects of different electoral systems in the UK; see also Game (2001). Past election statistics are available from a range of sources, including Butler and Butler (2000) *Twentieth-Century Political Facts 1900–2000* and (2006) *British Political Facts since 1979*.

Important books on voting behaviour in the UK include: Clarke et al. (2004) *Political Choice in Britain*, Clarke et al. (2009) *Performance Politics and the British Voter* and Whiteley et al. (2013) *Affluence, Austerity and Electoral Change in Britain*. Full accounts of particular UK elections are provided in the Nuffield series, with which David Butler has been associated since 1951. Books in the series include Butler and Kavanagh (1997, 2001, 2005) and, most recently, Kavanagh and Cowley (2010) and Cowley and Kavanagh (2016). Denver and Garnett's (2014) *British General Elections since 1964: Diversity, Dealignment and Disillusion* is also well worth a read. There are many other accounts of specific elections that can be consulted for comparison.

## USEFUL WEBSITES

The increasing number of publications of the Electoral Commission are useful, some of which can be consulted on its website: www.electoralcommission.org.uk.

*Further student resources to support learning are available at*
**www.macmillanihe.com/griffiths-brit-pol-3e**

# 14 POLITICAL PARTIES

The general election of 2017 saw Labour and the Conservatives win well over 80% of the popular vote and just under 90% of the seats in the House of Commons. Andreas Whittam Smith (2017), hedging his bets, proclaimed: 'After three decades of splintering, two-party politics is back – sort of.' Indeed, traditionally Britain was uncontroversially described as having a two-party system. Over the past 200 years, a two-party 'duopoly' has appeared to be the norm: first Whigs and Tories, then Liberals and Conservatives, and from the 1920s onwards Labour and Conservatives.

Only two parties formed governments between 1945 and 2010. The Conservatives and, to a lesser extent, Labour have dominated British politics since before the Second World War.

Indeed, the whole Westminster system of government assumes a confrontation between just two parties. There is a government and opposition, a Cabinet and a shadow Cabinet, a House of Commons with two sets of benches facing each other (compared with semi-circular assemblies, common elsewhere, including the Scottish Parliament).

The era of two-party politics was meant to be drawing to a close. Since the 1970s, there has been a gradual erosion of combined support for Labour and the Conservatives:

» In the 2015 general election, for example, just 67% of voters supported one of the big two parties.

» Class and partisan dealignment mean that voters associate much less strongly with political parties than they once did (see 'Social class and voting behaviour', pp. 278–79).

» Multiparty politics is already well established in Scotland, Wales and Northern Ireland, particularly in elections for the devolved assemblies. The SNP almost wiped the other parties off the electoral map in Westminster elections in 2015, winning 56 of Scotland's 59 seats.

» New parties (such as UKIP) and some older smaller parties (like the Greens) have also secured some electoral success. Indeed, UKIP – a party only founded in 1993 and which had never achieved more than 3% of the vote before – came third place in terms of votes at the 2015 general election.

The 2017 general election seemed to reverse a long-term trend. Party politics in Britain today is more fluid and unpredictable than ever before.

## THIS CHAPTER:

» Looks at the changing nature of party politics in the UK, and in particular in Westminster.

» Explores briefly the need for parties, reviews the party system in Britain, and goes on to explain how and why it is changing.

» Explores some of the main distinctions between different types of parties, as well as examining how much cohesion they have.

» Analyses the organisation of political parties in the UK, particularly the relationship between the party leadership, parliamentary parties, party members and voters.

» Considers the controversial issue of party finance.

» Asks if the 'two-party system' is here to stay.

# WHAT'S THE USE OF POLITICAL PARTIES?

Politics is commonly associated almost exclusively with 'party politics', a specialist and rather unpopular activity undertaken by party politicians. This very narrow interpretation of politics is misguided (as we discussed in Chapter 1), but it does underline how important parties have become in modern political systems.

It is not immediately obvious why political parties are necessary in a modern representative democracy. Why could voters not simply choose the best person for the job, regardless of party labels? Parties may seem to bring more division than necessary to politics. Often it is suggested that a certain issue should be 'taken out' of party politics, or that party politics should play no part in, for example, local government. Could we not dispense with parties altogether? The answer to that question is, almost certainly, no. Parties have developed in just about every political system involving representative democracy (see Comparing British Politics 14.1), which suggests that they are useful for the operation of the system.

Indeed, parties have many important functions, including:

» *Political choice*: parties are the principal means by which voters are given an effective choice between different teams of leaders, ideas and policies. Without parties, it would be very difficult for voters as a whole to have much influence on the shape of the government to emerge or the policies to be pursued.

» *Political recruitment*: parties recruit and train people for political office and government. Virtually all MPs and most councillors are first nominated as candidates by political parties. As such, selection committees within parties have significant control over who becomes an MP or councillor, which has, at times, led to discrimination against women or ethnic minorities, for example, who want a political career.

» *Political participation*: belonging to and taking an active role in political parties is one way in which ordinary citizens can participate in the political process besides voting. As party members, they can help to choose candidates for Parliament and local councils, join in the election of party leaders and other party positions, and influence party policy, both directly through party conferences and policy forums and indirectly through other channels of communication with the party leadership (see Chapter 16 for more on participation).

» *Reconciling and aggregating interests*: parties involve coalitions of interests. They bring together various sectional interests in society and assist in transforming a mass of demands into a relatively coherent programme that can be placed before voters at election times. They help to balance conflicting interests on the many issues confronting governments.

» *Communication*: parties provide a two-way channel of communication between political leaders and their supporters. The party leadership uses various channels of communication, including speeches, party publications, websites and social media, to persuade their members and voters that they are doing their best to meet their needs and aspirations. Members and supporters can express their concerns through, for example, representations to MPs and councillors, resolutions to party conferences and views voiced in party meetings, surveys, focus groups and the media.

» *Accountability and control*: parties effectively take control of the government of the UK and other levels of government. It is through parties that the government, at various levels, is held accountable for its performance, particularly at elections. Through parties, voters can clearly identify who is in charge and either reward them by giving them another term in office or reject them and elect a government of another party or parties.

## 🇬🇧 COMPARING BRITISH POLITICS 14.1 🌍
### Party systems around the world

» *No party systems*: These are now relatively rare and confined largely to traditional autocracies dominated by a ruling family, such as Saudi Arabia.

» *One-party systems*: In most communist states, such as China or North Korea, only one party is permitted. In some former colonial states, a nationalist party that led the struggle for independence achieved a virtual monopoly of political life. In both cases, there is no competition between parties, although there may be competition between candidates and factions within the party.

» *Dominant party systems*: In some states, more than one party may contest elections, but one party dominates membership of the legislature and government, and there seems little real prospect of a change in power (in the short term at least). This was the position for many years in post-independence India, where the Congress Party dominated, in Japan, where government was monopolised by the Liberal Democratic Party for most of the postwar period, and in South Africa today, where the African National Congress dominates.

» *Two-party systems*: Two parties win most of the seats in the legislature and alternate in government, such as competition between Democrats and Republicans in the USA. Third-party groups or candidates have sometimes challenged in US elections, but have not succeeded in changing the two-party duopoly.

» *Systems involving two major parties and smaller parties*: Two major parties compete to lead government, but may not be able to form a majority government alone without the support of a smaller third-party. This was the position in Germany for several decades. Christian democrats (CDU/CSU) and social democrats (SPD) are the two major parties who relied on the smaller Free Democratic Party (FDP) or Greens for support in coalition governments.

» *Stable multiparty systems*: Although many parties are represented and normally none can command a majority in the legislature, it is relatively easy to form stable coalition governments between parties, perhaps because ideological differences are not too deep. The Netherlands, France and Denmark might be included in this category.

» *Unstable multiparty systems*: It is difficult to form coalition governments, and once formed such governments often prove short-lived. Examples include France's Fourth Republic (1946–58), Italy for most of the postwar period and Israel. One problem may be the existence of substantial anti-system parties that are excluded from coalition-building.

An important question is how far party systems reflect particular electoral systems (of the kind discussed in Chapter 13) or significant divisions in society.

# THE DECLINE OF THE MASS PARTY?

British political parties (as in many western nations) developed in the eighteenth and early nineteenth centuries as cadre parties based on Parliament and dominated by elites, with only rudimentary organisation in the country. The growth of a mass electorate in the nineteenth century made it far more important for the Liberal and Conservative parties to recruit and identify supporters in the constituencies and ensure that those eligible were registered to vote. Both existing major parties went on to establish national organisations to look after their new mass membership. By contrast, the Labour Party (and other socialist and social democratic parties in other countries) was actually founded outside Parliament, as the Labour Representation Committee in 1900, and was organised from the beginning as a mass party.

Both Conservative and Labour could at one time fairly claim to be mass parties. Party membership figures rose to a peak in the early 1950s, but have generally declined significantly since. Conservative Party membership climbed steeply after the Second World War, from about 910,000 in 1946 to a record high of 2.8 million in 1953. The Conservative Party was for many people a way of socialising and meeting new people from a similar background, with new Conservative clubs created throughout the UK, and party membership soaring during a period of Conservative politics dominance of Westminster. The Labour Party also claimed over 1 million members in 1952–53 (Keen and Audickas, 2017). Labour could also rely on the support of the wider labour movement, organised by a strong trade union body, to aid its recruitment.

Arguably, the age of the mass party is waning. Conservative Party membership has plummeted from nearly 3 million in the 1950s to just 149,800 in 2013 (and the party is reluctant to publish more recent figures). The decline is particularly marked at the younger end. Once there was a thriving Young Conservative membership. Now half the party's members are retired. The fall is a response to many factors, including the increasing unpopularity of the Thatcher and Major governments, the effect of an ageing membership that failed to recruit new members and a wider disillusion with party politics (of the kind discussed in Chapter 16).

Labour Party membership has also dropped since the highs of the postwar period. The low point was between 2010 and 2014, when membership fell to around 190,000. However, in the run-up to the 2015 and 2016 leadership election, there was an amazing reversal of the historical trend, as new members signed up to vote in their thousands for Jeremy Corbyn (see Key Figures 14.1 for more on Corbyn and below for more on the election of Labour leaders). Labour membership rose to around 517,000 by March 2017 (Keen and Audickas, 2017). This is the highest number since the late 1970s and bucked a seemingly inexorable long-term, downwards trend. Labour is arguably re-entering the era of the mass party under Corbyn. The increased membership gives the party some significant benefits when it comes to campaigning, with members often willing to deliver leaflets and knock on doors to 'get the vote out'. Despite this recovery, the figures are relatively low by historical standards (as Figure 14.1 on p. 291 shows).

By contrast, smaller, 'niche' parties have increased their membership in recent years. Between December 2013 and July 2016, the SNP increased its membership from 25,000 to 120,000; the Green Party (in England and Wales) increased its membership from 13,800 to 55,000; and UKIP increased its membership from 32,000 to around 39,000 (although it had hit 47,000 in May 2015).

Overall, membership of any political party is something of a rarity across the population as a whole. The combined membership of the Conservative, Labour and Lib Dem parties was around 1.6% of the electorate in 2016, compared to a historic low point of 0.8 % in 2013. By contrast, in 1970, membership of these parties (or their predecessors) was around 5.5% of the electorate (Keen and Audickas, 2017).

The problem is perhaps worse than the membership figures suggest. Only a relatively small proportion of members are active, while many do nothing beyond paying their

# KEY FIGURES 14.1

Jeremy Corbyn

*Source*: JUSTIN TALLIS/AFP/Getty Images

A knitted doll of Labour leader Jeremy Corbyn attracted significant numbers of new supporters to Labour. He surprised many critics by dramatically reducing the Conservative majority at the general election that year.

**Jeremy Corbyn (1949–)** was elected leader of the Labour Party in 2015, a one-time rank outsider for the role. On the left of the party, he has been the MP for Islington North since 1983.

Corbyn was born in Chippenham, England. His middle-class parents were peace campaigners who met in the 1930s at an event supporting the republicans in the Spanish Civil War. Prior to becoming an MP, Corbyn worked for several trade unions and was elected a local councillor in Haringey, north London in the 1970s. As a backbench MP, he was a frequent rebel, often voting against the Labour whip, when the party was in government between 1997 and 2010. He was the chair of the Stop the War Coalition between 2011 and 2015.

Following Labour's defeat in the 2015 general election, Corbyn announced his candidacy for the Labour leadership. He was seen as a long shot, with little realistic chance of success. He secured the 35 nominations from fellow Labour MPs to get on to the members' ballot, when he was 'lent' votes at the last minute to broaden the debate. Corbyn was the only anti-austerity candidate and soon surged to be the favourite with members. He was elected leader in September 2015, with a first-round vote of 59.5%.

In June 2016, following what critics saw as a lacklustre campaign to stay in the EU, two-thirds of Corbyn's shadow Cabinet resigned, and Labour MPs passed a vote of 'no confidence' in his leadership by 172 votes to 40. In September 2016, following a second leadership contest, Corbyn increased his vote in a ballot of party members.

Despite this, the 2017 general election saw Labour finish as the second largest party in the Commons, with a hugely increased share of the popular vote and a gain of 32 seats, resulting in a hung Parliament. Corbyn, a serial rebel and backbencher, suddenly seemed a serious contender to be prime minister.

annual subscription. Local political meetings are commonly too poorly attended to be worth the time and expense of organising, and social events are not well supported. Some constituency parties are effectively run by a handful of members. Indeed, it may be questioned whether parties are, in any sense, still 'mass parties'.

Does the decline of the mass party matter? It has some serious consequences for the parties themselves. Members bring in money through subscriptions and other fundraising; they provide invaluable voluntary labour, particularly at election times, and an important sounding board for both MPs and the leadership. Yet there are more fundamental concerns. Some of the key functions of parties within a healthy system of representative democracy, notably recruitment, participation, reconciling and aggregating interests, and two-way communication can only be effectively performed by parties with a substantial membership.

## PARTIES AND PRESSURE GROUPS

Distinctions are commonly drawn between political parties and pressure groups (discussed in more detail in Chapter 16). One difference is said to be that parties pursue power by fighting elections and forming governments, while pressure groups seek influence over government and public policy. However, this distinction is problematic. Some interest groups may put up candidates at elections, but often more to win publicity than with the expectation of victory. Indeed, some single-

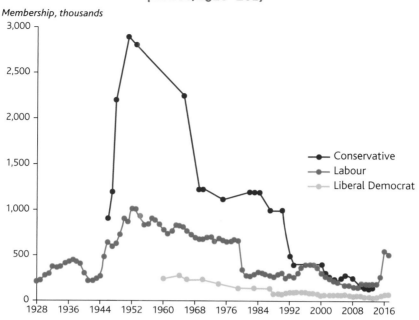

**Figure 14.1: Membership of the Conservative, Labour and Lib Dem\* parties, 1928–2017**

Note: \* including predecessor parties. Labour Party membership figures for 2015 to 2016 include Party members and affiliated supporters, but exclude registered supporters.

*Source*: Keen and Audickas (2017) *Membership of UK Political Parties*, Figure 1, p. 7, http:// researchbriefings .parliament.uk/ResearchBriefing/Summary/SN05125#fullreport. Contains Parliamentary information licensed under the Open Parliament Licence v3.0. www.parliament.uk/site-information/copyright/open-parliament-licence/

issue groups have occasionally been successful in winning seats at Westminster and for the Scottish Parliament. For example, Dr Richard Taylor was an MP between 2001 and 2010 for the Independent Kidderminster Hospital and Health Concern – a pressure group initially set up to restore the casualty unit at the local hospital (Berry, 2008).

Another difference is said to be that pressure groups commonly represent a single interest, while parties – if they are to be successful – must involve coalitions of interests. To use the academic terminology, groups 'articulate' interests while parties 'aggregate' them. Once more, the distinction is hardly watertight. There are 'niche' parties that are linked closely with a single interest. UKIP, for example, was set up specifically to secure Britain's withdrawal from the EU and focused almost entirely on that goal (Lynch et al., 2011).

The British Labour Party from its origins has had a close relationship with a particular interest – trade unions. (Trade unions, as a particular kind of interest group, are discussed in more detail in Chapter 16.) As they used to provide nearly all the party's membership and money, the relationship was a source of considerable strength to Labour, although it also provided ammunition for Labour's opponents, who have often argued that the unions controlled the party and its policies. The unpopularity of unions, particularly in the 1970s, the reduction in size and fragmentation of the old manual working class and the decline in union membership rendered the trade union connection a depreciating asset. Labour leaders from Wilson to Miliband – although not Corbyn – have sought to distance the party from the unions, to the extent that some unions have increasingly questioned the value of the Labour Party link. However, the 'contentious alliance'

(Minkin, 1992) between Labour and the unions survives because, on balance, both sides have more to lose than to gain from divorce.

The Conservative Party has been (less formally) linked with landed interests and subsequently business interests, and more broadly with the middle classes. Such interests provided the party with much of its finance and active membership. Yet if Labour needed to reach out beyond its class base to win and retain power, this was even truer for the Conservatives, as the interests with which they were linked involved a far smaller proportion of the electorate. To win power, the Conservatives needed to appeal to at least a sizeable minority of the working class, including trade union members. For much of the twentieth century, it was the breadth of the party's appeal that brought it considerable success.

# PARTY ORGANISATION

Modern political parties are complex organisations that operate at a number of levels. Key elements of their organisation normally include:

» A *parliamentary party* (assuming it has parliamentary representation), including party committees and a whip system to maintain party unity and discipline.

» A clearly identified *party leadership*, including a single acknowledged leader who has considerable prestige and authority, and commonly a deputy leader, surrounded by a team, which together constitute the collective party leadership.

» *Party conferences* to represent the party as a whole, supplemented increasingly by postal and online communications with party members.

» A *national organisation and party bureaucracy* involving both full- and part-time officials who serve the party and provide it with administrative, promotional and often research support.

» A *mass membership* in the country, which, for the major parties, is organised at regional, constituency and ward levels.

» A *viable source of funding* in order for the party to carry on its activities.

## THE ORGANISATION OF PARTIES IN PARLIAMENT

Parties in Britain began in Parliament, flourishing long before any formal party leadership roles were acknowledged. Although it is sometimes suggested that modern parliamentary parties are mere 'lobby fodder', coerced to troop through the division lobbies at the behest of their powerful leaders, they still retain a crucial role at the very centre of the modern party system. The most gifted politicians are powerless without a significant parliamentary party behind them. Lloyd George, perhaps the ablest orator and administrator in twentieth-century British politics, was effectively forced out of office in 1922, at the height of his powers, never to return, because he did not have a united parliamentary party with a majority behind him. His position depended on the support of the Conservatives, rather than his own Liberals, and this was withdrawn once Conservative backbenchers voted to fight the election as a separate party, against the advice of most of their leaders, who wanted to maintain the Lloyd George coalition.

The power of ordinary Conservative backbenchers, revealed then, was subsequently formally recognised with the establishment of what is known as the '1922 Committee'. Historically, this consisted of Conservative backbenchers, when the party was in government, and its elected officers remain figures of real status and influence within the party. It is the 1922 Committee that acts as the sounding board for ordinary Conservative MPs, alerts the leadership to the concerns of the backbenchers and organises leadership elections. David Cameron upset his backbenchers when he became prime minister in May 2010 by pushing through a change in the rules to allow ministers to attend the 1922 Committee, although he agreed, in a compromise, that they should not vote.

Until 2011, the Parliamentary Labour Party (PLP) performed a similar function within the Labour Party. When the party was in opposition, the PLP elected a parliamentary committee, which became, in effect, the shadow Cabinet. The leader was obliged to offer shadow posts to all those elected, although others who are not elected could be given a frontbench role as well. When the Labour Party is in government, the leader would choose their own Cabinet, although they were normally constrained initially to offer Cabinet posts to former elected shadow Cabinet members, and the PLP would choose a small Parliamentary Liaison Committee to provide a link between the parliamentary party and the government. Since 2011, the leader has been able to choose their own shadow Cabinet.

Party cohesion and discipline are promoted by the party 'whips', who play a key role in the modern parliamentary party, although the name and post date back to the eighteenth century. In the Commons, whips are MPs whose job it is to enforce discipline among their own party members, ensuring that they vote the way the leadership wants. Today, both major parties have a whip's office, led by a chief whip assisted by junior whips. The whips may use a combination of threats, bribes and cajolery to keep members of their party in line. A disaffected MP may risk losing some valued perks of the job, for example trips abroad on parliamentary delegations, membership of prestigious parliamentary committees, an honour, or the prospect of promotion. In more extreme circumstances, the whips may threaten to communicate their displeasure to an MP's constituency association, which could lead to their deselection as party candidate at the next election, or to withdraw the party whip, so that the MP is no longer considered a member of the parliamentary party. For offences that are regarded as particularly heinous, they may be expelled from the party, although the party cannot expel an MP from Parliament. Only the House of Commons or, ultimately, the voters can do that.

However, such weapons are not always effective, particularly against MPs who have no further political ambitions or realistic expectations of promotion. Even the withdrawal of the whip may not prove too damaging to an MP who retains the support of their constituency party. In 1994, the whip was withdrawn from eight Eurosceptic Conservative MPs who had consistently refrained from voting with the party on European issues and one sympathiser voluntarily resigned the whip. These 'whipless nine' continued to constitute a separate parliamentary grouping until the whip was restored without promises of future good behaviour a year later. Rebellion has not always proved a bar to promotion, and in retrospect has sometimes appeared a good career move. Former rebels who have gone on to become party leaders include Churchill, Macmillan and Duncan Smith among Conservatives, and Wilson, Foot and Corbyn on the Labour side.

Party splits are traditionally perceived as damaging to a party's electoral prospects and hence to the prospects for re-election of individual MPs, who normally owe their position almost completely to party endorsement. Although much party discipline is self-discipline, it has weakened of late, with more backbench rebellions. One possible explanation is that large government majorities (enjoyed by both Thatcher and Blair) allow the luxury of rebellion without any risk to the survival of the government, and also make it more difficult to satisfy the political ambitions of increased numbers of MPs, who may consequently become restive. Blair's government faced huge backbench revolts on some of its policies, notably on the Iraq War and student top-up fees (Cowley, 2005). Coalition government complicates the position further. Many backbench Lib Dems rebelled against their ministerial colleagues over university tuition fees in 2010. Jeremy Corbyn – who himself had been a serial rebel when Blair was prime minister – turned the perceived wisdom on its head, when he led a deeply divided Labour Party into a general election in 2017, but significantly increased Labour's share of the vote.

The power of ordinary backbench MPs is not to be measured by the size and frequency of rebellions. Much of their influence springs from the leaders and whips anticipating what backbenchers will not stand for, and altering course accordingly. While most MPs want their party to succeed and want to remain loyal, they all have a 'bottom line', issues of principle on which they are not prepared to budge, as party whips realise. Indeed, the whips' job is not just to persuade or coerce recalcitrant backbenchers, but often, more importantly, to convey backbench feeling to the party leaders, and warn them against proceeding with policies or decisions in the teeth of substantial opposition from their own MPs. A celebrated example was when Wilson's Labour government backed down from its proposed trade union reforms after the chief whip informed the Cabinet that he could not get the reforms through the parliamentary party. More recently, Brown was persuaded to reverse several decisions following backbench pressure on, for example, some of the tax changes he had proposed in his 2007 budget, such as the abolition of the proposed 10p starting rate for income tax. The Brown government also quietly dropped proposals to extend the 28 days of detention without charge for terrorist suspects to 42 days after a near-defeat in the Commons was followed by rejection in the Lords.

## Factions and tendencies

Any successful party arguably needs to involve a broad coalition of ideas and interests. Too narrow a focus will restrict its appeal and limit its chances of winning support. This is particularly the case in Britain where the electoral system in Westminster heavily penalises smaller parties (see Chapter 13, pp. 267–70). However, the range of interests and ideological perspectives within a single party can be a constant source of tension, with the periodic threat of open dissent, rebellion and even a fundamental party split. The appearance of party unity is important, as openly divided parties do not often win elections.

There are significant divisions, or **factions** and **tendencies** within all major British parties. These sometimes arise over particular issues; for example, the Conservative Party was deeply divided over membership of the EU, particularly from Major's period in office in the mid-1990s until the UK voted to withdraw in 2016. Sometimes, they have more to do with immediate tactics or medium-term strategies, such as Lib Dem attitudes to coalition with other parties. At other times, they reflect deeper ideological differences, for example between free-market and one-nation Conservatives, or between the radical, 'Trotskyist' Militant Tendency in the Labour Party during the early 1980s and more centrist and social democrats. Not infrequently, personal differences and rivalries complicate other divisions, as with Blair and Brown in the Labour Party.

A **party faction** is a more stable, enduring group, sometimes with a constitution and formal organisation and membership. Momentum, a group within the Labour Party that supports the leadership of Jeremy Corbyn, is an example.

A **party tendency** is sometimes defined as a loose and informal group within a party sharing a particular ideological perspective or policy stance.

If the internal tensions and divisions within a party develop, a split may result. Splits can be very damaging, perhaps even leading to the demise of the party as a serious political force. One cause of the rapid decline of the old Liberal Party was a series of damaging divisions, in 1886, 1916–18 and 1931–32. Labour's internal divisions, long a source of electoral weakness, led to a major split in 1981 when some leading Labour 'moderates' left the party to form the Social Democratic Party (SDP). Some commentators concluded that Labour was effectively finished as a credible party of government. However, after much initial attention, the SDP failed to break through and eventually merged with the Liberal Party to end up as the Liberal Democrats (Crewe and King, 1995). (The experience left Corbyn's critics in the Labour Party sceptical about their chances of success should they have decided to go it alone and split the Labour Party again.) Divisions within the Conservative Party severely weakened Major's government and contributed to the party's defeat in 1997. Some Conservative MPs, like Shaun Woodward, 'crossed the floor' to Labour, while others, including Emma Nicholson, joined the Lib Dems.

The Labour Party, in particular, has been periodically concerned about the dangers of infiltration or 'entryism' by groups or tendencies that do not share the party's commitment to parliamentary methods and its own moderate interpretation of socialism. Apart from the internal divisions and conflict caused by such groups, the perception that a party has been infiltrated by 'extremists' can be electorally damaging. Corbyn's critics often describe Momentum, the grassroots organisation set up by his supporters following his 2015 leadership campaign, in the same way. Although the Labour Party has suffered most from association with extremists, popularly described as 'reds under the beds', instances of former British National Party and National Front activists working within the Conservative Party have sometimes undermined its recent attempts to appear more inclusive and welcoming towards ethnic minorities.

## PARTY LEADERS

A credible and popular leader can make a substantial difference to the fortunes of a political party. The leader of a majority party who is also prime minister wields considerable power and responsibility and may change the course of history. It follows that the method of choosing leaders is extremely important both for parties and for the country as a whole. The selection or election of leaders has often been controversial and the major parties have all changed their rules, in some cases several times.

## Choosing the Conservative Party leader

The Conservative Party did not have a formal system for electing their leader until 1965. When a Conservative prime minister resigned other than because of an election defeat, the monarch invited another leading Conservative to head a new government, normally after consultation with senior figures in the party. This informal system operated without significant difficulties until Macmillan suddenly announced his resignation as prime minister on the eve of the 1963 Conservative Party conference. The resulting frantic competition for support by candidates for the succession and a somewhat flawed process of consultation led eventually to the emergence of Douglas-Home as prime minister and leader – and the refusal of two Cabinet ministers to serve in his government in protest against his appointment. This shambles reflected badly on the party, which, like the Labour Party, then moved to a system of formal election by MPs.

The new formalised system, relying on the votes of MPs, produced several close and bruising leadership contests. It was first used to elect Heath as party leader in 1965, Thatcher in 1975 and Major in 1990. The last time this system was used was in 1997, after Major resigned as leader following the Conservative defeat at the general election, when Hague defeated Clarke to become party leader.

The Conservative Party, which had been slow to introduce a formal system of electing its leader by MPs, became the only major party restricting the election of leader to MPs alone after 1981. In a reform aimed at giving more power and influence to ordinary members after the general election defeat in 1997, William Hague introduced a new method of election that gave them the final decision on the leadership. MPs would nominate candidates for the leadership, followed by ballots within the parliamentary party to narrow the choice down to two, with the final decision involving a ballot of ordinary party members. This system was used for the first time in 2001 when Hague resigned after the 2001 general election defeat. Iain Duncan Smith defeated Kenneth Clarke in the members' ballot by 61% to 39%. However, Iain Duncan Smith made little impact and was replaced as party leader in 2003 by Michael Howard, who, as the only candidate, avoided a ballot of party members. The system was used again after the 2005 general election, when Howard announced that he would resign. After Conservative MPs whittled the number of candidates down to two, party members had a choice between David Davis, the early frontrunner, and the relatively unknown David Cameron, who, after a strong performance at the Conservative Party conference, eventually triumphed by a margin of two to one.

Cameron resigned as party leader and prime minister in June 2016, following the referendum on Britain's membership of the EU, in which he had strongly campaigned to remain. After a frenzied few days of backroom deals and manoeuvring, where former mayor of London Boris Johnson, the favourite to win the race, dropped out, five Conservative MPs secured the necessary nominations from their peers to stand: Theresa May and Stephen Crabb, who had both campaigned to stay in the EU, and Andrea Leadsom, Michael Gove and Liam Fox, from the right of the party, who had campaigned to leave. After the first ballot, Fox was eliminated, after receiving the least votes from fellow MPs, and Crabb withdrew from

*Source*: Karwai Tang/Getty Images News/Getty Images

Theresa May became prime minister in July 2016, but her decision to call a general election in June 2017 greatly weakened her power.

the race. Gove was eliminated in the second ballot, leaving May and Leadsom to proceed to the ballot of party members around the UK. However, less than a week later, after a lacklustre campaign, Leadsom withdrew from the race, leaving May to become leader of the Conservative Party and prime minister in July 2016, before a ballot of members was held.

## Choosing the Labour leader

For most of the twentieth century the PLP elected its own leader and (subsequently) deputy leader. Where there were more than two candidates, a series of ballots was held, with the bottom candidate dropping out, until one candidate emerged with an overall majority. Some of these elections were very closely contested. When Wilson resigned as prime minister in 1976, there were six candidates to succeed him, and Callaghan eventually emerged as party leader and prime minister in the third ballot.

After considerable pressure for more internal party democracy within the Labour Party, a new leadership election process was adopted after a special conference held at Wembley in 1981. One problem for Labour was that the party had individual members, attached to parliamentary constituencies, and affiliated members (mainly from trade unions affiliated to the Labour Party). The rather clumsy solution was an electoral college in which

originally trade unions had 40% of the votes, constituency parties 30% and the PLP 30%. The system was first used in a contest for the deputy leadership in September 1981 when Dennis Healey very narrowly defeated left-winger Tony Benn. It was subsequently used when Kinnock and Hattersley were elected leader and deputy leader in 1983, and again in 1988, when they were unsuccessfully challenged. Using the same system, John Smith and Margaret Beckett were elected leader and deputy leader in 1992.

After the 1993 Labour Party conference, the system of election was slightly modified, adjusting the proportions in the electoral college to give one-third of the votes to each of the constituent elements. More significantly, unions and constituency parties were obliged to ballot members individually and divide their votes accordingly, meeting the demand for 'one member, one vote'. Using this modified system, Tony Blair and John Prescott achieved a clear majority in the 1994 elections for leader and deputy leader in each category as well as overall. When Blair resigned in 2007, Gordon Brown was elected without opposition, although Harriet Harman eventually defeated five other candidates for the post of deputy leader.

Following Brown's resignation as prime minister and party leader after the 2010 election, five candidates stood for the leadership. However, it soon became clear that it was essentially a two-horse race between the Miliband brothers. Following a four-month interregnum in which Harman was acting leader, Ed Miliband defeated his older brother David by the narrowest of margins, once the second preferences of those who voted for eliminated candidates were taken into account.

There was some criticism from inside and outside the party on the rules under which the contest was fought, particularly as it was clear that Ed Miliband owed his victory to trade union votes. Ed Miliband was supported by a minority of MPs and MEPs (46.57%) and party members (45.59%), but overtook David by securing 59.80% of the votes of members of affiliated organisations (largely trade unions). However, since the reforms of the 1990s, individual trade unionists who have not opted out of the political levy paid to the Labour Party vote individually in a secret ballot, just like other party members. Nevertheless, there is some legitimate criticism of the way in which some individuals can acquire multiple votes by qualifications in different categories. So a Labour MP is also a party member, and may have additional votes in other categories by being a member of one or more affiliated organisations.

After losing the 2015 general election, Ed Miliband stepped down. The leadership election took place under the rules set out in the 2014 *Collins Review into Labour Party Reform*, chaired by Ray Collins, a Labour peer. The review dropped the electoral college and moved, in line with other parties, to empower party members. The leader would be elected on a 'one member, one vote' system. To stand, candidates needed to be nominated by 15% of the PLP (after 2015 this meant that they had to secure the support of 35 Labour MPs). Four MPs made it onto the ballot in June 2015: Yvette Cooper and Andy Burnham, two former Cabinet members from the centre of the party, Liz Kendall from the right of the party and Jeremy Corbyn, a veteran socialist MP and long-time critic of New Labour.

Corbyn was seen as an outside bet in 2015. He only secured his nomination by gaining the support of MPs who disagreed with him politically, but who wanted to open up the debate. Over the next three months, the Labour Party changed. Corbyn's attack on the coalition government's austerity measures appealed to many Labour supporters, and meant he stood out from the other candidates, who equivocated on the need for cuts. New members signed up for the party in their thousands, many taking advantage of the offer to register as supporters for a reduced price, rather than as full party members. By the summer, it was clear that Corbyn was going to win the leadership. To Labour 'modernisers', Corbyn would be an electoral liability. Margaret Beckett, former foreign secretary and caretaker Labour leader, who had nominated Corbyn in order to widen the debate, accepted that she was a 'moron' for doing so (BBC News, 2015). Notable Labour politicians, including Blair, made public interventions to appeal to members not to vote for Corbyn. It was to no avail. Corbyn was announced Labour leader in September 2015 with almost 60% of the vote. Andy Burnham and Yvette Cooper, his two nearest rivals, gained 19% and 17% respectively. To Corbyn, this was a chance for a 'new kind of politics' (Wintour, 2015).

Less than a year later, in July 2016, Corbyn faced a leadership challenge from his fellow MPs, who argued that his presentation and polices would be electorally disastrous for the party. Owen Smith – who had been shadow secretary of state for work and pensions under Corbyn – was presented as a 'unity candidate' against Corbyn, after a wave of shadow Cabinet resignations, which were meant to undermine the leader's authority. Again, Corbyn was elected with a huge mandate from Labour Party members, gaining almost 62% of the vote. Seemingly from nowhere, the ascent of the left of the party was complete and the mantra of Labour politicians from Kinnock to Blair – to win elections, you had to govern from the centre – was ignored. Despite his victory, it was not until Labour's performance in the 2017 general election, in which the party massively exceeded almost all expectations, that Corbyn could begin to establish authority over his party.

## Party members and party leaders

All major parties now involve their ordinary party members in the election of the party leader. The Lib Dems, UKIP, the SNP and the Greens all ballot members to determine their leader. Green party members elected Caroline Lucas and Jonathan Bartley in 2016 to lead the party on a job share, for example. This move towards more internal party democracy raises challenges in an era after 'mass parties'. There is clearly a risk that parties may end up with leaders who enjoy neither the confidence of parliamentary colleagues nor the support of the wider electorate, which has the critical voice in the making of a prime minister at a general election. Conservative MPs and members repeatedly rejected Ken Clarke, the leadership candidate who had most support in the country. Jeremy Corbyn became Labour's leader in 2015, despite his views being perceived as far to the left of the wider electorate. As such, there is plenty of continuing potential for tensions between MPs, party members and voters. Yet open leadership elections help to secure legitimacy for leaders, and can help build support for them among voters.

## The power of party leaders

While the Conservative Party has traditionally emphasised the importance of leadership, historically Labour was suspicious of the leader's power and has sought to restrain it (see Spotlight 14.1).

It should not be forgotten that while most of the media attention is focused on the individual who is party leader, they are normally surrounded by other politicians with their own positions, power bases and popularity within the party. The leader has to try to satisfy the political ambitions of those who may be real or potential rivals, but also needs to draw on their talents so as to present a credible collective leadership of actual or potential ministers, and convince the voters of their collective competence. Within the leadership group, some politicians may come to seem indispensable, as Willie Whitelaw was to Margaret Thatcher, and Michael Heseltine became to John Major. Both were disappointed leadership candidates who gave full loyalty to the victors. By contrast, Gordon Brown, who was reluctantly persuaded to forego his own leadership hopes in 1994, evidently retained ambitions to lead the Labour Party, in which he remained a hugely important figure, with real power in his own right.

## PARTY CONFERENCES

Each party holds an annual conference for a week in the autumn, together with other occasional or more specialised conferences. In theory, there is a massive difference between the role of the Labour Party conference as the

## SPOTLIGHT ON ...    The authority of Labour and Conservative leaders compared    14.1

Labour leaders have historically appeared weaker in theory than their Conservative counterparts because:

» They are bound by conference decisions according to the Labour Party Constitution

» They are constrained by the National Executive Committee (NEC) between conferences, and have not always enjoyed a majority on the NEC

» They do not control the appointment of their own deputy who is separately elected

» Until 2010, they could not choose their own shadow Cabinet in opposition, which is formed from a parliamentary committee elected by a vote of the PLP

» They do not fully control the party bureaucracy.

However, in practice, Labour leaders have generally enjoyed considerable power over their parties – at times ignoring conference decisions. When Labour leaders have also been prime minister, they have enjoyed all the considerable constitutional powers associated with that office and have had as much authority as their Conservative counterparts.

Labour leaders have also been less vulnerable to formal challenges within the party. The only sitting Labour leaders who faced a leadership contest over the past 40 years were Kinnock, who easily saw off a challenge from Benn in 1988 and Corbyn, who defeated Smith in 2016. Over the same period, Heath, Thatcher, Major and Duncan Smith have all faced challenges, which only Major survived. Perhaps one reason for the greater vulnerability of Conservative leaders is that their party has grown accustomed to success, and is unforgiving of failure, or the prospect of failure.

party's own 'parliament', supreme over party policy, compared with that of the Conservative Party conference, which has no constitutional power. Indeed, Balfour, past Conservative prime minister, said he 'would rather take advice from his valet than the party conference' (cited in Peele and Francis, 2016, p. 155). In practice, however, the Labour conference was never as powerful as the party constitution suggested, while Conservative conferences were often influential despite their lack of formal power. Labour leaders could, and effectively did, disregard conference decisions they opposed, while the Conservative leadership was sometimes influenced by strong expressions of conference opinion, not always in the party's longer term interest. One example is Thatcher's ill-fated poll tax that helped to remove her from Downing Street, which proved popular with Conservative Party members at the conference, but less so with the wider electorate (see Chapter 10, pp. 198–200, for more coverage of the poll tax).

Even so, until recently, there were still considerable differences between the parties in the way in which the conferences were conducted. Labour Party conferences often involved furious rows and party splits. The party leadership lacked effective control of the agenda or who could speak (even leading Cabinet ministers had no right to speak). One celebrated example was in 1960, when the leader Hugh Gaitskell defiantly declared, to the jeers of his audience, that he would 'fight and fight and fight again' to reverse a Labour conference decision in favour of unilateral nuclear disarmament. Another came in 1985 when Neil Kinnock denounced Labour's (left-wing) Liverpool Council to a mixture of cheers and boos. All this made for dramatic television, but also reflected badly on a divided party. Similarly, the run-up to the 2016 Labour conference was dominated by the leadership challenge against Corbyn by the centrist candidate, Owen Smith. By contrast, Conservative annual conferences were generally carefully stage-managed and relatively docile. Contentious motions and issues were kept off the conference agenda. Essentially, they were viewed as rallies of the party faithful, rewarding loyal members with an opportunity to meet their leaders in a friendly social setting, and, more importantly, allowing leading politicians to display some effective platform oratory and secure abundant valuable free publicity for the party.

## PARTY BUREAUCRACY

From the late nineteenth century onwards, mass political parties appeared increasingly important as a means of participation by ordinary citizens in the political process, and potentially as a bridge between the political mass and the political elite, particularly as they became more open and inclusive. Internal party democracy would ensure that leaders served the mass membership rather than the other way around. However, in 1911, Robert Michels ([1911] 1968) argued that power in political parties (including those that strongly proclaim their attachment to democracy) naturally gravitates to the parliamentary leadership and permanent bureaucracy. This may be because large organisations are inevitably oligarchies, where power rests with a small group of people (the argument of Robert Michels), or because parties, particularly in Britain, operate within a centralised political system, or because of media focus on leading personalities, or perhaps because leaders betray (or more subtly manipulate) their followers.

The last argument has been most commonly heard within the Labour Party. 'Betrayal' has been a familiar theme since Ramsay MacDonald ignored his own party and formed a national government with the Conservatives in 1931. Much of the argument over organisational reforms in the 1980s barely concealed a battle for power between the moderate parliamentary leadership and a left-wing active membership. Giving power to the members was interpreted to mean giving power to activists who turned up to meetings, rather than those whose involvement was largely confined to paying their subscription. These battles are being repeated a generation later as Corbyn and his team push to give party members more power.

A problem for parties is that their members only constitute a tiny and unrepresentative minority of voters. Because many constituency parties are now effectively run by a few activists, there is even the possibility that a small unrepresentative group opposed to some of the party's core principles could take them over. This happened in the early 1980s, for example, when the Militant tendency – a group of radical Trotskyists – encouraged activists to join the Labour Party and gain key positions in an effort to shift its politics to the left, leading to expulsions and divisions within the party. While internal democracy within competing parties with an active mass membership may complement representative institutions and enhance democracy, grassroots power in parties that no longer involve the masses could deny them effective choice and subvert rather than assist the wider democratic process.

## Bureaucracy in the Conservative and Labour Party

Parties with a substantial mass membership require complex organisational structures to manage the relationship between the parliamentary leadership and the extra-parliamentary party, operating at various levels in the country. Major parties now require extensive permanent bureaucracies to meet their needs. This has meant employing increasing numbers of paid staff – particularly at the centre, but also in the regions and in constituencies – as well as using large numbers of unpaid party activists. Professional expertise is required for a range of purposes, such as raising money and controlling spending,

Electoral campaigning is an expensive and time-consuming business. Traditional campaign techniques, such as party political broadcasts and leaflets, are now been supplemented by the use of social media to win over voters.

marketing and advertising, policy-oriented research, legal advice, party management and administration. All major parties retain paid permanent agents in marginal constituencies, who play a crucial role in maintaining the party organisation at constituency level, and maximising the party's vote at election times.

At national level, the Conservative Party is organised from Conservative Central Office, founded in 1870. The party's chair is directly appointed by the leader, and Central Office has been described as 'the personal machine of the leader'. Its main tasks are fundraising, the organisation of election campaigns, assistance with the selection of candidates, research and political education. While Central Office has enjoyed substantial power and prestige in the past, it has become increasingly subject to criticism following poor election results and other evidence of the party's decline. Some party activists (e.g. in the Charter Movement) would like to see Central Office become more accountable and subject to democratic control. Pressure for reform and more internal democracy in the party following the landslide defeat of 1997 led William Hague to introduce a range of changes (published as *A Fresh Future for the Conservative Party*), although the increased influence given to a diminishing and elderly membership has sometimes proved problematic.

Labour's organisation was not always efficient and was subject to extensive change over the years. The party's headquarters were for a long time located at Transport House, in the offices of the Transport and General Workers Union, symbolising the close links of Labour with the trade unions. In 1955, Wilson famously described Labour's party machine as 'a rusty penny-farthing bicycle in the era of the jet plane' (cited in Pimlott, 1992, p. 194). In 1980, the party moved to its own modest headquarters in Walworth Road, but it was still criticised as ineffective, until a substantial reorganisation started under Kinnock's leadership (Minkin, 1992, Ch. 19). From 1995, key staff moved to the new campaign and media centre at Millbank Tower, which came to symbolise New Labour's slick public relations and 'spin doctoring' (discussed in Chapter 17), although the expense and the (increasingly unfavourable) image of Millbank led the party to find a new home in the heart of Westminster.

In the past, Labour leaders lacked the control over party organisation enjoyed by Conservative leaders. This is partly because the party's official governing body (between conferences) is not the Cabinet or shadow Cabinet or even the PLP, but the National Executive Committee (NEC). The NEC was once dominated by the trade unions and, to a lesser degree, members chosen by constituency associations (largely left-wingers). In the 1970s and early 1980s, the majority of the NEC was hostile to the party leadership. As the NEC had to approve the party manifesto and controlled key appointments in the Labour Party, including the post of general secretary, there was often division at the top.

In 1997, under New Labour, there was a significant reorganisation of the party's central machinery. The new NEC has caused fewer problems to the leadership (particularly since the introduction of postal ballots for party members), and the party appeared less divided under Blair. Since Corbyn's election as leader in 2015, however, the NEC is increasingly a battleground for control of the party between, on the one hand, the leader, his team and many Labour members around the country, and, on the other, the more moderate parliamentary party.

Whereas the Labour Party's national organisa-tion in the past often appeared divided and shambolic while the Conservative organisation seemed ruthlessly united and efficient, the image of the two parties was almost reversed from 1995 to 2005. The Conservatives sought to imitate aspects of Labour's successful electoral machine. Yet Labour paid a price for its greater discipline and professionalism. The Labour leadership was accused of acting like 'control freaks' (Jones, 2002), seeking to manipulate all key roles in the party, while the party's slick public relations had become increasingly identified with manipulation and 'spin' (see Chapter 17, pp. 368–70). Alastair Campbell, Labour's most formidable 'spin doctor', resigned as the prime minister's director of communications in 2003. Following the Phillis Report (2004) into government communications, the party became less reliant on 'spin' by anonymous spokespersons, with more direct communication by ministers in televised press briefings.

## PARTY MEMBERS

All major parties have recently sought (ostensibly at least) to give more power and influence to ordinary members. Labour in particular has seen a surge in membership since Corbyn's leadership election campaign. Party members have always had one very significant power: choosing party candidates for local and general elections. Although, in certain circumstances, the national party may seek to influence the choice of parliamentary candidate, and exceptionally may block the selection of a particular candidate, in general it is the members voting at constituency level who choose. Moreover, particularly in the Labour Party, members have sometimes exercised powers to deselect sitting MPs with whom they have become dissatisfied. Beyond that, as we have seen, all major parties over the past 30 years or so sought to involve party members in the choice of the party leader, and made some show of involving them more in the policy-making process.

Internal party democracy may not necessarily help a party to win elections, however, and can be positively detrimental. Most people who vote in elections are not members of a political party (indeed, we saw earlier how rare party membership was). Active party members almost by definition are unusual creatures with views and preferences that may be similarly untypical. Thus, the problem for parties is that they serve two very different political 'markets'. Green party members, for example, by their very decision to join the party, are much more likely to prioritise environmental concerns higher than an average voter. Policies that please active members may not appeal to ordinary voters. Labour Party members in the 1980s wanted left-wing policies (including more nationalisation and unilateral nuclear disarmament), which the electorate rejected in the 1983 general election. Critics argue that the surge in Labour Party members enthused by Corbyn, who tend to be against nuclear weapons and in favour of state intervention in the economy, will alienate the moderate voters whose support the party needs to win an election. Nicola Sturgeon's promise of a second referendum on independence during the 2017 general election campaign would have played well with SNP voters, but it seemed to alienate many voters who were not SNP party members, but who liked the party's wider policies.

The gap between party members and the rest of the electorate also causes potential problems for the Conservative Party too. Hague, Duncan Smith, Howard and, most of all, Cameron have all sought a broader, more inclusive party. However, its existing dwindling membership is elderly, overwhelmingly white and middle class. Although women are well represented among party activists, many hold very traditional views on gender relations and the role of women in society and the workplace. No Conservative leader has dared to introduce all-women shortlists, although Cameron's preferred 'A-list' candidates contained many career women and representatives of ethnic minorities whom he sought to advance. Yet central influence on candidate selection is still much resented and has led to rows and splits within constituency parties. The internal Conservative differences over policy have more generally been muffled in the interests of election victory. But the policies that appeal to members, such as tax and public spending cuts, a hard line on crime and immigration, and support for 'family values', alienate more liberal voters.

All main parties seem to have a problem recruiting and keeping younger members. Perhaps the real problem is that older forms of political activity, such as attending local party meetings, no longer appeal. Increasingly, the parties are pursuing other methods of communicating with their members through postal ballots and surveys and interactive websites. It seems most unlikely, however, that the long-term decline in active party membership will be reversed.

One pessimistic answer is that people are not interested in more participation in politics, despite the benefits that it might bring wider society. (This issue is discussed in much more depth in Chapter 16.) There are more diverting ways for people to spend their leisure time in a modern consumer society. Another possible answer is that insofar as people have the energy and inclination to participate in politics, it is increasingly in single-issue pressure groups rather than political parties (see Chapter 16). Parties, involving coalitions of interests, inevitably require compromise. Those whose ideals motivate them to become involved in politics may be turned off by the messy and sometimes grubby processes of accommodation and compromise within mainstream parties. For them, political parties are part of the problem rather than the solution, contributing to the sense that ordinary people are left behind from the political process rather than offering an opportunity for involvement. Whatever the explanation, the UK political system currently depends to a degree on competition between political parties, which no longer hold the sway over people's lives they once did.

## FUNDING POLITICAL PARTIES

The financing of political parties has become an important and controversial issue. Parties need money for many purposes, such as servicing their permanent organisation, paying administrators and agents, commissioning policy research, financing elections, political advertising and market research. There are three main possible sources of finance: subscriptions from ordinary members, donations from organisations and individuals, or state funding (Outhwaite, 2004).

Ideally, perhaps, money would come from party members, through ordinary party subscriptions, but it is difficult for the membership to provide the funds required. Much higher membership fees would deter potential recruits at a time when all parties are desperately seeking to encourage a larger and wider membership. Many 'unwaged' members (e.g. the large number who are retired) do not pay the full membership rates.

So additional sources of finance are solicited, from individual donors, business organisations, trade unions and other friendly bodies. Yet this can cause problems for parties, as has been only too evident in recent years. How far are contributors to party finances effectively buying influence or status? There is a long history of allegations of the award of honours in return for donations to political parties. Lloyd George,

Liberal leader and coalition prime minister (1916–22), sold honours almost openly. Recent Conservative and Labour governments have been accused of giving knighthoods and peerages to individual donors and directors of companies who have made party donations.

Most damaging are allegations of influence on policy. For many years, the Conservative Party routinely received contributions from particular sectors of business, such as brewers, tobacco companies and construction companies, and there were suggestions they were particularly open to influence in these areas as a result. Particularly controversial were contributions from wealthy foreign businessmen. Until Hague's leadership (1997–2001), most large donations to the Conservatives were secret – so there were allegations of hidden influence.

Labour had long openly depended financially on contributions from trade unions, but under Blair, Labour courted business as well, and Blair's Labour government was embarrassed by a large donation from Formula One boss Bernie Ecclestone in 1997. The subsequent exemption of F1 events from bans on tobacco companies sponsoring sporting events was thought by some to reflect his influence. The problems surrounding party donations led Blair to ask the Committee on Standards in Public Life to investigate party funding. The committee, led by Lord Neill, delivered its report, *The Funding of Political Parties in the United Kingdom*, in October 1998 (see Spotlight 14.2).

Scandals around donations have led to renewed interest in another possible source of party finance – state funding, ultimately out of taxation. Some countries already use state funding, such as Germany, Sweden, Austria, Spain, Israel, Canada and Australia. More recently, France, the Netherlands, Poland, Japan and Mexico also introduced state funding. In theory, state funding allows

## SPOTLIGHT ON ...    Recommendations of Neill Report (1998) into party funding    14.2

» Public disclosure of donations to parties of more than £5,000, or more than £1,000 to parties locally

» A £20 million cap on any party's general election campaign spending

» An end to 'blind trusts', where money is placed in a trust and given to parties without their knowledge of what money the trust holds or where it is from

» A ban on foreign donations by non-citizens

» A ban on anonymous donations to political parties of more than £50

» Scrutiny of nominations for honours where nominees have donated more than £5,000 to a political party within the past five years

» An independent and impartial Electoral Commission to monitor the new regulations

» More public money to finance political parties in Parliament.

Most of the recommendations of the Fifth Report of the Committee on Standards in Public Life (the Neill Report, 1998) were implemented, including the establishment of the impartial Electoral Commission. Labour hoped that more transparency would end allegations of 'sleaze' – a generic term for political scandals – that undermined Major's Conservative governments (see Chapter 3). Instead, the publication of donations has made it easier for journalists to allege some connection between gifts and a possible impact on policy. Publicity given to some donors has also sometimes upset party members. In 2002, the revelation that the new owner of the Express group of newspapers had given the Labour Party £120,000 aroused anger from party members (including some ministers) that the party had accepted money from an individual who also owned a number of pornographic publications.

parties to operate free from the influence of donors, such as unions, businesses or wealthy individuals. However, there is limited public appetite to fund parties from general taxation. In the UK, there is already some limited state financial help for opposition parties to fund their administration and policy research. This problem was addressed in 1975 by the then Labour government, which introduced payments to opposition parties to enable them to carry out their parliamentary role more effectively.

In the past, the Conservative Party regularly outspent the Labour Party, but these two far exceeded the financial resources of other parties. This raises questions about whether the best-financed parties have an unfair advantage. Particularly controversial was the 2010 election, where the Conservatives comfortably outspent Labour, both in the period leading up to the election and in the campaign itself, and benefitted from large sums donated by Lord Ashcroft, the non-domiciled, former Conservative peer, directed at the crucial marginal constituencies. The 2015 general election was fairly typical in terms of distribution of resources. The Conservatives spent £15.6 million and Labour £12 million. However, evidence shows that there is no simple link between funding and seats won;

the Lib Dems spent £3.5 million, but dropped from 57 to 8 seats, UKIP spent £5 million and won just 1 seat, while the SNP spent £1.5 million and went from 6 to 50 seats (Cowley and Kavanagh, 2016).

What does all this mean for Britain's two-party system? The unpredictability of contemporary British politics means that there is no way of knowing if the two-party system is back for good. The two main parties, which now dominate Westminster, as they did for much of the twentieth century, certainly benefitted from the collapse in support for third parties in 2017. The Lib Dems failed to recover from their decimation in 2015, while UKIP all but disappeared once their main reason for being was achieved. The SNP sends a considerable number of MPs to Parliament. Other smaller parties do attract popular votes – notably the Greens – but the voting system in Westminster prevents them from making a significant breakthrough (as we saw in Chapter 13). What is certain is that while party politics in Westminster, of the kind that this chapter largely focuses on, is, for the time being, seeing a return to the traditional norm, outside Westminster, multiparty politics is the reality – in local government, the devolved assemblies and, while the UK remains a member, in the European Parliament.

# SUMMARY

- » Political parties fulfil important functions in modern representative democracies.

- » Parties in Britain, as elsewhere, have experienced a significant decline in their active membership, although Labour membership has enjoyed a small resurgence related to Jeremy Corbyn's election as leader. Fewer than 1 in 40 voters are now party members. It is questionable how far British parties can still be described as mass parties. Party members are predominantly elderly and in other respects unrepresentative of the wider population.

- » Party leaders have considerable influence over policy and strategy. An effective and credible leader seems to be crucial for a party's electoral prospects. Methods of choosing new leaders

and challenging existing leaders are therefore important and often controversial. All major parties have moved towards involving ordinary members in leadership elections.

- » Party conferences are not generally occasions for important political decisions, and today rarely involve major controversy. All parties now seem to use their party conferences as, primarily, opportunities for promoting the party, its policies and leading personalities.

- » Local constituency members normally choose candidates for parliamentary and other elections, and have more recently been given a role in leadership elections. Their influence on policy is less easy to assess. Insofar as members are influential, they may damage a party's electoral prospects, as the views of party activists are generally untypical of those of voters.

» Parties need money to compete effectively, but their finances are very unequal. Subscriptions from a diminishing membership are inadequate, and parties rely on donations from corporate bodies, particularly businesses

and trade unions, and from rich individuals, leading to concerns over the purchase of influence. Reforms have made party funding more transparent, but this has raised further questions about the sources of party finance. One possible solution is state funding of political parties.

 QUESTIONS FOR DISCUSSION

» Is Britain's two-party system making a comeback?

» Is partyless democracy a realistic prospect?

» Could modern representative democracy operate successfully without political parties?

» In what sense, if any, are British political parties still mass parties?

» Do party systems come about because of particular electoral systems or because of significant divisions in society?

» Why might more internal party democracy possibly risk adverse electoral consequences?

» What are the arguments for and against the state funding of political parties?

 FURTHER READING

There are many good books on British party politics, although aspects of them quickly become dated. Driver (2011) *Understanding British Party Politics* provides a decent overview. On specific parties, there are many excellent books. Bale's (2012) *The Conservatives since 1945: The Drivers of Party Change* is a useful and readable source. Still worth consulting on the Labour Party is Minkin's (1992) *The Contentious Alliance: Trade Unions and the Labour Party*, a monumental study between the unions and Labour, and, more recently, *The Blair Supremacy: A Study in the Politics of Labour's Party Management* (2014). Shaw's (1996) *The Labour Party since 1945* is also a good introduction.

A new series on leaders of the main parties has many excellent essays. Clarke et al.'s (eds) (2015)

*British Conservative Leaders* and Clarke and James (eds) (2016) *British Labour Leaders* cover the two main parties. Brack et al. (eds) (2015) *British Liberal Leaders* and Mitchell and Hassan (eds) (2016) *Scottish National Party Leaders* cover the two smaller parties.

There is also a good analysis of UKIP in Goodwin and Milazzo (2015) *UKIP: Inside the Campaign to Redraw the Map of British Politics*. Bale (2017) *European Politics: A Comparative Introduction* (4th edn) has a helpful chapter on party politics around Europe. Useful sources for updating include journals such as *Political Quarterly* and *British Politics*, as well as the Political Study Association's magazine, *Political Insight*.

 USEFUL WEBSITES

Party websites can be consulted: www.conservatives.com, www.labour.org.uk, www.libdems.org.uk and www.greenparty.org.uk.

The Electoral Commission is a key source on party funding and electoral competition: www.electoralcommission.org.uk.

 *Further student resources to support learning are available at* **www.macmillanihe.com/griffiths-brit-pol-3e**

# 15 IDEOLOGY

As Labour leader, Jeremy Corbyn has frequently argued that Conservative policy on everything from the economy to schools and public broadcasting is part of an ideological attack. Similarly, former Labour minister Yvette Cooper (2015) attacked the Conservative government for making 'an ideological attempt to shrink the state and our public services'. In turn, former Conservative leader David Cameron claimed that Corbyn's views on terrorism were part of his 'Britain-hating ideology' (Bennett, 2015). Whatever the rights and wrongs of these claims, they are all based on the same assumption: that their opponents' actions are driven by an 'ideology', which informs their actions.

This chapter explores the concept of 'ideology' in more detail. What is 'ideology'? If to be 'ideological' is an insult, as the examples above imply, can we have politics without ideology? One view would be to contrast 'ideological' approaches to politics with more 'pragmatic' views. We ask if 'ideology' is necessary in politics. We also consider the relationship between ideologies, political parties and material interests. We look at the mainstream ideologies of liberalism, conservatism and socialism in British politics, the changing ideas and interests these ideologies represent, and their links to political parties. While these ideologies transcend national boundaries, their British interpretations are distinctive and have evolved over time, along with their internal tensions and differences. This chapter also discusses other ideologies outside the mainstream, including feminism, nationalism, racism and green thinking, some of which cut across or transcend the traditional 'left–right' ideological spectrum and have increasing implications for British government and politics. While some of these other ideologies also find expression in political parties, others are more clearly linked with pressure groups and less formally constituted broad political movements (see Chapter 16).

## THIS CHAPTER:

» Explores the role of ideas in British politics.
» Examines the competing mainstream ideologies and their evolution to review how far they have converged or remain distinctive.
» Explores other ideological perspectives that are outside the traditional mainstream.

# Do Ideas Matter in Politics?

The study of politics, from Plato in Ancient Greece onwards, assumed the importance of political ideas. It has been said that there is nothing so important as an idea whose time has come. 'Democracy', 'national self-determination', 'socialism', 'the free market' are all examples of powerful ideas that have, at one time or another, appeared to change the world. A new idea or, perhaps more commonly, the revival of an old idea may still seem to drive political change today. It is often suggested that political parties, or political leaders, need a 'big idea' if they are to succeed.

At various levels, however, the importance of ideas in politics has been questioned. To Marx, in particular, political ideas were just a rationalisation of the interests of different economic classes. In every age, the ruling ideas are the ideas of the ruling class. Plausibly, the dominant class, capitalists in a capitalist society, are in a strong position to influence or condition the thinking of subordinate classes, through, for example, the education system and the mass media. The manual working class may come to hold views that are not in their objective interests, and consequently they may reject socialism – very much in their objective interests from a Marxist perspective. By contrast, liberals and modern neoliberals assume that individuals act in their own rational self-interest (as voters and consumers). If they reject socialism, it is because they have concluded it is not in their interest or unworkable – correctly, from a neoliberal perspective.

Both Marxists and neoliberals in their different ways suggest that it is *interests* (of an individual or a class) that drive political behaviour. Yet both paradoxically illustrate the power of ideas. Marx's ideas inspired political movements around the world and revolutions in Russia, China and elsewhere, which did much to shape the issues and conflicts of the twentieth century. The revival of free-market ideas by modern neoliberals similarly transformed the government and politics of the western world, before going on to affect (with varying success) the economies and societies of the communist world, most of which spectacularly imploded after the collapse of the Berlin Wall in 1989. Ideas can still exert a powerful grip on our collective consciousness.

## SHOULD POLITICS BE ABOUT PRAGMATISM OR IDEOLOGY?

Political ideology involves any connected set of political beliefs with implications for political behaviour. This is the neutral understanding of the term as it is most commonly used today (Seliger, 1976; McLellan, 1995; Leach, 2015). On this definition, conservatism, liberalism, socialism, fascism, nationalism and feminism are all ideologies. However, the term 'ideology' has often been used – and is still sometimes employed – in a pejorative (hostile or negative) sense, and equated with rigid adherence to political dogma, which critics have sometimes associated with Marxism. Marxists, by contrast, have interpreted ideology as the rationalisation of material interests, particularly the interests of the ruling class.

Pragmatism is often contrasted to ideology. Pragmatists are more concerned with the pursuit of power than the implementation of programmes, and are prepared to adjust policies to the perceived preferences of voters, relying on common sense or 'what works' rather than theoretical assumptions.

Some argue that politics should be about 'pragmatism' and 'common sense' rather than being governed by an 'ideology'. In the past, Labour was seen as an ideological party, with its socialist objectives defined in the old clause IV of its constitution, which committed the party to the 'common ownership of the means of production', generally understood as nationalisation of a significant section of industry. By contrast, the Conservative Party was perceived as essentially pragmatic, mainly interested in the pursuit of power, and thus avoiding ideology and theory. Many Conservatives distrust 'ideology', which they sometimes see as an attempt to impose one thinker's abstract rational 'blueprint' on society, regardless of what other people want.

It is commonly argued that the distinction was reversed when Thatcher introduced ideology and 'conviction politics' into the Conservative Party. Under Blair, New Labour arguably transformed into a pragmatic party, prepared to steal the opposition's clothes. Blair emphasised their pragmatism in the slogan 'What matters is what works'. It was practical answers that were needed, not grand ideas. This seems to be at the root of the critical use of ideology at the start of this chapter: politicians ignoring common sense to drive through a dogmatic set of ideas, regardless of the consequence or context.

More recently, there seems to have been a reversion to the norm, with Conservative leaders Cameron and May both claiming to be pragmatists, while Labour's Corbyn is presented as an ideologically driven socialist. In practice, both parties have always involved a blend of ideology and pragmatism, particularly when in office.

The argument is also often made that claims to pragmatism conceal rather than remove ideology. Even when leaders claim to be acting pragmatically, they are driven by an often unstated or implicit set of ideological beliefs. This view was put forward by Hall and Jacques (1983), who argued that Thatcher's claims to be governing through 'common sense' and Blair's claims that he was only concerned with whatever policies worked were both deeply ideological and guided by 'neoliberal' ideas about the world in which we should live. (Neoliberalism is discussed in more detail later in this chapter.)

Even if it is possible to draw a distinction between ideology and pragmatism, it is common to argue that politics requires both. Politics can hardly be conducted without reference to values and principles (or ideology), but it also requires flexibility and compromise (or pragmatism) in pursuit of ideological goals. Indeed, a dogmatic insistence on pragmatism, and a denial of the possibility of radical change based on clear principles, reflects distinctive ideological assumptions over human nature, behaviour and motivation, and the scope and limitations of government. This is a view common in traditional conservative thought, as we see below.

## POLITICAL IDEOLOGIES

Many modern political differences arise from rival political perspectives or ideologies, reflecting distinctive assumptions and involving different political prescriptions. Most British political controversy, and much in the western world more generally, has long seemed to focus on the arguments between and within the mainstream ideologies of liberalism, conservatism and socialism.

Typically, a political ideology provides a description and interpretation of contemporary society, explaining why and how it has come to be as it is, and how far it might be changed. Conservatism, as the name suggests, traditionally involves suspicion of change, which may reflect broad satisfaction with the current social, economic and political system, or pessimism over the chances of securing any improvement. Socialism, by contrast, combines radical criticism of the existing social and political order with the hope and expectation that a fairer and better alternative is possible. However, some of the deepest ideological divisions are over strategy, the means to achieve desired ends. Thus socialists differ more over the means to achieve socialism than ends, Greens are split between fundamentalists and realists over how far they are prepared to compromise their principles, while conservatives disagree over the best way of preserving social and political stability.

Ideologies are neither uniform nor static. While they transcend national boundaries, the particular form they take is influenced strongly by the historical context and the prevailing culture of a country. The British interpretation of liberalism, conservatism and socialism is distinctive, reflecting British political circumstances (as we see below). Ideologies also adapt to changing conditions, frequently reinterpreting old values and principles. All mainstream British ideologies have evolved and changed over time, although this has often involved bitter debate between modernisers and their opponents over the 'real' meaning of conservatism, liberalism and socialism.

# MAINSTREAM IDEOLOGIES AND POLITICAL PARTIES IN BRITAIN

Accounts of political ideologies may include creeds such as nationalism, fascism, feminism, anarchism and environmentalism (or green thinking), but they commonly focus chiefly on three 'mainstream' ideologies: liberalism, conservatism and socialism. In Britain, these ideologies can be loosely linked to three historically significant political parties: the Liberals (and today's Liberal Democrats), the Conservatives and Labour. It is a mistake, however, to identify ideologies wholly within the parties with which they are linked. Those who call themselves socialists, both within and outside the British Labour Party, often disagree passionately over the nature and definition of socialism. Some would deny that Labour is, or ever has been, a socialist party, arguing that while it had socialists among its members, it was mainly concerned with the representation of working people and trade unions and sought to do nothing more than that. Similarly, both Conservatives and Liberals agonise over the true meaning of conservatism and liberalism. Such debates suggest some ideal conception of conservatism, liberalism and socialism against which the programmes, policies and performance of parties can be measured. Furthermore, although one ideology or another might be dominant in a party, individual members will differ in their views and interpretations and will often combine elements of different ideologies in their own thinking. Ideologies themselves are often overlapping, rather than hermetically sealed and entirely distinct from one another.

This implies that it might be better to examine political ideologies without linking them to parties. Yet this would not do either. The key point about political ideologies is that they are 'action-oriented'; they have implications for political behaviour. Political parties are key vehicles for translating ideas into practice. So parties that call themselves 'liberal' seek to bring about, over time, their own version of a liberal society.

Moreover, political ideologies are expressed at a number of levels – by leading thinkers, by practising politicians who adapt the ideas of more original minds in speeches and slogans, by parties in election manifestos and programmes, and by the masses, if often in simplified and perhaps vulgarised form. Indeed, some ideologies, such as nationalism, or fascism, are fairly thin in theoretical terms. While there are some important theoretical sources for British conservatism, much of it has to be inferred from the policy and practice of the British Conservative Party. So it is neither possible nor desirable to separate the study of mainstream political ideologies from their distinctive and sometimes highly contested expression by political parties.

## LIBERALISM
### Core interests and values of liberalism

It is particularly important not to identify liberalism entirely with the British Liberal Party of the nineteenth and early twentieth century and modern Liberal Democrats, as liberal ideas have been so influential that they have permeated all mainstream British political parties. The term 'liberalism' was not commonly used until the nineteenth century. However, the foundations of European liberal thought are much older, springing from the religious reformations of the sixteenth and seventeenth centuries, the eighteenth-century Enlightenment, the French Revolution, but most of all from the economic, social and political transformation brought about over time by industrialisation. Indeed, the growth of liberalism is closely linked with the growth of capitalism, representative democracy and the modern world. In that sense, it is the 'hegemonic' (or dominant) ideology of the modern age.

The core values of the liberal ideology are:

» *Individualism*: Liberal analysis starts with individual men and women, rather than nations, races or classes. Individuals, it is assumed, pursue their own self-interest. The interests or rights of individuals take priority over society or the state, which is only the sum of individuals composing it. Social behaviour is explained in terms of some fairly basic assumptions about individual human psychology.

» *Liberty (or freedom)*: Individuals must be free to pursue their own self-interest. Liberals demand full freedom of thought and expression, and particularly religious toleration. Yet liberals have often differed over the interpretation of freedom. Early liberals emphasised freedom *from* tyranny and oppressive government (negative liberty) and championed the free market. In the early twentieth century, New Liberals sought freedom *to* fulfil individual potential (positive liberty), which might require state welfare services and state intervention to secure full employment.

» *Rationalism*: Liberals assume that humans are rational creatures who are the best judge of their own self-interest. Many liberals followed Bentham in assuming that the universal pursuit of rational self-interest would promote the greatest happiness of the greatest number.

» *Political and legal equality*: Liberals generally emphasised an equality of worth, advocating equality before the law and political equality. In the economic sphere, liberals have advocated equality of opportunity, but not equality of outcome. Indeed, freedom in the economic sphere has commonly resulted in marked inequality.

Liberalism has been closely linked with the class interests of the industrial bourgeoisie (capitalists, or more loosely, the middle class). In early nineteenth-century Britain, following the arguments of classical economists such as Smith and Ricardo, liberals championed the free market and free trade, and opposed government intervention in the economy. They saw a very limited role for the state, summed up in the French expression *laissez faire* – suggesting government should refrain from interfering with individual freedom and the beneficial operation of free-market forces. Their political programme involved an extension of the vote and parliamentary representation to the new industrial centres, leading to a gradual transfer of power and influence from the old landowning aristocracy to the manufacturing classes.

To achieve power, however, Liberals increasingly had to appeal to a wider constituency, including the growing ranks of the professions and the skilled working class. The Liberal Party that Gladstone led, four times as prime minister, contained an awkward coalition of old Whig landowners and successful businessmen, supported by middle- and working-class religious nonconformists who favoured radical reform. This helps to explain some of the tensions within British liberalism as it evolved in the course of the nineteenth century. While early, or classical, liberalism advocated limited constitutional government and free markets, subsequently British liberalism became identified with full representative democracy, as advocated by John Stuart Mill (see Key Figures 15.1). However, the extension of the vote to the working classes increased pressures for more state intervention, for example, to provide free education for all children. Some liberals, such as Herbert Spencer (1820–1903), still vehemently opposed such state intervention.

## The new liberalism

Mill was a transitional figure between the classical free-market liberalism and the interventionist new liberalism of the late nineteenth and early twentieth centuries. New Liberals such as T.H. Green (1836–1882), Leonard Hobhouse (1864–1929) and John Hobson (1858–1940) argued that state intervention was not a restriction on liberty, but would enlarge the freedom of each individual to make the most of their own potential. The Liberal government of 1906–14 introduced old age pensions, labour exchanges for the unemployed and health and unemployment insurance, and laid some of the foundations for the welfare state.

The rise of the Labour Party and the First World War split the Liberals, who divided over competing leadership factions and declined rapidly. Many former Liberals moved to the Conservatives or Labour, and by the 1950s the party was reduced to just six MPs in the House of Commons. Yet New Liberal ideas permeated the other parties. Keynes and Beveridge, whose work and thought underpinned the postwar political consensus, were both small and large 'l' liberals. The inspiration of the policies pursued by postwar Labour and Conservative governments arguably owed more to new liberalism than to traditional conservative or socialist thinking.

# KEY FIGURES 15.1
## John Stuart Mill

**John Stuart Mill (1806–73)** survived an intensive education supervised by his father, James Mill, that turned him into an infant prodigy and provoked an early mental breakdown, to become the leading nineteenth-century liberal thinker, and a continuing source of inspiration to modern liberals. His essay *On Liberty* ([1859] 1972) was a passionate plea for full freedom of expression and toleration of difference. His *Considerations on Representative Government* ([1861] 1972) advocated the principle and practice of representative democracy, which Mill thought required extensive citizen participation beyond simply voting. Unlike his father, Mill argued that the vote should not be confined to males. As an MP, he introduced a bill to give votes to women. His feminism was influenced by his intellectual partnership with Harriet Taylor, whom he subsequently married. In *The Subjection of Women* ([1869] 1988), he compared the condition of Victorian wives to that of black slaves, denounced the violence and abuse suffered by many women, and advocated full and equal partnership between the sexes. His writings on political economy show a gradual shift from orthodox free-market economics towards some sympathy with trade unionism and even socialism.

*Source*: Hulton Archive/Stringer/Getty Images

Friedrich Hayek (1899–1992) made one of the most significant intellectual contributions to 'neoliberalism'.

## Neoliberalism

Ironically, when this ideological consensus was challenged in the 1970s, part of the challenge came from a revival of an older version of liberalism, the free-market liberalism derived from Adam Smith and the classical economists.

This 'neoliberalism' (not to be confused with new liberalism) was energetically promoted by key thinkers such as Friedrich Hayek and Milton Friedman and taken up by Conservative politicians such as Keith Joseph and Margaret Thatcher. The second half of the twentieth century in Britain can be interpreted as much as a conflict between different versions of liberalism as a battle between conservatism and socialism.

## Liberalism and the Liberal Democrats

The Liberal Party, and later its successor the Liberal Democrats, retained a characteristic liberal interest in individual rights and civil liberties, support for New Liberal-type welfare policies, a strong commitment to constitutional reform (particularly devolution and electoral reform) and an internationalist, humanitarian approach in foreign affairs. Many of the party's supporters felt themselves to be on the centre-left of British politics. Yet, as the discussion above shows, there are divisions within liberalism between left-leaning liberals, who often draw on the new liberalism of the early twentieth century, and those on the right of the party, who are closer to neoliberalism.

These old ideological divisions were made clear by the publication of *The Orange Book: Reclaiming Liberalism*, co-edited by David Laws, Lib Dem MP (Marshall and Laws, 2004), which called for a return to economic liberalism. According to Gray (2010, p. 3), the aim of this book was 'to reaffirm a version of liberalism they believed had been lost: one in which support for small government and the free market goes with a strong commitment to civil liberties and freedom of lifestyle'.

The decision to enter a coalition with the Conservatives between 2010 and 2015 seemed to mark the triumph of the 'Orange Book' liberals over the 'New Liberal' strand of liberalism within the party (Beech and Lee, 2015). Following their entry into the coalition government, Clegg and his fellow Lib Dem ministers moved away from the centre-left project of earlier Lib Dem leaders, such as Paddy Ashdown and Charles Kennedy. The consequence of joining the coalition was an electoral disaster for the party. Their former left-of-centre supporters deserted them, while their right-of-centre supporters drifted away to the Conservatives. In the 2015 general election, the party was reduced from 57 to 8 seats in the House of Commons and Nick Clegg, their leader, resigned. In 2017, the party failed to regain significant ground on their pre-2015 seat total in the House of Commons.

## CONSERVATISM

### Traditional conservatism

Whereas early liberalism favoured change and reform, nineteenth-century **conservatism** was generally suspicious of, and resistant to, change. The Conservative Party in Britain emerged from the old Tory party that originated in the seventeenth century. Tories supported the monarchy and the Church of England, and defended the rights and interests of landowners. While liberalism was a product of the eighteenth-century Enlightenment, the American and French Revolutions and, most of all, industrial capitalism, Toryism and subsequently conservatism involved a reaction against all these. It was suspicious of the Age of Reason and the threat this seemed to present to traditional religious and secular authority. It was hostile to the language of freedom, equality and fraternity. It was fearful of many of the changes resulting from industrialisation and the ideas associated with it. The eighteenth-century politician and writer Edmund Burke expressed many of these ideas (see Key Figures 15.2).

---

**Conservatism** *suggests 'conserving', keeping things as they are, resisting radical change. It implies a defence of the existing social and political order and of traditional institutions. However, British conservatives are prepared to accept limited reform that grows out of the past.*

---

## KEY FIGURES 15.2

Edmund Burke and the conservative tradition

**Edmund Burke (1729–97)**, a lifelong Whig politician rather than a Tory, is now regarded as a key source of inspiration for conservatives. Like all Whigs, he celebrated the Glorious Revolution of 1688 that had expelled James II and established limited constitutional monarchy. Like most Whigs, he also supported the American Revolution (1765–83). However, he broke with the leaders of his own party over the French Revolution (1789–99), which he condemned in his critical essay *Reflections on the Revolution in France* ([1790] 1975). Here, he argued for gradual reform that would grow out of tradition, rather than radical revolution inspired by 'naked reason' (Jones, 2017). His hostility to radical change, his reverence for tradition and his suspicion of rationalism became key elements of conservative ideas, as, for example, outlined by conservative thinker Michael Oakeshott (1901–90).

If liberalism was (initially at least) the ideology of the rising capitalist class, Toryism and conservatism at first reflected the interests of the declining but still powerful landed interest. Conservatives sought to maintain the current economic, social and political order against the pressures for change that could only result in a decline in their influence and power. Yet, had conservatism remained wedded to a declining landed interest, it would have fast faded as a political creed. Instead, it held its own in conflict with liberalism in the nineteenth century and proceeded to dominate twentieth-century politics in Britain. It achieved this remarkable success by flexible adaptation to new circumstances, although it can also be argued that some of its core principles have been fairly consistently maintained.

Thus, although British conservatives have opposed radical change, they have not generally been reactionary. They have often subsequently accepted changes introduced by their political opponents rather than seeking to turn the clock back, and indeed have sometimes initiated gradual reforms themselves. Flexibility, gradualism (a preference for gradual rather than radical reform) and pragmatism have been key aspects of British conservatism in action for most of the past two centuries.

To survive, Conservatives had to seek a wider base of support as the franchise was progressively extended to the middle classes, skilled workers and then the entire adult population. Increasingly, the Conservative Party came to be identified with the interests of property in general, rather than landed property, winning the support of many businessmen who once supported the Liberals. Moreover, from the late nineteenth century, the Conservatives under Benjamin Disraeli (1804–81) and subsequent leaders made a determined attempt to woo the working classes, particularly skilled workers, through social reform at home, combined with the pursuit of British national and imperial interests abroad (Beer, 1982). In the course of the twentieth century, they also sought to give the workers an increased stake in property by encouraging homeownership and wider share ownership.

Their political opponents saw this as a patent 'con trick', to persuade those with little or no property to support the Conservative cause and reject policies of social reform and redistribution advocated by socialists. Conservatives themselves have generally argued that the various classes are bound together by ties of mutual dependence in an organic society, which is more than the sum of its individual parts. This organic theory of society and the state (derived from Burke) has often been contrasted with the individualism of liberalism. Disraeli had sought to transcend class differences and create 'one nation'. He argued that wealth carries with it obligations, including an obligation to assist those less fortunate. This 'paternalism' might entail a duty of voluntary charity, or an acceptance of state-sponsored social reform.

Such an approach marks off traditional conservatism from older forms of liberalism. While early liberals thought individual human beings could achieve social progress by pursuing their own rational self-interest in a free market, traditional conservatives did not generally share this optimistic faith in human reason, goodness and progress. Conservatism has been described as a 'philosophy of imperfection' (Quinton, 1978). Most conservatives do not believe in the perfectibility of humankind, but rather assume that there is an 'evil streak' (which Christians might describe as 'original sin') in human nature. This implies a need for authority – a strong state and strong government to maintain law and order and restrain violent and antisocial behaviour (Leach, 2009, pp. 54–67).

Conservatives were once far from being enthusiastic supporters of the free market and free trade. They supported the protection of British agriculture from cheap imports from abroad as opposed to 'free trade' in the nineteenth century. In the early twentieth century, the party was converted by Joseph Chamberlain to tariff reform and 'imperial preference', in which the British Empire would ideally act as a vast free-trade area, a policy which his son Neville Chamberlain sought to put into practice as chancellor and later prime minister in the Conservative-dominated national government of the 1930s (Beer, 1982, Ch. 10).

In the postwar era, modernisers in the Conservative Party adopted Disraeli's 'one-nation' slogan to embrace social reform and state intervention. This one-nation conservatism became the new party ortho-doxy. Thus, Conservative governments bet-ween 1951 and 1964, particularly that of Harold Macmillan (1957–63), supported Keynesian demand management, state welfare provision, the mixed economy, and consensus and compromise in industrial relations. These policies did not seem far removed from those of the Labour Party (see Chapter 2 for more on the Conservatives during this period). Indeed, Macmillan had written a book entitled *The Middle Way* in 1938 and had once provocatively declared that conservatism was a kind of paternal socialism. For some modern Conservatives, this whole period is an aberration in the long history of the party, although for others it remains the very essence of the authentic Tory and conservative tradition (Gilmour, 1992; Gilmour and Garnett, 1997). According to one influential interpretation, however, British conservatism involves an ongoing tension between two rival libertarian and collectivist strands of thought, with each appearing to be dominant at different periods (Greenleaf, 1973, 1983; Seawright, 2010; Heppell, 2014).

There are significant internal tensions and contending schools of thought within conservatism – as there are within all major ideologies. Thatcher and her successors rejected much of this one-nation conservatism in pursuing neoliberal or New Right free-market ideas. While there were important elements of continuity between Thatcherism and older conservative thinking, Thatcher's leadership marked a watershed in the development of British conservatism.

## Thatcherism, conservatism and the New Right

The controversy over the nature of conservatism is at the heart of the continuing debate over the modern Conservative Party. It is difficult to discuss conservatism after 1975 without extensive reference to 'Thatcherism'. For some, Thatcher and her allies hijacked the Conservative Party, and introduced alien, individualist, free-market ideas at odds with the one-nation tradition of social reform (Gilmour, 1978, 1992; Gilmour and Garnett, 1997). For others, Thatcherism involved the rediscovery of true conservatism. Both critics and true believers perhaps exaggerated the break with the immediate past.

Margaret Thatcher broke with the consensus politics of the postwar era, and rejected traditional conservative pragmatism for the ideology of the free market and competition. There is clearly some truth in this picture. Under Thatcher's leadership, the neoliberal ideas of Hayek and Friedman became the new orthodoxy. Keynesian demand management was rejected and Adam Smith's 'invisible hand' of the free market restored to favour. Many of the policies pursued by her governments, such as the sale of council houses, the privatisation of nationalised industries, the injection of competition into the public sector, and the attempts to 'rein back' the state and cut public spending and taxation, reflected free-market ideas (Kavanagh, 1990).

However, Thatcherism can be seen as the consequence rather than the cause of the breakdown of Keynesianism and the postwar consensus. Keynesian policies had been applied with some apparent success in the postwar decades, but by the late 1970s they no longer seemed to work – with the economy sluggish and inflation and unemployment rising – and had been effectively abandoned by Callaghan's Labour government, which lasted from 1976 to 1979. Similarly, concerns over the growth of government, the cost of the welfare state, trade union power and poor industrial relations were already widespread before Thatcher became leader of the Conservative Party in 1975. The party and its new leader adapted to altered circumstances as British Conservatives had managed to so successfully in the past. (The 'crisis of the 1970s' is discussed in Chapter 2.)

Moreover, while in office (1979–90), Thatcher was generally more pragmatic and cautious than is sometimes imagined. Although she embraced the rhetoric of the free market with some fervour, she rejected replacing the NHS with an insurance system, avoided the privatisation of British Rail and the Post Office, and continued policies of state-financed urban regeneration (while slashing regional aid). Despite some real cuts in spending programmes and significant changes in the distribution of taxation, Conservative governments after 1979 were not particularly successful in reducing public spending and the overall burden of taxation. The state was restructured rather than 'reined back'. It was only towards the end of her premiership that she dogmatically and disastrously pursued policies such as the poll tax, which ultimately helped to bring her down (see Chapter 10, pp. 198–200).

Indeed, Thatcherism or the New Right is best seen not as a pure free-market ideology but as a blend of neoliberalism and traditional conservatism, 'the free economy and the strong state' – the latter was used to impose the former, often against the resistance of local government and organised labour in the trade union movement (Gamble, 1988). 'Reining back the state' in the economic sphere did not entail weakening government. On the contrary, Thatcherism involved a reaffirmation of the traditional Tory commitment to strong government, leadership, defence, law and order and the authority of the state. Thatcher and her successors continued to exploit the sentiments of nationalism and patriotism, which had appealed so well in the past to the British electorate, most obviously in relation to the Falklands, the Gulf War and Europe. Thatcher and her successor John Major strongly opposed devolution and continued to champion the union of the UK. Both also employed the rhetoric of traditional family values that always played well with their party.

For a period, Thatcherism played well with the electorate. Ideologies are held at various levels. While the sophisticated version of Thatcherism reflected the economic theories of Smith, Hayek and Friedman, the popular version was more about vivid imagery and slogans: 'the Iron Lady', 'Stand on your own two feet', 'the nanny state', 'Get on your bike' (to look for work). Some of this rhetoric appealed to sections of the working class as well as the Conservative Party rank and file, although the popularity of Thatcherism can be

exaggerated. Indeed, parliamentary landslides depended more on the electoral system and weaknesses and divisions in the opposition rather than positive support for Thatcher's brand of conservatism.

Moreover, this blend of conservative and neoliberal ideas inevitably involved some tensions and contradictions. One important illustration of the problems of reconciling free-market and traditional conservative ideas was over Britain's relations with Europe. Thatcher had supported joining the European Community and was an enthusiastic advocate of the single market, which seemed to fulfil her own free-market values. Indeed, membership of the EC had been sold to the Conservative Party and the British people as a Common Market entailing economic benefits for Britain. However, closer European integration threatened another core conservative value, national and parliamentary sovereignty. Conservative schizophrenia over Europe was intensified by the Maastricht Treaty, signed by John Major, and subsequently the issues of monetary union and the European constitution.

Altogether, Thatcherism and Margaret Thatcher herself were rather more compatible with the mainstream Tory and conservative tradition than is sometimes imagined. Even so, in one respect at least Thatcher was untypical. Her instincts were radical rather than gradualist.

## The Conservative Party since Thatcherism

Although John Major, Thatcher's successor, won the 1992 general election, the Conservative Party seemed to enter a period of crisis. Major's political style was more consensual, but otherwise his premiership did not mark a significant break from Thatcherism. After almost 18 years in power, the Conservatives were defeated in a landslide victory for New Labour in 1997. Despite the electoral limits of Thatcherism, the next three Conservative Party leaders – William Hague (1997–2001), Iain Duncan Smith (2001–03) and Michael Howard (2003–05) – neither wished nor dared to challenge the Thatcher legacy in any significant way.

The electoral failure of the Conservative Party gave David Cameron, the next leader, more freedom to try a different approach than his predecessors. Cameron positioned himself as the 'heir to Blair', a politician who would win elections from the centre (cited in Pierce, 2005, 9).

Some people, such as Theresa May (2002), commented that many people still saw the Conservatives as the 'the nasty party', pushing forward 'uncaring' Thatcherite policies despite their social cost. Cameron set about 'decontaminating' the Conservative Party brand (Stelzer, 2007). Some people predicted that Cameron would mark a return to one-nation conservatism (Wilson, 2006). He spoke of the importance of the 'Big Society' – in contrast to Thatcher's claim that there was no such thing – encouraging citizens to play a fuller part in social life. He also seemed to draw on so-called progressive 'red Tory' ideas (Blond, 2010), which in turn seemed heavily dependent on the early twentieth-century Catholic thinkers Hilaire Belloc and G.K. Chesterton, and notions of community, voluntary endeavour and mutual aid rather than state intervention (Raban, 2010).

In office from 2010 to 2015, the Conservative-led coalition argued that the government needed to make cuts to government spending – 'austerity' – in response to the economic downturn. (For more on the 2007–08 economic crisis, see Chapter 19, pp. 412–15.) The policies of the Conservative-led governments since 2010 have led to differing interpretations. For some commentators, they were a pragmatic response to difficult economic circumstances, which necessitated making cuts to balance the books (Seldon and Finn, 2015). For other writers and politicians, as we saw in the introduction to this chapter, Cameron was guided by an ideological belief that the state should spend less and do less and that the private sector was the best provider of services. Under this view, Cameron in office marked a return to Thatcherism (Hall, 2011; Lakin, 2013; Griffiths, 2014; Beech, 2015). May is yet to set out a clear ideological position, but appears to draw on a more traditional form of conservatism.

## BRITISH SOCIALISM AND SOCIAL DEMOCRACY

While the ideology of 'liberalism' is found in Parliament in the name of the Lib Dems and 'conservatism' in the Conservative Party, the link between socialism and the Labour Party is less clear. The Labour Party was in part set up to represent organised labour, by providing parliamentary representation to the trade unions (as we discussed in Chapter 14). However, for many party members, the best way of doing this was through socialism. The Labour Party has always contained a mixture of supporters, some of whom want nothing more than a fairer deal for working people and others with the more radical and ambitious goal of creating a socialist society. This section examines what that would mean, and looks at the sometimes ambiguous relationship between the Labour Party and socialism.

### Early socialism

While conservatism – if not necessarily the modern Conservative Party – involved a defence of traditional social arrangements, and liberalism a justification for moderate constitutional and social reform, European socialism developed as a radical or revolutionary ideology involving a funda-mental challenge to traditional interests and industrial capitalism. As Britain was the first country to industrialise, at some initial cost to the living conditions of the labouring poor, it might appear a fertile environment for revolutionary ideas. Yet the British working class largely rejected the revolutionary and Marxist movements that swept through much of the European continent (McKibbin, 1984).

### Socialism and the Labour Party

The mainstream British version of socialism, the socialism of the Labour Party, developed relatively late and was distinctly unusual. Indeed, some question whether it should be called socialism at all. The Labour Party was effectively formed in 1900 from an alliance between some trade unions seeking parliamentary

## KEY FIGURES 15.3
Robert Owen

**Robert Owen (1771–1858)** secured some popular support for his interpretation of socialism, derived initially from his own experiences of running a model factory, but subsequently from his involvement in early British trade unionism in the 1830s and the cooperative movement from the 1840s. His socialism depended on grassroots working-class self-help rather than the total overthrow of the existing economic and political system demanded by revolutionary socialists. He was criticised by Marx as a 'utopian socialist' with no realistic strategy for achieving socialism. Yet Marx's own socialism found less support in Britain, the country where he spent the bulk of his working life, than in Germany, France, Italy or even (but ultimately especially) Russia.

representation to protect union rights and three small socialist societies, of which one, the Marxist-inspired Social Democratic Federation, left within a year. The other two were the tiny but influential Fabian Society, committed to gradual, parliamentary state-sponsored socialism, and the Independent Labour Party (ILP), which preached a quasi-religious ethical socialism based on the universal brotherhood of man rather than the revolution arising from inevitable class conflict taught by Marxists. In practice, Labour's reformist ideas were not so dissimilar from those of the New Liberals, for example both supported pensions, welfare payments and unemployment insurance; indeed, some of whom were to switch subsequently to the new party (Bevir, 2011).

Trade union ideas and interests dominated the early history of the Parliamentary Labour Party, which was created in part to serve the wider interests of the labour movement. Trade unions were more concerned with improvements in wages and conditions through 'free collective bargaining' rather than the radical overthrow of capitalism.

While socialists of sorts were part of the broad labour coalition from the start, the Labour Party only became formally committed to a socialist programme in 1918 with the adoption of clause IV of the Labour Party's constitution, which committed the party to the 'common ownership of means of production, distribution and exchange', that is, greater nationalisation (discussed in Chapter 20). However, the detailed plans for implementing this ambitious goal were

never formulated. Instead, the Labour Party in practice remained committed to gradual parliamentary reform rather than a fundamental transformation of the economic, social and political order. This was demonstrated by the cautious record of the two minority Labour governments of 1924 and 1929–31, as well as the whole labour movement's peaceful and constitutional record in the 1926 general strike. Socialism for the Labour Party was a distant aspiration, dependent on the achievement of a parliamentary majority and step-by-step gradual reform. Other variants of socialism, including Marxism, syndicalism, guild socialism, cooperation and local socialism, were rejected or marginalised by the Labour Party, although, arguably, they had a greater impact on culture and society (Smith and Worley, 2014). Radical critics, such as Ralph Miliband (the father of Ed Miliband, Labour leader from 2010 to 2015, and David Miliband, foreign secretary under Gordon Brown), suggested that the Labour Party was always more committed to the parliamentary representation of the labour movement and the trade unions than it was to socialism.

Labour achieved its first parliamentary majority in 1945. The record of the Attlee government (1945–51) has come to define the Labour interpretation of socialism, both what it was and what it was not. Nationalisation of the 'commanding heights of the economy' (largely energy and transport) involved an extensive and controversial extension of the role of the state, although not the wholesale common ownership envisaged by some socialists. The

## Figure 15.1 Influences on the ideology of the Labour party

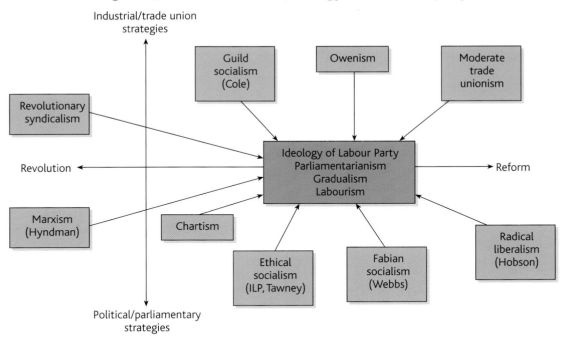

*Source*: Reprinted from Leach (2015), p. 113.

industries taken into state ownership were already largely municipalised (electricity, gas) and/or perceived to be declining (gas, rail, iron and steel). Left-wing critics complained that the method of nationalisation (through public corporations) involved 'state capitalism' rather than workers' control. Labour's economic policy followed the principles of Keynesian demand management rather than the detailed socialist planning of a command economy (see Chapter 2). Labour operated a mixed but essentially still capitalist economy, albeit with more government regulation. The government's most important achievement was the establishment of the welfare state. It not only largely implemented the welfare proposals of the 1942 Beveridge Report, but also established the NHS, and expanded municipal housing. (For more on all of this, see Chapter 20, pp. 423–30.)

## Socialism and 'revisionist' social democracy

The second half of the twentieth century saw a long battle between the Labour left and right, which began with the resignation of Aneurin Bevan, Harold Wilson and John Freeman from the Attlee government, in protest against the Labour Chancellor Hugh Gaitskell's imposition of charges for teeth and spectacles in 1951. Bevan became the unofficial leader of the left, which championed more nationalisation and opposed German rearmament and Britain's independent nuclear deterrent. Revisionists or social democrats on the right of the party were convinced that Labour had to modernise and abandon further nationalisation, which was electorally unpopular. Gaitskell, who defeated Bevan for the leadership of the party in 1955, sought to scrap clause IV, and even considered changing the party's name. He fought to reverse a 1960 party conference decision in favour of unilateral nuclear disarmament. The 'revisionist' argument for social democracy (made by the right of the party) was most clearly set out by Anthony Crosland, in *The Future of Socialism* (1956), and discussed in Key Figures 15.4.

If anything, the conflict became more bitter following the deaths of Bevan in 1960 and Gaitskell in 1963, after which Harold Wilson, the candidate of the left, became leader, while Roy Jenkins eventually emerged as the standard bearer of the Gaitskellites. The problems faced by the Wilson and Callaghan governments further polarised opinion within the party. Left-wing socialists favoured more nationalisation, unilateral nuclear disarmament and internal party democracy, and mostly opposed membership of the European Community. The right supported NATO, nuclear weapons and Europe, while opposing further nationalisation. After the election of Michael Foot, the old Bevanite, as leader in 1980, some 'moderates' left Labour to form the new Social Democratic Party (Crewe and King, 1995) – which eventually merged with the Liberals to form today's Liberal Democrats – while others such as Denis Healey and Roy Hattersley stayed to fight from within. Healey narrowly defeated Tony Benn (by now the standard bearer of the left) for the deputy leadership in 1981, but the party went on to its most disastrous defeat in 1983 on a left-wing manifesto, which included commitments to further nationalisation, nuclear disarmament and leaving Europe.

# KEY FIGURES 15.4
## Anthony Crosland and revisionism in the Labour Party

**Anthony Crosland (1918–77)** was the most influential thinker on the social democratic right of the Labour Party. In his key book *The Future of Socialism* (1956), he argued that Marx 'has little to offer the contemporary socialist either in respect of practical policy, or of the correct analysis of our society, or even of the right conceptual tools or framework'. Pure capitalism had been replaced by a mixed economy. Socialism thus needed revising and updating. Ownership of industry was irrelevant. Instead, socialists should pursue greater equality through progressive taxation and improved welfare provision. Crosland served in Wilson's government, promoting comprehensive schools and the expansion of higher education. He opposed cuts in public spending at the time of the 1976 IMF loan crisis. Crosland died in office as foreign secretary under Callaghan, but continues to exert a powerful intellectual influence on the Labour Party to this day (Hain, 2015; Diamond, 2016).

## From 'New Labour' to Corbynism and the rebirth of socialism?

Under the leadership of Neil Kinnock (1983–92), John Smith (1992–94) and finally Tony Blair (1994–2007), the Labour Party gradually restored its electoral fortunes. Kinnock faced down the hard-left Militant tendency that had infiltrated the party – seeing it as a vehicle for radical 'Trotskyite' left-wing policies – and instituted a policy review that led to the abandonment of the pledges which some considered had lost the party support, and modernised the image and presentation of the party. Smith introduced 'one member, one vote', weakening the power of trade union leaders over the party. Blair persuaded the party to change clause IV, which earlier revisionist social democrats had sought, and (unofficially) rebranded the party as 'New Labour'.

Much has been written on the transition from old to New Labour. The party's programme clearly changed considerably from the election defeat in 1983. Blair initially described his ideology as part of a 'third way', beyond the 'old left' and the 'new right', and drew on the work of Anthony Giddens (1998). The third way was seen as an attempt to renew the social democracy of Crosland and others, for an age of globalisation and increased individualism. However, critics accused Blair of abandoning not just socialism but social democracy too, so that he was effectively Thatcher's heir (Hay, 1999; Heffernan, 2000).

Certainly, Blair accepted the free market. His government from 1997 onwards did not reverse the Conservative privatisations, and made controversial use of public–private partnerships and the private finance initiative to fund public sector investment (see Chapter 3). Whichever interpretation one follows, New Labour achieved considerable electoral success, securing an unprecedented three terms of government.

When Gordon Brown took over from Blair as prime minister in 2007, some hoped that

Brown's leadership would involve a return to old Labour or a reinvigorated social democracy. Initially, this was not to be the case, and – as Blair's chancellor for ten years – Brown was hardly likely to depart in a radically different direction. It took a global banking crisis to force a change. In response, Brown's government effectively took a large slice of the British banking industry into temporary public ownership, imposed more controls over financial services, and raised income tax for higher earners. He did this, not to demonstrate his socialist convictions, but in response to the worst economic crisis the world had faced since 1929. If any ideas were resurrected, it was not Labour's old clause IV, and still less Marxism, but the economic analysis and prescriptions of Keynes (see Chapter 19, pp. 412–15). Thus, Brown borrowed heavily to inject more demand into the economy, by cutting taxes and maintaining public spending.

Labour's election loss in 2010 gave Ed Miliband, its new leader, a 'five year mission' to take the party back to power (Bale, 2015). Miliband, critics argued, never developed a clear ideological narrative. Was he 'Red Ed' (BBC News, 2013), a radical like his father Ralph, returning Labour to socialism, or a moderate social democrat like his predecessor Gordon Brown. Indeed, on the big issue of the economy, Miliband was criticised both for not taking the deficit seriously enough, and for not offering an alternative to austerity, leaving voters uncertain as to Labour's position. Despite this, Miliband went into the 2015 general election with almost every poll pointing to a hung Parliament with no clear winner, so the outright victory of the Conservatives was a surprise for many, and Miliband stepped down.

Jeremy Corbyn's overwhelming victory in the subsequent leadership elections was one of the biggest political surprises in decades. Corbyn was, after all, seen as a veteran of Labour's hard left and a follower of Tony Benn. Yet a blend of dissatisfaction with the record of New Labour, an 'anti-political' rejection of the governing elite (of the kind discussed in Chapter 16) and a growing rejection of austerity swept Corbyn to victory over more mainstream contenders for the leadership. For commentators, this marked a revival of the more radical tradition of socialism, which had been marginalised in the Labour Party since

*Source*: Dan Kitwood/Getty Images News/Getty Images

For many of his supporters, Jeremy Corbyn has returned the Labour Party to its socialist roots since his election in 2015.

Kinnock became leader in the 1980s. Corbyn's ideological vision draws on an egalitarian form of Keynesian social democracy, and a belief that capitalism works for the few, not the many. His relative success at the 2017 general election, where the Labour Party significantly improved the number of seats and proportion of the popular vote, shocked nearly all political commentators, who believed, following the Blairite model, that elections are won in the centre-ground of politics. Yet Corbyn's challenge to 'neoliberalism' and austerity clearly found more of a chord with voters than many experts thought.

# OTHER IDEOLOGIES: BEYOND LEFT AND RIGHT

A marked feature of British politics over the past 40 years or so has been the development of political ideas that cut across the traditional left–right ideological spectrum. Most of these new ideological currents have little in common, except that they are not primarily concerned with the interests and values of traditional ideologies centred on attitudes to state intervention, but reflect other issues and priorities. While some of these non-mainstream ideologies are represented by political parties, others are largely articulated by pressure groups or social movements.

## FEMINISM

Feminism is another ideology that can be found in different varieties across the political spectrum. Although some leading figures are associated with the left, feminists can arguably also be found on the right and centre, bound together by the common aim of securing justice for women and combating **sexism**. Today, politicians who at least describe themselves as feminists are found among the leading figures of all the main parties.

---

**Sexism** *involves attitudes and behaviour that discriminate against women or demean them. Unequal pay and prospects for women, demeaning images of women in the media or pornography, and the use of language that neglects or diminishes women are all examples of sexism.*

---

Feminism has a long history, fuelling ultimately successful demands for property rights, education and opportunities at work, as well as votes for women. However, in Britain as in most of the western world, a 'second wave' of feminism from the late 1960s onwards drew attention to the continuing severe disadvantages suffered by women despite their formal political and legal equality. Thus few women reached the top in business, government or the professions, while women's average pay lagged well behind that of men. Moreover, women continued to bear the major responsibility for child-rearing, housework and care for elderly relatives. An important influence on second wave feminism was the French thinker, Simone de Beauvoir (discussed in Key Figures 15.5).

Conventionally, three principal strands of modern feminism are distinguished – liberal feminism, socialist or Marxist feminism and radical feminism (see Table 15.1), although there is, in practice, considerable overlap between these categories, while some feminists are difficult to categorise and resist labelling.

Liberal feminism goes back a long way. Early feminists like Mary Wollstonecraft (1759–97) sought to extend the rights liberals demanded for men to women. They built on liberal assumptions and values but sought to apply them to both sexes. They sought equal rights for women, on the assumption that (apart from some obvious physical differences) women were much the same as men in terms of their nature and capacities. Liberals also assumed that they could persuade both men and women of the justice of the demand for equal rights by rational argument. Liberal feminism was largely responsible for the formal establishment of women's legal and political equality, and other advances such as the expansion of education opportunities for females. Modern liberal feminists have continued to press for better policies for women – such as better maternity rights or an end to the gender pay gap where men tend to earn more than women – as well as increased political representation for women. Yet they have had some difficulty in explaining why formal legal and political equality has fallen well short of achieving

## Table 15.1 Strands of feminism

| | Liberal feminism | Socialist or Marxist feminism | Radical feminism |
|---|---|---|---|
| **Who?** | *(first wave)* | *(first wave)* | Germaine Greer |
| | Mary Wollstonecraft | William Thompson | Kate Millett |
| | John Stuart Mill | Friedrich Engels | Shulamith Firestone |
| | Harriet Taylor | *(second wave)* | Eva Figes |
| | The suffragettes | Juliet Mitchell | Susan Brownmiller |
| | *(second wave)* | Michelle Barrett | Angela Dworkin |
| | Betty Friedan | | 'Ecofeminists' |
| **Key ideas and terms** | Application of liberal principles to women; gender equality; freedom of opportunity | Economic exploitation of women as 'industrial reserve army'; women's role in reproduction of labour | Patriarchy and male dominance; 'the personal is political'; sexual politics; celebration of women's difference |
| **Aims** | Extension of rights of man to women; legal and political rights; women's education; equal opportunities; equal pay | Politicisation and unionization of women; nurseries and workplace crèches; wages for housework | Alternatives to nuclear family; a woman's right to choose (on abortion); end of violence against women; end of pornography; lesbian rights; green issues; peace |

actual equality for women. Today, key figures in all the most significant political parties – with the possible exception of UKIP – would describe themselves as feminist.

Socialist or Marxist feminists were arguably the most important strand in the UK. They explained women's inequality in terms of social pressures and in the context of wider inequality in a capitalist society. Low wages in what was once a predominantly male full-time paid workforce could only be sustained through the unpaid domestic and childcare labour provided by women. Women in the workforce, many part time and not members of trade unions, also constituted an 'industrial reserve army', particularly important when there were labour short-ages, but always useful to employers in keeping wages down. Working-class women were doubly exploited, both as members of a subordinate class, and because of their gender. Socialist feminists sought to raise the political consciousness of women, persuade them to join trade unions and secure more

effective protection for part-time and casual work. One contentious proposal, wages for housework, was opposed by some feminists because it appeared to legitimise the unfair domestic burden placed on women. Thus many socialist feminists saw the solution in terms of a dramatic extension of paid maternity leave and nursery provision. While Marxism provided a body of theory that could explain some of women's subordinate role in modern western society, it could not explain all of it, nor inequality in other non-capitalist societies.

Radical feminists had less influence on UK party politics than socialist feminists. Radical feminists argued that the real problem was not the lack of formal political and legal rights for women, nor inequality in society generally, but simply men and men's power over women, **patriarchy**, in the family and society more generally. Male power was exercised sometimes through crude physical force and violence against women (including rape), often through more subtle social and educational

# KEY FIGURES 15.5
Simone de Beauvoir

*Source: DPA/DPA/PA Images.*

**Simone de Beauvoir (1908–86)** was an influential French feminist whose key work *The Second Sex* ([1949] 1972) anticipated much of the analysis of 'second-wave' American, Australian and British feminists some 20 years later. She sought to explain why women constituted a 'second' or inferior sex in society with less freedom to shape their own destiny. She attacked contemporary images of passive femininity, and advocated full equality for women in a balanced relationship between the sexes, in which both men and women enjoyed freedom.

conditioning. One radical feminist target was the images of women in the media and pornography, another the subliminal messages conveyed by everyday language (chair*man*, business*man*, *his*tory), and by literature from Jane Austen onwards, suggesting that women's ultimate fulfilment lay in love and marriage to a man.

---

**Patriarchy** *means literally 'rule of the father'. The term is used by feminists to mean the habitual domination of men over women in the family and wider society, even in states where equal rights are enshrined in law.*

---

Liberal feminists (and subsequently most socialist feminists) had sought equality and partnership with men and were only too happy to campaign alongside sympathetic men, such as John Stuart Mill. Radical feminists argued that women had to achieve their own liberation. While liberal and socialist feminists assumed that there were no fundamental differences between the minds and mental capacities of men and women, some radical feminists celebrated the differences between the sexes. Women thought and behaved differently. While men were inherently competitive and prone to violence, women were more cooperative and pacific. Thus men were largely excluded from the women's movement and from some women's

political initiatives, such as the Greenham Common women's peace camp (1981–2000).

Radical feminism has helped transform the way people think about politics. No longer is politics confined to the public sphere. Radical feminists argued that much of women's oppression takes place in the private sphere – in the family and in personal and sexual relationships. A particular concern remains continuing violence against women, especially rape (including rape within marriage). Thus, for radical feminists, 'the personal is political'. Radical feminists have been behind the UK events, such as Take Back the Night and SlutWalk, originally imported from North America, which highlight sexual violence against women.

Recent developments in feminism have stressed 'intersectionality' – a term originally imported from the USA. **Intersectional feminism** is the view that women experience oppression in varying degrees of intensity depending on their identity. Cultural patterns of oppression, such as racism, capitalism and patriarchy, are interrelated (Crenshaw, 1989, 2012). Women who are black, disabled or from

---

**Intersectional feminism** *stresses that patterns of oppression, such as racism, capitalism and patriarchy, are interrelated and therefore women experience oppression differently depending on their identity.*

---

*Source*: Cary Welling

The women's movement often campaigned for peace and against militarism, as shown in the 1980s by their protests against the siting of nuclear weapons at the US nuclear base at RAF Greenham Common, Berkshire.

poorer backgrounds, for example, experience oppression differently than white, able-bodied or wealthier women. Part of the move to intersectional feminism comes from the claim that the feminist movement has for too long been dominated by white, heterosexual, middle-class women, and neglected the experience of those with other identities. In some respects, these differences and even conflicts within the women's movement testify to its richness and diversity, although they also raise a question mark over the direction of feminism (Evans, 2015; Mügge and Erzeel, 2016).

Although feminism has been incorporated in different ways into the platforms of all the main political parties, until recently there was not an obviously feminist party that sought to push these ideas forward. This changed with the creation of the Women's Equality (WE) Party in 2015 (although they have shied away from describing themselves as a 'feminist' party). It was founded by journalist Catherine

Mayer and comedian and presenter Sandi Toksvig. As such, it was able to capitalise on the networks and public appeal of its founders. Led by Sophie Walker, the WE Party has over 65,000 members and supporters, with over 50 branches across the UK. It fielded candidates in the devolved and London mayoral elections in 2016. As a party, it campaigns on seven recognisably feminist policy areas: equality in healthcare, representation, pay, parenting, education, media treatment and an end to violence against women (Women's Equality Party, 2017). In this, it perhaps owes more to liberal feminism than other strands. The surprise 2017 general election rather caught the party off guard and they fielded only a handful of candidates, gaining greatest success in Shipley, West Yorkshire, where Walker stood against Philip Davies, the sitting Conservative MP and an avowed anti-feminist. However, Walker received just 1.9% of the vote, finishing last (Evans and Kenny, 2017).

## GREEN THINKING

Green thinking is often referred to as 'environmentalism' or 'ecologism'. As the name and colour 'green' have become almost universally identified with concern for the environment, there seems little point in using less familiar terms for what has become an important and distinctive political ideology. Other ideologies focus on the interests and needs of humankind in general or a particular section of humanity – a class, a nation, a race or gender. The green slogan 'Earth First!' subordinates the future of humankind to the future of the planet, although greens would argue that the futures of both planet and people are bound up together.

Key points of the green ideology are:

» *'Earth first!'*: The needs of the planet should have priority over the needs and wishes of humankind. This is sometimes called an *ecocentric* approach rather than an *anthropocentric* approach, putting ecology ahead of humanity.

» *Limits to growth*: There are limits to the increases in productivity that can be derived from the exploitation of finite natural resources – an argument distantly derived from eighteenth-century economist Thomas Malthus. Greens have also identified significant costs to the pursuit of growth in terms of potentially irreversible damage to the environment.

» *Sustainability*: Humans should only pursue policies that can be sustained in the long run without irreversible damage to the resources on which the human species and other species depend. Any growth has to be sustainable.

» *Protect future generations*: Those alive today may not pay the price for unsustainable policies, but our descendants will. We need to consider the interests of future generations, and should leave the earth in no worse shape than we found it. Climate change from human activity could ultimately make the earth uninhabitable.

» *Animal rights*: Many (but not all) greens are strong supporters of animal rights, and refuse to eat or wear dead animals.

Greens also argue that the production of meat consumes too many resources compared with the production of cereals and vegetables.

» *'Think global, act local'*: While greens believe environmental issues and problems are global, they stress the need for action at the local level. Many greens are suspicious of central government and the state, and believe, with economist E.F. Schumacher (1973), that 'small is beautiful'.

Although many green activists are associated more with the left, they draw support across the political spectrum. Indeed, the green slogan 'not left, not right but forward' transcends conventional political divisions. While mainstream ideologies and parties from left to right welcome economic growth as a means of satisfying conflicting human interests and demands without necessarily making anyone worse off, greens insist that there are limits to growth. Many of the resources on which our current standard of living depends are non-renewable and thus finite. Unless renewable energy resources are utilised to replace the dwindling stocks of fossil fuels, humans will ultimately exhaust those supplies. Pollution is also causing irreversible damage to the environment and climate change that could prove catastrophic. The relentless pursuit of growth to satisfy the needs of a still fast-expanding human population threatens not only other species but future generations.

While some green thinking has permeated all major parties and sections of big business, radical greens suggest that much of this is relatively superficial 'greenspeak'. It falls well short of the massive changes in policy and lifestyles they feel are necessary to avoid further irreversible damage to 'planet earth' through pollution and climate change. The rise of the Green Party is discussed in more detail in Chapter 21.

Neither feminism nor green thinking are concerned primarily with the relationship of the individual to the state, or the argument over how far the state can and should interfere with free-market forces, which are major concerns of the traditional mainstream ideologies. Insofar as these ideologies are concerned with equality and social justice, it is with other divisions of the human race than social class, or in the case of greens, future generations, other species and the planet. Together, they have enlarged political discourse, extending ideological debate well beyond the confines of established party politics, reflecting a wider range of political interests and conflicts.

## NATIONALISM

**Nationalism** has been defined as 'a political principle which holds that the political and the national unit should be congruent' (Gellner, 1983). In other words, **nations** should form independent sovereign states, and states should consist of nations or **nation states**. The simple principle of **national self-determination** had dangerous implications for old dynastic states that included various national or ethnic groups, such as nineteenth-century Austria or Russia. Nationalists demanded political unification for Germany and Italy, and independence for nations then subject to foreign rule, such as Greece, Poland, Hungary or Norway. In the twentieth century, nationalist movements demanded and secured independence for the colonies of imperial powers, including Britain.

**Nationalism** *is a political ideology that holds that nations should form independent sovereign states.*

*A* **nation** *is a community of people bound together by some common characteristics (real or imagined).*

*A* **nation state** *is an independent sovereign state whose inhabitants belong to a single national community.*

**National self-determination** *requires that a nation should be able to pursue its own future, normally involving a free and independent sovereign state.*

Many nationalists were less concerned with nationalism as a universal principle than the advance of their own specific nation, which might involve the rejection of other nationalist claims. Indeed, for Breuilly (1993, p. 2), a basic assertion

of nationalism is that the interests and values of the nation take priority over all other interests and loyalties, although some forms of nationalism seem more prepared to accommodate multiple identities and allegiances.

What precisely is a nation? There are no easy definitions or clear criteria. Language, ethnicity, religion, culture and history may all contribute to a sense of nationhood, but ultimately a nation exists in the minds of its members; it is an 'imagined community' (Anderson, 1991), although it is also clear that a sense of national identity can evolve and change over time.

Nationalism was associated with liberalism in the early nineteenth century, and more closely linked with conservatism and the right subsequently. Over the past century, it has sometimes been associated with racism and fascism (see Spotlight 15.1), defining membership of the nation in racist terms or glorifying the nation. Alternatively, anticolonial nationalism was often socialist and sometimes explicitly Marxist, arguing for the liberation of a nation from colonial oppression. Thus nationalism is something of a chameleon ideology, taking colour from the political context in which it develops. In Britain, nationalist ideas were absorbed into the mainstream parties, particularly the Conservatives, and at one time seemed to reinforce the British political system and culture.

The impact of nationalism on British politics has changed significantly over the past forty years or so. From the late 1960s, support for separatist nationalism in Northern Ireland, Scotland and Wales posed an increasing threat to the survival of the British state. From 2007, nationalist parties shared power in Northern Ireland, Scottish nationalists ran the government in Edinburgh, and Welsh nationalists briefly joined a coalition with Labour in the Welsh Assembly (Sandry, 2011). In Scotland, where the Scottish nationalists dominate politics, a referendum on independence was held and narrowly defeated in 2014. The nationalism of the SNP is combined to a centrist, or centre-left form of social democracy, rather than to the right. (For more on the SNP, see Chapter 11.) Thus separatist nationalism has appeared stronger than ever in the non-English territories of the United Kingdom. At the same time, there has been a resurgence of

English nationalism, which leads to questions about the exact role of England in the United Kingdom (Kenny, 2014). With strong support for nationalism in Scotland and parts of Northern Ireland, nationalism could be the ideology that pulls the United Kingdom apart.

Populism, an ideology that has both left- and right-wing variants and derives from a view of 'the people', has burst onto the scene in Europe and the USA in recent years (see Comparing British Politics 15.1), threatening old ideological certainties.

## SPOTLIGHT ON ...

### Fascism and the far right in British politics     15.1

Before the Second World War, Oswald Mosley's British Union of Fascists was subsidised by Mussolini and Hitler and attracted some initial media support, notably from the *Daily Mail*. Fascism, it was claimed, offered a middle way between capitalism and communism, but its main appeal was to xenophobia and anti-Semitism. After the war, Mosley attempted a political comeback, exploiting concerns over 'coloured' immigration rather than anti-Semitism. However, fascism has never had much appeal for most British voters, partly because it is associated with Britain's wartime enemies. Insofar as extreme right-wing parties have achieved significant support in parts of Britain from time to time, this has been because of their racism rather than their connection to the politics of Germany and Italy during the Second World War.

Quasi-fascist and racist parties like the National Front (support for which peaked in the 1970s) and the British National Party (which won a seat in the London Assembly in 2008 and two seats in the European Parliament in 2009 before electorally collapsing) also attracted publicity and support (Goodwin, 2014).

More recently, members of the 'counter-jihadist' English Defence League (a pressure group rather than a party, which organises marches and demonstrations) often express racist views against Muslims (Goodwin, 2013). Although advances in by-elections, local elections and European Parliament elections have sometimes raised alarm, none of these extreme right-wing groups have come remotely close to winning a seat at Westminster.

## COMPARING BRITISH POLITICS 15.1

### The rise of right-wing populism in Europe

Much of the rhetoric of right-wing parties in Britain is populist – it is highly sceptical of the political 'establishment'. This is in line with the rise of similar right-wing populism elsewhere in Europe. These parties raise difficult questions of definition and classification.

Some populist parties, like Austria's Freedom Party and the National Front (FN) in France, have ditched some of their more obviously extremist positions and project a more professional image (Akkerman et al., 2016). The leader of the FN, Marine Le Pen, came second in the French presidential election in 2017, gaining considerable support from a largely white section of the French working class, and pledging strict immigration controls, attacking 'radical Islam' and invoking French nationalism. In Britain, UKIP (discussed in Chapter 14) comes closest to these groups. All these parties are xenophobic and nationalist, and reject European integration. They might best be described as radical right-wing parties.

Other parties, like Jobbik in Hungary and Golden Dawn in Greece, are overtly racist and might be fairly described as neofascist or far right. All these parties are likely to have charismatic leaders, and are populist and anti-establishment in their appeal.

# MAINSTREAM AND OTHER IDEOLOGIES

Ideology is a pervasive part of party politics. Even those politicians who claim to be pragmatists, far removed from grand ideological theory, are often unconsciously informed by years of ideological debates that find their way into their assumptions about 'human nature', 'individual freedom' or 'human equality', for example. The political parties that dominate British politics owe something to the ideologies of conservatism, liberalism, socialism and nationalism. But these ideologies do not map clearly onto each party: conservative ideology onto the Conservative Party, liberalism to the Lib Dems and so on, although conservatism and liberalism are important to both those parties. In particular, the Conservatives and the Labour Party have also drawn on different strands of liberal ideology. Other ideologies, which do not neatly map onto party politics, are increasingly playing a part in British party political life, including feminism and green political thinking, as well as a variety of right-wing ideologies.

## SUMMARY

»   In Britain the mainstream ideologies of liberalism, conservatism and socialism have developed within a British context, and show distinctive features.

»   British liberalism is a broad ideology that has evolved over time, with some tension between older free-market liberalism and the more interventionist new liberalism of the late nineteenth and twentieth centuries. These ideas are still important for the Liberal Democrats, but have also influenced Conservatives and Labour.

»   British conservatism has generally sought to preserve the existing social and political order and resist radical change, emphasising tradition, authority and the interdependence of classes against the individual freedom and rational self-interest of liberalism. Yet, from Disraeli onwards, Conservatives have favoured limited social reform to benefit the less fortunate.

»   The New Right (which influenced Thatcherism) combined some traditional conservative themes (patriotism, leadership, law and order) with free-market liberalism (competition and privatisation). Thatcher's successors were unable to escape from her shadow.

»   David Cameron, and to some extent, Theresa May, distanced themselves from elements of the Conservative Party's 'Thatcherite' past. The extent to which this was merely a presentational, rather than substantial move, is debatable.

»   British socialism (or 'labourism') has been gradualist rather than revolutionary, influenced by progressive liberalism and moderate trade unionism, but with a tension between its more socialist and reformist (or social democratic) wings. From 1945 onwards, Labour was associated with the welfare state and a mixed economy.

»   New Labour under Blair and Brown formally abandoned its commitment to nationalisation, and embraced market competition, but also increased spending on public services and pursued constitutional reform.

»   The banking crisis and recession has forced Labour and the Conservatives in particular to re-examine their positions on state intervention and regulation, particularly with respect to management of the economy. There was a brief revival of Keynesian ideas. Yet the nationalisation of banks was seen as a temporary measure.

»   Outside the traditional mainstream, other political perspectives that prioritise different concerns beyond the role of the state and the market are attracting increasing interest and support, with continuing implications for British politics, government and policy.

»   Feminism has prioritised gender issues, while radical feminism in particular has extended the sphere of politics to encompass personal and family relations.

» Greens raise issues over the relationship between humankind and the environment that transcend old issues and conflicts within current human society, concerning generations yet unborn, other species and the very survival of the planet.

» Nationalists have reopened debates over the borders and nature of the state, whereas populists have defended 'the people' against a variety of perceived outside threats.

## QUESTIONS FOR DISCUSSION

» Is it possible to hold a view of politics without ideology?

» How did the new liberalism differ from older liberalism?

» What are the core values of traditional conservatism?

» How far was Thatcher more a nineteenth-century liberal than a traditional conservative?

» Did Cameron's progressive conservatism involve anything really different from Thatcherism?

» What is socialism? Has the British Labour Party ever been a socialist party?

» How might New Labour be distinguished from old Labour?

» Did the election of Jeremy Corbyn as Labour leader mark a return to Labour's socialist roots?

» Where do other ideologies, such as feminism, green thinking and nationalism, fit on the left–right ideological spectrum?

» Are the terms 'left' and 'right' still meaningful?

» How far has feminism or green thinking redefined what politics is about?

## FURTHER READING

McLellan (1995) has written a good brief introduction to the contentious concept of ideology. For a fuller analysis, see Seliger (1976) and Freeden (1996). Definitions of key terms and brief accounts of important thinkers can be found in specialist dictionaries of politics and political thought, such as Williams (1976), Miller (1991), Bottomore (1991) and Scruton (2007).

There are now many useful introductions to political ideologies in general, such as Heywood (2017). Leach (2015) relates ideologies specifically to British politics. More extensive interpretations of British political thinking can be found in Greenleaf (1983), Freeden (1996) and Barker (1997). The literature on specific ideologies is massive and just a small proportion of it can be found referenced in this chapter.

## USEFUL WEBSITES

The websites of political parties generally set out the ideas and core beliefs: the Conservatives: www.conservatives.com/manifesto; the Labour Party: www.labour.org.uk and the Lib Dems: www.libdems.org.uk.

Smaller parties, such as UKIP and the Women's Equality Party are also worth exploring: www.ukip.org; www.womensequality.org.uk.

*Further student resources to support learning are available at*
**www.macmillanihe.com/griffiths-brit-pol-3e**

# 16 PARTICIPATION

Toilet paper. A garlic peeler. Work on a bell tower. A 'duck island'. In 2009 *The Daily Telegraph's* revelation that all these items had featured in recent MP expenses claims caused widespread outrage. It was not just the size of the claims (some substantial) that made headlines but often their frivolity. Claims for duck islands and moat cleaning illustrated the gulf between the lifestyles of some MPs and their constituents, while others for more mundane items like dog food and toilet seats simply appeared petty. A more serious criticism was of the apparently widespread practice of MPs 'flipping' their main residence and second home to maximise their expenses and minimise their tax bills. The House of Commons' Speaker Michael Martin was effectively forced out after his perceived mishandling of the crisis.

These revelations led to numerous humiliating public apologies and repayments of wrongly claimed expenses by MPs. All parties suffered from the allegations, and many parliamentary careers were effectively ended as some members, voluntarily or under pressure, declined to stand for re-election. The most serious cases of false claims led to prison sentences. Few MPs came out well, although *The Telegraph* (n.d.) listed some fifty 'saints' whose claims were modest and reasonable.

The scandal seemed to crystallise a longer term sense of mistrust in politics and politicians and a drop in the desire to engage with the political process. A poll in 2016 showed that politicians were the least trusted professional group, scoring lower than estate agents and journalists – just 15% of people trusted them to tell the truth, compared to 93% for nurses (Ipsos MORI, 2016). There was pressure not just to reform the system of parliamentary expenses, but the House of Commons more generally. Politicians were increasingly seen as corrupt, 'in it for themselves' rather than the public, and disconnected from the lives of their constituents. Politics seemed to be in crisis.

Academic literature picked up on this feeling and analysed it. Recent titles appearing in book-shops include: *Why We Hate Politics; Don't Vote for the Bastards! It Just Encourages Them; Is Democracy a Lost Cause?* and *Can Democracy be Saved?* (Flinders, 2015 and reviewed in more detail in Ercan and Gagnon, 2014). A substantial number of people it seems are fed up with politics.

This chapter explores how we participate – or decide not to participate – in politics. We examine what could be summarised as a crisis in representative democracy. It also looks at the role that pressure groups perform in modern democracies. While elections and parties are crucial to the theory and practice of representative democracy, they do not necessarily involve much popular participation in day-to-day government and decision-making. Involvement in pressure groups is a more direct way in which political participation is now often carried out. This chapter analyses their role in the political system as well as examining the emergence of 'new social movements', which often operate outside, or at least at arm's length from, representative politics.

## THIS CHAPTER:

» Examines various kinds of political participation, including voting and party membership.

» Asks who participates in politics, and why this varies between groups.

» Discusses the rise of negative attitudes towards politics, often summed up in the term 'anti-politics', and examines some of the main explanations for that.

» Looks at other ways in which people do participate: through involvement with pressure groups and examines various types of pressure group, their targets and methods.

» Introduces other forms of activism, including involvement in 'new social movements' that challenge conventional politics.

## REPRESENTATIVE DEMOCRACY AND THE 'CRISIS OF PARTICIPATION'

The most basic form of **political participation** in a representative democracy is voting. The political system depends on the readiness of people to exercise their right to vote. Substantial non-voting reduces the legitimacy of any elected individual or authority. Low turnout, the proportion of the eligible population that actually vote, in elections has become a matter of concern in Britain. Turnout in general elections has declined since the 1950s when it averaged over 80%. In 1992, turnout was 77.7%, in 1997 it was 71.5% and in 2001 it was down to 59%. In general elections since then, it has staged something of a recovery, but it only reached 69% by 2017. Turnout is lower still in elections for the European Parliament and local elections (see Figure 16.1 overleaf).

---

**Political participation** *can be described as citizen involvement in politics through, for example, voting, or pressure group and party activity aimed at influencing government and public policy.*

---

### VOTING AND NON-VOTING

Britain is hardly alone in registering relatively low levels of electoral participation. Indeed, they appear to be a feature of most western democracies (Hague et al., 2016, Ch. 13). Recent US presidential elections have only involved around half of American citizens. Although it is sometimes argued that non-voting reflects contentment, the more general view is that low turnout is a serious cause of concern as it suggests disengagement. Whiteley et al. (2001, p. 222), reviewing the 59% turnout in the 2001 general election, observed: 'If this is not a crisis of democratic politics in Britain, then it is hard to know what would be.' For Bill Jones (2003, p. 24), large-scale abstentions indicate that 'worryingly large numbers of people have little faith in the political system'. Although the number of people voting in general elections has increased since the low in 2001, the proportion of people turning out for other elections remains low. Suggested remedies for low and declining electoral turnout depend to a degree on some very different perceptions of the causes of non-voting (see Table 16.1 on p. 333).

All the suggested causes of non-voting have a certain plausibility and most of these suggested

## Figure 16.1: Turnout for recent elections, %

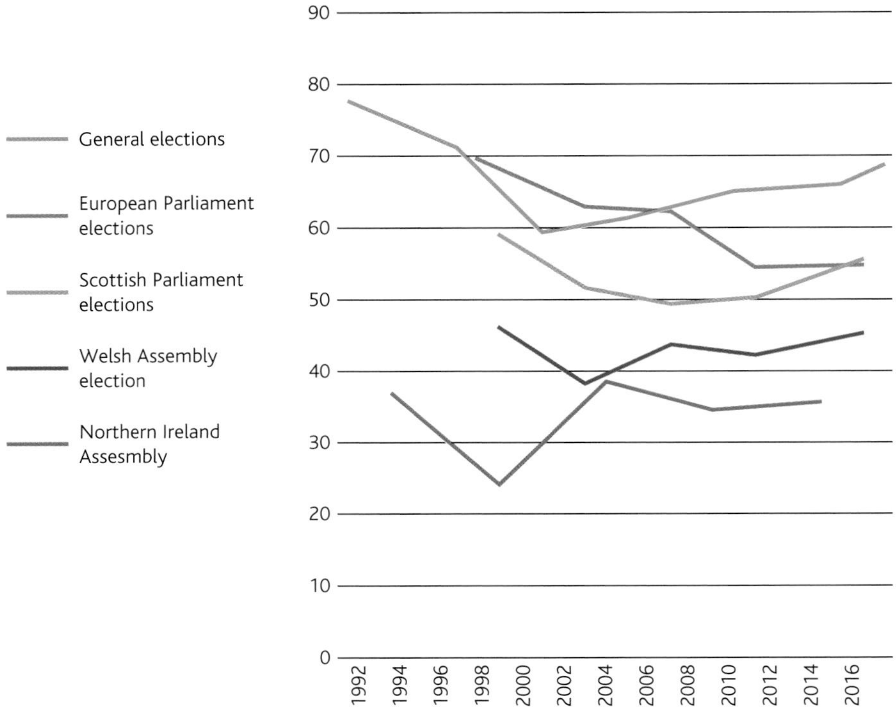

Note: Turnout for local elections is often considerably lower, but like-for-like comparisons are difficult, because of different areas holding elections. Turnout for other, specific votes varies considerably. For example, the turnout on local 'police and crime commissioner' in 2012 was just 15.1%. Turnout on the referendum on the alternative vote in 2011 was 42%. Turnout in the Scottish independence referendum in 2014 was 84.6%.

*Source*: Compiled using data from *Voter Engagement in the UK: Political and Constitutional Reform*, www.publications.parliament.uk/pa/cm201415/cmselect/cmpolcon/232/23202.htm. © Parliamentary copyright 2014. Contains Parliamentary information licensed under the Open Parliament Licence v3.0, www.parliament.uk/site-information/copyright/open-parliament-licence/

remedies have already been tried, many in Britain, and others elsewhere. Those who are better educated are more interested and more likely to vote, which makes political education important. There have been efforts to improve the level of political education in Britain with the introduction of citizenship classes in schools, and through the efforts of campaigning individuals and societies. But political education is also intrinsically controversial. Many are worried that it could involve political indoctrination. Yet if it is confined to the safer ground of the political system and process rather than more controversial political issues, it risks being boring. The impact of more political education can only be judged in the longer term, but to date the results are unimpressive.

Arguably, low knowledge of, and interest in, politics may be blamed more on the mass media than on any deficiency in political education. Certainly, there is evidence of reduced political coverage in the popular press and on the main TV news programmes. Much of the coverage is also superficial and, in the case of the press, nakedly partisan. There has also been a rise in 'fake news' giving an untrue picture of political events and an increasing tendency for voters to obtain their political education from their personal social media networks, which merely reinforces existing prejudices. Yet those involved in the media might reasonably claim only to be reacting to demand, or in this case the lack of it. (These issues are discussed in more detail in Chapter 17.)

### Table 16.1 Low electoral turnouts: possible causes and remedies

| The cause? | The cure? |
|---|---|
| Voter ignorance of politics and government in general, and local government and the EU in particular | More political education in schools and colleges. Improved media coverage of government and politics |
| Lack of confidence that voting changes anything, particularly for non-Westminster elections. Lack of a clear impact of voting on government | More powers for local and devolved government. Increase accountability of European institutions to the elected European Parliament |
| Potential voters deterred by limited effective choice in British elections and 'unfair' relationship between votes cast and the result in terms of seats won | Reform the electoral system to provide a more proportionate relationship between votes cast and election outcomes, and more effective choice |
| Citizens disillusioned by party politics, elections and the processes of representative democracy | More direct democracy. New forms of politics involving more direct action and involvement from local groups and communities |
| Voters put off by perceived lack of representativeness in the political system – the idea that the political class are all the same and/or unable to relate to the average voter | Avoid selecting 'professional politicians' in favour of candidates who have proved themselves outside politics. Use 'all women shortlists' to select candidates |
| Potential voters put off by 'low-tech', antiquated and inconvenient means of registering choice, by marking a ballot paper in a remote polling station | Penalties (e.g. fines) for non-voting. More convenient polling stations (e.g. in supermarkets). Reform voting methods by introducing more postal voting, telephone voting and internet voting |

Some non-voting might reflect not so much political ignorance as a (reasonably accurate?) belief that voting is unlikely to make much difference for anything other than Westminster elections. (Even here, the low turnout in 2001 especially could be blamed on the widespread assumption that the result was a foregone conclusion and that Labour would win comfortably over the Conservatives, as indeed they did.) Thus low turnout in local elections may be because local councils do not seem to have much power, and perhaps also in many cases because elections are unlikely to lead to a change in party control (see Chapter 10 for more on local elections). Voters may also perceive that the European Parliament lacks power. Although it has gained increased influence over legislation, the budget and even the composition of the European Commission, it does not effectively control the government of Europe (see Chapter 12, p. 254), which

might be why the British public turned against it when given the chance in 2016. Nationalists would argue that one reason for the lower turnout in elections for the Scottish Parliament and, particularly, the Welsh Assembly is that these bodies still do not have enough power. Indeed, the turnout for the vote on Scottish independence was high, at nearly 85% – arguably because the vote did matter so much to so many people (see Chapter 11). Whether turnout would be markedly higher in elections for local councils, devolved assemblies and the European Parliament if these bodies had more power seems debatable, however.

Voting might be encouraged by rewards and/or punishments. Some countries, like Belgium, fine non-voters. Unsurprisingly, this encourages very high turnout (over 90%), yet such a solution has not generally found favour. Compulsion involves some interference with freedom. Moreover, the constrained voter may vote arbitrarily or perversely. Alternatively, voters might be rewarded with a modest tax rebate. There may also be some merit in allowing positive abstention as an option in elections, for example allowing voters to put a cross next to 'none of the above' under the parties or candidates listed.

Electoral reform might do more to ensure that each vote counts, and thus increase the incentive to vote. At present, turnout is higher in marginal constituencies, and lower in those unlikely to change hands. So it is at least plausible that a more proportional electoral system would lead to a higher turnout. Yet more proportional electoral systems introduced for elections for the European Parliament, Scottish Parliament and Welsh Assembly have not produced high turnouts. It is even possible that these more complicated electoral systems have confused some electors and put them off. This is arguably reflected in the turnout for the referendum on electoral reform in 2011, in which only 42% of eligible people voted. (The AV referendum is discussed in more detail in Chapter 13.)

In Britain, more emphasis has been placed on modernising and simplifying voting procedures, particularly by facilitating postal voting. While a generation used to communicating through mobile phones and internet-driven tablet devices may find marking a ballot paper with a pencilled cross in a remote schoolroom requisitioned as a polling station both antiquated and inconvenient, there are continuing security concerns over alternatives. Among these, only the relatively 'old-tech' postal voting has led to significantly higher turnout levels, at the cost of increased allegations of electoral fraud, which the Electoral Commission and, in some cases, the police have investigated. There have also been experiments with rather more user-friendly polling stations, sited in supermarkets. Having elections on a Sunday or public holiday (as in other countries) instead of a Thursday, when elections are traditionally held, might encourage higher turnout in Britain.

## PARTY MEMBERSHIP

Voting is only the simplest and most basic form of political participation in a modern representative democracy. A rather higher level of political commitment than voting in the UK is registered by joining a political party. (Party membership is discussed in more detail in Chapter 14.) The modern political parties that developed and flourished in the twentieth century had substantial mass membership, and most voters strongly identified with specific parties. Both active party membership and strong party loyalty have declined markedly over the past half-century over most of the western world and in Britain in particular. Accurate membership figures are difficult to obtain, but the latest figures at the time of writing are set out in Table 16.2.

Altogether, only 1–2% of voters are party members, and fewer still are actively involved in party meetings, fundraising and canvassing. Party membership thus does not necessarily

### Table 16.2 Membership of main political parties in UK

| Party | Membership number | Date recorded |
|---|---|---|
| Labour | 517,000 | March 2017 |
| Conservative Party | 149,800 | December 2013 |
| Scottish National Party | Approx. 120,000 | July 2016 |
| Liberal Democrat Party | 82,000 | February 2017 |
| The Green Party (England and Wales) | 55,500 | July 2016 |
| UKIP | 39,000 | July 2016 |
| Plaid Cymru | 8,273 | July 2016 |

*Source*: Data from Keen and Audickas (2017)

indicate active participation in politics. Many members do no more than pay subscriptions by direct debit, and some join for the social facilities offered by Conservative or Labour clubs.

## PARTICIPATION: WHO DOES, WHO DOES NOT AND HOW?

Evidence from the Hansard Society (a UK charity working around the world to promote democracy and strengthen parliaments) shows that political activists (as defined in Figure 16.2) are found disproportionately among the higher social classes. Thus those in the A and B social groups (higher or intermediate managerial, administrative or professional) have a mean score of 5.23 for the number of activities they mention being willing to undertake if they felt strongly about an issue. This is significantly above the national average 3.39 mean score. Those in social group C1 (lower middle class) are marginally above the national average, with a mean score of 3.56, whereas C2s (skilled

## Figure 16.2: Political activities

Activities that people have done in the past 12 months vs would do if felt strongly enough about an issue in the future

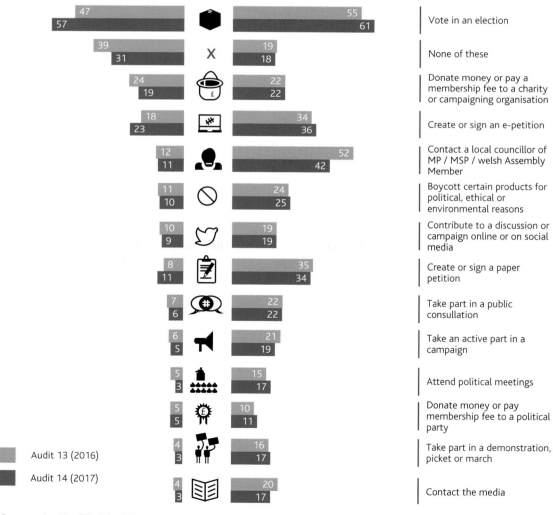

Source: Audit of Political Engagement 14, Figure 24, reproduced with permission of the Hansard Society, https://assets.contentful.com/xkbace0jm9pp/1vNBTsOEiYciKEAqWAmEKi/cgcc36b98f60328c0327e313ab37ae0c/Audit_of_political_Engagement_14__2017_.pdf

manual workers) and D and Es are below the average at 2.35 and 2.0 respectively (semi-skilled and unskilled manual workers) and Es (state pensioners or widows, casual or lowest grade employees and long-term unemployed) (see Chapter 4, pp. 59–62, for more on this class categorisation). White citizens are more politically active (with a mean score of 1.7) than those from non-white ethnic minorities (1.03). Gender differences in political participation, once significant, have largely disappeared. The propensity of women to be political participants is marginally higher than that for men (Hansard Society, 2017, p. 44).

Why do some people participate more in politics than others? Political activists may be more confident that their efforts may make a difference. The Hansard Society survey (2017, p. 47) found that just 32% of the public agreed that 'when people like me get involved in politics they really can change the way that the UK is run'. Those believing political participation is futile and ineffective may not even try to influence decisions that affect them. They are thus unlikely to have their interests taken into account, confirming the view that 'no one takes any notice of people like us'. They may be right, at least in part. Governments may be more responsive to some interests than others, while some sections of the population lack the resources and skills – in terms of connections, knowledge about politics, or a public platform – to allow them to participate effectively in the current system. There seems to be a fairly widespread dissatisfaction with popular influence on government and policy, and considerable mistrust of Parliament and politicians.

Research also indicates that young adults are less interested in politics, less knowledgeable about it and less likely to vote than older generations. This has aroused considerable concern over the alleged political apathy and alienation of young adults, and the prospects for democratic politics in Britain, although some argue that this is simply a life-cycle problem – young people will become more politically engaged as they grow older. Another possible explanation is that the young are 'turned off' by conventional party politics but are interested instead in a new politics agenda involving single-issue pressure groups and new social movements.

A survey of young people eligible to vote in elections for the first time found that they had a rather narrow view of politics, involving government, running the country, politicians and political parties. They considered the government unresponsive to the needs and wishes of young people, and had little confidence in their ability to influence parties or the government. Although the research indicated that young people 'had a general attachment to and confidence in the democratic process', they were sceptical about the outcome of elections, and showed 'a deep-seated scepticism towards the political parties and politicians who vie for their votes and political office' (Henn et al., 2005, p. 567). However, the young adults surveyed showed similar levels of interest in political issues to the population as a whole – public services, war, the economy, law and order. Henn et al. (2005, p. 569) concluded that:

> at the heart of young people's declining election turnout and their apparent disenchantment with Westminster politics is a strong sense of political alienation rather than political apathy – the political system in Britain is failing to provide the stimuli necessary for young people to take a greater role in political life.

Higher than average political participation may also be related to political values. Those holding strong or extreme political views tend to participate well above average, with overall participation in all fields of political activity highest on the extreme left. By contrast, the moderate centre tends to underparticipate. This may be because they are more satisfied with the way the country is run, and so less inclined to indulge in political activities to secure change. The Hansard Society survey (2017, p. 47) found that just three in ten people (31%) are satisfied with the way our system of governing works, with almost two-thirds (65%) saying that it needs improvement.

Political values associated with the 'new' or 'post-materialist' politics of environmentalism, peace and feminism are linked to higher than average participation, although this may be expressed through collective and direct action far more than through more conventional forms of participation. **Civil disobedience** and **direct action** strategies have been most evident in anti-poll tax demonstrations in the 1980s and early 1990s, and more recently in animal rights protests and campaigns against new roads, airport runways, nuclear and coal-fired power stations and similar environmental protests. While a majority only support orderly, peaceful methods of political protest, willingness to engage in forms of direct action such as site occupations, destruction of crops, refusals to pay taxes and blocking roads appears to have increased.

---

**Civil disobedience** *is a political act disobeying the authority of the government, on the grounds of a moral objections, in order to create a more 'just' society.*

---

**Direct action** *is a form of protest aimed at getting change, which bypasses conventional channels, such as Parliament or bureaucracy.*

---

## A CRISIS IN REPRESENTATIVE DEMOCRACY?

Despite a slight improvement in recent years, the numbers of people voting or joining a political party membership have not recovered to their postwar high, and are often seen as part of a wider dissatisfaction with politics. Much of this dissatisfaction is demonstrated each year in the Hansard Society's Audit of Political Engagement. The organisation's polling has consistently revealed public scepticism about the political system. Focus groups also reveal strong negative associations with the term 'politics', which participants often viewed as something they were not involved with and which was the preserve of an elite, acting in their own interests (Stoker, 2011, p. 152).

All this reflects negative perceptions of politics, politicians and traditional political institutions.

Yet, dissatisfaction with the political process is not new. In perhaps the first major study to look at attitudes to politics, carried out in 1959, 3 in 10 people reported never talking about politics with friends or acquaintances, while 8 in 10 were doubtful of the promises made by candidates in elections (reported in Stoker, 2011, p. 159). The claim that is sometimes made that things were once different ignores this evidence. However, the depth of disengagement with traditional political institutions and activities does seem to be different to the past.

## THE RISE OF ANTI-POLITICS?

One consequence of disengagement from traditional politics is that those politicians who have succeeded in recent years have often done so by presenting themselves as outsiders, who are critical of 'the ruling elite'. Nigel Farage (2014), the leader of UKIP in the run-up to the UK's decision to leave the EU, for example, would frequently criticise 'the Westminster bubble' of politicians and journalists that, he argued, dominated British politics. Donald Trump, in his successful presidential campaign in the USA, would similarly talk about how he would 'drain the swamp' in Washington of professional politicians, lobbyists and bureaucrats (*Time*, 2016). From a very different political position, Jeremy Corbyn's success as Labour leader can in part be put down to his status as an outsider. He is not part of the Westminster elite, and certainly not an 'identikit' professional politician. The language and presentation of all these men is purposefully designed to sound different to those they rejected as practised, professional politicians. This disengagement with the traditional ways of doing politics and political institutions is often summed up by the term **anti-politics**.

---

**Anti-politics** *is a strong, negative outlook towards politicians and a disengagement from the formal institutions and practice of politics.*

---

## Problems with the political system

One set of explanations for the rising dissatisfaction with formal politics places the blame at the door of politicians and political institutions (Stoker, 2011), for the following reasons:

1 *Citizens do not engage because they feel powerless to make a change*: Indeed, one vote is unlikely to make any difference (and for many citizens in safe seats, it is clear in advance which candidate will win in their constituency – as we discuss in Chapter 13). If one person's vote is unlikely to make any difference, why bother? The Power Report, *Power to the People* (2006), set out an argument along these lines and argued that electoral reform would at least ensure that votes were not wasted.

2 *The process of politics turns people off*: The confrontational rhetoric in the House of Commons, particularly at Prime Minister's Question Time, is often dismissed as 'Punch and Judy' politics, after the old puppet show, that is, based on point-scoring, personal attacks and jeering. This approach to discussion would be widely viewed as unprofessional in other workplaces, particularly when discussing issues of importance, and can alienate the watching public.

3 *The partisan divisions in modern politics, that is, those to do with political parties*: The main parties in Westminster emerged over a century ago to represent voters in a very different society to the one we live in today. This explanation would note that the divisions between the main political parties do not reflect the social, economic or other divides in our society. As such, it is no longer clear which political party represents us best as citizens.

4 *The performance of the political institutions we have*: The biggest problems the world faces today cannot be solved in Westminster or in the devolved administrations. Global warming, international terrorism, the power of global financial institutions and the spread of nuclear weapons cannot be controlled through the actions of any one national or subnational government. The problems we face today are bigger than the ability of our traditional political

*Source*: Oli Scarff/Getty Images

An expenses claim for a duck island came to symbolise the parliamentary expenses crisis of 2009 as well as wider unease with politics and politicians more broadly.

institutions to solve them and that turns voters off traditional politics.

5 *Some voters have questioned the proficiency of politicians*: For example, the people who become MPs, so the argument goes, are not up to the job, instead focusing on their own interests or feeding their own egos. The parliamentary expenses scandal back in 2009 provided one very obvious example of politicians who seemed to be 'in it for themselves'.

## The decline in social capital and political engagement

An alternative explanation for the decline in engagement with politics focuses instead on social changes, rather than the failure of politicians or political institutions. We are no longer connected to the political process. Robert Putnam (1995, 2000), in particular, has linked the decline of political participation with a reduction in 'social capital', a more general decline in social interaction and engagement in the modern western world. Basically, social capital reflects how much individuals interact with each other face to face as neighbours, members of clubs and other forms of association. High levels of such interaction encourage the development of civic attitudes, including voting in elections. The more individuals play passive, isolated roles in society, such as staying at home, watching TV and videos and surfing the internet, the more likely they are to withdraw from public activities such as voting, and from active involvement in political parties and pressure groups. Putnam supports his theory with a wealth of research in the USA, indicating a strong correlation between a decline in social capital and decline in active citizenship and political engagement.

Some critics suggest that Putnam has been too pessimistic and one-sided over the social changes he has described. Social capital theorists have tended to see innovation in communications as a threat to participatory democracy, through the reduction in face-to-face communication and social interaction. Yet it can be argued that they offer new forms of communication and opportunities for increased participation, through, for example, internet chat rooms (Margetts, 2002) and social media. Other critics suggest that Putnam's American findings do not necessarily apply to Britain. So Maloney (2006, pp. 114–15) cites evidence of increased political engagement and involvement in the voluntary sector in Britain and relatively high levels of social and political trust.

# Pressure Groups and Participation

It is sometimes argued that the decline in involvement in political parties has been balanced by a rise of participation in single-issue pressure groups. Pressure groups offer opportunities for ordinary people to participate in the political process on a continuous basis over specific issues that concern them. Pressure groups normally seek influence over, rather than direct control of, government. Indeed, the membership of some groups runs into millions, and far exceeds the membership of political parties. However, these figures are hardly reliable indicators of active participation in politics. Members of pressure groups can join for a host of reasons, beyond a desire for political participation – including a general interest, advice or some other benefit of membership. A more reliable indicator is perhaps provided by membership of campaigning groups such as Greenpeace, Friends of the Earth or Amnesty International (all between 100,000 and 200,000). However, even much of this support involves 'cheque book participation', with many members only prepared to make a donation to a cause with which they sympathise, but not to involve themselves further in active campaigning (Maloney, 2006).

## WHAT ARE PRESSURE GROUPS?

A simple definition of **pressure groups** will serve as an introduction, but some aspects remain problematic. Many pressure groups are highly organised, with formal constitutions, containing clearly stated aims and objectives, rules and procedures, including the election of officers and the management of resources. Yet some groups may begin with a much looser informal structure, while others may prefer to retain non-hierarchical organisations from ideological preference or practical considerations. Thus radical green or feminist groups may consciously reject formal structures with leadership roles for a flatter and more democratic means of operating, while groups on the fringe of the law (such as some animal rights groups) prefer informal and clandestine procedures. (The clandestine nature of these meetings is in part because several of these groups have been subject to controversial and at times illegal police infiltration and surveillance in recent years.)

---

A **pressure group** is any organised group that seeks to influence government and public policy at any level: they are not just a section of the public with an interest in common. Pressure groups seek influence rather than formal positions of political power (unlike political parties) and are outside rather than inside government.

---

While pressure groups (unlike parties) do not normally contest elections, they may seek to influence elections, for example advising voting against particular candidates, and occasionally may fight (and even win) elections in pursuit of a particular interest or cause. The Campaign for Nuclear Disarmament (CND) did sporadically put up candidates for elections, while more recently members have been elected to the Westminster Parliament and the Scottish Parliament on pressure group platforms. Moreover, some formally constituted political parties are essentially single-issue pressure groups – hence the debate over the future of UKIP after its main goal, Britain's withdrawal from the EU, was met in 2016.

Although pressure groups are formally outside government, some groups work so closely with government that they are part of the process of governance. Government, both at national and local level, may seek the active cooperation and partnership of business groups and voluntary organisations. Such groups may continue to put pressure on government, but as recipients of government contracts, grants and other benefits they are also clients of government. Decisions may emerge as a result of an ongoing debate within a network of public, private and voluntary organisations, all with an interest in a particular area of policy (see discussion of policy networks in Chapter 18). It may even be possible on occasion for a government department or agency to be effectively captured by the interests they are responsible for regulating. It is also worth noting that some parts of government seek to influence other parts of government, often using familiar pressure group tactics. Thus local councils and local government in general (through the local government association and appropriate professional bodies) often seek to influence the decisions of central government and the EU.

## TYPES OF PRESSURE GROUP

Pressure groups are so numerous and varied that many attempts have been made to distinguish between types of group, to bring some order into the analysis of a crowded field.

### 'Political' and 'non-political' groups

One distinction for political scientists is that between groups with a clear political purpose, such as Plane Stupid or the Taxpayers Alliance, and groups that exist primarily for social purposes and engage in politics rarely, if at all. However, even an allotment association or sports club, ostensibly non-political, may from time to time seek political influence, over ground rents or council grants for example, or more seriously over plans for roads or buildings that might threaten their survival. Charitable organisations, such as Oxfam or the RSPCA, may frequently engage in political lobbying – seeking to influence key political actors on an issue – as part of their primary purpose, although they have to be careful not to endanger their charitable status.

### Local, national or global groups

Another simple distinction might be made about the level at which groups operate. Some are purely local, seeking to influence decisions and services in the immediate community. Others are national, although they might have local or regional branches (e.g. the National Farmers' Union (NFU), the National Union of Students, the National Union of Teachers (NUT)). An increasing number of groups operate at the European level (e.g. European Automobile Manufacturers Association). Some of these groups act as **peak** or **umbrella groups**, which represent a large number of similar organisations. Finally, some groups are genuinely international in their membership and concerns (e.g. Amnesty International, Greenpeace), although such groups commonly have links with national organisations or national branch structures.

---

**Peak** *or* **umbrella groups** *involve formal associations of a large number of similar groups. In the UK, the most well known of these are the Trades Union Congress (TUC), to which nearly all British trade unions are affiliated, and the Confederation of British Industry (CBI), of which most (but not all) large and medium-sized firms are members.*

---

## Interest and cause groups

This approach classifies groups by what or who they represent. It distinguishes between interest groups, seeking to defend the interests of a particular section of the population (alternatively, these may be described as 'sectional' or 'defensive' groups); and cause (or promotional) groups. **Interest groups** include business firms, trade associations, professional bodies and trade unions and other groups involved with industry and employment. Examples include the CBI, the TUC, the British Medical Association (BMA), the Law Society and the NUT. Members of churches, sports bodies, residents' associations and groups representing particular minority communities may also be described as groups concerned primarily, although not exclusively, with defending their own interests.

**Cause groups**, by contrast, come into existence to promote some belief, attitude or principle. They are also referred to as promotional, attitude, ideological or preference groups. Examples are Greenpeace, the Child Poverty Action Group, the League Against Cruel Sports, Amnesty International, Liberty and Plane Stupid.

---

**Interest groups** *are concerned to defend or advance the interests of their members.*

---

**Cause groups** *are based on a shared attitude or values.*

---

There are two main differences between the two types of group. First, whereas membership of a sectional group is limited to those with a shared background, membership of a cause group is open to all those sharing the same values. Second, whereas the purpose of the sectional group is to protect the interests of its own members, the aim of the cause group is generally to advance other interests (the environment, children, animals, prisoners of conscience) or the public welfare as perceived by its members.

The distinction between interest and cause groups is not, however, always clear-cut. First, interest groups may pursue causes. The BMA, for example, not only looks after the professional interests of doctors but also campaigns on more general health issues such as drinking and smoking. Second, while in terms of their overall goals and motives many groups are clearly cause groups, such groups also often have material interests to defend. A charity such as Oxfam owns property and employs professional staff with careers to advance.

Many groups may combine a mixture of self-interest and more altruistic concerns. Thus groups opposed to specific developments (e.g. a new airport runway or a bypass) can involve both those promoting the broad cause of environmental conservation and others with a more self-interested objection to the proposed development's impact on their personal wellbeing and their property values. While some opponents reject almost all new roads or airports as part of a radical alternative transport strategy, others simply want the proposed development somewhere else – the NIMBY, 'not in my back yard', view. Moreover, as a matter of tactics, to win wider public support, particular sectional interests often claim they are acting in the wider public interest. University lecturers seeking to protect their pensions, for example, stress the benefits to higher education and the country. Foxhunters opposing a ban on their leisure pursuits broadened the debate to encompass the cause of rural protection (the Countryside Alliance). Despite these complications, the straightforward classification of groups into sectional and cause remains useful.

## Insider and outsider groups

An additional distinction between **insider** and **outsider groups** is also employed (Grant, 2000, p. 19). One important virtue of this typology is that it sets groups firmly within a relationship with government. It refers to the strategy pursued by a group – whether or not it seeks acceptance by government – and to the status achieved or not achieved as a result of its efforts. This distinction is also not clear-cut. While insider groups operate mainly behind the scenes, as we explore later in this chapter, rather than indulging in the politics of protest, in part because they do not want to put at risk their good relations with government and their influence in the 'corridors of power', they may on occasion campaign publicly. Indeed, some groups that are too powerful or important to ignore, such as the BMA and NFU regularly use behind the scenes influence and public campaigns.

---

**Insider groups** *are consulted on a regular basis by government.*

---

**Outsider groups** *either do not want to become closely involved with government or are unable to gain government recognition.*

---

However, other groups dependent on government funding or official recognition may become 'client' or 'prisoner' groups. Some outsider groups may lack the contacts and skills to become insiders, while others may be potential insiders, who seek to be consulted and may achieve this over time. Others may fear that a close relationship with government could jeopardise their independence and blunt their capacity for radical criticism and action. Radical groups committed to direct action, for example the Animal Liberation Front or Plane Stupid, may reasonably suspect their aims and methods will make them unacceptable to government in any case.

This classification cuts across the interest/cause distinction. Interest groups are perhaps rather more likely to be insiders than cause groups. However, some cause groups have managed

*Source*: Stefan Rousseau/PA Archive/PA Images
Some groups, such as Plane Stupid, have used direct action to further their cause.

to achieve insider status (e.g. MENCAP, which works with people with learning difficulties, and the Howard League for Penal Reform), while some interest groups (e.g. Fathers 4 Justice, which campaigned for fathers' rights to see their children after relationship breakdowns) have been conspicuously excluded from government consultation (understandably given the illegal nature of many of their protests). Status can also change over time. Trade unions were regularly consulted on employment issues, incomes policies and economic and social policy generally by both Labour and Conservative governments up until the election of a hostile Conservative government in 1979 when they lost much of their insider status. By contrast, many radical environmental groups, such as Greenpeace, began as outsiders. Questions of definition and perception as well as apparent changes over time illustrate some problems with the insider/outsider distinction as a basis for classifying groups.

## PRESSURE GROUP TARGETS AND METHODS

Whom do pressure groups seek to influence and what methods do they use? It is reasonable to consider these together as the methods adopted may clearly depend on potential targets. Moreover, in choosing their strategy, much depends on the aims and resources of particular groups and the level at which they are operating. Potential targets are many of those institutions discussed elsewhere in this book, including:

» the 'core executive' – government ministers (including the prime minister) and civil servants (Whitehall)

» Parliament (both houses)

» political parties

» informed opinion – more disrespectfully described as 'the chattering classes'

» wider public opinion – mainly through the mass media

» local institutions, including local government

» the European Union – while the UK remains a member.

## Influencing the government

Why do groups seek to influence the government and why is the government ready to listen? The answer to the first question is perhaps fairly obvious. Groups seek to defend and advance their own interest or cause, and government policy or specific government decisions may affect them, adversely or beneficially. Therefore they have a strong motive to seek to influence government, especially as power in the British political system is heavily concentrated within the core executive. Thus a change in taxation may significantly affect business profitability or the living standards of particular sections of the population. A change in the law may similarly affect business costs, employment opportunities or individual freedom. So pressure groups will generally seek to lobby the Westminster government or that of the relevant devolved parliament or assembly.

Government decisions on benefits, grants and subsidies and specific projects, such as hospitals, schools, roads and airports, may profoundly affect particular sections of society and specific communities. Those groups affected want information on the government's early thinking and draft proposals, because it is often easier to influence the government before it has gone public and committed itself. They want the chance to influence both the substance and detail of government policy, for if they cannot change the government's mind on the principle, they will want to ensure that the detailed implementation damages their interests as little as possible. Once a law is passed, a tax introduced or a planning decision announced, affected interests may continue to seek its amendment or repeal. Influence on the core executive is commonly the most direct and effective way to look after those interests, and groups may only seek to influence Parliament, political parties or public opinion when this direct route fails.

There can also be risks involved in becoming too close to government. Groups may fear to criticise government for fear of losing their valued insider status. In so doing they may risk upsetting some of their own members, who may feel their interests and views are being ignored or unrepresented.

At first sight, it is perhaps less easy to see what the government gains from contacts with pressure groups, although this is at least as important. Government needs, first, information and specialist knowledge and advice, which is not generally available in Whitehall. Second, government will want some idea of the potential reaction to specific initiatives from those likely to be affected. Prior consultation may avoid potential trouble later. Third, if possible, government wants support from relevant interests. If a minister can claim that those with an interest in a particular policy or initiative have been fully consulted and support the proposals, this will help win the argument in Parliament, the media and the country. Finally, on many issues the government needs the active cooperation of outside bodies, if it is to be successful.

Much effective influence may not involve high-profile meetings with ministers, but routine behind the scenes discussions with officials. Many group representatives sit with civil servants on the large number of committees advising government. Many group spokespersons will have frequent formal and informal contacts with their 'opposite numbers' in Whitehall.

## Influencing Parliament

Attempts by pressure groups to influence Parliament often secure more media publicity than attempts to influence the executive (because much of this is behind the scenes). Thus TV news frequently broadcasts pictures of particular groups lobbying Parliament, and occasionally more dramatic interventions; for example, when Fathers 4 Justice campaigners threw a condom filled with purple dye into the Commons chamber in 2004. Although Parliament has long been seen by most established groups as a less effective target for influence than the executive, there seems to be a growing use of parliamentary channels. Reasons for this include the increase in backbench independence and the growth in size and number of backbench revolts, the increasing importance of departmental select

committees that provide another channel for influence, and the growth of Westminster-based professional consultancies, often employing MPs or their researchers. The semi-reformed House of Lords has also become an increased target of pressure group influence, particularly as it has demonstrated more readiness to amend and delay government legislation.

Groups may seek to influence Parliament by submitting petitions, lobbying Parliament and individual MPs, circulating all MPs and peers with letters and information packs, and using friendly MPs to ask questions, raise issues, and introduce amendments to legislation, or sometimes even a bill (through Private Members' legislation). Much of this activity is open and legitimate, although sometimes it has involved more questionable inducements, which have led to scandals and increased scrutiny, particularly from the Committee on Standards and Privileges. Indeed, former cabinet members Sir Malcolm Rifkind (a Conservative) and Jack Straw (Labour) were both secretly filmed seeming to offer access to key contacts in exchange for cash in 2015. Both denied wrongdoing, saying that they were working within the rules Parliament sets down for lobbyists.

Groups may seek to influence the legislative process at every stage. As nearly all the legislation passed by Parliament is government bills, much of this influence is targeted at the executive, particularly in the formative pre-parliamentary stages when the need for new legislation is discussed and the government is consulting outside interests. However, while a bill is going through Parliament, groups will seek to target both government and Parliament, particularly with regard to the details of legislation, often at the committee stage using sympathetic MPs or peers to introduce amendments drafted for them. On controversial bills, groups will hope to influence the votes of MPs, particularly backbench MPs on the government side, who may be persuaded to defy the government whips. Even after a bill is passed and becomes an Act of Parliament, groups may often be involved in the crucial implementation of the Act, and in influencing delegated legislation (although much of this influence will be directed at the executive rather than Parliament). If a group remains dissatisfied with the law as it stands, it will campaign for new legislation, using the channels of influence, and the whole process may start again.

Groups may particularly target Parliament and individual MPs and peers on Private Members' legislation (bills introduced by MPs who are not members of the government). Although very few of these succeed, certain controversial political questions, particularly those involving moral issues, have often been left to Private Members' legislation, such as changes in the laws on homosexuality, divorce and abortion, partly because these cut across party lines. As such issues are normally left to a free vote of MPs, there is more scope for pressure group influence. Sometimes, outside groups draft whole bills and seek to persuade MPs who have won a place in the annual ballot for a chance to present Private Members' bills to introduce their measure (see Figure 16.3).

## Influencing political parties

Influencing Parliament and individual MPs inevitably involves influencing parties, as generally all MPs and most peers belong to parliamentary parties. But groups may seek to influence parties more directly and in a number of ways. The most obvious way is to make donations to political parties, as do both the trade unions (to Labour, which was set up as a party largely to provide trade union representation in parliament.) and business (mainly to the Conservatives).

Some cause groups, such as the anti-hunting and anti-abortion lobbies, try to influence parties' choice of parliamentary candidates. Others attempt to persuade parties to include detailed commitments in their manifestos. In return for influence, such groups campaign for the party supporting their cause. Sometimes, group and party membership overlaps, and

**Figure 16.3: Pressure group influence on Whitehall and Westminster: the main stages**

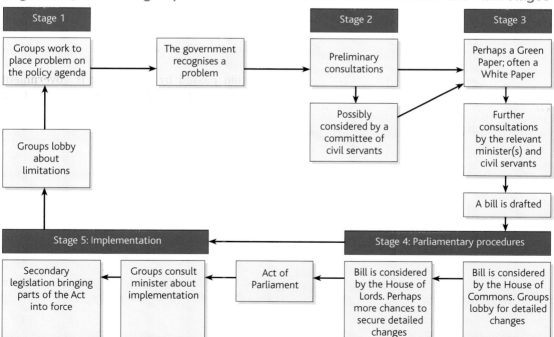

*Source:* Grant (1995) *Pressure Groups, Politics and Democracy in Britain,* Figure 3.1, p. 48, Macmillan Publishers Ltd. Reproduced with permission of Macmillan Publishers Ltd

this may help the groups achieve a favourable reception from parties.

Targeting a particular party may have drawbacks for a group, however. It may alienate opinion in other parties and is only likely to be successful if the targeted party is in power or has reasonable prospects of reaching power, and even then past commitments may not be honoured. However, Labour was more receptive to some interests when it was in power between 1997 and 2010, as they fitted with the party's overall outlook (e.g. trade unions, ramblers, groups opposed to blood sports) and it made sense for relevant groups to target the party to fulfil prior commitments on the minimum wage, access to the countryside and hunting legislation after 1997. Other organisations, such as the Countryside Alliance and the Taxpayers' Alliance, have found a more sympathetic audience from Conservatives.

## Influencing informed opinion

Because many public policy issues are relatively specialist and do not attract much interest from the mass media or the wider public, it may often be more important to target what might be called 'informed opinion' – sometimes more disrespectfully called 'the chattering classes'. This may be achieved, for example, through influencing important professional bodies, and through more specialist media, including minority TV channels and programmes, the 'quality' daily press, and weeklies, such as *The Economist*, *The Spectator* or *New Statesman*. Such bodies and media outlets may be far more influential than their membership or audience figures may suggest, as they are noticed by leading 'opinion-formers' in Parliament, journalism and elsewhere. This group may often prove decisive in the long run in swaying the decisions of ministers, civil servants and MPs, even sometimes where the popular media and wider public opinion is pushing in another direction. For example, while the mass media dramatised a possible link between the triple MMR (measles, mumps and rubella) inoculation programme and autism in the late 1990s, health professionals and informed opinion reached a clear consensus that there was no such link and the government held firm, despite an initial panic.

## Influencing wider public opinion

Much of the most visible pressure group activity involves influencing public opinion, to gain further support for their cause and to pressure key actors, although this can be time-consuming and expensive in resources, and may be less effective than other channels. Thus groups can seek to raise public awareness of an issue by various forms of protest and direct action (Jordan and Mahoney, 1997). These include legal and non-violent methods including public petitions, marches and demonstrations, such as those by the Stop the War Coalition against the invasion of Iraq in 2003, or consumer boycotts of goods, such as the long-running boycott of Nestlé products from the 1970s onwards for selling baby milk formula in the developing world, rather than advocating breastfeeding. But they can also include the disruptive but nonviolent tactics used by radical campaigning groups such as Greenpeace or Plane Stupid. More rarely, the use of violence and intimidation is employed; for example, supporters of the Animal Liberation Front have broken into laboratories, released animals, and targeted the persons and property of any individual remotely connected with experiments on animals.

Some experienced pressure group campaigners make only sparing use of public demonstrations, because they can be not only ineffective but even counterproductive, particularly if they get out of hand and alienate public opinion and decision-makers. Yet more disciplined peaceful mass demonstrations can have relatively little effect. Thus the CND annually organised massive four-day marches between the nuclear research establishment at Aldermaston and London from the late 1950s onwards without having any appreciable impact on government defence policy. More recently, what was estimated to be the largest public demonstration ever, that against the Iraq War in March 2003, did not succeed in its objective of stopping the war.

Rather more successful in influencing public opinion have been much smaller, more targeted demonstrations, such as those employed by Greenpeace. One of the most successful of these was the brief occupation by protestors of the Brent Spar oil rig in 1995, in protest against proposed plans to dump it at sea. The episode was filmed and shown on the main TV news. The publicity embarrassed the Shell oil company and the government to such an extent that the plans to dispose of the rig at sea were abandoned. The demonstration was successful in changing policy (Jordan, 2001).

This example illustrates the importance of the mass media (see Chapter 17) if a pressure group demonstration is to be effective in influencing public opinion. Without the free publicity given by the media, only those few people directly involved would have known about the occupation of the Brent Spar oil rig. Other protests have been taken up and extensively amplified by the tabloid press, particularly those by the Countryside Alliance from 1997 onwards, the fuel protests of September 2000, the anti-council tax protests of 2003–04, and chef Jamie Oliver's campaign to improve the nutritional value of school dinners in the 2000s, which illustrates the value of a prominent public celebrity to a cause in securing news coverage and the attention of politicians.

## Influencing local government and other local institutions

Many important decisions that affect people's lives are still made locally (see Chapter 10). Small local community groups with relatively few resources can sometimes be very effective in influencing these local decisions, such as the proposed closure of a school or hospital, or decisions on planning applications, or policy on roads and traffic regulation.

An organisation can spring up very quickly, and can often tap local expertise to mount a professional campaign. There are some clear targets for influence. The local MP may be a potentially useful and influential ally, even if the issue involves local institutions rather than central government. Individual councillors, local government officers and the council as a whole are obvious targets for issues that are a local authority responsibility, although sometimes a government department may also be contacted if a minister has the final say. Doctors, nurses and other health service professionals, together with affected patients, readily attract sympathetic coverage on any health service issue. Meetings and demonstrations can invariably attract free publicity from the local press and radio, and sometimes also regional TV if a story is deemed newsworthy.

## Influencing the EU

At the other extreme, many decisions that affect people in Britain are currently made by the EU (for more on Britain's exit from the EU, see Chapter 12). Although this seems to many Britons a remote body – part of the reason Britain voted to leave in 2016 – it is still highly susceptible to influence from organised groups. Business and farming interests, trade unions, professional associations such as the BMA and the Law Society, and environmental groups all lobby at EU level. Some British groups have offices in Brussels and lobby directly, and many others employ consultancy firms to lobby on their behalf. Commonly, British groups seek allies in other EU member states and work through Europe-wide umbrella groups such as BusinessEurope (formerly the Union of Industrial and Employers' Confederations of Europe), ETUC (European Trade Union Confederation), COPA (Committee of Professional Agricultural Organisations), BEUC (the European Consumer Organisation) and EEB (European Environmental Bureau). A potential disadvantage of such Europe-wide groups, however, is that they sometimes find it hard to agree on policy because of national differences. Pressure groups have long sought primarily to influence the European Commission, but as the powers of the European Parliament have increased, that too has become an important target. It is rarely possible for groups to have any direct influence on the Council of Ministers, so here they have to rely on their national government to protect their interests. However, they may be able to influence the Committee of Permanent Representatives, which serves the Council of Ministers and prepares papers on which Council decisions are made. Relatively few groups seem to make much use of the Economic and Social Committee in Brussels, which was an institution designed to reflect the interests of employers, employees and consumers.

Some British groups (such as the fishing industry) undoubtedly feel they have little or no influence over decisions made in Brussels that affect their livelihoods. Other groups, however, make use of EU directives and regulations to put pressure on their own government, and cite examples of practices in other EU member states to demand improved services and higher standards in Britain (see Chapter 12, pp. 257–58, for more on pressure groups and the EU). Britain's decision to leave the EU in 2016 will lead to a withdrawal from this area of lobbying, but EU regulations will remain important for British politics, not least because most of our foreign trade is done with EU countries.

## Pressure groups, power and democracy

The debate over the role of pressure groups in the political process is closely bound up with arguments over the distribution of power and the extent of democracy, both in Britain and in other modern western political systems. Pluralists argue that power is effectively dispersed in modern western democracies in large part through the activities of countless freely competing groups (see Chapter 1, pp. 9–13, for more on pluralism). They point to the apparent influence of pressure groups in numerous case studies of decision-making. They claim that pressure groups promoting one interest or cause (such as legalised abortion, a ban on blood sports or low taxes) stimulate the growth of rival groups to counter their arguments, as has happened in Britain. These rival groups, through their activities, promote democratic debate, help educate the public on the issues and lead to better informed decisions, which reflect the net sum of influence and the balance of public opinion. So pressure group activity is the very essence of a free democratic society. Indeed, some modern theories of democracy (notably those of Robert Dahl, see Key Figures 16.1) depend heavily on the role of pressure groups.

# KEY FIGURES 16.1
## Robert Dahl and pluralism

**Robert Dahl (1915–2014)** was a leading US political scientist, particularly associated with the study of power. He was a key figure in the community power debate between pluralists, who argued power was widely dispersed, and elitists, who claimed it was concentrated in the hands of the few. His 1961 book *Who Governs?* (a study of decision-making in New Haven, Connecticut) concluded that there was no single elite guiding decisions, but that power was dispersed through the influence of numerous groups on specific policy areas. His theory of democracy (he preferred the term 'polyarchy') rested heavily on the ability of ordinary people to influence government decisions through their participation in pressure group activity.

Elitists, by contrast, argue that power remains concentrated in the hands of the few. The contest between groups, they claim, remains profoundly unequal, in part because of massive differences in resources. (See Chapter 1, pp 9–13 for more on elitism.) Some have abundant finance, effective leadership and communication skills, but above all access to decision-makers, while others do not. Much of the most effective influence takes place behind the scenes rather than in the open. Government listens to some interests and ignores or rejects others. Within a capitalist system, business groups have much more influence than groups representing labour or consumers not only because of their greater resources and access to government, but also because their role is crucial if the economy is to be managed successfully. Some interests (the poor, the sick, the elderly) are more difficult to organise than others.

Although the numbers involved in some pressure groups are impressive, and far larger than those involved in parties, group policy is commonly determined by leaders and spokespersons. Some group leaders are elected by members, but most are not, and can be virtually self-appointed. Although some, like the once influential Mary Whitehouse, who, appalled by what she saw as immorality on TV and radio, formed the National Viewers' and Listeners' Association, claim to speak for the 'silent majority', while the majority remains silent there is no way of testing such claims. Moreover, much of the most effective influence is behind the scenes in the 'corridors of power' rather than in the open. Some of the most effective pressure groups are 'hidden persuaders' rather than contributors to a democratic public debate.

While some of the criticism of the role of pressure groups in modern politics has come from the left, because of marked inequalities in group resources and influence, some has come from the right, particularly the New Right (which is discussed in more detail in Chapter 15). New Right thinkers and politicians have argued that increases in public spending and taxation have been pushed by an alliance of unions of public sector workers and dependent client groups with a vested interest in higher spending, against the interests of the broad mass of voters and taxpayers. The excessive influence of these groups, it was argued, interfered with the operation of free-market forces, to the detriment of economic efficiency and prosperity. The Thatcher government, in particular, reacted against a particular form of economic decision-making involving 'peak organisations' representing employers and workers, known as 'tripartism' or 'corporatism' (see Chapter 2, p. 32). The election of the Thatcher government virtually ended corporatism. Lord Young, a leading member of her Cabinet, claimed: 'We have rejected the TUC; we have rejected the CBI. We do not see them coming back again. We gave up the Corporate State' (*Financial Times*, 9 November 1988).

Finally, it may be noted that pressure groups are viewed differently in other political cultures. While pressure groups are widely seen as integral to the process of democracy in the USA, they tend to be viewed rather differently in a country like France (see Comparing British Politics 16.1).

# 🇬🇧 COMPARING BRITISH POLITICS 16.1 🇺🇸 ▮ ▮

## Pressure groups in the USA and France

The academic study of pressure groups goes back a long way in the USA, at least as far back as the work of Bentley (1908). They have been viewed as not only a necessary but also a highly beneficial part of the political process, increasing competition and spreading influence. Under Robert Dahl, they have become the vital ingredient of a modern theory of democracy or 'polyarchy'. Among the national pressure groups considered particularly well supported and influential in the US political system are the National Rifle Association, the National Organization of Women, and the American Association for Retired Persons.

In France, the political culture seems less compatible with pressure group politics, perhaps reflecting a tradition of thought going back to Rousseau, who saw special interests as articulating a 'partial will' opposed to the 'general will' of the French people. Thus, the Fifth French Republic – 'one and indivisible' – is less responsive to special interests than the US political system with its elaborate checks and balances. Groups representing labour and business are smaller and weaker than elsewhere in northern Europe. Although some French workers are often involved in disruptive action, such as strikes, obstruction and boycotts, this may reflect their relative lack of influence in government circles. However, farmers remain an important exception to the relative lack of influence of special interests in French politics, partly because of the historical significance of agriculture in the French economy (and its society) and the power of the farmers' lobby (*The Economist*, 2005).

# ACTIVISM AND PARTICIPATION IN NEW SOCIAL MOVEMENTS

Pressure group membership has sometimes been seen as a limited form of political participation, distanced from involvement in the traditional practices and institutions of representative democracy, such as voting or party membership. To critics, it is a problematic alternative. Dismissively termed 'clicktivism', support for pressure groups is often characterised as a 'light-touch' alternative to traditional political activism – a click of a mouse to sign a petition on Facebook or highlight a donation signifying to others that you care about an issue, without ever taking the time to fully engage in or debate the issue. There are certainly concerns that pressure group participation, discussed above, does not involve the same depth of participation that other forms of political engagement might have. However, this is rarely said of participation in social movements.

The term 'social movement' has been employed to describe a much looser and less organised coalition of individuals or groups supporting a broad interest or cause. It is customary to define a pressure group as an organisation that aims to influence policy by seeking to persuade decision-makers by lobbying rather than by standing for election and holding office. By contrast, Paul Byrne (1997) described a social movement as something that is relatively disorganised. While a pressure group is a formal organisation with members, a social movement is an informal and loosely organised network, with supporters rather than members. Examples of what are termed **new social movements** are the women's movement, the peace movement, the green movement and the anti-capitalist movement (to be contrasted with older social movements such as the labour movement) (see Spotlight 16.1). (There is more discussion on these new social movements in Chapter 16.) All these include some specific organised groups, and many individuals who may be members of one or more such groups, but also others who may not belong to any organised group but still identify strongly with the interest or cause. Thus the women's movement is much more than a coalition of interest groups, but represents a broad swathe of interests and opinion in society that has already promoted significant social change.

---

**New social movements** *describe a diverse set of popular movements, characterised by a departure from conventional methods of organisation and expression. In recent decades, women's movements and green movements have been seen as examples.*

---

A loose informal movement may be preferred to a formal organisation for ideological reasons. Some feminists associate formal organisations, with their rules and hierarchies, with a male preference for order, authority and status, and seek more spontaneous and cooperative methods of working. Similarly, some peace campaigners or green activists positively reject leadership roles as part of a wider rejection of the existing social and political order based on traditional values.

Radical social movements favour alternative ways of organising politics and society and want changes that will fundamentally change the existing order. Rather than working through parliamentary parties, which accept and reinforce 'traditional' channels of influence (as pressure groups do), social movements instead advocate supporters to lead their own private lives in ways shaped by their alternative values and ideologies and encourage them to challenge the values of the governing elite, question its authority and replace conventional politics with the 'new' politics of direct action.

Social movements come from across the political spectrum. Recently, there has been a resurgence of populist far-right political movements, such as the English Defence League, ostensibly formed in 2009 to counter militant Islam, but whose provocative demonstrations have appeared indiscriminately Islamophobic and racist, and have commonly led to violent confrontations with anti-fascist groups.

Perhaps we are less fed up with politics than is frequently stated. We do, however, seem to have lost some faith in representative democracy, as the beginning of this chapter shows. The

## The anti-capitalist movement and Occupy    16.1

Anti-capitalist protests and direct action against multinational companies have grown. This new social movement has no established leaders, and no organisation (in the sense of having a headquarters staffed by office workers), but involves a loose international network linked by the internet. Naomi Klein described it as a 'global, anarchic and chaotic' body (quoted in Viner, 2000), but it has nevertheless become a significant political force. Much campaigning takes place against the 'iron triangle' of global capitalism: the World Trade Organization, the International Monetary Fund and the World Bank. Much additional grassroots campaigning takes place against multinational companies such as McDonald's, Coca-Cola, Nike, Texaco, Shell, Microsoft, Disney and Gap. The protesters' causes range from anti-consumerism and environmentalism to anti-slavery and the promotion of human rights. Some oppose junk food replacing locally produced 'real' food. Some oppose the use of 'sweatshop labour' by women and children in the third world to produce expensive designer label products in the West.

A recent example of this activity is 'Occupy' – a broad movement against social inequality and lack of 'real' democracy around the world. They have often used the slogan 'We are the 99%' to highlight the issue of inequality. Occupy has held protests around the world, and created encampments in various locations in the UK, most notably outside St Paul's Cathedral in London in 2011–12.

*Source*: CARL COURT/AFP/Getty Images

An Occupy camp outside St Paul's Cathedral in London, set up to protest against social inequality and injustice.

long-term fall in party membership and the decline in people voting give some evidence for this. However, the election of Jeremy Corbyn as Labour Party leader in 2015 went some way to challenging these assumptions. As Chapter 15 shows, Labour members joined the party in their thousands to get Corbyn elected leader. Despite a torrid two years for Corbyn, his relative success at the 2017 general election surprised commentators. Corbyn's Labour managed to attract new social movements, such as green protestors, feminists, disabled groups, peace activists, into campaigning for a traditional political party (Chadwick, 2017). Whether this coalition of supporters can hold together to push Corbyn closer to Downing Street remains to be seen, but one thing is clear: the claim that we are disengaging from politics looks a far less solid one than it might first appear.

 ## SUMMARY

» Democracy appears to require higher levels of political interest, knowledge and involvement than other political systems.

» Nevertheless, up to half of British adults have little knowledge of or interest in politics. A substantial minority do not vote, and the majority of the population do not participate in traditional, parliamentary politics beyond voting.

» This rejection of traditional means of political participation is often described as 'anti-politics'. For some theorists, the problem lies in the political system itself, which doesn't meet the needs of the citizens. For other theorists, declining political participation is part of a wider decline in 'social capital' in modern society.

» Some argue that a decline in traditional political engagement through voting, parties and representative institutions has been offset by a rise in new forms of political activity involving social movements, campaigning groups and more direct action.

» Pressure groups offer more scope for direct involvement in the political process than political parties.

» Pressure groups may operate at various levels. Distinctions are commonly made between interest (or sectional or defensive) groups and cause (or promotional) groups, and between insider and outsider groups.

» Insider groups may enjoy a mutually beneficial relationship with government, although there may be a risk that groups get too close to government and become effectively emasculated. Government departments or agencies may sometimes be effectively captured by their client groups.

» Groups may have a variety of targets, including ministers, civil servants, Parliament or the wider public. In the British political system, influence on the executive is generally seen as more effective than influence on the legislature, although some policy areas can be exceptions.

» For pluralists, pressure groups help promote democracy by dispersing power in society.

» A more recent phenomenon has been the growth of broad, loosely organised 'new social movements' often involving the politics of direct action. Although these have generally been associated with the left, under the Labour government there was some increased use of direct action by groups and movements on the right.

 ## QUESTIONS FOR DISCUSSION

» How far do low and declining turnout figures in elections suggest a crisis for democracy?

» Should voting be compulsory? How else might people be encouraged to vote? Does voting change anything?

» How else can individuals participate in politics beyond voting? How many do in fact participate significantly beyond voting?

» Are younger people less interested in politics, and if so, why, and how might this be remedied?

» Has there been a general decline in social interaction and engagement in modern Britain, and what are the implications for politics?

» How far is the distinction between interest groups and cause groups valid and useful?

» How far do most pressure groups have a choice in becoming an insider or outsider group? Are there any disadvantages to insider status?

» Why do most pressure groups prefer to target the executive rather than the legislature in the British political system? What exceptions are there to this general rule?

» What is a 'new social movement' and how might such a movement be distinguished from a pressure group?

» How far is power effectively dispersed and democracy assisted through the activities of pressure groups?

 ## FURTHER READING

On political participation, a key source is still Parry et al. (1992) *Political Participation and Democracy in Britain*. For a valuable survey of participation, citizenship and associated academic debates, see Margetts (2002) and Frazer (2002). For more specific analysis of political culture and voting participation, see Evans (2003). For a good discussion of anti-politics, see Stoker (2011).

Good texts on pressure groups in Britain are those by Grant (2000) *Pressure Groups and British Politics*, Byrne (1997) *Social Movements in Britain* and Coxall (2001) *Pressure Groups in British Politics*. Richardson (1993) *Pressure Groups* affords a useful comparative perspective, as does Chapter 13, 'Political Participation', in Hague et al. (2016).

 ## USEFUL WEBSITES

Print material should be supplemented by the British Social Attitudes surveys: www.natcen.ac.uk produced annually, and the annual reports on political engagement produced by the Hansard Society from 2004 onward, which can be consulted on their website: www.hansardsociety.org.uk.

More information on specific groups can be found from their websites: the British Medical Association: www.bma.org.uk; the Campaign for Nuclear Disarmament: www.cnduk.org; Greenpeace: www.greenpeace.org.uk, among many others.

 *Further student resources to support learning are available at*
**www.macmillanihe.com/griffiths-brit-pol-3e**

# 17          THE MEDIA

In the wake of Theresa May's unexpected failure to win an outright majority in the 2017 election, the Conservative-supporting *Sun* newspaper began to look for answers. One aspect, they argued, was the impact of 'fake news' on the election campaign. The popular newspaper complained that there were a large number of false statements about the Tories circulated on social media by Labour campaigners during the election run-up. One example they found used a poster that contained the official logos of Public Health England and the NHS. A question read: 'Have you bought your NHS insurance? From January 2018 the NHS will no longer be a free service' (Tolhurst, 2017). The false claims in the poster, *The Sun* argued, were designed to scare voters into thinking the Tories were planning to privatise the NHS.

The much-reported rise in these kinds of 'fake' news stories led Oxford Dictionaries to select 'post-truth' as its word of the year for 2016. 'Post-truth' is defined as a state of affairs when 'objective facts are less influential in shaping public opinion than appeals to emotion and personal belief'. It came to be associated with a particular noun: 'post-truth politics'. In the UK, the term began to be used to describe some of the claims made by both sides of the debate on the consequences of Britain leaving the EU and the general election of 2017. Fake news caused enough worry in the UK that the Commons Select Committee on Culture, Media and Sport began an investigation into the practice in 2017.

Fake news consists of false stories, often digitally manipulated to look like credible journalistic reports. They can be easily spread online to large audiences, particularly those whose opinions they confirm. They became a major feature of the debates around the US presidential election in 2016 and from there the term entered debate in the UK. One US story that gained widespread coverage was the rumour that Hillary Clinton and an aide were running a child sex ring out of a Washington pizza shop. The story was widely shared on social media. There was, of course, absolutely no credible evidence to support the claim.

It is the spread of social media that makes the dissemination of fake news so easy. Facebook, by far the world's largest social media platform, introduced tools after the 2012

US presidential election that allowed users to share news and stories, perhaps hoping to create a better informed public. However, some individuals soon found they could create content that was false, but sensationalist enough that it would be widely shared. This allowed creators to make money through the automated advertising that rewards high traffic to websites. The incentives were therefore to create content that would be shared with as many people as possible rather than content that was most accurate or informative. For readers, it can be difficult to know a fake news story from a real one, especially if the story itself confirms their wider worldview. In an ironic twist, after his election, President Trump flipped the term and began to use it to refer to the traditional media, particularly those newspapers and TV networks that had been hostile to his presidency.

Communication is inseparable from politics and a vital part of any political system in any age. However, the development of the mass media in the course of the twentieth century hugely enlarged the scope of political communication. Dictators like Hitler, Mussolini or Stalin, with almost exclusive control of the press, film and radio, as well as the education system, could shape how people thought about politics. Democratic leaders also realised that a supportive media could help them. Social media has changed the terms of the debate, as we saw above. It breaks the power of the traditional media, who, in many cases, prided themselves on journalistic integrity and truth. But it also gives groups who have previously had no say in society a voice and an outlet for expression.

## THIS CHAPTER:

» Examines the way in which the internet and social media are interacting with more traditional media in the UK, such as radio, television and newspapers.

» Reflects on the changing political media in Britain, including issues of technological change, political bias and ownership.

» Explores questions of the power, influence and bias of the media on British politics, and whether it needs further regulation to control its excess or if politics should stay out of the media in a free society.

## BRITISH POLITICS AND THE MEDIA

Most of what people think they know about government and politics comes through the mass media. Relatively few people participate much in politics (see Chapter 16, pp. 330–39). Government and politicians do not, most of the time, communicate directly with voters, but through the prism of the **mass media**. The mass media enables government and politicians to reach far more people, but the message is shaped and sometimes transformed in the process. Moreover, those who own and control the media may have their own political agenda.

---

*The **mass media** refers to all those forms of communication where large numbers of people are exposed to an identical message. The mass media does not just convey news and current affairs, but includes the press, film, radio and television, the internet and even the education system, according to some analysts. The mass media provides the ideas and images that help most people to understand the world they live in and their place in that world.*

---

## TRADITIONAL MEDIA, NEW MEDIA – AND NEW HYBRIDS

Political communication in the UK, and elsewhere, has undergone rapid change since the mid-2000s. The mass media includes newspapers, magazines, cinema, video, radio and television, the internet and social media. This growth implies greater choice for the individual as well as easier access to global mass communication. Newspapers and television are still the most important media through which the British public gets its information about politics. However, the internet has increasingly changed the way in which various groups – politicians, the public and journalists – produce and consume media, as we will see in this chapter (Chadwick and Stanyer, 2011, p. 215).

New media channels allow individuals access to a far wider range of information, including political information, but also provide scope for new ways of political involvement. Recent advances in media technology have increased opportunities for more specialist communication to niche audiences. The move from analogue to digital has reshaped TV, with many more channels made available. An expansion of subgenre themed interactive channels has replaced what was once a choice from only a few national or regional channels.

Even more important has been the massive expansion of access to the internet. This has already had important consequences for traditional media. Television faces a formidable rival in the production of up-to-date news and comment, and a rival not subject to the same controls (as we saw in the introduction to this chapter). The BBC is now as well known for its website as its TV and radio channels. The internet has further accelerated the decline in newspaper circulation. Although traditional newspapers are still printed, circulated, purchased and read, younger readers in particular have become used to getting most of their news online, and many may never acquire the habit of buying newspapers. The major national papers publish extensively online, and their websites are a major source of news, opinion and information. They also allow readers to engage with stories, by allowing comments 'below the line', after the article and on Facebook, Twitter and other social media platforms. For some analysts, the rise of social media has a profound effect on politics, creating a much more 'turbulent' politics, where the old certainties and methods of predicting what will happen next are out of date (Margetts et al., 2016).

Some optimistic political scientists have speculated that, driven by this technological change, the world of media conglomerates will be replaced by a 'marketplace of ideas', leading to a massive growth in decentralised, grassroots politics. In this new media world, some have argued, any individual with access to the web has the same potential political power as *The Sun*. Add to this the mobilising impact of the internet for bringing together individuals who share political values, then it is possible to argue that technological change in the media will result in a new, more democratic political order. Indeed, in non-democratic regimes, like Egypt and Iran, where mainstream news media supports autocratic elites, social media like Twitter and Facebook can help mobilise opposition by providing a medium to organising protest and resistance (Heffernan, 2016).

However, while the new media has the capacity to transform political communication and encourage different forms of political behaviour, it also provides a vehicle for trolling (anonymous online abuse), 'fake news' and propaganda. So far, the capacity of the internet to create a more democratic society where the powerless are given a voice has been exaggerated (Morozov, 2011).

What is certain is that political communication and the mass media have been revolutionised in the past 20 years. When Alan Rusbridger, *The Guardian* editor, retired in 2015, he reflected that: 'the essentials of newspaper life were the same in 1995, when I took over from Peter Preston, as they had been in 1821' (Rusbridger, 2015). Today, newspapers still tell stories in text and pictures, but they also use live blogs, streamed content, audio, data graphics, interactive content and live discussion. Deadlines are no longer once a day in time for the print run, but every minute. Online provision of news blurs the distinction between print and broadcast journalism

(Heffernan, 2016, pp. 183–4). More broadly, we are now in a new 'hybrid' environment, characterised by a complex intermingling of traditional and new media. News stories that begin on blogs or social media are reported by the traditional media, while the mainstream media informs comment on social media (Chadwick and Stanyer, 2011, p. 215).

## THE MEDIUM IS THE MESSAGE?

Marshall McLuhan (1964), celebrated media guru from the 1960s, coined the snappy formula: 'the medium is the message'. What he meant by this is that each medium of communication has its own distinctive characteristics that shape the message that is put across. There are some obvious differences between the media. Some are wholly or largely visual, for example posters or silent films, while radio is wholly aural – your mind has to supply the pictures. Some, like film and television, are visual and aural, although arguably the main message comes through the visual images rather than the soundtrack, and pictures have more impact than the spoken word.

It has been argued that radio manages serious political debate better than television. Yet radio abhors silence, even for a few seconds. Questions have to be answered instantly – there is no time for reflection or rephrasing. Ideas and complex arguments may be better expressed in print, where the writer has time to develop and refine their ideas, perhaps through a succession of drafts, and readers can digest matter at their own speed, rereading what they may not have grasped initially.

There are also major differences in the circumstances in which the audience receives communications. Although the term 'mass media' implies a mass audience, that mass is generally made up of countless individuals and small groups. A national newspaper may have a huge circulation but each copy is usually read by just one person at a time. Radio and television may have an audience of millions, but normally this is made up of individuals and families who receive the same message in separate households. Prime Minister Harold Macmillan observed of his own TV broadcasts: 'Someone once said to me "there will be twelve million people watching tonight". I just had the sense to say to myself, no, no, two people, at the most three. It is a conversation, not a speech' (cited in Goddard, 2001, p. 120). He grasped that television was essentially an intimate domestic medium. It was necessary to talk to people in a quiet relaxed fashion, as if he was a guest in the room, rather than speak at them as if he was addressing a mass meeting.

Television may be contrasted with films, viewed by large audiences in cinemas, at least before the video age. Hundreds and sometimes thousands in cinemas all over Germany would have viewed together Leni Riefenstahl's film of the Nazi Party rally at Nuremberg, *Triumph of the Will*, and been moved by collective emotion, as if they had been part of the crowds at the rally themselves, carried away by the experience. However, one could argue that Hitler's style of presentation would not have been successful in the TV age, as the gestures and rhetoric would seem even more over-the-top, comical and ridiculous on the small screen.

Each medium works differently. Politicians adept at one form of communication may never master another that requires a different approach. Looking and sounding good on television has become a crucial skill that ambitious politicians have to learn. The former Labour leader Michael Foot was a powerful platform and parliamentary orator, and an engaging writer, but he never mastered television. By contrast, the more relaxed conversational style of James Callaghan or John Major was well suited to 'the box'. Harold Wilson became a good TV performer after his advisers persuaded him to replace his emphatic hand gestures with a calming pipe that became his trademark. Margaret Thatcher's appearance, clothes and strident voice were initially off-putting, especially to those for whom a female prime minister was anathema until she sought advice, learned to soften her image and became an effective TV performer. Blair was a more natural communicator, adopting a conversational style. Cameron self-consciously adopted some of the rhetorical techniques that Blair had used, as well as embracing the internet through the release of 'WebCameron' videos online and, despite early scepticism, an active Twitter feed, to try and reach new audiences. May, as yet, has not defined a clear style.

## THE CHANGING POLITICAL MEDIA IN BRITAIN

### The decline of the print press

The traditional print media is struggling in the UK, with the financial model – selling hard copies of newspapers – rendered obsolete by the new media (and there are many freely circulated newspapers, such as the *Evening Standard* in London, which is funded by advertising). Between 2010 and 2015, there was a 31% drop in the daily circulation of print copies of newspapers and a 36% drop in Sunday newspaper circulation (Deacon and Wring, 2016, p. 303). This is mitigated by the growth in online readership for many newspapers. Here, however, the financial model is less obvious. Traditional newspapers are now experimenting with new financial models, giving most of their readers access to their content online. Most sites use advertising to compensate for the drop in sales of hard copies. *The Times* follows a 'paywall' model, with readers expected to subscribe to read content. *The Guardian* appeals to its readers' loyalty by asking for financial contributions towards its time-intensive investigative journalism.

Despite the decline in newspaper sales, the UK press still has considerable reach. Daily readership of hard copy newspapers (excluding the *Financial Times*) still averaged 16.7 million in April 2015. Press readership is also skewed towards older people, with 80% of readers over the age of 35 – the demographic most likely to vote in elections (Deacon and Wring, 2016, p. 305).

While over 1,000 newspaper titles are published in Britain, more than half being 'free papers' wholly dependent on advertising for revenue, the press remains dominated by nine national daily papers (plus linked Sunday papers). Scotland has its own dailies alongside the London press, but the few regional morning dailies elsewhere in Britain have a relatively small circulation. This is in marked contrast to some other countries, where the regional press is stronger than the national press.

The rack of papers seen outside any newsagents symbolises the British class system. *The Times*, *The Daily Telegraph*, *The Guardian* and the *Financial Times* are read overwhelmingly by the higher socioeconomic groups. These papers used to be known as the 'broadsheets' from the size of paper used, although this term is no longer applicable, as *The Times* and *Guardian* are now available in tabloid size. Two papers, the *Daily Mail* and the *Daily Express*, compete in the midmarket area for middle-class readers, while the mass circulation papers, *The Sun*, *Daily Mirror* and *Daily Star*, have predominantly working-class readers. The resizing of former broadsheet newspapers has meant that the term 'populars' is now more often used than 'tabloids' for these newspapers. There is relatively little crossover in readership between these different titles (Sparks, 1999, pp. 47–50), and thus little effective competition.

Treatment of the news varies enormously between papers. The so-called 'quality' papers (*The Times*, *The Telegraph*, *Financial Times* and *The Guardian*) contain much more of what might be described as 'hard news', in addition to comment and editorial. The mass circulation papers contain more 'soft news' and features that have interest but not immediate newsworthiness. Much space is taken up with photographs and large-print headlines. Where the quality press covers international events and city news, the mass circulation papers rarely fail to devote considerable space to 'scandal' of one sort or another, often involving celebrities. The quality press survive on a much smaller circulation than the populars (see Table 17.1) because their readers come predominantly from the higher social classes and enjoy more income and spending power, which is significant for advertising revenue.

Other publications are also worth mentioning, for they have influence on elite thinking beyond their circulation figures. These include weeklies, like the Conservative-leaning *Spectator* magazine, once edited by Boris Johnson, who later became mayor of London and foreign secretary. The magazine takes a generally pro-American and Eurosceptic position. *The New Statesman*, set up by influential socialists Beatrice and Sidney Webb

**Table 17.1 Major daily newspaper circulation, ownership and party support**

| | Editor, 2017 | Media owner | Party support, 2017 | Total, overall, Jan 2016 |
|---|---|---|---|---|
| *The Sun* | Tony Gallagher | News UK | Conservative | 1,787,096 |
| *Daily Mail* | Paul Dacre | Associated Newspapers Ltd | Conservative | 1,589,471 |
| *Daily Mirror* | Lloyd Embley | Trinity Mirror plc | Labour | 809,147 |
| *Daily Telegraph* | Chris Evans | Telegraph Media Group Ltd | Conservative | 472,033 |
| *Daily Star* | Dawn Neesom | Express Newspapers | Largely non-political | 470,369 |
| *Daily Express* | Hugh Whittow | Express Newspapers | Conservative | 408,700 |
| *The Times* | John Witherow | News UK | Conservative | 404,155 |
| *i* | Oliver Duff | Independent Print Ltd | None | 271,859 |
| *Financial Times* | Lionel Barber | Financial Times Ltd | Conservative | 198,237 |
| *Daily Record* | Murray Foote | Scottish Daily Record & Sunday Mail Limited | Labour | 176,892 |
| *The Guardian* | Katharine Viner | Guardian News and Media | Labour | 164,163 |

*Source*: Adapted from abc.org.uk, July 2017

in the first half of the twentieth century, has long had an influence on Labour thinking. The satirical magazine *Private Eye*, edited by Ian Hislop, is read by many journalists and parliamentarians, partly for its insider gossip. The liberal *Economist* also has considerable influence, much greater sales figures, and international appeal.

## TV and radio in a digital age

Radio and television began in Britain as state-sponsored services financed by a licence fee paid by listeners and viewers, controlled by the BBC, an arm's-length public corporation. The BBC's constitution is set out in a Royal Charter, while an accompanying agreement between the BBC and the secretary of state recognises the BBC's editorial independence and sets out its public obligations in detail. The first Charter Review was in 1927, with subsequent reviews approximately every ten years. For the first time in 2017, the BBC was regulated by Ofcom, an external, independent regulator, to ensure it meets its public obligations. How Ofcom

interprets its role could limit the freedom of the BBC in a way it has not previously had to contend with.

The BBC monopoly was broken in the 1950s with the inauguration of commercial television and radio, with programmes financed by advertising revenue, although the statutory obligation on the Independent Broadcasting Authority (from 1990 replaced by the Independent Television Commission, and later by Ofcom) of balanced political coverage remained. So the BBC monopoly was replaced by a BBC/ITV duopoly. This was only marginally affected by the slow emergence of new TV channels, BBC2, Channel 4 and finally Channel 5, before the arrival of satellite, cable and digital television considerably expanded the range of choice open to viewers. In the context of this explosion of options, the continued survival of the BBC as a public service broadcaster with a global reputation is remarkable. In most other countries, public service broadcasting has shrivelled in the face of competition (Curran and Seaton,

2003, p. 231). (Britain's experience of a state-regulated national broadcaster is very different to that of many nations.)

The TV audience is now far more segmented than it was. The same can be said of radio audiences. While the number of people listening to the radio each week has not changed significantly in recent years, more stations are listened to than before, with younger people in particular more likely to listen to commercial stations, rather than the BBC. At one time, a large part of the population viewed the same national events and news at the same time, often as a family, in front of the single radio and then TV set in the house. This helped to create what was substantially a shared national political culture. Today, many households have several devices that can access content – TVs, radios, laptops, tablets and phones – with individual household members viewing programmes geared to their tastes at a time of their choosing. Thus television and radio no longer bring the nation together, as they once did. It is also easier now to avoid material that individuals may prefer not to see. Viewers are more likely to watch what they want, when they want to, and are no longer forced to sit through political programmes, which they have little or no interest in, through lack of an alternative. So it is possible for those who are apathetic or antagonistic towards politics to avoid overt political communication almost entirely, because there is always something else to watch, even for those who rarely consider the drastic alternative of switching the set off.

## POWER WITHOUT RESPONSIBILITY?

Conservative leader Stanley Baldwin once famously observed that newspaper proprietors exercised 'power without responsibility, the prerogative of the harlot throughout the ages' – a phrase apparently suggested by his cousin, writer Rudyard Kipling (cited in Curran and Seaton, 2009, p. 37). Few would deny that the press and the media generally do have political power and influence, although there is considerable debate about its nature and extent.

In one interpretation, perhaps the media do not have as much power as might be imagined.

It has been persuasively argued that people do not just passively accept the political communication imparted by the media, but 'filter out' messages that do not match their own preconceived ideas, and only accept communications that reinforce those ideas. They do this through a process of selective exposure, selective perception and selective retention. People tend to read newspapers or watch programmes that support their own political viewpoints. They reinterpret the hostile material they do encounter to fit in with their own preconceptions. Moreover, they remember selectively, only recalling evidence and arguments that fit in with their own ideas and forgetting those that do not (Trenaman and McQuail, 1961; Blumler and McQuail, 1967; Denver et al., 2012). In an age of social media, this becomes even easier with arguments that fit with, rather than challenge, your worldview just a click or swipe away.

As Denver et al. (2012) point out, the key research supporting the filter model was carried out a long time ago, and largely focused on television and, more specifically, on party election broadcasts and their influence on voting. The bias in party election broadcasts is both transparent and generally unsubtle and, perhaps, consequently less influential. Outside the special case of party broadcasts, TV coverage is constrained by obligations to balance, particularly in election campaigns, and thus largely follows the parties' own agendas, rather than the independent judgement of TV programme producers and reporters. However, television may still influence political choice in some respects. Media that involve visual presentation, (e.g. television and photographs in print media) mean the physical appearance, clothes and body language of candidates and leaders may influence voters, consciously or unconsciously. In today's media era, politicians are expected to dress and present themselves in a particular way. This has a particularly strong 'gendered' element to it, with male and female politicians treated very differently. The first meeting between Scottish First Minister Nicola Sturgeon and British Prime Minister Theresa May, after the latter became prime minister, was greeted in *The Mail* with the headline 'Never mind Brexit, who won

Legs-it!' and a photo of the two leaders' legs, which led to much criticism of the paper (see Oppenheim, 2017). The need to 'look good' had also been particularly apparent in the party leaders' debates in 2010, when Gordon Brown, then prime minister, fared worse than David Cameron and Nick Clegg, his more telegenic, younger rivals.

Although most people trust television more than newspapers as a reliable source of news, the press may still be more politically influential, in part because it is uninhibited by any obligation towards balance. Moreover, it is not just editorials and comment columns that show bias, but the way in which news is selected and interpreted. Even those who turn straight to the sport pages can hardly help registering, if only subconsciously, headlines that carry a strong political message. While people may believe they are uninfluenced by papers showing a manifest bias, they also think they are not influenced by commercial adverts. If this were the case, companies could save money by scrapping their extensive advertising budgets. They advertise because their market research indicates it is effective, if sometimes subliminally. It is also difficult to believe that the 'drip, drip, drip' of political propaganda has no effect on readers over a period of years, rather than the three or four weeks of an official election campaign. As Denver et al. (2012, p. 174) point out, this influence is likely to be stronger still now that fewer people identify strongly with particular parties. They conclude that 'the conditions are ripe' for increased media influence on voters' opinions 'with the development of a more free-floating and easily mobilized electorate'.

Political scientists have put forward three broad models of the role and power of the media:

1  The *pluralist model* suggests that Britain has a free press, with other media not controlled by the government. The media presents a wide diversity of views, aiding public debate and the democratic process, enabling people to make up their own minds on important political issues. The media also has an important 'watchdog' role on behalf of the people, over government and powerful interests in society, and promotes more effective public accountability.

2  The *dominant values model* suggests that the media portrays news and events in such a way as to support the dominant values of political elites. As Marxists have argued, the ruling ideas in every age are the ideas of the ruling class. Ownership and control of the media are heavily concentrated, reflecting the concentration of wealth, income and power in society. The media reflects only a relatively narrow range of views, and minority perspectives are given little space or airtime. The media also 'scapegoats' minority social groups perceived as 'deviant' from prevailing norms – single mothers, social security scroungers, striking workers, asylum seekers.

3  The *market model* suggests that the media is driven largely by market or commercial considerations. Owners, editors, and producers seek to maximise profits by increasing circulation or audience share. Thus the media delivers what the public wants. The reduction of serious political content and overseas news in the press and mainstream news programmes reflects public taste and preference.

It is also plausible that the press helps to determine the political agenda, and influences public opinion on specific issues, such as attitudes towards the EU, crime, or asylum seekers. The press can show bias that television, which is far more tightly regulated, cannot. On particular issues, the press can distort, and publish scare stories and even plain untruths. Past examples include allegations that 'loony left' councils (a much-used derogatory term used by the press to describe left-wing Labour councils in the early 1980s) had banned black bin liners as racist, or that the EU was going to ban curved bananas. Such stories seem harmless nonsense, but perhaps it has an effect; the relentless hostility and mockery of most of the press towards the EU, for example, goes some way towards explaining the prevailing Euroscepticism in Britain. Come the referendum on Britain's membership of the EU, attempting to take an opposing line to much of the popular press proved a struggle for Cameron (Oliver, 2016; see also Chapter 12).

## POLITICAL BIAS, DEMOCRACY AND THE MEDIA

A free and diverse media expressing a range of political views is widely seen as a necessary condition for democracy. The media assists the workings of a democratic system by facilitating free speech and unrestricted public debate. In Britain, a variety of political opinions are aired in the media, and many of them are hostile to the government of the day. However, it is often argued that there is a political bias in the media that inevitably influences public opinion.

Much of the debate over media bias is around the issue of overt or covert party political bias. Here, there is a clear difference between the broadcast media and the press. Both commercial radio and television as well as the BBC are bound by charter and by law to show balance between parties and impartiality in reporting and treating the news. This is interpreted to mean balance between the major parties and opinions within the political mainstream. The only programmes exempted from this requirement to political impartiality are party political broadcasts and party election broadcasts (see Comparing British Politics 17.1).

## COMPARING BRITISH POLITICS 17.1

### Political advertising in Britain and the USA

A marked feature of US election campaigns is the volume of political advertising on US television. Candidates, parties and special interests can buy TV time to promote themselves, just like the advertising of commercial goods and services. Thirty-second or one-minute political commercials are a familiar feature of the US political scene. Candidates who run out of cash to finance advertising campaigns lose visibility. Well-funded groups, like the National Rifle Association or those with a vested interest in private medicine, are able to purchase substantial airtime to communicate their message in debates over gun control or healthcare. However, not all groups have the financial resources to enable them to put across their case.

In Britain, parties, candidates for elections and political groups are not allowed to buy advertising time on radio and television. British political parties are, however, allotted a number of party political broadcasts (and, during an election campaign, party election broadcasts), on a formula that takes into account the seats they contest and the votes they secure at elections. (Thus the far-right British National Party first qualified for a party election broadcast during the 2005 election campaign.) The broadcasting time and basic studio facilities are free, although parties may purchase the services of filmmakers, advertising agencies or public relations consultants to secure more professional promotion of their cause. A few party election broadcasts have made sufficient impact to become important news stories, with a measurable immediate effect on party support. Normally, they have little impact and are generally treated by viewers as a 'kettle opportunity' – to take a break from viewing to make coffee or tea. Some question their continuing value. They do, however, continue to provide an opportunity for relatively poorly financed parties (like the Lib Dems) to put their case to the public, helping to provide a more level playing field between competing parties. But it is now widely reckoned that the televised leader debates, introduced into British politics for the first time in 2010 and a feature of the 2015 and 2017 general elections, have further marginalised party election broadcasts.

Despite the obligation to maintain political balance, smaller parties and minority interests often feel broadcasters disregard their views. Moreover, the major parties may allege party bias in individual broadcasters or programmes. The left has long been critical of television's coverage of political news, particularly industrial disputes, where they detect an anti-union bias. By contrast, some on the political right have portrayed the BBC as a hotbed of radicalism, hostile to mainstream conservative values. Tensions between government and the BBC peaked in 2003, when a major and bitter conflict between Alastair Campbell, the Labour government's former director of communications, and the BBC arose over its coverage of the government's case for war with Iraq. This conflict resulted in the resignations of the BBC's chairman and director-general after the publication of the Hutton Report (2004) (see Spotlight 17.1).

## SPOTLIGHT ON ...

### Alastair Campbell, the BBC and the Hutton Report    17.1

In the events leading up to the invasion of Iraq, Alastair Campbell, then the government's director of communications and strategy, had a key role in the presentation of the government's case for war. A political storm broke after Andrew Gilligan, BBC journalist, alleged on the *Today* programme on 29 May 2003 that the government had embellished or 'sexed up' the case for war based on intelligence reports. Campbell demanded that the BBC apologised for the claim. Gavyn Davies, BBC chairman, and Greg Dyke, director-general, stood by their reporter. The row became a major crisis after David Kelly, the source of Gilligan's allegation, a scientific adviser to the Ministry of Defence and a former weapons inspector, committed suicide shortly after giving evidence to the Commons Foreign Affairs Committee. An official inquiry set up under Lord Hutton to investigate the circumstances surrounding Kelly's death exonerated the government, and criticised the BBC. Campbell declared: 'What the report shows very clearly is this: the Prime Minister told the truth, the government told the truth, I told the truth. The BBC, from the Chairman and Director General down, did not' (quoted in

Morris, 2004). Both Davies and Dyke resigned, a consequence that the government had not initially expected or desired. Ironically, the earlier appointment of both men had been criticised by the Conservative Party because of their known Labour connections. Events proved that the 45-minute claim was wrong, although the government continued to argue it was based on available intelligence. (Other inquiries into the Iraq War are discussed in Chapter 22.)

*Source*: Matthew Fearn/PA Archive/PA Images

The Hutton Report (2004) investigated the conflict between the government and the BBC, after the death of Dr David Kelly, UN weapons inspector.

By contrast, the press has no obligation to maintain impartiality, and indeed most British national newspapers make no secret of their own political sympathies and party preferences, freely selecting and interpreting the news in accordance with these. The political bias of newspapers often reflects the established preferences of its readers. Most *Daily Telegraph* readers are Conservative, while *Mirror* readers are predominantly Labour. In 2015, these figures stood at 72% and 62% respectively (Deacon and Wring, 2016, p. 331). Thus editorial policy arguably reflects market considerations. Any attempt to turn *The Daily Telegraph* into a staunch Labour paper would spell disaster for its circulation.

Yet most people do not buy papers for their politics, and may notice only subliminally, if at all, shifts in their political stance. So, although *The Sun* arose from the ashes of the old *Daily Herald*, which was a Labour paper when

Rupert Murdoch acquired it in 1974, he turned it into a highly partisan supporter of Margaret Thatcher's Conservatives, an allegiance initially maintained when Major succeeded Thatcher. By 1997, however, Murdoch had switched to support Blair and New Labour, and *The Sun* endorsed Labour again in 2001 and once more in 2005. But, *The Sun* became increasingly critical of the Labour government after Brown succeeded Blair, and it was no surprise when it dramatically announced it was abandoning its support for the party in the midst of the Labour conference in 2009. In the 2010 election campaign, its coverage was markedly pro-Conservative and critical of both Labour and the Lib Dems. *The Times* also switched to the Conservatives, as did the *Financial Times*, while the left-leaning *Guardian* endorsed the Lib Dems. By 2010, only the *Mirror* still backed Labour. The 2015 and 2017 elections saw *The Guardian* return to Labour. In general, the final years of New Labour saw a massive swing in the political coverage of the press, back to the anti-Labour bias of the pre-1997 period.

Ownership of the press is concentrated in the hands of a few major groups, often with an influential controlling proprietor, such as Rupert Murdoch today or Lord Beaverbrook in the early twentieth century (see Key Figures 17.1). Some of these have other extensive media interests. Thus Rupert Murdoch's News Corporation owns papers in many other western countries, and also has major interests in satellite and digital television, radio, cinema and books. The Mirror Group has extensive magazine interests, and controls many regional and local papers. Richard Desmond also has a major stake in magazines (including a number of 'soft porn' titles).

# KEY FIGURES 17.1
## Rupert Murdoch

*Source*: PA/PA Archive/PA Images

There are tensions about the role and power of media moguls in society. Here, Rupert Murdoch, the owner of News International, gives evidence to a House of Commons select committee over his organisation's involvement in phone hacking.

**Rupert Murdoch (1931–)** is an Australian-born media owner and billionaire. His father was also a journalist and newspaper executive. In the 1950s and 60s, Murdoch bought a number of newspapers in Australia and New Zealand. By the late 1960s he had expanded into the UK, taking over well-known titles, including the *News of the World*, *The Sun* and later *The Times*. In the mid-1980s, Murdoch consolidated his UK printing operations in Wapping and moved to new electronic publishing technology, causing a bitter dispute with printers and industrial action.

In 1981, Murdoch became a US citizen in order to satisfy the legal requirement for US TV network ownership. He continued to expand his empire, acquiring Twentieth Century Fox, HarperCollins and *The Wall Street Journal* in the 1980s, and extending his reach into South America and Asia in the 1990s.

Murdoch keeps a very close eye on the editorial stance of his publications, which in the UK – aside from a brief dalliance with New Labour – have strongly backed the Conservatives and been highly critical of the EU. Some Murdoch-owned newspapers were involved in the phone-hacking scandal, which forced the closure of the *News of the World*.

Does the concentration of media ownership matter? Editors have responsibility for the overall style and content of papers, but owners appoint (and can sack) editors, and this alone gives them substantial influence. Some owners, like Rupert Murdoch, have a more hands-on approach, and enjoy the power they wield that extends to the party political allegiance of their papers. Indeed, giving evidence to the Leveson Inquiry (discussed below), John Major, former prime minister, said that at a private meeting before the 1997 general election, Murdoch had warned Major to take a more sceptical policy position on the EU or his papers, including *The Sun*, would not support him. Major did not and several Murdoch-owned papers switched their support to Labour at the next general election (see Spotlight 17.2 overleaf).

So far, bias has been explored almost exclusively in terms of party bias. It has often been alleged, however, that the British media display other forms of political bias. Feminists have long complained that the media portrays women in a demeaning or degrading way, reinforcing and perpetuating their inferior status in society, sometimes even stimulating, through pornography, the degrading or violent treatment of women. Ethnic minority groups used to complain that they were invisible in the media, or shown in subordinate, stereotypical roles, although this is now less evident than before. People who are gay were shown, if at all, as comic figures. 'BBC English' once reflected southern middle-class accents, in a way that appeared to marginalise other parts of Britain and other social backgrounds.

More generally, the media, it has been argued, tends to reflect dominant interests in society, the views of the establishment, of business rather than the workers, of 'the haves' rather than 'the have nots' and of private enterprise and free-market capitalism. This is perhaps more particularly the case for newspapers and commercial television, substantially dependent on advertising revenue, and both directly and indirectly celebrating commercial values. Some have claimed that a globalised media reflects the interests of global capitalism.

One group has become particularly well known for its criticism of media ownership. The Glasgow Media Group is a group of researchers based at the University of Glasgow. Beginning with *Bad News* in 1976, a group of academics, including John Eldridge, David Miller and Greg Philo, have argued that TV news is consistently biased in favour of the most powerful in society and places the blame for society's problems at the door of the most vulnerable, despite all evidence to the contrary. In short, the Glasgow Media Group's various publications (e.g. 1976, 1980), make the argument that the media reinforces, protects and advances dominant class interests in society. As such, they draw on influential Marxist ideas about the dominance of ideas, discussed in Chapters 1 and 15.

The British media are thus far from neutral. News does not just happen, rather it is made. News items are selected and placed in order, in an implicit hierarchy of importance. Selection and ordering inevitably reflects bias of some kind. This may be a bias in favour of home rather than foreign news, of stories with 'human interest', and, for television, a bias in favour of visually interesting material. Some of this bias may substantially reflect what it is assumed readers, listeners and viewers want. Thus the sex life of a minor British celebrity, particularly if accompanied by revealing pictures, may command more media space and time than a humanitarian disaster in a remote continent, and this reflects and, in turn, influences people's values. The theoretical influence of the media is discussed in Spotlight 17.3 on p. 367.

## THE 'DUMBING DOWN' OF POLITICS?

Some suggest that the media, and particularly the press, influence more general attitudes towards politics and government in Britain. The media have been blamed both for 'dumbing down' political coverage, and encouraging a cynical negative attitude to parties, politicians and politics generally, with damaging consequences for political participation and the democratic process (Lloyd, 2004). This dumbing down is seen as one cause of the rise in scepticism about politics more generally and the rise of 'anti-politics', discussed in more detail in Chapter 16.

Today, there is more political information in the public domain than ever before, as a

## SPOTLIGHT ON ...
## Press influence on voting: 'It's The Sun wot won it'?    17.2

Perhaps the best-known claim that the media influences politics comes from Rupert Murdoch's *The Sun*. In 1992, opinion polls predicted victory for Labour and its leader, Neil Kinnock. *The Sun* campaigned ruthlessly against both Labour and particularly Kinnock himself. On the eve of the election, *The Sun* published a nine-page special fronted with the banner headline 'Nightmare on Kinnock Street' graphically predicting the horrors to come if Labour won. On polling day itself, *The Sun* announced to its readers that if Kinnock won, 'We'll meet you at the airport.' After the Conservatives won, and Kinnock resigned the Labour leadership, Murdoch's paper boasted 'It's The Sun wot won it' on 11 April 1992. Five years later *The Sun* transferred its allegiance to Tony Blair's Labour.

Was it really 'The Sun wot won it'? Do popular newspapers have significant influence on the voting habits of their readers? The change in party support by *The Sun* between 1992 and 1997 from strong Conservative support to lukewarm Labour support allowed political scientists to assess this claim, by comparing the voting habits of *Sun* readers to non-*Sun* readers. If *Sun* readers switched to Labour in significant numbers, but non-*Sun* readers did not, perhaps the *Sun*'s recommendation influenced that decision.

Paul Whiteley (2012) compared readers of *The Sun* and *Mirror* newspapers between 1992 and 1997, both of which had similar largely working-class readerships. Whereas *The Sun* switched its support, *The Mirror* remained pro-Labour. Whiteley found that one big change between the two elections was the number of *Sun* readers who did not vote in 1997. Whereas only about a fifth of *Sun* readers did not turn out in 1992, that increased to nearly a third by 1997. By contrast, the increase in non-voting among *Mirror* readers was very small. It seems that the *Sun*'s switch from the Conservatives to Labour did not persuade its readers to vote Labour, but it did discourage them from voting Conservative. Perhaps newspapers are better at mobilising readers to vote (or abstain) than they are at changing their voting habits (Whiteley, 2012, 107 ff.).

*The Sun* remained weakly pro-Labour in 2005, but switched its allegiance back to the Conservatives in 2010, 2015 and 2017. In 2015 and 2017, in particular, *The Sun* ran brutal campaigns against the Labour leadership. The *Independent* newspaper reported that Rupert Murdoch had visited staff at *The Sun* in the months before the 2015 election to instruct staff to get their 'act together' and prevent Ed Miliband becoming prime minister (Sherwin and Wright, 2015). In the months before the election, *The Sun* ran various stories about the perceived forces that would control Miliband as prime minister, including the trade unions and Scottish and Irish nationalists. It was speculated that Murdoch was seeking to undermine Miliband for his support for press regulation (see below). The eve of poll edition of *The Sun* was given over to an unflattering photograph of Miliband eating a sandwich from the year before (Deacon and Wring, 2016, p. 308). In 2017, *The Sun* urged readers not to 'chuck Britain in the Corbin' and described the Labour leader as a 'terrorists' friend', 'useless on Brexit', 'puppet of unions' and 'Marxist extremist' (*The Sun*, 2017). Despite the onslaught from the traditional media, Corbyn's Labour Party shocked many to wipe out the Conservative Party's majority, perhaps implying that the power of traditional media is on the wane and that social media is increasingly influential.

## SPOTLIGHT ON ...    Media influence: agenda-setting, priming and framing    17.3

Many people claim that the media is influential. But how does it influence us? Academics have put forward three interrelated but separate theories that help explain the influence of media on society: agenda-setting, priming and framing (Scheufele, 2000; Smith, 2013, pp. 142–4):

1   The media is influential because it is *agenda-setting*. It does not just tell us what to think about a particular issue, but also which issues to think about (McCombs and Shaw, 1972). Although the mass media is arguably not very successful in telling us what to think about a particular issue, it is very effective at persuading us which issues are newsworthy and which are not. The media's decision to focus on scandals, substance abuse, climate change, fuel costs, terrorism or the funding crisis in the public services, among thousands of other issues, sets the agenda for public debate.

2   The media is influential because it *primes* us to respond in a particular way to an issue, by providing the context for public discussion and understanding (Iyengar et al., 1982). The time and space that the media spends on a particular issue primes us of its importance. For example, the announcement of a general election was covered as the main story on the evening news and high levels of coverage of the campaign primed us that this was an important event, even if we were uninterested in politics.

3   The media is influential because it frames issues a particular way, influencing how we understand them (Goffman, [1974] 1986). Framing is part of how we 'socially construct' the world around us. Journalists, for example, provide their own rhetorical analysis of an issue, presenting it and interpreting it in a particular way – the metaphors they use and their choice of words help to frame the issue. Framing has been called an exercise in power (who tells the story first) and persuasion (manipulation of audiences). For example, during Tony Blair's premiership (1997–2007), it was common for journalists to frame news stories through an account of tensions between the prime minister and his chancellor, Gordon Brown. To journalists, these divisions were the story, not the policy announcement itself. In the run-up to the 2017 general election, it was common that any story about the Labour Party was framed through a discussion of the unpopularity of its leader Jeremy Corbyn. It was only when Corbyn did much better than journalists predicted in the election itself that they had to reframe the issues.

consequence of the proliferation of new media channels and the continuing pressures for more open government. Yet, while there is far more information out there for those who want to access it, paradoxically, the majority of the public are less exposed to politics than they were and, unsurprisingly, feel less well informed. For all the growth of new media channels and new sources of information, most people still learn about politics from newspapers and mainstream television. However, serious political coverage by the popular press has declined markedly in recent

decades, to be replaced by gossip, scandal and features. The private lives of politicians can attract a vicious media feeding frenzy, while their ideas and policies are relatively neglected, unless they upset the prejudices of journalists or readers. Even the so-called 'quality press' devotes far less space to some aspects of politics than previously, most notably parliamentary business. Full coverage of parliamentary proceedings, including summaries of speeches, has been replaced by short humorous reviews of (most commonly) Prime Minister's Questions. The main TV news programmes have also moved down market, devoting more time to celebrities, sport and idiosyncratic items. Most members of the public have scarcely ever heard a full-length political speech involving a developed argument, only **soundbites** – memorable sentences or phrases plucked out of context (Franklin, 2004).

---

**Soundbites** *are short, snappy, memorable phrases, frequently extracted from the broader context of a speech or document. Mainstream television rarely broadcasts whole speeches or even substantial extracts from speeches but brief 'soundbites'. Research suggests that soundbites are becoming shorter.*

---

Some consider that the mass media has steadily reduced the intellectual demands made on readers, listeners and viewers. Americans call this process 'dumbing down'. Serious political coverage is reduced to increase market share. Within ITV, for example, 'there are undoubtedly pressures to reduce and popularize news output' (Crisell, 1999, p. 69). The BBC is affected by similar pressures, despite its role as a non-commercial public service broadcaster, partly because if its market share declines significantly it becomes politically more difficult to justify finance through the licence fee. Of course, it can be argued that far more news is now available on a 24-hour basis on minority channels for those who want it. But the channels that most people watch have cut their serious news content, and it is much easier for the politically apathetic to avoid informing themselves about politics.

Others argue that the growth of cynical hostile interrogation of politicians and negative reporting has encouraged a general distrust of the political process and democracy (Lilleker et al., 2003; Lloyd, 2004). If interviewers assume that all politicians are crooks or liars, it is hardly surprising that viewers and listeners come to share the assumption. Politicians have hardly helped to improve their own image by the strategy they commonly adopt when confronted by sneering cross-examinations by 'rottweiler' interviewers, simply repeating their own prepared 'soundbites', almost regardless of the questions posed. Such confrontations may sometimes make good television but rarely contribute much to the sum total of public political knowledge.

## POLITICIANS AND THE MEDIA: THE USES AND ABUSES OF IMAGE AND SPIN

So far the emphasis in this chapter has been on the power and influence of the media on government and the political process. However, government and political leaders generally are far from being helpless victims of the mass media. As they inevitably make news by their pronouncements and decisions, they can seek to control the news, by the timing and manner of the release of information. They can seek to manage the media, to use whatever channels of communication are available to put their message across. When politicians cannot manage the media, they can now turn to social media.

Politicians and their advisers can also manage the presentation of their own image. Graham Wallas ([1908] 1920, p. 31), the pioneering British social scientist, grasped the value of photographs in projecting a favourable image of candidates for political office: 'Best of all is a photograph which brings his ordinary existence sharply forward by representing him in his garden smoking a pipe or reading a newspaper.' More recently, Nigel Farage, the former leader of UKIP, was rarely photographed without a pint of bitter in his hand, giving the carefully cultivated appearance of an 'everyday bloke'. The casual, seemingly spontaneous appearance would, in reality, be carefully posed, the background, clothes and props deliberately chosen, the body language conveyed by expression and posture considered. Later, the posed photograph was replaced by the televised 'photo opportunity', the context providing an appropriate political message – Tony Blair beginning an election campaign at a school to show the importance of education to Labour and David Cameron with huskies on a Norwegian glacier to show the Conservative's environmental credentials. All these photo opportunities were professionally stage-managed to create an impression of informal spontaneity. More recently, politicians and their advisers have learned how to project their own image more effectively through websites. The technology may change, and some of the skills, but the essential art of image projection is as old as politics.

Similarly, skilful leaders and politicians have always grasped the importance of putting a favourable gloss on events, of getting their version of the story accepted. This is essentially what **spin** is about. 'Spin doctors' are those skilled in presentation and interpretation. The use of the term in British politics is relatively new, but the activity is very old. Although 'spin' became particularly associated with New Labour, it was effectively practised in British politics long before. Indeed, one of the old Labour Party's problems was that they were not as good at political communication as their opponents. While the Conservatives hired the best advertising agencies available to put their message across, Labour was distrustful of advertisers and 'selling politics like cornflakes' (Tench and Yeomans, 2009, p. 90). Moreover, Labour had to contend with a generally hostile press, particularly in the 1980s and early 1990s. Labour's 'spin machine' grew from the bitter experiences of opposition. They learned the importance of good political communication, of party unity and 'staying on message' – agreeing the story and sticking to it. They also appreciated the need for better relations with the media, particularly the press. While many in the party loathed Rupert Murdoch and *The Sun* newspaper, Blair and his advisers actively sought to win and retain Murdoch's support, in the process converting a substantially anti-Labour press into a generally supportive press.

---

**Spin** *means putting a favourable gloss on events, or getting one's version of a story accepted.*

---

Moreover, spin is not confined to politicians, parties and their advisers. Radio, television and newspaper journalists are constantly putting their own interpretation, or spin, on news stories. Confronted with a complex mosaic of facts and unsubstantiated rumour, journalists try to reveal the 'real story'. Often the first in the field determines what the story is, unless a rival can provide a convincing new interpretation. Far from being some kind of New Labour invention, spin may be seen as a universal activity.

Ultimately, New Labour spin became counterproductive. The most successful and effective spinning is that which is so unobtrusive as not to be noticed; people are led to believe that they are given the plain unvarnished and incontrovertible truth, rather than a selective and partisan interpretation of events. The problem with Labour's spin doctors was that they became too high profile. Rather than anonymously and successfully purveying good stories, they themselves became the story and in the process damaged the product they were hired to promote (see Key Figures 17.2).

Political communication is important in any political system, but particularly crucial in those states claiming to be democratic. Democracy requires more than effective government communication, for it implies a two-way interactive communication between government and people. A government that does not listen is unlikely to remain long in power. However, western democracy also assumes a continuous competitive struggle for power and influence by individuals, interests and parties, in which those who manage to put across the most persuasive stories are more likely to prevail. The stakes can be high, helping to determine 'who gets what, when, how' in Lasswell's terse definition of politics (see Chapter 1, p. 6). Effective communication of the message of a politician, party or group may make the difference between winning and losing. In a complex world, there are inevitably many sides to difficult questions, not a single version of the truth. Effective communication generally requires selection, simplification and graphic illustration, which can easily lead to accusations of manipulation and spin. While the media can perform a watchdog role, they are also participants, with their own interests to defend and their own conflicting but strongly held interpretations of the public interest to advance. In such circumstances it is difficult for the public to know whom to believe. Routine accusations of deliberate deception on the part of government or the media undermine public

## KEY FIGURES 17.2
### The spin doctors

**Peter Mandelson (1953–)** has been credited with successfully rebranding the Labour Party as New Labour, and making it electable. A successful backroom operator, he had political ambitions of his own, becoming Labour candidate for Hartlepool, which he won in 1992. He played a key role in the emergence of Blair as leader in 1994, and in the revision of clause IV of Labour's Constitution, to abandon the party's commitment to nationalisation of industry. Curiously, he was much less effective in spinning himself than his party, and was twice obliged to resign Cabinet posts in controversial circumstances in 1998 and 2001. His return to the Cabinet as business secretary under Gordon Brown in 2008, after a period as a European commissioner, was a real surprise. However, selling Brown to the public proved beyond him.

**Andy Coulson (1968–)** became the director of communications and planning for the Conservative Party in 2007, after he had resigned from his post as editor of the *News of the World* after journalists at the paper were involved in phone-hacking the royal family, politicians and celebrities. Coulson denied any personal knowledge of phone-hacking when he appeared before a Commons select committee in July 2009. When *The Guardian* made fresh allegations about the extent of phone-hacking by *News of the World* journalists, Cameron was urged to sack Coulson. He refused, saying he believed in giving people a second chance. Ultimately, Coulson felt obliged to resign in January 2011. The spinner had become the story. Coulson was imprisoned for his role in the phone-hacking scandal in 2014.

trust, are corrosive of democracy and increase alienation from the whole political process (Lloyd, 2004).

## REGULATING THE PRESS: LEVESON AND AFTER

During the 2010–15 coalition, a press scandal exploded into a full-blown crisis in the British press, ending in calls for much tighter press regulation. The cause of the crisis went back to the early 2000s. Around that time, newspapers increasingly began to use private detectives to help with tasks that were not suited to conventional investigative journalists. Private investigators could trace car registrations or discover private telephone numbers, for example. A few offered to go beyond this and illegally provide transcripts of messages left on mobile phones. This was the beginning of the phone-hacking scandal.

An article in the Murdoch-owned *News of the World,* which revealed innocuous but little-known details of Prince William's medical history, led to a police investigation into royal phone-hacking and the jailing of Clive Goodman, the newspaper's royal editor, and Glen Mulcaire, a private detective, in 2007. Andy Coulson, the paper's editor, professed innocence, but stood down at the time the offending article was published. It soon became clear that this was not an isolated case, and a trickle of victims came forward with evidence that their messages had illegally found their way into the press. This included Gordon Taylor, head of the Professional Footballer's Association, and Max Clifford, the publicist, both of whom received substantial compensation. However, there was relatively little public concern at the time.

The scandal then moved closer to Westminster. In 2007, David Cameron, the leader of the opposition, was looking for an experienced spin doctor in the mould of Alistair Campbell. Andy Coulson fitted the bill and was appointed Conservative Party communications director shortly after his resignation from the *News of the World*, despite private warnings to Cameron.

Public feeling changed in March 2011, when it became clear that the *News of the World* had also hacked into the voicemail of the murdered teenager Milly Dowler, giving her devastated parents false hope that she was alive and picking up messages. Andy Coulson stepped down from his role, still protesting that he knew nothing of the practices of the newspaper that he had edited. (He was later sentenced to 18 months' imprisonment for his knowledge of the scandal in July 2014, serving five before release.) Murdoch closed down the *News of the World* – a paper with a history that dated back to 1843. David Cameron, the prime minister, was forced to act. He responded by calling on Lord Justice Leveson to carry out an inquiry into the behaviour of the press, and relationships between the press, police and politicians (Preston, 2015, pp. 564–8).

The Leveson Inquiry reported in November 2012. It called for much tougher self-regulation of the press by a new body independent of serving editors, government and business. This new body should, controversially, be backed by legislation designed to assess whether it was doing its job properly. For many editors, this seemed to be suspiciously close to state regulation of a free press. Leveson also recommended that an arbitration system should be created through which people who say they have been victims of unjust press treatment can seek redress without having to go through the courts. The report also provided substantial evidence that politicians and the press had become too close – with politicians spending a disproportionate amount of time, attention and resource on this relationship in return for the hope of favourable treatment by the press. Indeed, the phone-hacking inquiry made clear the close personal relationships between politicians and journalists. For example, it was revealed that Cameron was good friends with Rebekah Brooks, and lived close by in Oxfordshire. Brooks, then editor of *The Sun*, and Andy Coulson, who went from being editor of the *News of the World* to being Cameron's press spokesman, were involved in

*Source*: Howard McWilliam/The Week

The close friendship between David Cameron and Rebekah Brooks, the former editor of *The Sun*, was criticised during Cameron's premiership.

a long-term extramarital affair. Brooks was also close to Rupert Murdoch, the owner of *The Sun* and *News of the World*, who sought to protect her in her editorship during the scandal. And Tony Blair, former prime minister, was godson to one of Murdoch's children, before their relationship soured. All this gave an impression of a cosy elite composed of press and politicians. Leveson also argued that press behaviour had, at times, been 'outrageous', as was clearly the case in the phone-hacking scandal, or their treatment of the parents of Madeleine McCann, a British girl who went missing on holiday in Portugal in 2007. However, Leveson (2012) found no widespread evidence of corruption by the press.

Perhaps unsurprisingly, the full recommendations of the Leveson Inquiry (2012) have met with strong opposition from the press. Impress, the new press regulator, was recognised by the government in 2016. However, its membership was confined largely to small community papers. Britain's main newspapers refused to sign up to the system, arguing that Leveson's call for a regulator 'recognised' by the state (even though it is a body at arm's length) is too close to the state regulating the press, which has no place in a free society. The implementation of the policies recommended by the Leveson Inquiry had stalled.

Nevertheless, Leveson raises a number of unresolved questions about political communication: over the appropriate relationship between the state and the media; the relationships between particular politicians and the journalists who rely on them for stories; and the role of press ownership in a free society. But, in some ways, Leveson was an inquiry for an earlier age. In a 'post-truth' era, many of the questions examined in this chapter over the rise of social media and the spread of 'fake' news are far less possible to regulate and control than traditional media.

# SUMMARY

» Most of what people think they know about politics and government does not come from direct personal experience. Political communication between government and people is largely through the mass media.

» Traditional and new media are increasingly blurring, so that stories in the traditional press are reproduced on social media, which in turn feed the traditional press.

» The British print press is dominated by a few national dailies (and associated Sunday papers) competing in segmented markets. The rise of online news has led to a decline in newspaper sales and challenges the traditional financial model that made newspapers profitable through hard copy sales. Ownership of the press is substantially concentrated, and some proprietors have other extensive media interests.

» British radio and television have charter and statutory obligations to maintain political balance, unlike the highly partisan national press.

» The handling of party and government communications and the management of the media have also come under increasing criticism. New Labour, in particular, became associated with 'spin', putting a favourable interpretation on events and developments. However, all big political parties spend considerable resources on spin, often paying highly paid professionals to get the party's story across to the media, with varying degrees of success.

» The extent of media power and influence is contentious. It has been argued that media influence on voting is limited, although not everyone agrees. Others suggest that there is a pervasive media bias in favour of the establishment or free-market capitalism.

» The media has been accused of reducing and 'dumbing down' political coverage, and more recently of encouraging alienation and apathy.

» The discovery that the *News of the World* had paid investigators to hack phones to get stories led to the Leveson Inquiry. Leveson called for better self-regulation of the press, backed by legislation. Newspapers have so far resisted what they see as attempts at state regulation.

# ? QUESTIONS FOR DISCUSSION

» How far does the concentration of ownership of the press and media generally pose problems for democracy?

» How far and in what ways are the British press and British television biased?

» In what ways might television trivialise political debate?

» In what ways has social media transformed political communication in Britain? How far does social media facilitate genuine two-way communication between citizens and government? How might it transform democracy? Does social media pose any problems for politics?

» How much real political power and influence does the media have?

» Should the state have any role in regulating the press?

» What evidence is there that the British press, or the media generally, have significantly influenced political views and party choice?

» To what extent has media coverage of British politics been 'dumbed down'?

» What is spin and how new is it? How far was New Labour's approach to spin effective? Why did the party make such extensive use of spin?

 **FURTHER READING**

Curran and Seaton (2009) *Power without Responsibility: Press, Broadcasting and the Internet in Britain* (7th edn) remains one of the best guides to the British media. Kuhn's (2007) *Politics and the Media in Britain* provides an excellent overview that contains extremely useful summaries of most of the relevant research and controversies around political communication over the past 40 years.

On media influence on British politics, and specifically voting, see the discussion in Chapter 6 of Denver et al. (2012). On the growing literature on government communication and news management, see Franklin (1994, 2003, 2004),

Jones (1996, 1999), Gaber (2003) and Jones (2003). Wring (2006) covers New Labour's political communication. Lloyd (2004) is critical of the influence of media political reporting on the style and content of British politics. Morozov (2011) is provocative on the internet and democracy, as is Heffernan (2016).

The influence of the media on recent general elections is discussed extensively in chapters in the Nuffield election studies. See especially relevant material in Cowley and Kavanagh (2016) on the 2015 election. Preston (2015) is good on the media and the 2010–15 coalition.

 **USEFUL WEBSITES**

One hope of this chapter is that readers will take a more critical and analytical look at some of their existing online web sources. Hybrids of online and traditional news now dominate how we get our news.

The Oxford Media Convention brings together many of the key opinion-formers each year: oxfordmediaconvention.com. More critical sources, like the Glasgow Media Group, are still active: www.glasgowmediagroup.org.

 *Further student resources to support learning are available at*
**www.macmillanihe.com/griffiths-brit-pol-3e**

# PART IV

# POLITICS AND POLICY-MAKING

Part IV explores the policy-making process in the UK, setting out some of the theoretical approaches to policy and examining the framework in which policy-makers operate. We then explore some of the big policy questions that the UK faces today: how to create a successful economy; provide welfare and public services; and protect the environment. This part concludes with an exploration of foreign policy.

## POLITICS IN ACTION

Simon Griffiths, one of the authors of this book, provides an overview of some of the key questions and themes in this Part.

Patrick Diamond explores how policy is made, discusses some of the big policy challenges facing the UK today, and examines the gulf between academic debates and the practice of policy-making.

Watch the videos at **www.macmillanihe.com/griffiths-brit-pol-3e**

# 18  THE POLICY-MAKING PROCESS

In their book, *The Blunders of Our Governments* (Crewe and King, 2014) – a phrase taken from James Madison, the American statesman and philosopher – Ivor Crewe and Anthony King pick some policies that they argue were 'blunders'. These include:

» The community charge (or 'poll tax') introduced by the Thatcher government in 1989 and 1990. It was evaded by a substantial minority, and eventually abandoned after riots in the streets and the replacement of Margaret Thatcher by John Major (for more on this see Chapter 2).

» The Child Support Agency, set up in the 1990s. This failed to obtain maintenance payments from absent fathers, was fraught with administrative errors and alienated both the single parents it had initially been set up to help and the absent parents who had to deal with its ineptitude.

» The decision to join the European Exchange Rate Mechanism (ERM) in 1990. The decision valued the pound at almost three deutschmarks. (This was before the euro was introduced.) Sterling was overvalued and vulnerable to currency speculation, something that happened on 'Black Wednesday', 16 September 1992, when private investors made a fortune betting against the success of the pound, and Britain's economic policy collapsed. (The ERM is discussed in more detail in Chapter 18.)

» Among more recent policies, Crewe and King (2014) were also highly sceptical about the coalition government's Health and Social Care Act 2012; its abolition of the Audit Commission; the establishment of police commissioners; the coalition's close relations with News International; the introduction of tuition fees; and immigration policy.

Of course, whether a policy is a failure or not is often in the eye of the beholder. Those in favour of a policy are likely to claim it as a success, while political opponents are likely to see it as a failure. For pro-Europeans, for example, Cameron's decision to hold a referendum on membership of the EU appears to be a major policy blunder. No doubt Cameron, who fought to remain in the EU, thought that he would never have to deliver on the referendum, because of the Lib Dem veto on decisions during the 2010–15 coalition. The unexpected overall majority gained by the Conservatives at the 2015 general election changed that, but Cameron was confident of getting a deal from EU partners that would receive popular support in the UK and keep Britain in the EU. The answer is often more 'grey', with policies succeeding according to some criteria and failing on others (Marsh and McConnell, 2010).

Crewe and King (2014) point out that there are policy blunders in the private sector too, which also have devastating consequences on people's lives, but they restrict their analysis to the public sector and to domestic policies; so there is no mention of any of the UK's 'blunders' on the international stage – from the occupation of the Suez canal in 1956 to the invasion of Iraq in 2003. They offer a range of explanations for these blunders from human errors, such as the 'cultural disconnect' between a policy-maker in government and the person that a policy affects, to the systematic, such as the constant replacement of ministers, who do not become experts, but feel that they have to act to make a contribution.

So far, this book has focused on political and governmental institutions and processes, and only incidentally on issues, problems, policies and outcomes – on whether the institutions and process of UK politics create good policy. In this chapter, we explore these questions in more detail and examine how issues and problems get onto the political agenda, how they are analysed, decided and approved, how policies are implemented (or in some cases not implemented), monitored and reviewed. We will see that issues and problems are regularly addressed, but seldom solved. While the chapter draws on the analysis in earlier chapters of key political and governmental institutions and processes, it also serves as an introduction to subsequent chapters on particular issues and policies. These chapters are not purely illustrative. On the contrary, they focus on problems that are at the very heart of British politics. In considering the outcomes of the policy process, they address the crucial questions asked by Lasswell: 'Who gets what, when, how?' (see Chapter 1, p. 6).

## THIS CHAPTER:

»    Examines what policy-making is and how decisions are made in local and national government.

»    Looks at the policy-making 'cycle', taking us – in theory, although often not in practice – from an idea to implementation and thereafter to monitor and review.

»    Analyses how real-world issues, problems and politics get in the way of the models of policy-making.

»    Explores the changing context within which policy-making takes place, including the claims that the state is increasingly 'hollowed out' and that it can at best 'steer' rather than 'row' in a particular policy direction.

## POLICY-MAKING AND DECISION-TAKING

Governments at all levels make policy and take decisions. Policy is about aims, objectives or ends, while decisions are means to an end. Policy provides a framework within which particular decisions can be taken. Thus a transport policy should provide a framework for decisions on particular road proposals. In practice, the distinction between policy-making and decision-making is not clear-cut, but one of interpretation and degree.

**Policy-making** *involves taking up a clear position on a function, service or issue that will provide a framework for decision-making, such as an integrated transport policy or an ethical foreign policy.*

**Decision-making** *involves making particular decisions, often within an overall policy framework. Thus an ethical foreign policy may provide a framework for decisions on arms exports to particular countries. Decisions often involve selecting from a range of options, such as the site of a new hospital or the route of a bypass.*

Both governing and opposition parties are expected to have a range of policies on, for example, taxation, health, education, transport, the environment, defence, immigration and foreign affairs, and often on more specific issues, such as the renewal of Britain's Trident nuclear programme, the development of high-speed rail links or student fees.

Government policies are designed to be implemented. Indeed, any problems in the policy may soon be apparent as it is implemented, and any inconsistency between particular decisions and the broad policy will also be noticed. Yet governments can hardly avoid having policies (declared or inferred) for virtually all the functions and services for which they are responsible.

Opposition policies, by contrast, involve pledges that will only have to be implemented should the party gain power. They may never have to find the money to implement them, nor discover the potential snags. Moreover, opposition parties lack the resources of government for a full investigation of possible costs and consequences. So, many opposition policies may be a 'wish list' of hopeful aspirations. But, if their policy proposals are not costed and potential difficulties not considered, the governing party will happily do it for them to show its flaws and cost. Policies are hostages to fortune. Thus oppositions may prefer to play it safe with as few policy pledges as possible, but there are dangers here also. If a party does not have a declared policy on an issue that is deemed important, their opponents will soon invent a damaging one for them, and challenge them to deny it.

Indeed, there can be a significant gap between policies declared in opposition and what is possible in office. Before becoming prime minister in 2010, for example, David Cameron pledged to reduce net migration to the 'tens of thousands' (Prince, 2010) – a radical policy commitment. In government, he found that the policy was extremely difficult to bring about, particularly while Britain remained a member of the EU, which promised free movement of people within its borders. When Cameron left office six years later, immigration levels remained in the hundreds of thousands. A policy made in opposition, for better or worse, was not easily achievable in government.

## THE POLICY CYCLE

Policies may be declared in a speech, government document or party election manifesto, but they commonly emerge over a period. Policy-making is sometimes theoretically thought of as a process or cycle, involving a number of stages (see Figure 18.1). This suggests a much more orderly process than often occurs in reality. Governments facing an unexpected turn of events, for example the 2008 credit crunch or even the 2016 vote to leave the EU, may have to respond quickly and make up policy as they go along. Some of the stages in the policy process may be brief or perfunctory. There may not be time to appraise all the options. Implementation can be problematic, and on occasion may not even happen. Monitoring and review may be thorough, superficial or almost nonexistent. Even so, the stages of the policy cycle provide a useful conceptual framework for examining policy-making in theory and in reality, and will serve as the structure for the sections below. It may also help to identify shortcomings. Above all, the policy-making cycle serves to emphasise that making policy is an iterative process. Problems are rarely solved. The 'end' of one policy cycle is commonly the beginning of the next, as difficulties in implementation, revealed by monitoring and review, or exposed by critics, lead to attempts to modify or transform established policy.

## Figure 18.1: The policy cycle

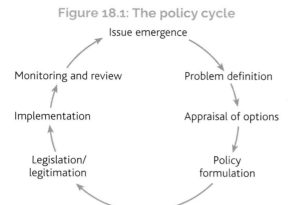

## ISSUES, PROBLEMS AND THE POLITICAL AGENDA

At any one time, there appears to be a limited number of issues that the political system can address. A useful analogy is with the agenda for any formal meeting. The agenda comprises a list of items to be considered, so determining not only what is to be discussed but also the order in which things are to be discussed. A common experience is that long agendas result in some items being discussed briefly or not all. Often only the items that are high on the agenda are really considered. Some other items might be hastily approved without discussion, and the rest postponed for consideration at a subsequent meeting, if at all.

While there is a formal agenda for meetings of particular political institutions, such as the Cabinet or Parliament and their numerous committees, an agenda for the whole British political process does not exist. But, at any one moment, there are a number of issues on that broad 'political agenda' that seem to have a high profile with politicians, the media and the wider public. (The media's role in agenda-setting is discussed in Chapter 17.)

This is particularly obvious at elections, where certain issues dominate the agenda. Take the British general election of 2015. The issues that seemed to dominate political debate between the parties were the economy and how to deal with the deficit, welfare spending, immigration and public services, particularly the NHS. The Conservatives, Labour and the Lib Dems talked less about the EU, perhaps because it was, in different ways, a problem for them all. David Cameron had promised that the Conservatives would hold a referendum on EU membership, knowing that his party was divided over the issue. Ed Miliband, for Labour, and Nick Clegg, for the Lib Dems, were aware that the general population was less keen on membership than most of their party members and MPs, so did not feel that it would be helpful to push the issue up the agenda. UKIP, in contrast, focused their campaign on withdrawal from the EU and the control of immigration, which they hoped would occur as a result.

Some big issues from previous decades have disappeared almost completely from the electoral radar screen, for example the balance of payments deficit, control of inflation, trade union power, or nationalisation and privatisation. Some no longer seem to matter. In other cases the problem still exists, but the media and public have lost interest. They are low on the political agenda, until something happens to make them newsworthy again.

Of course, one reason why an item may be high on the political agenda is that leading politicians have put it there, in manifestos, speeches and photo opportunities. Competing parties seek to emphasise those issues they feel are to their advantage, and try to ignore other more awkward issues that might be potential vote losers. They may be successful in shaping the agenda, although sometimes they find that the media and the public are not particularly interested in the issues they want to focus on, but are concerned about something else. Events such as the 2011 London riots, the unexpectedly close vote in Scotland over independence in 2014, or the UK's surprise vote to leave the EU in 2016 can take politicians by surprise and force new issues onto the agenda (or, more commonly, old issues back onto the agenda). It may take a food scare or a rail crash to push food or rail safety up the agenda. An issue long neglected suddenly seems to strike a chord with the public. The mass media may reflect public concerns, but often may effectively stimulate them.

At any one time, there are many issues and interests competing for the attention of politicians and other decision-makers. Getting an issue onto the agenda is the crucial first step. Maintaining it there may be more difficult. After a time it is no longer news. The problem may appear more difficult than first realised. It may be too expensive to make an appreciable impact. There may be conflicting interests to take into account. Proposed remedies may even seem worse than the disease, something pointed out by Anthony Downs (1973) in his five-stage model of the way in which issues grab our attention.

## DEFINING THE PROBLEM

An issue may be raised by a particular event, but it is often far from self-evident what the problem really is. In summer 2011, for example, riots broke out in London and other English cities following the police shooting of Mark Duggan, in Tottenham, north London, as police tried to arrest him. During the riots, people were seriously injured and property worth billions of pounds was destroyed. It is an issue that must be addressed, but what really is the problem? Why did the riots take place? Only if the causes are understood can the real problem be addressed. Yet there are often competing explanations, implying very different remedies. Was it essentially a 'race riot' arising from ethnic tensions, sparked by police mistreatment of young black men like Mark Duggan? Was it more the consequence of urban deprivation and unemployment?

Source: CARL DE SOUZA/AFP/Getty Images
Sporadic looting and clashes continued for several nights in August 2011, after the killing of Mark Duggan by armed police in an attempted arrest.

Was the physical environment a contributory factor? Did it reflect a breakdown in community, or the collapse of family life? Was it simply the consequence of poor, inadequate or overly aggressive policing? On the definition of the problem depends the policy response.

Different interests may try to 'capture' the problem, defining it in such a way as to suggest more resources for the police, urban planners, inner-city schools, social services or housing. They are not necessarily cynically pushing their own interests. Different professionals – police officers, economists, planners, teachers and social workers – naturally view the world through the prism of the assumptions involved in their own professional training and experience. They will be sincerely convinced that the 'real answer' is more trees, more jobs, better educational resources, more police and increased police powers, improved community resources and so on.

The 'riot' itself is a form of political behaviour that commands political attention, but political values and interests also help shape how the problem is defined and addressed. Some interests may seek to play down or marginalise potential contributory factors, such as alcohol or drugs, ethnic tensions or discriminatory policing, while others may want to exaggerate them. Commonly, there will be an investigation, involving the collection of evidence, the publication of a report with recommendations for action, some of which may lead to a response. After the 2011 riots, for example, reports were published by the Riots Communities and Victims Panel, the Metropolitan Police and the Home Affairs Select Committee, among others. These reports may be thorough and their analysis sensible, but it is not holy writ, and can never be the whole truth. Different interests will emphasise different parts of the report and put their own interpretation on the conclusions. Then, the riot and its possible causes may be largely forgotten until another riot happens, perhaps somewhere else in rather different circumstances, and the whole anguished debate will start up again.

A similar process will follow any significant political event – from the run on the Northern

Rock bank in 2007 to the London Bridge terrorist attack in June 2017. The 'real issue' will be defined according to underlying ideological assumptions and political interests. There is no objective interpretation, and normally no single ideal solution.

## APPRAISING OPTIONS

Nevertheless, attempts may be made to analyse a range of options more thoroughly, at least when governments enjoy the luxury of time, for sometimes an immediate decision is required. In such circumstances, governments have to act fast and work out some rational justification for their actions afterwards. On other occasions, governments may be able to explore a range of options or appoint a commission to do it for them (see Spotlight 18.1).

A variety of techniques may be used in an ostensibly rational appraisal of possible

## SPOTLIGHT ON ...

## Government by commission?

18.1

Faced with a particular problem, a government may decide to appoint an independent commission or committee of experts to examine the issues, collect opinions, commission research and make recommendations in a final report. Most of this can be done anyway, using the normal resources and contacts of government, but there may be political advantages to an independent royal commission:

» The government may be genuinely undecided, or internally divided, on a particular issue, and a commission may be a useful way of trying to resolve the issue.

» On controversial issues likely to cause political trouble, the conclusions of a prestigious royal commission, backed by extensive research, may add authority and legitimacy to a difficult decision the government needs to make.

» Although the commission may be independent, the government can influence or substantially determine the outcome by the choice of chair and members, and by setting the terms of reference. The final report may then come up with what the government thinks is the 'right' answer.

» Alternatively, the government is not obliged to accept the recommendations (particularly if they lead to a political outcry). They can 'pick and mix', accepting some recommendations and rejecting others. Critics of the report may be relieved if the government decides not to implement all its proposals.

» Appointing a commission may sometimes be a way of avoiding the need to declare a policy. The government can then fairly say that they are awaiting the outcome of a report, which it would be unreasonable to prejudge.

» Finally, appointing a commission may be a way of burying a difficult or politically damaging issue. With any luck, media and public attention will be transferred elsewhere when it finally reports.

Even so, it can be embarrassing if an independent commission or committee comes up with the 'wrong' or politically unacceptable answer. There are numerous examples of recommendations by high-profile commissions or committees being rejected, including the Roskill Commission (1971) on the site of London's third airport, the Layfield Committee (1976) on local government finance, the Jenkins Commission (1998) on electoral reform and the Airports Commission (2015) on airport expansion. The conclusions of Roskill and Layfield were ignored, while the Jenkins Report was effectively 'kicked into the long grass' by the Blair government. The Airports Commission (2015) recommended the expansion of Heathrow Airport, despite it being contrary to prevailing government policy.

options. Economists have sometimes used cost–benefit analysis to assess particular projects or alternative possibilities. This involves putting a monetary value on all the identifiable costs and benefits to the community (not just the direct financial costs and benefits) to decide whether a project should go ahead, or which of several options is the best buy. Accountants have argued in favour of more overtly rational techniques for managing and controlling the budgetary process, such as zero-based budgeting, which forces planners to justify each piece of expenditure for every new period and was influential in the 1980s. These rational systems have been advocated precisely because much policy-making in practice has not always appeared particularly rational, but instead commonly involves relatively small shifts (or increments) from past policy, without any real analysis of how far various options meet clear aims and objectives. Some argue, however, that what has come to be called 'incrementalism' is not just the way in which most policy is made in practice, but is actually preferable to more ostensibly rational approaches (see Key Figures 18.1).

It has been claimed that the budgetary process is almost inevitably incremental. Commenting on the UK budgetary process, observers suggest that the next budget can only involve a shift of around 2.5% at most from the previous budget. The chancellor of the exchequer does not start with a blank sheet, but with past revenue and expenditure involving continuing programmes, with commitments and expectations that can only be ignored at considerable political costs. Understandably, successive governments have sought to make the process more rational, by linking spending to clear objectives, and planning spending over a longer period than the budgetary year. Inevitably, plans are blown off course by unanticipated developments and political pressures. Although governments since the financial crisis of 2008 have accepted the need for cuts to public spending, past spending commitments will remain a significant constraint on planned future spending (as Chapter 19 shows).

Many other areas of policy are inevitably substantially incremental. Hospitals and schools depend on past decisions on training and investment. Staffing, buildings and equipment cannot be transformed overnight. Yet radical shifts can and do take place in British government. Whatever might be said about the privatisation programme of the Thatcher government or New Labour's devolution programme, neither could be characterised as incremental.

## POLICY FORMULATION

Sooner or later a policy emerges or a key decision is taken. Once a policy has been declared it is difficult to retreat, at least until the policy has been tried and perhaps found wanting. It is not always easy, however, to determine exactly when a new policy is established. It may be announced in a speech, a government circular or sometimes a White Paper (described in Chapter 6). This provides a convenient firm date, but a decision will normally have been made inside government, sometimes well ahead of any public announcement. Although the policy will be associated with the appropriate departmental minister and, under the assumption of collective Cabinet responsibility, with the government as a whole, its real instigator may be someone else, perhaps the prime minister or chancellor, possibly a civil servant or a special adviser. More commonly, a new policy may have been developed from the contributions of many prominent and less prominent individuals, over a period of time.

Some policies, however, emerge almost by default, as other options are rejected or become discredited, and it gradually becomes clear that there is no realistic alternative. There may be no formal announcement, and indeed the policy may only become clear in retrospect. Thus, after a long debate over the location of London's proposed third airport from the 1970s onwards, a number of proposed sites were rejected. As a consequence, Stansted, a small airport rejected at an early stage by the official Roskill Commission (1971), gradually grew to become, in effect, London's third airport as a result of the failure of successive governments to reach a decision. Since then, Luton and City Airports also take far more

# KEY FIGURES 18.1

## Herbert Simon and Charles Lindblom: rationalism versus incrementalism

One of the most important debates in policy-making is between rationalists and incrementalists. Depending on which side you agree with, your approach to public policy will start from a very different place. Two American political scientists define the debate: Herbert Simon and Charles Lindblom. However, the approach is as important in the UK.

**Herbert Simon (1916–2001)** is the leading theorist of rationalism. One common version of the rational model emphasises the importance of first determining the ends or objectives of policy and then exploring all possible means to securing those ends, and choosing the best (the ends–means model). Simon argued that, ideally, the decision-maker should start from the situation, trace through all possible courses of action and their consequences, and choose the one with the greatest net benefits. However, he recognised that, in practice, administrators are limited by time, information and skills, so that they cannot find the optimum solution, and search until they find a tolerably satisfactory solution. Thus they 'satisfice' rather than optimise. Simon described this approach as involving 'bounded rationality'.

**Charles Lindblom (1917–)**, by contrast, argued that, in practice, policy-makers choose between relatively few options. Most policy-making involves small-scale extensions of past policy. This is the theory of incrementalism. It does not commonly involve a single decision-maker impartially sifting options, but requires accommodation and compromise between different interests, a process Lindblom described as 'partisan mutual adjustment'. He also argued that much policy-making does not follow any coherent plan, but proceeds rather disjointedly ('disjointed incrementalism'). Lindblom argued not only that his model better fitted the reality of policy-making, so was a better description of what was going on, but also that it led to better results than attempts at rationalism. Incremental policy-making, building on the past, was more likely to be successful than radical shifts. It was also more likely to be acceptable because it was based on consultation and compromise. Thus it was a prescriptive model. Provocatively, Lindblom (1959) referred to his model as the 'science of muddling through'.

The debate begun by Simon and Lindblom continues. Critics of Lindblom argue that we should aspire to more than 'muddling through'. They also argue that there is an inbuilt conservative bias in incrementalism. Sometimes radical change is necessary. Lindblom has responded that a series of incremental shifts can achieve a radical change in policy over a period, although he has conceded the case for some forward planning and 'strategic analysis' in later versions of his model. There have also been attempts to construct a model incorporating elements of rationalism and incrementalism, such as Amitai Etzioni's 'mixed scanning' (1967).

commercial passengers, while Heathrow and Gatwick have expanded to cope with increased traffic. Faced with strong local political opposition to any new airport in the 'home counties' that surround London, governments have tended to prevaricate, and have, in practice, preferred the rather less politically contentious expansion of existing airports. Even the strategy of 'muddling through' (set out by Lindblom) ran into problems, when a proposed new runway for Heathrow encountered strenuous objections from environmental groups and local campaigners, and was scrapped by the coalition government in 2010, only to be recommended again by the Airports Commission in 2015.

After an issue has aroused strong public emotions and demands for action, a government may eventually decide to take no action, because of the economic or political costs. Some analysts suggest that non-decision-making may tell us more about the exercise of power in western society than decision-making.

## The politics of non-decision-making

Much of the debate on power and decision-making has been conducted by American academics using US examples, although the analysis has also been applied to British politics. Robert Dahl (1961) concluded from his own studies of decision-making in New Haven, Connecticut that power was dispersed rather than concentrated in the hands of the few. Bachrach and Baratz (1970) argued that there were 'two faces of power'. One involved overt conflicts of interest on key political issues, of the kind analysed by Dahl. The second face of power involved the suppression of conflict and the effective prevention of decisions. This is sometimes described as the 'restrictive face of power' and involves the 'dynamics of non-decision-making'. Influence is used to limit the scope of discussion or to prevent conflicts from ever being brought to the forefront. Sometimes, there can be a secret element to this, when it is unclear where and by whom a decision is being made (which government committee, when and so on).

Steven Lukes ([1974] 2005) argued that there was a 'third dimension of power' involving the shaping of people's preferences so that neither overt nor covert conflicts of interests exist. People are so conditioned by the prevailing economic and social system that they cannot imagine alternatives. Thus potential political issues do not even get onto the political agenda. Lukes drew particularly on the work of

Crenson (1971), who had shown that the issue of pollution control had not even come up for debate in some US cities whose economies were dominated by a major industry with a pollution problem. This was not because of the use of direct power and influence by employers, but because the bulk of the community had become conditioned to think that pollution was a natural and inescapable by-product of the employment and prosperity created by the industry.

There are some obvious problems in analysing 'non-decisions'. Moreover, Lukes and others assume that people's 'real' interests may differ markedly from their 'felt' interests. While this is plausible, it does conflict with the assumption of liberal democracy that individuals are the best judges of their own self-interest.

## LEGISLATION AND LEGITIMATION

Government may decide what it wants to do, the policy may have been determined, but policy generally requires some form of official ratification if it is to be widely accepted as legitimate. This may involve legislation. Government policy may have been announced in a speech or White Paper, but it still may need to become the law of the land for it to be accepted by courts, media and public. Thus the transfer of the judicial functions of the House of Lords to a new Supreme Court was established as government policy in 2003, but it took until 2005 for it to become law, and until 2009 for the policy to be implemented. A policy of that importance clearly required legislation, and indeed there is always the possibility that a policy may be substantially modified or even abandoned as a bill proceeds through Parliament. (These stages are set out in Chapter 6.)

Other forms of legitimation may effectively derail a policy. The Labour government instituted what has been described as a 'rolling programme of devolution' for the English regions, involving directly elected regional assemblies. However, they gave voters an effective veto with a commitment to referendums in the regions concerned. Referendums initially announced for three regions were reduced to one, the northeast, where there was a well-established lobby for regional government. The subsequent overwhelming rejection of an assembly in a 2004 referendum by voters in the northeast has seemingly buried the policy for the foreseeable future. Similarly, while all the main parties were officially committed to the policy of remaining in the EU, the result of the 2016 referendum in favour of 'exit' was largely accepted as a legitimate challenge to that policy, and would lead Theresa May (2016a), who had previously supported the 'remain' campaign, to argue that the will of the British people must be respected – 'Brexit means Brexit'. (For more on the EU referendum, see Chapter 12.)

By no means all important government decisions require legislation, and only major constitutional issues are thought to require a referendum. Other decisions do normally depend on some kind of formal authorisation or ratification, perhaps in the form of a Cabinet minute or a circular, order or regulation issued by a departmental minister under delegated authority. Important decisions in local government require formal council approval. On planning decisions, there is normally a right of appeal, followed by a public inquiry. This can be an important part of the legitimation process, although some argue that the whole inquiry system is weighted against objectors. Constitutionally, some of the most important powers of government, including making war, are part of the 'prerogative powers of the Crown', exercised in practice by the prime minister, and although it is questionable whether a prime minister who took a country to war without the support of Cabinet and Parliament could survive in the job, strictly speaking do not require special authorisation or legislation.

## IMPLEMENTATION

Implementation is perhaps the most underregarded part of the policy-making process but the most important. The passing of a law in Parliament or a policy pronouncement by a minister is often regarded as the end of the policy process when it may be just the beginning. Cabinet decisions may be taken,

laws may be passed, but the policy is not necessarily implemented as intended. There is often a considerable 'implementation gap' when it comes to applying policy (Hogwood and Gunn, 1984, Ch. 11). Why?

A policy may break down because of significant strong opposition from the public or a section of the public (as some of the examples of 'policy failure' at the start of this chapter). Yet the explanation for imperfect implementation can often be rather less dramatic. One reason is that ministers often rely on individuals or organisations outside central government to implement policy. Much government policy is implemented not by civil servants, but by local authorities, hospital trusts and a range of quangos. In health and education, successive governments have made a virtue of devolving control to local professionals and the community. Competition and choice require some autonomy for local producers and consumers. Local councils are elected bodies, retaining some significant discretion over priorities and spending. They are often controlled by different parties with different priorities from those of the government. Even where the law seems clear, councils may 'drag their feet' on policies to which they or local communities are opposed.

Public officials may often have significant discretion in administering policies. Terms such as 'street-level bureaucracy' (see Hudson, 1997) or 'street-level policy-making' suggest that quite low-level staff who deal with the public at the sharp end of policy, for example teachers, doctors or social workers, may have significant discretion over decisions. Such people may be 'gatekeepers', effectively controlling access to resources.

The problem is clearer still in areas where central government is reliant on organisations and interests outside government altogether for implementation. This was one of the difficulties with incomes policy (discussed in Chapter 19) pursued by both Labour and Conservative governments in the 1960s and 70s, where pay rises were capped in an effort to keep inflation down, sometimes backed by the authority of the law. Yet whether the policy was 'voluntary' (agreed voluntarily by the unions) or

*Source*: www.imagesource.com
These 'street-level bureaucrats' often have the last say in implementing policy.

'statutory' (given a legal basis), it still depended on the cooperation of employers and unions for implementation, and this was not always forthcoming. Much industrial, agricultural and environmental policy relies on private sector firms if it is to succeed. Much social policy depends heavily on the local community and the voluntary sector. While much can be done by central government through the stick of regulation and the carrot of grants, the implementation of policy is, ultimately, often in the hands of people who are outside the line management control of central departments.

However, the biggest obstacles to effective policy implementation are generally resources. Governments will lay out the ends, but do not always provide adequate means. There may be lack of finance, lack of skilled staff, lack of usable land or lack of sufficient powers. Even where government is prepared to provide additional resources, it takes time for these to be converted into usable resources on the ground. It takes many years to train new teachers, doctors, nurses or police officers, often longer still to plan, build and equip new hospitals and schools. There is no tap that can be turned on to provide an instant supply of additional resources.

Over and above all this there are problems with coordination. Many programmes require cooperation between different levels of government, between different agencies and departments and between the public, private and voluntary sectors. Issues such as drugs, vandalism, school truancy and drink-fuelled violent disturbances require cooperation between the police, schools, social workers and community organisations. Frequently, there are difficulties in achieving coordination, arising from the different organisation, processes and cultures of the services and agencies involved. The problem of coordination is not new. David Marsh and Rod Rhodes (1992) focus on the 'implementation gap' during the Thatcher governments of the 1980s. Partly as a response, a New Labour mantra was 'joined-up government' that could focus on implementation, or 'delivery', of policy. Indeed, a special Prime Minister's Delivery Unit was established inside the Cabinet Office to monitor the implementation of government policy during the New Labour years, although it was later abolished by the coalition government in 2010, as part of its cost-saving measures.

Finally, it is important to acknowledge that policy can have unintended as well as intended effects. A distinction can be drawn between policy outputs, the direct and intended result of inputs of resources, and policy outcomes, including the unintended consequences of policy. Thus some welfare payments intended to help the low-paid and unemployed involved a perverse disincentive against seeking work or higher paid employment, insofar as it would entail the loss of means-tested benefits, and in some cases even leave them worse off. Critics claim that the tax and benefit system can create a 'poverty trap' from which it is difficult to escape, although the politicians and civil servants who had designed the policy had certainly neither expected nor intended this outcome.

## MONITORING AND REVIEW

To judge whether a particular policy is working, its implementation must be thoroughly monitored and reviewed. This appears common sense, but it has not always happened in the past, nor is it necessarily practised effectively today.

Many organisations ostensibly build internal monitoring and review into their own processes, to check that they are meeting their own aims and targets. Many local councils established performance review committees to monitor their own policies. Other public sector organisations formally review their own performance. This is very much in their own interest as there are all kinds of external reviews that will draw attention to problems, and it is better to identify weaknesses internally and seek to remedy them to forestall more damaging criticism.

From the nineteenth century onwards, various inspectorates were established by central government to measure performance. More recently, central government's performance review has been reformed and extended. The auditing of public spending used to be concerned primarily with the legality of expenditure – was money being spent as voted by Parliament? It is now much more concerned with achieving value for money, and the 'three Es' – economy, efficiency and effectiveness:

» *Economy*: minimising the cost of resources, or inputs (e.g. land, labour, capital) involved in producing a certain level of service (e.g. reducing the cost of providing a hospital bed for a patient).

» *Efficiency*: securing maximum quantity of outputs for a given quantity of inputs (e.g. treating more patients in the NHS without an increase in resources).

» *Effectiveness*: securing effective outcomes, (e.g. improved health in the community). While economy is about reducing costs and efficiency about increased productivity, effectiveness is about realising objectives – but this is the most difficult to measure. If a school teaches more pupils without any increases in resources, this implies increased economy (reduced costs per pupil) and increased efficiency, if results appear unaffected. But, both teachers and parents assume that larger classes in some way involve less effective education, which is plausible but difficult to measure and prove. Similarly, the quantity of patients treated in the NHS may increase, perhaps at the expense of quality of care.

The National Audit Office (NAO) reviews performance in government departments and associated quangos. The Audit Commission monitored the performance of local authorities in England and Wales. This was closed down by the coalition government in 2015, with its functions passed to local councils and private accounting firms. Critics have argued that these private firms do not have the expertise necessary to monitor local government performance.

In addition, the government may set up inquiries or commissions to review a particular service and recommend reforms. Parliament now has its own comprehensive system for monitoring the performance of all government departments and services through the departmental select committees, as well as the Public Accounts Committee. Professional bodies such as the Chartered Institute of Public Finance and Accountancy have also long published their own performance statistics.

There is no doubt that all this performance review has had a massive impact on government at every level. There are sanctions on poor performance. Pay, prospects and sometimes jobs are on the line. Comparative performance indicators can throw up some substantial variations in costs and standards, for example the money spent on school meals or death rates arising from particular medical conditions in different hospitals or areas of the country. Poor performance can be addressed and remedied. Good practice can be analysed and copied. Often, performance indicators can be ranked in league tables, as they are for schools and hospitals. Some object that the publication of comparative league tables can distort priorities, concentrating on the easily measurable at the expense of more important but less easily quantified outcomes. While there is some truth in the argument, the answer lies not in less performance review but better and more sensitive performance review. Government, service users and voters can hardly assess whether the large sums devoted to public services are efficient and effective without it. Finally, performance review can throw up evidence that existing policy is not working, and new thinking is required. Thus the end of one policy cycle can provide the stimulus for the beginning of the next.

# POLICY-MAKING IN A 'HOLLOWED-OUT' STATE

Policy-making now takes place in the context of continuing ideological debate over the nature and extent of the British state. According to Rod Rhodes (1997), there has been a 'hollowing out of the state'. By this, he means that the state has ceded former responsibilities in different directions. Some previous responsibilities have been shifted upwards to supranational organisations (such as the EU). Others have gone downwards to devolved bodies in Scotland, Northern Ireland and Wales. In other areas, the state's former responsibilities have moved 'sideways'. Since the 1980s, for example, significant areas of the economy, once run by the state, have been privatised, while public services formerly run by the state are increasingly run by private companies or partnerships between the state, the private and the not-for-profit sectors. In this section, we look at changing views of the state and ask how this affects policy-making. Many of the changes that Rhodes describes as a 'hollowing out' of the state are discussed elsewhere (see Chapter 11 on devolution or Chapter 12 on Europe, for example). We look at some of the other main developments now.

## PRIVATISATION

A major theme in political theory, and perhaps the most significant divide between (and sometimes within) mainstream political ideologies is over the respective roles of the state and the market (as we saw in Chapter 15). Classical liberalism involves leaving as much as possible to free-market forces, with only a residual role for the state. Yet from the Second World War until the 1970s, there was a prevailing cross-party consensus in favour of state intervention and planning. It was widely assumed by policy-makers that the state had a major role, not only in influencing the macroeconomy along Keynesian lines, but in managing extensive welfare provision and major nationalised industries. From the later 1970s onwards, this consensus supporting state intervention gave way to a new consensus favouring the free market, which eventually included the Conservatives under Cameron and May, parts of New Labour, as well as the New Right (also discussed in Chapter 15). This new consensus involved a very different role for policy-makers, with the abandonment of Keynesianism, state planning and incomes policies, the privatisation of former state-owned industries and the introduction of market competition into the management of public services. A presumption in favour of state intervention was replaced by a presumption in favour of the private sector and free-market forces.

The Thatcher and Major governments certainly saw a significant transfer of assets and activities from the public sector to the private sector. Most significant here was the privatisation of nearly all the former nationalised industries that the 1945–51 Labour government had transferred to state control (although some had previously been municipally owned and run). After a few relatively minor privatisations, gas, steel, telecommunications, water, electricity, coal and railways were all sold off between 1984 and 1995.

One of the interesting aspects of privatisation is that the transfer of assets from the public to the private sector has not removed these industries from the sphere of public policy, or even significantly reduced pressures on government to remedy perceived problems. Government is still held to account for the problems and deficiencies of rail transport, despite the removal of the industry from state ownership and control. This is hardly surprising, as whether state-owned, privatised or controlled by a not-for-profit organisation, the rail network still requires massive injections of public money that ultimately come from taxpayers. Rail users continue to agitate over prices, punctuality and reliability. Rail crashes provoke legitimate public concerns over rail safety, and demands for government action and tougher safety regimes. The state may divest itself of the ownership of troublesome industries, but not, it seems, of their problems.

## COMPETITION

Besides such massive transfers of assets, the Conservative governments from 1979 to 1997 also attempted to introduce more competition into the provision of public services. One mechanism was the introduction of **compulsory competitive tendering (CCT)** into parts of the NHS and local government. The deregulation of bus transport also led to a substantial shift from publicly owned and controlled bus companies into the hands of private operators. So, many services previously provided almost exclusively by public organisations were now undertaken by private firms for profit, although they remained the statutory responsibility of local or health authorities, who laid down the terms of contracts and monitored their implementation (Walsh, 1995).

*Source:* Brand X

The rail network still involves massive public subsidies from taxpayers, despite being privatised in the 1990s.

> **Compulsory competitive tendering (CCT)** *was introduced by the UK Conservative government of the 1980s. It required public sector organisations to allow private sector firms to bid for the delivery of services (e.g. refuse collection or transport) in competition with any internal provision by the organisation itself.*

In addition, further competition was introduced through internal markets (or quasi-markets) in health and, to a lesser extent, education. State grants were based on patients treated and pupils enrolled. As a consequence, hospitals were competing for patients and schools for pupils. This was part of an attempt to inject more competition and private sector values into the public sector, through new public management. This involved not only a substantial change in culture for public servants, but major developments in administrative institutions, affecting not only the Civil Service, but the health service and local government.

## QUANGOS AND EXECUTIVE AGENCIES

Although much New Right rhetoric was anti-government and appeared to involve a 'rolling back' or 'hollowing out' of the state (Rhodes, 1997, 2000), it did not involve a significant shrinking of the size of the state as measured by public spending as a percentage of GDP. Indeed, for some commentators, Thatcherism involved a strong state rather than the minimal state lauded by neoliberals (Gamble, 1988), and centralisation rather than the decentralisation to consumers and service users claimed in some government rhetoric. The apparent contradiction was sometimes explained by the suggestion that the government was seeking 'more control over less' (Rhodes, 2000, p. 156).

In practice, the state was substantially restructured rather than reduced, although this restructuring involved significant implications for the traditional British system of government, or Westminster model, as well as for the functions and scope of the state. In terms of administrative machinery, restructuring meant increased reliance on quangos, executive agencies, new single purpose bodies and state-aided voluntary bodies rather than government departments and elected local authorities.

One aspect of this restructuring was the growth in the number of **quangos**, appointed public bodies not directly controlled by elected politicians. Quangos were not new. There were always persuasive reasons for putting some government-sponsored or funded activities in the hands of an appointed body rather than party politicians and civil servants. In some cases, it was particularly important that certain bodies were seen to be impartial and independent of the government of the day. Older examples include the BBC or Independent Television Authority, the Equal Opportunities Commission or the Commission for Racial Equality (the last two now combined in the Equality and Human Rights Commission). In other cases, a key motive was to attract the services of relevant experts as advisers. While some quangos have important executive responsibilities, employ numerous staff and manage multi-million pound budgets, many others are purely advisory, and experts provide part-time services for little or nothing. Indeed, it may often be much cheaper to establish a quango than run an activity as part of a government department.

---

*Quango is an acronym for (originally) quasi-autonomous nongovernmental organisation. Quangos are, however, normally funded, appointed and ultimately controlled by the state (so are part of government). They are appointed rather than elected, and not directly accountable to elected politicians. National quangos are officially described as 'non-departmental public bodies' and are thus distinguished from executive agencies, which have some managerial autonomy but are attached to departments.*

---

There can be good reasons for establishing independent public bodies. However, the main criticisms of quangos are over the issues of patronage and accountability. Many positions on non-departmental public bodies are effectively in the gift of ministers, and there has been considerable criticism of the criteria by which appointments are made. In the past, Labour governments appointed leading trade unionists to many quangos, partly because some organisations needed representatives of 'labour' to balance business representatives. Conservative governments were sometimes accused of stuffing health authorities and urban development corporations with people from the private sector (often Conservative supporters), although they too could respond that such people brought essential management expertise to running these organisations. It is difficult to evade accusations of political partisanship in appointments, particularly where an organisation may be seen as inherently party political.

Even more clearly, many quangos are not very accountable (Plummer, 1994). Not only are they unelected, their proceedings are often held in secret, and even if reports and accounts are published, they receive little effective public scrutiny, although the Freedom of Information Act 2000 has recently had some impact here. Ministers are traditionally responsible for what goes on within their own departments, but it is harder to hold a particular minister to account for the failures of quangos that run services in the area for which that minister has responsibility. Thus, in practice, quangos also weaken the convention of individual ministerial responsibility, in which a minister is held ultimately responsible for what goes on in their department. Few ministers now see themselves as beholden to it and will take full responsibility for mistakes made in quangos. (For more on ministerial responsibility, see Chapter 8, pp. 152–53.)

Parties in opposition often criticise quangos, but establish their own in government. Thatcher promised a bonfire of quangos, and indeed some were abolished as the result of the Pliatzky Report (1980) into non-departmental bodies. However, her governments proceeded to establish a wide range of new appointed bodies, although they generally refused to accept that these were 'quangos' because of the term's pejorative associations. Many new quangos were created as a result of the Thatcher government's determination to 'hive off 'activities from the

Civil Service and traditional local government. Indeed, some argued that the proliferation of quangos was part of a deliberate strategy to make the centre appear smaller – a somewhat cosmetic attack on 'big government'. Other new quangos were established to provide some regulation of pricing and investment of the privatised bodies running the former nationalised industries, for example the Office of Water Services and the Office of Gas and Electricity Markets (Ofgem).

In the 1980s, more financial delegation and commercial disciplines were also introduced into the Civil Service. From 1988, the introduction of executive agencies involved more managerial autonomy but also obliged civil servants to reach prescribed targets and operate in a more commercial manner. One consequence was that ministerial responsibility and Civil Service anonymity were both eroded. Increasingly, heads of executive agencies were named and blamed for perceived shortcomings.

The transformation of most of the old unified Civil Service into a diverse collection of executive agencies with substantial managerial autonomy has also made British government more complex and confusing. Although distinctions can be drawn between older non-departmental public bodies (or quangos) and the new executive agencies, variations within both types of organisation seem rather more significant than the differences between them. Indeed, even some leading participants appear confused over the formal status of their own organisation. In effect, this programme has created many more public bodies with variable autonomy from direct ministerial control.

---

*Executive agencies are still part of the Civil Service, subject to Civil Service conditions and codes of practice. They are organised within government departments, and are subject to ministerially imposed policy objectives, budgets and performance targets. Yet they are headed by chief executives and operate within framework documents that give them considerable operational autonomy. Examples include the Child Support Agency and HM Passport Office.*

---

Similarly, successive reforms of the health service, education and the police service increased managerial delegation and reduced local democratic control. Local councils lost much of their control over schools formally to school governing bodies, but in practice to head teachers and senior management teams.

In government, Labour in turn created a range of new quangos to meet its own policy objectives, or meet specific problems. Thus the Food Standards Agency was established in the wake of the BSE and foot and mouth crises. Labour also set up a number of cross-cutting agencies designed to improve the coordination of government services and secure better policy delivery, such as the Social Exclusion Unit, Better Regulation Task Force and New Deal Task Force. They renamed and partially reconstituted some independent public bodies and controversially amalgamated others.

As part of its programme to cut the budget deficit, the coalition government conducted an extensive review of quangos. In October 2010, Francis Maude, then Cabinet Office minister, announced that 901 quangos would be reduced to 648, with another 40 still under review. Some major decisions, such as the scrapping of the Audit Commission, the UK Film Council, the 10 strategic health authorities and 152 primary care trusts, had been made earlier. Other quangos abolished included British Nuclear Fuels Ltd, the Youth Justice Board, Consumer Focus, the Renewable Fuels Agency and Cycling England. Still others were merged (the Competition Commission and Office of Fair Trading became the Competition and Markets Authority), converted into charities (British Waterways) or taken over by government departments or, in some cases, the private sector. In many cases, the functions will be carried on in another way, and there will be few savings, particularly when payment of pensions, redundancies and contractual liabilities are taken into account. Some advisory quangos cost very little and their abolition will save next to nothing. Other quangos (e.g. the Equality and Human Rights Commission, the World Service, the British Council and the British Library) have been reprieved, although some are facing a substantial cut in funding. Maude argued that the changes would 'restore accountability and responsibility' to public life. Critics fear some of the functions of the axed quangos will be performed less effectively or not at all. A report by the Commons Public Administration Select Committee, chaired by Conservative MP Bernard Jenkin, suggested that the 'bonfire of the quangos' had been botched and would lead to neither significant savings nor improved accountability (House of Commons, 2011).

Whether quangos, executive agencies and a range of other new public bodies involve more or less government and central control, they remain an area of legitimate concern. Once, the only government bodies that seemed to count in the UK were government departments, headed by ministers and staffed by civil servants, and (second in importance), elected local authorities. Lines of responsibility and accountability were fairly clear, and, ultimately, elected politicians were responsible for policy, accountable to Parliament or a local council, and they carried the can for failure. When things go wrong, it is now more often agency managers or officers who are blamed rather than politicians. Old central departments and local councils have increasingly lost out to these other public bodies. Indeed, some have argued that the proliferation of appointed bodies reflected a purposeful bypassing of democratic institutions, particularly elected local government, in favour of a 'new magistracy', so-called after the appointed local magistrates who administered much of county government until 1888 (Skelcher and Davis, 1996). Whatever judgement is made, government has certainly become more complex and less subject to direct control by elected politicians.

## PARTNERSHIP WITH THE PRIVATE AND VOLUNTARY SECTOR

Increased private sector investment in the public sector was provided through a particular form of public–private partnership, the private finance initiative (PFI). Many new PFI hospitals, schools and prisons have already been built, using the money and expertise of the private sector, paid for by the relevant public authority over a period, commonly 25 years. The main attraction for government of PFIs is that they increase the funds available for public sector capital investment (chronically underfunded in the past) without requiring public sector borrowing. Some argue that there are also efficiency gains arising from private sector involvement. Critics contend that PFIs are more expensive than traditional public sector borrowing, because of the pursuit of profit and the need to provide a return to shareholders. They also argue that there is little effective transfer of risk to the private sector, as the state cannot afford to allow the projects to fail. The long record of PFI hospitals, schools and prisons remains contentious and includes some claimed successes and failures. Perhaps a more balanced verdict on the costs and benefits of PFIs will only be obtainable as projects reach the end of their 25-year agreements, and the ownership and maintenance of building reverts to the public sector.

---

*The **private finance initiative (PFI)** is a specific and controversial form of partnership, under which the private sector funds, builds and maintains public sector investment in, for example, hospitals, schools, prisons and roads. The relevant sponsoring public authority (local council or hospital trust) makes annual payments, typically for a period of 25 years, after which the assets become its property.*

---

Although much of the ideological debate has been over the relative merits of public provision and private provision for profit, there has been some focus on a third way – provision by mutually owned or voluntary organisations. The most important example of 'mutuals' used to be the building societies, which were owned by the members and not run for profit. However, after banking deregulation, most of the largest building societies became public limited companies with shareholders instead of members, who were generally happy to vote for the legal transfer of assets and pocket (often substantial) sums in recompense. Some of these staid and respectable former building societies became highly speculative banks that contributed significantly to the financial crisis from 2007 onwards.

The most significant example of voluntary provision of public services is now the housing associations, which were favoured as a 'third force' in the supply of rented accommodation by the Thatcher Conservative government (the other two being the council and private landlords). While most Labour councils opposed the sale of council houses in the 1980s, many voluntarily cooperated in the transfer of much of their remaining housing stock to housing associations, which have, over time, become major providers of rented 'social housing'.

Voluntary provision of public services is far from new in the UK. Indeed, in the nineteenth century it was generally the preferred method of provision. Thus schools were provided by voluntary religious organisations, with increasing state subsidy, and many hospitals were initially established on a voluntary basis. This suited Victorian opinion, which was suspicious of state intervention, and it remains more ideologically acceptable today to both free-market advocates hostile to direct state provision and to many within the Labour Party who retain an aversion to private provision of public services for profit.

'Voluntary organisations' conjure up images of small-scale operations by well-meaning but inexpert amateurs. However, many voluntary associations today are big businesses, employing substantial numbers of well-paid professional staff. Although they are 'not for profit', they are run on commercial lines, and while they are not part of government, they rely substantially on state financial support. They thus inhabit a grey area between the public and private sectors. However, while they lack some of the disadvantages of each, they may also lack some of their advantages. They may be less susceptible to the private sector discipline of market competition and less publicly accountable than mainstream government organisations. Nevertheless, they remain attractive to those seeking a third or middle way between the state and the market.

The Conservative governments of Thatcher and Major, the Labour governments of Blair and Brown and the Conservatives under Cameron emphasised the need for partnership with the private and voluntary sector. While Labour in opposition strenuously opposed most of the Conservative privatisation programme, CCT and many of the changes introduced into the health and education services, including internal markets, in government Labour generally proved unable or unwilling to put the clock back. The major Conservative privatisations were not reversed, and Labour itself proceeded with the part-privatisation of air traffic control. Although CCT was replaced by the more flexible 'best value' regime, the provision of key local government services was still subject to competition, and many remain privately provided. Labour effectively endorsed greater managerial delegation and autonomy by continuing the use of executive agencies and proceeding with further significant decentralisation and delegation within the NHS.

New Labour also enthusiastically embraced partnership with the private sector, through **public–private partnerships (PPPs)**, under which government departments, local authorities and other public bodies enter into partnership agreements with private firms on key developments and initiatives. Perhaps the most politically controversial of these schemes were the partnership agreements funding an extensive programme of new investment in the London Underground system, despite the strong opposition of Ken Livingstone, the then London mayor.

---

**Public–private partnerships (PPPs)** *involve formal partnership between government bodies (such as local councils), private firms and sometimes voluntary organisations to manage a specific initiative or deliver a policy.*

---

While PFIs were introduced by Major's Conservative government, they were endorsed and extensively utilised by Blair's Labour government. Under a PFI, the ownership and maintenance of the building (e.g. school or hospital) usually remains the responsibility of the private consortium, while the relevant public authority runs the service, employing and paying for professional staff, and meeting other day-to-day service costs. Some PFI prisons, however, were both built and run by the private sector.

Overall, New Labour did not challenge the trend towards the proliferation of agencies and fragmentation of government. It continued the roll-out of executive agencies, and replaced some older quangos with newer quangos of its own, although it cut or amalgamated others. However, it placed rather more emphasis on collaboration and cooperation between agencies and sectors. To counteract some of the problems of coordination arising from increased institutional fragmentation, it established a number of cross-cutting units or task forces in the interests of 'joined-up government', such as the Social Exclusion Unit.

## 'STEERING, NOT ROWING': NETWORKS, ENABLING AND GOVERNANCE

The cumulative impact of all these changes has transformed the character of the British state. While many services are still publicly funded, they are often no longer provided or controlled by government departments and local authorities but by all kinds and combinations of organisations, including private firms, voluntary bodies or decentralised quasi-autonomous public sector bodies. This has been described as a 'hollowing out' of the state. Yet it also suggests that the state is performing an essentially different role – an 'enabling' role, to borrow a term first used in Britain to describe the new role of local government, but which can also be applied to the role of the state as a whole. The key point is that the state is no longer necessarily providing services directly but 'enabling' others to do so – business, public–private partnerships, the voluntary sector, the community itself. An analogous term employed by the Americans Osborne and Gaebler (1992) is the notion of the state 'steering' rather 'rowing'. Governments should facilitate and coordinate rather than attempt to do everything themselves (see Table 18.1).

Instead of the old 'command and control' state, involving formal hierarchies and highly centralised decision-making, policy and decisions emerge today from complex partnerships or less formal networks of public, private and voluntary and hybrid organisations, working cooperatively together with relevant community groups and interests.

### Table 18.1 From old government to new governance: the shifting focus

| Old government | New governance |
| --- | --- |
| • The state | • The state and civil society |
| • The public sector | • Public, private and voluntary (or third) sectors |
| • Institutions of government | • Processes of governing |
| • Organisational structures | • Policies, outputs, outcomes |
| • Providing ('rowing') | • Enabling ('steering') |
| • Commanding, controlling, directing | • Leading, facilitating, collaborating, bargaining |
| • Hierarchy and authority | • Partnerships and networks |

*Source*: Adapted from Leach and Percy-Smith (2001) *Local Governance in Britain*, Palgrave. Reproduced with permission of Palgrave

The fashionable term 'governance' emphasises the process of governing rather than the institutions of government, and blurs the distinction between government and governed. Governance does not just include those who, as ministers, civil servants or elected councillors, are part of 'government', but business and the voluntary sector, as well as parties and pressure groups insofar as they contribute to the process of governance and the delivery of services to the community. No one is 'in charge'. Governance necessarily involves collaboration between agencies and sectors, and partnership working rather than the clear lines of authority and responsibility found in more traditional management hierarchies (Rhodes, 1997; Pierre and Stoker, 2002; Bevir and Rhodes, 2003). It draws on the agenda of Osborne and Gaebler in *Reinventing Government* (1992), some of the ideas of new public management (see Chapter 8, p. 154), together with strands of New Labour and third way thinking (Giddens, 1998; Newman, 2001).

Networks, almost by definition, require cooperation and collaboration, needing patience and diplomacy. Governance through networks involving a range of organisations and interests resembles a pluralist vision of widely dispersed power and influence. While a large number of organisations may be formally associated with the process of decision-making, some are commonly far more closely involved and count far more than others. In practice, those who bring useful resources to the table, such as money, land, expertise and legal authority, are more likely to 'call the shots'. Politics is still about power, and some inevitably have more effective influence than others.

Some organisations may indeed be only token participants in networks. Perhaps this is as well, for a large number of partners in any enterprise can be a recipe for procrastination. Yet decisions that emerge through networks raise other problems of responsibility and accountability. Formal partnerships may clearly determine respective responsibilities, commonly in legal documents. More complex and informal networks may not locate who is responsible and accountable, and real decision-makers may be able to hide behind the cloak of collective responsibility if things go wrong.

## THE REGULATORY STATE

There is nothing essentially new in regulation. Governments have long been in the business of regulating, although the extent of regulatory activity and regulatory bodies seems to have increased dramatically over the past 30 years or so, sufficiently to justify the term 'regulatory state'. Michael Moran (2000, 2001, 2003, 2005) has been particularly associated with the concept of the regulatory state involving a substantial shift in emphasis from state provision and control to state regulation, through a diverse range of bodies, such as the Competition Commission, the Health and Safety Executive, the NAO, Ofgem and many, many more.

Providers, public, private and voluntary, cannot be relied on to regulate themselves. External regulation of services provided by the state appears necessary to measure performance and ensure value for money. Voluntary bodies entrusted with taxpayers' money to provide public services need monitoring. Where former state-run enterprises or services have been privatised, there is a continuing need to regulate quality, prices, safety and efficiency in the wider public interest, particularly where there are monopoly elements or continuing state subsidies. Parts of the private sector, such as banks and the financial sector generally, require state regulation and support to maintain public confidence in the banking system. Beyond all this, the state is increasingly called upon to regulate all kinds of aspects of our lives in the wider public interest, including health and safety, hygiene, drug and alcohol consumption, childcare, care of the elderly, food standards, labelling and advertising and much else besides. The state may be providing less, but certainly appears to be regulating more. Thus there are a huge number of regulatory bodies of all kinds looking after us, some now facing abolition or merger following the coalition government's review.

## 🇬🇧 COMPARING BRITISH POLITICS 18.1 🇺🇸

### Regulatory capture in the USA

'Regulatory capture' is a term long used by observers of regulatory agencies in the USA. A particular agency established to regulate a profession or industry may become effectively captured by the interests it is supposed to regulate, instead of looking after the interests of consumers or the wider public. A notorious early example was the Interstate Commerce Commission established in the USA to prevent rail companies from collaborating to fix prices and exploit their customers, which instead became the protector and advocate of the railway interests. Regulatory capture can arise from the practice of appointing regulators with relevant knowledge and expertise, most easily found among those employed by the industry being regulated. Thus the US

Environmental Protection Agency was staffed by officials who had worked previously for known polluting firms, leading to a scandal and resignations when Congress investigated its ineffective enforcement of anti-pollution policy (Denenberg, 1996, pp. 159–60).

Critics would argue that some British regulatory bodies have similarly 'gone native', adopting the perspective of those whose activities they were expected to police. Moran pointed out that the Financial Services Authority (FSA), which was meant to regulate the financial services industry, was captured by the private interests that it was designed to regulate (Moran, 2005, pp. 158–9). Indeed, in the aftermath of the financial crisis, the FSA was closed down.

Regulation implies a less positive and constructive role for the state than the notion of enabling. An enabling state may initiate, encourage, sponsor or stimulate others (in the public, private or voluntary sectors) to work together to achieve some positive outcome. Moreover, the state is an active partner. Regulation suggests a more negative control function. The provision of goods and services is left to others. Managers in the public, private and voluntary sectors are given substantial discretion, autonomy and 'freedom to manage', but the state establishes appropriate regulatory authorities to inspect and measure their performance and police their activities. Rather more positively, governments can pursue policy objectives by rewarding success and punishing failure in meeting performance targets.

Moran (2005, pp. 158–9), however, argues that the regulatory state has created some serious problems. He notes problems for traditional ministerial and parliamentary accountability, particularly because of what he calls the 'ambiguous legal status' of some regulatory bodies. He also questions the effectiveness of some regulation, alluding to the danger of regulatory capture and pointing out: 'in the

case of the Financial Services Authority ... the regulated actually "own" the regulator'. These comments appear prophetic in the light of the failure of 'light-touch' regulation of the banks by the FSA, contributing to the banking crisis of 2007–08. But if some regulation appears weak and ineffective, critics suggest that other regulation is damaging and counterproductive, particularly the extensive monitoring of the health and education services through targets (see Chapter 20, pp. 430–33). Thus the new 'regulatory state' may be no more successful in achieving policy objectives than the old 'welfare' or 'control' state. While the media seize on ludicrous examples of overregulation, particularly on grounds of health and safety, they are quick to seize on failures of regulation, when relevant regulators have not picked up serious problems in hospitals, schools or social services. If much regulation is either heavy-handed or ineffective, the whole concept of a regulatory state seems suspect.

## CONCLUSION

So why does government blunder, as Crewe and King ask at the start of this chapter? In part, because policy-making is difficult. It rarely follows the tidy 'policy cycle' set out in the early stages of this chapter: policies are ill-conceived, policy-makers respond to events and are pulled by special interests in one direction or another. They are also guided by ideological assumptions they make about the world around them.

Indeed, changes in the past few decades – economic and ideological – have meant that the very remit and size of the state has been rethought. The ideas that dominated the immediate postwar world, in which policy-makers assumed that they could pull Keynesian economic levers to control the economy and the state should be responsible for a significant proportion of industry, were shunted aside in the 1980s by a belief in the market. Policy-makers became increasingly focused on commissioning services from private providers, overseeing the creation of arm's-length bodies, and on regulation of the market. The choices open to policy-makers in government and the approaches they used were very different to those used by their predecessors. It remains to be seen what happens next: whether the pendulum will swing back to greater state control; and how different policy-makers will cope with the many levels and tiers of government after devolution, not just to Scotland, Wales and Northern Ireland, but to city regions like Manchester too. Policy-making in government, and outside, is a complex and uncertain process.

 **SUMMARY**

»   Policy-making may be analysed as a cycle involving a number of stages, including issue emergence, problem definition, option appraisal, policy formulation, legislation and legitimation, implementation, monitoring and review. In practice, policy-making is far less likely to proceed in the orderly manner than the 'cycle' theory might imply.

»   The crucial first stage is for an issue to get onto the political agenda, and to be identified as a priority.

»   Once an issue is on the agenda, it is not necessarily self-evident what the 'real problem' is. Some familiar and recurring problems have been defined very differently. The problem may be 'captured' and defined by a particular interest in its own terms.

»   Various options or proposed solutions may be appraised using a variety of ostensibly rational techniques.

»   However, much policy-making in practice appears incremental rather than rational, and some argue that the incremental approach may be preferable.

»   A policy may be clearly announced, or emerge over time. Some analysts suggest that non-decision-making explains more about the nature and distribution of power than decision-making.

»   A policy is normally decided well in advance of legislation or some other form of formal legitimation.

»   However, legitimation is crucial for public acceptance and democratic accountability. Sometimes, problems with legitimation may effectively derail a policy.

»   Policies may not always be effectively implemented for a variety of reasons, including inherent problems, lack of resources, dependence on other agencies or interests for implementation, and political difficulties.

»   There is extensive machinery for the monitoring and review of policy. This may not always work as well as it might and can be counterproductive, but is essential in measuring efficiency and effectiveness. It can reveal that existing policies are not working, and thus inaugurate a new policy cycle.

»   The boundaries of the state have become blurred. In academic literature, there has been some switch in emphasis from considering the institutions of government to the process of governing (or 'governance'), which can involve the private and voluntary sectors.

» Under Conservative governments from 1979 to 1997, the rhetoric was about reining back the state. Some state assets and activities were privatised and others subjected to competition either from the private sector or through the introduction of internal markets.

» New Labour has emphasised partnership with the private and voluntary sectors and 'joined-up government'. Much new capital investment

for the public sector has been financed through the controversial private finance initiative (PFI).

» Under all governments there has been a growth in importance of appointed public bodies (quangos), for a variety of reasons.

» Under both recent Conservative and Labour governments the state's role has changed from providing to 'enabling'. A centralised and largely uniform welfare state has been replaced by more diversity of provision, and supervised by what has been described as a 'regulatory' state.

 **QUESTIONS FOR DISCUSSION**

» How and why do issues get onto the policy agenda? What kinds of issues might be relatively neglected?

» Why are some familiar issues, such as crime or inner-city poverty, so variously defined and explained?

» Are some policies kept off the agenda? Which policies and why?

» Why does it often appear that past policy is the most important factor influencing future policy? What radical shifts in policy have occurred in recent years and why?

» Do the issues that are not debated tell us more about power in Britain than those issues that are debated?

» In what ways are policies legitimated? How might problems in legitimation derail a policy?

» Why are some policies not implemented effectively and, sometimes, not implemented at all? How might governments secure fuller implementation?

» In what ways has the state been 'hollowed out'?

» How far does the growth of appointed public bodies threaten the principle and practice of representative democracy?

» How far and how successfully have the free-market principles of competition and choice been introduced into the running of public services?

» Has the old welfare state been replaced by a new regulatory state? Why has regulation grown? What are the difficulties associated with regulation?

 **FURTHER READING**

There is an extensive literature on policy-making and policy analysis. Dorey (2014) *Policy Making in Britain: An Introduction* (2nd edn) and Cairney (2011) *Understanding Public Policy: Theories and Issues* are both excellent introductions. Hill (2013) *The Public Policy Process* (6th edn) provides a more advanced overview of the policy process, while Hill has edited *The Policy Process: A Reader* (1997, 2nd edn), which contains extracts from some of the sources referred to here, and many others besides.

On quangos and the 'democratic deficit', see Weir and Hall (1994), Weir (1995), Skelcher (1998) and Weir and Beetham (1999). On privatisation and marketisation, see Ascher (1987), Self (1993) and Walsh (1995).

On governance, see Rhodes (1997, 2000) and Bevir and Rhodes (2003). On regulation and the regulatory state, see Moran (2000, 2001, 2003, 2005).

## USEFUL WEBSITES

Paul Cairney, mentioned above, runs a particularly good website, with lots of useful information, including a '1000 words' section, which sets out key policy theories and concepts: paulcairney.wordpress.com/1000-words.

*Further student resources to support learning are available at*
**www.macmillanihe.com/griffiths-brit-pol-3e**

# 19

# MANAGING THE ECONOMY

'It's the economy, stupid!' Bill Clinton's campaign manager declared in the 1992 US presidential election, explaining the importance of effective economic management to electoral success (Pryce et al., 2015). This is borne out in British electoral fortunes too. A generation before, in 1959, British Prime Minister Harold Macmillan boasted that the growing postwar economy meant 'You've never had it so good!', while advertisements for his party proclaimed 'Life's better under the Conservatives. Don't let Labour ruin it'. Labour's Harold Wilson won the 1964 and 1966 elections largely on his perceived economic mastery, only to lose in 1970 after the devaluation of sterling. Economic problems contributed substantially to the defeats of Heath in 1974, Callaghan in 1979 and Major in 1997. Labour's wins in 2001 and 2005 can be attributed to Gordon Brown's apparently successful management of the economy. By 2006, the authors of this book felt that Labour had 'captured the record of economic competence previously enjoyed by the Conservatives, with a record of low inflation and relatively low unemployment' (Leach et al., 2006, p. 358). Yet Brown was undermined by the impact of the global economic crisis of 2008. Thus management of the economy has often seemed to determine, or at least strongly influence, the outcome of elections and the fate of governments and politicians.

Some have claimed that recent political shell shocks, such as the UK referendum vote to leave the EU in June 2016 and the victory of Donald Trump in the US presidential election in November 2016, were further evidence of economic factors determining political outcomes. These largely unexpected results were widely attributed to a revolt by the poor white working class, left behind by the collapse of industry and decline of jobs in the US rust belt or much of the English north and Midlands, following the pressures of globalisation.

Not everyone agrees. Eric Kaufmann (2016) argues: 'It's not the economy, stupid.' He denies that Brexit and Trump's election 'had much to do with personal economic circumstances'. Instead, he distinguishes 'between those who prefer order and those who seek novelty'. Thus 'diversity and differences tend to alarm right-wing authoritarians, who seek order and stability'. He notes a close correlation between support for Brexit and support for the death penalty, which he claims both reflect right-wing authoritarian attitudes. Kaufmann's rejection of economic explanations in electoral success and the priority he gives certain values in politics has been controversial. However, it remains highly plausible that economic circumstances still matter: that the loss of jobs, income and material wellbeing, for example, are a factor in some voters' concerns about immigration and multiculturalism. People may accept change when it is linked with growth and prosperity, but reject it when it appears to involve a threat to their material circumstances. So the economy still seems critical to electoral and political choice.

## THIS CHAPTER:

» Explores who makes economic policy and how to assess outcomes.

» Examines the instruments policy-makers use, and the theoretical assumptions that influence decision-making.

» Discusses the use of the market to drive growth.

» Examines the record of recent British governments on the economy.

» Considers how the economic crisis has reshaped debates between economists and parties about growth.

## WHO MAKES AND SHAPES ECONOMIC POLICY IN BRITAIN?

Within British government, the chancellor of the exchequer and the Treasury traditionally dominate the framing of economic policy. From time to time, there have been attempts to separate longer term economic policy from immediate decisions on budgets and public finance (e.g. Wilson's creation of a separate Department of Economic Affairs when he was prime minister in 1964). Other departments, such as trade and industry or more recently business, have sometimes briefly appeared to have a major proactive role in various aspects of economic policy. Many prime ministers, particularly those with some claim to economic expertise (Wilson), strongly held economic assumptions (Heath, Thatcher), or who have previously served as chancellor (Churchill, Macmillan, Callaghan, Major and Brown), have taken a particular interest in economic policy. Indeed, some chancellors appeared effectively subservient to dominant prime ministers (Lloyd to Macmillan, Barber to Heath), while others have been forced out because their economic policies diverged from those of Number 10 (e.g. Thorneycroft by Macmillan

and Lawson by Thatcher). Among postwar premiers, only Attlee, Eden, Home, Blair and, most recently, Cameron have been content to leave economic management substantially to their chancellors. In the case of Blair, this self-denying ordinance allegedly went back to a deal in 1994, under which Brown agreed not to challenge for the Labour leadership in return for a free hand in economic policy and related areas. (Many of these relationships are discussed in more detail in Chapters 2 and 3.)

The Treasury's power has sometimes been perceived as largely negative, responsible for cutting down the creative policies and spending plans of other departments. This has particularly been the case during recurrent periods of economic crisis in Britain. Brown's role as chancellor was much more proactive, extending over welfare, labour and industrial policy, Europe and international development. Indeed, critics complained that 'the Treasury had become the Department of Social Policy' (Sampson, 2005, p. 130). Brown dominated much of the Labour government's domestic policy-making, and increasingly appeared co-equal with Blair, before he succeeded him as prime minister.

Within the Treasury, chancellors have sometimes appeared to be the mouthpiece for their officials, the formidable 'Treasury mandarins' – those civil servants working in the Treasury (the role of the Civil Service is discussed in much more detail in Chapter 8). Others, such as Jenkins, Healey, Howe, Lawson, Clarke, Brown and Osborne, have dominated the Treasury from the start and put their personal stamp on government economic policy. Following Labour's election victory in 1997, Treasury officials discovered that Gordon Brown, their new chancellor, 'had already taken the decisions that would set the new government's economic course' (Stephens, 2001, pp. 187–8). Much the same could be said of George Osborne in 2010. It is perhaps too early to judge the relative influence of Theresa May and her chancellor, Philip Hammond, on critical economic decisions.

Among other institutions, the Bank of England (formally nationalised by Labour in 1946, but operating as an independent body) has long loomed large in economic policy. Brown's decision to hand over decisions on interest rates to the bank's Monetary Policy Committee (MPC) in 1997 was balanced by the transfer of most of the bank's former regulatory power over the financial sector to the new Financial Services Authority (FSA). Osborne later decided to phase out the FSA and restore regulatory authority to the Bank of England, which now appears more powerful than ever (see below). Mark Carney, governor of the Bank of England, also remains a key figure.

Government economic policy-making, although normally dominated by the prime minister, chancellor and Treasury, is still strongly influenced and constrained by forces outside government. There are often tensions between elected politicians and unelected experts. For example, Conservative MPs repeatedly criticised Mark Carney over his economic warnings against Brexit ahead of the EU referendum in 2016. In her time as prime minister, May has also been critical of the bank over its decision to inject cash into the economy in the wake of the financial and economic crisis of 2008, a policy known as 'quantitative easing', and its decision to keep interest rates low to encourage borrowing. Carney, an unelected official, commented: 'Politicians have done a very good job of setting up the system. Where it can be difficult sometimes is if there are political comments on our policies as opposed to political comments on our objectives' (Dominiczak et al., 2016).

Influence is also sometimes attributed to important or colourful male entrepreneurs such as Richard Branson, Alan Sugar, Philip Green or Rupert Murdoch, although rather more significant are impersonal institutions, interests and markets, many of which transcend national boundaries. Among these are business interests in general and financial interests in particular. Recently, financial services, which focus on the lending, management and investment of money and assets, have appeared to be the engine of Britain's economic growth, and both Brown and Conservative shadow chancellors endorsed a 'light-touch' regulatory regime over bankers. The influence of the banks on policy has remained strong even after banking profits were replaced by massive losses, as the government could not allow them to fail without undermining confidence.

Major business firms, including multinational corporations, may exert a direct influence on government. Various sectors of the economy are represented by their own organisations, such as the Society of Motor Manufacturers and Traders. There are powerful health and education lobbies to which any government would be advised to pay some attention. Key business groups, such as the Confederation of British Industry and the Institute of Directors, have a high public profile and also exert influence behind the scenes. Prestigious think tanks, professional associations and some academic institutions are also listened to. Of course, economists weigh in with their own analysis and prescriptions, and this often underpins policy; for example, the influence of monetarism (discussed below) and public choice theory (discussed in Chapter 8) on the Thatcher government's economic management. More recently, divisions among economists have perhaps limited their influence.

Trade unions recovered some of their former influence with a Labour government from 1997 to 2010, but they remained much less powerful than in the immediate postwar decades. 'One of the things that struck most visitors to 11 Downing Street during the first Blair Parliament was that they were as likely to meet a departing venture capitalist as a trade unionist' (Stephens, 2001, p. 198). Trade union influence on the economic policies of the coalition and ensuing Conservative government appears limited. Out of office, under Jeremy Corbyn, the trade unions had a close relationship to the Labour leadership.

Beyond the ranks of organised business and labour, the influence of more specialist interests can be amplified considerably if they secure significant media publicity and public support, as was the case with truckers' protests in the fuel crisis of September 2000, which led to some modification of fuel taxation. Behind these particular institutions and interests are the wider public as voters, taxpayers and consumers of goods and services, including public services. Governments that ultimately must seek re-election ignore wider public concerns at their peril.

International obligations, as represented through such bodies as G7/G8 (and also more recently G20), the WTO, the International Monetary Fund (IMF) and of course the EU (at least up until the 2016 referendum), inevitably constrain British economic policy and effectively rule out some options. Credit rating agencies can downgrade the ratings of sovereign states, making it more expensive for them to borrow money. (A state's credit rating represents how likely they would be to default in paying back a bond – a **debt** mechanism, similar to a government taking out a loan. An 'AAA' rating would mean, for example, that a government has an extremely strong capacity to meet its financial commitments. Credit ratings are carried out by private companies, although the market is dominated by a few big agencies, notably Moody's and Standard & Poor's. Beyond all this, impersonal global markets can have a massive impact on national economies, particularly the British economy that is so locked into the global economy.

Wyn Grant (2002, pp. 8–9) recalls a seminar of international economic decision-makers. Someone asked, 'Who calls the shots?' The international financial institutions answered it was not them but the finance ministers of the major economies. The finance ministers argued that it wasn't them, it was the markets. Indeed, governments often appear helpless in the face of market forces. Yet markets are not quite as impersonal as they sometimes appear. While some markets consist of countless virtually powerless price-takers, others comprise a few very powerful price-makers.

---

**Debt** *is the total amount of money owed by a government. This can be built up over many years.*

---

## ASSESSING ECONOMIC POLICY

Simply describing who makes economic policy and the main tools they use is relatively easy. Assessing the effectiveness of economic policy is more difficult. All British governments have generally sought to maintain economic prosperity, encourage growth, pursue low inflation and unemployment and encourage what they consider a fair distribution of income and wealth. How far they have succeeded is commonly hotly contested, by their political opponents, the media, economists, business interests, trade unions and public opinion generally. Moreover, verdicts on prime ministers, chancellors, budgets and overall economic performance may vary over time. In retrospect, some may appear better or worse than they did at the time, in the light of subsequent developments.

One test is comparative. Are Britain's economic growth, inflation and unemployment rates better or worse than those in similar countries or among its main competitors? An annual growth rate of 2% may seem healthy, but less so if other countries are achieving 4% or more. Again, there may be plausible reasons for an apparently poorer record. Other countries may be starting from a lower base, perhaps recovering from the devastation of war (one possible reason why some countries in Western Europe had higher growth than Britain in the 1950s). Still others may have a particular concern over

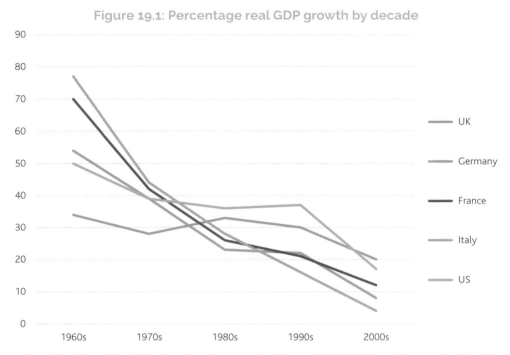

Figure 19.1: Percentage real GDP growth by decade

*Source*: Compiled from World Bank national accounts data and OECD National Accounts data files, http://data.worldbank.org/indicator/NY.GDP.MKTP.KD.ZG?page=

maintaining price stability because of past experience of hyperinflation (e.g. Germany).

There have long been some fundamental questions over the health of the British economy. Britain was the first country to industrialise and was once the world's leading economic power. And although the British economy has continued to grow over the past century or more, other countries have grown faster and Britain has suffered a relative economic decline. This relative economic decline began in the late nineteenth century, was manifest between the two world wars, and became the subject of heated economic and political argument in the postwar period. Productivity, growth and living standards were higher not only in North America but also among Britain's main competitors in Europe until the end of the 1970s (see Figure 19.1), with real GDP growth much slower than its main competitors after the Second World War. Successive governments sought to diagnose and address Britain's economic problems, but largely failed. No government had managed

to achieve steady economic growth for long, and none had ultimately been able to escape from the 'stop-go' boom and bust cycle of the postwar years.

## THE TOOLS OF ECONOMIC MANAGEMENT

If political fortunes rest substantially on successful economic management, how, then, do governments seek to manage the economy? They can intervene directly to control key aspects of the economy. They can use fiscal policy (taxation and government spending). They can use monetary policy (control of the money supply and interest rates). Generally, governments have employed a mix of these economic management tools, although the balance has varied over time, and, more recently, government rhetoric has generally emphasised the need for reduced state intervention and regulation, and more encouragement for free-market forces and business enterprise.

## DIRECT INTERVENTION

Governments can manage the economy through direct controls and intervention. In Britain, such direct control of the economy has been most evident in wartime. In directing the wartime economy, the coalition government led by Winston Churchill assumed massive powers of intervention in controlling the labour force, deciding on the location of industry, requisitioning economic assets, rationing the supply of raw materials to factories and so on. Some of these controls were briefly retained in the immediate aftermath of war, but largely disappeared during the 1950s. Nevertheless, peacetime governments have since attempted to control aspects of the economy through direct intervention.

A contentious example was the 1945–51 Labour government policy of nationalisation, involving the compulsory acquisition by the state of a number of key industries. Had Labour pursued a policy of wholesale nationalisation of industry, as implied in clause IV of its constitution (see Chapter 2, p. 22), this might have involved the kind of direct state management of the economy long advocated by many socialists. In practice, Labour only nationalised what they described as 'the commanding heights of the economy', and industries that were either already substantially municipally owned (gas, electricity, water) or appeared to be declining or in trouble (coal, gas again, railways, iron and steel). Moreover, the government did not seek to manage these industries, nor were they owned and run by workers, as some socialists had demanded. While government intervened to own these industries, the day-to-day running was placed in the hands of 'arm's-length' public corporations. While governments could and sometimes did lean on the chairs of boards to influence decisions on pricing or investment, they never sought to use state-owned industries to manage the economy.

With the exception of steel, the maintenance of a mixed economy with a substantial state sector remained a bipartisan policy from the 1950s through to the 1970s. This policy was sharply reversed by the Thatcher and Major governments, which privatised virtually all the former nationalised industries. New Labour accepted these privatisations, and even marginally extended them. Later, part-nationalisation of the banks in the wake of the 2008 financial crisis was presented as a necessary but strictly temporary expedient (see below).

Both major parties pursued other policies involving direct intervention in the economy. For example, in the fight against inflation, Labour and Conservative governments implemented prices and incomes policies (see Spotlight 19.1 overleaf). Both Labour and Conservative governments from 1945 through to 1979 pursued an industrial policy involving incentives to encourage investment and growth. Impressed by the success of economic planning in France, a Conservative government in 1962 set up the National Economic Development Council (familiarly known as 'Neddy') as a forum in which governments and both sides of industry discussed plans to improve Britain's industrial efficiency and international competitiveness. Later Labour governments set up other interventionist bodies – the Industrial Reorganisation Corporation in 1966 and the National Enterprise Board in 1975 – with a view to restructuring and strengthening Britain's industrial base. Labour and Conservative governments also strove to help economically depressed areas of Britain, particularly the former manufacturing regions, with an interventionist regional policy to attract new investment through grants and other financial incentives. During Thatcher's years in office, her governments pursued a more free-market and less interventionist approach to the problems of the British economy, not only privatising the former state industries, but abandoning incomes policy, cutting regional aid, scrapping interventionist bodies and allowing unemployment to rise and manufacturing industry to contract. (Urban policy, however, remained interventionist.)

From 1997 onwards, New Labour's direct economic intervention, if it can be so-called, involved incentives for investment and training, the micromanagement of the delivery of public services and tax and welfare policies designed to increase incentives to work and reduce child poverty.

# SPOTLIGHT ON ...    Incomes policies in the 1960s and 70s    19.1

In 1961 a Conservative chancellor, Selwyn Lloyd, introduced the 'pay pause', designed to hold down pay awards and help restrain inflation. Between 1965 and 1969, Labour pursued a prices and incomes policy, and the Conservative government that followed converted an informal incomes policy into a statutory policy which controlled all incomes between 1972 and 1974. Then, Labour, back in power from 1974 to 1979, developed a voluntary incomes policy, known as the 'social contract', under which trade unions accepted wage restraint in return for welfare benefits (the 'social wage'). But incomes policy proved ineffective in holding down wages for long. The social contract finally broke down in the 'winter of discontent' of 1978–79, a factor in the 1979 Conservative election victory. Since then, governments of both parties have avoided any formal incomes policy (either statutory or voluntary). Labour, however, introduced a statutory minimum wage in 1997, which later governments have continued.

## FISCAL POLICY

**Fiscal policy** is about the management of public finances and the economy through taxation and government spending. All governments have to raise taxes to finance their spending, commonly amounting to over two-fifths of national income since the Second World War. This government spending inevitably has a major influence on the wider national economy. Through their own spending, governments may seek to influence aggregate (or total) demand in the economy. As just one example, the government's decision to build the new HS2 rail link, at a cost of billions of pounds, will create thousands of new jobs (see Chapter 21, p. 452). Sometimes, fiscal policy is also used purposely to redistribute income and wealth.

---

*Fiscal policy* is about the management of public finances and the economy through taxation and government spending.

---

Gladstonian public finance (named after William Gladstone, the great nineteenth-century Liberal chancellor and prime minister) involved 'balancing the books' in the annual budget, ensuring that planned government expenditure over the coming year was met by planned government revenue from taxation and other sources. Later, Keynes argued that governments should not always seek to balance the books, but should deliberately aim to affect total or aggregate demand in the economy (see below). Subsequently, particularly under Thatcher, there was a return to balancing the books and controlling the money supply. This was carried out to reduce inflation, which reached close to 25% a year in 1975.

The budgetary process has always involved awkward choices between the calls on the public purse from different departments with spending needs, and between different means of raising taxation, with varying implications for individual taxpayers and businesses. Successive governments have sometimes sought to reduce income tax and raise pensions before elections, hoping they will be rewarded by voters. Governments may also use fiscal policy to achieve other objectives, to influence the behaviour of individuals and businesses by providing financial incentives, for example for green energy saving, or disincentives, for example to deter spending on goods deemed harmful (e.g. alcohol and tobacco).

## KEYNESIANISM AND DEMAND MANAGEMENT

From the 1940s through to the 1970s, governments of both parties used fiscal policy as a key tool of Keynesian demand management policies. Keynes himself was never a socialist, but a progressive liberal who believed in capitalism and free enterprise (see Key Figures 2.1). He sought not direct state intervention and detailed control of the economy but a system of managed capitalism. His theories involved a crucial distinction between **microeconomics** and **macroeconomics**. The government should leave microeconomics, the behaviour of individuals, households and firms, substantially to free-market forces. It would seek instead to influence macroeconomics and aggregate (or total) demand, through fiscal and monetary policy to secure full employment, stable prices and steady growth.

---

**Microeconomics** *involves theories about the behaviour of individual consumers, households and firms in the economy. Basic microeconomic theory assumes free markets, although goes on to examine the effects of imperfect competition and government intervention on market forces.*

---

**Macroeconomics** *is mainly concerned with the performance of the national economy, including levels of inflation, employment, growth and the balance of payments, and techniques for influencing or controlling these. It focuses on aggregate (or total) demand and supply in the economy.*

---

Keynes argued that economic depressions are caused by a lack of sufficient demand in the economy to purchase all goods and services when total economic resources (and particularly labour) are fully utilised. Falls in output and employment result in lower government revenue, higher welfare cost and budget deficits. In such circumstances, raising taxes and cutting public spending to reduce the deficit will cut demand still further and worsen the depression. Nor will cuts in wage rates help to raise demand for labour, as lower wages will reduce purchasing power and demand for goods and services and thus labour. The Keynesian remedy is to stimulate demand using fiscal policy (if necessary incurring a temporary budget deficit) and monetary policy (lower interest rates and easier credit). Inflation, on the other hand, is caused by excessive demand in the economy – too much money chasing too few goods. If the economy is already operating at full employment, it

*Source*: Tophams/Topham Picturepoint/Press Association Images

John Maynard Keynes.

is not possible to increase supply to meet excess demand and the consequence will be higher prices. Here, the Keynesian remedy is to reduce aggregate demand by taking purchasing power out of the economy through fiscal policy (through a budgetary surplus) and monetary policy (higher interest rates and credit restrictions).

Although Keynes's theory was developed in a period of depression for the British and the wider world economy, with policy implications for achieving economic recovery, it also involved remedies for inflation. Deficit finance, a deliberate surplus of government expenditure over income, was only supposed to be applied for a specific purpose for a limited period. However, the ideas of Keynes have sometimes been misinterpreted to justify government borrowing in general. Moreover, haunted by the memories of depression in the 1930s, governments of both parties in the early postwar period tended to respond to any rise in unemployment with measures to increase demand. They were also tempted to use Keynesian remedies for political purposes, to engineer a boom before an election, which commonly required deflation afterwards, with cuts in spending and higher taxation and interest rates (the familiar 'stop-go' economic cycle). When, in the 1970s, Keynesian remedies appeared to lead to steeply rising inflation *and* unemployment (or 'stagflation', as it was termed), as well as a mounting deficit in public finances, a Labour government, under James Callaghan, effectively abandoned Keynesianism.

Keynesianism was to remain out of fashion until the credit crunch and recession of 2007–09 led to a revival of arguments for deficit finance to encourage recovery (Skidelsky, 2010). Indeed, many countries, including Britain, initially sought to kick-start their economies by cutting taxes and maintaining spending. However, financial markets, credit ratings agencies and central banks together provided strong pressures for a rapid reduction in deficits almost everywhere. In Britain, after Labour's defeat in 2010, it was soon clear that the 'hawks', who wanted tough cuts to government spending to bring down the government's deficit, led by Chancellor George Osborne, dominated the Cameron coalition's economic policies, marginalising Keynesian economics once more, although the argument is by no means over. The May government, which took power in 2016, seems, for now, to have postponed reduction of the deficit.

## MONETARY POLICY AND MONETARISM

Just as all governments inevitably use fiscal policy, they can also hardly avoid having a monetary policy. The issue and control of money has long been a government function, with substantial implications for the economy. In the early sixteenth century, King Henry VIII expanded the money supply by debasing the coinage, with serious inflationary consequences. In 1923, the German government provoked hyperinflation by issuing too many banknotes, which were ultimately not worth the paper they were printed on. Today, it is rather more difficult to define, let alone control, the money supply,

but it is still the case that a failure in monetary policy can have dire consequences.

---

*Monetary policy is about influencing the money supply and the cost and/or availability of credit. Other things being equal, high interest rates may deter consumers from buying houses, cars and other goods, and businesses from making new investments. Low interest rates may encourage consumption and investment. Monetary policy, like fiscal policy, which deals with tax and spending, can also be used to reduce or stimulate aggregate demand in the economy, although it was subsequently advocated as an alternative to Keynesian demand management. Some economists (e.g. Milton Friedman) argued that effective control of the money supply was the key to the control of inflation.*

---

In the immediate postwar period, British governments often tried to restrict the availability of credit, for example requiring a substantial down payment as a condition of a bank loan or 'hire purchase'. More generally, governments have sought to influence the cost of borrowing by influencing or determining interest rates. Higher interest rates may deter borrowing and encourage saving, thus damping down demand in the economy, while lower interest rates may encourage spending and investment, stimulating an economy in recession. British governments have also sometimes felt obliged to increase interest rates to encourage foreigners to hold sterling when there is pressure on the currency in international money markets. Yet governments can only normally alter interest rates within fairly narrow limits set by market forces. Moreover, as a major borrower, government is not above the market but part of it. If the government seeks to increase its own borrowing by issuing more bonds, it will normally have to offer higher rates of interest to attract savers.

Overall, however, there are limits to the effect of changes in interest rates on behaviour. Very low interest rates will not encourage consumption and investment if households and businesses remain pessimistic about the future. Very high interest rates may similarly be ineffective.

The apparent discrediting of Keynesianism, deficit finance and 'tax and spend' policies led to more emphasis on monetary policy as a means to manage the economy, and in particular to restrain inflation, which had appeared 'out of control' in the early and mid-1970s. The economic policy of the Thatcher government was described as 'monetarism'. In narrow terms, monetarism meant controlling the money supply as the means to control inflation. It also entailed a return to Gladstonian public finance and the need to 'balance the books', in part because persistent government borrowing to finance current spending leads to inflationary pressures. The Thatcher government saw the control of inflation rather than the prevention of unemployment as the paramount aim of economic policy. To control the money supply, interest rates were kept high, which pushed up the value of the pound against other currencies. However, 15% interest rates did not discourage the selling of sterling on 16 September 1992, so-called 'Black Wednesday'; indeed, it had almost the opposite effect (see Spotlight 19.2 overleaf). Currency speculators saw it as a panic measure, confirming that the depreciation of sterling was inevitable, and sold pounds in the expectation of being able to buy them back later at a lower price. High interest rates and a high pound depressed investment and exports, with disastrous consequences for British manufacturing industry. Moreover, monetarism in the narrow sense proved unsuccessful. Whatever definition of the money supply was used, it did not seem to have much direct impact on inflation and the overall performance of the economy. If the Thatcher government achieved any success in the economic sphere, it was in spite of its failure to control the money supply or secure significant cuts in overall public spending.

Interest rates began to come down after Black Wednesday, in the latter years of Major's government and have remained historically low since. The New Labour government appeared to abandon any control of monetary policy with its surprise decision to hand over control of the minimum lending rate to the MPC of the Bank of England. This was a clever political move that gained the all-important confidence of business and the markets. But the government retained influence over monetary policy through its appointments and, more importantly, through its broader economic policy, which provided the background to the decisions of the MPC.

## ENCOURAGING MARKET FORCES

Behind the debates over Keynesianism and monetarism lies an older and wider argument over the whole role of government and the state in the economy. In the immediate postwar decades, there was a presumption in favour of state intervention to provide work, welfare 'from the cradle to the grave' and greater equality. This presumption was shared by one-nation Conservatives (discussed in Chapter 2) as well as Labour. Yet from the 1970s, it was increasingly challenged by many on the New Right, who argued that the state had grown too big, that high taxation destroyed incentives and enterprise and that state welfare encouraged a 'dependency culture'. A radical remedy was needed, which went beyond tinkering with fiscal and monetary policy. The state must be 'reined back' and market forces allowed to work.

Advocacy of the free market by the Thatcher government never involved a wholesale rejection of state intervention, public spending and public services. To this extent, her economic policies disappointed the more enthusiastic apostles of the free market. However, three key policy areas involved a shift towards the free market:

1   A reduction in the power and influence of trade unions led to a freer labour market.

2   The privatisation of state-owned assets promoted wider share ownership, homeownership and 'popular capitalism'.

3   Elements of competition and quasi-markets were introduced into the management of public services, particularly health and education (see Chapter 20).

# SPOTLIGHT ON ...

## The legacy of Black Wednesday, 16 September 1992

19.2

Thatcher was reluctantly persuaded by Cabinet colleagues in 1990 that Britain should enter the European Community's Exchange Rate Mechanism (ERM). This meant the government undertook to maintain the exchange rate of sterling against the currencies of other member states of the European Community (the forerunner to what is now the EU). It was recognised that this might cause some economic hardship in the short term, particularly if inflation made British goods uncompetitive abroad, but the longer term benefits of ERM membership would be low inflation and low interest rates.

However, the depth and length of the recession that had begun in the late 1980s surprised the government. At first it was dismissed as a blip in the economy; later, it was clear that the UK was in the middle of its deepest recession since the 1930s. By December 1990, Chancellor of the Exchequer Norman Lamont (1999, p. 140 ff.) claimed he could see the 'green shoots of recovery' and reassured the public that the recession would be 'relatively short-lived and relatively shallow'. But the persistent poor performance of the British economy, coupled with a growing conviction in world money markets that the pound appeared overvalued, led to increased pressure on sterling.

The crisis came to a head in mid-September 1992. Currency markets began a mass sell-off of the pound, believing it would not be able to remain within the ERM. The government tried to defend the pound by using almost all its reserves of foreign currency to buy sterling in a desperate attempt to maintain the exchange rate. On Wednesday 16 September, interest rates were raised to an unprecedented 15%. It all provided fruitless, and Lamont, backed by a young David Cameron as his special adviser, had to announce that evening the withdrawal of sterling from the ERM and a consequent devaluation of the pound. The episode was widely viewed as a political disaster for the Conservative Party, destroying their economic strategy, and became known as 'Black Wednesday'.

This may appear increasingly remote history – especially as the economic recession of the 1990s was dwarfed by that of the crisis that took hold of the economy in the UK and around the world in 2007–08. But it proved a pivotal moment in people's confidence in the economic competence of the major parties. Previous economic disasters, such as the 1931 crisis, the devaluations of 1949 and 1967, and the 1976 IMF crisis had taken place under Labour governments, although arguably Labour was not to blame for the underlying problems. By contrast, the Conservatives were credited with stable handling of the economy. But Black Wednesday destroyed the Conservative Party's reputation for economic competence almost overnight. The turnaround played a significant part in New Labour's huge election victory in 1997 and their subsequent dominance of British politics; until well after the economic crisis of 2007–08, Labour became the party most trusted by voters to manage the economy.

In some ways, the Conservatives, like Labour earlier, were unfairly blamed for Black Wednesday; after all, the Labour opposition had supported ERM entry in 1990. Just as almost two decades later, when the latest financial crash came, Labour again lost their reputation for economic competence, despite the Conservatives supporting many of the economic policies Labour had put forward beforehand. The Conservative Party endured five more years in office until the 1997 general election, when they lost heavily to New Labour. The Conservative's reputation for economic management took years to recover. The Black Wednesday crisis demonstrates the importance of economic credibility to a political party's electoral success.

Admirers credit the Thatcher government (1979–90) with addressing long-standing problems with the British economy: poor industrial relations partly reflecting trade union power, inflation, escalating public spending, lack of incentives for enterprise and overreliance on subsidies. Critics argue that the economic, social and political costs of Conservative remedies were worse than the disease. High interest rates led to two recessions that further reduced British manufacturing industry, and led to over 3 million unemployed. Boom and bust in the housing market led to repossessions and ruin for many. The defeat of union power, symbolised by the bitter miners' strike of 1984–85, coupled with divisive tax and welfare policies, split the country and intensified social and political opposition to Thatcherism.

The intellectual climate was transformed. A presumption in favour of state intervention and state provision, which had dominated postwar politics, was replaced by a presumption in favour of the free market and private enterprise. Even the Labour Party leadership was largely converted. Although Labour had opposed the Thatcher government's trade union reforms, the privatisation of public utilities, the sale of council houses and the marketisation of public services, they did not subsequently seek to reverse them and indeed embraced the language of competition and choice. New Labour, first in opposition and then in government, courted business and was no longer seen as hostile to their interests.

# NEW LABOUR: ECONOMIC GROWTH AND PUBLIC SERVICE INVESTMENT

Labour inherited a sound economy, which they maintained for a decade. Gordon Brown as chancellor immediately and unexpectedly announced the transfer of decisions on interest rates to the MPC of the Bank of England. He also signalled his determination to keep inflation low by announcing a 2.5% target rate, and announced that government would stick to what economists have referred to as a 'golden rule' of only borrowing to finance investment, and keeping public debt at a stable and prudent proportion of national income over the economic cycle. Labour honoured two pre-election pledges, to sign up to the Social Chapter of the Maastricht Treaty (from which Major had secured an opt-out) and to introduce a national minimum wage. Neither proved as damaging to business as critics had feared. Indeed, they had little if any measurable impact on inflation and unemployment. While Blair appeared keen for Britain to join the euro, Brown was more cautious, supporting entry only if five economic tests could be met. However, the main problem was perhaps political; winning a referendum in the face of a largely hostile British public.

The commitment to keep within Tory spending plans constrained Labour's policies in the first two years. However, Brown did raise some additional revenue from a windfall tax on the privatised utilities, raising national insurance contributions and removing some forms of tax relief. These 'stealth taxes', as the opposition called them (e.g. BBC News, 1998), enabled him to pursue some (limited) redistribution of income, inject some (initially fairly modest) additional money into public services and finance his New Deal to move the young unemployed 'from welfare to work'. Investment was encouraged through the establishment of regional development agencies (with limited budgets, however) and, more controversially, enthusiastic encouragement of the private finance initiative (PFI), developed under the previous government. A major attraction was that PFIs enabled substantial additional investment in new hospitals, schools and prisons without increasing public sector borrowing, although critics objected that the long-term costs would be far higher, as, indeed, proved the case.

Subsequently, the self-imposed shackles on public spending were partially removed, and substantial new money was made available for public services, particularly health and education. Increased spending was achieved partly through economic growth (resulting in a higher tax take) and expectation of further growth, although some extra revenue was raised through more 'stealth taxes' with a less immediately visible impact. Thus while the standard rate of income tax was actually reduced, along with some business taxes, national insurance contributions and indirect taxes were increased. Although the Conservative opposition criticised the 'stealth taxes', they promised to match Labour's increased spending on health and education.

Hence Labour captured the record of economic competence previously enjoyed by the Conservatives. Chancellor Gordon Brown claimed he had broken the cycle of boom and bust of earlier years, achieving steady economic growth for 40 consecutive quarters (Lee, 2008, p. 33). In marked contrast to earlier decades, Britain's economic performance appeared rather better than most of its leading competitors. By the time Brown moved from Number 11 to Number 10 Downing Street in 2007, some admirers were hailing him as Britain's most successful chancellor for a century or more. Through his long period at the Treasury, the British economy experienced low inflation, low interest rates, relatively high employment and continuous economic growth higher than most of Britain's major competitors, a combination many previous chancellors of any party would have died for. Moreover, Brown had also appealed to progressive opinion by achieving some modest redistribution to benefit poor families and mothers, and by taking a lead in cancelling third world debt and supporting international trade and development.

However, Brown always had his critics. Business interests had become increasingly critical of the rise in public spending and the economic consequences in terms of higher taxation, although others suggested that Labour had not raised taxation sufficiently to cover necessary increases in spending on health and education. Left of centre critics argued that Labour had not significantly reduced inequality in general, and had only tinkered with the substantial inequality among pensioners. Green critics deplored Labour's uncritical pursuit of economic growth, its concessions to the road lobby on fuel taxes and its refusal to make the aircraft industry bear the full cost of its fuel consumption and environmental pollution.

Indeed, many of the old problems in the British economy remained. There was still a substantial balance of payments deficit, a lack of skills and lack of investment in manufacturing industry and a persistent productivity gap compared with Britain's main competitors (Lee, 2008, pp. 17–33). A more immediate concern was the alleged developing 'black hole' in Britain's public finances. Many independent critics suggested that the government's economic forecasts were overoptimistic, and that further tax increases or spending cuts were required to maintain Brown's 'golden rule' of balancing taxation and expenditure over the economic cycle and only borrowing to fund new investment. Britain was not ideally placed to face the economic storms ahead.

## NEW LABOUR AND THE GLOBAL FINANCIAL CRISIS

Soon after Brown became prime minister in 2007, his government faced mounting problems with, first, the banks and then the economy as a whole. The financial crisis, which few had anticipated, substantially originated in the USA, where a housing boom collapsed, with increasing defaults on home mortgages, particularly 'subprime' mortgages, that is, mortgages given to high-risk borrowers, sometimes described as NINJA loans (no income, no job or assets). This led to serious cash flow problems for the financial institutions involved, both in the USA and elsewhere (Lanchester, 2010). The crisis rapidly became global; particularly badly affected were Iceland, Ireland, Greece, Spain and Portugal.

The root causes of the financial crisis have been much analysed. The answer to who or what was responsible varies widely, is shaped by ideological assumptions about the role of the market and the state and coloured by partisan bias. Three broad narratives of blame are common:

1 The first account views the crisis as international, stemming from the USA. This view stresses the indebtedness of many US banks, which had issued mortgages to home buyers who were unable to pay them back. These banks then repackaged their debts and sold them on to other financial institutions, spreading the 'subprime' crisis across the world.

2  A second narrative suggests that the policies of New Labour generated the crisis. The Conservatives popularised this view after 2010, blaming the UK's economic vulnerability on Labour's 'overspending' on public services when in office (see the brief review of the debate in Chivers and Perraton, 2015). As David Cameron, former prime minister, frequently noted, in a metaphor that resonated with voters, the government had failed to 'fix the roof when the sun was shining' (BBC News, 2014), that is, they borrowed too much and failed to create an economy that was ready for future shocks (see Comparing British Politics 19.1 below for Reinhart and Rogoff's account of this).

3  A final account sees the crisis as stemming from the 1980s and the policies of Thatcherism, particularly Thatcher's 'right to buy' scheme, which created an unsustainable property boom, and the Big Bang financial deregulation of 1986 (both discussed in Chapter 3). To critics, this shifted the economy towards overdependence on financial services, which paved the way for the crisis (Kirkland, 2015).

The 2007–08 crisis was dramatically illustrated by a series of failures or near failures of major banks, with bailouts by governments (and ultimately taxpayers) to prevent a collapse in confidence in the whole banking system. However, the financial crisis and the measures taken to cope with it precipitated recession in the global economy. Although interest rates were historically low, bank lending was reduced and loans called in, house prices and consumer spending dropped, businesses failed and output and employment fell. All this inevitably meant lower government revenue from taxes and higher public spending on unemployment and other benefits. Coupled with other measures taken by governments to boost the economy and take countries out of recession, this led to mounting government deficits, to an extent that disturbed international financial institutions (Skidelsky, 2010, Ch. 1).

The Labour government could, not unreasonably, blame Britain's financial crisis and recession on global forces outside its control. Moreover, Brown acted energetically to deal with the crisis and save the banking system in 2008, and then took a lead role in securing concerted international action. Gordon Brown's long experience in managing economic policy and the extensive contacts he had built up around the world were significant assets here. He dominated the deliberations of the G20 emergency summit in London in 2009. Political journalist Andrew Rawnsley (2010, pp. 633–4), no fan of Brown, comments that the British prime minister successfully assumed the role of global chancellor, which 'played to his strengths ... garnered approving headlines and won the applause of his international peer group'. However, he adds: 'The missing ingredient was making it relevant to voters.'

Brown may have helped avert catastrophe, but he was hardly blameless for the problems Britain faced. He and the regulatory system he put in place had done nothing to curb the rise in credit card debt and overgenerous 120% mortgage loans (which, in some cases, relied on self-certified declarations of borrowers' income), practices comparable to the disastrous subprime mortgages offered in the USA. By October 2007, there was £1,200 billion outstanding on mortgage debt and £222 billion on unsecured consumer credit. In seven years, personal debt had risen by 115%, while over the same period earnings had risen by less than 30% (Elliott and Atkinson, 2009, p. 176). Many had incurred levels of debt that they were in no position to repay, particularly if faced with a drop in income. This meant that financial institutions were left holding 'assets' (mortgages and loans) on their balance sheets that were overvalued and could not be realised if their customers defaulted. Many of these 'toxic' mortgages and loans were packaged up and sold on to other financial institutions in a process misleadingly described as 'securitisation', which affected the whole financial sector and not just those banks responsible for the initial unsound loans. Britain's reliance on financial services was no longer a benefit. Indeed, for critics of the UK, the oversized financial sector had become a 'curse' on the UK's economy, reducing economic diversity and entrepreneurialism, and creating unemployment, economic instability, inequality, conflict and corruption (Christensen et al., 2016).

Meanwhile, the government's own finances had become more suspect, as Brown abandoned his earlier prudence in his years as chancellor, and relied on optimistic forecasts of growth and government revenue to meet dramatic increases in public spending. He only avoided breaking his own 'golden rule' to finance new investment out of revenue by changing the accounting period. So the government was not ideally placed to deal with the crisis it soon faced. An early harbinger of the troubles to come was the run on the Northern Rock bank in September 2007, not long after Brown himself moved from Number 11 to Number 10 Downing Street, and Alistair Darling became chancellor.

Northern Rock had been a respectable building society based in Newcastle, offering mortgages financed by the savings deposited by its members, like other mutual societies. In common with many other mutuals, it took advantage of Conservative government legislation allowing building societies to convert into banks, a process that gave windfall profits to members in the form of shares, often sold on. The new bank expanded rapidly, more than tripling its share of the UK mortgage market from 6% to 19%, sometimes by offering up to 120% of a house's value (compared with 75% or 80% traditionally offered by building societies). However, its cash reserves were soon insufficient to meet potential demands arising from its very liquid liabilities and highly illiquid assets (in the shape of bricks and mortar). Faced with a funding crisis, the bank was forced to seek help from the Bank of England, the lender of last resort, in September 2007. This failed to restore confidence, leading to the first major run on a British bank for more than a century. The immediate crisis only ended when Darling guaranteed all Northern Rock deposits, and was virtually forced to nationalise the bank in February 2008.

*Source*: Johnny Green/PA Archive/PA Images

The collapse of Northern Rock in 2007, the UK's fifth biggest mortgage lender, led to the country's first bank run since the nineteenth century as customers queued to withdraw their savings.

Northern Rock provided an early warning of problems in the banking system in Britain and many other countries. Financial institutions in the USA, France, Belgium, Iceland, Ireland and elsewhere faced similar liquidity crises. Some were rescued by mergers and takeovers, others by state bailouts, while a few, like the massive US investment bank Lehman Brothers, were allowed to fail. Bank regulation in the USA and other countries besides Britain appeared to be ineffective.

In September 2008, HBOS (formed from a merger of Halifax, another former building society, and the Bank of Scotland) was taken over by Lloyds TSB, a marriage arranged and supported by the government. Bradford & Bingley, another former building society, was virtually nationalised after it had expanded rashly into providing mortgages in the buy-to-let market. In October, the government took a controlling stake in the Royal Bank of Scotland (which also owns NatWest) and a 40% share in Lloyds TSB and HBOS. Among the major British banks, only Barclays and HSBC avoided part-nationalisation. While there was all-party agreement that state support was necessary to preserve public confidence, there was public anger at the failure of light-touch regulation of the banks, the 'bonus culture' in the city that provided incentives for the aggressive marketing of risky loans and the apparent inability of the government to curb extravagant bonuses and pensions, even in banks they virtually owned.

Labour's strategy for dealing with the recession was similar to that of governments in many other leading economies. There was initially broad agreement that cutting public spending and increasing taxation to reduce mounting deficits too early would only make the recession worse and delay recovery. Although the deficits would eventually have to be tackled, this would have to wait until the return of growth. This was one lesson learned from the earlier Wall Street Crash of 1929.

The severity of the downturn that began in 2007–08 has been compared with the earlier Great Depression of 1929 onwards. There are some obvious similarities. Both started in the USA with rash speculation in property and shares leading to a stock market crash and a banking crisis. However, the Great Depression was far deeper and lasted much longer (Skidelsky, 2010, p. 15). Unemployment rose much faster and higher, and remained high, with enduring social consequences. Major bank failures in the USA and around the world triggered a huge crisis in confidence. World GDP fell by 12% from 1929 to 1930, but only by 1.37% in 2008–09. The later recession was less damaging because policy-makers had learned from the mistakes made in 1929 and to some degree the lessons of Keynes. So central banks slashed interest rates, governments propped up the banks with public money and G20 leaders agreed to stimulate national economies and avoid economic protection of the kind that led to a major contraction of world trade in the 1930s. However, it can also be argued that the later crisis happened because one lesson of 1929 had been forgotten – the need for tight regulation of financial services and controls over the growth of credit. Curiously, while both recessions involved a crisis of capitalism, the main political beneficiaries were parties of the right or far right. In Britain, the obvious political losers were Labour, who happened to be in government during both crises. The Conservative Party, which became the largest party in 2010, was highly effective at blaming the financial crisis and economic crash on Labour.

## CONSERVATIVE-LED GOVERNMENTS AND 'THE POLITICS OF AUSTERITY'

The 2010 election led to the first coalition government in Britain since the war. While Lib Dems held the positions of business secretary (Vince Cable) and chief secretary to the Treasury (David Laws and then Danny Alexander), government economic policy remained firmly in the hands of Osborne, who had the full confidence of Cameron, the prime minister. Osborne had been shadow chancellor since 2005, and had managed Cameron's campaign to become Conservative leader. Osborne was to remain chancellor from 2010 to 2016, when he was not reappointed by May, the new prime minister, after the vote for Brexit. As shadow chancellor and chancellor, however, Osborne was at the centre of debate over economic policy for almost as long as Gordon Brown, and enjoyed the full support of Cameron. In 2007, Osborne pledged that the Conservatives would match Labour's public spending plans for the next three years, a pledge that was soon overtaken by events.

As chancellor of the coalition government that took office in 2010, Osborne moved swiftly to make institutional changes that were foreshadowed before the 2010 election, including the creation of the independent Office for Budget Responsibility (OBR: see Spotlight 19.3) and the Financial Conduct Authority to replace the FSA

established by Labour. Overall responsibility for regulating banks and financial services was handed back to the Bank of England, and the new Financial Policy Committee was established within the Bank of England to oversee the whole financial sector. The Independent Commission on Banking, under the chairmanship of Sir John Vickers, was appointed to look into the possible breakup of large banks, which advised that banks should be made to 'ring-fence' their retail banking from their investment banking arms. In addition, a new Prudential Regulation Authority was created as a part of the Bank of England by the Financial Services Act 2012 to regulate banks and the Competition and Markets Authority was set up to look after the interests of consumers (see Figure 19.2).

## SPOTLIGHT ON ...    The Office for Budget Responsibility    19.3

The OBR was set up ostensibly to provide economic forecasting independent of government, although initially it was staffed largely by a team of staff seconded from the Treasury. This initiative of Osborne has been compared with the earlier decision of Brown in 1997 to transfer responsibility for setting interest rates to the MPC of the Bank of England. Both moves were well received by the markets and commentators, and

were politically astute. Osborne argued that the earlier Treasury forecasts were often overoptimistic, influenced by government hopes and aspirations. Critics argued that the OBR was not truly independent, however, as it was not responsible to Parliament, like the Office for National Statistics and the National Audit Office. It remains questionable whether its forecasts are more accurate than earlier Treasury forecasts.

## THE COALITION AND DEFICIT REDUCTION

These institutional reforms were soon overshadowed by the main thrust of the coalition government's economic policy, set out in the emergency budget of 22 June 2010. This followed the outgoing Labour chancellor's budget of March 2010, which had raised national insurance contributions, announced £11 billion spending cuts and conceded the need for substantial future spending cuts, without specifying details. Previous Labour budgets had introduced a new 50% tax rate and reduced tax relief for pension contributions for high earners. None of this, apart from the increased employer's national insurance contributions, was substantially altered by Osborne, although his tax changes and

proposed cuts went much further, amounting to a significant change in direction for British economic policy.

Osborne initially promised a programme of spending cuts and tax rises that would transform the massive **deficit** to a surplus within the life of a Parliament. The UK entered a new age of 'austerity', where the government would reduce its deficit largely through cuts to public spending. Indeed, austerity became the watchword of the Conservative Party under Cameron and Osborne. One issue was how far this larger and faster programme of cuts might

---

**Deficit** is the difference between a government's day-to-day spending and the revenues it receives in taxes and other income.

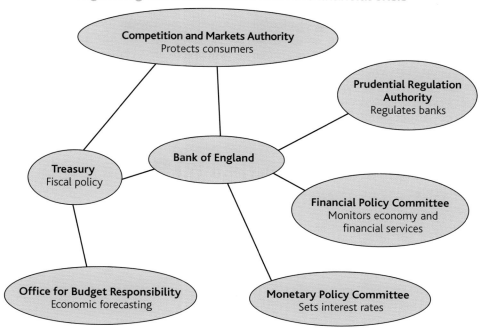

Figure 19.2: The system for managing the economy and regulating financial services after the financial crisis

endanger the fragile economic recovery and threaten a double-dip recession. Economists influenced by Keynes worried that the rapid reduction of government spending would reduce demand and slow the economy further. Osborne, by contrast, seems to have convinced his coalition partners, including the previously sceptical Cable, that a more rapid reduction of the deficit was necessary to reassure markets and the all-important credit rating agencies to avoid increases in interest on government debt (see Comparing British Politics 19.1 overleaf). Even more controversial was the balance between planned spending cuts (77%) and tax increases (23%) to achieve the deficit reduction. The size of the additional proposed cuts, on top of Labour's, implied an average reduction in the budgets of all departments not ring-fenced (principally health and international development) of 25%. Extensive changes in taxes and benefits were spelt out. Key measures included:

» Raising VAT from 17.5% to 20% from 2011

» Raising capital gains tax for higher rate taxpayers to 28%

» Increasing personal income tax allowances by £1,000 to £7,475

» Cutting corporation tax by 1% for four years successively from 28% to 24%

» A new levy on banks to raise £2 billion

» Freezing child benefit for three years

» Freezing public sector pay for two years, except for those earning less than £21,000

» Restoring the link between the basic state pension and earnings rather than prices

» Reducing tax credits for families earning more than £40,000

» Restricting housing benefits to £400 a week

» Reviewing disability allowances

» Reviewing public sector pensions.

The government described the budget as 'tough but fair' (BBC News, 2010). The toughness was undisputed, although the claim to fairness was more contentious. Lib Dems hailed the higher personal tax allowances as the first stage in a programme to take all those earning under £10,000 out of income tax, a key plank in their election manifesto. (However, several previous chancellors had similarly taken lower earners out of income tax, only for wage inflation to bring them back in.) The new government also argued that the major tax changes would affect mostly high earners. However, the Institute for Fiscal Studies pointed out that much of this was the responsibility of the outgoing Labour government, while the cuts in public spending and reductions in welfare benefits (particularly housing benefits) would clearly impact mostly on poor families and poor regions. Moreover, the increase in VAT (for which Cameron claimed there were 'no plans' before the election), while affecting everyone, impacts more on those who have little choice but to spend all their income, although food and children's clothes remained exempt.

## ⚏ COMPARING BRITISH POLITICS 19.1 ⚏

### Public debt and the Reinhart-Rogoff controversy

Governments around the world responded to the financial and economic crisis of 2007–08 by going into debt. Banks were bailed out and public spending continued, despite the economic slowdown significantly reducing tax income. Governments in Europe and the USA pursued Keynesian stimulus programmes to get the economy moving again. This raised the question, is this a problem? Can economies be healthy, while being in debt?

In a controversial article, Carmen Reinhart and Kenneth Rogoff (2010), two Harvard professors, presented their answer. Using a huge international dataset, Reinhart and Rogoff found that economic growth slows to a snail's pace once government debt levels exceed 90% of GDP. The 90% figure was picked up by politicians on the right of the political spectrum. In the USA, Republican congressman Paul Ryan cited Reinhart and Rogoff's 'conclusive empirical evidence' to provide support for austerity measures – notably, rapid cuts in public spending.

Ryan was critical of the Obama administration's economic stimulus. Shortly before the 2010 general election, George Osborne, then shadow chancellor, drew on the authors' arguments to justify big cuts in government spending.

The problem was that Reinhart and Rogoff had their numbers wrong (Herndon et al., 2013). The dataset they used left important years and countries out of the analysis. When they were included, the 90% threshold became meaningless. There was a correlation between high debt and low growth, but it was nothing like as stark as Reinhart and Rogoff had argued. Nor was there evidence about the direction of causation. It was no clearer that high debt caused slow growth, than it was that slow growth led to debt. The direct link between significant national debt and slow economic growth was far less clear than many advocates of austerity had assumed. In the USA under President Obama, Reinhard and Rogoff's claims never really made it into policy. In Britain, since 2010, they have.

As far as the impact on people was concerned, there was a planned cut of £18 billion from welfare, including pensions, child benefit, housing benefit and a range of incapacity and disability benefits. Among the obvious losers were the poor and women, who lost benefits and services and saw their retirement age planned to rise rapidly to 66 (the same as for men) by 2020. Employee contributions to public sector pensions also rose. The elderly emerged from the review comparatively unscathed – their free bus passes, winter fuel allowances and free TV licences all survived the cuts, while the earnings link of the state pension was restored. However, the elderly and infirm suffered from cuts in social services. Some critics argued that the real government objective was an ideological project to shrink the state and dramatically reduce the scope and scale of Britain's public services. The size of the budget deficit provided a plausible excuse for doing what they wanted to do anyway.

*Source:* Leon Neal/Getty Images
Food banks have become a part of everyday life for many people since the economic crisis.

But, both Cameron and Osborne lamented the need for cuts and described themselves as progressive one-nation Conservatives, while their Lib Dem partners in government largely supported welfare spending.

The introduction of austerity politics fundamentally changed British politics. It led to the election of Jeremy Corbyn as Labour leader, a one-time rank outsider who easily beat his rivals for the job in 2015 (and again in 2016 when he was challenged) in large part because of his unequivocal rejection of 'austerity'. This position galvanised a surprising amount of support, particularly among younger voters, in the 2017 general election.

It is too early to make any judgement on Osborne's successor as chancellor, Philip Hammond, the former foreign secretary. He, like Cameron and Osborne, supported the UK remaining in the EU, but now has the awkward responsibility for managing the UK economy throughout negotiations over Brexit, and planning for an economic future for Britain outside the EU. This will be partly shaped by

other Conservative politicians, including Prime Minister May, Foreign Secretary Boris Johnson, International Trade Minister Liam Fox and Brexit Secretary David Davis (the last three of whom campaigned to leave the EU). It will probably be influenced even more by political leaders in EU states, and others around the world. As negotiations on the UK's terms of withdrawal from the EU continue, the biggest questions are economic, concerning the UK's access to the EU market and the ability of EU members to work in the UK and vice versa.

Altogether, Britain currently faces a more difficult and contentious economic future than at any time since the Second World War. However, one of Osborne's commitments has apparently been shelved. The new government seems to have postponed, for the foreseeable future at least, his plans to eliminate the deficit by 2020, which perhaps makes some sense while the cost of borrowing remains low and new investment is urgently needed. However, even this apparent change of direction will be at the mercy of external markets and the dreaded credit rating agencies. Apart from that there was little to comfort those who are 'just about managing' – coining a newly fashionable acronym (the jams) and a focus of the prime minister's concern (Butler and Syal, 2016). Perhaps for them there will be jam tomorrow. Above all else, the future of the British economy now rests on the final shape of Brexit and the success of negotiations with other countries. To that extent, Chancellor Philip Hammond has perhaps less control of UK economic policy than almost any of his predecessors. The words of Bill Clinton, 'it's the economy, stupid', seem to remain as important a mantra as ever for any political party's success.

# SUMMARY

» The Treasury and the chancellor of the exchequer remain at the heart of British economic policy-making, along with the prime minister, a few other ministers and their advisers, and other appointed officials, such as the governor of the Bank of England.

» Governments have limited powers to influence economies shaped by market forces. The British economy is part of an increasingly globalised economy, affected by global trends.

» The main tools of government economic policy are direct intervention, fiscal policy and monetary policy. The balance between them has changed over the years, with less direct intervention and less reliance on fiscal policy to manage the economy, and rather more emphasis on monetary policy, with interest rates determined by the Monetary Policy Committee of the Bank of England.

» Although the Thatcher governments and the Blair governments have been credited with halting and reversing Britain's relative economic decline, the record of both is now rather more contentious.

» New Labour presided for a decade over low inflation, low interest rates and (until the credit crunch) relatively high employment and steady growth, deep-seated problems in the British economy. However, underinvestment, poor training and low productivity were not resolved.

» The financial crisis and recession faced by Brown's government were global in scope and also severely affected other leading western countries. Overdependence on financial services and the growth of personal and government debt left the British economy vulnerable.

» The 2010–15 coalition government initially planned to reduce the deficit faster than Labour intended, largely through public spending cuts. While these were made with the general approval of bankers, they caused controversy over the possible impact on economic recovery, and on poorer communities and regions in Britain.

» The vote to leave the EU in the 2016 referendum has compelled a rethink of economic policy, under a new prime minister and chancellor (who is not in charge of negotiating the details of Britain's exit from the EU). Deficit reduction has again been postponed. Long-term, economic prospects remain unclear.

# QUESTIONS FOR DISCUSSION

» What are the enduring problems of the British economy and how might they be remedied?

» Who 'calls the shots' on decisions over the British economy?

» Why did Keynesian demand management become less fashionable? In what respects does the analysis of Keynes remain relevant?

» How far and with what success did New Labour embrace markets as a means of economic growth?

» Who or what was to blame for the 2008 banking crisis and ensuing recession? Why did few see it coming? How successful were the measures taken to deal with it? Could it happen again?

» Why were plans to eliminate the UK deficit by 2015 and later, by 2020, abandoned? What are the possible consequences?

» What are the prospects for the British economy outside the EU?

» Does anyone really 'manage' the economy?

» When asked to explain the reasons behind electoral success, one reply politicians have made was: 'It's the economy, stupid!' Is it?

 **FURTHER READING**

Some pre-recession sources remain useful. Grant (2002) *Economic Policy in Britain* examines postwar economic policy and policy-making. The economic management of earlier Labour governments is usefully discussed by Thomas (1992) *Government and the Economy Today*. Gamble (1994) *The Free Economy and the Strong State: The Politics of Thatcherism* (2nd edn) examines the political context of Thatcherism. There is useful analysis of New Labour's economic management by Stephens (2001), Smith (2005), Coates (2005), Lee (2008) and Mullard and Swaray (2008).

There are numerous sources on the global banking crisis and economic recession, although some of these focus principally on the USA.

For the impact on Britain, see, among others, Gamble (2009), Cable (2009), Elliott and Atkinson (2009), Lanchester (2010) and a symposium in *Political Studies Review* (2010). Skidelsky (2010, Ch. 1) provides a useful brief 'anatomy of the crisis', and discusses who (or what) is to blame for it. More recent sources include Smithers (2013) *The Road to Recovery*, Berry (2016) *Austerity Politics and UK Economic Policy* and King (2017) *The End of Alchemy: Money, Banking and the Future of the Global Economy*. Hood and Himaz (2017) take the long view in *A Century of Fiscal Squeeze Politics: 100 Years of Austerity, Politics, and Bureaucracy in Britain*, comparing how policy-makers have dealt with the current crisis with earlier times.

 **USEFUL WEBSITES**

Useful official websites on economic policy include the Treasury: www.gov.uk/government/organisations/hm-treasury, Downing Street: www.gov.uk/government/organisations/prime-ministers-office-10-downing-street, the Cabinet Office: www.gov.uk/government/organisations/cabinet-office, and the Bank of

England: www.bankofengland.co.uk. Further analysis can be derived from the websites of think tanks, such as the Institute of Fiscal Studies: www.ifs.org.uk, the financial press, business and trade unions.

 *Further student resources to support learning are available at*
**www.macmillanihe.com/griffiths-brit-pol-3e**

# 20 WELFARE AND PUBLIC SERVICES

The Channel 4 show *Benefits Street* depicts the lives of residents of James Turner Street in Winson Green, Birmingham, England. The area was selected because newspapers had reported that 90% of the residents in the area were 'on benefits'. The programme shows residents committing crimes, including shoplifting, and presents a picture of people who lack the motivation to look for paid work and are dependent on state welfare payments to get by.

The show was hugely controversial when it was first broadcast in 2014. It sparked a national debate about the British welfare state. *Benefits Street* was discussed in the Houses of Parliament, in national newspapers and in the community in which it was set. Channel 4 was accused of trivialising the lives of people in need, depicting the participants of the documentary in a negative light, and blurring the lines between entertainment and documentary-making in a misleading way. The negative depiction of welfare in *Benefits Street* fitted with a long-term public decline in support for welfare spending in the UK. In 1989, 61% of people agreed that more should be spent on welfare benefits. By 2009, this figure had fallen to 27%, and remained low, at 30%, in 2014 (British Social Attitudes, 2015). What was striking was how different the depiction of welfare was to the immediate postwar period when the 'welfare state' was created.

William Beveridge, whose 1942 report led to the creation of the welfare state, identified five 'giant evils' as obstacles on the road to progress: 'want, disease, ignorance, squalor and idleness' (Timmins, 1995). Accordingly, he assumed the state should be active in relieving poverty, delivering health and education and providing housing and environmental services. A state that did this would ensure that individuals could lead a life of dignity and freedom – a stark contrast to the caricature presented in *Benefits Street*. These two different interpretations of welfare have deep underlying ideological differences (recall the kind of debates discussed in Chapter 15 on ideology). These views on welfare contain, among other things, radically different assumptions about why people use the benefits system, how people fall into poverty, whether welfare is the responsibility of the state or individuals and their families, where responsibility for providing welfare lies and what incentives the welfare system creates. We look at some of these questions in this chapter, which examines postwar welfare and public services.

## THIS CHAPTER:

- » Examines the birth of the welfare state: looking at the period of consensus and the controversies of the 1980s.
- » Discusses New Labour's programme of 'choice' and investment in the public services – a third way?
- » Debates public services after the economic crisis – from the coalition spending cuts to the present day.
- » Considers recent attempts to 'shrink the state'.

## THE WELFARE STATE

Although the state had in the past been partially involved in the provision of some public services, it was the unemployment and misery of the economic slump of the 1930s, but more especially the ensuing Second World War, that provoked new thinking on welfare reform. War had led to far more government control over people's lives and also substantial increases in state spending and taxation. Many hoped that government intervention could also help win the peace, once the war was over. The 1942 Beveridge Report, *Social Insurance and Allied Services*, published in the midst of war, became an unlikely bestseller. It recommended a comprehensive system of welfare benefits for all, paid for by flat-rate national insurance contributions, although later critics have argued that it was based around male-headed households (see Spotlight 20.1). Beveridge also emphasised the need for government maintenance of full employment, as recommended by the economist John Maynard Keynes, and a national health service, free at the point of use. (Beveridge is discussed in Key Figures 20.1 overleaf.)

## SPOTLIGHT ON ...    Gender and the welfare state    20.1

The Beveridge Report (1942) formed the basis of the modern welfare state. It assumed a model of welfare provision based on men being the 'breadwinner', while women stayed at home to be the main carers. Economic and demographic change since the 1940s has made this model increasingly out of date. Later critics have argued that Beveridge 'wrote gender difference into the social security system' (Pascall, 2012, p. 8). Jill Pascall has argued that policy has been slow to adapt. She argued that governments have tried to make women 'equal to men' in the workplace, for example, with little thought for the other side of the 'male breadwinner/female caregiver' model. Pascall (2012, p. 4) argues for 'an idea of equality in which women's lives are enabled to become more like men's, and men's lives to become more like women's'. She argues for a new model of welfare based on a 'universal caregiver approach', in which care is seen as the equal responsibility of men and women, in the same way that paid employment is for most people in the UK today.

# KEY FIGURES 20.1
William Beveridge

**William Beveridge (1879–1963)** was a Liberal social reformer who chaired the Committee on Social Insurance and Allied Service during the Second World War. The Beveridge Report (1942) proposed a system of national insurance that is widely described as 'cradle to the grave'. The report was enthusiastically endorsed by the public and the Labour Party, which promised 'Beveridge Now' at the 1945 general election, winning by a landslide. It was realised that the cost of the scheme could only be kept within reasonable bounds by the maintenance of close to full employment. This depended on the pursuit of state management of economic demand, as urged by John Maynard Keynes. (See Key Figures 2.1 for more on Keynes.)

Hans Wild/The LIFE Picture Collection/Getty Images

No one political party was entirely responsible for the postwar welfare state. Some important developments, such as the introduction of old age pensions and unemployment insurance, were introduced by the Liberal government before the First World War. Two of the main post-war founders of the welfare state, Keynes and Beveridge, were both lifelong Liberals. Some reforms were instituted by the wartime coalition government, notably the 1944 Education Act, which modernised the education system. The Family Allowances Act 1945, which provided child benefit, was introduced by the brief caretaker Conservative government at the end of the war. However, the vast bulk of the legislation was brought in by Attlee's postwar Labour government, including a series of National Insurance Acts to implement the Beveridge Report and the National Health Service Act 1946, presided over by Aneurin ('Nye') Bevan. Although Labour lost power in 1951, a new generation of Conservatives appeared fully committed to the welfare state and the provision of public services, which now enjoyed cross-party support. Harold Macmillan as housing minister presided over a major programme of private and council house building. Conservative governments in the 1950s maintained Keynesian economic demand management to secure close to full employment and steady if unspectacular economic growth. Indeed, across Europe, in the years after the Second World War a variety of welfare systems developed (see Comparing British Politics 20.1).

---

*The **welfare state** is one where the state plays an important role in the protection and promotion of the social and economic wellbeing of citizens. The welfare state is seen as a broader, more comprehensive description than simply a welfare 'system'.*

---

*Public services are those that are provided by government to people living within its jurisdiction, directly through the public sector or by indirectly financing provision of services. Major public services include welfare, health and education, among many others.*

---

## MEETING THE COST OF SERVICES

The implication of the Beveridge scheme was that national insurance contributions would pay for social security payments, as private insurance contributions pay for successful claims on policies. It never worked out quite like that. The amount of total national insurance raised from those in work was relatively fixed, while claims for benefits depended on fluctuating economic circumstances. In practice, national insurance became just another tax, with social security funded from general taxation.

# 🇬🇧 COMPARING BRITISH POLITICS 20.1 🇺🇸 ⬛ 🇩🇰

## 'Three worlds of welfare capitalism'

Most modern western states developed welfare services (including health and unemployment insurance, pensions and family allowances) in the course of the twentieth century, although the type and extent of welfare provision varies considerably. Esping-Andersen (1990, 1999) distinguishes between three welfare models, liberal, conservative and social democratic:

» *The liberal model*: Also known as the classical or free-market model, it assumes that citizens insure themselves, privately or through company schemes against ill health, accident, unemployment and the costs of old age (e.g. USA). The state provides only means-tested basic support for those who are uninsured.

» *The conservative model*: This involves occupational insurance schemes to which

employers and employees contribute, and protects claimants' incomes (and therefore social position) if they lose their job or fall ill (e.g. Germany).

» *The social democratic model*: This involves universal state welfare provision funded out of taxation and free at the point of use (e.g. Sweden, although some aspects of the Swedish system have been eroded). Britain largely falls within the social democratic model, although charges are made for prescriptions, glasses, dentistry and much care of the elderly, while state pensions are inadequate and, in practice, topped up by occupational and private pensions, or supplementary benefits.

Although there had been an initial understanding that national insurance would also contribute to funding the new health service, that too was largely financed from general tax receipts. It had been anticipated that the costs of healthcare would rise initially, to cope with a backlog of untreated illness from those who had been too poor to pay for treatment, but then costs were predicted to fall among a now healthier population, once the new NHS was fully established. But increasing longevity (in part a consequence of the NHS) and the development of new treatments led to ever-expanding demands and escalating costs. Thus Gaitskell, Labour's chancellor, introduced charges for teeth and spectacles in 1951, abandoning the principle of an NHS free at the point of use, and prompting the resignation of Bevan and Harold Wilson, the future prime minister. The Conservative government that followed introduced prescription charges. But such contentious innovations made only a small contribution to NHS costs, which continued to rise throughout the postwar period. The cost of social care for the elderly and infirm also grew as people lived longer. The welfare state was, in part, a victim of its own success.

Costs rose for other services too. Education costs rose throughout the postwar period as pupils stayed at school longer, seeking better qualifications and entry to university. There was also a continuing huge expansion in the number and size of universities, as new institutions were founded and some polytechnics and colleges of education secured university status. For several decades after the war, university students not only enjoyed free tuition but generous maintenance grants, although the latter were dependent on parental income. This stimulated some debate over how the rising expense should be met. While school education remains substantially universal and compulsory, enjoyed or endured by all children, higher education still only benefits a minority (although now close to half of the age group), but can yield lasting advantages in careers subsequently. While it seemed reasonable that the whole community should bear the costs of health services, social services, school education and the relief of poverty, there was some questioning over poor working-class taxpayers effectively subsidising the expensive education of (largely) the children of the middle classes. Even so, the sense of outrage among students who were later forced to bear the high costs of courses that were free for their predecessors is easy enough to understand. In recent years, it has been a major factor in loss of student support for, first, Labour in 2010 and then the Lib Dems for their changing stance on student fees.

## THE ROLE OF CENTRAL AND LOCAL GOVERNMENT

Before the 1945 Labour government, much of the management and finance of welfare services was originally not down to central government but to elected local authorities (see also Chapter 10). Local government had long managed school and further education, and had an expanding role in the delivery of social services in the community, including providing institutional care and domestic support for the elderly and disabled. It also had a major role in planning and housing, and in the postwar years designed and built many extensive council estates, with affordable rents.

Beveridge argued that an expanded health service should continue to be run by the local authorities that were, at the end of the war, already responsible for some personal health provision. In contrast, Bevan firmly believed in the role of the central state as the most efficient way of providing services and, in line with this view, the new NHS, created in 1948, was centrally managed and controlled. However, in a compromise, doctors and surgeons were contracted to provide their services, rather than acting as full state employees. Indeed, surgeons were allowed to continue to have lucrative private patients and beds in NHS hospitals to accommodate them. Bevan commented that he had 'stuffed their mouths with gold' (Timmins, 1995) to secure their participation in the NHS. Meanwhile, the new national insurance system was centrally controlled from the start. The payment of benefits followed nationally prescribed rules with no scope for local discretion.

Even so, elected local authorities initially continued to have a major role in the provision of other welfare services in the postwar decades, particularly in housing, planning, personal social services and schools and

further education. There was some local democratic accountability for these services, many of which were efficiently managed, for example the housing policies of the old London County Council or the educational services run by the former West Riding County Council.

## HOUSING AND LOCAL GOVERNMENT FINANCE

Since the 1980s, the responsibility of local government to provide welfare services has been eroded. In particular, the 'right to buy' council houses, introduced by the Thatcher government (1979–90), dramatically reduced councils' once extensive housing functions. Council tenants were enabled to buy the properties they had formerly rented, at a substantial discount against the market price. Over a million council houses were sold to their tenants, who often sold them on at a substantial profit, sometimes to private landlords. This not only decimated councils' existing stock of rented accommodation, but also almost halted new council building. Within a few years, house building, letting and maintenance, which had been a major function of (particularly) urban councils, were destroyed. Beneficiaries included the Conservative Party (council tenants predominantly voted Labour, while homeowners favoured Conservative) and private landlords. Rents spiralled beyond many tenants' ability to pay, leading to higher housing benefit payments, borne by government and, ultimately, taxpayers. Some former council houses were at first transferred to voluntary housing associations, which provided low-cost social housing for those in need, then the government's preferred supplier of rented social housing. The Conservative government proposed in its 2015 election manifesto to extend the right to buy to tenants of housing associations. Housing, it seems, is no longer part of state welfare, except insofar as taxpayers will continue to pick up the bill for increases in housing benefit, resulting from higher rents demanded by private landlords.

Besides promoting homeownership by selling council houses, Thatcher also transformed the finance of local government by replacing domestic rates with the community charge,

**KEY FIGURES 20.2**

T.H. Marshall and Richard Titmuss: defenders of the welfare state

T.H. Marshall and Richard Titmuss were two of the best-known advocates for the new welfare state in the postwar years.

**T.H. Marshall (1893–1981)** was a British sociologist and academic, who was influenced by New Liberals, such as Hobson and Hobhouse (see Chapter 15, p. 310) and later Beveridge. Marshall's most famous work was *Citizenship and Social Class and Other Essays* (1950). In this book, Marshall set out the historical development of rights in England that came with greater citizenship. He argued that the eighteenth century saw the development of civil rights, such as greater equality before the law. The nineteenth century saw the expansion of political rights, such as the right to vote (for most men). The twentieth century, for Marshall, saw the expansion of social rights, such as those provided by the welfare state.

**Richard Titmuss (1907–73)** was born to a farming family and left school with no qualifications, but went on to become one of the pioneers of social policy, as an academic discipline. Several themes are brought out in his *Essays on the Welfare State* (1958) and later works. Titmuss was writing in a context where he believed that the five 'giants' that Beveridge identified could and would be slain. The abolition of poverty was an achievable and sensible goal.

Like many scholars at the time, Titmuss assumed that Keynesian economics would ensure constant economic growth (see Key Figures 2.1 for more on Keynes). As such, social policy was more about distribution (who gets what when) rather than production (how to ensure growth). He argued for the 'universality' of welfare. The system must be for all, not just those in need – a welfare system solely for the poor is destined to become a poor welfare system. Titmuss was confident that the general public could be relied on to accept progressive taxation and to vote for parties that support an enhanced welfare state. The party political attacks on 'welfare' and the negative connotations it now has for some critics (of the kind set out in the introduction to this chapter) would have surprised him. In *The Gift Relationship: From Human Blood to Social Policy* (1970), Titmuss looked at the economics of blood donation. But he drew much wider conclusions about the importance of altruism and the limits of the market. He found that in voluntary systems, such as the UK, where people donated their blood for altruistic reasons, the blood supply was of a much better quality than in market systems, such as the USA, where people are paid for their donations. The conclusion was that markets crowd out altruism and worsen the quality of services. By implication, Titmuss would argue that we should worry about the marketisation of our welfare and public services.

better known as the poll tax, later scrapped by John Major who introduced the rather less regressive community charge (see Chapter 10, pp. 198–200). Subsequent central government controls over increases in council tax have reduced the financial resources of local government still further.

The cumulative impact is that local government revenue is now much reduced, particularly for poorer councils with the most needs. It has become progressively more difficult for local authorities to finance their remaining services, including social welfare (see below). While councils still retain extensive responsibility for social services, these have become so underfunded that levels of care are inadequate and social workers demoralised. Indeed, a crisis in social care has already had knock-on implications for the NHS, with hospitals unable to release patients and free up beds because of a lack of adequate care in the community. Reports now suggest that the recently instituted Better

Care Fund, set up in 2013, is failing: '58% of targets for improving care in people's homes and local communities were missed' (*The Guardian*, 2016). Some propose that health and social services should be controlled and funded together. Indeed, the new Greater Manchester Combined Authority already combines responsibility for both. However, as the medical profession remains as hostile as ever to local government control, it seems unlikely that this solution could become universal.

Consequently, local government now has a much-diminished role in running public services and the welfare state. Indeed, latterly, even education has been largely taken out of effective local authority control with the growth of academies and 'free' schools, and, most recently, the threat (for the moment rescinded) of the removal of all remaining state schools from local authorities.

## THE MANAGEMENT OF WELFARE: THE ROLE OF THE STATE AND THE MARKET

While advocates of comprehensive social welfare sometimes differed over whether services should be controlled by central or local government, it was widely assumed, not just by Labour and progressive Liberals (including Beveridge and Keynes) but by centrist, one-nation Conservatives in the 1950s and 60s (such as Macmillan, Butler and Macleod), that this was a legitimate role for the state in some shape or form, as indeed the term 'welfare state' implies. (One-nation conservatism is discussed in more detail in Chapter 15.) However, as the rising cost of public services became more burdensome to taxpayers, it was increasingly questioned whether particular services were really delivering the anticipated benefits. In the 1960s and early 70s, enduring problems, such as child poverty, inner-city deprivation, homelessness and care of the elderly, indicated that the welfare state was not providing effective security 'from the cradle to the grave' (Timmins, 1995).

Advocates of the free market had more fundamental criticisms. They claimed that state welfare provision actually made social problems worse, by encouraging what critics viewed as a 'culture of dependency' (a controversial description for a way of life dependent on state benefits) and stifling initiative. Neoliberal economists argued that services free at the point of use were bound to stimulate an excess of demand. Moreover, what they described as 'bureaucratic oversupply' satisfied the interests of the pay and careers of public service workers. Thus an alliance of welfare-dependent benefit claimants and public service professionals would provoke an ever-expanding growth of public spending and taxation. Increasingly, a broad cross-party consensus in favour of state welfare was, over time, challenged by free-market economists who argued that state provision was inherently inefficient, involving monopoly powers and wasteful oversupply.

While some were opposed in principle to the supply of services free at the point of use, viewing this as unjustified interference in the free market, others argued that, at the very least, the provision of care should be open to competition, including from the private sector. Indeed, it was claimed that the skills and experience of the private sector could be used to cut costs and improve performance. Arguments in favour of a shift towards market forces and the private sector were aired by some Conservatives, such as Enoch Powell in the 1960s and Keith Joseph in the early 1970s, but only became dominant in the Thatcher government (1979–90).

By the 1980s, there had been significant shift from state to market – or to the running of public and welfare services in ways similar to how companies operating under market conditions would be run. While housing was substantially removed from state welfare services (see above), the management of other services was reformed through the introduction of more competition and increased private provision. Residential care for the elderly was substantially privatised, with local authorities providing regulation and much of the funding. Ancillary services in health and education (e.g. cleaning, catering, laundry, ground maintenance) were subjected to compulsory competitive tendering, leading to increased private sector provision, often at lower cost, but with poorer conditions of service for the workers involved. For core services, such as education and medical services, 'internal markets' or 'quasi-markets' were introduced to provide more consumer choice (in theory at least) and promote more efficiency and drive down costs through the stimulus of competition between rival providers. This involved a more private sector approach to the management of public services, termed the 'new public management' in place of traditional public administration (see Table 20.1).

### Table 20.1 Contrasting administrative cultures in provision of public services

| Traditional public administration | New public management |
|---|---|
| • Informed by a 'public service ethos' | • Informed by private sector principles |
| • Services delivered according to written rules, minimum managerial discretion | • Services delivered more flexibly with more managerial autonomy, and competition between providers |
| • All citizens in the same circumstances receive the same service – equity and uniformity | • Services tailored more to the requirements of consumers and local circumstances – variations in services |
| • Service delivery audited to ensure strict legality, the spending of money as authorised | • Service delivery audited to measure economy, efficiency and effectiveness (the 3 'E's) |

## The private finance initiative

The private sector has long been involved in public sector capital projects. In the past, while the private sector built many new schools, hospitals and prisons, it was the public sector that had to raise the loans (for example through the issue of government bonds) and the public sector that owned and maintained the new buildings once they were completed.

From the 1990s onwards, both major political parties came to favour increased private sector involvement in new capital investment in school and hospital building through PFI (private finance initiative). PFI was launched by a Conservative chancellor, Norman Lamont, but eagerly adopted by New Labour as a way of improving the infrastructure of public services.

Hospitals, schools and prisons built under PFI involve a private consortium raising capital, designing and constructing the buildings and, commonly, subsequently maintaining them too. The public sector does not have to provide upfront finance and leases the buildings for a period of years (commonly 25 or 30 years), after which ownership is transferred.

The big attraction for the government was that PFIs allowed a massive and much-needed

*Source*: Arcaid/UIG via Getty Images

Many schools, such as this one in Slough, hospitals and prisons have been rebuilt using money from Private Finance Initiatives.

increase in public sector investment without this showing as part of public borrowing. Indeed, nearly all recently built hospitals and many new schools have been financed and built through PFIs. It was also argued that PFIs brought new expertise to public sector investment with potential efficiency savings, and transferred risk to the private sector. However, critics argued that PFIs were, in the long run, more expensive than traditional public sector finance of capital investment, that risk was not transferred, as schemes were effectively underwritten by government, and that many PFI schemes were badly designed and did not provide value for money (Pollock, 2004). Many hospitals are still burdened by considerable ongoing costs arising from new building completed decades ago.

## NEW LABOUR: 'CHOICE' AND INVESTMENT

The Labour Party, returned to office in 1997, had long seen itself as the champion of the welfare state and public service provision. Health and education were seen as key Labour issues and priorities for the new Blair government. Yet Labour struggled to satisfy the sometimes conflicting demands of voters, taxpayers, service users and, particularly, public service workers, who looked to Labour to reverse the market-oriented reforms introduced by the Conservatives and to substantially improve public service pay and conditions. In practice, New Labour provided additional resources for some public services, but also maintained much of the thrust of Conservative management reforms.

While there was little extra money available for public services in New Labour's early years, as its first priority was to establish its credentials for sound management of the national economy, later, substantial additional sums were promised and delivered for health and education. Britain's health expenditure had lagged well below the European average, following decades of underfunding and underinvestment, and Blair had pledged to raise health spending from 6.8% of GDP to the EU average (then 8%)

by 2006. This target was reached, and Gordon Brown's three-year spending plan for 2005 involved a further rise to 9% of GDP. Indeed: 'public expenditure on health, education and social security increased more rapidly under New Labour than under previous Conservative and Labour governments' (Mullard and Swaray, 2008, p. 48).

As always, however, it is debatable how far additional spending secured value for money. Increased spending simply involves additional inputs into a service. It does not guarantee a commensurate improvement in outputs and outcomes. Critics of high public spending had long argued that problems cannot be solved by simply providing more and more money. So it was politically necessary for Labour to demonstrate that additional money involved real improvements in public services, rather than additional waste and bureaucracy. This meant that the government had to publish clear targets and measures for achieving those targets.

Moreover, a government committed to the choice in public services had to provide more evidence to enable service users to make informed decisions. Thus 'league tables' of hospital and school performance were published. Those that met government targets were given star ratings, those that did not were 'named and shamed'. However, some measures, it was suggested, were misleading and unfair. Some hospitals appeared to have poorer success rates in surgical operations because they were treating patients with more difficult conditions. Some schools had poorer exam results because their pupils came from disadvantaged backgrounds, with fewer skills on entry. The government tried to respond to these criticisms by providing more sophisticated measures of performance, for example providing measures for 'added value' in school league tables, which aim to show how well a school has brought on a pupil between one test and another.

For public sector managers and staff, the stakes could be high. Failure to meet government targets and performance indicators might lead to the dismissal of those individuals deemed responsible, and sometimes even the takeover or closure of failing institutions. By contrast, success might be rewarded not only with additional resources, but also with more discretion over their use. Labour promoted the notion of 'earned autonomy' through the introduction of new 'foundation hospitals' for successful 'three star' hospital trusts. Foundation hospitals were freed from detailed control by the Department of Health, and could manage their own assets and raise private funds for investment purposes (Coates, 2005, p. 125). In education, more power was devolved to successful schools, particularly the new private sector-backed city academies (Driver, 2008, p. 61). However, there was always some tension at the heart of Labour's management of public services. While they emphasised the need for greater flexibility, choice and the delegation of more discretion to institutions and frontline staff, it was also politically essential to be able to demonstrate improved service delivery and performance, which meant they could not afford to give up detailed regulation and control.

New Labour promised a 'third way of running the NHS based on partnership and driven by performance', and their White Paper, *The New NHS: Modern, Dependable*, declared: 'There will be no return to the old centralised command and control system of the 1970s ... But nor will there be continuation of the divisive internal markets of the 1990s' (Department of Health, 1997). The new buzzwords were partnership, cooperation and networks, implying collaboration rather than competition. However, the Labour government wanted to maintain elements of competition between providers, as a spur to efficiency and to give more choice for consumers.

So although Labour claimed that it had scrapped the Conservative's internal market in the NHS, this was 'more superseded than abolished' (Denham 2003, p. 288). The hospital trusts established by the Conservatives continued, and subsequently the best performers were allowed to apply for foundation hospital status (see below). The Conservatives had also encouraged groups of doctors in general practice to apply for fundholder status, to control their own budgets. Labour abolished GP fundholders, and made all GPs and other 'primary care' health workers, such as community nurses, midwives and chiropodists, join new primary care trusts (PCTs), with control of their own budgets as suppliers and purchasers of healthcare. These PCTs contracted with hospitals of their choice for the supply of further healthcare, although some work previously performed in hospitals, including some simple operations, could now be performed in PCT clinics. A new central body, the National Institute for Clinical Excellence (NICE) was established in 1999 to advise on common standards of health treatment and best medical practice. (After the Health and Social Care Act 2012, it was renamed the National Institute for Health and Care Excellence, still abbreviated as NICE.) Another body, the Commission for Health Improvement, advised on the quality of local services (this was replaced in 2004 by the Healthcare Commission and then in 2009 by the Care Quality Commission). These new arrangements were designed to reduce some of the differences and inequalities in healthcare provision.

It was over the delivery of public services that New Labour parted company from its union allies and 'old Labour' critics, for whom public services have to be delivered by the public sector. For New Labour (Brown as well as Blair), 'a sharp distinction is drawn between how services are funded and how they are delivered' (Denham, 2003, p. 282). While still committed to state funding of public services, delivered free at the point of use, New Labour also sought more private sector involvement in the delivery of public services, breaking up the old public sector monopoly. In part, this was simple pragmatism – 'what matters is what works'. If there was unsatisfied demand for health services – for example for the removal of cataracts from eyes or hip replacements – and this demand could not be met within the public sector, it made sense to buy in resources from the private sector to meet demand and reduce waiting times. NHS patients wanted free and effective treatment as soon as possible, and it hardly mattered to them who provided it.

Much the same went for the provision of state education. School pupils and their parents wanted good facilities and good teaching, without having to pay for private education, but precisely how this was provided was regarded as a secondary consideration. Thus businesses and voluntary organisations were encouraged to sponsor new city academies in poor areas. For New Labour, private sector involvement in the delivery of public services stimulated competition and choice, but also exemplified the principle of partnership between the public and private sectors. While Labour introduced academies to deal with the specific problem of underperforming schools in inner-city areas, the coalition government that took office in 2010 later encouraged many other schools to apply for academy status and effectively opt out of local government control.

To critics, private sector involvement in the provision of state services was a Trojan horse, threatening the future of the welfare state through the creation of a two-tier system. Public service providers feared that the private sector would 'cream off' the most potentially profitable parts of the system, leaving them with the most difficult and expensive patients, pupils and consumers. So, the private sector would perform routine uncomplicated surgery, leaving NHS staff and facilities to cope with the more problematic cases, incidentally involving a much lower potential 'success rate'. Similarly, it was feared that the new city academies would not take their share of pupils with special needs or marked behavioural problems, who would be left in what one New Labour insider controversially dismissed as 'bog standard comprehensives' (BBC News, 2005). Those who defended Labour's reforms pointed out there had always been a 'two-tier' or indeed a 'multi-tier' NHS and state education system, with marked differences in performance between schools and health treatments across the country. Additional resources, wherever they come from, public, private or voluntary sector, could only raise standards of provision.

Did Labour improve public services? Toynbee and Walker (2005, 2010) deliver a mixed verdict. Labour certainly increased capital and current spending on health and education, evident in a huge school and hospital building programme, remedying decades of underinvestment. By 2010, only one-fifth of hospitals dated from before 1948. Labour reduced waiting times in the NHS, and presided over an expansion of nursery education and university education. However, there remain questions over value for money. Toynbee and Walker (2010) suggest that the NHS probably got too much extra funding too quickly and it was not always spent wisely. There were generous pay rises for GPs. Many criticised the government's micromanagement through targets and its repeated reorganisations.

Major problems in funding some public services persisted. Social care for the growing numbers of elderly and infirm remained chronically underfunded, NHS dentistry was unavailable in many areas, while successive governments had not succeeded in adequately financing the huge growth in university education (explored further in Spotlight 20.2).

Labour's increased spending on health and education was closely linked with Brown's apparently successful management of the British economy. Brown himself appeared well placed to maintain his party's dominance when he succeeded Blair in 2007. Indeed, the Conservative opposition, now led by Cameron, with Osborne as shadow chancellor, could initially only promise to match Labour's spending on health and education. Cameron explicitly disagreed with Thatcher (1987), asserting that 'there is such a thing as society', but adding that it was not the same as the state. In the period leading up to the 2010 election, he championed the 'big society' as opposed to 'big government', stressing the need for community action, voluntary work and mutual aid. He argued that many services could be delivered by voluntary groups, community self-help and user or producer cooperatives. Cooperation was an ideal commonly linked with Labour, but Cameron attempted to steal Labour's clothes by advocating cooperatives in the delivery of Britain's public services. He argued that this would empower frontline staff, give them a real sense of ownership of their own schools and hospitals, raise morale and productivity and thus improve the quality of services for consumers and service users. However, less was heard of the big society after Cameron exchanged opposition for government in 2010.

## THE FINANCIAL CRISIS AND RECESSION

Mounting budget deficits, resulting from the financial crisis and recession of 2008 onwards, and pressure for massive cuts in public spending from central banks and the markets created a cold economic climate for public services. (The background of the financial crisis is discussed in more detail in Chapter 19.) Many countries like Britain sought cuts in public spending (notably Canada and Ireland). Before the 2010 election, the main parties agreed to reduce the deficit over time, but without specifying details. The Conservatives emphasised the need for early cuts, but promised to ring-fence health spending, Brown argued that although the deficit was serious and must be reduced, premature spending cuts could endanger economic recovery.

In the aftermath of the election, the mood changed rapidly, with veiled threats to the UK's credit rating and dire warnings from business leaders and bankers. The new Conservative/Lib Dem coalition government swiftly agreed a massive programme of spending cuts, involving average reductions in departmental budgets of 25%, but with the continued commitment not to cut health or international development. Much of the detail remained unclear until the results of the government's comprehensive spending review were announced on 20 October 2010. Even then, much subsequent detailed analysis was necessary to discern the real impact of the cuts on public services.

The coalition government pledged a small real increase in spending on the NHS (1.3% per annum). However, rising demand for services, coupled with the extra costs of another controversial NHS reorganisation (Labour's PCTs were replaced by new commissioning bodies headed by GPs), ensured costs rose faster. Education also fared relatively well, with only a predicted 3.4% per annum cut in spending. Although the schools budget was supposedly ring-fenced, it was widely reckoned to be insufficient to cover rising numbers of primary schoolchildren. There were other cuts in the education budget, including capital spending, 16–19 education, school sports and extracurricular activities. However, the most significant change was that the new government encouraged a huge increase in

## SPOTLIGHT ON ...    Academies and free schools    20.2

Labour had introduced city academies as charitable trusts with business sponsors, outside local authority control, largely to turn round failing schools in poor areas. Additional resources and new management led to some high-profile success stories, although the general record of performance was more contentious. The Cameron government allowed successful primary and secondary schools (rather than failing schools in deprived areas) to secure academy status, arguing this would give more autonomy to schools and teachers, removed from local authority control. Michael Gove, then secretary of state for education, was not only committed to a massive expansion of academies, but also the introduction of new 'free schools', based on Swedish and US models. Parents, teachers or voluntary groups could apply to run their own 'free schools', receiving government funding for each pupil recruited equivalent to spending in state schools. Critics suggested that 'pushy' middle-class parents and their children were the most likely beneficiaries, with poorer children left in worse-resourced local authority schools the potential losers (Griffiths, 2015). The debate about free schools in Sweden, USA and now Britain remains contentious.

the number of academies, removed from local government control (see Spotlight 20.2).

The biggest cuts in education were in university teaching budgets, with state spending on higher education planned to fall from £7.1 billion to £4.2 billion, with arts and humanities hardest hit. Science, technology, engineering and maths (so-called 'STEM' subjects) were better protected, as they were deemed more 'useful' (Morgan, 2014). Most politically contentious was the introduction of much higher student fees, financed by loans repayable as and when graduates secure sufficiently adequately paid jobs. This was particularly controversial, and politically damaging for the Lib Dems who had fought the 2010 election on a pledge to oppose tuition fees (see Spotlight 20.3).

## SPOTLIGHT ON ...    Financing higher education    20.3

Spending on higher education had failed to match the substantial postwar growth in student numbers, causing a crisis for university finance. Labour had sought to raise overall access to higher education still further, to 50% of the age group, but largely failed to increase access for those from poorer backgrounds. According to Toynbee and Walker (2005, p. 122), 'the top social class sent 80% of its sons and daughters to university while the bottom sent only 7%'. This differential had implications for funding university education. It seemed unfair to expect taxpayers, including the low paid, few of whose children benefitted from university, to bear all the escalating costs. Labour initially introduced flat-rate tuition fees, covering only a small proportion of course costs, and abolished maintenance grants, leading to an accumulation of student debt. However, elite universities, disturbed at their increasing difficulty in competing internationally, wanted to be able to charge more for their degrees. As part of a package of reforms, Labour allowed variable fees, with interest-free loans, repayable by students after graduation, and reintroduced non-repayable maintenance grants for students from poorer families. Labour's U-turn on fees caused the party huge political difficulties. The Lib Dems, who opposed tuition fees in 2005 and 2010, were the main beneficiaries.

In government with the Conservatives from 2010–15, Lib Dem ministers reversed their previous pledges to abolish tuition fees and largely accepted the recommendations of the Browne report, commissioned by the previous Labour government with the agreement of the Conservatives, involving a substantial increase in fees, coupled with more help for poorer students, and the indefinite deferral of loan repayments for low-paid graduates. Universities now act increasingly like businesses, trying to attract students who bring funding with them. However, student leaders denounced this turnaround as a betrayal. Support for the Lib Dems plummeted (Griffiths, 2015). In 2010 they had won 57 seats, in 2015 just 8. (The 2017 election saw only a modest increase to 12 seats.)

Among other services, there were major planned cuts in policing (a 20% cut in central funding over four years) and the prison service. The government proposed to reduce by a massive 60% the budget for building affordable houses, with new tenants facing rents of 80% of market value. As most social housing tenants are on benefits (65%), they are heavily dependent on housing benefits, which were also being squeezed. Overall, local government faced a major cut in central funding (27% over four years). The budget for local authority social care was severely constrained; despite the government providing an extra £2 billion for care of the elderly, this was widely reckoned to be insufficient to meet rising demand. Cuts in social care had significant knock-on effects for the NHS, particularly hospitals, which were often unable to discharge elderly patients because of the lack of suitable care in the community. Other local authority services, especially libraries, sports and leisure facilities, suffered extensive cuts and closures. In March 2016, the BBC reported that at least 343 libraries (of 4,290) had closed since 2010, with at least another 111 closures planned for the following financial year (Crewe, 2016).

The coalition government stressed its intention to protect, as far as possible, frontline services supplied by doctors, nurses, teachers, police and others, by cutting back-office staff, sometimes described, more derogatively, as 'pen-pushers'. Yet the scope for such savings is limited. Most clerical workers are relatively low paid and provide valuable resources for better paid professionals, who are thus freed to concentrate on the work that only they are qualified to do. Cuts to clerical staff therefore effect the frontline workers who lack the help they previously had, while the efficiency of all parts of the NHS also clearly depends on easy access to accurate patient records. Similar points could be made about local authority social services.

However, the biggest cuts were to welfare benefits. Between 2010 and 2015, the coalition government's benefit reforms were estimated to have reduced welfare spending by over £16 billion (Hood and Phillips, 2015). Speaking to the Conservative Party conference in 2009, Cameron had announced that, while cuts would have to be made, they would also demonstrate that we were 'all in this together'. There were changes that did largely affect higher income families, the most notable being the removal of child benefit from 1.5 million households where there was a higher rate taxpayer. There were also savings made on pensions, with a rise in pension age for both men and women to 66 and higher pension contributions for public sector workers (except the very low paid and members of the armed forces).

But, far from being felt equally across the board, there were clear distributional patterns to the cuts to welfare spending made by the coalition government. Increasing the generosity of the state pension in fact left spending on pensioners £7 billion higher by 2015. The biggest spending reductions fell on children and adults in the poorest working age households. Alongside cuts to the value of housing benefits, disability benefits and working and child tax credits, new measures such as the 'benefit cap' challenged some of the long-standing principles of the welfare state. Under this policy, non-working households who were not eligible for disability benefits could not receive more than £26,000 per year in benefits, regardless of their other circumstances. This ended the link between demonstrated need and entitlement to benefits for the first time. The Conservatives believed that these measures had widespread popular support – their manifesto for the 2015 general election promised to cut a further £12 billion from welfare benefits if they were elected.

The coalition government also introduced a radical overhaul of the working age benefit system through universal credit. Universal credit replaces six different working age benefits with a single payment, becoming the main benefit for people in and out of work. Iain Duncan Smith, the former work and pensions secretary, believed that universal credit would tackle many of what he viewed as the long-term problems of Britain's welfare system, particularly the idea that it 'trapped' people in cycles of poverty and benefit dependency. Universal credit is intended to provide stronger incentives for people to move into work and increase their hours and earnings. However, the new system is proving hugely complicated to administer and full implementation has been subject to numerous delays.

## WELFARE AND AUSTERITY: FROM CAMERON TO MAY

Despite a widespread expectation that voters would punish Cameron and his chancellor, George Osborne, for austerity, the 2015 election surprisingly resulted in an overall Conservative majority after the collapse of the Lib Dem vote. Seemingly, voters bought into the Conservative narrative that the deficit and resulting economic problems were the fault of the last Labour government and that Cameron's administration was simply 'clearing up Labour's mess'.

Cameron's triumph proved short-lived. The vote to leave the EU in the 2016 referendum led immediately to his resignation and, soon after, the departure from government of Osborne. One explanation for the referendum decision was public hostility to rising immigration and its impact on overstretched health, social and educational services, although it was largely workers from overseas who were filling vacancies in these services. Robert Ford (2015) has found that in the UK 'white majority' survey respondents discriminate against foreign-born or ethnically different welfare claimants and favour co-ethnic welfare claimants. His analysis of surveys found that both race and migrant status trigger discrimination and the impact of these is cumulative, so a foreign-born Muslim claimant suffers a 'double disadvantage'.

Headed by Theresa May, the former home secretary, who had been counted as a supporter of remaining in the EU but had played little part in the public debate, the new Conservative government seemed content to implement the preference of voters, particularly the need for stronger border controls. Indeed, May emphasised the protective functions of the state associated with her old Home Office responsibilities (Davies, 2016). She also spoke of the need to look after those who were 'just about managing' (Sodha, 2016). Philip Hammond, her new chancellor, effectively abandoned plans to eliminate the deficit even by 2020. This makes some sense in the current economic climate where low interest rates keep the cost of borrowing and new investment relatively cheap. In other respects, austerity seems likely to continue. So far, Hammond has promised little to help either those who were 'just about managing' or those not managing at all.

*Source*: Matthew Chattle/Barcroft Images/Barcroft Media via Getty Images
Tens of thousands of people gathered to protest against the austerity cuts and the privatisation of services in July 2017 in London.

## THE DECLINE OF THE WELFARE STATE?

What would the founders of Britain's welfare state – the Liberals, Beveridge and Keynes, Labour's Attlee, Bevan and Morrison, and Conservatives such as Butler, Macmillan and Macleod – make of the evolution of welfare provision? The visions that spanned 'from the cradle to the grave', for which they had such high hopes, have been followed by the virtual disappearance of council housing and the current crisis in the provision of personal social services.

Other services have admittedly continued to expand in the postwar period. But, while state education has grown, it is no longer subject to any coherent accountability to, and control by, public authorities. Britain's NHS survives, although it has suffered from periodic dysfunctional reorganisations that are as bewildering to health professionals as to the wider public. While there remains strong public support for the NHS, free at the point of use, voters appear less willing to pay for it with higher taxes.

In part, some of the difficulties in welfare and public services could be attributed to underestimating problems and costs. It is also a failure of will. Periodic crises, such as the most recent from 2008 onwards, have been addressed principally by cuts in services rather than tax rises, supported by popular concerns about welfare, backed up by the media and many politicians, who view welfare not through Beveridge's and Titmuss's optimism for a better postwar world, but through a belief that programmes like *Benefits Street*, discussed in the introduction to this chapter, provide an accurate depiction of welfare in the UK today. It remains to be seen if new forces can challenge these beliefs and rekindle the optimism of the past.

 ## SUMMARY

» In the period immediately after the Second World War, there was a cross-party consensus over the need for a comprehensive range of welfare services supplied by central and local government.

» Britain's welfare state in the postwar decades gave way to increased questioning of the efficiency of public services, and attempts to introduce more competition and private sector methods into their management.

» The right of tenants to buy their council houses, introduced by the Thatcher government, led to the sale of a million houses and a substantial reduction of housing provision by local government.

» Changes in local government taxes introduced by the Thatcher and Major governments substantially cut local authority financial resources.

» New Labour continued much of the Conservative reform process, including partnership with the private sector, while increasing spending on public services such as health and education.

» Labour set numerous targets for public services and extensively monitored performance, publishing 'league tables' on the record of schools and hospitals and other institutions. Some argued that targets and league tables were dysfunctional and distorted priorities.

» There is a continuing tension between politicians' rhetoric on decentralisation and delegation and (both Conservative and Labour) government intervention in specific areas of public service management.

» Although there have been substantial increases in spending on health and education especially, by successive governments, there remain doubts whether value for money has always been achieved.

» The recession from 2008 and mounting government debt have led to substantial further cuts in spending, especially on welfare benefits, further and higher education and local government social care, although by the election of 2017, growing public opposition to austerity was acknowledged by leading Conservatives as one of the reasons they failed to secure a majority.

 ## QUESTIONS FOR DISCUSSION

» What do you understand by the term 'welfare state'? How far does Britain still have a welfare state providing security 'from the cradle to the grave'?

» How far are there significant differences between the main political parties in the delivery and management of public services?

» Why have some services been removed from local government control?

» How far do targets and league tables in health and education serve any useful purpose?

» Why is it apparently so difficult for governments to devolve the management of services to local communities, service users and/or frontline staff?

» How should higher education be funded?

» Overall, did New Labour's 'choice and investment' approach deliver improved public services?

» How far have governments from 2010 onwards offered alternative ideas for delivering public services?

» How do Britain's welfare services compare with those of other countries?

 ## FURTHER READING

On the development of the welfare state, see Fraser (2009).

On the NHS, there are two well-established books, Klein (2013) and Ham (2009).

Books on social policy include Alcock with May (2014) *Social Policy in Britain* (2014), Dwyer and Shaw (eds) *An Introduction to Social Policy* (2013) and Spicker (2014) *Social Policy: Theory and Practice* (3rd edn).

Griffiths et al. (eds) (2013) *Public Services: A New Reform Agenda* contains a variety of essays examining how public services might be reformed in response to economic and social change.

For recent events, see Bochel and Powell (2016) *The Coalition Government and Social Policy: Restructuring the Welfare State*. Toynbee and Walker (2010) provide a readable audit of Labour's successful and failures between 1997 and 2010.

 ## USEFUL WEBSITES

Many think tanks carry out interesting, forward-looking work on welfare and public services. On the centre-left, the Institute of Public Policy Research: www.ippr.org/research/topics/public-services, has carried out a variety of interesting projects on welfare and public services over the years, as has Reform, on the centre-right: www.reform.uk/our-work/area/welfarereform/.

Citizens Advice carries out some well-informed policy work in this area, building on the advice it gives to citizens dealing with public services and welfare: www.citizensadvice.org.uk/about-us/policy/.

*Further student resources to support learning are available at*
**www.macmillanihe.com/griffiths-brit-pol-3e**

# 21    THE ENVIRONMENT

In 2016 the new prime minister, Theresa May, backed the building of a third runway at London's Heathrow Airport, following the recommendations of the Airports Commission a year before. The decision was controversial and will face legal and political challenges before the first bulldozers can begin work. But May was swayed by the benefits a new runway would bring, allowing more goods and people easily in and out of London. The Airports Commission (2015) argued that the expansion would boost the UK economy by £147 billion and create 70,000 jobs by 2050 – a powerful incentive for any prime minister.

But the new runway had encountered strenuous objections from environmental groups and local campaigners. Plans for expansion were originally scrapped by the coalition government in 2010 and they continued to create controversy for May. Her decision to back expansion generated such strong feelings that it even led to the resignation of one of her own backbenchers, Zac Goldsmith, the Conservative MP for Richmond Park in west London and a former editor of the *Ecologist* magazine.

A big part of this debate was the issue of climate change. Increasing emissions – including those from planes – have long been connected to the gradual increasing of global temperatures (Intergovernmental Panel on Climate Change, 2014). If this continues unchecked, oceans will warm and ice at the polar caps will melt. In some parts of the world, flooding and desertification will lead to mass migration. Even in the UK, weather patterns will become less predictable, with more likelihood of violent floods, such as those caused by Storms Desmond and Eva in the north of England in early 2016.

The issues around the expansion of Heathrow Airport provide an example of some of the challenges facing any government when confronting this issue (Griggs and Howarth, 2013). Is economic growth more important than our environment? Do governments have more responsibility to the wealth of current voters or the long-term 'health' of the planet for future generations? Is economic growth compatible with a clean environment, or must we trade off one against the other? Can local, devolved or national government act to solve environmental problems, or must 'green' regulation be supported by international bodies, such as the EU or the UN. If so, what impact does the UK's decision to leave the EU have on its environmental policy? The answers to these questions have been transformed by the impact of 'green' approaches to politics in recent decades.

440

## THIS CHAPTER:

» Examines the rise of the Green Party, as well as the 'greening' of the mainstream UK political parties.

» Considers the response of UK governments from the 1990s to the present day in dealing with environmental problems and concerns, including energy supply and nuclear power, agriculture, transport and climate change.

» Looks at some of the obstacles facing environmental policy in the UK and elsewhere.

## THE ENVIRONMENT IN BRITISH POLITICS

Much of the postwar consensus in British politics was built on the assumption common to Labour and Conservatives that economic growth would provide the extra resources for higher living standards and an expanding welfare state, without the need for higher taxation. Maximising growth and promoting affluence was seen as the key to economic and political success. Yet growth was based substantially on the exploitation of non-renewable resources and commonly involved more environmental pollution.

The modern environmental debate began with the publication of Rachel Carson's book *Silent Spring* in 1962, which drew attention to the deadly impact of pollution on the natural environment. In 1972, the Club of Rome report *The Limits to Growth* argued that current rates of economic growth were unsustainable (Meadows et al., 1972). Their projections suggested that non-renewable resource depletion, population growth and environmental pollution would lead to a collapse of the world system. The new concerns over the environment spurred by these and other warnings led to the establishment of the major international radical pressure groups Friends of the Earth in the USA in 1969 and Greenpeace in Canada in 1972. Membership expanded rapidly in Britain, where the new groups became part of a growing environmental lobby. Today, this includes some traditional well-established organisations such as the National Trust, the Council for the Protection of Rural England and the Royal Society for the Protection of Birds, as well as some newer, more radical groups, such as the Campaign for Better Transport and Frack Off, which campaigns against fracking in the UK (see Spotlight 21.2 below). Over the years, these groups have helped draw the attention of the British public and politicians to a number of important environmental issues in British politics.

---

**Non-renewable resources** *are those that will run out or will not be replenished. Most non-renewable energy sources are fossil fuels, such as coal, petrol and natural gas. Carbon is the main element in fossil fuels.*

---

**Fracking** *is a way of extracting shale gas, for use in the home and to provide power.*

---

However, as political scientist Anthony Downs theorised, it can be easier to raise the alarm than find politically acceptable remedies. In his five-stage model for environmental issues, Downs (1973) argued that political concern about the environment would pass through the following processes:

» Stage 1: *The pre-problem stage*: The problem exists and is recognised by experts, but the public is unaware, the media are uninterested and only interest groups are alarmed. (Interest groups are discussed in more detail in Chapter 16.)

» Stage 2: *Alarmed discovery and euphoric enthusiasm*: The public are alerted to the issue, often by a dramatic event (e.g. the 1986 Chernobyl nuclear disaster in Ukraine, then part of the USSR). The public demand solutions and politicians promise action.

» Stage 3: *Realising the cost of significant progress*: Over time, the public and politicians come to realise that the cost of proposed solutions is likely to be high and involve sacrifices.

» Stage 4: *Gradual decline of public interest*: Public and media interest declines, either from boredom or a realisation of the scale of changes necessary and the costs involved.

» Stage 5: *Post-problem stage*: The issue has lost its previously high position and receives only spasmodic attention. (Derived from Downs, 1973; Richardson and Jordan, 1979; Savage and Robins, 1990.)

Downs' model has often proven to be broadly accurate in terms of a range of environmental concerns, such as oil pollution, carbon dioxide ($CO_2$) emissions and nuclear waste, although some clear progress has been made on others, such as lead in petrol, salmonella and BSE. As we saw in the introduction, part of the problem when tackling green issues is that there are often marked conflicts of interest between different sections of the public – between road users and residents in the building of new road bypasses, or between local communities and the wider public in the creation of new wind farms.

Only relatively recently have British governments accepted an explicit responsibility for the environment. In 1970, Peter Walker became the first secretary of state for the environment in Heath's Conservative government. A number of other senior politicians, including Anthony Crosland, Michael Heseltine and Chris Patten, later held the post in subsequent Labour and Conservative Cabinets. In 1997, Labour's Deputy Prime Minister John Prescott was given responsibility for a new Department of the Environment, Transport and the Regions (DETR). While there was some logic in the combination of these functions, they were perhaps too extensive for any single minister or department. In 2001, environment was joined with agriculture in the new Department for Environment, Food and Rural Affairs (Defra), while transport became part of the Department of Transport, Local Government and the Regions for a year, and then, in 2002, the Department of Transport.

Other departments, such as agriculture, trade (or more recently business) and energy, whether formally linked or not, have always had major implications for the environment. The crucial importance of energy policy for the environment was explicitly recognised in 2008 when Gordon Brown made Ed Miliband – Labour leader from 2010 to 2015 – the secretary of state for energy and climate change, and in effect the lead minister on environmental policy, despite the survival of Defra. The 2010–15 coalition government changed some departmental titles and responsibilities but retained Defra and the Department of Energy & Climate Change (DECC). However, after July 2016, DECC became part of the Department for Business, Energy & Industrial Strategy, a move that was criticised for downplaying the importance of climate change by Theresa May's critics, including the Conservative's former coalition partners, the Lib Dems, and many environmental groups (Vaughan, 2016).

Government policy towards the environment is also substantially influenced by a range of interests, some of which may not be actuated mainly or at all by environmental concerns. For example, major businesses and industry bodies routinely lobby ministers and civil servants, and they have far more financial and other resources to influence government, parliamentary and public opinion than the green pressure groups. Energy suppliers, manufacturers, builders and retailers (including the major supermarkets) all make sure their voice is heard, as do the agriculture, fishing and aviation industries and the road transport lobby.

The government also has to coordinate its environmental policies with other lower levels of government and administration. Since 1999, environmental policy has been a 'devolved power', although international agreements are still decided by Westminster. This has led to policy divergences within the UK, as Scotland, Wales and Northern Ireland have been able to develop different models and standards for environmental policy, as long as they are the same or higher than the minimum required by EU rules. For example, Scotland and Wales have both adopted more ambitious policies in relation to climate change. (For more on devolution, see Chapter 11.)

Also, local authorities have extensive environmental responsibilities for regulating pollution and for waste collection and disposal. In some cases, the actions of councils may reflect pressure from the British government or EU directives (until we leave the EU). In others, local action may be innovative, providing examples to be followed elsewhere, and perhaps adopted as national policy.

Because much environmental policy transcends state boundaries, the UK government also seeks to influence, and is influenced by, the governments of other states, multinational business corporations and all kinds of international organisations, governmental and nongovernmental. Issues such as poverty, energy and climate change have inevitably become globalised, so governments have to respond to this international pressure and public opinion as well as to their own domestic electorate. Environmental policy necessarily involves multi-level governance (a term introduced in Chapter 1, p. 16). Over the course of Britain's membership, the EU was increasingly a key player and EU decisions and laws often had significant implications for the UK environment (see Spotlight 21.1 overleaf).

# THE RISE OF GREEN POLITICS

## THE MAINSTREAM PARTIES

As environmental concerns rose up the issue agenda, mainstream parties sought to address them. At times, each party developed its own green organisations – Labour has the Socialist Environment and Resources Association and the Lib Dems have the Green Liberal Democrats. The Conservative Party has less well-established 'green' organisations, but at various times the Tory Green Initiative, active during the early days of David Cameron's leadership, and more recently the 2020 Group have pushed a green agenda. Such groups have tried to place green issues higher up each party's policy agenda, although with rather limited success.

The most apparently dramatic conversion was of Margaret Thatcher, who startled the 1988 Conservative Party conference with a speech in which she proclaimed that Conservatives are 'not merely friends of the Earth', but its 'guardians and trustees' (Thatcher, 1988b). Thatcher was a science graduate and appears to have been convinced of the scientific arguments on the dangers of population growth, global warming and environmental pollution. Her conversion helped bring environmental concerns into the British political mainstream.

More recently, David Cameron initially put the environment at the forefront of his efforts to transform the image of his party. He changed the party logo from the old 'freedom torch' to a green tree, adopted the slogan 'Think Green, Vote Blue', and appointed Zac Goldsmith as an adviser. He also pursued a personal green lifestyle, fixing a wind turbine on his house and cycling to work, albeit, as the media revealed, with a car following to carry his papers. (Indeed, many critiques have pointed out that the Conservative's commitment to the environment was more lukewarm in office than out, as we note below.)

While all mainstream parties began to show more concern for environmental issues, there were conflicts of interest and ideas within each of them that prevented a wholehearted commitment to a green philosophy. For example, while it was true that conservatism involved conservation and within the party there were strong interests committed to the preservation of the countryside, Thatcherism had also strongly emphasised the free market and deregulation (discussed in Chapter 3), whereas many environmental issues appeared to require more regulation.

In practice, in Britain as elsewhere, greens are more likely to be found on the left than the right, and Labour contains some radical environmentalists. Yet Labour was historically committed to economic expansion, high growth and full employment. Both Labour and its trade union allies were more concerned to defend jobs, and with that industry, rather than the environment. The Lib Dems, minority players in coalition between 2010 and 2015, have often appeared more sensitive to environmental issues than the other major parties, but even they have felt obliged to make concessions to conflicting interests, for

# SPOTLIGHT ON ...

## The environmental consequences of Brexit    21.1

It was estimated that 'over 80% of British environment policy originates in the EU' (Jordan, 2002, p. 262). Of course, the British government has also often played a proactive role in the shaping of EU environmental policy, notably over the Kyoto Protocol and emission targets.

While past UK governments were prepared to accept the EU's ambitious targets for recycling waste, they sometimes seemed unable to deal with the detailed problems of implementing EU directives on recycling, which should help meet these broad targets. As a consequence of this failure, crises have arisen, for example over indiscriminate car, fridge and freezer dumping and fly tipping generally, which the UK media often blame on EU directives rather than the UK government (Humphrey, 2003, pp. 314–16).

While the green lobby generally approves of the EU approach to recycling, there are other aspects of EU policy that have been criticised as less environmentally friendly, including much of the Common Agricultural Policy, which leads to overproduction, intensive farming and the draining of wetlands and some environmentally damaging major civil engineering schemes.

The UK's decision to leave the EU is likely to have a significant, but as yet unclear, impact on UK environment policy. For Burns et al. (2016), the decision to leave the EU raised three consequences:

1  They argued that environmental policy is being downgraded. Theresa May did not mention the environment in her speeches on Brexit, for example. It seems that the environment is not a policy priority in the current negotiations.

2  Brexit could lead to greater calls for deregulation, as laws to protect the environment are dismantled. This has long been a desire for many politicians, particularly in the Conservative Party, who are wary of the impact of environmental legislation on the economy. For green campaigners, Brexit has increased concerns that environmental policy is at risk of being weakened. As it stands, the government's EU (Withdrawal) Bill, which will begin to pull apart UK and European legislation, will maintain the body of law accumulated by the EU even after the European Communities Act no longer applies. After this, environmental policies might be revised, removed or left to grow out of date. However, this does not mean that the UK has complete freedom when it comes to environmental policy – it will still have to negotiate an exit deal with its EU partners. It is not yet known what position EU negotiators will take on what counts as a trade-related environmental measure and what does not and which environmental policies the EU will want to see maintained in the UK.

3  Environmental policy after Brexit faces internal challenges within the UK from devolution (see Chapter 11). Before Brexit, Scotland, Wales and Northern Ireland were able to pursue their own environmental policy, providing it met minimum EU standards. It is an open question how environmental policy will develop in Wales, Scotland and Northern Ireland after Brexit, and whether we see greater policy divergence between different parts of the UK once the EU is not setting the minimum standards for environmental policy (Burns et al., 2016).

example concerns in rural areas over rising fuel costs. All mainstream parties are wary of offending motorists by advocating higher car taxes or restrictions on car use.

The problem is that mainstream parties have generally competed by promising to make people better off, whereas a more thorough green philosophy might entail making them materially worse off, at least in the public perception, and this is an intrinsically difficult message to sell to voters. So the major parties prefer to express a generalised concern for the environment, particularly the global environment, and only emphasise some relatively easy, voter-friendly environmental issues, such as recycling and energy conservation, that will not cost too much nor upset significant vested interests.

## THE GREEN PARTY

The Green Party would claim that it is the only party wholeheartedly committed to a green agenda. So far, it has not made the same progress as some green parties in other countries (notably Germany; see Comparing British Politics 21.1 below), although the British Green Party can trace its origins back further than the more successful German Greens. The party began as the People Party in 1973, changed its name to the Ecology Party in 1975, and finally to the Green Party in 1985. In the early years, it only secured 1–1.5% of the vote in general elections, although rather more in local elections, and was a marginal player in British politics.

Then, in 1989, the Green Party appeared to make a decisive breakthrough in electoral politics, winning 15% of the vote in the elections for the European Parliament, although no seats under the single member plurality system then used in Britain for European elections (for more details on electoral systems, see Chapter 13). It proved a false dawn. The circumstances in 1989 were unusual. The centre was in disarray as the old Liberal Party and its recent electoral partner the SDP had proceeded to a clumsy and hotly contested merger after the 1987 election, and the Green Party attracted protest votes from those who did not want to support either of the two main parties.

They have never approached their 1989 performance in any subsequent election. However, they have benefitted modestly from the introduction of more proportional representation into elections for Europe and devolved assemblies. In 1999, 2004 and 2009, they won two seats in the European Parliament, and three in 2014 on 6% of the vote (a much smaller share than in 1989). In 2016, they won six seats in the Scottish Parliament (on 7% of the regional list vote) and two seats in the London Assembly (on 8% of the vote). This representation has given the Green Party a rather higher profile, but perhaps their biggest breakthrough in recent times was winning a seat at Westminster under 'first past the post'. In 2010, Caroline Lucas was elected in Brighton Pavilion, becoming the first Green MP. She then retained the seat in 2015 and 2017 general elections (see Key Figures 21.1 overleaf).

Indeed, the 2015 general election, in particular, was rather successful for the Green Party. They quadrupled their vote around the country and were a significant presence in the campaign, taking part in the televised leaders debates. They were the only credible party in England to campaign on a radical anti-austerity manifesto, arguing against cuts to public services and government spending, and attracted significant numbers of younger voters and disenchanted former Labour and Lib Dem supporters. In England and Wales, membership rose from 14,000 in January 2014 to nearly 67,000 by the May 2015 general election (Carter, 2015). But with only one MP, the Greens are penalised by the 'first past the post' electoral system.

In the past, the Green Party have perhaps not helped their cause by refusing to behave like a 'normal political party', reflecting some ambivalence towards conventional parliamentary politics. Until 2007, they declined to choose a single party leader, preferring to nominate several spokespersons. All this is reminiscent of the behaviour of the early German Greens as an 'anti-party party' (see Comparing British Politics 21.1 overleaf). It is worth noting, however, that their level of support (over 6%) in recent elections held under proportional representation is very close to that of the German Greens who were in the German government from 1998 to 2005. By comparison, the Green Party is marginal to British politics and is arguably less influential than the major pressure groups, Greenpeace and Friends of the Earth. However, the election of Lucas as an MP after 2010 and Green Party participation in the leadership debates ahead of the 2015 general election has raised the party's profile.

# KEY FIGURES 21.1
## Caroline Lucas

**Caroline Lucas (1960–)** is Britain's most successful green politician. She was elected as the Green Party's first MP in 2010 and re-elected in the 2015 and 2017 general elections with increased majorities. Lucas was leader of the Green Party from 2008 to 2012 and returned to the role as co-leader in 2016. Born to Conservative parents, at university Lucas became involved with the Campaign for Nuclear Disarmament and the Greenham Common women's peace camp, which protested against US nuclear missiles in the UK. She joined the Green Party in 1986 and was seen as a moderniser, stressing the importance of a professional media image and message. She later represented the party as a local councillor and Member of the European Parliament (MEP). Lucas campaigns for green economics, alternatives to globalisation, animal welfare, fair trade and electoral reform. She has argued that left of centre parties should work together to form a 'progressive alliance'.

# COMPARING BRITISH POLITICS 21.1
## The German Greens (Die Grünen)

The green movement developed in Germany in the late 1970s. Green candidates won election to state parliaments and in 1983 the Green Party won 5.6% of the vote and 28 seats in the German federal parliament (the Bundestag). The new Green representatives caused a stir by turning up in jeans and T-shirts and placing potted plants on their desks in the chamber. Petra Kelly, their best-known early leader, proclaimed that they were an 'anti-party party'. However, the Greens were soon split between *realos* (realists), who were prepared to make compromises and form alliances with other parties, and *fundis* (fundamentalists), who were not. Some Greens joined the Social Democrats in 'red–green' coalitions in state parliaments. Party fortunes subsequently fluctuated at national level, until, in 1998, they won 6.7% of the vote and joined in a coalition government with the Social Democrats under Gerhard Schröder. The Green leader Joschka Fischer became foreign minister, and three other Greens entered the Cabinet. As part of this, environmental laws and practices in Germany are among the strongest in Europe. Defying predictions, the red–green coalition remained in power after fresh elections in 2002, but lost office in 2005. Since then, it has struggled electorally at federal level, perhaps because so many of its concerns have found their way into the politics of the main parties.

The German Greens show what the British Green Party could achieve, particularly if a more proportional electoral system was introduced at Westminster. However, the internal tensions and splits among German Greens also indicate the problems in moving from an anti-party of protest to a party of government.

# ENVIRONMENTAL POLICY

Environmental policy has become an increasingly significant area of policy. Blair and New Labour came to power in 1997 committed to placing the environment at the heart of its policy-making. Indeed, Labour embraced sustainability and announced a number of targets: to meet 10% of UK energy needs from renewable resources by 2010, to cut the 1990 level of greenhouse gas emissions by 23% by 2010, and to recycle 35% of all household waste by 2015. Recycling of food, paper, glass and plastics became the norm in British homes in a way they had never been before.

---

Greenhouse gases, such as $CO_2$, trap heat in the atmosphere, keeping the earth's surface warmer than it would be if they were not present. Increases in the amount of greenhouse gases in the atmosphere cause climate change. Carbon dioxide is released when fossil fuels are burnt.

---

David Cameron placed commitment to the environment at the centre of his own rebranding of the Conservative Party after his election as party leader in 2005. As such, the environment was not a significant problem in the formation of the Conservative–Lib Dem coalition in 2010. The Lib Dems under Nick Clegg had continued their own identification with environmental concerns, and in the inter-party bargaining following the election secured the key environmental Cabinet post – secretary of state for energy and climate change – for Chris Huhne and later Ed Davey.

Nevertheless, within a few years of coalition government, tensions began to surface over climate change between the Lib Dems and the Conservatives, and between Cameron and his own Conservative backbench MPs, many of whom – urged on by the right-wing press – were sceptical over the evidence for global warming (Carter and Clements, 2015). Theresa May has tended to deprioritise the environment in her record to date as prime minister, although some of her most significant policy decisions, including the commitment to withdraw from the EU, will have huge environmental effects (see Spotlight 21.1 on p. 444).

## CLIMATE CHANGE

The issue that has come to dominate UK, EU and international environmental policy is climate change and, more specifically, humanity's contribution to climate change and efforts to halt or slow it by reducing emissions of $CO_2$ and other greenhouse gases. Yet it has proved difficult to secure full cooperation from all national governments, including some of those with the most significant emissions levels.

A significant step forward was taken in 1997, when the Kyoto Protocol (which came into force in 2005) set targets for 186 states (including 38 developed states), binding them to reduce their emissions of $CO_2$ and other greenhouse gases by 2012. The EU committed all member states to keep to their targets by law. However, the USA unilaterally withdrew from the Kyoto Protocol. While President Clinton was supportive, the Senate rejected the agreement. The election of George W. Bush in 2000 destroyed early hope of US participation in international cooperation to stem climate change.

Despite international difficulties, climate change rose rapidly up the UK political agenda and the Labour government, with cross-party support, introduced major changes in domestic climate and energy policy. As chancellor of the exchequer, Gordon Brown commissioned the economist Nick Stern to examine the economic impact of climate change. The Stern Review, published in 2006, argued that the benefits of tough, early action on climate change hugely outweighed the costs of doing nothing. According to Stern, the results of inaction on climate change would be equivalent to losing over 5% of the world's GDP every year. When he included a wider range of risks and impacts, he found that this figure could be as high as 20% of global GDP annually. Stern argued that an increase of 5–6$^0$C in global average temperatures was a real possibility. However, he believed it could be avoided. By investing 1–2% of global GDP in various measures to mitigate climate change a year, he argued we could avoid global warming's worst effects (Stern Review, 2006).

Influenced by Stern, among others, Labour passed the Climate Change Act in 2008, which represented an important step toward the UK becoming a low carbon economy. The Act, steered through parliament by future Labour leader Ed Miliband, at the time secretary of state for energy and climate change, made it the duty of the secretary of state to ensure that the net UK carbon account for all six Kyoto greenhouse gases for the year 2050 is at least 80% lower than the 1990 baseline.

The 2009 UN Climate Change Conference met at Copenhagen, amid high hopes of securing new binding targets on reducing greenhouse gas emissions and checking global warming, particularly as the US government, now headed by President Barack Obama, was an active participant. Yet the outcome was widely reckoned a failure. Delegates only agreed to 'take note of the Copenhagen Accord'. Thus while the scientific arguments for keeping global temperature rises below 2⁰C were acknowledged, there were no legally binding commitments. Some blamed the richer nations for not offering more assistance to developing nations in reducing emissions. Others blamed the reluctance of major developing powers such as China and India to commit to restrictions on emissions, for fear that this might adversely affect their own rapid growth, based substantially on coal.

One possible contributory factor to the difficulty of achieving binding global agreements to limit carbon emissions is public, and to some extent governmental, scepticism over the reality and implications of climate change. This is despite the almost unanimous consensus of the international scientific community that significant global warming is occurring, that human activity significantly contributes to global warming and that action is urgently required to prevent potentially calamitous effects. In part, this public scepticism reflects difficulty in accepting the reality of long-term climate trends against direct experience of short-term climate fluctuations. It can be hard to convince a British public that continues to experience relatively cold and rainy summers that the world is dangerously heating up. This is one reason why the terminology of the debate has subtly altered from 'global warming' to 'climate change'. It may be easier to convince British (and US) opinion that we are now experiencing more extreme variations in climate such as the 2016 floods (mentioned in the introduction to this chapter), at the same time as a long-term trend towards global warming, the thawing of polar ice caps and rises in sea levels. Indeed, debates over flood defences became a significant political factor in the UK after recent periods of high rainfall. However, the existence of 'climate change deniers' continues to affect public opinion.

Only a small minority of scientists dispute the link between human activity and climate change, but there are some. They also have some high-profile political supporters, such as Nigel Lawson, the former Conservative chancellor. One problem here is that the media thrive on controversy and attempt to present arguments with counterarguments. This approach has been criticised for disregarding the gross disparity in numbers of those who affirm and deny climate change and the weight and quality of the evidence on each side.

In the UK, the coalition government of 2010–15 had a mixed record when it came to the environment. On the big issue of climate change, David Cameron swung between identifying climate change as a priority for his government and undermining that claim. He promoted John Hayes, an opponent of wind farms, to the role of junior energy minister. (Wind is one of the main alternatives to greenhouse gas producing energy.) It was also reported that Cameron had demanded that his civil servants 'get rid of all the green crap', that is, the levies and regulations, that he regarded as responsible for pushing up energy prices. Nor did Cameron, despite his own championing of the environment after becoming Conservative Party leader, challenge the growth of climate change denial in his own party (Carter and Clements, 2015). Indeed, by the end of the Parliament, the environment had become one of the most significant sources of tension between the Conservatives and Lib Dems (Carter, 2016).

The Department of Energy & Climate Change also suffered significant cuts after 2010 in the coalition government's spending review, and after 2016 its responsibilities were subsumed by the Department for Business, Energy & Industrial Strategy. The government still appears committed to investment in renewables and carbon capture and storage, and is establishing a new green investment bank, which it is hoped will attract substantial private sector finance, although the size of the government contribution (reported to be £1 billion) remains somewhat unclear and controversial.

---

*Carbon capture and storage is the process of trapping $CO_2$, a greenhouse gas produced by burning fossil fuels or other chemical or biological processes, and storing it in such a way that it is unable to affect the atmosphere, normally deep underground.*

---

Internationally, a major step to mitigate the effects of climate change seemed to have been made in Paris in 2015, when 197 parties – including the UK – acting within the UN Framework Convention on Climate Change agreed that, by 2020, countries would begin a process to determine, plan and report their own contribution to mitigate global warming. Known as the Paris Agreement, it has been ratified by 168 parties. Although the Paris Agreement contained no mechanism to force a country to set a specific new target, it was agreed that each new target a country set should go beyond that previously agreed. The election of Donald Trump as US president in November 2016 shifted the debate on climate change significantly. Trump's cabinet is highly sceptical of the science behind climate change, and many have backgrounds in the oil and gas industries. In June 2017, Trump announced that the USA was pulling out of the Paris Agreement as 'a reassertion of America's sovereignty', adding he was 'elected to represent the citizens of Pittsburgh, not Paris' (Shear, 2017). The move led to worldwide condemnation, including from the EU and China, although the UK prime minister at the time, Theresa May, was notably less critical than many other world leaders, hoping to avoid upsetting the 'special relationship' between Britain and the USA (see Spotlight 22.2).

## ENERGY

The Labour government, elected in 1997, took over at a time when the decline of coal-fired power stations and the 'dash for gas' to replace them was already far advanced. Labour sought to arrest the decline in the coal industry and maintain competition in energy supply. While the switch from coal to gas helped the UK to meet its climate change emission targets, it made the country dangerously dependent on gas, and, increasingly, imported gas, as Britain's own supply of gas from the North Sea is rapidly declining, although fracking presents an alternative option, as discussed in Spotlight 21.2 overleaf.

The UK's ageing nuclear power stations were also providing a declining contribution to electricity generation. Initially, the Labour government were reluctant to build new or replacement nuclear power stations, because of the high cost of nuclear power, the problems and expense of disposing of nuclear waste and fears on security and safety grounds.

The Labour government sought, on the one hand, to cut energy consumption, by the encouragement of more efficient use of energy by industry and households, and, on the other hand, to seek new renewable energy resources. Neither made an appreciable impact. It was hoped that wind farms would help the government reach its target of meeting 10% of energy needs from renewable resources, but electricity produced by wind farms is irregular and expensive. Moreover, the location of large numbers of giant windmills on attractive countryside aroused increasing opposition from local pressure groups, leading to more emphasis on more expensive offshore wind farms.

Other bold schemes to generate electricity through the use of wave power, such as the proposed Morecambe Bay barrage, have yet to get off the ground. In the circumstances, the Labour government began to 'think the unthinkable' and recommit to nuclear power, previously ruled out on cost and security grounds. Despite the massive problems of nuclear waste disposal and eventual plant decommissioning, atomic power stations are relatively 'greenhouse-friendly' (Jordan, 2002, p. 283). So, as dependence on imported gas and oil rose, the Labour government actively sought to construct a new generation of nuclear power stations.

# SPOTLIGHT ON ...

## Fracking

With the gradual decline of North Sea oil and the UK's dependency on imported gas, fracking is seen by its advocates as a viable option. The fracking process involves drilling deep into the earth, then injecting a mixture of water, sand and chemicals into the rock beneath to extract shale gas. Doing this at high pressure fractures the rock (hence the term fracking), forcing the gas to the surface. Fracking is now widely used to meet energy needs in the USA, but its extension to the UK has been controversial.

Fracking uses powerful, sometimes cancer-causing chemicals. There have been concerns these could escape and contaminate the wider area. The process also requires huge amounts of water, a particular issue in places where it is scarce. In some areas, fracking has also been linked to earth tremors; in 2011, a 1.5 magnitude earthquake near Blackpool was linked to fracking activities close by. Environmental campaigners want governments to focus resources on generating renewable sources of energy, rather than investing in what they view as an expensive, harmful and resource-intensive means of extracting more fossil fuel.

The UK government has awarded over 100 licences, allowing firms to start exploratory activities at certain sites in the UK. Companies also require permission from the local authority. Tests were paused after the earth tremors in Blackpool in 2011. However, in 2016, several more sites received the go-ahead to carry out explanatory work. North Yorkshire County Council approved further tests, and in October, Sajid Javid, secretary of state for communities and local government, overturned Lancashire County Council's rejection of a planning application for fracking activity, making possible four new 'wells' for drilling.

The gradual expansion of fracking activity has led to protests at local and national levels. As well as opposition from major environmental charities such as Greenpeace, large numbers of local pressure groups have formed to oppose fracking in their areas. Many of these groups are linked together by networks such as Frack Off, which tries to alert people to activities they can take part in and coordinate action against fracking.

*Source*: www.frackoff.org.uk

Fracking licences cover over 10 million acres of the British Isles. Over 300 anti-fracking community groups are currently active in the UK, causing costly delays and bad publicity for the industry nationwide.

The election of a Conservative–Lib Dem coalition in 2010 led to new tensions on energy policy: despite general agreement on the environmental agenda, there was one important issue on which the two parties appeared divided. While the Conservatives broadly sided with the outgoing Labour government on the need for nuclear power as part of Britain's energy mix, the Lib Dems were strongly opposed. This was not an issue that was resolved by the talks leading up to the formation of the new government. There was effectively an agreement to disagree. The outgoing Labour government had chosen eleven sites for new nuclear power stations – almost all close to existing nuclear power stations, where it was expected there would be less opposition. In October 2010, Chris Huhne rejected three of these sites on environmental grounds but identified eight others as potential sites for new nuclear power stations (all already producing nuclear energy). Huhne declared: 'I'm fed up with the stand-off between advocates of renewables and of nuclear which means we have neither … I am making it clear that new nuclear will be free to contribute as much as possible with the onus on developers to pay for the clean-up' (*The Independent,* 2010).

In 2016, despite reservations and after much delay, May's government announced an agreement that would lead to the building of the first new nuclear power station in the UK for 20 years at Hinkley Point in Somerset, partly financed by the French and Chinese governments. Critics raised national security concerns about allowing the national energy supply to rely so heavily on foreign spending and development. But the Conservative governments under Cameron and May confirmed Britain's commitment to nuclear energy (Ward et al., 2016).

Greenpeace, the key environmental group, remains implacably opposed to nuclear power, although a few prominent environmentalists, including writer James Lovelock (2007) and journalist George Monbiot, are now advocates of nuclear power as the only way to meet Britain's (and the world's) energy needs without destroying the planet. Others have become reluctant converts, although many still remain strongly opposed. The impact of the

*Source*: Getty

Radioactive leaks have led to concerns over the long-term safety of nuclear power in many nations, including the UK.

Japanese earthquake and tsunami of March 2011 on the nuclear power plant at Fukushima and the serious radioactive contamination of the surrounding environment and food and water supplies has reawakened concerns over the safety of nuclear power, particularly in Japan, but also elsewhere.

## TRANSPORT

Not only is transport a major consumer of energy, but its infrastructure – roads, airports, railways – has a major impact on the physical environment, and almost all new developments are politically contentious. Noise pollution, with massive effects on the quality of life and physical and mental health, is an important factor here, but there are also invariably concerns over the impact on the landscape and flora and fauna. So transport and the environment have become closely linked.

In 1997, it was hoped that the large and high-profile DETR under John Prescott would place environmental concerns at the centre of government, and build an integrated transport system in which public transport would no longer suffer neglect and underinvestment. However, the new department proved too large for effective control. After the 2001 election, it was broken up, and the environment was combined with food and rural affairs in a new ministry (Defra) to replace the old Ministry of Agriculture, Fisheries and Food, while transport re-emerged as a separate department.

Labour's planned integrated transport policy soon ran into trouble, compelling a U-turn. John Prescott had boldly announced in 1997: 'I will have failed if, in five years' time, there are not many more people using public transport and far fewer journeys by car' (Cahill, 2010, p. 26). Yet it was clear that Labour was reluctant to upset motorists for electoral reasons. After the September 2000 fuel protests, the government abandoned regular increases in fuel duty as a policy instrument to deter car use, and Brown fought shy of increasing petrol taxes substantially. Moreover, it was London, and not central government, that was responsible for the only significant curb on car use. Congestion charges, introduced in London in 2003 by the London mayor Ken Livingstone, proved reasonably successful in reducing congestion and raising revenue, and led to interest in other cities, although residents in Edinburgh and elsewhere later voted against following London's example. Meanwhile, Labour's hopes of boosting rail transport were dealt a major blow by the emergence of serious problems in the rail management system they had inherited. The Hatfield crash in 2000 forced a rethinking of priorities, led to substantial delays because of new safety restrictions and contributed to the collapse of Railtrack – the group of companies that owned the railway tracks and other infrastructure after privatisation. Labour effectively abandoned any prospect of reducing car use, which has continued to increase.

More recently, and tardily, all parties have expressed support for new high-speed rail links between Britain's major cities – known as High Speed 2 (HS2). Even if these lines are eventually built (and there is strong local opposition), Britain remains well behind other European countries such as France and Spain in the development of high-speed rail. Meanwhile, Labour did nothing to deter the expansion of air travel and backed proposals for a third runway at Heathrow, opposed not only (and predictably) by local residents and greens, but also by the Conservatives and Lib Dems. As the introduction to this chapter showed, the issue became controversial once more, with the Conservative government slowly moving towards approving Heathrow expansion, after much delay, in 2016.

Elsewhere, the coalition government approved a number of expensive transport capital investment plans around the country, including the Crossrail project in London, high-speed rail links between London, the Midlands and the north, a new Mersey bridge, and a revamp for the Tyne and Wear Metro. While the green lobby may be encouraged by the commitment to investment in rail transport, they and passenger groups are much less happy with projected substantial increases in rail and bus fares. These will do nothing to encourage the use of public transport, ease road congestion or reduce carbon emissions.

## FOOD, AGRICULTURE AND THE COUNTRYSIDE

Agriculture and food production in Britain has become big business. Small farms have become increasingly uneconomic as farming has become more mechanised and capital-intensive. An already small agricultural workforce has shrunk to less than 1% of the working population (Jones, 2013). Although the countryside has increasingly attracted people seeking refuge from the pressures of urban life, many of those who now live in the more rural parts of Britain no longer work there. While farmers and landowners claim to be the custodians of the natural environment, they are, like those engaged in other kinds of business, also, and primarily, intent on securing the maximum return on their investment, regardless of the environmental consequences. Major supermarkets increasingly dominate food production, because of their purchasing power and marketing. Thus most British agricultural produce is not consumed locally but transported, sometimes hundreds of miles, to be processed, packaged and promoted. Consumers predominantly want cheap and convenient food and most are not concerned where it comes from, although there are periodic food scares – salmonella in eggs, BSE and contaminated beef, pesticides on fruit and vegetables, food with genetically modified (GM) ingredients – that cause alarm and lead to consumer boycotts.

British governments have not generally sought radical change in food policy. Cheap food helps keep inflation low. Beyond that, much of the regulation of British agriculture now lies primarily with the EU, whose subsidies, for all their proclaimed interest in small farms, largely reward the big 'agribusinesses'; although, more recently, some financial assistance has been directed towards environmental conservation and organic farming. Britain's decision to withdraw from the EU is likely to significantly alter farming practices around the UK. The 1997–2010 Labour governments sought to give rather more priority to these areas, although like their predecessors, they necessarily became involved with periodic food scares and crisis management, particularly over GM foods and the foot and mouth outbreak in 2001. These concerns ultimately resulted in the creation of the Food Standards Agency and Defra.

In 2004–05, concerns over obesity, particularly child obesity, linked with concerns over diets and 'junk food' with high sugar and salt content, and numerous additives for colour and flavouring, increased pressure for more regulation of the food industry and healthier school meals. However, EU proposals to require bolder warnings on foods, with a traffic light system (red for high calories, yellow for medium and green for low), were dropped in 2010 after intense lobbying by food manufacturers, despite pressure from health experts worried about the consequences of a high-sugar diet for the NHS and patient health in general.

Labour had a troubled relationship with rural interests, who accused the party of urban bias. The government's most significant achievement involved opening up the countryside to walkers under the Countryside and Rights of Way Act 2000. This had the support of not only the Ramblers Association but also the green lobby, whose environmental concerns were largely met, although the measure was resisted by most farmers and landowners. Increased access to the countryside largely serves the leisure needs of urban dwellers, although it can be argued that it is they who pay through their taxes for substantial subsidies to agriculture, and the countryside should be for the benefit of all.

It was, however, the hunting issue that stoked up rural resentment against the Labour government and led to the creation of the Countryside Alliance in 1997, covering a number of rural grievances, although hunting always remained the chief motivating force. The Countryside Alliance was defending traditional rights and a traditional way of life and, they argued, the countryside itself. Yet most of the environmental lobby was on the other side. Hunting is a highly emotive but essentially peripheral concern to environmental conservation. The real political issues are: Why and how to preserve the countryside, and for whom?

## OBSTACLES FACING ENVIRONMENTAL POLICY

As the introduction to this chapter showed, environmental policy frequently conflicts with other policy objectives. Is it possible for a government to be in favour of both airport expansion to provide jobs and economic growth and measures to limit climate change that more flights cause? These tensions are part of all policy-making. Different departments and the policy areas for which they are responsible are frequently in competition with each other for government priority and resources. However, environmental policy, in particular, cuts across any government's broad economic objectives for growth, high employment and low inflation, and the aim of business to maximise profits in a free market, with minimum regulation. Indeed, within government, environmental calls are often drowned out by the demands of the bigger, more prestigious, high-spending departments, such as the Treasury and the Foreign Office. Even the substantial environmental lobby often comes up against a well-organised, influential and highly resourced business lobby, which can often argue that particular restrictions and regulations will damage their competitiveness in world markets. This is an argument that can be highly persuasive with politicians and governments, and also with workers and ultimately consumers and voters. Politicians may be quite sincere in the concerns they express for the environment, but in the real world they have to balance these concerns against other desirable objectives relating to jobs, services and living standards.

There is another particular problem with environmental issues and policies. Their impact is frequently long term and sometimes contentious, while politicians deal primarily with the short term and the immediate impact on the economy and political prospects. Many of the presumed beneficiaries of environmental conservation are not current voters and have little weight in the political marketplace. There often appears to be an urgent need to satisfy present demands. The horizons of us all, not just politicians, tend to be short term. It is often difficult to persuade people, in their own interests, to forgo current consumption for some future benefit, such as a comfortable retirement. It is much more difficult to persuade them to forgo current consumption for the benefit of unknown peoples in distant continents, still less for future generations yet unborn. So the green lobby has its work cut out. The political process, not just in Britain but more generally, has an inbuilt bias against their concerns. In the wake of the immediate problems caused by the financial crisis and economic recession that began in 2008–09, and working out the consequences of how to implement Britain's decision to leave the EU, longer term environmental issues have slipped down the national and global political agenda.

 **SUMMARY**

» Governments face competing calls for resources and critics have long argued that the environment is neglected compared to economic concerns.

» It is only relatively recently that environmental issues and policies have become a more important focus of British politics and government.

» The main impact on British politics was initially through green pressure groups rather than mainstream parties, although all these have increasingly sought to address environmental concerns.

» The Green Party had negligible political influence until quite recently, partly because it has been underrepresented through the British 'first past the post' electoral system. It gained its first MP in 2010 when Caroline Lucas was elected in Brighton Pavilion. The party has also benefitted from the introduction of more proportional voting systems for the European Parliament, Scottish Parliament and London Assembly.

» New Labour claimed that the environment was central to its programme, yet its record on energy, transport and agriculture was mixed and contentious, reflecting other political pressures.

» Both parties in the 2010–15 Conservative–Lib Dem coalition government claimed a commitment to the environment. In office, however, the relationship became strained. Backbench Conservative MPs, sceptical of the evidence on climate change and the burden of environmental regulation, often pushed Cameron towards a less 'green' agenda.

» There is a question over the extent to which environmental issues are best dealt with at national level, with many problems needing international responses. A significant part of the UK's environmental legislation comes from the EU. Brexit potentially threatens to weaken UK environmental protection measures, while debates over the UK's future relationship with the EU have distracted policy-makers in Westminster away from environmental policy.

» The environment is a devolved issue in the UK, with policy divergence occurring between Scotland, Wales and Northern Ireland. This divergence is likely to be even greater once the EU no longer sets minimum standards for environmental legislation in the UK.

» Longer term green issues and problems are not well served in a democratic political system that (perhaps inevitably) reflects the immediate concerns and demands of current voters.

## ? QUESTIONS FOR DISCUSSION

» Why is it difficult for mainstream British parties to pursue environmental policies wholeheartedly?

» How far is sustainability compatible with a real increase in living standards in countries like Britain?

» Should governments focus on economic growth or environmental protection?

» What impact could leaving the EU have on the UK's environmental policy?

» How far should the Green Party engage in traditional politics?

» Why has the German Green Party apparently been so much more successful than the British Green Party?

» How might Britain's dependence on imported fossil fuels be reduced? Is renewable energy a convincing answer to Britain's energy needs? Should Britain be building a new generation of nuclear power stations? Can the nuclear option be safe?

» Is the democratic political process ill-equipped for addressing environmental concerns?

» Who or what is the British countryside for? Who can be best trusted to look after it?

## FURTHER READING

Green classics include Carson (1962) *Silent Spring*, the Club of Rome's *The Limits to Growth* (Meadows et al., 1972), Schumacher (1973) *Small is Beautiful*, O'Riordan (1976) *Environmentalism* and Lovelock (1979) *Gaia: A New Look at Life on Earth*. The latter may be compared with Lovelock's more recent *The Revenge of Gaia* (2007).

There are useful short chapters on green ideas and policies in several general books on contemporary ideologies, including Eccleshall et al. (2003), Heywood (2017) and Leach (2015).

Green thinking is explored further in Goodin (1992), Eckersley (1993) and Dobson (2007). Some older accounts are still useful for the growth of green politics in Britain and more generally, including Porritt and Winner (1988), McCormick (1991), Robinson (1992) and Garner (2000). Accounts of the early environmental policy of the

Blair government are provided by Jordan (2002) and Humphrey (2003). Foster (2001) discusses the Blair government's transport policy. Bale (2010) is useful on Conservative environmental policy. Carter (2015, 2016) has written widely on the environmental policies of the coalition and Conservative Party since 2015. Connelly (2015) also provides a succinct overview of the coalition's record on the environment.

## USEFUL WEBSITES

Many environmental lobby groups provide information on green causes. Friends of the Earth and Greenpeace are the two biggest: www.greenpeace.org.uk; www.foe.co.uk. Their websites set out their latest campaigns and research.

The Green Party website contains useful information on the party: www.greenparty.org.uk.

The impact of Brexit on the environment is discussed by experts on the blog: http://environmenteuref.blogspot.co.uk.

The Intergovernmental Panel on Climate Change (IPCC) issues weighty and scientifically rigorous reports on the impact of climate change: www.ipcc.ch.

*Further student resources to support learning are available at*
**www.macmillanihe.com/griffiths-brit-pol-3e**

# BRITAIN AND THE WORLD

Donald Trump was elected president of the USA in 2016 promising to put 'America First'. What he meant by this challenged many of the basic assumptions of US foreign policy, including its commitment to the North Atlantic Treaty Organization (NATO), which America had led since soon after the Second World War, cool relations with Russia, and a willingness to use military intervention. During his campaign, Trump's speeches shocked many commentators. Trump was conciliatory towards Russia and its president, Vladimir Putin (and alleged links between the Trump campaign and Russia caused severe problems for Trump during his presidency). The previous administration has imposed sanctions on Russia in punishment for its military intervention in Ukraine. Trump accused China of stealing American jobs and questioned the legitimacy of the Beijing government. He praised Britain's decision to leave the EU, and was seen with Nigel Farage, one of the leading figures in the campaign to get Britain out of the European Union. In contrast, Trump's predecessor President Obama had argued for the importance of Britain's continuing involvement in the EU for global peace. Trump argued that the USA should never have been involved in the Iraq War and criticised the Obama administration's peace agreement with Iran. Trump's election has challenged many of the assumptions in international relations and created new questions for the UK in how it responds to Trump's new world order.

During the Cold War and subsequently, Britain has claimed a 'special relationship' with the USA. Trump's election, and the seemingly new direction in foreign policy, placed new strains on the relationship. Indeed, Theresa May, British prime minister, was fiercely criticised for rushing to meet Trump in the months after his election. Membership of the European Community (later Union) from 1973 provided another focus for British policy. The vote in a referendum to leave the EU in 2016 (discussed in Chapter 12) raises new questions for Britain's foreign policy. British governments have often been torn between the special relationship with America and ties with Europe. Both of these relationships have become increasingly strained in recent years.

This chapter examines the making of British foreign policy in the context of international relations in which Britain's strongest alliances are under pressure, and where independent sovereign states are no longer the main or even necessarily the most important players.

## This chapter:

» Examines how foreign policy is made.

» Explores the debates about, and tensions between, Britain's 'national interests' and international obligations.

» Studies the tension in British foreign policy between pro-European and pro-American views.

» Assesses New Labour's interventionist foreign policy, involvement in war and response to the new threat of 'global terrorism'.

» Reviews the foreign policy response of Conservative-led governments since 2010 to events around the world.

## Making and Influencing Foreign Policy

In constitutional terms, responsibility for foreign policy lies with the secretary of state for foreign affairs and is implemented directly by the Foreign and Commonwealth Office (FCO: commonly referred to as the Foreign Office) and British embassies and missions abroad. The FCO promotes the UK's interests overseas. It has responsibility for:

» Safeguarding the UK's national security, by countering terrorism and weapons proliferation and working to reduce conflict.

» Building prosperity by increasing exports and investment, opening markets, ensuring access to resources and promoting sustainable global growth.

» Supporting British nationals around the world through modern and efficient consular services (Foreign and Commonwealth Office, 2017).

Defence, trade and aid – the responsibilities of the Ministry of Defence, the Department for Business, Innovation & Skills and the Department for International Development – are closely linked with foreign policy and require careful coordination. Indeed, in the context of austerity, discussed in Chapter 3 and 19, there has been pressure on government to get more out of the 'aid' money it provides for international development by ensuring that, at the very least, it creates a favourable impression of the UK in recipient states. Other departments, such as the Department for Environment, Food & Rural Affairs (Defra), whose responsibilities are primarily domestic, may be frequently involved in international or EU negotiations.

Most prime ministers have had a major role in foreign policy, and some have overshadowed their foreign secretaries. A few prime ministers, such as Churchill, Eden or Macmillan, could claim some special prior experience or expertise to justify their dominant role in foreign policy. However, neither Margaret Thatcher nor Tony Blair, who both substantially controlled Britain's foreign policy from 10 Downing Street, had any special preparation for that role. Yet it is difficult for prime ministers to avoid involvement in foreign affairs. In the modern world, any head of government is expected to represent their country abroad. The relationships that they can establish with other national leaders may be crucial in shaping informal alliances and agreements, as well as more formal treaties.

At times, a prime minister with strong convictions on foreign affairs may be in conflict with the prevailing view among senior officials and career diplomats in the Foreign Office. As PM, Margaret Thatcher was noted for her long-running hostility towards the FCO and occasional bitter battles with her own foreign secretary. There were complex reasons for this antagonism, but of central importance among them was the clash between Thatcher's Atlanticist (or pro-American) foreign policy outlook and the Europeanism of the FCO. Similarly, Blair's foreign policy, particularly his close alliance with George W. Bush, did not always have the full support of senior officials in the Foreign Office and the Ministry of Defence, as became clear from some of the evidence reported in the Hutton (2003) and Chilcot (2016) Reports (the first of which is discussed in more detail in Chapter 17, while the second is found below).

The influence of the chancellor of the exchequer on foreign and defence policy should not be underestimated. Part of this influence is essentially negative. It is the Treasury that has to fund foreign policy as well as domestic policy. The implicit support of the chancellor is therefore essential for international commitments, defence spending and, above all, war. Financial constraints have played a key role in shaping and limiting Britain's diplomatic and defence commitments; leading, for example, to the closure of bases 'east of Suez' in the postwar period and the abandonment

of specific weapons programmes. Moreover, the strength or weakness of the British economy substantially determines the extent of British influence in Europe and the world. The responsibility of the chancellor for the health of the national economy and their role in European and international economic decision-making necessarily involves them in foreign policy at the highest level. For example, Gordon Brown, as Labour chancellor from 1997 to 2007, effectively vetoed any moves to early UK membership of the euro, played a leading role in advocating more competitive labour markets within the EU, and took the lead in cancelling debt owed by poorer nations and promoting international development to help the African continent. All these policies were maintained when he became prime minister.

The distinction between foreign and domestic policy is often blurred and involves multiple actors, at Cabinet level and elsewhere (see Figure 22.1). There are occasions when foreign policy influences domestic policy. Foreign policy, such as the military intervention in Iraq, was driven forward by the prime minister, Tony Blair. However, the intervention certainly

Figure 22.1: The British foreign policy process

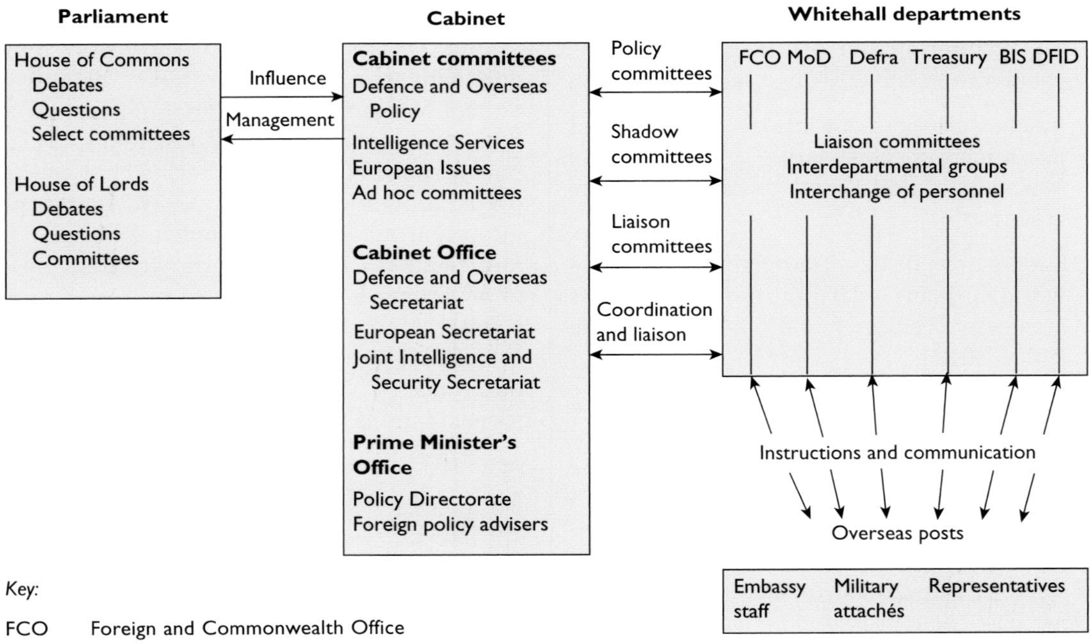

Key:

FCO     Foreign and Commonwealth Office
MoD     Ministry of Defence
Defra   Department for Environment, Food & Rural Affairs
BIS     Business, Innovation and Skills
DFID    Department for International Development

contributed to the radicalisation of some Muslims in the UK and an increase in anti-western attitudes, which, in turn, led to UK anti-extremist programmes that are largely under the remit of the home secretary and are part of domestic policy.

Parliament also has a role in many foreign policy decisions. Until recently, the power to commit troops in armed conflict was one of the remaining royal prerogatives, that is, those powers derived from the Crown, rather than conferred by Parliament. As such, there is no codified parliamentary procedure that formally requires the government to seek approval before taking military action. The prime minister and Cabinet retain the constitutional right to decide when and where to authorise action (Rosara, 2013). In recent years, however, where practical, Parliament has voted on military intervention. Blair's government won a vote over the decision to invade Iraq in March 2003, while Cameron's government won a vote over enforcing a no-fly zone in Libya in March 2011, but lost one over military intervention in Syria in September 2013. (These events are discussed in more detail below.) In 2006, Blair acknowledged that he could not 'conceive of a situation in which a Government ... is going to go to war – except in circumstances where militarily for the security of the country it needs to act immediately – without a full parliamentary debate' (quoted in Haddon, 2013). A new constitutional convention seems to have emerged. Parliament appears to have a role in foreign policy that it did not once have.

Citizens also influence foreign policy. Protests, in particular, may not decide an issue, but they can demonstrate and shape public opinion and constrain foreign policy. Thus, although popular opposition to the Vietnam War in Britain did not lead to any official condemnation of US policy by the British government, it was perhaps one reason why Harold Wilson's Labour government declined to send any troops in support. However, while Blair committed Britain to war on Iraq despite considerable public opposition in 2003, the decision appreciably weakened his position and was a major factor in Labour's reduced electoral support in 2005, and perhaps Blair's subsequent resignation in 2007. It did not stop the war. The prospect of further public and

*Source*: Peter Macdiarmid/Hulton Archive/Getty Images

The huge marches around the world against the invasion of Iraq in 2003, including this one in London, did nothing to stop the invasion.

party opposition may inhibit any similar initiatives in the future. Foreign policy, particularly the decision to go to war, in the absence of broad public support is a risky undertaking.

A rising number of multinational and international institutions also play an important role in foreign policy and regulate interstate relations. They include the International Court of Justice, the UN, the IMF, the World Bank, the WTO, the International Criminal Court, the G8 (the Group of Eight advanced industrial states) and, more recently, the G20 (the Group of Twenty industrialised and emerging economies). The jurisdiction of these international institutions has been recognised by increasing numbers of states, including the UK, although not always by their peoples. Thus the World Bank, the WTO and the G8 have been increasingly targeted by demonstrators opposed to global capitalism (see Spotlight 22.1 overleaf).

# SPOTLIGHT ON ...

## International organisations

22.1

» *The International Court of Justice* (sometimes the 'World Court') was established in 1946 under the auspices of the UN as the successor body to the Permanent Court of International Justice, established at The Hague (Netherlands) in 1922. Using international law, it adjudicates on disputes between states.

» *The United Nations* (UN) is a voluntary association of states who have signed the UN Charter (1945), committed to the maintenance of international peace and security, the solution of problems through international cooperation and the promotion of human rights. Based in New York, it is headed by a secretary-general, with a Security Council of five permanent members (each of whom can use a veto on decisions) and ten further members elected by the General Assembly representing all states. UN peacekeeping is dependent on troops and finance from member states. Its reputation for effective peacekeeping was blighted by the failure of UN troops to prevent the massacre in Srebrenica, Bosnia in July 1995. The US government – the UN's largest financial backer – has become critical of the UN in recent years, particularly since the UN failed to back the US-led invasion of Iraq in 2003.

» *The International Monetary Fund* (IMF) was set up following the Bretton Woods agreement in 1944 to oversee currency exchange rates and the international payments system. Governments could borrow from the IMF to defend their currencies, but often with onerous conditions attached on state finance and economic policy (e.g. the UK loan from the IMF in 1976). As a promoter of sound finance and economic liberalisation (often with harsh consequences for particular economies), the IMF has attracted criticism and protest.

» *The World Bank* (strictly speaking, the International Bank for Reconstruction and Development, along with affiliated organisations) was established in 1945. It is owned by the governments of member states, and makes loans to developing countries, although the conditions the bank insists on to make those loans – historically involving an insistence on cuts to public spending – made the bank a target for anti-globalisation protestors.

» *The World Trade Organization* (WTO) emerged in 1995 from the former General Agreement on Tariffs and Trade. The WTO regulates world trade, promoting free trade and adjudicating on disputes between countries involving restrictions on trade and on 'dumping' surplus goods on world markets. Anti-globalisation protestors argue that free trade does not always benefit developing countries.

» The *G7* is a group of seven advanced industrialised states that meet every year to discuss important economic and political issues. The present G7 includes the USA, the UK, Germany, France, Japan, Italy and Canada. They were joined by Russia between 1998 and 2014 to make the G8. It has attracted criticism from anti-globalisation protestors as a 'rich man's club'. At Gleneagles in 2005, representatives of African states attended the G8 meeting that discussed aid, trade and debt cancellation in Africa.

» The *G20* is a wider group, including some developing nations, that is becoming increasingly important.

» *The International Criminal Court* was created following an agreement in Rome in 1998, and formally established in 2002 in The Hague, Netherlands. Whereas the International Court of Justice is concerned with disputes between states, the International Criminal Court is able to bring to justice individuals, including former heads of state, accused of war crimes or atrocities. The US government has not recognised it.

Such international institutions may offer opportunities to national governments to wield influence in the wider world on issues of concern, such as security, trade, development and the global environment, but also may limit or control their relations with other states and even aspects of their domestic policy. The British government, as a permanent member of the UN Security Council, and a founder member of G8, has some influence on the decisions of these bodies. But these and other international institutions, such as the WTO and the IMF, have also, from time to time, acted as significant constraints on British policy; for example, when the IMF placed strict constraints on Britain's 1976 loan (see Chapter 2, p. 32).

There are other powerful actors in the global economy and the international political system, which influence foreign policy. Multinational corporations (MNCs) operating across state boundaries can move capital across frontiers and manipulate transfer prices and costs between their subsidiaries, minimising the effects of particular countries' business taxation and regulation. Indeed, they can be far more powerful than the states that have the theoretical authority to control them. The revenue of some of these MNCs exceeds the national income of many of the supposedly independent sovereign states represented at the UN and has far more influence on the operation of global capitalism.

Alongside the MNCs, there is the growing influence of nongovernmental organisations (NGOs), global pressure groups representing a range of interests and causes that also transcend national boundaries and influence foreign policy. NGOs are defined by the UN as 'any international organization which is not established by a government entity or international agreement'. The UN already recognises around 2,000 NGOs, many of which have also established relationships with other international governance institutions, such as the WTO and the IMF. Although there are inevitably some problems with the democratic accountability and legitimacy of NGOs, they can put pressure on states, MNCs and international institutions to consider the moral and humanitarian implications of their behaviour. So foreign policy in the UK is made and influenced by a wide variety of actors, nationally and internationally.

---

*Multinational corporations (MNCs) are business firms that operate in many countries and across national boundaries. They can shift their operations between countries to maximise profits.*

---

*Nongovernmental organisations (NGOs) are international organisations or pressure groups not established by governments or international agreements.*

---

## NATIONAL INTERESTS AND INTERNATIONAL OBLIGATIONS

The account above of the many actors that shape foreign policy implies that the field is nothing more than a scrap between competing groups, each with their own demands, responding to periodic outbreaks of war or revolution. In fact, there are several different theoretical responses to international relations, which are worth setting out briefly – each view provides a different understanding of the relationship between the UK and the rest of the world:

» *Idealism*: The slaughter of the First World War provided a catalyst for a more liberal (or idealist) theory of international relations, associated with US President Woodrow Wilson. Collective security, where states recognise that the security of one state is the concern of all, and international law would replace anarchy and war. However, the failure to prevent aggression, culminating in the Second World War, led to some disillusionment with the liberal approach to international relations (Carr, [1939] 2001). Labour and the Lib Dems (and Liberals before them) have rhetorically at least been guided by idealism in international relations.

» *Realism*: Hans Morgenthau ([1948] 1978) promoted an alternative realist theory of international relations involving 'states pursuing interests in terms of power'. Peace and security could not be preserved by diplomacy and international institutions but only by the realistic threat of force, backed by strong military capability. This realist perspective on international relations underpinned foreign and defence policy for the Cold War period. The Conservative Party has tended towards a realist approach to international relations (although views cut across the main parties).

» *Neorealism*: Kenneth Waltz (1979) developed Morgenthau's approach during the Cold War and perceived a fairly stable bipolar balance of power between the USA and USSR with their respective allies, rather than a more volatile anarchy. Neorealists stressed the importance of building alliances between states to balance the power of other states or alliances.

» *Constructivism*: The sudden end of the Cold War (not predicted by international relations theorists) has spawned other approaches, including constructivism (Wendt, 1999), which criticises the 'crude materialism' of neorealist approaches that view power in international relations as a fact, based, for example, on the size on a state's economy or the number of nuclear warheads they have. Instead, Wendt argues that power in international relations is 'constructed' by human understandings and, as such, can be transformed by human practice.

» *Liberal institutionalism*: A revived liberal approach, drawing inspiration from early twentieth-century idealism, recognises the increasing importance of international governmental organisations, such as the EU or the IMF, and NGOs, such as the Red Cross or Amnesty International. Those responsible for acts of genocide or illegal war should be punished in international courts according to international law.

---

*The* **Cold War** *was a state of political and military tension after the Second World War between the western bloc countries, notably the USA, its NATO allies and others, and those of the eastern bloc, in particular the USSR and its satellite states.*

---

There has long appeared an inherent conflict in foreign policy between the pursuit of national interest and the honouring of international obligations. A realist interpretation of international relations suggests that state power and state interests determine foreign policy. From this perspective, international obligations are only accepted when they appear to be in the national interest, and are freely broken when this no longer seems to be the case. Might is right, a concept sometimes illustrated by the German words *machtpolitik* (power politics) or *realpolitik* – the politics of the real, of the world as it is, as opposed to the world as one might prefer it to be. Alliances should depend on advantages to the national interest rather than ethical considerations or ideological sympathies. Such an approach has often seemed to guide states' foreign policies. Thus republican France forged an alliance with Tsarist Russia in the lead-up to the First World War to protect it against invasion from Germany, while Nazi Germany signed a non-aggression pact with the communist Soviet Union in 1939 so that it could continue its war with France without being invaded from the east. Both the Nazi–Soviet pact and its subsequent violation with the German invasion of Russia appeared to validate *realpolitik*.

National interest, however, is a rather nebulous concept. It appears to suggest that nations or states have a single exclusive objective interest that can be determined. This national interest is not the same as the public interest. It cannot be simply identified with the expressed interests of the majority of the population of a state. It may indeed be the case that among the citizens that belong to a state there are diametrically opposed views over what is in the national interest. In the postwar period, Britain has been pulled between those who have argued that it is in Britain's national interest to engage fully with the EU, and those who argue that it is in Britain's interest to disengage from Europe and pursue a close alliance with the USA. Even the debates following Britain's decision to leave the EU in 2016 were, and continue to be, shaped by claims and counterclaims about the extent to which it was, and still is, in Britain's national interest to engage in a single European market. In practice, the national interest is what leading politicians and officials with responsibility for foreign policy declare it to be. Whatever foreign policy is pursued by ministers or their civil servants, it will inevitably be accompanied by claims that this decision or that treaty is 'in the national interest'.

Others argue that the recognition of international law and obligations is in the interests of states and peoples, in the same way as acceptance of the rule of law and freely entered agreements is in the interests of individuals within states. Just as rational individual self-interest and the wider public interest may coincide within communities, so state interests and international interests may coincide in the global community.

In the context of a more complex and interdependent world involving layers of governance and a variety of NGOs transcending national boundaries, the pursuit of national interest, even if it can be discerned, inevitably involves compromise and negotiation. This is particularly the case when the 'national interest' of any state, such as the UK, runs counter to the interest of other states, or major MNCs, or the wider international community. There are, moreover, political costs if the authority of international bodies is flouted or the views of influential NGOs are ignored. A state, an MNC, or even an international institution loses moral and political credibility when it appears to reject the consensus of the global community. For example, after Russia's military intervention in Ukraine, which began in February 2014, the EU, the USA and a number of other governments imposed sanctions against Russian individuals, businesses and officials, which cost the Russian economy billions of dollars. Thus a more 'ethical' foreign policy, in line with the international consensus, may be in the national interest.

## BETWEEN EUROPE AND THE USA

Reflecting on Britain's role in the world in the aftermath of the Second World War, Winston Churchill argued there were three interlinked circles that mattered in foreign policy: the British Commonwealth and Empire; the English-speaking world, notably the USA; and Europe. For Churchill, speaking in 1948, Britain had to remain at the point where these circles overlapped in order to maintain its global role (Churchill, 2013). Through geography, language and military power Churchill argued it was in a position to do so. These three circles have dominated British foreign policy in the postwar period, particularly the UK's relationship with America and Europe, although Brexit has led some Conservative politicians, in particular, to demand more focus on the Commonwealth too (see Blitz, 2017).

In the past, British national interest often appeared to require a balance of power in Europe to prevent the emergence of a dominant continental state that might threaten Britain's commerce and industry. Thus British governments sought allies to resist French dominance of Europe in the eighteenth and early nineteenth centuries, German dominance in the first half of the twentieth century and Soviet Russia's dominance after the Second World War. The relative decline of Britain's economic and military strength in the postwar era obliged Britain (as well as other Western European states) to accept US leadership in NATO, an alliance founded to contain the perceived threat of Soviet expansion. See further details in Spotlight 22.2 overleaf.

The Soviet threat appeared to require the development and retention of nuclear weapons to deter aggression through the prospect of **mutually assured destruction (MAD)**. It could be argued that this 'balance of terror' worked, and kept the two great powers out of direct military conflict with each other. Nuclear

*Mutually assured destruction (MAD) was the basis of nuclear deterrence throughout the Cold War. It rested on the premise that if the USA and the USSR had nuclear parity, that is, each posed an identical risk to the other, then neither would risk a first strike as this would guarantee destruction of the attacking side. MAD demanded a second-strike capacity, which accounted for the thousands of warheads stockpiled by the superpowers during the Cold War.*

# SPOTLIGHT ON ...

## The special relationship

22.2

Britain's 'special relationship' with the USA involved the leaders of both countries working together closely. It developed out of the close cooperation between the two states during the Second World War. Subsequently, Labour Foreign Secretary Ernest Bevin helped draw the USA into a postwar European defence commitment with the establishment of the North Atlantic Treaty Organization (NATO). America continued to contribute directly to Britain's defence when, after the failure of Britain's own nuclear weapons programme, the USA provided Britain with the most modern systems in the shape of Polaris and Trident, advanced submarine-launched intercontinental ballistic missiles. This underlines the point that the relationship was always unequal, reflecting the unequal military and economic strength of the two countries, and meant more to the British as the weaker, dependent partner. Indeed, former German Chancellor Helmut Schmidt once drily observed that the relationship was 'so special that only one side knows it exists' (quoted in Garton Ash, 2005, p. 199).

The special relationship was never altogether a myth. It was facilitated by a common language and the notion of an 'English-speaking union' that can be found in Churchill's 'three circles'. The ideological and party affinities of particular national leaders and the development of close personal ties, between Thatcher and Reagan, Blair and Clinton and, more surprisingly, Blair and George W. Bush, sometimes further strengthened it. While Blair hoped to provide a 'bridge' between Europe and America, in practice he chose the American alliance over working more closely with Britain's European partners, notably over Iraq. Later British PMs – Brown, Cameron and May – have not achieved the same personal connection as Blair or Thatcher with their American counterparts, Bush, Obama and Trump respectively.

*Source*: ODD ANDERSEN/AFP/Getty Images

Theresa May was criticised for her close relationship to US President Donald Trump.

war did appear close at several points, however, particularly during the Cuban missile crisis of 1962, where the two superpowers faced off over the USSR's aborted decision to house nuclear missiles just off the US coast. Although the USSR armed and encouraged resistance to the USA in Korea and Vietnam while the USA similarly armed and financed opposition to the USSR in Afghanistan, both superpowers avoided steps that might have engaged them directly with each other in a war neither could win.

For those responsible for Britain's foreign policy, there initially appeared to be no realistic alternative to the American alliance – certainly not the new Commonwealth, replacing the fast vanishing British Empire, which was little more than a loose association of independent states with different interests. Nor did closer European cooperation offer a viable substitute, at least in the postwar decades. Early attempts to build a European Defence Community had failed. Not just Britain but Western Europe generally depended on American arms and NATO for its defence. The one occasion when Britain and France risked independent military action in defiance of American opinion, over Suez in 1956, ended in a humiliating withdrawal (see Chapter 2, p. 25). British membership of the European Community, when it was sought and eventually obtained in 1973, was not perceived as an alternative to Britain's 'special relationship' with the USA, which then welcomed closer European integration as another bulwark against communism. Indeed, in the run-up to the 2016 referendum on whether Britain should remain in the EU, Barack Obama, then American president, intervened to urge Britons to vote to remain, largely because of the mutual trading benefits that membership brings both nations.

The abrupt end of the Cold War following the destruction of the Berlin Wall, the reunification of Germany and the re-establishment of independence for states in Eastern Europe removed the perceived Soviet threat that had dominated British and Western European foreign policy for more than three decades. There was no longer a single clear enemy, a single obvious threat to prepare against. The

democratic revolutions that swept through Eastern Europe ended the ideological division of the continent that had existed since the end of the Second World War. The old bipolar certainties of the Cold War disappeared very rapidly: Germany reunited, the communist Warsaw Treaty dissolved and President Yeltsin announced that he wanted Russia to join NATO. Some optimistically predicted a 'peace dividend' as defence spending was diverted to more productive purposes. In practice, the Cold War was replaced by a series of more localised but brutal conflicts in outlying parts of the former communist bloc, the Middle East and Africa. This increasingly looked not so much like the 'end of history' celebrated by Fukuyama (1992) (see Key Figures 22.1 overleaf) but a return to the petty nationalist and ethnic conflicts of the era before the First World War in place of the ideological conflict between liberal capitalism and communism.

The end of the Cold War also increased the potential for conflict between the USA and an enlarged EU pursuing closer European integration in economic and monetary policy and reviving aspirations for a distinctive European foreign and defence policy. The old European Community had appeared to some as the economic underpinning for NATO. The new EU seemed to aspire to become an alternative to NATO, whose whole role and purpose appeared problematic following the end of the Cold War. Indeed, the role of NATO today is contested (see Spotlight 22.3 overleaf).

During the late 1990s and 2000s, the EU itself sought to develop more effective common foreign and defence policies. Part of the rationale for this was the recognition that the EU had failed to deal with crises on its own doorstep, such as the wars in the Balkans in the 1990s. To an extent, it reflected a realisation that the USA could not be expected to sort out all Europe's problems and a fear, prior to 9/11, that the USA might retreat into isolationism, as it had done previously between the two world wars. Thus the Maastricht Treaty (signed in 1992) incorporated the objective of a common foreign policy. The Treaties of Amsterdam (signed in 1997) and Nice

# KEY FIGURES 22.1

## Fukuyama, Huntington and Kagan

**Francis Fukuyama (1952–)** provocatively announced the 'end of history' (1989, 1992). The end of the Cold War, he argued, marked the decisive victory of economic and political liberalism over its ideological rivals, and the end of the contests that had dominated the history of the twentieth century (although he later went on to renounce this claim).

**Samuel Huntington (1927–2008)** maintained in *The Clash of Civilisations and the Remaking of World Order* (1996) that ideological conflicts between superpowers would be replaced by broader struggles between cultures, such as between Islam and the West. His analysis acquired greater resonance with the growth of the threat of Islamic fundamentalism and al-Qaeda terror.

**Robert Kagan (1958–)** asserts in *Paradise and Power: America and Europe in the New World Order* (2004, p. 3) that 'on major strategic and international questions today, Americans are from Mars and Europeans are from Venus'. Europeans prefer to rely on international law and diplomacy to deal with crises because of their military weakness, while Americans are prepared to use force, if necessary unilaterally, because they have the military resources. But, Kagan argues, European peace and security continue to depend on America's readiness to use force to defend western values and democracy from real threats (see Comparing British Politics 22.1).

# SPOTLIGHT ON ...

## NATO in and after the Cold War

22.3

The North Atlantic Treaty Organization (NATO) was founded in 1949 in the face of what appeared to be a threat from the USSR and its allies or satellites, which established the rival Warsaw Pact in 1955. The original member states of NATO included the USA, Canada and twelve European countries, including the UK, with Greece and Turkey joining in 1952. Members of the alliance were obliged to assist each other if attacked.

Following the end of the Cold War and the dissolution of the Warsaw Pact in 1991, it was not immediately clear whether NATO still had a role. Post-communist Russia was no longer perceived as the enemy. Yet NATO has grown. The former communist states of Poland, Hungary and the Czech Republic joined in 1999, five years before they joined the EU. Since then, seven other former communist states have joined, bringing the total membership to 26 states. NATO today is a US-led coalition of countries prepared to intervene if deemed necessary in trouble spots around the world. So, the war on Serbia in 1999 to assist the Muslim majority in Kosovo was a NATO operation. NATO countries also supplied most of the coalition military force in the First Gulf War in 1991 and, since 2001, the war in Afghanistan. In 2011, they enforced a no-fly zone in Libya, to protect those involved in the uprising against Muammar Gaddafi.

Russia's increasingly militaristic turn has seen NATO's importance increase. NATO suspended cooperation with the country in 2014, in response to the Russian annexation of part of Ukraine. In 2017, NATO strengthened its presence in the Baltic states in response to Russian activities. NATO's future also became a subject of debate during the US presidential campaign of 2016, when Donald Trump questioned its continuing relevance in the post-Cold War era, and suggested that it hindered closer ties with Russia. Trump was also highly critical of the levels of spending many NATO members contributed to the organisation, although the UK does meet the NATO target that 2% of GDP is spent on defence. In office, Trump's personal relations with the Russian government have been controversial, although he has reigned back on his criticism of NATO.

(signed in 2001) involved the development of a Common Foreign and Security Policy and European Security and Defence Policy. The Lisbon Treaty, finally ratified in 2009, involved the appointment of an EU foreign minister, a post for which Blair was once widely tipped, but which was eventually secured by the relatively unknown Lady Ashton. Comparing British Politics 22.1 examines the contrasting

theoretical approaches of the US and EU in more detail.

However, it has to be said that the EU has never played a large role in British foreign and defence policy, and will most likely play far less after Britain's decision to leave the EU in 2016. This is perhaps because Britain, along with most other EU members, belongs to NATO.

## 🇬🇧 COMPARING BRITISH POLITICS 22.1 🇺🇸 🇪🇺

### Venus or Mars? Soft, hard or smart power?

Robert Kagan (2004), US foreign policy adviser, offered an explanation of why Americans are more willing to go to war than Europeans. His argument was timely, given the difference of global opinion on the impending Iraq War, with France and Germany opposed to the American-led invasion.

Kagan argued that since the end of the Cold War, Europe and the USA have developed different views of just what sort of place the world is and should be. Americans have a lower level of tolerance for insecurity than Europeans. This is largely because they have the military capability to take on their enemies. After the terrorist attacks in New York in 2001, Americans have, in the main, been willing to use the power they have in international relations. Particularly under President George W. Bush, the USA saw the world as an essentially anarchic and violent place, where military power is sometimes needed. Trump shares much of this view, although he has been highly critical of Bush's interventionism and, so far, Trump seems less keen to commit to troop deployments.

In contrast, Kagan argues that Europeans, traumatised by the bloody history of the twentieth century and used to US protection during the Cold War, have turned to a model of EU-style negotiation. Kagan notes that the EU regularly defends the idea of a world where the rule of law, rather than military power, should decide how things are done. This is why it has supported initiatives such as the Kyoto Protocol on global warming (see Chapter 21, p. 447) or

the International Criminal Court. Referring to the Roman gods of war and peace, Kagan (2004, p. 3) argued, in a famous phrase, that 'on major strategic and international questions today, Americans are from Mars and Europeans are from Venus: they agree on little and understand one another even less'.

A related concept is the distinction between 'hard' and 'soft power', set out by Joseph Nye (2004), US political scientist. In international relations, 'hard power' is the use of military or economic means to influence the behaviour of other states. This form of political power is often aggressive and coercive and is most effective when it is imposed by one state upon a lesser power. This contrasts with 'soft power', which relies on diplomacy, culture and history. Soft power is the ability to shape the preferences of others through appeal and attraction. Grix and Houlihan (2014) have argued that states are increasingly using sports mega-events, such as the London Olympics, as part of their 'soft power' strategies. In contrast to hard power, it is non-coercive.

In his latest works, Nye (2008, p. 43) has argued for the importance of 'smart power'. Smart power comes at the interplay of hard and soft power, which he described as: 'The ability to combine hard and soft power into an effective strategy.' International leadership involves drawing strategic benefit from both – knowing when to use hard or soft power depending on context and opportunity. In foreign policy, Britain has been pulled between Mars and Venus and between hard power and soft.

Many strategic thinkers do not believe that the EU structures have the potential to be the basis of Britain's foreign or defence policy. The EU has been described as an 'economic giant but a military worm' (Kegley and Wittkopf, 1999, p. 168). The massive spending gap between the USA and its Western European NATO allies sets the two apart. Others have commented that a common security and defence policy to include Britain remains impractical for the EU because it is too diverse an organisation, unable to take on a robust defensive military role for the foreseeable future. So Britain's foreign and defence policies continue to be developed within an Atlanticist framework. Even so, most leading British politicians have never wanted or expected to make a choice between Europe and America, believing that they could and should preserve the special relationship with the USA along with involvement in Europe (Gamble, 2003).

The circles that Churchill argued foreign policy was carried out for are shifting. Britain's decision to leave the EU reduces its influence over its continental neighbours, regardless of the arrangement that will replace EU membership. President Trump's 'America First' rhetoric, set out in the introduction to this chapter, and his desire to protect US workers and to ask more of its military allies shifts the second circle. Both of these shifts undermine Britain's influence in the world. The emergence of new global players, notably China, also allows new relations to be formed in foreign policy (as we discuss in Spotlight 22.4). Britain faces an uncertain future in foreign policy. Brexit and Trump have undermined those relationships that Britain has relied on to try and maintain its global status.

Having examined Britain's relationship with the US and Europe, the next section looks more closely at the foreign policy of governments since 1997, reflecting on the different approaches they have taken and the issues they have faced.

## NEW LABOUR: ETHICAL FOREIGN POLICY AND LIBERAL INTERVENTIONISM

Labour's return to power in 1997 might have been expected to herald a marked change of direction in the conduct of foreign affairs. Indeed, Robin Cook, Labour's new foreign secretary, proclaimed in a mission statement that Britain would 'once again be a force for good in the world'. No longer 'could the national interest be defined by realpolitik'. Instead, there would be a new 'ethical dimension' to Britain's foreign policy (quoted in Rawnsley, 2001, p. 169). The centrepiece of this approach was the promise not to sell arms to repressive regimes that might use them to suppress their own civilian population or aggressively against neighbouring countries. Britain signed and ratified the Ottawa Convention that banned the use, production, stockpiling and export of anti-personnel landmines, which came into force in 1999. However, the wider arms trade remained big business for Britain, the second largest supplier of arms in the world behind the USA. Export earnings and jobs were at stake. The international arms industry was highly competitive with, arguably, little room for ethics. Thus arms continued to be exported to Indonesia, then engaged in the brutal suppression of a revolt in East Timor. Indeed, Buller (2001, p. 231) concluded that Labour's record showed 'a rather depressing continuity with the activities of previous governments'.

Neither Robin Cook nor Jack Straw, Margaret Beckett or David Miliband, his successors at the Foreign Office, proved able to put their own personal stamp on their government's foreign policy, which was substantially dominated by Blair and subsequently Brown. Labour prime ministers were as committed to the US alliance as their Conservative predecessors, developing a strong relationship with US Presidents Clinton, Bush and, to a less extent, Obama. Yet Blair also initially appeared to be the most enthusiastically pro-European premier since Heath. To Blair this involved no contradiction because, in a favourite metaphor, he saw Britain as a bridge between Europe and America.

### BLAIR'S LIBERAL INTERVENTIONISM

The enduring close alliance with the USA surprised many, not least inside the Labour Party. The early good relationship between Blair and Clinton was not so surprising. New Labour had copied some of the campaigning techniques of Clinton's Democrats, with whom

## SPOTLIGHT ON ...

## Britain's turn towards China: Sinophiles and Sinophobes

**22.4**

The staggering economic growth of China in recent decades has made it an increasingly important player in economic and foreign policy. This raises new question of Chinese–British (or 'Sino–British') relations. Journalist George Eaton (2015) has argued that the growing power of China is such that in a few years' time we might talk of Sinophiles and Sinophobes as we do now of Europhiles and Europhobes.

Closer economic ties with China became an important piece of government policy for Sinophiles, particularly David Cameron and his chancellor, George Osborne, who saw in them the potential to boost the British economy at a time of austerity. Welcoming Chinese President Xi Jinping to the UK in 2015, Cameron claimed that the UK was entering a 'golden era' in relations with China (Reuters, 2015). The main benefit of this was economic. It was estimated that China will invest £105 billion in British infrastructure by 2025 (Centre for Economics and Business Research, 2014), most controversially by allowing China a role in building new nuclear power stations in the UK. Osborne also announced his desire to 'formally connect' the London and Shanghai Stock Exchanges. British

exports to China are also growing, albeit from a low base.

But Sinophobes have concerns with the rapid reorientation of foreign and economic policy. Nick Timothy, joint chief of staff to Theresa May until just after the 2017 general election, raised concerns over national security in giving Chinese state-owned companies a stake in the British nuclear power stations planned for the UK. There are concerns that the Chinese could use their role to build weaknesses into computer systems, which would allow them to shut down Britain's energy production (Timothy, 2015). Indeed, one of May's first acts as prime minister in 2016 was to review Cameron and Osborne's decision on China's role in this industry until national security worries had been allayed. Other Sinophobes have questioned China's human rights record, noting that the 'golden era' of trade relations has come at the cost of 'turning a blind eye' towards China's poor human rights record (Eaton, 2015). Whatever one's position, the growth of the Chinese economy means China is an increasingly important part of any future government's foreign and economic policies.

---

they shared some ideological inspiration. The Republican Party of George W. Bush, however, was never a natural ally of the British Labour Party. Yet Blair, apparently encouraged by Clinton, sought to establish good relations with Bush, and these were cemented by the '9/11' terrorist attacks on New York in September 2001, which led to British forces joining the American-led invasions of Afghanistan in 2001 and Iraq in 2003. One argument advanced for the strong support Blair gave to the government of George W. Bush was that it gave Britain a restraining influence on US policy. Blair was able to persuade his ally to seek a second UN resolution authorising the use of force in Iraq – unsuccessfully, as it turned

out. Critics, however, have suggested there is little evidence that Blair had much influence on the Bush administration, for example on the Palestinian question or the issue of global warming.

Even before 9/11, however, Blair's Labour government had been prepared to resort to arms. In December 1998, it had supported Operation Desert Fox – US airstrikes against Iraq. From March 1999, British planes had joined with the USA and other NATO allies in bombing Serbia in response to their treatment of Albanian Muslims in Kosovo. Finally, after a prolonged civil war in Sierra Leone, the British government took unilateral action in 2000, sending a small force, initially to protect British citizens, but ultimately to support the elected government against rebel forces.

While the latter two wars could be criticised as involving unwarranted outside interference in the internal affairs of independent states, they were substantially justified in Britain and the wider world in terms of humanitarian intervention to prevent further atrocities and 'ethnic cleansing'. In the 1990s, the failure of the international community to prevent a series of massacres, sometimes amounting to systematic ethnic cleansing, in Rwanda, Bosnia, the Congo and Chechnya, had led to much agonised soul-searching in Britain and elsewhere in Europe. So most Europeans subsequently supported the NATO attack on Serbia over Kosovo in 1999: 'They believed Europe in particular had a moral responsibility to avert another genocide on the European continent' (Kagan, 2004, p. 124). Blair had been a passionate advocate of war over Kosovo, and during that war advanced the case for humanitarian (or liberal) intervention.

For Blair, Kosovo was 'a just war, based not on any territorial ambition but on values'. He argued that: 'We cannot let the evil of ethnic cleansing stand.' While Blair conceded that non-interference in another country's internal affairs was an 'important principle of international order', which 'we would not want to jettison too readily', he argued that: 'the principle of non-intervention must be qualified ... Acts of genocide can never be a purely internal matter' (cited in Kampfner, 2004, pp. 36–61). The 'international community' should be prepared to act. As a consequence, the Kosovan refugees were able to return home and the Serbian leader Milosevic was toppled and put on trial for war crimes, while an elected government and a measure of peace was restored in Sierra Leone. Many would argue that in these two cases, the ends justified the means.

Similar justifications were voiced to justify intervention in Afghanistan, where the Taliban government had breached human rights, most notably in their denial of the rights of women, and Iraq, where Saddam Hussein had massacred many thousands of opponents of his regime, particularly Kurds and Shia Muslims. However, the humanitarian argument for 'regime change' (passionately argued by the Labour left-winger Ann Clwyd in the case of Iraq) remains highly contentious. It could justify further intervention against numerous other repressive governments around the world, but, in practice, western governments have not rushed to intervene to protect human rights in Burma, China and North Korea (Hill, 2005; Cox and Oliver, 2006; Plant, 2008).

The attack by al-Qaeda terrorists on New York's Twin Towers and the Pentagon on 11 September 2001 had a dramatic impact on the foreign and defence policy of the USA and Britain, its closest ally. It led directly to the invasion of Afghanistan in the same year, and the overthrow of the Taliban government that was providing shelter and training facilities for Osama bin Laden's terrorists. Less directly, it led to the far more controversial invasion of Iraq in 2003 and the removal from power of Iraqi leader Saddam Hussein, although there was no significant link between Saddam Hussein's regime and al-Qaeda, despite claims to the contrary. After Saddam Hussein's removal from power, Iraq did become a recruiting ground for Islamic fundamentalist organisations. While British involvement in the war in Afghanistan had substantial cross-party and public support, the subsequent Iraq War divided Parliament and the public. Robin Cook, former foreign secretary, resigned from the government immediately (March 2003) along with two junior ministers; Clare Short, the secretary of state for international development, resigned subsequently (May 2003), and 139 Labour MPs broke ranks and rebelled on an anti-war motion in the Commons, including Jeremy Corbyn, future Labour leader. They were joined by the Lib Dems and a small number of Conservatives, including Kenneth Clarke. (The main body of the official opposition sided with the government.) A majority of the public was initially against war, although this briefly changed once British troops were in action. The decision to go to war had a profound effect on Britain's Muslim population, many of whom saw them as an attack on Islam. The controversy over British involvement in Iraq has persisted, kept alive by the continued bloody insurgency there. It was a significant issue in the 2005 election, and some were quick to link the terrorist attacks on London in July 2005 with the Iraq War.

It is difficult to summarise briefly and dispassionately events and policies that have proved so divisive. Few would have anticipated that a Labour government (a party linked traditionally with idealism rather than realism) would have involved Britain in a series of wars – five, if the airstrikes on Iraq and the intervention in Sierra Leone are included. Some have argued that the Iraq War, and perhaps others, were illegal under international law. According to the 1945 UN Charter, Article 2(4), the threat or use of force against another sovereign state is illegal and Article 51 confers the right to self-defence. The Bush administration argued that some rogue states justified pre-emptive action as they were developing weapons of mass destruction that threatened their neighbours and the wider international community. Both before and increasingly after 9/11, it was maintained that these states were also harbouring and exporting terrorism. The case for pre-emptive self-defence could be argued more convincingly in the case of Afghanistan, where the link with al-Qaeda terrorism was clear.

In the case of Iraq, there was no evidence of a link with al-Qaeda in 2003. There were, however, reasonable grounds for suspecting that Saddam Hussein had dangerous weapons: some had been earlier sold to him by the West, and he had used them against neighbouring Iran and Kuwait and against his own people. Moreover, the Iraqi government's failure to cooperate with the UN weapons inspectors gave grounds for suspicion that there were continuing programmes to develop weapons of mass destruction. The threat posed by these weapons was the main justification for war. But, after Saddam Hussein's regime was overthrown, no such weapons were discovered.

The number of casualities caused by the war and subsequent insurrection is difficult to know for sure, but was huge. Iraq Body Count, a web-based database (www.iraqbodycount. org/database), which uses newspapers and other sources to estimate the number of violent deaths in Iraq, found 179,240 Iraqis were reported killed between 2003 and 2013, the vast majority of whom were civilians. The number of additional deaths resulting from the damage to basic infrastructure such as water and healthcare is far higher: in the same period, 5,272 US and coalition military personnel and foreign contractors died. The number of British military deaths in Iraq was 179.

In the UK, two particularly significant inquiries were held over the decision to go to war. The Butler Review, led by former Cabinet Secretary Robin Butler, examined why the intelligence services had got it wrong about the threat posed by Iraq's weapons of mass destruction (WMDs). Butler (2004) confirmed that the intelligence was unreliable, but cast no blame, and found that Blair honestly stated what he believed to be true about WMDs before the 2003 invasion. A second inquiry run by Sir John Chilcot, which ran from 2009 to 2016, was more critical. It found, among other things, that war was pursued before peaceful means had been exhausted, that the threat from Iraq was exaggerated and that Blair had given unqualified commitment to support George W. Bush before weapons inspectors had finished their search in Iraq (Chilcot Report, 2016). (A third report, the 2003–04 Hutton Inquiry into the suicide of the weapons inspector David Kelly, is discussed in Chapter 17.)

The British and American governments interpreted conflicts in Afghanistan and Iraq in the context of an ongoing war against terrorism. The global reach of the new terrorism, threatening states and peoples across continents, is a new phenomenon, requiring new kinds of responses by governments. Some critics have argued that the USA and Britain have exaggerated the threat of terrorism to justify repressive measures at home and aggressive action abroad. This new terror threat has, however, led to atrocities in the UK, notably the 7 July 2005 London bombings, when terrorists detonated three bombs on underground trains and one on a bus, which killed over 50 and injured hundreds. (A second similar attack on 21 July caused further disruption but no deaths when bombs failed to explode.) Bloody attacks have occurred in several other European cities, including Madrid in 2004, Paris in 2015, Nice in 2016 and London and Manchester in 2017. The terrorist threat is more potent because of its indiscriminate nature and the abundance of 'soft' targets that are difficult to protect. The knowledge and technology to kill hundreds is now relatively widespread and fairly simple. Some critics suggest that western actions have intensified rather than diminished the threat of terrorism, not least because many Muslims perceive the wars with Afghanistan and Iraq as part of a western war against Islam. This perception is questionable. In Kosovo, the US-led NATO intervention was in support of Muslims. Afghanistan was attacked not because it was Muslim but because it was harbouring terrorists, while Saddam Hussein's regime was essentially a secular dictatorship opposed by many Muslims.

Even so, the long-running failure to reach a peaceful settlement in Palestine, coupled with US support for repressive regimes in the Middle East and elsewhere, lends support to the grievances of Muslims against the West. These and other grievances have been fed by the insurgency against the western occupation of Iraq, which continued in military terms until 2011 (although most of the victims of this insurgency have been other Muslims). The American raid on Pakistan that killed Osama bin Laden in May 2011, hailed as a triumph by US opinion, may suggest that al-Qaeda is now less relevant, but extremist groups often linked to so-called 'Islamic State of Iraq and the Levant' (ISIL or just 'Islamic State', IS) remain powerful.

## Reacting to Events? Foreign Policy Since 2010

Did the election of a Conservative-led coalition government in 2010 mark a new direction in foreign policy? The Conservative's

*Source*: Nikini Jayatunga

Flowers and messages of solidarity and support were left after the terrorist attack at London Bridge in June 2017, in which eight people were killed and many more injured.

election manifesto from 2010 claimed that their policy would be based on 'liberal Conservative principles', supporting human rights, democracy and the rule of law. But, the manifesto continued, 'policy must be hard-headed and practical, dealing with the world as it is and not as we wish it were'. The last section of the manifesto was an implicit critique of New Labour's interventionism, which played well with the Lib Dems when the two parties sat down to negotiate a coalition deal (Conservative Party, 2010, p. 109).

Despite the theory, there still appeared to be a yawning gulf between the Coalition parties on foreign policy. While the Conservative frontbench and most of its backbenchers had supported the Iraq War, the Lib Dems were united in opposition to it. (It helped the coalition that the bulk of British troops had already

**Timeline 22.1 Britain's major military involvements since 1945**

| | |
|---|---|
| 1950–53 | Korean War. Under the UN, UK military forces fought against the communist expansion in Korea. The action was supported by the leadership of the Labour and Conservative Parties |
| 1952–60 | UK forces fight the Mau Mau Uprising in Kenya. The ruling Conservative Party saw this as a defence of empire |
| 1956–57 | Suez Crisis. UK, French and Israeli forces fight the Egyptians over the Suez Canal (see Chapter 2, p. 25). In power in the UK, Conservatives justified the action on grounds of national interest and opposition to the 'tyrannical' Egyptian regime. |
| 1968–98 | The Troubles. UK forces involved in Northern Ireland (see Chapter 11) |
| 1982 | Falklands War. UK military fight Argentinian forces over Falkland Islands. In power, the Conservatives saw this as an attack on a British community (see Chapter 3, p. 40) |
| 1990 | Gulf War. UK joins a US-led force overturning the Iraqi occupation of neighbouring Kuwait |
| 1999 | US/UK NATO-sponsored bombing of Serbia secures withdrawal of Serbian forces from Kosovo and eventually the fall of Serb leader Milosevic and his trial for war crimes and genocide. In power, Labour justified the intervention to prevent genocide |
| 2000 | UK troops sent to Sierra Leone initially to release UN hostages and evacuate expatriates caught up in civil war. The ruling Labour government then supported continued intervention to assist the elected government to defeat rebellion |
| 2001 | UK joined US-led attack on Afghanistan following 9/11. After an apparently easy defeat of the Taliban, the latter launched increasingly effective guerrilla war against the occupiers. In power, Labour justified the action against fundamentalism |
| 2003 | US and UK forces invaded Iraq and overthrew Saddam Hussein's regime, but faced a long and bloody insurgency. In power, Labour justified the action on Iraq's human rights record and, more controversially, because of the threat of Iraq's WMDs |
| 2011 | UK involvement enforcing no-fly zone during uprising in Libya. There was no involvement with troops on the ground. The action was justified to protect the civilian population against the Gaddafi regime |
| 2014 | Military intervention against so-called 'Islamic State', following a formal request for assistance by the Iraqi government. This was extended into Syria a year later. The Conservative government again provided air support, but no troops on the ground |

left Iraq by 2009.) While the Conservatives sought increased defence spending and the replacement of Trident with an upgraded nuclear deterrent, the Lib Dems were attacked as soft on both issues. (Labour is also divided on nuclear weapons, with Jeremy Corbyn, leader since 2015, a long-term supporter of unilateral disarmament in contrast to most of his backbenchers.) While the Conservatives had become more Eurosceptic than Labour, the Lib Dems were solidly committed to the EU.

There were thus clear differences on foreign and defence policy that caused tensions during the coalition.

Foreign policy, however, often has to react to the unexpected. Few predicted the dramatic upheavals that spread through the Arab world in the first months of 2011, now known as the 'Arab Spring', which led to regime change in Tunisia and Egypt, followed by rebellion in Libya and challenges to the regimes in Yemen and Syria. These upheavals caught Britain and its coalition government unprepared and reawakened the debate over intervention in foreign affairs.

Although British foreign policy in theory favoured democracy and human rights, it had often supported regimes who abused the human rights of their own people. This was compatible with the realist approach to international relations, involving the pursuit of national interest and accepting the world as it is, and not as one would like it to be, refraining from interfering with the internal affairs of other states. By contrast, Blair justified humanitarian intervention to prevent genocide and crimes against humanity. Yet the controversy over Blair's wars provoked a reaction in favour of a less interventionist approach. Blair himself sought to bring Libya's dictator Gaddafi into the international fold, to secure the abandonment of his nuclear ambitions and support for international terrorism, as well as trade benefits. In opposition, Cameron had been critical of the attempts to rehabilitate the Gaddafi regime in Libya. However, the coalition government initially appeared to favour a more cautious and realist approach to foreign policy, which seemed to accord more closely with the national interest.

Yet the popular Arab uprisings against repressive governments forced a rapid reappraisal. Doing business with dictators no longer appears in the national interest when revolution leads to regime change. Indeed, British interests are now arguably better served by support for democracy and human rights. Cameron, along with the French government, ultimately secured US and Arab League backing for a UN resolution that authorised a no-fly zone over Libya, to protect the civilian population from Gadaffi's forces: an intervention that had domestic cross-party support. Military action began in March 2011 with attacks on Libya's air defence systems by a coalition of ten states including the UK, France and the USA. The action substantially weakened Gadaffi's regime and empowered rebel groups. Despite his earlier scepticism about military intervention, within a year of taking office, Cameron had committed Britain to military intervention that basically had regime change as its aim (Vickers, 2015, p. 232).

Cameron received a hero's welcome during a trip to Benghazi, Libya's second city, in September 2011. But, by 2016, Libya had become a fragile state dominated by warring militia groups on the edge of civil war. The cross-party Foreign Affairs Committee (2016) produced a scathing report on the Libyan intervention, arguing that it was carried out without proper intelligence analysis, had drifted in its mission from humanitarian action to regime change and had failed to consider postwar reconstruction. The report echoes criticisms widely made of Blair's intervention in Iraq after 2003.

At the time, intervention in Libya appeared to galvanise Cameron's support for intervention in the same way Kosovo had for Blair. In a short time, Cameron had turned from being 'a reluctant to a passionate interventionist' (Wintour and Watt, quoted in Vickers, 2015, p. 232).

Yet Cameron found that his room for action was far more limited when it came to the civil war in Syria and the subsequent rise of so-called 'Islamic State' (IS). In Syria, unrest after the 'Arab Spring' uprisings in 2011 quickly developed into full-blown civil war between government and opposition, which triggered a refugee crisis on the borders of Europe. By 2013, increasing concern at the use of chemical weapons against the opposition by Bashar al-Assad's regime led Cameron's Conservative-led government to seek support for a motion allowing a military response for humanitarian action, subject to strict limits and qualifications. The motion was defeated in the House of Commons by 285 votes to 272, with 30 Conservative and 9 Lib Dem MPs voting against the government. William Hague described the defeat as his worse moment as foreign secretary. The defeat demonstrated the lack of faith MPs and the public seems to have that limited military action would remain limited and would achieve its goals. By 2013, a decade after the beginning of the Iraq War, there was little appetite for more military involvement among the public in the UK (Vickers, 2015, p. 234).

As the Syrian civil war continued, the opposition groups fighting on the ground became increasingly radicalised. Some fighters crossed the border from Iraq in support of extremist groups such as so-called Islamic State. Islamic State (IS), a non-state actor, took control of much of the region with incredible speed. Within a few months, IS fighters controlled nearly a third of neighbouring Iraq, moving to within 500 miles of the Iraqi capital Baghdad. In June 2014, Cameron declared IS a threat to Britain. The beheading of several western hostages, including the murder of an American hostage by a militant with a British accent, resulted in a shift in public opinion in favour of action against extremist forms of Islamism. In September 2014, Cameron again went to the House of Commons, this time seeking support for a limited use of military force in Iraq to tackle the rise of IS. This time, the motion was overwhelmingly passed, by 524 votes to 59 (Vickers, 2015, p. 236). By December 2015, the Conservative government was back in the House of Commons (by now governing without the Lib Dems) asking for support to extend authorisation for airstrikes against IS in Syria. Again, the motion was supported. Just as under New Labour, the UK was dragged into a war, if not on terror, certainly against organisations like IS that were prepared to use terrorism to further their ends.

Foreign policy is largely determined by events. The 'Arab Spring' and its often bloody aftermath, Russian intervention in Ukraine, or North Korea's nuclear weapons programme demand a response of some kind – although not necessarily a military one. Indeed, largely because of the legacy of the Iraq War, the public and many MPs are warier of committing the UK to military intervention than before. Scarred by the experience of Afghanistan and Iraq, Parliament and the public seem more tolerant of some forms of intervention than others. Airstrikes, although controversial, have caused fewer protests than troop deployment – in part because airstrikes kill far fewer UK military personnel, despite their effects on civilian populations abroad. It might be that the election of Trump in America, explicitly more sceptical about US involvement abroad, will quieten some of the hyperactivity in foreign policy and the desire for military intervention in recent years. But, as this chapter shows, events can overtake intentions, no matter how firmly stated.

## SUMMARY

» Although foreign policy is often perceived as a relatively specialist and elitist field, it can have massive consequences for the wider public, with considerable potential implications for British politics.

» British prime ministers have often appeared more important in shaping foreign policy than their foreign secretaries.

» There is persistent tension in foreign policy between the pursuit of national interests and the acceptance of international obligations and international law. This reflects the continuing disagreement between realist and liberal (or idealist) theories of international relations.

» Increasingly, international institutions, multinational corporations and nongovernmental organisations have become influential players alongside state governments in global politics.

» During the Cold War between the two superpowers of the USA and the USSR, British foreign policy was shaped by the North Atlantic Treaty Organization (NATO) and the special relationship with the USA. The European Community was perceived as complementary with (rather than competing against) the American alliance.

» The end of the Cold War posed new threats, with implications for the role of an enlarged NATO and EU and the potential tensions between the two, and for British foreign policy, caught 'between Europe and America'.

» International terrorism, particularly after 9/11, strengthened the pro-American tendencies in the Labour government's foreign policy, as America's closest ally in the invasions of Afghanistan and Iraq, with far-reaching consequences for British politics and British society.

» The Conservatives, in coalition with the Lib Dems and later alone, initially seemed to support a more limited and realist direction in foreign policy. Events, particularly following the 'Arab Spring', led to a more interventionist approach. In this, there has not been a sharp change of direction for Britain's foreign policy since New Labour. However, the experience in Iraq has made politicians and the public more sceptical about intervention.

## ? QUESTIONS FOR DISCUSSION

» Is foreign policy inherently more elitist and less subject to effective democratic control than other areas of policy?

» Why is it that prime ministers often appear more important in making and shaping British foreign policy than foreign secretaries?

» How far do international institutions and a body of accepted international law effectively restrain state governments from pursuing their national interest? Are international relations essentially determined by *realpolitik*?

» Consider the perspectives of Fukuyama, Huntington and Kagan on the end of the Cold War and the post-Cold War world. Which, if any, is the most persuasive and illuminating?

» For what purposes is there still a role for NATO following the end of the Cold War?

» Why does there appear to be a growing rift between Europe and America? How far can Britain be a 'bridge' between the two?

» How far has Britain's 'special relationship' with the USA imposed obligations on both sides?

» Account for the growth of international terrorism. Why has it proved so difficult to combat? How far have British and American policies contributed to a diminution or increase of the terrorist threat?

» How far is there a case for humanitarian intervention, involving force if necessary, to prevent atrocities or genocide?

## FURTHER READING

There are several good overviews of the issues raised in this chapter. Gaskarth (2013) is particularly useful on the making of foreign policy. Self (2010) and Sanders and Houghton (2017) also provide good analyses. A thought-provoking overview that is illuminating on the foreign policy dilemmas facing Britain (although it covers far more than foreign policy) is Gamble's *Between Europe and America* (2003). Vickers (2015) and Clarke (2015) provide summaries of policy between 2010 and 2015. Useful surveys of the foreign policy of the Blair government are also provided by Daddow and Gaskarth (eds) (2011) *British Foreign Policy: The New Labour Years*.

Some of the wider issues of international relations are rather beyond the scope of a book on British politics, although some readers might wish to consult some of the texts that have been influential and widely quoted, such as Fukuyama (1992) *The End of History and the Last Man*, Huntington (1996) *The Clash of Civilizations and the Remaking of World Order* and Kagan (2004) *Paradise and Power*. Garton Ash's (2005) *Free World* is a thought-provoking British contribution to the debate on modern global politics and Britain's role within it.

## USEFUL WEBSITES

Useful websites include government departments, such as the Foreign and Commonwealth Office: www.gov.uk/government/organisations/foreign-commonwealth-office, the Ministry of Defence: www.gov.uk/government/organisations/ministry-of-defence and the Department for International Development: www.gov.uk/government/organisations/department-for-international-development, and various international organisations such as NATO: www.nato.int, the European Union: www.europa.eu, and the United Nations: www.un.int.

*Further student resources to support learning are available at*
**www.macmillanihe.com/griffiths-brit-pol-3e**

# BIBLIOGRAPHY

Addison, P. ([1975] 1994) *The Road to 1945: British Politics and the Second World War* (London: Random House).

Airports Commission (2015) *Final report* [online]. Available at: www.gov.uk/government/news/airports-commission-releases-final-report [Accessed 2 Oct. 2017].

Akkerman, T., de Lange, S. and Rooduijn, M. (2016) *Radical Right-Wing Populist Parties in Western Europe* (Abingdon: Taylor & Francis).

Alcock, P. and May, M. (2014) *Social Policy in Britain*, 4th edn (Basingstoke: Palgrave Macmillan).

Anderson, B. (1991) *Imagined Communities* (London: Verso).

Annesley, C. and Gains, F. (2010) 'The Core Executive: Gender, Power and Change', *Political Studies*, 58(5): 909–29.

Arblaster, A. (1987) *Democracy* (Buckingham: Open University Press).

Ascher, K. (1987) *The Politics of Privatisation* (London: Macmillan).

Asthana, A. and Elgot, J. (2017) *Theresa May ditches manifesto plan with 'dementia tax' U-turn* [online]. Available at: www.theguardian.com/society/2017/may/22/theresa-may-u-turn-on-dementia-tax-cap-social-care-conservative-manifesto [Accessed 1 Oct. 2017].

Atkins, J. (2015) '(Re)imagining Magna Carta: Myth, Metaphor and the Rhetoric of Britishness', *Parliamentary Affairs*, 69(3): 603–20.

Bache, I. et al. (2015) *Politics in the European Union*, 4th edn (Oxford: Oxford University Press).

Bachrach, P. and Baratz, M. (1970) *Power and Poverty: Theory and Practice* (New York: Oxford University Press).

Bagehot, W. ([1867] 1963) *The English Constitution* (London: Fontana).

Bains Report (1972) *The New Local Authorities: Management and Structures* (London: HMSO).

Bale, T. (2010) *The Conservative Party from Thatcher to Cameron* (Cambridge: Polity).

Bale, T. (2012) *The Conservatives since 1945: The Drivers of Party Change* (Oxford: Oxford University Press).

Bale, T. (2015) *Five Year Mission* (Oxford: Oxford University Press).

Bale, T. (2017) *European Politics: A Comparative Introduction*, 4th edn (London: Palgrave).

Bandelj, N. and Sowers, E. (2013) *Economy and State* (Oxford: Wiley).

Barker, R. (1997) *Political Ideas in Modern Britain*, 2nd edn (London: Routledge).

Barnett, A. (1997) *This Time: Our Constitutional Revolution* (London: Vintage).

Barnett, A. (2012) *Iron Britannia: Time to Take the Great out of Britain* (London: Faber and Faber).

Barnett, H. (2009) *Constitutional and Administrative Law*, 7th edn (Abingdon: Routledge-Cavendish).

Barnett, H. (2017) *Constitutional and Administrative Law*, 12th edn (Abingdon: Routledge-Cavendish).

Barry, B. (2001) 'Multicultural Muddles', *New Left Review*, 8(2): 49–71.

BBC (1976) *Lord Hailsham: Elective Dictatorship, The Richard Dimbleby Lecture* [online]. Available at: www.bbc.co.uk/programmes/p00fr9gh [Accessed 1 Oct. 2017].

BBC News (1998) *Maude warns of spending 'black hole'* [online]. Available at: http://news.bbc.co.uk/1/hi/uk_politics/194663.stm [Accessed 2 Oct. 2017].

BBC News (2005) *Writer's 'bog standard' regrets* [online]. Available at: http://news.bbc.co.uk/1/hi/education/4243035.stm [Accessed 2 Oct. 2017].

BBC News (2006) *Cameron places focus on optimism* [online]. Available at: http://news.bbc.co.uk/1/hi/uk_politics/5396358.stm [Accessed 1 Oct. 2017].

BBC News (2010) *Osborne on 'tough but fair' welfare state* [online]. Available at: www.bbc.co.uk/news/av/uk-politics-11468623/chancellor-george-osborne-on-tough-but-fair-welfare-state [Accessed 2 Oct. 2017].

BBC News (2012) *Clegg: Coalition contract 'broken'* [online]. Available at: www.bbc.co.uk/news/av/uk-politics-19151879/nick-clegg-lords-reform-failure-breaks-coalition-contract [Accessed 1 Oct. 2017].

BBC News (2013) *Miliband: Red or not so Red Ed?* [online]. Available at: www.bbc.co.uk/news/uk-politics-24280701 [Accessed 1 Oct. 2017].

BBC News (2014) *PM attacks Labour's economy 'gamble'* [online]. Available at: www.bbc.co.uk/news/uk-politics-30470126 [Accessed 5 Nov. 2017].

BBC News (2015) *Beckett: I was a moron to nominate Corbyn* [online]. Available at: www.bbc.co.uk/news/uk-politics-33625612 [Accessed 1 Oct. 2017].

BBC (2016a) *Tearing Up the Politics Textbook, Analysis* [online]. Available at: www.bbc.co.uk/programmes/b07w9km7 [Accessed 29 Sept. 2017].

BBC News (2016b) *Euroscepticism on rise, poll suggests* [online]. Available at: www.bbc.co.uk/news/uk-politics-eu-referendum-36471989 [Accessed 1 Oct. 2017].

BBC News (2017a) *Corbyn: We need political solution to Syria* [online]. Available at: www.bbc.co.uk/news/av/uk-politics-39730986/jeremy-corbyn-we-need-a-political-solution-to-syria [Accessed 29 Sept. 2017].

BBC News (2017b) *Election delivers most diverse Parliament* [online]. Available at: www.bbc.co.uk/news/election-2017-40232272 [Accessed 1 Oct. 2017].

BBC News (2017c) *Baroness Hale: The legal trailblazer* [online]. Available at: www.bbc.co.uk/news/uk-40679299 [Accessed 1 Oct. 2017].

BBC News (2017d) *A guide to the EU Withdrawal Bill* [online]. Available at: www.bbc.co.uk/news/uk-politics-39266723 [Accessed 1 Oct. 2017].

Beech, M. (2015) 'The Ideology of the Coalition: More Liberal than Conservative', in M. Beech and S. Lee (eds) *The Conservative-Liberal Coalition: Examining the Cameron-Clegg Government* (London: Palgrave).

Beech, M. and Lee, S. (eds) (2008) *Ten Years of New Labour* (Basingstoke: Palgrave Macmillan).

Beech, M. and Lee, S. (eds) (2010) *The Brown Government: A Policy Evaluation* (Basingstoke: Palgrave Macmillan).

Beech, M. and Lee, S. (eds) (2015) *The Conservative-Liberal Coalition: Examining the Cameron-Clegg Government* (London: Palgrave).

Beer, S. (1982) *Modern British Politics* (London: Faber and Faber).

Beers, L. (2012) 'Thatcher and the Women's Vote', in B. Jackson and R. Saunders (eds) *Making Thatcher's Britain* (Cambridge: Cambridge University Press).

Bell, D. (1960) *The End of Ideology* (New York: Free Press).

Bennett, A. (2015) *David Cameron's attack on 'Britain-hating' Jeremy Corbyn has painfully hit home* [online]. Available at: www.telegraph.co.uk/news/politics/Jeremy_Corbyn/11918926/David-Camerons-attack-on-Britain-hating-Jeremy-Corbyn-has-painfully-hit-home.html [Accessed 1 Oct. 2017].

Bennister, M. and Heffernan, R. (2011) 'Cameron as Prime Minister: The Intra-Executive Politics of Britain's Coalition Government', *Parliamentary Affairs*, 65(4): 778–801.

Berry, C. (2016) *Austerity Politics and UK Economic Policy* (London: Palgrave).

Berry, R. (2008) *Independent: The Rise of the Non-aligned Politician* (Exeter: Societas).

Beveridge, W.H. (1942) *Social Insurance and Allied Services*, Cmnd 6404 (London: HMSO).

Bevir, M. (2011) *The Making of British Socialism* (Princeton: Princeton University Press).

Bevir, M. and Rhodes, R.A.W. (2003) *Interpreting British Governance* (London: Routledge).

Bingham, T. (2010) *The Rule of Law* (London: Allen Lane).

BIS (2015) Trade Union Membership [online]. Available at: www.gov.uk/government/uploads/system/uploads/attachment_data/file/525938/Trade_Union_Membership_2015_-_Statistical_Bulletin.pdf [Accessed 1 Oct. 2017].

Black, L. (2010) *Redefining British Politics: Culture, Consumerism and Participation, 1954–70* (Basingstoke: Palgrave Macmillan).

Blackstone, W. ([1827] 1979) *Commentaries on the Laws of England* (Chicago: University of Chicago Press).

Blair, T. (1995) *Leader's speech, Brighton 1995* [online]. Available at: www.britishpoliticalspeech.org/speech-archive.htm?speech=201 [Accessed 1 Oct. 2017].

Blair, T. (1998) *Leading the Way: A New Vision for Local Government* (London: Institute for Public Policy Research).

Blair, T. (2010) *A Journey* (London: Hutchinson).

Blick, A. (2016) *The Codes of the Constitution* (London: Bloomsbury).

Blick, A. and Jones, G. (2010) *Premiership: The Development, Nature and Power of the Office of the British Prime Minister* (Exeter: Imprint Academic).

Blitz, J. (2017) 'Post-Brexit delusions about Empire 2.0', *Financial Times*, 7 March.

Blond, P. (2010) *Red Tory: How Left and Right Have Broken Britain and How We Can Fix It* (London: Faber and Faber).

Blumler, J.G. and McQuail, D. (1967) *Television in Politics* (London: Faber and Faber).

Bochel, H. and Powell, M. (2016) *The Coalition Government and Social Policy: Restructuring the Welfare State* (Bristol: Policy).

Bogdanor, V. (2001) 'Constitutional Reform', in A. Seldon, (ed.) *The Blair Effect: The Blair Government 1997–2001* (London: Little, Brown).

Bogdanor, V. (2009) *The New British Constitution* (Oxford: Hart).

Bogdanor, V. (2011) *The Coalition and the Constitution* (Oxford: Hart).

Bottomore, T. (1991) *A Dictionary of Marxist Thought* (Oxford: Blackwell).

Brack, D., Little, T. and Ingham, R. (eds) (2015) *British Liberal Leaders* (London: Biteback).

Breuilly, J. (1993) *Nationalism and the State*, 2nd edn (Manchester: Manchester University Press).

British Social Attitudes (2015) *Benefits and welfare: Long-term trends or short-term reactions?* [online]. Available at: www.bsa. natcen.ac.uk/media/38977/bsa32_welfare. pdf [Accessed 2 Oct. 2017].

Brooke, R. (1989) *Managing the Enabling Authority* (Harlow: Longman/LGTB).

Buller, J. (2001) 'Interpreting New Labour: Constraints, Dilemmas and Political Agency', in S. Ludlam and M.J. Smith (eds) *New Labour in Government* (Basingstoke: Palgrave).

Bulmer, S. and Burch, M. (2000) 'The Europeanisation of British Central Government', in R.A.W. Rhodes (ed.) *Transforming British Government*, vol. 1: *Changing Institutions* (London: Macmillan).

Burch, M. and Holliday, I. (1996) *The British Cabinet System* (London: Harvester Wheatsheaf).

Burke, E. (1975) *On Government, Politics and Society*, including *Reflections on the Revolution in France* [1790] and other writings, ed. B.W. Hill (London: Fontana/Harvester Press).

Burns, C., Jordan, A., Gravey, V. et al. (2016) *The EU Referendum and the UK Environment: An Expert Review* [online]. Available at: http:// environmentEUref.blogspot.co.uk/ [Accessed 8 Oct. 2017].

Bush, S. (2017) *Theresa May's magic money tree is growing in Northern Ireland* [online]. Available at: www.newstatesman.com/politics/ uk/2017/06/theresa-mays-magic-money-tree-growing-northern-ireland [Accessed 8 Oct. 2017].

Butler, D. and Butler, G. (2000) *Twentieth-Century British Political Facts 1900–2000* (Basingstoke: Palgrave Macmillan).

Butler, D. and Butler, G. (2006) *British Political Facts since 1979* (Basingstoke: Palgrave Macmillan).

Butler, D. and Kavanagh, D. (1997) *The British General Election of 1997* (London: Macmillan).

Butler, D. and Kavanagh, D. (2001) *The British General Election of 2001* (Basingstoke: Palgrave).

Butler, D. and Kavanagh, D. (2005) *The British General Election of 2005* (Basingstoke: Palgrave Macmillan).

Butler, D. and Stokes, D. (1969) *Political Change in Britain: Forces Shaping Electoral Choice* (London: Macmillan).

Butler, D., Adonis, A. and Travers, T. (1994) *Failure in British Government: The Politics of the Poll Tax* (Oxford: Oxford University Press).

Butler, P. and Syal, R. (2016) *'Just about managing' families to be £2,500 a year worse off by 2020 – study* [online]. Available at: www.theguardian. com/politics/2016/nov/20/just-about-managing-families-to-be-2500-a-year-worse-off-by-2020-study [Accessed 2 Oct. 2017].

Butler, R. (1971) *The Art of the Possible* (London: Hamilton).

Butler, R. (2004) *Review of Intelligence on Weapons of Mass Destruction: Report of a Committee of Privy Counsellors*, HC898 (London: TSO).

Byrne, G. (2017) *Ethnicity in the Civil Service in 2016* [online]. Available at: www. instituteforgovernment.org.uk/blog/ethnicity-civil-service-2016 [Accessed 1 Oct. 2017].

Byrne, P. (1997) *Social Movements in Britain* (London: Routledge).

Byrne, T. (2000) *Local Government in Britain* (Harmondsworth: Penguin).

Cabinet Office (1997) *Ministerial Code: A Code of Conduct and Guidance on Procedures for Ministers* (London: TSO).

Cabinet Office (2001) *The House of Lords: Completing the Reform*, White Paper, Cm 5291 (London: TSO).

Cabinet Office (2016) *Ministerial Code* (London: TSO).

Cable, V. (2009) *The Storm: The World Economic Crisis and What it Means* (London: Atlantic Books).

Cahill, M. (2010) *Transport, Environment and Society* (Maidenhead: Open University Press).

Cairney, P. (2011) *Understanding Public Policy: Theories and Issues* (Basingstoke: Palgrave Macmillan).

Cairney, P. and McGarvey, N. (2013) *Scottish Politics*, 2nd edn (Basingstoke: Palgrave Macmillan).

Callaghan, J. (1987) *Time and Chance* (London: Collins).

Cameron, D. (2005) *Speech to Launch Leadership Bid* [online]. Available at: www.ukpol.co.uk/ david-cameron-2005-speech-to-launch-leadership-bid/ [Accessed 29 Sept. 2017].

Cameron, D. (2006) *Cameron places focus on optimism* [online]. Available at: http://news. bbc.co.uk/1/hi/uk_politics/5396358.stm [Accessed 29 Sept. 2017].

Campbell, B. (1987) *The Iron Ladies: why do women vote Tory?* (London: Virago).

Campbell, R. (2006) *Gender and the Vote in Britain* (Colchester: ECPR Press).

Campbell, R. and Childs, S. (2015) 'All Aboard the Pink Battle Bus? Women Voters, Women's Issues, Candidates and Party Leaders', *Parliamentary Affairs*, 68(1): 206–23.

Carr, E.H. ([1939] 2001) *The Twenty Years Crisis, 1919–1939*, ed. M. Cox (London: Macmillan).

Carrell, S. (2011) *Identity crisis: are we becoming a disunited kingdom?* [online]. Available at: www.theguardian.com/uk/blog/2011/oct/06/national-identity-disunited-kingdom-debate [Accessed 1 Oct. 2017].

Carson, R. (1962) *Silent Spring* (Harmondsworth: Penguin).

Carter, N. (2015) 'The Greens in the UK General Election of 7 May 2015', *Environmental Politics*, 24(6): 1055–60.

Carter, N. (2016) 'The Coalition Government's Climate and Energy Policy: From Consensus to Conflict', *Journal of Liberal History*, 92: 46–50.

Carter, N. and Clements, B. (2015) 'From "Greenest Government Ever" to "Get Rid of all the Green Crap": David Cameron, the Conservatives and the Environment', *British Politics*, 10(2): 204–25.

Castells, M. (1977) *The Urban Question* (Cambridge, MA: MIT Press).

Castle, B. (1980) *The Castle Diaries, 1974–1976* (London: Weidenfeld & Nicolson).

Centre for Economics and Business Research (2014) *Chinese investment into UK infrastructure* [online]. Available at: cebr.com/reports/chinese-investment-into-uk-infrastructure/ [Accessed 2 Oct. 2017].

Chadwick, A. (2017) *Corbyn, Labour, Digital Media, and the 2017 UK Election* [online]. Available at: medium.com/@andrew.chadwick/corbyn-labour-digital-media-and-the-2017-uk-election-ac0af06ea235 [Accessed 2 Oct. 2017].

Chadwick, A. and Heffernan, R. (eds) (2003) *The New Labour Reader* (Cambridge: Polity).

Chadwick, A. and Stanyer, J. (2011) 'The Changing News Media Environment', in R. Heffernan, P.J. Cowley and C. Hay (eds) *Developments in British Politics 9* (Basingstoke: Palgrave Macmillan).

Chilcot Report (2016) *Report of the Iraq Inquiry* (London: TSO).

Chivers, D. and Perraton, J. (2015) *Fact Check: did Labour overspend and leave a deficit that was out of control?* [online]. Available at: http://theconversation.com/fact-check-did-labour-overspend-and-leave-a-deficit-that-was-out-of-control-41118 [Accessed 2 Oct. 2017].

Christensen, J., Shaxson, N. and Wigan, D. (2016) 'The Finance Curse: Britain and the World Economy', *British Journal of Politics and International Relations*, 18(1): 255–69.

Churchill, W. (2013) *Never Give In! Winston Churchill's Speeches* (London: Bloomsbury).

Clarke, C. and James, T.S. (eds) (2015) *British Labour Leaders* (London: Biteback).

Clarke, C., James, T.S., Bale, T. and Diamond, P. (eds) (2015) *British Conservative Leaders* (London: Biteback).

Clarke, H., Sanders, D., Stewart, M. and Whiteley, P. (2004) *Political Choice in Britain* (Oxford: Oxford University Press).

Clarke, H., Sanders, D., Stewart, M. and Whiteley, P. (2009) *Performance Politics and the British Voter* (Cambridge: Cambridge University Press).

Clarke, M. (2015) 'The Coalition and Foreign Affairs', in A. Seldon and M. Finn (eds) *The Coalition Effect, 2010–2015* (Cambridge: Cambridge University Press).

Clarke, M. and Stewart, J. (1988) *The Enabling Council* (Luton: Local Government Training Board).

Coates, D. (2005) *Prolonged Labour* (Basingstoke: Palgrave Macmillan).

Cochrane, F. (2013) *Northern Ireland: The Reluctant Peace* (New Haven, CT: Yale University Press).

Cockburn, C. (1977) *The Local State* (London: Pluto).

Cole, A., Meunier, S. and Tiberj, V. (eds) (2013) *Developments in French Politics: FIVE* (Basingstoke: Palgrave Macmillan).

Colley, L. (2003) *Britons: Forging the Nation 1707–1837* (London: Pimlico).

Connelly, J. (2015) 'The Coalition: How Green was My Tally?', in M. Beech and S. Lee (eds) *The Conservative-Liberal Coalition: Examining the Cameron-Clegg Government* (London: Palgrave).

Conservative Home (2008) *Eric Pickles: I'll have a pearl-handled revolver waiting in my drawer for the first civil servant who suggests another local government re-organisation* [online]. Available at: www.conservativehome.com/localgovernment/2008/12/eric-pickles-th.html [Accessed 1 Oct. 2017].

Conservative Party (2010) *The Conservative Manifesto 2010* (London: Conservative Party).

Cooper, Y. (2015) *I will deliver a radical – and credible – Labour alternative to Tory austerity* [online]. Available at: www.theguardian.com/commentisfree/2015/aug/23/my-radical-labour-alternative-tory-austerity-corbyn-print-money-deficit [Accessed 1 Oct. 2017].

Councillors Commission (2007) *Representing the future* [online]. Available at: http://webarchive.nationalarchives.gov.uk/20121029115445/http://www.communities.gov.uk/documents/localgovernment/pdf/583990.pdf [Accessed 1 Oct. 2017].

Cowburn, A. (2016) *David Cameron rated the third worst prime minister of the past 71 years* [online]. Available at: www.independent.co.uk/news/uk/politics/david-cameron-worst-prime-minister-ranking-third-since-ww2-a7358171.html [Accessed 29 Sept. 2017].

Cowley, J. (2017) *The May Doctrine* [online]. Available at: www.newstatesman.com/2017/02/-theresa-may-method-interview-jason-cowley [Accessed 29 Sept. 2017].

Cowley, P. (2005) 'Whips and Rebels', *Politics Review*, 14(3): 2–5.

Cowley, P. (2006) 'Making Parliament Matter?', in P. Dunleavy, R. Heffernan, P. Cowley and C. Hay (eds) *Developments in British Politics 8* (Basingstoke: Palgrave Macmillan).

Cowley, P. (2015) *The most rebellious parliament of the post-war era* [online]. Available at: www.psa.ac.uk/insight-plus/blog/most-rebellious-parliament-post-war-era [Accessed 1 Oct. 2017].

Cowley, P. and Kavanagh, D. (2016) *The British General Election of 2015* (Basingstoke: Palgrave Macmillan).

Cowley, P. and Stuart, M. (2008) 'A Rebellious Decade: Backbench Rebellions under Tony Blair, 1997–2007', in M. Beech and S. Lee (eds) *Ten Years of New Labour* (Basingstoke: Palgrave Macmillan).

Cox, M. and Oliver, T. (2006) 'Security Policy in an Insecure World', in P. Dunleavy, R. Heffernan, P. Cowley and C. Hay (eds) *Developments in British Politics 8* (Basingstoke: Palgrave Macmillan).

Coxall, B. (2001) *Pressure Groups in British Politics* (Harlow: Pearson Longman).

Crenshaw, K. (1989) 'Demarginalizing the Intersection of Race and Sex: A Black Feminist Critique of Antidiscrimination Doctrine, Feminist Theory and Antiracist Politics', *University of Chicago Legal Forum*, 140: 139–67.

Crenshaw, K. (2012) 'Postscript', in H. Lutz, M.T.H. Vivar and L. Supik (eds) *Framing Intersectionality: Debates on a Multi-Faceted Concept in Gender Studies* (Farnham: Ashgate).

Crenson, M.A. (1971) *The Un-politics of Air Pollution: A Study of Non-decision Making in the Cities* (Baltimore: Johns Hopkins Press).

Crewe, E. (2015) *Commons and Lords: a short anthropology of Parliament* (London: Haus Publishing).

Crewe, I. and King, A. (1995) *SDP: The Birth, Life and Death of the Social Democratic Party* (Oxford: Oxford University Press).

Crewe, I. and King, A. (2014) *The Blunders of Our Governments* (London: Oneworld).

Crewe, T. (2016) *The strange death of municipal England: Assault on local government* [online]. Available at: www.lrb.co.uk/v38/n24/tom-crewe/the-strange-death-of-municipal-england [Accessed 1 Oct. 2017].

Crick, B. (1993) *In Defence of Politics*, 4th edn (Harmondsworth: Penguin).

Criddle, B. (2010) 'More Diverse, Yet More Uniform: MPs and Candidates', in D. Kavanagh and P. Cowley, *The British General Election of 2010* (Basingstoke: Palgrave Macmillan).

Crisell, A. (1999) 'Broadcasting: Television and Radio', in J. Stokes and A. Reading (eds) *The Media in Britain: Current Debates and Developments* (London: Macmillan).

Crosland, C.A.R. (1956) *The Future of Socialism* (London: Jonathan Cape).

Crossman, R. (1963) 'Introduction' to W. Bagehot: *The English Constitution* (London: Fontana).

Crossman, R. (1975, 1976, 1977) *Diaries of a Cabinet Minister,* three vols (London: Hamish Hamilton and Jonathan Cape).

Curran, J. and Seaton, J. (2003) *Power without Responsibility: The Press, Broadcasting, and New Media in Britain* (London: Routledge).

Curran, J. and Seaton, J. (2009) *Power without Responsibility: Press, Broadcasting and the Internet in Britain*, 7th edn (London: Routledge).

Curtice, J. (2003) 'Changing Voting Systems', in P. Dunleavy, A. Gamble, R. Heffernan and G. Peele (eds) *Developments in British Politics 7* (Basingstoke: Palgrave Macmillan).

Curtice, J., Fisher, S. and Ford, R. (2010) 'An Analysis of the Results', in D. Kavanagh and P. Cowley, *The British General Election of 2010* (Basingstoke: Palgrave Macmillan).

Curtice, J., Fisher, S. and Ford, R. (2016) 'The Results Analysed', in D. Kavanagh and P. Cowley, *The British General Election of 2015* (Basingstoke: Palgrave Macmillan).

Curtis, C. (2017) *How Britain voted at the 2017 general election* [online]. Available at: https://yougov.co.uk/news/2017/06/13/how-britain-voted-2017-general-election/ [Accessed 1 Oct. 2017].

Daddow, O. and Gaskarth, J. (eds) (2011) *British Foreign Policy: The New Labour Years* (Basingstoke: Palgrave Macmillan).

Dahl, R.A. (1961) *Who Governs?* (New Haven, CT: Yale University Press).

Davies, N. (2000) *The Isles: A History* (Basingstoke: Palgrave Macmillan).

Davies, W. (2016) 'Home Office Rules', *London Review of Books*, 38(31): 3–6.

Deacon, D. and Wring, D. (2016) 'Still Life in the Old Attack Dogs: The Press', in P. Cowley, and D. Kavanagh, *The British General Election of 2015* (Basingstoke: Palgrave Macmillan).

Dearlove, J. (1973) *The Politics of Policy in English Local Government* (Cambridge: Cambridge University Press).

De Beauvoir, S. ([1949] 1972) *The Second Sex* (Harmondsworth: Penguin).

Denenberg, R. (1996) *Understanding American Politics* (Waukegan, IL: Fontana Press).

Denham, A. (2003) 'Public Services', in P. Dunleavy, A. Gamble, R. Heffernan and G. Peele (eds) *Developments in Politics 7* (Basingstoke: Palgrave Macmillan).

Denver, D. (2003) '2003 Scottish Parliament Elections: Messages for Unpopular Parties', *Politics Review*, 13(2): 28–30.

Denver, D., Carman, C. and Johns, R. (2012) *Elections and Voters in Britain*, 3rd edn (Basingstoke: Palgrave Macmillan).

Denver, D. and Garnett, M. (2014) *British General Elections Since 1964: Diversity, Dealignment, and Disillusion* (Oxford: OUP).

Department of Health (1997) *The New NHS: Modern, Dependable*, White Paper, Cm 3807 (London: TSO).

Department for Work and Pensions/Office for Disability Issues (2014) *Disability facts and figures* [online]. Available at: www.gov.uk/government/publications/disability-facts-and-figures/disability-facts-and-figures#about-these-statistics [Accessed 1 Oct. 2017].

De Smith, S.A. and Brazier, R. (1998) *Constitutional and Administrative Law*, 8th edn (Harmondsworth: Penguin).

De Tocqueville, A. ([1835, 1840] 2003) *Democracy in America* (Harmondsworth: Penguin).

Devine, T. (2012) *The Scottish Nation* (London: Penguin Books).

Devine, T. (2016) *Independence or Union: Scotland's Past and Scotland's Present* (London: Allen Lane).

Diamond, P. (2011) *Beyond the Westminster model* [online]. Available at: www.renewal.org.uk/articles/beyond-the-westminster-model/ [Accessed 1 Oct. 2017].

Diamond, P. (2014) *Governing Britain: Power, Politics and the Prime Minister* (London: I.B. Tauris).

Diamond, P. (2016) *The Crosland Legacy: The Future of British Social Democracy* (Bristol: Policy).

Dicey, A.V. ([1885] 1959) *Introduction to the Study of the Law of the Constitution* (London: Macmillan).

Dobson, A. (2007) *Green Political Thought*, 4th edn (London: Routledge).

Dominiczak, P., Hughes, L. and Chan, S. (2016) *Do not tell me what to do, Mark Carney warns Theresa May* [online]. Available at: www.telegraph.co.uk/news/2016/10/14/mark-carney-says-he-will-not-take-instruction-after-theresa-may/ [Accessed 2 Oct. 2017].

Dorey, P. (2008) *The Labour Party and Constitutional Reform: A History of Constitutional Conservatism* (Basingstoke: Palgrave Macmillan).

Dorey, P. (2014) *Policy Making in Britain: An Introduction*, 2nd edn (London: Sage).

Dorey, P. (2016) '"Should I Stay or Should I Go?": James Callaghan's Decision Not to Call an Autumn 1978 General Election', *British Politics*, 11(1): 95–118.

Dowding, K. (2013) 'The Prime Ministerialisation of the British Prime Minister', *Parliamentary Affairs*, 66(3): 617–35.

Downs, A. (1973) 'Up and Down with Ecology', in J.S. Bain (ed.) *Environmental Decay: Economic Causes and Remedies* (Boston, MA: Little, Brown).

Driver, S. (2008) 'New Labour and Public Expenditure', in M. Beech and S. Lee (eds) *Ten Years of New Labour* (Basingstoke: Palgrave Macmillan).

Driver, S. (2011) *Understanding British Party Politics* (Cambridge: Polity).

Dunleavy, P. (1991) *Democracy, Bureaucracy and Public Choice* (London: Harvester Wheatsheaf).

Dunleavy, P. (2006) 'The Westminster Model and the Distinctiveness of British Politics', in P. Dunleavy, R. Heffernan, P. Cowley and C. Hay (eds) *Developments in British Politics 8* (Basingstoke: Palgrave Macmillan).

Dunleavy, P. and Diwakar, R. (2013) 'Analysing Multiparty Competition in Plurality Rule Elections', *Party Politics*, 19(6): 855–86.

Dunleavy, P. and O'Leary, B. (1987) *Theories of the State* (London: Macmillan).

Dunleavy, P. and Rhodes, R.A.W. (1990) 'Core Executive Studies in Britain', *Public Administration*, 68(1): 3–28.

Dutton, D. (1997) *British Politics since 1945: The Rise and Fall of Consensus* (Oxford: Blackwell).

Duverger, M. (1964) *Political Parties: Their Organization and Activity in the Modern State*, trans. B. and R. North (London: Methuen).

Duverger, M. (1972) *The Study of Politics*, trans. R. Wagoner (Sunbury on Thames: Nelson).

Dwyer, P. and Shaw, S. (eds) (2013) *An Introduction to Social Policy* (Thousand Oaks, CA: Sage).

Eaton, G. (2015) *The Tories' embrace of China has created a new divide in British politics* [online]. Available at: www.newstatesman.com/politics/uk/2015/10/tories-embrace-china-has-created-new-divide-british-politics [Accessed 2 Oct. 2017].

Eccleshall, R., Geoghegan, V., Jay, R. et al. (2003) *Political Ideologies*, 3rd edn (London: Routledge).

Eckersley, R. (1993) *Environmentalism and Political Theory: Towards an Ecocentric Approach* (London: UCL Press).

EHRC (Equality and Human Rights Commission) (2017) *What is the difference between the gender pay gap and equal pay?* [online] Available at: www.equalityhumanrights.com/en/advice-and-guidance/what-difference-between-gender-pay-gap-and-equal-pay [Accessed 1 Oct. 2017].

Elgot, J. (2017) *Osborne says Theresa May is a 'dead woman walking'* [online]. Available at: www.theguardian.com/politics/2017/jun/11/george-osborne-says-theresa-may-is-a-dead-woman-walking [Accessed 29 Sept. 2017].

Elliott, L. and Atkinson, D. (2009) *The Gods That Failed* (London: Vintage Books).

Ercan, S. and Gagnon, J. (2014) 'The Crisis of Democracy: Which Crisis? Which Democracy?', *Democratic Theory*, 1(2): 1–10.

Esping-Andersen, G. (1990) *Three Worlds of Welfare Capitalism* (Princeton, NJ: Princeton University Press).

Esping-Andersen, G. (1999) *Social Foundations of Postindustrial Economies* (Oxford: Oxford University Press).

Etzioni, A. (1967) 'Mixed-Scanning: A "Third" Approach to Decision-Making', *Public Administration Review*, 27(5): 385–92.

Evans, E. (2015) *The Politics of Third Wave Feminisms* (London: Palgrave).

Evans, E. and Kenny, M. (2017) *The Women's Equality Party and the 2017 General Election* [online]. Available at: www.electionanalysis.uk/uk-election-analysis-2017/section-4-parties-and-the-campaign/the-womens-equality-party-and-the-2017-general-election/ [Accessed 1 Oct. 2017].

Evans, G. (2003) 'Political Culture and Voting Participation', in P. Dunleavy, A. Gamble, R. Heffernan and G. Peele (eds) *Developments in British Politics 7* (Basingstoke: Palgrave Macmillan).

Evans, G. and Tilley, J. (2017) *The New Politics of Class: The Political Exclusion of the British Working Class* (Oxford: Oxford University Press).

Evans, M. (2008) 'New Labour and the Rise of the New Constitutionalism', in M. Beech and S. Lee (eds) *Ten Years of New Labour* (Basingstoke: Palgrave Macmillan).

Farage, N. (2014) *The main parties don't listen to the working classes* [online]. Available at: http://webcache.googleusercontent.com/search?q=cache:GYDkm54wRIQJ:www.standard.co.uk/comment/comment/nigel-farage-the-main-parties-don-t-listen-to-the-working-classes-9181460.html+&cd=1&hl=en&ct=clnk&gl=uk [Accessed 2 Oct. 2017].

Fawcett Society (2016) *Sex Equality: State of the Nation 2016* [online]. Available at: www.fawcettsociety.org.uk/sex-equality-state-of-the-nation-2016 [Accessed 1 Oct. 2017].

Flinders, M. (2006) 'The Half-hearted Constitutional Revolution', in P. Dunleavy, R. Heffernan, P. Cowley and C. Hay (eds) *Developments in British Politics 8* (Basingstoke: Palgrave Macmillan).

Flinders, M. (2015) 'The Problem with Democracy', *Parliamentary Affairs*, 69(1): 204–6.

Foley, M. (1993) *The Rise of the British Presidency* (Manchester: Manchester University Press).

Foley, M. (2000) *The British Presidency: Tony Blair and the Politics of Public Leadership* (Manchester: Manchester University Press).

Foley, M. (2013) 'Prime Ministerialisation and Presidential Analogies: A Certain Difference in Interpretive Evolution', *Parliamentary Affairs*, 66(3): 655–62.

Foreign Affairs Committee (2016) *Libya: Examination of Intervention and Collapse and the UK's Future Policy Options* [online]. Available at: https://publications.parliament.uk/pa/cm201617/cmselect/cmfaff/119/119.pdf [Accessed 2 Oct. 2017].

Foreign and Commonwealth Office (2017) *About us* [online]. Available at: www.gov.uk/government/organisations/foreign-commonwealth-office/about [Accessed 2 Oct. 2017].

Ford, R. (2015) 'Who Should We Help? An Experimental Test of Discrimination in the British Welfare State', *Political Studies*, 64(3): 630–50.

Foster, C. (2001) 'Transport Policy', in A. Seldon (ed.) *The Blair Effect: The Blair Government, 1997–2001* (London: Little, Brown).

Foucault, M. ([1975] 1991) *Discipline and Punish: The Birth of a Prison* (London: Penguin).

Francis, M. (2012) '"A Crusade to Enfranchise the Many": Thatcherism and the "Property-owning Democracy"', *Twentieth Century British History*, 23(2): 275–97.

Franklin, B. (1994) *Packaging Politics* (London: Edward Arnold).

Franklin, B. (2003) 'The Hand of History: New Labour, New Management and Governance', in A. Chadwick and R. Heffernan (eds) *The New Labour Reader* (Cambridge: Polity).

Franklin, B. (2004) *Packaging Politics*, 2nd edn (London: Edward Arnold).

Fraser, D. (2009) *The Evolution of the British Welfare State*, 4th edn (Basingstoke: Palgrave Macmillan).

Frazer, E. (2002) 'Citizenship and Culture', in P. Dunleavy, A. Gamble, R. Heffernan, I. Holliday and G. Peele (eds) *Developments in British Politics 6*, rev. edn (Basingstoke: Palgrave Macmillan).

Freeden, M. (1996) *Ideology and Political Theory* (Oxford: Clarendon Press).

Fukuyama, F. (1989) 'The End of History?', *National Interest*, 16: 3–18.

Fukuyama, F. (1992) *The End of History and the Last Man* (London: Hamish Hamilton).

Fulton Report (1968) *The Civil Service Vol. 1. Report of the Committee 1966–68*, Cmnd 3638 (London: HMSO).

Gaber, I. (2003) 'Lies, Damn Lies … and Political Spin', in A. Chadwick and R. Heffernan (eds) *The New Labour Reader* (Cambridge: Polity).

Gamble, A. (1979) *The Free Economy and the Strong State* [online]. Available at: http://socialistregister.com/index.php/srv/article/view/5431#.Wc5_IBNSzBI [Accessed 29 Sept. 2017].

Gamble, A. (1981) *Britain in Decline* (London: Macmillan).

Gamble, A. (1988) *The Free Economy and the Strong State: The Politics of Thatcherism* (London: Macmillan).

Gamble, A. (1994) *The Free Economy and the Strong State: The Politics of Thatcherism*, 2nd edn (London: Macmillan).

Gamble, A. (2000) 'Theories and Explanations of British Decline', in R. English and M. Kenny (eds) *Rethinking British Decline* (Basingstoke: Palgrave Macmillan).

Gamble, A. (2003) *Between Europe and America* (Basingstoke: Palgrave Macmillan).

Gamble, A. (2009) *The Spectre at the Feast: Capitalist Crisis and the Politics of Recession* (Basingstoke: Palgrave Macmillan).

Gamble, A. and Wright, T. (eds) (2009) *Britishness: Perspectives on the British Question* (Chichester: Wiley-Blackwell).

Game, C. (2001) 'The Changing Ways We Vote', in S. Lancaster (ed.) *Developments in Politics*, vol. 12 (Ormskirk: Causeway Press).

Garland, J. and Terry, C. (2015) *The 2015 General Election: A voting system in crisis* [online]. Available at: www.electoral-reform.org.uk/wp-content/uploads/2017/06/2015-UK-General-Election.pdf [Accessed 1 Oct. 2017].

Garland, J. and Terry, C. (2017), *The 2017 General Election: Volatile voting, random results* [online]. Available at www.electoral-reform.org.uk/wp-content/uploads/2017/08/2017-UK-General-Election-Report.pdf [Accessed 8 Feb 2018].

Garner, R. (2000) *Environmental Politics: Britain, Europe and the Global Environment* (Basingstoke: Palgrave Macmillan).

Garton Ash, T. (2005) *Free World* (Harmondsworth: Penguin).

Gaskarth, J. (2013) *British Foreign Policy* (Cambridge: Polity).

Geddes, A. (2003) *The European Union and British Politics* (Basingstoke: Palgrave Macmillan).

Gee, G., Malleson, K., Hazell, R. and O'Brien, P. (2015) *The Politics of Judicial Independence in the UK's Changing Constitution* (Cambridge: Cambridge University Press).

Gellner, E. (1983) *Nations and Nationalism* (Oxford: Basil Blackwell).

George, S. (1998) *An Awkward Partner: Britain in the European Community* (Oxford: Oxford University Press).

Giddens, A. (1998) *The Third Way: The Renewal of Social Democracy* (Cambridge: Polity).

Gifford, C. (2014) *The Making of Eurosceptic Britain: Identity and Economy in a Post-imperial State*, 2nd edn (Aldershot: Ashgate).

Gilmour, I. (1978) *Inside Right* (London: Quartet Books).

Gilmour, I. (1992) *Dancing with Dogma* (London: Simon & Schuster).

Gilmour, I. and Garnett, M. (1997) *Whatever Happened to the Tories? The Conservatives since 1945* (London: Fourth Estate).

Glasgow Media Group (1976) *Bad News* (London: Routledge & Kegan Paul).

Glasgow Media Group (1980) *More Bad News* (London: Routledge & Kegan Paul).

Goddard, P. (2001) 'Political Broadcasting in Britain: System, Ethos and Change', in J. Bartle and D. Griffiths (eds) *Political Communications Transformed: From Morrison to Mandelson* (Basingstoke: Palgrave).

Goffman, E. ([1974] 1986) *Frame Analysis* (Boston, MA: Northeastern University Press).

Goodin, R. (1992) *Green Political Theory* (Cambridge: Polity).

Goodwin, M. (2013) *The roots of extremism: The English Defence League and the counter-Jihad challenge* [online]. Available at: www.chathamhouse.org/publications/papers/view/189767 [Accessed 2 Nov. 2017].

Goodwin, M. (2014) 'Forever a False Dawn? Explaining the Electoral Collapse of the British National Party (BNP)', *Parliamentary Affairs*, 67(4): 887–906.

Goodwin, M. and Milazzo, C. (2015) *UKIP: Inside the Campaign to Redraw the Map of British Politics* (Oxford: Oxford University Press).

Grant, W. (1993) 'Pressure Groups and the European Community: An Overview', in S. Mazey and J.J. Richardson (eds) *Lobbying in the European Community* (Oxford: Oxford University Press).

Grant, W. (1995) *Pressure Groups, Politics and Democracy in Britain*, 2nd edn (Hemel Hempstead: Prentice-Hall/Harvester Wheatsheaf).

Grant, W. (2000) *Pressure Groups and British Politics* (Basingstoke: Palgrave Macmillan).

Grant, W. (2002) *Economic Policy in Britain* (Basingstoke: Palgrave Macmillan).

Gray, J. (2010) 'Progressive, Like the 1980s', *London Review of Books*, 32(20): 3–7.

Green, D.A. (2018) *Brexit: What Everyone Needs to Know* (Oxford: Oxford University Press).

Greenleaf, W.H. (1973) 'The Character of Modern British Conservatism', in R. Benewick, R.N. Berkhi and B. Parekh (eds) *Knowledge and Belief in Politics* (London: Allen & Unwin).

Greenleaf, W.H. (1983) *The British Political Tradition,* vol. 2*: The Ideological Heritage* (London: Methuen).

Griffith, J.A.G. (2010) *The Politics of the Judiciary*, 5th edn (London: Fontana).

Griffiths, S. (2014) 'What was Progressive in "Progressive Conservatism"?', *Political Studies Review*, 12(1): 29–40.

Griffiths, S. (2015) 'Education Policy: Consumerism and Competition' in M. Beech and S. Lee (eds) *The Conservative-Liberal Coalition: Examining the Cameron-Clegg Government* (Basingstoke: Palgrave Macmillan).

Griffiths, S., Foley, B. and Prendergast, J. (2009) *Assertive Citizens* (London: Social Market Foundation).

Griffiths, S., Kippin, H. and Stoker, G. (eds) (2013) *Public Services: A New Reform Agenda* (London: Bloomsbury Academic).

Griggs, S. and Howarth, D. (2013) *The Politics of Airport Expansion in the United Kingdom: Hegemony, Policy and the Rhetoric of 'Sustainable Aviation'* (Manchester: Manchester University Press).

Grix, J. and Houlihan, B. (2014) 'Sports Mega-Events as Part of a Nation's Soft Power Strategy: The Cases of Germany (2006) and the UK (2012)', *British Journal of Politics and International Relations*, 16(4): 572–96.

Haddon, C. (2013) *Voting 'No' on Syria: What now for the Role of the UK Parliament in Approving Military Action* [online]. Available at: www.e-ir.info/2013/09/10/voting-no-on-syria-what-now-for-the-role-of-the-uk-parliament-in-approving-military-action/ [Accessed 2 Oct. 2017].

Hague, R. et al. (2016) *Comparative Government and Politics,* 10th edn (London: Palgrave).

Hain, P. (2015) *Back to the Future of Socialism* (Bristol: Policy).

Haldane Report (1918) *Report of the Machinery of Government Committee under the chairmanship of Viscount Haldane of Cloan*, Cd. 9230 (London: HMSO).

Hall, M. (2004) 'Nationalism in the UK', *Talking Politics*, 16(3): 148–53.

Hall, S. (2011) 'The Neoliberal Revolution', *Soundings*, 48: 9–27.

Hall, S. and Jacques, M. (1983) *The Politics of Thatcherism* (London: Lawrence & Wishart).

Ham, C. (2009) *Health Policy in Britain*, 6th edn (Basingstoke: Palgrave Macmillan).

Hammond Perry, K. (2016) *London is the Place for Me: Black Britons, Citizenship and the Politics of Race* (Oxford: Oxford University Press).

Hansard Society (2017) *Audit of Political Engagement* [online]. Available at: https://assets.contentful.com/xkbace0jm9pp/1vNBTsOEiYciKEAqWAmEKi/c9cc36b98f60328c0327e313ab37ae0c/Audit_of_political_Engagement_14_2017_.pdf [Accessed 2 Oct. 2017].

Harman, H. (2017) *A Woman's Work* (London: Allen Lane).

Hastings, A., Bailey, N., Bramley, G. et al. (2015) *The Cost of the Cuts: The Impact on Local Government and Poorer Communities* (York: Joseph Rowntree Foundation).

Hay, C. (1999) *The Political Economy of New Labour: Labouring Under False Pretences?* (Manchester: Manchester University Press).

Hay, C. (2007) *Why We Hate Politics* (Cambridge: Polity).

Hay, C. (2009) 'The Winter of Discontent Thirty Years On', *Political Quarterly*, 80(4): 545–52.

Hayek, F. A. (1944) *The Road to Serfdom* (London: Routledge & Kegan Paul).

Hayes, M. (2010) 'Access to Justice', *Studies: An Irish Quarterly Review*, 99(393): 29–42.

Hazell, R. (ed.) (1999) *Constitutional Futures: A History of the Next Ten Years* (Oxford: Oxford University Press).

Hazell, R. (ed.) (2000) *The State and the Nations* (Thorverton: Imprint Academic).

Hazell, R. (ed.) (2003) *The State of the Nations 2003: The Third Year of Devolution in the United Kingdom* (Thorverton: Academic Imprint).

Hazell, R. and Melton, J. (eds) (2015) *Magna Carta and its Modern Legacy* (Cambridge: Cambridge University Press).

Headey, B. (1974) *British Cabinet Ministers: The Roles of Politicians in Executive Office* (London: Allen & Unwin).

Heffernan, R. (2000) *New Labour and Thatcherism: Political Change in Britain* (Basingstoke: Palgrave Macmillan).

Heffernan, R. (2013) 'There's No Need for the "-ization": The Prime Minister is Merely Prime Ministerial', *Parliamentary Affairs*, 66(3): 636–45.

Heffernan, R. (2016) 'Politics and the News Media', in R. Heffernan, M. Russell, P. Cowley and C. Hay (eds) *Developments in British Politics 10* (London: Palgrave).

Held, D. (1987) *Models of Democracy* (Cambridge: Polity).

Henn, M., Weinstein, M. and Forrest, S. (2005) 'Uninterested Youth? Young People's Attitudes towards Party Politics in Britain', *Political Studies*, 53(3): 556–78.

Hennessy, P. (1990) *Whitehall*, 2nd edn (London: Fontana).

Hennessy, P. (1993) *Never Again: Britain 1945–51* (London: Vintage).

Hennessy, P. (2000) *The Prime Minister: The Office and its Holders since 1945* (London: Allen Lane).

Hennessy, P. (2006) *Having It So Good: Britain in the Fifties* (London: Penguin Books).

Heppell, T. (2014) *The Tories* (London: Bloomsbury Academic).

Herndon, T., Ash, M. and Pollin, R. (2013) 'Does High Public Debt Consistently Stifle Economic Growth? A Critique of Reinhart and Rogoff', *Cambridge Journal of Economics*, 38(2): 257–79.

Heywood, A. (2009) *The Essentials of UK Politics by Andrew Heywood, Companion website* [online]. Available at: https://he.palgrave.com/companion/Heywood-Essentials-Of-Uk-Politics/resources/Update-material/ [Accessed 1 Oct. 2017].

Heywood, A. (2013) *Politics* (Basingstoke: Palgrave Macmillan).

Heywood, A. (2017) *Political Ideologies*, 6th edn (Basingstoke: Palgrave Macmillan).

Hickson, K. (2004) 'The Postwar Consensus Revisited', *Political Quarterly*, 75(2): 142–54.

Hill, C. (2005) 'Putting the World to Rights: Tony Blair's Foreign Policy Mission', in A. Seldon and D. Kavanagh, *The Blair Effect 2001–5* (Cambridge: Cambridge University Press).

Hill, M. (ed.) (1997) *The Policy Process: A Reader*, 2nd edn (Hemel Hempstead: Prentice-Hall).

Hill, M. (2013) *The Public Policy Process*, 6th edn (Harlow: Pearson Education).

Hix, S. (2002) 'Britain, the EU and the Euro', in P. Dunleavy, A. Gamble, R. Heffernan, I. Holliday and G. Peele (eds) *Developments in British Politics 6*, rev. edn (Basingstoke: Palgrave Macmillan).

Hix, S. and Høyland, B. (2011) *The Political System of the European Union*, 3rd edn (Basingstoke: Palgrave Macmillan).

HM Government (2012) *Civil Service Reform Plan* (London: HMSO).

HM Treasury (1991) *Competing for Quality*, White Paper, Cm 1730 (London: HMSO).

Hogwood, B.W. and Gunn, L. (1984) *Policy Analysis for the Real World* (Oxford: Oxford University Press).

Holliday, I. (2002) 'Executives and Administrations', in P. Dunleavy, A. Gamble, R. Heffernan, I. Holliday and G. Peele (eds) *Developments in British Politics 6*, rev. edn (Basingstoke: Palgrave Macmillan).

Hood, A. and Phillips, D. (2015) *Benefit Spending and Reforms: The Coalition Government's Record*, Institute for Fiscal Studies, Briefing note BN160.

Hood, C. and Himaz, R. (2017) *A Century of Fiscal Squeeze Politics: 100 Years of Austerity, Politics, and Bureaucracy in Britain* (Oxford: Oxford University Press).

House of Commons (2011) *Smaller Government: Shrinking the Quango State*, report of the Public Administration Select Committee (London: TSO).

House of Commons Reform Committee (2009) *Rebuilding the House*, HC 1117 (London: TSO).

Howard, M. (2005) *Judges must bow to the will of Parliament* [online]. Available at: www.telegraph.co.uk/comment/personal-view/3618954/Judges-must-bow-to-the-will-of-Parliament.html [Accessed 1 Oct. 2017].

Hudson, B. (1997) 'Michael Lipsky and Street Level Bureaucracy: A Neglected Perspective', in M. Hill (ed.) *The Policy Process: A Reader*, 2nd edn (Hemel Hempstead: Prentice Hall).

Humphrey, M. (2003) 'Britain and the International Arena', in P. Dunleavy, A. Gamble, R. Heffernan and G. Peele (eds) *Developments in Politics 7* (Basingstoke: Palgrave Macmillan).

Huntington, S.P. (1996) *The Clash of Civilizations and the Remaking of World Order* (New York: Simon & Schuster).

Hutton Report (2004) *Report of the Inquiry into the Circumstances Surrounding the Death of Dr David Kelly*, HC 247 (London: TSO).

Hutton, W. (1996) *The State We're In*, rev. edn (London: Jonathan Cape).

Ibbs, R. (1988) *Improving Management in Government: The Next Steps* (London: HMSO).

IFS (2017) *A time of revolution? British local government finance in the 2010s* [online]. Available at: www.ifs.org.uk/uploads/publications/comms/R121.pdf [Accessed 1 Oct. 2017].

Intergovernmental Panel on Climate Change (2014) *Climate Change 2014 Synthesis Report Summary for Policymakers* [online]. Available at: www.ipcc.ch/pdf/assessment-report/ar5/syr/AR5_SYR_FINAL_SPM.pdf [Accessed 2 Oct. 2017].

Ipsos MORI (2015) *Northern Ireland Border Poll* [online]. Available at: www.ipsos.com/ipsos-mori/en-uk/Assets/Docs/Polls/ipsos-mori-northern-ireland-border-poll-2016-tables.pdf [Accessed 1 Oct. 2017].

Ipsos MORI (2016) *Veracity Index 2016* [online]. Available at: www.ipsos.com/sites/default/files/migrations/en-uk/files/Assets/Docs/Polls/ipsos-mori-veracity-index-2016-topline.pdf [Accessed 1 Oct. 2017].

Iyengar, S., Peters, M.D. and Kinder, D.R. (1982) 'Experimental Demonstrations of the "Not-So-Minimal" Consequences of Television News Programs, *American Political Science Review*, 76(4): 848–58.

Jackson, D., Thorsen, E. and Wring, D. (2016) *EU Referendum Analysis 2016: Media, Voters and the Campaign* (Poole: Centre for the Study of Journalism, Culture and Community Bournemouth University).

James, S. (1992) *British Cabinet Government* (London: Routledge).

Jeffery, C. (2003) 'Devolution: What's It All For?', *Politics Review*, 13(2): 10–13.

Jeffery, C. (2010) 'An Outbreak of Consensus: Scottish Politics after Devolution', *Political Insight*, 1(1): 32–5.

Jenkins Commission (1998) *Report of the Independent Commission on the Voting System* (London: HMSO).

Jenkins, R. (2001) *Churchill* (Basingstoke: Palgrave Macmillan).

Jennings, I. ([1941] 1966) *The British Constitution*, 5th edn (Cambridge: University Press).

Jones, A. (2013) *Less than 1% of British workers now employed in agriculture for first time* [online]. Available at: www.independent.co.uk/news/uk/home-news/less-than-1-of-british-workers-now-employed-in-agriculture-for-first-time-in-history-8645324.html [Accessed 2 Oct. 2017].

Jones, B. (2003) 'Apathy: Why Don't People Want to Vote?', *Politics Review*, 12(4): 23–7.

Jones, E. (2017) *Edmund Burke and the Invention of Modern Conservatism, 1830–1914* (Oxford: Oxford University Press).

Jones, N. (1996) *Soundbites and Spin Doctors* (London: Indigo).

Jones, N. (1999) *Sultans of Spin* (London: Gollancz).

Jones, N. (2002) *The Control Freaks* (London: Politico's).

Jones, N. (2003) 'Sultans of Spin: The Media and the New Labour Government', in A. Chadwick and R. Heffernan (eds) *The New Labour Reader* (Cambridge: Polity).

Jones, O. (2015) *The Establishment and How They Get Away with It* (London: Penguin).

Jones, R.W. and Scully, R. (2012) *Wales Says Yes: Devolution and the 2011 Welsh Referendum* (Cardiff: University of Wales Press).

Jordan, A. (2002) 'Environmental Policy', in P. Dunleavy, A. Gamble, R. Heffernan, I. Holliday and G. Peele (eds) *Developments in British Politics 6*, rev. edn (Basingstoke: Palgrave Macmillan).

Jordan, G. (2001) *Shell, Greenpeace and Brent Spar* (Basingstoke: Palgrave Macmillan).

Jordan, G. and Mahoney, W. (1997) *The Protest Business* (Manchester: Manchester University Press).

Jowell, J., Oliver, D. and Ocinneide, C. (2015) *The Changing Constitution*, 8th edn (Oxford: Oxford University Press).

Judd, D. (1996) *Empire: The British Imperial Experience from 1765 to the Present* (London: Fontana).

Judt, T. (2005) *Postwar: A History of Europe since 1945* (London: William Heinemann).

Judt, T. (2010) *Ill Fares the Land* (London: Allen Lane).

Kagan, R. (2004) *Paradise and Power: America and Europe in the New World Order* (London: Atlantic Books).

Khan, O. (2015) *Diversity and Democracy: Race and the 2015 General Election* [online]. Available at: www.runnymedetrust.org/uploads/GE2015.pdf [Accessed 1 Oct. 2017].

Kampfner, J. (2004) *Blair's Wars* (London: Free Press).

Kaufmann, E. (2016) *It's NOT the economy, stupid: Brexit as a story of personal values* [online]. Available at http://blogs.lse.ac.uk/politicsandpolicy/personal-values-brexit-vote/ [Accessed 1 Oct. 2017].

Kavanagh, D. (1990) *Thatcherism and British Politics*, 2nd edn (Oxford: Oxford University Press).

Kavanagh, D. and Cowley, P. (2010) *The British General Election of 2010* (Basingstoke: Palgrave Macmillan).

Kavanagh, D. and Seldon, A. (eds) (1994) *The Major Effect* (London: Macmillan).

Keen, R. and Audickas, L. (2017) *Membership of UK political parties* [online]. Available at: http://researchbriefings.parliament.uk/ResearchBriefing/Summary/SN05125 [Accessed 1 Oct. 2017].

Kegley, C. and Wiitkopf, E. (1999) *World Politics* (New York: Worth).

Kelley, N., Khan, O. and Sharrock, S. (2017) *Racial prejudice in Britain today*, NatCen and Runnymede Trust, Available at: http://natcen.ac.uk/media/1488132/racial-prejudice-report_v4.pdf?_ga=2.113235332.125617652.1512470676-1934898503.1465207162 [Accessed 17 December 2017].

Kelly, L., Lovett, J. and Regan, L. and the Child and Woman Abuse Studies Unit, London Metropolitan University (2005) *A Gap or a Chasm? Attrition in Reported Rape Cases* (London: Home Office Research Study 293).

Kelso, A. (2013) *Parliamentary Reform at Westminster* (Manchester: Manchester University Press).

Kenny, M. (2011) 'The Political Theory of Recognition: The Case of the "White Working Class"', *British Journal of Politics and International Relations*, 14(1): 19–38.

Kenny, M. (2014) *The Politics of English Nationhood* (Oxford: Oxford University Press).

Keynes, J.M. (1936) *The General Theory of Employment, Interest and Money* (London: Macmillan).

King, A. (ed.) (1985) *The British Prime Minister: A Reader*, 2nd edn (London: Macmillan).

King, A. (2007) *The British Constitution* (Oxford: Oxford University Press).

King, M. (2017) *The End of Alchemy: Money, Banking and the Future of the Global Economy* (London: W.W. Norton).

Kirkland, C. (2015) 'Thatcherism and the Origins of the 2007 Crisis', *British Politics*, 10(4): 514–35.

Klein, R. (2013) *The New Politics of the NHS*, 7th edn (Oxford: CRC Press).

Kuhn, R. (2007) *Politics and the Media in Britain* (Basingstoke: Palgrave Macmillan).

Kumarasingham, H. (2016) *Constitution-making in Asia* (Abingdon: Routledge).

Kynaston, D. (2008) *Austerity Britain, 1945–51* (London: Bloomsbury).

Kynaston, D. (2010) *Family Britain, 1951–57* (London: Bloomsbury).

Kynaston, D. (2015) *Modernity Britain 1957–62* (London: Bloomsbury).

Lakin, M. (2013) 'The Ideology of the Coalition: More "Muscular" than "Liberal"?', *British Politics*, 8(4): 476–90.

Lamont, N. (1999) *In Office* (London: Little, Brown).

Lanchester, J. (2010) *Whoops! Why Everyone Owes Everyone and No One Can Pay* (London: Allen Lane).

Langer, A. (2011) *The Personalisation of Politics in the UK: Mediated Leadership from Attlee to Cameron* (Manchester: Manchester University Press).

Lasswell, H. (1936) *Politics: Who Gets What, When, How?* (New York: McGraw-Hill).

Layfield Committee (1976) *Committee of Inquiry into Local Government Finance*, Cmnd 6453 (London: HMSO).

Lazarsfeld, P., Berelson, B. and Gaudet, H. (1944) *The People's Choice* (New York: Duell, Sloane and Pearce).

Leach, R. (1998) 'Local Government Reorganisation RIP?', *Political Quarterly*, 69(1): 31–40.

Leach, R. (2004) 'Democracy and Elections', in S. Lancaster (ed.) *Developments in Politics* (Ormskirk: Causeway Press).

Leach, R. (2009) *Political Ideology in Britain*, 2nd edn (Basingstoke: Palgrave Macmillan).

Leach, R. (2015) *Political Ideology in Britain*, 3rd edn (London: Palgrave).

Leach, R. and Lightfoot, S. (2018) *The Politics and IR Companion* (London: Palgrave).

Leach, R. and Percy-Smith, J. (2001) *Local Governance in Britain* (Basingstoke: Palgrave Macmillan).

Leach, R., Coxall, B. and Robins, L. (2006) *British Politics* (Basingstoke: Palgrave Macmillan).

Lee, S. (2008) 'The British Model of Political Economy', in M. Beech and S. Lee (eds) *Ten Years of New Labour* (Basingstoke: Palgrave Macmillan).

Lee, S. and Beech, M. (eds) (2009) *The Conservatives under David Cameron: Built to Last?* (Basingstoke: Palgrave Macmillan).

Leftwich, A. (ed.) (2004) *What is Politics?* (Oxford: Polity).

Lester, A. and Clapinska, L. (2004) 'Human Rights and the British Constitution', in J. Jowell and D. Oliver (eds) *The Changing Constitution*, 7th edn (Oxford: Oxford University Press).

Leston-Bandeira, C. and Thompson, L. (2018) *Exploring Parliament* (Oxford: Oxford University Press).

Leveson Inquiry (2012) *Leveson Inquiry: Culture, Practice and Ethics of the Press* [online]. Available at: http://webarchive.nationalarchives.gov.uk/20140122144906/http://www.levesoninquiry.org.uk/ [Accessed 2 Oct. 2017].

Lewis, J. (1992) *Women in Britain Since 1945* (London: Wiley-Blackwell).

Lilleker, D., Negrine, R. and Stanyer, J. (2003) 'Media Malaise: Britain's Political Communication Problems', *Politics Preview*, 12(3): 29–31.

Lindblom, C. (1959) 'The Science of "Muddling Through"', *Public Administration Review*, 19(2): 79–88.

Lloyd, J. (2004) *What the Media are Doing to Our Democracy* (London: Constable).

Lodge, M. and Hood, C. (2011) 'Into an age of multiple austerities?: public management and public service bargains across OECD countries' *Governance*, 25 (1).

Loughlin, M. (2013) *The British Constitution: A Very Short Introduction* (Oxford: Oxford University Press).

Loughlin, M. and Viney, C. (2015) 'The Coalition and the Constitution', in A. Seldon and M. Finn (eds) *The Coalition Effect, 2010–2015* (Cambridge: Cambridge University Press).

Lovelock, J. (1979) *Gaia: A New Look at Life on Earth* (Oxford: Oxford University Press).

Lovelock, J. (2007) *The Revenge of Gaia* (Harmondsworth: Penguin).

Lowe, R. (2011) *The Official History of the British Civil Service: Reforming the Civil Service, Volume I: The Fulton Years, 1966–81* (Abingdon: Routledge).

Lukes, S. ([1974] 2005) *Power: A Radical View* (Basingstoke: Palgrave Macmillan).

Lynch, P. and Whitaker, R. (2008) 'A Loveless Marriage: The Conservatives and the European People's Party', *Parliamentary Affairs*, 61(1): 31–51.

Lynch, P., Whitaker, R. and Loomes, G. (2011) 'The UK Independence Party: Understanding a Niche Party's Strategy, Candidates and Supporters', *Parliamentary Affairs*, 65(4): 733–57.

McCombs, M. and Shaw, D. (1972) 'The Agenda-Setting Function of Mass Media', *Public Opinion Quarterly*, 36(2): 176–87.

McCormick, J. (1991) *British Politics and the Environment* (London: Earthscan).

McCormick, J. (2017) *Understanding the European Union*, 7th edn (London: Palgrave).

McEvoy, J. (2008) *The Politics of Northern Ireland* (Edinburgh: Edinburgh University Press).

McGarry, J. and O'Leary, B. (2006) 'Consociational Theory, Northern Ireland's Conflict, and its Agreement. Part 1: What Consociationalists Can Learn from Northern Ireland', *Government and Opposition*, 41(1): 43–63.

McKenzie, R.T. (1955) *British Political Parties* (London: Heinemann).

McKercher, B. (2017) *Britain, America, and the Special Relationship since 1941* (London: Routledge).

McKibbin, R. (1984) 'Why Was There No Marxism in Great Britain?', *English Historical Review*, 99(391): 297–331.

Mackintosh J. (1962) *The British Cabinet* (London: Stevens).

McLean, I. (2001) 'The National Question', in A. Seldon (ed.) *The Blair Effect: The Blair Government, 1997–2001* (London: Little, Brown).

McLellan, D. (1995) *Ideology*, 2nd edn (Buckingham: Open University Press).

McLuhan, M. (1964) *Understanding Media: The Extensions of Man* (New York: McGraw-Hill).

Macmillan, H. (1938) *The Middle Way: A Study of the Problem of Economic and Social Progress in a Free and Democratic Society* (London: Macmillan).

Macpherson, C.B. (1977) *The Life and Times of Liberal Democracy* (Oxford: Oxford University Press).

Macpherson, Sir W. (1999) *The Stephen Lawrence Inquiry*, Cm 4262 (London: TSO).

McSmith, A. (2011) *No Such Thing as Society: A History of Britain in the 1980s* (London: Constable).

Macwhirter, I. (2013) *Road to Referendum* (Glasgow: Cargo).

Madgwick, P. (1991) *British Government: The Central Executive Territory* (London: Philip Allan).

Madgwick, P. and Rawkins, P. (1982) 'The Welsh Language in the Policy Process', in P. Madgwick and R. Rose (eds.), *The Territorial Dimension in United Kingdom Politics* (London: Macmillan).

Major, J. (1999) *John Major* (London: Harper-Collins).

Malleson, K. (2016) *The New Judiciary* (Abingdon: Routledge).

Maloney, W. (2006) 'Political Participation Beyond the Political Arena', in P. Dunleavy, R. Heffernan, P. Cowley and C. Hay (eds) *Developments in British Politics 8* (Basingstoke: Palgrave Macmillan).

Margetts, H. (2002) 'Political Participation and Protest', in P. Dunleavy, A. Gamble, R. Heffernan, I. Holliday and G. Peele (eds) *Developments in British Politics 6*, rev. edn (Basingstoke: Palgrave Macmillan).

Margetts, H., John, P., Hale, S. and Yasseri, T. (2016) *Political Turbulence: How Social Media Shape Collective Action* (Princeton: Princeton University Press).

Marmot, M. (2015) *The Health Gap: The Challenge of an Unequal World* (London: Bloomsbury).

Marr, A. (1996) *Ruling Britannia: The Failure and Future of British Democracy* (Harmondsworth: Penguin).

Marsh, D. and McConnell, A. (2010) 'Towards a Framework for Establishing Policy Success', *Public Administration*, 55(2): 564–83.

Marsh, D. and Rhodes, R.A.W. (eds) (1992) *Policy Networks in British Government* (Oxford: Oxford University Press).

Marshall, P. and Laws, D. (eds) (2004) *The Orange Book: Reclaiming Liberalism* (London: Profile Books).

Marshall, T.H. (1950) *Citizenship and Social Class and Other Essays* (Cambridge: Cambridge University Press).

Marx, K. and Engels, F. ([1848] 2017) *The Communist Manifesto* (London: Pluto Press).

Mason, R. and Asthana, A. (2016) *Ken Clarke caught on camera ridiculing Conservative leadership candidates* [online]. Available at: www.theguardian.com/politics/2016/jul/05/ken-clarke-caught-camera-ridiculing-tory-leadership-candidates-theresa-may-michael-gove [Accessed 29 Sept. 2017].

Massey, A. (ed.) (2011) *International Handbook on Civil Service Systems* (Cheltenham: Edward Elgar).

Maud Report (1967) *Report of Committee on Management of Local Government* (London: HMSO).

May, E. (1844) *A Treatise on the Law, Privileges, Proceedings and Usage of Parliament* (London: Charles Knight & Co.).

May, E. (2011) *Erskine May: Parliamentary Practice*, 24th edn, ed. Malcolm Jack et al. (London: Butterworths Law).

May, T. (2002) *Full text: Theresa May's conference speech* [online]. Available at: www.theguardian.com/politics/2002/oct/07/conservatives2002.conservatives1 [Accessed 1 Oct. 2017].

May, T. (2016a) *Theresa May: Brexit means Brexit* [online]. Available at: www.bbc.co.uk/news/av/uk-politics-36764525/no-second-eu-referendum-if-theresa-may-becomes-pm [Accessed 29 Sept. 2017].

May, T. (2016b) *Theresa May's conference speech in full* [online]. Available at: www.telegraph.co.uk/news/2016/10/05/theresa-mays-conference-speech-in-full/ [Accessed 1 Oct. 2017].

Mazey, S. and Richardson, J.J. (eds) (1993) *Lobbying in the European Community* (Oxford: Oxford University Press).

Meadows, D.H., Meadows, D.L., Randers, D.L. and Behrens III, W. (1972) *The Limits to Growth* (New York: Universe Books).

Michels, R. ([1911] 1968) *Political Parties* (New York: Free Press).

Mill, J.S. ([1859] 1972) *On Liberty*, ed. H.B. Acton (London: Dent).

Mill, J.S. ([1861] 1972) *Considerations on Representative Government*, ed. H.B. Acton (London: Dent).

Mill, J.S. ([1869] 1988) *The Subjection of Women*, ed. S. Okin (Indianapolis: Hackett).

Miller, D. (1991) *The Blackwell Encyclopaedia of Political Thought* (Oxford: Blackwell).

Ministry of Justice (2015) *Race and the criminal justice system: 2014* [online]. Available at: www.gov.uk/government/statistics/race-and-the-criminal-justice-system-2014 [Accessed 9 Oct. 2017].

Minkin, L. (1992) *The Contentious Alliance: Trade Unions and the Labour Party* (Edinburgh: Edinburgh University Press).

Minkin, L. (2014) *The Blair Supremacy: A Study in the Politics of Labour's Party Management* (Manchester: Manchester University Press).

Mitchell, J. and Hassan, G. (eds) (2016) *Scottish National Party Leaders* (London: Biteback).

Moore, C. (2013) *Margaret Thatcher: The Authorized Biography, Volume One: Not For Turning* (London: Allen Lane).

Moore, C. (2016) *Margaret Thatcher: The Authorized Biography, Volume Two: Everything She Wants* (London: Penguin).

Moran, M. (2000) 'From Command State to Regulatory State', *Public Policy and Administration*, 15(4): 1–13.

Moran, M. (2001) 'Not Steering but Drowning: Policy Catastrophes and the Regulatory State', *Political Quarterly*, 72(4): 414–27.

Moran, M. (2003) *The British Regulatory State: High Modernism and Hyper-innovation* (Oxford: Oxford University Press).

Moran, M. (2005) *Politics and Governance in the UK* (Basingstoke: Palgrave Macmillan).

Moran, M. (2015) *Politics and Governance in the UK*, 3rd edn (London: Palgrave).

Morgan, J. (ed.) (1981) *The Backbench Diaries of Richard Crossman* (London: Hamish Hamilton).

Morgan, K.O. (2014) *Revolution to Devolution: Reflections on Welsh Democracy* (Cardiff: University of Wales Press).

Morgan, N. (2014) *Nicky Morgan speaks at launch of Your Life campaign* [online]. Available at: www.gov.uk/government/speeches/nicky-morgan-speaks-at-launch-of-your-life-campaign [Accessed 2 Oct. 2017].

Morgenthau, H.J. ([1948] 1978) *Politics Among Nations: The Struggle for Power and Peace*, 5th edn (New York: Kopf).

Morozov, E. (2011) *The Net Delusion: How Not to Liberate the World* (London: Allen Lane).

Morris, N. (2004) *Campbell: 'I told the truth. The BBC, from the chairman down, did not'*, [online]. Available at: www.independent.co.uk/news/uk/politics/campbell-i-told-the-truth-the-bbc-from-the-chairman-down-did-not-75928.html [Accessed 2 Oct. 2017].

Mount, F. (1992) *The British Constitution Now* (London: Heinemann).

Mügge, L. and Erzeel, S. (2016) 'Double Jeopardy or Multiple Advantages? Intersectionality and Political Representation', *Parliamentary Affairs*, 69(3): 499–511.

Mullard, M. and Swaray, R. (2008) 'New Labour and Public Expenditure', in M. Beech and S. Lee (eds) *Ten Years of New Labour* (Basingstoke: Palgrave Macmillan).

Mullin, C. (2009) *A View from the Foothills* (London: Profile Books).

Nairn, T. (1981) *The Break-up of Britain: Crisis and Neo-nationalism* (London: NLB/Verso).

Nairn, T. (2000) *After Britain* (London: Granta Books).

Nairn, T. (2001) 'Post Ukania', *New Left Review*, 7: 71.

Neill Report (1998) *The Funding of Political Parties in the United Kingdom* (London: HMSO).

Newman, J. (2001) *Modernising Governance: New Labour, Policy and Society* (London: Sage).

Newton, K. (1976) *Second City Politics* (Oxford: Oxford University Press).

Niskanen, W.A. (1971) *Bureaucracy and Representative Government* (Chicago: Aldine-Atherton).

Niskanen, W.A. (1973) *Bureaucracy: Servant or Master?* (London: Institute of Economic Affairs).

Nolan Report (1995) *First Report of the Committee on Standards in Public Life*, Cm 2850 (London: HMSO).

Norris, P. and Lovenduski, J. (1995) *Political Recruitment: Gender, Race and Class in the British Parliament* (Cambridge: Cambridge University Press).

Northcote-Trevelyan Report (1854) *Report on the Organisation of the Permanent Civil Service* (London: HMSO).

Norton, P. (2001) 'Parliament', in A. Seldon (ed.) *The Blair Effect: The Blair Government 1997–2001* (London: Little, Brown).

Norton, P. (2005) *Parliament in British Politics* (Basingstoke: Palgrave Macmillan).

Norton, P. (2008) 'Tony Blair and the Office of Prime Minister', in M. Beech and S. Lee (eds) *Ten Years of New Labour* (Basingstoke: Palgrave Macmillan).

Norton, P. (2013) *Parliament in British Politics*, 2nd edn, (Basingstoke: Palgrave Macmillan).

Nugent, N. (2017) *The Government and Politics of the European Union*, 8th edn (London: Palgrave).

Nye, J. (2004) *Soft Power: The Means to Success in World Politics* (New York: PublicAffairs).

Nye, J. (2008) *The Powers to Lead: Soft, Hard and Smart* (New York: Oxford University Press).

Oliver, C. (2016) *Unleashing Demons: The Inside Story of Brexit* (London: Hodder & Stoughton).

ONS (2010) *Average Briton highlighted on UN World Statistics Day* [online]. Available at: www.ons.gov.uk/ons/...ons/.../-average-briton-highlighted-on-un-world-statistics-day [Accessed 1 Oct. 2017].

ONS (2011a) *Ethnicity and National Identity in England and Wales: 2011* [online]. Available at: www.ons.gov.uk/peoplepopulationandcommunity/culturalidentity/ethnicity/articles/ethnicityandnationalidentityinenglandandwales/2012-12-11 [Accessed 1 Oct. 2017].

ONS (2011b) *Religion in England and Wales 2011* [online]. Available at: www.ons.gov.uk/peoplepopulationandcommunity/culturalidentity/religion/articles/religioninenglandandwales2011/2012-12-11 [Accessed 1 Oct. 2017].

ONS (2013) *Women in the Labour Market: 2013* [online]. Available at: www.ons.gov.uk/employmentandlabourmarket/peopleinwork/employmentandemployeetypes/articles/womeninthelabourmarket/2013-09-25 [Accessed 1 Oct. 2017].

ONS (2015a) *Main results from the Wealth and Assets Survey: July 2012 to June 2014* [online]. Available at: www.ons.gov.uk/peoplepopulationandcommunity/personalandhouseholdfinances/incomeandwealth/compendium/wealthingreatbritainwave4/2012to2014/mainresultsfromthewealthandassetssurveyjuly2012tojune2014 [Accessed 1 Oct. 2017].

ONS (2015b) *Civil service numbers decline, but women increase as a proportion* [online]. Available at: www.ons.gov.uk/news/news/civilservicenumbersdeclinebutwomenincreaseasaproportion [Accessed 1 Oct. 2017].

ONS (2015c) *Police workforce, England and Wales: 31 March 2015* [online]. Available at: www.gov.uk/government/publications/police-workforce-england-and-wales-31-march-2015/police-workforce-england-and-wales-31-march-2015#police-workforce [Accessed 1 Oct. 2017].

ONS (2016a) *Population Estimates for UK, England and Wales, Scotland and Northern Ireland* [online]. Available at: www.ons.gov.uk/peoplepopulationandcommunity/populationandmigration/populationestimates/bulletins/annualmidyearpopulationestimates/latest [Accessed 1 Oct. 2017].

ONS (2016b) *Economic Review: April 2016* [online]. Available at: www.ons.gov.uk/economy/nationalaccounts/uksectoraccounts/articles/economicreview/april2016 [Accessed 1 Oct. 2017].

Oppenheim, M. (2017) *Daily Mail accused of 'appalling sexism' over Theresa May and Nicola Sturgeon front page* [online]. Available at: www.independent.co.uk/news/uk/home-news/daily-mail-front-page-legs-it-theresa-may-nicola-sturgeon-sexism-compare-sarah-uk-prime-minister-a7653556.html [Accessed 2 Oct. 2017].

O'Riordan, T. (1976) *Environmentalism* (London: Pion).

Osborne, D. and Gaebler, T. (1992) *Reinventing Government* (Reading, MA: Addison-Wesley).

Outhwaite, D. (2004) 'How Should Parties be Funded?', *Politics Review*, 14(2).

Page, R. (2015) *Clear Blue Water? The Conservative Party and the Welfare State since 1940* (Bristol: Policy).

Parekh, B. (2000) *Rethinking Multiculturalism: Cultural Diversity and Political Theory* (Basingstoke: Palgrave Macmillan).

Parker, S. (2015) *Taking Power Back: Putting People in Charge of Politics.* (Bristol: Policy).

Parker, S., McClory, J., Paun, A. and Blatchford, K. (2010) *Shaping up: a Whitehall for the future* [online]. Available at: www.instituteforgovernment.org.uk/publications/shaping [Accessed 1 Oct. 2017].

Parry, G., Moyser, G. and Day, N. (1992) *Political Participation and Democracy in Britain* (Cambridge: Cambridge University Press).

Pascall, G. (2012) *Gender Equality in the Welfare State?* (Bristol: Policy).

Pateman, C. (1970) *Participation and Democratic Theory* (Cambridge, Cambridge University Press).

Paxman, J. (1998) *The English* (London: Michael Joseph).

Peck, T. (2017) *Theresa May was asked not to use soundbites. She lasted just 30 seconds* [online]. Available at: www.independent.co.uk/news/uk/politics/theresa-may-lasts-30-seconds-when-asked-on-marr-not-to-use-soundbites-a7710021.html [Accessed 1 Oct. 2017].

Peele, G. and Francis, J. (2016) *David Cameron and Conservative Renewal* (Manchester: Manchester University Press).

Phillips, A. (1998) *The Politics of Presence*: Political Representation of Gender, Ethnicity, and Race (Oxford: Oxford University Press).

Phillips, T. (2015) *Ethnicity labels are divisive, says Phillips* [online]. Available at: www.thetimes.co.uk/article/ethnicity-labels-are-divisive-says-phillips-qptswxk3l93 [Accessed 1 Oct. 2017].

Phillis Report (2004) *An Independent Review of Government Communications* (London: HMSO).

Pierce, A. (2005) *Horror as Cameron brandishes the B word* [online]. Available at: www.thetimes.co.uk/article/horror-as-cameron-brandishes-the-b-word-rfjm9v3xhsh [Accessed 2 Nov. 2017].

Pierre, J. and Peters, B.G. (2000) *Politics, Governance and the State* (Basingstoke: Palgrave Macmillan).

Pierre, J. and Stoker, G. (2002) 'The Restructuring of the British Polity: Towards Multi-Level Governance', in P. Dunleavy, A. Gamble, R. Heffernan, I. Holliday and G. Peele (eds) *Developments in British Politics 6*, rev. edn (Basingstoke: Palgrave Macmillan).

Piketty, T. (2013) *Capital in the Twenty-First Century* (Cambridge, MA: Harvard University Press).

Pimlott, B. (1992) *Harold Wilson* (London: HarperCollins).

Pimlott, B. (1994) 'The Myth of Consensus', in B. Pimlott, *Frustrate Their Knavish Tricks: Writings on Biography, History and Politics* (London: HarperCollins).

Pitkin, H. (1967) *The Concept of Representation* (Berkeley, CA: University of California Press).

Plant, R. (2008) 'Blair's Liberal Interventionism', in M. Beech and S. Lee (eds) *Ten Years of New Labour* (Basingstoke: Palgrave Macmillan).

Pliatzky, L. (1980) *Report on Non-Departmental Bodies*, Cmnd 7797 (London: HMSO).

Plummer, J. (1994) *The Governance Gap: Quangos and Accountability* (London: Demos/Joseph Rowntree Foundation).

*Political Studies Review* (2010) 'Symposium on the 2008 Financial Crisis and its Repercussions', 8(1): 1–144.

Pollock, A.M. (2004) *NHS plc: The Privatisation of our Health Care* (London: Verso).

Porritt, J. and Winner, D. (1988) *The Coming of the Greens* (London: Fontana).

Power Report (2006) *Power to the People: The Report of Power, an Independent Inquiry into Britain's Democracy* (York: Joseph Rowntree Reform Trust).

Preston, P. (2015) 'The Coalition and the Media', in A. Seldon and M. Finn (eds) *The Coalition Effect, 2010–2015* (Cambridge: Cambridge University Press).

Prime Minister's Office (2017) *Prime Minister's letter to Donald Tusk triggering Article 50* [online]. Available at: www.gov.uk/government/publications/prime-ministers-letter-to-donald-tusk-triggering-article-50 [Accessed 1 Oct. 2017].

Prince, R. (2010) *David Cameron: net immigration will be capped at tens of thousands* [online]. Available at: www.telegraph.co.uk/news/politics/6961675/David-Cameron-net-immigration-will-be-capped-at-tens-of-thousands.html [Accessed 2 Oct. 2017].

Pryce, V., Ross, A. and Urwin, P. (2015) *It's the Economy, Stupid* (London: Biteback).

Pulzer, P. (1967) *Representation and Elections in Britain* (London: Allen & Unwin).

Putnam, R. (1995) 'Bowling Alone: America's Declining Social Capital', *Journal of Democracy*, 6(1): 65–78.

Putnam, R. (2000) *Bowling Alone: the Collapse and Revival of American Community* (New York: Simon & Schuster).

Pyper, R. and Burnham, J. (2011) 'The British Civil Service: Perspectives on "Decline" and "Modernisation"', *British Journal of Politics and International Relations*, 13(2): 198–205.

Quinton, A. (1978) *The Politics of Imperfection* (London: Faber and Faber).

Raban, J. (2010) *Cameron's Crank: 'Red Tory'* [online]. Available at: www.lrb.co.uk/v32/n08/jonathan-raban/camerons-crank [Accessed 1 Oct. 2017].

Radice, G. (2008) *The Tortoise and The Hares* (London: Politico's).

Rathbone, M. (2005) 'The November 2004 Referendum in the North East', *Talking Politics*, 17(2): 61–5.

Rawnsley, A. (2001) *Servants of the People: The Inside Story of New Labour* (Harmondsworth: Penguin).

Rawnsley, A. (2010) *The End of the Party* (Harmondsworth: Penguin).

Redcliffe-Maud Report (1969) *The Future of Local Government in England*, Cmnd 4040 (London: HMSO).

Reinhart, C and Rogoff, K. (2010) *Growth in a Time of Debt*, NBER Working Paper No. 15639 [online]. Available at: www.nber.org/papers/w15639 [Accessed 2 Oct. 2017].

Renwick, A. (2015) 'A British Constitutional Convention?', *Political Insight*, 6(2): 8–11.

Reuters (2015) *China, Britain to benefit from 'golden era' in ties - Cameron* [online]. Available at: http://uk.reuters.com/article/uk-china-britain/china-britain-to-benefit-from-golden-era-in-ties-cameron-idUKKCN0SB10N20151017 [Accessed 2 Oct. 2017].

Rhodes, R.A.W. (1981) *Control and Power in Central-Local Government Relations* (Farnborough: Gower).

Rhodes, R.A.W. (1988) *Beyond Westminster and Whitehall: The Sub-Central Governments of Britain* (London: Allen & Unwin).

Rhodes, R.A.W. (1997) *Understanding Governance* (Buckingham: Open University Press).

Rhodes, R.A.W. (ed.) (2000) *Transforming British Government*, vol. 1: *Changing Institutions* (Basingstoke: Palgrave Macmillan).

Rhodes, R.A.W. (2015) *Everyday Life in British Government* (Oxford: Oxford University Press).

Richard, Lord (2004) *Report of the Richard Commission: Commission on the Powers and Electoral Arrangements of the National Assembly for Wales* (Cardiff: National Assembly for Wales).

Richards, D. and Smith, M.J. (2004) 'Interpreting the World of Political Elites', *Public Administration*, 82(4): 777–800.

Richards, S. (2010) *Whatever it Takes: The Real Story of Gordon Brown and New Labour* (London: Fourth Estate).

Richardson, J.J. (ed.) (1993) *Pressure Groups* (Oxford: Oxford University Press).

Richardson, J.J. and Jordan, G. (1979) *Governing Under Pressure* (Oxford: Martin Robertson).

Riddell, P. (1991) *The Thatcher Era* (Oxford: Blackwell).

Riddell, P. (2001) 'Blair as Prime Minister', in A. Seldon, (ed.) *The Blair Effect: The Blair Government, 1997–2001* (London: Little, Brown).

Robinson, M. (1992) *The Greening of British Party Politics* (Manchester: Manchester University Press).

Robson, W. (1966) *Local Government in Crisis* (London: Allen & Unwin).

Rosara, J. (2013) *The War Prerogative: History, Reform and Constitutional Design* (Oxford: Oxford University Press).

Rose, R. (2001) *The Prime Minister in a Shrinking World* (London: Polity).

Rosamond, B. (2003) 'The Europeanization of British Politics', in P. Dunleavy, A. Gamble, R. Heffernan and G. Peele (eds) *Developments in British Politics 7* (Basingstoke: Palgrave Macmillan).

Roskill Commission (1971) *Report, Commission on the Third London Airport* (London: HMSO).

Runciman, D. (2010) 'Is This the End of the UK?', *London Review of Books*, 32(10): 3–10.

Rusbridger, A. (2015) *'Farewell, readers': Alan Rusbridger on leaving the Guardian after two decades at the helm* [online]. Available at: www.theguardian.com/media/2015/may/29/farewell-readers-alan-rusbridger-on-leaving-the-guardian [Accessed 1 Oct. 2017].

Russell, M. (2005). *Building New Labour* (Basingstoke: Palgrave).

Russell, M. (2011) '"Never Allow a Crisis Go To Waste": The Wright Committee Reforms to Strengthen the House of Commons', *Parliamentary Affairs*, 64(4): 612–33.

Russell, M. (2013) *The Contemporary House of Lords* (Oxford: Oxford University Press).

Ryan, M. (2004) 'A Supreme Court for the United Kingdom?', *Talking Politics*, 17(1): 18–20.

Sampson, A. (2005) *Who Runs This Place?* (London: John Murray).

Sandbrook, D. (2005) *Never Had It So Good: A History of Britain from Suez to the Beatles* (London: Abacus).

Sandbrook, D. (2006) *White Heat: A History of Britain in the Swinging Sixties* (London: Abacus).

Sandbrook, D. (2010) *State of Emergency: The Way We Were: Britain, 1970–1974* (London: Allen Lane).

Sanders, D. and Houghton, D. (2017) *Losing an Empire, Finding a Role*, 2nd edn (London: Palgrave).

Sandry, A. (2011) *Plaid Cymru* (Cardiff: Ashley Drake).

Särlvik, B. and Crewe, I. (1983) *Decade of Dealignment* (Cambridge: Cambridge University Press).

Saunders, P. (1980) *Urban Politics: A Sociological Interpretation* (Harmondsworth: Penguin).

Savage, M. et al. (2013) 'A new model of social class? Findings from the BBC's Great British Class Survey experiment', *Sociology*, 47 (2).

Savage, M. (2009) *Cameron admits U-turn on Lisbon* [online]. Available at: www.independent.co.uk/news/uk/politics/cameron-admits-u-turn-on-lisbon-1813615.html [Accessed 29 Oct. 2017].

Savage, S. and Robins, L. (eds) (1990) *Public Policy under Thatcher* (London: Macmillan).

Scarman, Lord (1981) *The Brixton Disorders 10–12 April, 1981: Special Report* (London: HMSO).

Scheufele, D. (2000) 'Agenda-Setting, Priming, and Framing Revisited: Another Look at Cognitive Effects of Political Communication', *Mass Communication and Society*, 3(2/3): 297–316.

Schumacher, E.F. (1973) *Small is Beautiful* (London: Sphere Books).

Scruton, R. (2007) *Dictionary of Political Thought*, 3rd edn (Basingstoke: Palgrave Macmillan).

Seawright, D. (2010) *The British Conservative Party and One Nation Politics* (New York: Continuum).

Seldon, A. and Collings, D. (2000) *Britain under Thatcher* (Harlow: Longman).

Seldon, A. and Finn, M. (eds) (2015) *The Coalition Effect, 2010–2015* (Cambridge: Cambridge University Press).

Self, P. (1993) *Government by the Market? The Politics of Public Choice* (London: Macmillan).

Self, R. (2010) *British Foreign and Defence Policy since 1945: Challenges and Dilemmas in a Changing World* (Basingstoke: Palgrave Macmillan).

Self, R. (2017) *Neville Chamberlain: A Biography* (London: Routledge).

Seliger, M. (1976) *Ideology and Politics* (London: Allen & Unwin).

Shaw, E. (1996) *The Labour Party since 1945* (Oxford: Blackwell).

Shear, M. (2017) *Trump Will Withdraw U.S. From Paris Climate Agreement* [online]. Available at: www.nytimes.com/2017/06/01/climate/trump-paris-climate-agreement.html [Accessed 2 Oct. 2017].

Shepherd, J. (2011) *Gove loses court battle over cancelled school building projects* [online]. Available at: www.theguardian.com/education/2011/feb/11/gove-school-building-court [Accessed 1 Oct. 2017].

Shepherd, J. (2013) *Crisis? What Crisis? The Callaghan Government and the British 'Winter of Discontent'* (Manchester: Manchester University Press).

Sherwin, A. and Wright, O. (2015) *Rupert Murdoch berated Sun journalists for not doing enough to attack Ed Miliband and stop him winning the general election* [online]. Available at: www.independent.co.uk/news/media/rupert-murdoch-berated-sun-journalists-for-not-doing-enough-to-attack-ed-miliband-10191005.html [Accessed 2 Oct. 2017].

Skelcher, C. (1998) *The Appointed State* (Buckingham: Open University Press).

Skelcher, C. and Davis, H. (1996) 'Understanding the New Magistracy: A Study of Characteristics and Attitudes', *Local Government Studies*, 22(2): 8–21.

Skidelsky, R. (2010) *Keynes: The Return of the Master* (Harmondsworth: Penguin).

Sky News (2017) *May on Brexit: No deal better than a bad deal* [online]. Available at: http://news.sky.com/video/may-on-brexit-no-deal-better-than-a-bad-deal-10897952 [Accessed 1 Oct. 2017].

Smith, D. (2005) 'The Treasury and Economic Policy', in A. Seldon and D. Kavanagh (eds) *The Blair Effect 2001–5* (Cambridge: Cambridge University Press).

Smith, E. and Worley, M. (2014) *Against the Grain: The British Far Left from 1956* (Manchester: Manchester University Press).

Smith, M. (2003) 'The Core Executive and the Modernization of Central Government', in P. Dunleavy, A. Gamble, R. Heffernan and G. Peele (eds) *Developments in Politics 7* (Basingstoke: Palgrave Macmillan).

Smith, M. (2006) 'Britain, Europe and the World', in P. Dunleavy, R. Heffernan, P. Cowley and C. Hay (eds) *Developments in British Politics 8* (Basingstoke: Palgrave Macmillan).

Smith, M. (2017) *Voting Intention: Conservatives 43%, Labour 25% (26-27 Mar)* [online]. Available at: https://yougov.co.uk/news/2017/03/29/voting-intention-conservatives-43-labour-25-26-27-/ [Accessed 29 Sept. 2017].

Smith, R. (2013) *Strategic Planning for Public Relations*, 4th edn (New York: Routledge).

Smithers, A. (2013) *The Road to Recovery* (Chichester: John Wiley & Sons).

Sodha, S. (2016) *Will Theresa May's 'just about managing families' fall for the rhetoric?* [online]. Available at: www.theguardian.com/commentisfree/2016/nov/21/theresa-may-jams-rhetoric-just-managing-families-autumn-statement [Accessed 2 Oct. 2017].

Solomos, J. (2003) *Race and Racism in Britain*, 3rd edn (Basingstoke: Palgrave Macmillan).

Sparks, C. (1999) 'The Press', in J. Stokes and A. Reading (eds) *The Media in Britain: Current Debates and Developments* (London: Macmillan).

Spicker, P. (2014) *Social Policy: Theory and Practice*, 3rd edn (Bristol: Policy).

Stelzer, I. (2007) 'The Characters behind the Promises', *The Spectator*, 7 February.

Stephens, P. (2001) 'The Treasury under Labour', in A. Seldon (ed.) *The Blair Effect: The Blair Government, 1997–2001* (London: Little, Brown).

Stern Review (2010) *The Economics of Climate Change - HM Treasury* [online]. Available at: http://webarchive.nationalarchives.gov.uk/+/http://www.hm-treasury.gov.uk/sternreview_index.htm [Accessed 2 Oct. 2017].

Stoker, G. (1991) *The Politics of Local Government* (London: Macmillan).

Stoker, G. (2000) *The New Politics of British Local Governance* (Basingstoke: Palgrave Macmillan).

Stoker, G. (2011) 'Anti-politics in Britain', in R. Heffernan, P.J. Cowley, and C. Hay (eds) *Developments in British Politics 9* (Basingstoke: Palgrave Macmillan).

Stoker, G. (2017) *Why Politics Matters: Making Democracy Work*, 2nd edn (London: Palgrave).

Stoker, G. and Wilson, D. (eds) (2004) *British Local Government into the 21st Century* (Basingstoke: Palgrave Macmillan).

Sylvester, R., Watson, R. and Thomson, A. (2013) *No, Minister: Whitehall in 'worst' crisis* [online]. Available at: www.thetimes.co.uk/article/no-minister-whitehall-in-worst-crisis-fjkzfczqkqz [Accessed 1 Oct. 2017].

Tench, R. and Yeomans, L. (2009) *Exploring Public Relations* (Harlow: Prentice Hall).

Thane, P. (2010) *Happy Families?* (London: British Academy).

Thatcher, M. (1987) *Interview for Woman's Own ('no such thing as society')* [online]. Available at: www.margaretthatcher.org/ document/106689 [Accessed 2 Oct. 2017].

Thatcher, M. (1988a) *Speech to the College of Europe ('The Bruges Speech')* [online]. Available at: www.margaretthatcher.org/ document/107332 [Accessed 1 Oct. 2017].

Thatcher, M. (1988b) *Speech to Conservative Party Conference* [online]. Available at: www. margaretthatcher.org/document/107352 [Accessed 6 Nov. 2017].

Thatcher, M. (1993) *The Downing Street Years* (London: HarperCollins).

*The Economist* (2005) *Europe's farm follies* [online]. Available at: www.economist.com/ node/5278374 [Accessed 2 Oct. 2017].

*The Economist* (2017) *Britain's local councils face financial crisis* [online]. Available at: www. economist.com/news/britain/21715673-amid-painful-fiscal-squeeze-some-authorities-may-soon-be-unable-meet-their-statutory [Accessed 1 Oct. 2017].

*The Guardian* (2016) *Shock figures show Tory plans are 'making social care worse'* [online]. Available at: www.theguardian.com/society/ 2016/dec/10/tory-plans-making-social-care-worse [Accessed 2 Oct. 2017].

*The Independent* (2010) *Barrage ditched as new nuclear plants get green light* [online]. Available at: www.independent.co.uk/news/ uk/home-news/barrage-ditched-as-new-nuclear-plants-get-green-light-2109887. html [Accessed 1 Oct. 2017].

*The Sun* (2017) *Don't chuck Britain in the Cor-bin: vote Tory unless you want a friend of terrorists who's ready to open our borders and hike up taxes as your next PM* [online]. Available at: www.thesun.co.uk/news/3748893/the-sun-says-vote-conservative-dont-chuck-britain-corbyn/ [Accessed 2 Oct. 2017].

*The Telegraph* (n.d.) *MPs' expenses: The saints* [online]. www.telegraph.co.uk/news/news topics/mps-expenses/5342811/MPs-expenses-The-saints-Part-i.html [Accessed 2 Nov. 2017].

Thomas-Symonds, N. (2014) *Nye: The Political Life of Aneurin Bevan* (London: I.B. Tauris).

Thomas, G.P. (1992) *Government and the Economy Today* (Manchester: Manchester University Press).

Thucydides ([5th century BCE] 1972) *History of the Peloponnesian War*, trans. R. Warner (Harmondsworth: Penguin).

*Time* (2016) *Read Trump's Remarks on the Clinton Email Investigation* [online]. Available at: http://time.com/4550004/hillary-clinton-email-fbi-reopen-donald-trump-transcript/ [Accessed 2 Oct. 2017].

Timmins, N. (1995) *The Five Giants: A Biography of the Welfare State* (London: HarperCollins).

Timothy, N. (2015) *The Government is selling our national security to China* [online]. Available at: www.conservativehome.com/ thecolumnists/2015/10/nick-timothy-the-government-is-selling-our-national-security-to-china.html [Accessed 2 Oct. 2017].

Titmuss, R.M. (1958) *Essays on the Welfare State* (London: George Allen & Unwin).

Titmuss, R.M. (1970) *The Gift Relationship: From Human Blood to Social Policy* (London: George Allen & Unwin).

Tolhurst, A. (2017) *Fake viral post claiming healthcare would no longer be free under Theresa May could have stopped voters backing Tories - and Labour campaigners spread the post* [online]. Available at: www. thesun.co.uk/news/3770085/did-labours-facebook-fake-news-stop-people-voting-tory-nhs-denounce-viral-post-claiming-healthcare-would-no-longer-be-free-under-theresa-may/ [Accessed 2 Oct. 2017].

Tomlin Commission (1931) *Commission on the Civil Service*, Cmd 3909 (London: HMSO).

Tonge, J. (2014a) *Comparative Peace Processes* (Cambridge: Polity).

Tonge, J. (2014b) *The Democratic Unionist Party* (Oxford: Oxford University Press).

Tonge, J. (2016) 'The Impact of Withdrawal from the European Union upon Northern Ireland', *Political Quarterly*, 87(3): 338–42.

Toye, R. (2011) 'The Rhetorical Premiership: A New Perspective on Prime Ministerial Power Since 1945', *Parliamentary History*, 30(2): 175–92.

Toynbee, P. and Walker, D. (2005) *Better or Worse? Has Labour Delivered?* (London: Bloomsbury).

Toynbee, P. and Walker, D. (2010) *The Verdict: Did Labour Change Britain?* (Cambridge: Granta).

Travers, T. (2003) *The Politics of London: Governing an Ungovernable City* (Basingstoke: Palgrave Macmillan).

Travers, T. (2015) *London's Boroughs at 50* (London: Biteback).

Trenaman, J. and McQuail, D. (1961) *Television and the Political Image* (London: Methuen).

Tucker, R.C. (ed.) (1978) *The Marx-Engels Reader* (New York: W.W. Norton & Co.).

Turner, A. (2013) *Rejoice! Rejoice! Britain in the 1980s* (London: Aurum Press).

Turner, A. (2014) *A Classless Society: Britain in the 1990s* (London: Aurum Press).

Understanding Society (2016) *Poverty: How does ethnicity matter?* [online]. Available at: www.understandingsociety.ac.uk/2016/05/09/poverty-how-does-ethnicity-matter [Accessed 9 Oct. 2017].

Vaughan, A. (2016) *Abolition of DECC 'major setback for UK's climate change efforts'* [online]. Available at: www.theguardian.com/environment/2016/jul/15/decc-abolition-major-setback-for-uk-climate-change-efforts [Accessed 5 Nov. 2017].

Vickers, R. (2015) 'Foreign Policy and International Development', in M. Beech and S. Lee (eds) *The Conservative-Liberal Coalition: Examining the Cameron–Clegg Government* (London: Palgrave).

Viner, K. (2000) *Naomi Klein: Hand-to-brand-combat* [online]. Available at: www.theguardian.com/books/2000/sep/23/society.politics [Accessed 2 Oct. 2017].

Wadham, J. (1999) 'A British Bill of Rights', in R. Blackburn and R. Plant (eds) *Constitutional Reform: The Labour Government's Constitutional Reform Agenda* (London: Longman).

Wadham, J., Mountfield, H., Edmundson, A. and Gallagher, C. (2007) *Blackstone's Guide to The Human Rights Act 1998*, 4th edn (Oxford: Oxford University Press).

Wakeham Report (2000) *A House for the Future: Royal Commission on the Reform of the House of Lords* (London: TSO).

Wallas, G. ([1908] 1920) *Human Nature in Politics* (London: Constable).

Waller, P. (2014) *Understanding Whitehall: A short introduction for special advisers* [online]. Available at: www.ucl.ac.uk/constitution-unit/spadsresources/understanding_whitehall_peter_waller [Accessed 1 Oct. 2017].

Walsh, K. (1995) *Public Services and Market Mechanisms* (London: Macmillan).

Waltz, K. (1979) *Theory of International Politics* (Reading, MA: Addison-Wesley).

Ward, A., Pickard, J. and Stothard, M. (2016) *Hinkley go-ahead after 'national security' safeguards* [online]. Available at: www.ft.com/content/0cde26b6-7b66-11e6-b837-eb4b4333ee43?mhq5j=e6 [Accessed 1 Oct. 2017].

Ward, A.J. (2000) 'Devolution: Labour's Strange Constitutional "Design"', in J. Jowell and D. Oliver, *The Changing Constitution* (Oxford: Oxford University Press).

Webb, P. and Poguntke, T. (2013) 'The Presidentialization of Politics Thesis Defended', *Parliamentary Affairs*, 66(3): 646–54.

Weber, M. ([1946] 1991) *From Essays in Sociology* (London: Routledge).

Weir, S. (1995) 'Quangos: Questions of Democratic Accountability', in F.F. Ridley and D. Wilson (eds) *The Quango Debate* (Oxford: Oxford University Press).

Weir, S. and Beetham, D. (1999) *Political Power and Democratic Control in Britain: The Democratic Audit of Great Britain* (London: Routledge).

Weir, S. and Hall, W. (eds) (1994) *Ego Trip: Extra Governmental Organisations in the UK and their Accountability* (Colchester: University of Essex Human Rights Centre).

Wendt, A (1999) *Social Theory of International Politics* (Cambridge: Cambridge University Press).

Whiteley, P. (2012) *Political Participation in Britain: The Decline and Revival of Civic Culture* (Basingstoke: Palgrave Macmillan).

Whiteley, P., Clarke, H., Sanders, D. and Stewart, M. (2001) 'Turnout', in P. Norris (ed.) *Britain Votes, 2001* (Oxford: Oxford University Press).

Whiteley, P., Clarke, H., Sanders, D. and Stewart, M. (2013) *Affluence, Austerity and Electoral Change in Britain* (Cambridge: Cambridge University Press).

Whittam Smith, A. (2017) *Two-party politics is back – sort of* [online]. Available at: www.independent.co.uk/voices/election-results-hung-parliament-two-party-politics-back-return-labour-conservative-tory-jeremy-a7781256.html [Accessed 1 Oct. 2017].

Wilkinson, R. and Pickett, K. (2010) *The Spirit Level* (Harmondsworth: Penguin).

Willetts, D. (2010) *The Pinch: How the Baby Boomers Took Their Children's Future – And Why They Should Give It Back* (London: Atlantic).

Williams, R. (1976) *Keywords: A Vocabulary of Culture and Society* (London: Fontana).

Wills, C. (2017) *Lovers and Strangers: An Immigrant History of Post-War Britain* (London: Allen Lane).

Wilson, A. and Wilson, K. (2002) '"Ethnicity", "Race" and Racism', in G. Blakeley and V. Bryson (eds) *Contemporary Political Concepts* (London: Pluto Press).

Wilson, D. and Game, C. (2006) *Local Government in the United Kingdom*, 4th edn (Basingstoke: Palgrave Macmillan).

Wilson, D. and Game, C. (2011) *Local Government in the United Kingdom*, 5th edn (Basingstoke: Palgrave Macmillan).

Wilson, G. (2006) *Cameron 'heir to Disraeli as a One Nation Tory'* [online]. Available at: www.telegraph.co.uk/news/uknews/1537995/Cameron-heir-to-Disraeli-as-a-One-Nation-Tory.html [Accessed 1 Oct. 2017].

Wilson, H. (1976) *The Governance of Britain* (London: Weidenfeld & Nicolson/Michael Joseph).

Wintour, P. (2015) *Jeremy Corbyn: it's time for a new kind of politics* [online]. Available at: www.theguardian.com/politics/2015/sep/11/jeremy-corbyn-aims-to-throw-out-theatrical-abuse-in-parliament [Accessed 1 Oct. 2017].

Wolfenden, J. (1957) *Report of the Committee on Homosexual Offences and Prostitution* (London: HMSO).

Women's Equality Party (2017) *Party objectives* [online]. Available at: www.womensequality.org.uk/objectives [Accessed 1 Oct. 2017].

World Bank (2017) *GDP ranking* [online]. Available at: https://data.worldbank.org/data-catalog/GDP-ranking-table [Accessed 9 Oct. 2017].

Wring, D. (2006) 'The News Media and the Public Relations State', in P. Dunleavy, R. Heffernan, P. Cowley and C. Hay (eds) *Developments in British Politics 8* (Basingstoke: Palgrave Macmillan).

Yong, B. and Hazell, R. (2014) *Special Advisers: Who They Are, What They Do and Why They Matter* (Oxford: Hart).

Young, H. (1989) *One of Us: A Biography of Margaret Thatcher* (London: Macmillan).

Young, H. (1998) *This Blessed Plot: Britain and Europe, from Churchill to Blair* (London: Macmillan).

# INDEX